RAF Bomber Command Squadron Profiles

106 Squadron

RAF Bomber Command Squadron Profiles

106 Squadron

by Chris Ward

with Herman Bijlard

First published 2016 by Mention the War Ltd., 32 Croft Street, Farsley, Yorkshire, LS28 5HA.

Second edition published 2022 by Mention the War Limited.

Copyright © 2016 and 2022 Chris Ward.

The right of Chris Ward to be identified as Author of this work is asserted by him in accordance with the Copyright, Designs and Patents Act 1988.

The original Operational Record Book of 106 Squadron and the Bomber Command Night Raid Reports are Crown Copyright and stored in microfiche and digital format by the National Archives.

All rights reserved. No part of this publication may be reproduced, stored in a retrieval system, transmitted in any form or by any means, electronic, mechanical or photocopied, recorded or otherwise, without the written permission of the copyright owners.

This squadron profile has been researched, compiled and written by its author, who has made every effort to ensure the accuracy of the information contained in it. The author will not be liable for any damages caused, or alleged to be caused, by any information contained in this book. E. & O.E.

Photo layout, editing and captions by Clare Bennett.

Cover design: Topics - The Creative Partnership www.topicsdesign.co.uk

A CIP catalogue reference for this book is available from the British Library.

ISBN 978 1 915335 00 5

Also by Chris Ward from Bomber Command Books:

Casualty of War: Letters Home from Flight Lieutenant Bill Astell DFC

Dambuster Deering: The Life and Death of an Unsung Hero

Dambusters : The Complete WWII History of 617 Squadron
(with Andy Lee and Andreas Wachtel)

Other RAF Bomber Command Profiles:

10 Squadron (with Ian MacMillan)
35 (Madras Presidency) Squadron
44 (Rhodesia) Squadron
50 Squadron
75(NZ) Squadron (with Chris Newey)
83 Squadron
101 Squadron
103 Squadron (with David Fell)
106 Squadron (with Herman Bijlard)
115 Squadron
138 Squadron (with Piotr Hodyra)
207 Squadron (with Raymond Glynne-Owen)
300 Squadron (with Grzegorz Korcz)
467 Squadron RAAF
514 Squadron (with Simon Hepworth)
617 Squadron
619 Squadron

Contents

Introduction ... 8
Dedication ... 10
Section One: Narrative WWII History ... 11
Narrative History ... 12
1939/40 ... 12
1940 ... 12
1940 Final Quarter ... 15
January 1941 ... 23
February 1941 ... 23
March 1941 ... 24
April 1941 ... 27
May 1941 ... 32
June 1941 ... 37
July 1941 ... 42
August 1941 ... 49
September 1941 ... 56
October 1941 ... 61
November 1941 ... 65
December 1941 ... 68
January 1942 ... 84
February 1942 ... 88
March 1942 ... 92
April 1942 ... 98
May 1942 ... 104
June 1942 ... 109
July 1942 ... 113
August 1942 ... 120
September 1942 ... 127
October 1942 ... 133
November 1942 ... 139
December 1942 ... 144
January 1943 ... 183
February 1943 ... 190
March 1943 ... 196
April 1943 ... 203
May 1943 ... 211

June 1943	216
July 1943	223
August 1943	230
September 1943	239
October 1943	243
November 1943	249
December 1943	254
January 1944	287
February 1944	293
March 1944	297
April 1944	306
May 1944	313
June 1944	321
July 1944	329
August 1944	337
September 1944	348
October 1944	354
November 1944	359
December 1944	363
January 1945	401
February 1945	405
March 1945	411
April 1945	416
Stations	433
Commanding Officers	433
Flight Commanders	433
Aircraft	434
Operational Record	435
Aircraft Histories	436
Roll of Honour	445
Key to Abbreviations	467

Introduction

RAF Bomber Command Squadron Profiles first appeared in the late nineties, and proved to be very popular with enthusiasts of RAF Bomber Command during the Second World War. They became a useful research tool, particularly for those whose family members had served and were no longer around. The original purpose was to provide a point of reference for all of the gallant men and women who had fought the war, either in the air, or on the ground in a support capacity, and for whom no written history of their unit or station existed. I wanted to provide them with something they could hold up, point to and say, "this was my unit, this is what I did in the war". Many veterans were reticent to talk about their time on bombers, partly because of modesty, but perhaps mostly because the majority of those with whom they came into contact had no notion of what it was to be a "Bomber Boy", to face the prospect of death every time they took to the air, whether during training or on operations. Only those who shared the experience really understood what it was to go to war in bombers, which is why reunions were so important. As they approached the end of their lives, many veterans began to speak openly for the first time about their life in wartime Bomber Command, and most were hurt by the callous treatment they received at the hands of successive governments with regard to the lack of recognition of their contribution to victory. It is sad that this recognition in the form of a national memorial and the granting of a campaign medal came too late for the majority. Now this inspirational, noble generation, the like of which will probably never grace this earth again, has all but departed from us, and the world will be a poorer place as a result.

RAF Bomber Command Squadron Profiles are back, the basic format remaining, but, where needed, additional information has been provided. Squadron Profiles do not claim to be comprehensive histories, but rather expanded operations record books in narrative form detailing every operation undertaken by the subject squadron. There is insufficient space to mention as many names as one would like, but all aircraft losses are accompanied by the name of the pilot. Fundamentally, the narrative section is an account of Bomber Command's war from the perspective of the bomber group under which the individual squadron served, and the deeds of the squadron are interwoven into this story. Information has been drawn from official records, such as group, squadron and station ORBs, and from the many, like myself, amateur enthusiasts, who dedicate much of their time to researching individual units, and become unrivalled authorities on them. I am grateful for their generous contributions, and their names will appear in the appropriate Profiles. The statistics quoted in this series are taken from The Bomber Command War Diaries, that indispensable tome written by Martin Middlebrook and Chris Everitt, and I am indebted to Martin for his kind permission to use them.

Finally, let me apologise in advance for the inevitable errors, for no matter how hard I and other authors try to write "nothing but the truth", there is no such thing as a definitive account of history, and there will always be room for disagreement and debate. Official records are notoriously unreliable tools, and yet we have little choice but to put our faith in them. It is not my intention to misrepresent any person or RAF unit, and I ask my readers to understand the enormity of the task I have undertaken. It is relatively easy to become an authority on single units or even a bomber group, but I chose to write about them all, idiot that I am, which means 128 squadrons serving operationally in Bomber Command at some time between the 3rd of September 1939 and the 8th of May 1945. I am dealing with eight bomber groups, in which some 120,000 airmen served, and I am juggling around 28,000 aircraft serial numbers, code letters and details of provenance and fate. I ask not for your sympathy, it was, after all, my choice, but rather your understanding if you should find something with which you disagree. My thanks to you, my readers, for making the original series of RAF Bomber Command Squadron Profiles so popular, and I hope you receive this new incarnation equally enthusiastically.

When I first wrote this 106 Squadron Profile in the late nineties, I was afforded much assistance by the late and much-missed Des Richards, the acknowledged expert on 106 Squadron. He generously gave of his time to answer my questions, proof-read my original manuscript, and purge it of errors. He also provided additional information to enable me to complete the work, and ensure that the deeds of the gallant air and ground crews of this magnificent squadron are accurately represented. The second time around I was equally indebted to my friend, Herman Bijlard, from the Netherlands, who knows more about 106 Squadron than anyone else on the planet. He kindly shared his research information with me, sending me copious amounts of data and some photos, all of which has been put to good use. It is thanks to the dedication of archivists like Des and Herman that we can read today of the gallantry of the amazing generation that contested the Second World War and saw this country through to victory. I was also assisted greatly by the trustees of the Metheringham Aviation Heritage Centre at Westmoor Farm, Martin Moor, Metheringham, who granted me access to the photo archive, and my special thanks were due then to curator and archivist Rod Sanders, who assisted in selecting the pictures and then processed them for me. For this third edition of the wartime history of 106 Squadron, I have drawn on additional photographs from the Lincolnshire Aviation Heritage Centre at East Kirkby. As always, I am encouraged in my work by my gang members, Andreas Wachtel in Germany, Greg Korcz in Poland and my "old mucker" Steve Smith, without whose contribution I would flounder. I make a particular mention of Clare Bennett, who costs me a fortune in pub lunches, but cares deeply about the subject and invests much time and effort into locating, collating, editing and laying out the photos we include. Finally, my appreciation to my publisher, Simon Hepworth of Mention the War Ltd., for his belief in my work, untiring efforts to promote it, and for the stress I put him through to bring my books to publication.

Chris Ward. Skegness. October 2021.

Dedication

This WWII history of 106 Squadron is dedicated to the memory of Peter and Zena Scoley who, along with likeminded others, notably the Wright family, were co-founders of the Friends of Metheringham Airfield (FOMA), now known as the Metheringham Airfield Visitors Centre (MAVC). Peter and Zena lived at Westmoor Farm, the home to the Visitors Centre, from 1967 and were only too aware of RAF Metheringham, the last home to 106 Sqn, slowly succumbing to both nature and agriculture. They both felt that soon there may be very little left to mark the service of those brave and dedicated airmen and women who served at RAF Metheringham with many paying the ultimate sacrifice. Something had to be done to keep their memory alive. Thanks to their and many other volunteers' efforts, in 2020, FOMA/MAVC celebrated its 25th anniversary amid another global event, the COVID Pandemic, a crisis that has also changed the world. In those 25 years, FOMA/MAVC has gone from strength to strength and now has full museum status with its future secured for many years to come. Zena sadly passed in 2014 with Peter following only two years later. Their efforts though have indeed borne fruit. Generations to come will be able to visit the centre, understand what happened there during WW2, learn that freedom has a cost, and what ordinary people are capable of when called to defend democracy against extreme ideologies and authoritarian regimes. *Photo courtesy of Jennie Wilson.*

Zena Marjorie Scoley MBE DL 4th June 1931 – 22nd November 2014
Edward Peter George Scoley   6th May 1935 – 11th February 2016

Section One: Narrative WWII History

Narrative History

1939/40

First formed on the 30th of September 1917, 106 Squadron fulfilled a corps reconnaissance role, moving to Ireland in May 1918, before becoming one of a vast number of squadrons to be disbanded in late 1919. It remained on the shelf until being resurrected at Abingdon on the 1st of June 1938. W/C Montgommerie had been appointed to command the squadron on the 8th of October, and during his periods of absence S/L Sheen stepped up. The squadron was initially equipped with Hawker Hinds, which were replaced by Fairey Battles, and a number of Ansons and Oxfords were also taken on charge. In May 1939, Hampdens arrived, and this type would remain with the squadron until well into 1942. The outbreak of war on the 3rd of September 1939 found 106 Squadron at Cottesmore in the county of Rutland, where it had resided for just two days. Each of Bomber Command's operational groups had been ordered to designate one squadron for group pool training duties, to feed new crews into the front line. This important role was handed to 106 Squadron, and it would be thus occupied for the entire first year of war.

The squadron consisted of two flights, with F/O Johnson in command of A Flight and S/L Parker in command of B Flight. The training role took its toll of Hampdens during 1939 and 1940, and the accidents began on the 24th of October, when L4175 undershot a night landing and hit trees and a hut. No one was killed but the pilot, P/O Dier, did sustain injuries. S/L Sheen took over command of A Flight at the start of November for what would be a short-lived tenure. On the 11th of November, L4186 stalled and crashed in Lincolnshire during a low level bombing exercise in the hands of P/O Loew, and one member of the crew was injured. On the 2nd of December, S/L Sheen was posted from his role as A Flight commander, and moved to Scampton to replace W/C Johnnie Chick as the commanding officer of 49 Squadron. The vacancy as A Flight commander at 106 Squadron was filled by S/L Weir.

1940

The winter of 1939/40 was particularly harsh, and seemed to deepen as the year progressed. As a consequence, flying was extremely restricted, and in the context of what the Americans dubbed "the "Phoney War", there was very little to occupy the Command's front-line squadrons. It was the end of February before conditions had improved sufficiently for limited operations to be conducted, and these amounted predominantly to reconnaissance and leafleting (nickelling) sorties. The first experience of a bombing operation for the frontline squadrons of 5 Group came on the night of the 19/20th of March, when twenty Hampdens followed a force of Whitleys in an attack on the German seaplane base at Hörnum on the island of Sylt. This was in response to the inadvertent slaying by a stray bomb of a British civilian on the island of Hoy, during a Luftwaffe raid on elements of the Royal Navy at Scapa Flow two nights earlier. Despite enthusiastic claims of success by the returning crews, photographic reconnaissance on the 6th of April failed to detect any signs of damage, and the over-optimistic assessments of results would eventually return in eighteen months' time to haunt the Command. Not until the German landings in southern Norway, and the simultaneous unopposed march into Denmark by German troops on the 9th of April, did the Command gird its loins for a major battle. However, restricted by the range from directly supporting the British response at Narvik in the north, its attention fell upon southern Norway and its forays against the airfields at Oslo and Stavanger and the shipping in coastal waters, were both heroic and largely futile. It was an ill-fated campaign, which was lost before it began, but during its course, on the night of the 13/14th, Hampdens of 5 Group carried out the first mining operation of the war, when sowing mines in the sea lanes between Germany and Norway. This would represent the initial tentative steps in a new departure for Bomber Command operations, which would prove to be hugely successful, and, by war's end, would have sunk or damaged more enemy ships than the Royal Navy. The laying of parachute mines by air was given the code-name "gardening", and the entire enemy-held coastline from the Pyrenees in the south-west to the Baltic port of Königsberg in the north-east, and even the northern Italian coast, was divided into gardens, each with a horticultural or marine biological name. The process of delivery was known as planting, and the mines, themselves, were referred to as vegetables, and it would not be long before the other bomber groups joined in to create a spiders' web of mines in chains across all of the sea-lanes employed by the enemy. Gardening was a task to which the Hampden was to prove itself eminently suited.

Events in Scandinavia were superseded by others closer to home in the early hours of the 10th of May, when the German advance into the Low Countries ended the pretence and shadow boxing of the Phoney War, and pitched the Battle and Blenheim squadrons of the French based Advanced Air Striking Force (AASF) into a ferocious and unequal fight against impossible odds. This conflict also dragged in the Blenheim squadrons of Bomber Command's home-based 2 Group, and, within days, both had suffered grievous casualties. A number of the Battle squadrons were effectively knocked out of the conflict altogether, while the others would struggle on for a further month. The heavy bomber groups played their part by attacking communications and industrial targets behind enemy lines, principally in the Ruhr, and this resulted in the first bombs falling on mainland Germany. They were also employed in support of the desperate efforts to stem the tide of enemy troops and armour advancing across the Low Countries into France, and this would go on until Dunkerque.

It had been a relatively uneventful year thus far for 106 Squadron, which continued in its training role throughout the ill-fated campaign across the Channel. P1336 was lost on the night of the 24th of May, when it struck a barrage balloon cable over Coventry during a training flight, and crashed into the city, killing P/O Irvine and the others on board. On the 31st, L4174 came down near Finningley without injury to the crew of Sgt Wilkes, and P/O Potts and the occupants of L4181, likewise, escaped damage when it crashed through tented accommodation on the airfield during night training on the 6th of July, but sadly, three men inside were killed. By this time W/C Montgommerie had concluded his tenure as commanding officer, and had been temporarily succeeded on the 16th of June by S/L Stubbs. As events were to prove, he would still be at the helm at the time of the transition from training to operational status a few months hence.

The fall of France brought with it invasion fever, and the next four months would see the Command directing its efforts against German industry, airfields in the occupied countries, and ports, while a proportion of the Hampden forced continued to ply its mining trade in the major sea-lanes. August brought just one casualty to 106 Squadron, L4187 crashing in Lincolnshire during night flying training on the night of the 7/8th, killing Sgt Dalgress and the other three men on board. As the Battle of Britain began to gain momentum overhead, a campaign began to destroy the barges and other marine craft, which were being gathered in the occupied ports to ferry the enemy invasion force across to Britain. The Hampden crews were among those thrust into the cauldron of flak protecting these concentrations, and many heroic actions took place, resulting in numerous Hampdens failing to return. On the night of the 12/13th of August, S/L Learoyd of 49 Squadron was among a force of Hampdens attempting to breach an aqueduct section of the Dortmund-Ems Canal at its junction with the River Ems north of Münster. Attacking last in the face of the most hostile searchlight and flak defence, and, after witnessing the loss of two 83 Squadron Hampdens, 49 Squadron's F/L Learoyd breached the channel, and made it home to become the first from Bomber Command to be awarded a Victoria Cross. *(At the time of the posthumous awards of the VC to F/O Garland and Sgt Gray of 12 Squadron in May, the AASF was not technically part of Bomber Command.)*

September was the month in which 106 Squadron acceded to the front-line and began conducting mining operations, while retaining its training function. It started inauspiciously with the loss during a night training exercise of L4188, which exploded over Buckinghamshire on the 1st and crashed, and there were no survivors from the crew of Sgt Duncan. S/L Cooper was posted in from 14 O.T.U at Cottesmore on the 4th, and he would succeed S/L Weir as A Flight commander. Sgt Mills was carrying out night circuits and landings in P1254 on the 5th, when attacked by an enemy aircraft. The Hampden sustained damage, but, happily, there were no crew casualties. On the 7th, London was heavily bombed over a period of more than nine hours, and the squadron received Invasion Alert Warning No1, which required its aircraft to be bombed up and at readiness.

The main focus of the Command's attention at this point continued to be the build-up of invasion craft in the occupied ports. As the Battle of Britain reached its climax towards mid-month, invasion fever increased its grip the nation, and plans were put in place to repel landings by sea, although this was a campaign in which 106 Squadron would not take part. The squadron was briefed for its first offensive action on the 9th, but the crews of S/Ls Weir and Parker and P/O Altman were not to be among the twenty-one from 5 Group detailed to attack a special target in the Blohm & Voss shipyards in the Altona district of Hamburg to the west of the city centre. The actual aiming point was recorded as lying five hundred yards south-east of the centre of the yards, and was identified in the 44 Squadron Operations Record Book (ORB) as D2, dockland installations, but may have been a capital ship, perhaps, Bismarck. This had also been the target twenty-four hours earlier for forty-nine Hampdens on a night of excellent weather conditions, with clear skies and a quarter moon to light the way and aid map-reading. However, searchlight dazzle and gun flashes had created challenges of their own and, although returning crews were mostly confident that they had landed the bombs in the target area, no confirmation was forthcoming. For its operational debut, the 106 Squadron trio faced a long round-trip to the Deodars garden in the Gironde estuary north of the important port of Bordeaux on France's southern Biscay coast. They departed Finningley in fine weather conditions between 20.00 and 20.20, and all returned safely around eight hours later from successful if uneventful sorties. Typically, the ORB entries in 5 Group squadrons at this stage of the war provided meagre information, and it would be some time before the designated scribes became more expansive in their style.

More than a hundred aircraft were in action on the 10th, eighteen of them 5 Group Hampdens assigned mostly to invasion barges at Ostend and Calais. The operation against the Blohm & Voss shipyards was repeated on the night of the 11/12th, while the 106 Squadron crews of S/Ls Stubbs and Cooper and F/L Eustace departed Finningley between 19.45 and 20.10 bound for the Deodars garden. The weather was again fine, and they landed back home between 03.30 and 03.50 with nothing of significance to report. The 15th was the day on which the Battle of Britain reached its climax, and, by dusk, enemy losses had been sufficient to persuade Hitler to call off Operation Sealion, the invasion of Britain. This would not be apparent to the British authorities, however, and anti-invasion operations would continue, as would the Battle of Britain, at a reduced intensity for another six weeks.

On the 18th, X2960 was written off in a crash-landing near Finningley by P/O Grant during training, happily without injury to those on board, but that night, the inevitable first operational casualty came as the result of a mining sortie. P1259 departed Finningley at 19.40 as one of three Hampdens involved, and it was brought down by flak, the chief enemy of low-level mine-layers, while planting its vegetables in the Eglantine garden in the Elbe estuary on Germany's north-western coast. There were no survivors, and P/O Watkin and his crew thus became the first from the squadron to be killed as a result of enemy action. P/Os Howell and Hall and their crews were the others taking part in this operation, and they returned safely. Finningley was excluded from operations over the ensuing days while other elements of

5 Group and the Command continued the anti-invasion campaign, and the next operation for 106 Squadron came on the night of the 26/27th, when P/Os Howell and Hall and Sgt Huggins took off between 19.10 and 19.30 to lay mines in French coastal waters in the Cinnamon garden off la Rochelle. Returning during the early hours of the 27th, X2914 ran out of fuel and was abandoned by its pilot, Sgt Huggins, over Weston Zoyland airfield in Somerset, but his crew failed to leave the aircraft and perished in the ensuing crash. Later that day, P1256 crashed near Finningley while on a training flight, and P/O Lowe of 44 Squadron and his passenger died. It was another training crash that killed Sgt Gow and two of his crew on the last day of the month, when L4189 crashed into high ground near Buxton in Derbyshire during a navigation exercise. That night, P/Os Howell and Hall took off at 18.30 to join others to lay mines in the Eglantine garden in the mouth of the Elbe, and good weather conditions helped them to complete a successful operation. During the course of the month, the squadron carried out five operations and dispatched fourteen sorties for the loss of one Hampden and crew, and lost an additional five Hampdens to non-operational crashes that claimed five lives.

1940 Final Quarter

October was a kinder month for the squadron, perhaps largely because operations were curtailed somewhat by unfavourable weather conditions. The first operation involved three aircraft taking off in the early evening to lay mines in the Elbe Estuary on the night of the 11/12th. P/Os Hall and Howells and Sgt Stevenson took off either side of 18.00 in doubtful weather conditions, which prevented accurate identification of the target area, and only one vegetable was successfully delivered in the face of intense anti-aircraft fire from shore batteries and a flak ship. The only incident of note thus far in the month was an undercarriage collapse suffered by L4184 during training on the 13th, but Sgt Grainger and the other occupants were unharmed. P/O Howell and Sgt Stevenson took off at 18.00 and 18.10 respectively to lay mines in the Forget-me-not garden off the Baltic port of Kiel on the night of the 15/16th, but encountered low cloud in the garden area and intense anti-aircraft fire. One mine was successfully planted, but the other was brought home. P/O Street and Sgt Stevenson took off at 01.50 and 02.00 respectively on the 25th for a mining operation in the Jellyfish garden off Brest, enjoying favourable weather conditions throughout with no opposition of any kind, and they returned safely at 08.00.

On the 28th the squadron's stand-in commanding officer, S/L Stubbs, was posted to 144 Squadron at Hemswell. On the 18th of February 1941 he would be posted to Waddington to take over as B Flight commander at 207 Squadron, the first Avro Manchester unit, before moving on again with the rest of his flight on the 27th of February to form the nucleus of the newly-reforming 97 Squadron, which was to be the second Manchester unit. After a successful tour, S/L Stubbs would be promoted to the rank of wing commander, and eventually be given command of 49 Squadron at Scampton on the 17th of July. Also posted out on the 28th were P/O Hall to 61 Squadron at Hemswell and P/O Howell to 49 Squadron at Scampton. S/L Norris succeeded S/L Stubbs as B Flight commander at 106 Squadron.

While the other 5 Group squadrons were assigned to bombing operations over Germany, 106 Squadron continued to focus exclusively on mining, and provided three of five Hampdens to be dispatched to the Baltic to lay mines in the Verbena garden off Copenhagen on the night of the 29/30th. F/O Hill led them away at 23.40, to be followed by P/O Price at 23.45 and Sgt Stammers at 23.59. P1220 developed engine trouble, forcing P/O Price to turn back, and he landed safely at 01.30. The weather was very bad, and included severe icing conditions, as a result of which, neither of the remaining Hampdens reached the target area. L4180 was fixed at 05.50, and crashed into the North Sea twenty miles off Spurn Head at around 07.00 without survivors from the crew of F/O Hill. Three aircraft were sent on a sea search later in the morning, and another on the 31st, but no trace of the aircraft or crew was found. During the course of October, the squadron carried out just four gardening operations and dispatched ten sorties for the loss of one Hampden and its crew.

November would bring a similar pattern of activity for the squadron, but the first event of note in 5 Group took place on the 1st with the reformation of 207 Squadron to introduce the new twin-engine Avro Manchester into operational service. The new month's operations began for 106 Squadron that very night with three sorties to lay mines in the Jellyfish garden off Brest. P/O Streat, Sgt Stammers and S/L Norris took off either side of 02.00, and all reached the garden area, where two mines were successfully planted. Technical problems prevented the third from being released, and it was brought back to store after an otherwise uneventful trip. W/C Lindlay was posted in from 16 O.T.U at Upper Heyford later on the 2nd, and installed as the new commanding officer.

There were three further mining sorties on the night of the 7/8th, one of them in the Artichoke garden off Lorient, which was successfully undertaken by S/L Norris after departing Finningley at 18.30. The other two, by P/O Wilson and Sgt Stammers, were to the Jellyfish garden off the port of Brest, one of them being completed as briefed, while the other was thwarted by an electrical failure. F/L French DFC was posted to 207 Squadron on the 10th, where he would be joined shortly by F/O Eustace. There are contradictory entries in the squadron and group ORBs for the period of the 15th to the 17th. Three crews took part in gardening operations, those of P/O Wilson, and Sgts Stammers and Galloway, and the squadron ORB recorded them as taking off in the early hours of the 16th to lay mines in the sea lanes off Brest and Lorient, (Jellyfish and Artichoke), while the 5 Group record stated that the target area was the mouth of the Elbe (Eglantine). The squadron ORB stated that two of the sorties were successful, but that the third crew was unable to locate the garden area and brought its mine home. It then claims that three further sorties were carried out on the 17th, on a night when 5 Group operations were cancelled because of unfavourable weather conditions. It seems clear that there were not two nights of operations, but just one.

On the night of the 16/17th the main operation was against Hamburg, for which 130 aircraft were made ready. The three 106 Squadron Hampdens were to follow up this attack by laying mines in the Elbe estuary (Eglantine), and P/O Wilson took off first at 02.00 in X2970 in rain and poor visibility. While outbound he encountered icing conditions, which forced him to turn back, and he crashed on landing at 03.40, although without injury to himself or his crew. Meanwhile, Sgts Stammers and Galloway had taken off at 02.30 and 02.35 respectively, and one of them delivered a mine successfully in the face of heavy anti-aircraft fire from a shore battery and a flak ship, while the other was unable to locate the garden area and brought the mine home. S/L Weir was posted to 61 Squadron on the 21st, to fulfil the role of flight commander, and he was succeeded as commander of the Operational Flight at 106 Squadron by S/L Threapleton, who arrived from 14 O.T.U at Cottesmore.

Another mining operation in the coastal waters around Lorient involved three of the squadron's Hampdens on the night of the 22/23rd. Sgts Galloway, Osborne and Ward took off between 17.00 and 17.25, and the first two-mentioned successfully carried out their brief, one also attacking a railway junction at St Brieve with 250lb wing-mounted bombs, both of which were seen to explode on the target. L4194 failed to make it home, and is believed to have fallen victim to the heavy anti-aircraft fire reported by the other crews on their return. It crashed into the sea in the target area, killing Sgt Ward and his crew. On the 25th, P1320 spiralled into the ground just north of Stamford in Lincolnshire, after Sgt Bagnall lost control while engaged in night training, and, although he and one other survived with injuries, two of his crew were killed. The summary section (Form 540) of the squadron ORB mentioned two crews being dispatched to lay mines off the Brittany coast on the night of the 27/28th, but the detailed section (Form 541) carried no such entry, and the 5 Group ORB made no mention of Finningley operating on this night.

Sgts Galloway and Osborne went mining off Brest (Jellyfish) on the evening of the 29th, departing Finningley between 16.35 and 16.45. Perhaps the erroneous entry for the 27/28th, which described one crew finding its target area under ten-tenths cloud with a base as low as 1,200 feet, applied to this occasion, and was the reason one of them attacked an aerodrome, before returning safely to report observing bomb bursts on the edge of it. During the course of November, the squadron carried out six mining operations and dispatched seventeen sorties for the loss of one Hampden and crew, and another to a training crash costing two lives.

Fog curtailed all flying at the start of December, and it was the early hours of the 5th before operations from Finningley could be resumed. Sgts Topping and Osborne took off shortly after 04.00 bound for Brest (Jellyfish), where they successfully delivered a mine each before returning safely home. An unfortunate training incident on the 7th of December cost the life of Sgt Shilling and crew, who were on detachment from 50 Squadron, after L4103 lost a propeller to a lightning strike, and crashed close to the airfield. The squadron began sending freshman crews out on daylight North Sea sweeps at this time, and one on the 11th had a more serious intention, to search for a missing crew from 50 Squadron at Lindholme, which, it was falsely believed, may have come down in the sea. Sgts Osborne, Topping and Howard took off in a fifteen-minute slot from 03.00 on the 16th to lay mines off Lorient (Artichoke) and Brest (Jellyfish), and, although one failed to locate the garden area, the two others successfully carried out their briefs. Sgt Howard then attacked with wing bombs a merchant ship estimated to be of two to three thousand tons, and the rear gunner reported a direct hit on the starboard after deck.

Sgts Osborne, Galloway and Howard departed Finningley in the late afternoon of the 19th and headed for the waters off Brest (Jellyfish). All successfully planted their vegetables, before Sgt Galloway attacked the airfield at Plouescat, near the Brittany coast, and saw both wing bombs explode close to the flare path. Two further training accidents had vastly different outcomes on the 21st, P1304 hitting trees in Yorkshire, and crashing at 20.40 without injury to the crew of Sgt Wells, while the entire crew of P/O Hubbard perished when X3154 struck high ground near Chapel-en-le-Frith in Derbyshire. Four Hampdens took off from Finningley either side of 03.00 on the 23rd, bound for the Elbe estuary (Eglantine) to lay mines, and carrying the crews of Sgts Osborne, Galloway, Howard and Sidebotham, but Sgt Sidebotham was back within an hour with engine problems. The remaining aircraft pressed on to the target area, where one was unable to pinpoint the dropping zone because of poor visibility, and returned with mine and wing bombs. Sgt Howard met with no such difficulties, and planted his vegetables accurately, while Sgt Galloway was still outbound when he encountered a convoy off Wangeroog, and claimed two near misses with his wing bombs. Neither he nor his navigator were certain of their precise position, however, and, while searching for the dropping zone, they stumbled into fierce defensive fire from the ground. They ultimately planted the mine in an incorrect, but probably useful spot, before returning safely home. At 19.30 that same day, P2071 apparently crashed three miles from Market Drayton in Shropshire while training, but Sgt Sowden and the other occupant walked away unscathed. The 106 Squadron ORB made no mention of this incident in the general summary of events.

Just one further crew was lost during the year, and that was as the result of a mining sortie. 106 Squadron provided four of thirteen Hampdens sent to the Beech garden off St Nazaire on the night of the 27/28th. Sgts Sidebotham, Howard, Galloway and F/O Burr-Thomas took off between 02.35 and 02.50, and one attacked a flak ship with bombs on the way out, although without observing the result. Otherwise, the three returning crews reported an uneventful trip with only slight opposition. P2098 did not arrive back with the others, however, and disappeared without trace with the crew of Sgt Sidebotham. During the course of December, the squadron carried out five operations and dispatched sixteen sorties for the loss of one Hampden and its crew, while four other Hampdens were written off in non-operational incidents.

Since beginning its offensive career in early September, 106 Squadron had launched fifty-four Hampdens on exclusively mining operations, and five had failed to make it home, a loss rate of almost 11%. It had been a strange year for the Command, characterized by relative inactivity at either end, and a period of unbelievable ferocity in the middle. It had been a backs-to-the-wall struggle until the Battle of Britain was won, and the threat of invasion had been banished, but then had come the realisation that the road ahead was long and arduous, and for the time being at least, the best that the Command could hope to do was to present a defiant and belligerent face to the, as yet all-conquering enemy.

106 Squadron in 1938 at Abington

Fairey Battle of 106 Squadron 1938

106 Squadron Hampden

Kiel Naval Base 1940

F/L R O Altmann
Despite his Germanic name, F/L Reginald Otto Altmann (second from right), became one of one of the squadron's senior pilots. He went on to become a Wing Commander, receiving the DSO and sustained wounds whilst flying a Dakota glider tug at Arnhem. (Simon Sanders)

Barges being made ready for the invasion of Britain. (Aircrew Remembered)

A British airman is amongst a group of civilians crowded around the window of a shop in Holborn, London, to look at a map illustrating how the RAF is striking back at Germany during 1940.

Hampden Cockpit

January 1941

Another harsh winter heralded the arrival of the New Year, which began for 106 Squadron with a continuation of the training function, interspersed with gardening operations. The Command targeted the city of Bremen on each of the first three nights of the new year, on the night of the 1/2nd by an initial force of 141 aircraft, of which the 5 Group stations of Scampton, Waddington and Lindholme provided ten Hampdens between them. On the following night, Hemswell and Scampton put up eight aircraft, while Scampton alone represented the group with fifteen Hampdens twenty-four hours later. 106 Squadron would incur no operational losses during January, but would register one training accident involving the forced-landing of P4314 near the airfield in the hands of Sgt Mapp of 61 Squadron on the 3rd, happily without casualties. That night, training included sweeps over the North Sea, which passed without incident. It was at this time that the new bomber station at Coningsby opened on a care-and-maintenance basis, and would soon become home to 106 Squadron. The Command's attention during the period remained focused on German and French ports, Bremen, as already mentioned, at the start, and Wilhelmshaven at the end. The first operational activity for 106 Squadron came on the evening of the 4th, when four Hampdens took off to lay mines in the Artichoke garden off Lorient. Sgts Galloway, Topping, Osborne and West were airborne between 17.00 and 17.40, and three of them successfully delivered their stores, while the fourth was unable to locate the dropping zone and brought the mine back. Four 106 Squadron Hampdens were sent to lay mines in the Forget-me-not garden in Kiel Bay on the night of the 9/10, Sgts Howard, Topping, West and P/O Wareing all getting away safely either side of 17.00. Again, three were successful, and one planted his vegetable in the Elbe estuary (Eglantine) as an alternative, after failing to locate the briefed dropping zone. Sgt Howard also attacked Flensburg aerodrome with his wing bombs, but was unable to determine the result.

The same four crews were on duty again on the evening of the 12th to lay mines off Lorient, and they departed Finningley at 17.00 to carry out their brief successfully. P/O Wareing also attacked an aerodrome near the Brittany coast, and saw his bombs burst in the centre of the landing field. All four from the squadron were diverted to St Eval on return, and landed safely either side of 23.00. On the 15th, the commander-in-chief of Bomber Command, Sir Richard Peirse, who had been in post since succeeding Sir Charles Portal in October, received a new directive from the Air Ministry setting out the latest bombing policy. It was believed that Germany's oil situation was approaching a critical period, and that attacks on its synthetic oil production over the next six months would impact heavily upon its war effort. Accordingly, a list of seventeen targets had been prepared, the top nine of which represented around 80% of output. All but one of these plants were situated in two main areas, at Gelsenkirchen and Scholven-Buer in the Ruhr, and Leuna, Politz, Ruhland, Böhlen, Zeitz, and Lützkendorf near Leipzig, with the ninth at Magdeburg some sixty miles to the north, and they would represent the sole, primary aim for Peirse's forces until further notice. Peirse would wait until February before implementing the campaign, and would continue with his policy of one large-scale attack per month against a major industrial city. Sgts Howard and Topping carried out mining sorties in the Jellyfish garden off Brest on the evening of the 16th, and returned without incident. It was at this point that the weather closed in, and no operations were possible for twelve straight nights. 106 Squadron concluded the month with a tally of fourteen sorties without loss from four operations.

February 1941

February began as January had ended, with ports occupying the bulk of the Command's attention, although the accent shifted to those in France and Belgium. 106 Squadron opened its operational account with a record number of sorties on the evening of the 4th. The 5 Group ORB mentioned six of seven

Finningley mining sorties being carried out successfully in the Beech garden off St-Nazaire. The 106 Squadron ORB cited six crews, including those of the usual suspects, Sgts Galloway, Topping, Osborne and West, and they all got away safely at 17.00. One of the other crews was that of F/O Burr-Thomas, who failed to return after AD750 crashed near Nantes. Four mines were delivered successfully, and two crews then turned their attention upon a nearby airfield at Chateau Rougnon, which they attacked with their wing bombs. Bomb bursts were observed on hangars, and also on a factory north-east of the aerodrome. It seems that some aircraft landed at St Eval, and returned to Finningley on the 6th. During the course of this transit, AD736 was force-landed near the airfield through fuel shortage, and Sgt Osborne and his crew walked away unscathed. Some quite sizeable operations took place against German cities during the month, the first of which was Peirse's "big" raid, directed at Hannover on the night of the 10/11th, for which over two hundred aircraft were dispatched.

The oil directive was finally implemented on the night of the 14/15th, when the Nordstern (Gelsenberg A. G.) refinery at Gelsenkirchen was attacked by Wellingtons, while Wellingtons and Blenheims tried their hand at a similar target at Moers/Homberg, situated on the West Bank of the Rhine opposite Duisburg. Both of these massively important plants were vital to the German war effort, and employed the Bergius process, the hydrogenation of highly volatile bituminous coal, to refine high-grade petroleum products such as aviation fuel. It was on this night that 207 Squadron had hoped to launch its maiden sorties, but the modifications to the Manchesters had taken twice the time planned for, and the aircraft had not been tested.

Finningley was transferred from 5 to 7 Group on the 20th, and over the 22nd and 23rd, 106 Squadron moved into Coningsby, the new station situated about three miles to the south-east of Woodhall Spa. The crews spent the remainder of the month familiarizing themselves with their new home, and identifying important landmarks like the nearby Tattershall Castle. The squadron would not be the sole resident for long, as a new squadron, 97, was about to be reformed as an offshoot of 207 Squadron to be the second Manchester unit, and would shortly also take up residence at Coningsby. 106 Squadron's operational record for the month was just the above-mentioned single operation involving six sorties and one missing crew. News came through from the International Red Cross on the 28th, that the Burr-Thomas crew members had all lost their lives.

March 1941

March was to bring an increase in activity and a shift in accent for 106 Squadron from mining to bombing operations. The new month began with a return to Cologne on the night of the 1/2nd by an initial force of 131 assorted aircraft, of which forty-four Hampdens were provided by 5 Group from its stations at Coningsby, Hemswell, Lindholme and Scampton. 106 Squadron provided five aircraft in an overall force of 131, and this would be the first time that the squadron's bomb bays had contained bombs rather than mines. F/O Price and P/O Altmann, the latter of German extraction, were the senior pilots on duty, and they joined the three NCO crews in taking off between 20.00 and 20.30. They enjoyed favourable weather conditions as they made their way via corridor "G" over the North Sea, and were able to firmly establish their positions as they made landfall over the Scheldt estuary, before heading inland across Holland. They arrived in the target area to find clear skies and easily identifiable ground features, predominantly the distinctive bends in the River Rhine, which provided most with the references they required to run in on the briefed aiming point. Bombs were delivered from a variety of altitudes up to 16,000 feet in the face of an intense defensive response, and returning crews claimed a successful operation. This was confirmed by local sources, which reported extensive damage in central districts, particularly in the docks areas on both banks of the Rhine. Four of the 106 Squadron participants reported observing their bombs bursting within sight of the aiming point, while the fifth was unsuccessful through the failure of its bombs to release. Photo-reconnaissance revealed some useful damage in the docks area in return for the loss of six aircraft, but fourteen others were abandoned over England after fog made landing impossible. Later, on the 2nd, S/L Nelms arrived from 14 O.T.U at Cottesmore, and was installed as the new A Flight commander.

The threat of adverse weather conditions caused a reduction in the 5 Group force briefed to attack the Admiral Hipper at Brest on the night of the 2/3rd, and, ultimately, it was left to eight crews from 44 Squadron at Waddington to achieve what they could. A force of seventy-one aircraft was assembled on the 3rd to send once more against Cologne, for which Coningsby and Scampton provided the 5 Group element, while Waddington made ready three Hampdens and two Manchesters for a return to the Admiral Hipper at Brest. W/C Polglase had been appointed by this time to command the squadron, and the first mention of his name in the squadron ORB appeared in the Order of Battle for this night, when he took the opportunity to lead the squadron for the first time, supported by S/L Parker. A new squadron record of nine Hampdens departed Coningsby either side of 20.00, and arrived in the target area to find large amounts of cloud with gaps, but generally fair conditions, which allowed them to gain glimpses of the city. Bombing took place from between 10,000 and 12,000 feet in the face of considerable searchlight activity, but little flak, and returning crews reported a positive outcome, when, in fact, only a few locations in the western fringes of the city had been hit. Sgt Howard was thwarted by ten-tenths cloud and bombed Eindhoven aerodrome as an alternative on the way home, while Sgt Galloway experienced W/T failure soon after take-off and was unable to complete the operation. X3002 failed to return to Coningsby having crashed near Antwerp in Belgium, and Sgt Good and his crew were killed, thus becoming the first to be posted missing from 106 Squadron as the result of a bombing operation.

Thereafter, the weather took a hand to keep most of the Command on the ground for the next week, and it was during this period, on the 9th, that the Air Ministry responded to the urgent and burgeoning threat posed by U-Boots, which were claiming a massive tonnage of shipping crossing the Atlantic in convoys with vital war supplies. A new Directive was issued, which would unleash a concerted campaign against this menace and its partner in crime, the Focke-Wulf Kondor long-range maritime reconnaissance bomber. These two threats were to be attacked where-ever they could be found, at sea, in their bases in the occupied ports, and at their point of manufacture in the shipyards and in the assembly and component factories. A new target list was drawn up, which was headed by Kiel, Hamburg and Vegesack (Bremen), all of which were home to U-Boot construction yards, and Bremen itself, which also boasted a Focke-Wulf aircraft factory in its south-eastern Hemelingen district. Other related targets included the diesel engine plants at Mannheim and Augsburg, aircraft factories at Dessau, and, of course, the U-Boot bases at Brest, Lorient and St-Nazaire. Until otherwise instructed, this was to be the focus of Peirse's efforts, and, only occasionally, would he be able prosecute the oil campaign.

106 Squadron welcomed new neighbours at Coningsby on the 10th, when 97 Squadron moved in from Waddington with its Avro Manchesters. The new directive would be implemented first on the night of the 12/13th, at the end of a day of hectic activity across the Command, as aircraft were made ready for three major raids to be conducted that night. Eighty-eight aircraft were to attack the Blohm & Voss shipyards at Hamburg, while eighty-six other crews were briefed for the Focke-Wulf factory and the city of Bremen, and, finally, seventy-two aircraft were prepared for the long slog to Berlin to target two aiming points. 5 Group was to support the first-mentioned with forty Hampdens and four Manchesters, and the last-mentioned with thirty Hampdens, and, with the addition of a single freshman crew on gardening duties, this represented the largest effort undertaken by 5 Group thus far in the war. 106 Squadron briefed seven crews for Hamburg, and they hopped over to Lindholme for bombing-up before taking off either side of midnight with F/Ls Altmann and Boylan the senior pilots on duty. F/O Price and

crew were forced to return early with engine trouble, leaving the remainder to press on to find good visibility in the target area, where bombing took place from between 10,000 and 15,000 feet in the face of considerable opposition from the ground. They returned to Coningsby, where they expressed confidence that the attack had been effective, and damage to two slipways containing U-Boots in the Blohm & Voss shipyards was confirmed.

Weather conditions remained favourable as preparations were put in hand on the 13th to return to Hamburg that night with a force of 139 aircraft, including a contribution from 5 Group of thirty-four Hampdens and five Manchesters from Scampton, Hemswell, Waddington and Lindholme. 106 Squadron sat this one out, but, on the following day, made ready four Hampdens to contribute to a 5 Group element of twenty-one provided by Scampton, Hemswell, Lindholme and Coningsby in an overall force of a 101 aircraft to target the Hydriewerk-Scholven synthetic oil refinery at Gelsenkirchen, along with a number of similar objectives in this oil-dominated Ruhr city. S/L Nelms took the lead for the first time, and led the way at 19.15, with F/L Boylan bringing up the rear forty-five minutes later. Crews reported that haze made it difficult to identify ground detail, but this was an ever-present problem over the Ruhr, and a solution would not be found for a further two years. The defences were highly active, but all from Coningsby reported bombing as briefed and observing explosions and large fires. In fact, the raid turned out to be the most successful yet on this industry, resulting in some sixteen bomb loads hitting the oil plant and temporarily halting production. S/L Tudor was posted in on the 16th to assume command of B Flight as successor to S/L Parker, who departed for a post at the Air Ministry. S/L Tudor, who possessed a high-pitched voice, would bear the nickname "Mary" throughout his career in a reference to the first-born daughter of Henry VIII.

It fell to Scampton and Coningsby to provide eighteen Hampdens on the 17th for a force of fifty-seven aircraft targeting shipyards in Bremen, while another element of the Command focused its attention upon the naval port of Wilhelmshaven. 106 Squadron supported the former operation with seven Hampdens led by W/C Polglase and S/L Nelms, who departed Coningsby after midnight, with the commanding officer last away at 01.00. They had been briefed to aim for the shipyards, which five located in excellent weather conditions and bombed from between 10,000 and 11,000 feet, observing many explosions. S/L Nelms was attacked by a Me110 and a Ju88 over the Dutch coast on the way home, the former bursting into flames after being hit by the Hampden's return fire, while the latter broke off the attack. P/O Wareing returned to discover that he and his crew had attacked Oldenburg in error, while Sgt Osborne and crew had been forced to abandon their sortie because of W/T failure.

Coningsby was not represented in the force of thirty-eight Hampdens and two Manchesters detailed by 5 Group on the 18th for an operation that night against the Deutsche Werke U-Boot yards at Kiel, which would also involve fifty-seven Wellingtons and Whitleys. A relatively large mining effort by 5 Group on the night of the 20/21st involved forty-two Hampdens from Lindholme, Waddington, Hemswell and Coningsby, seven of them belonging to 106 Squadron. The garden areas were off the ports of Brest (Jellyfish), Lorient (Artichoke) and St-Nazaire (Beech), and 106 Squadron was assigned to the first-mentioned. S/Ls Nelms and Tudor were the senior pilots on duty, the latter undertaking his first operation with the squadron. They began taking off at 18.30, and all reached the target area, but S/L Nelms and crew were unable to locate their dropping zone and brought their mine back to base. S/L Tudor and crew planted their mine successfully, before dropping the wing bombs among vessels moored close to a jetty on the west coast of the island of Ushant off the Brittany coast. While the above was in progress, three Manchesters and twenty-one Whitleys turned their attention upon U-Boots at the base being built on the Keroman peninsula on the southern extremity of Lorient. The first phase of the massive construction project had begun just weeks earlier, and would continue until January 1942, by which time K1, K2 and K3 would be completed and capable of sheltering thirty vessels and their crews under cover. The complex would boast a revolutionary lift system, which could raise U-Boots from the water and transport them across the facility to repair and servicing bays. The thickness of the concrete roofs would render the structure impervious to the bombs available to Bomber Command at the time, and attacks would be directed predominantly at the town and its approaches to prevent access by road and rail.

The night of the 23/24th was moonless and attended by marginal weather conditions. On such nights, the policy was to send small forces to a number of targets to cause as much damage and disruption as possible, although in truth, these operations were generally ineffective and could be costly in aircraft and crews. Over sixty aircraft were sent to Berlin on this night, while thirty 5 Group Hampdens from Hemswell, Scampton, Lindholme and Coningsby targeted Kiel with little effect. 106 Squadron supported the operation with seven aircraft, which took off either side of 18.00 led by S/L Nelms. Sgt Topping and crew ran into severe icing conditions early on during the outward flight, compelling them to turn back, and they landed safely at Coningsby at 19.35. The remainder reached the target area to find intense searchlight activity and anti-aircraft fire that prevented an accurate assessment of their efforts. S/L Nelms and crew bombed from 12,000 feet, aiming at marshalling yards to the west of the inner docks basin, and, although F/L Boylan and crew could not make out their bomb bursts, they estimated that they fell also upon railway lines.

On the 29th, W/C Lindlay was posted to HQ 4 Group, although, it seems that he had already left 106 Squadron by this time. Also, on the 29th, the German cruisers Scharnhorst and Gneisenau were reported to be off Brest, and 50 Squadron was ordered to dispatch six Hampdens from Lindholme to carry out a cloud-cover daylight attack, a type of operation that would come to be known as "moling". The arrival of the vessels must have been expected, because Lindholme had been standing-by at two-hours readiness for seven days when the order was received. They flew out in two vics over the Lizard, until insufficient cloud cover over the Channel forced them to turn back. That night, twenty-five Hampdens were dispatched from Scampton, Waddington and Coningsby to mine the waters of the Jellyfish garden, the approaches to the port, thus beginning a long-running saga which would occupy the Command's attention for the next ten-and-a-half months. It was to become almost an obsession, and the first major operation against the raiders was mounted on the night of the 30/31st, when over a hundred aircraft were despatched, but scored no hits. 106 Squadron did not take part in the main attack, but contributed seven of ten Hampdens laying mines off the port. It was a late take-off either side of 01.00, with S/L Nelms again taking the lead. P/O Wareing and crew had to return early after experiencing W/T failure even before reaching the south coast, but the remainder pressed on in ten-tenths cloud and sleet showers to reach the target area. It was an intensely dark night, and this contributed to the inability of S/L Nelms and crew to locate the dropping zone and the return of their mine to store. F/O Price DFC was posted to 97 Squadron during the final week of the month, a move which kept him at Coningsby. During the course of the month the squadron participated in six bombing and two mining operations, and launched fifty-three sorties for the loss of a single aircraft and crew.

April 1941

The first week of the new month was reserved exclusively for operations on and around Brest with the intention of disabling its lodgers. It began with 5 Group launching a dozen Hampdens from a forward base at St Eval in Cornwall for a daylight attack on the 1st, when all but one turned back in the absence of cloud, and the one that continued on failed to return. 49 and 83 Squadrons sent six Hampdens each from their Scampton base to St Eval for another attempt on the 3rd, with similar results. Ninety other aircraft were made ready on the 3rd to attack the German cruisers that night, and returning crews reported that it had proved difficult to identify them. While that raid was in progress, 5 Group Hampdens conducted mining sorties in the waters off Brest (Jellyfish) and La Rochelle (Cinnamon).

On the 4th, Gneisenau entered a dry dock, which was to be drained on the following day for an inspection of the vessel, while, over at Coningsby and Waddington, eleven Hampdens and four Manchesters were called into action for yet another attempt on the enemy cruisers that night as part of a force of fifty-four aircraft. The relevance of the coming operation was made clear at briefings, when mention was made of the importance of winning the Battle of the Atlantic, and the "pep-talk" highlighted the heavy toll of merchant ships being lost to U-Boots, "even before surface raider are let loose upon our convoys". Also referred to were the recent mining operations off Brest to prevent Scharnhorst and Gneisenau from escaping into open sea, and the importance of destroying or crippling these enemy assets was made clear. The plan called for six of the eleven participating Hampdens to carry out standard high-level bombing runs, while five others, all volunteers, including the 106 Squadron crews of W/C Polglase, Sgts Topping and Osborne and P/O Wareing, sneaked in at low-level with 500lb semi-armour-piercing bombs (SAP). They got away from Coningsby between 19.00 and 19.20, and, on reaching the target area, P/O Wareing glided down to 1,000 feet, unfortunately, misjudging his approach, and bravely decided to go round again, this time to deliver an accurate attack. Sgt Topping dived down to just 50 feet, where his aircraft was hit by tracer, wounding the navigator, and he was forced to drop his bombs too early. Sgt Osborne arrived late on target, and chose not to go in at low level, while W/C Polglase, who, in the finest traditions of leadership, had put himself at the head of the low-level element, died with his crew after AD738 was hit by flak and crashed at Saint-Renan, some seven miles north-west of the target, presumably after carrying out an attack. One 44 Squadron crew claimed a direct hit on Scharnhorst, which was recognised in the flash of the detonation as being in a dry dock precisely as depicted in the reconnaissance photos shown to the crews at briefing. The rear gunner confirmed the success, but it was impossible to determine which part of the vessel had been hit. The crews in the medium to high-level element carried out their attacks from between 6,000 and 11,000 feet shortly after 22.00, and some of their bombs hit the Continental Hotel in the town just as dinner was being served, killing a number of naval officers.

When Gneisenau's dry dock was drained on the following day, the 5th, a single unexploded 500lb bomb was found nestling at the bottom, and the ship's captain, Kapitän-zur-See Otto Fein, decided to move his vessel out into the harbour while it was dealt with. The dock was refilled to allow Gneisenau to vacate it, and she was spotted by a reconnaissance aircraft at some point, which led to the planning of an operation by Coastal Command to be carried out at first light on the 6th. In the meantime, a daylight attack by elements of 5 Group on the 5th was thwarted by insufficient cloud cover. The Coastal Command operation took place in poor weather conditions, which led to the six Beauforts of 22 Squadron becoming separated while outbound, and F/O Kenneth Campbell and his crew alone pressed home an attack, which caused damage to Gneisenau that would require six months to repair. In the face of the most concentrated anti-aircraft fire, the Beaufort stood little chance of getting away with it, and was shot down without survivors. F/O Campbell was posthumously awarded a Victoria Cross for his actions. That evening, fifteen Hampdens from Scampton were dispatched to the Jellyfish garden off Brest, while four others were sent to one of the three Nectarine gardens off the Frisians and five from Waddington targeted the Beech garden off St-Nazaire.

The A Flight commander, S/L Nelms, stepped up to the helm, and remained temporarily in charge of 106 Squadron until the appointment of a new commanding officer. Sixty-one Hampdens were among a force of 229 aircraft sent to Kiel on the night of the 7/8th, and ten of them were contributed by 106 Squadron. F/Ls Boylan and Altmann were the senior pilots on duty, and they took off with the others between 19.50 and 20.15. They were to cross the English coast near Skegness, before setting course for Rømø Island on Denmark's western coast, where they would turn east to a position north of Flensburg to approach Kiel from the north. P/O Paramore and crew experienced W/T failure shortly after crossing the coast and turned back, leaving the others to encounter cloud at 6,000 feet for the first fifty miles of the North Sea crossing, but then clear skies for the remainder of the outward flight. Sgt Wotherspoon and crew were north of Heligoland when oxygen-supply failure curtailed their sortie, but the remainder pressed on to reach the target, which was bathed in brilliant moonlight, and all delivered their bombs in the face of a spirited flak defence, before returning home safely. It should be borne in mind that this period preceded the advent of the bomber stream, which would largely dictate routes, bombing heights and times-on-target. Currently, attacks could be spread over many hours, and the details left to the crew, squadron or group to determine. On this occasion, bombs were falling for five hours, and resulted in many fires and widespread damage. Two U-Boot yards suffered damage and loss of production, the eastern docks area was badly affected, and naval, industrial and civilian housing also suffered destruction.

Twenty-nine Hampdens and twelve Manchesters were included in a force of 160 aircraft made ready to send back to Kiel on the following night, four of the latter belonging to 5 Group's latest addition, 97 Squadron, which would be operating for the first time. 106 Squadron provided ten Hampdens, and they departed Coningsby between 20.15 and 20.30 with S/L Tudor the senior pilot on duty. Sgt Topping and crew returned early after a photo-flash device exploded on the wing, and they believed the problem to be more serious that it later turned out to be. The remainder followed a similar route to that of the previous night, passing through a band of icing-bearing cloud extending from the coast at between 3,000 and 6,000 feet, but this dispersed from 5 degrees east to leave clear skies and bright moonlight that enabled them to map-read after making landfall on the Jutland coast. They found the target in good visibility and well-defended, and some made glide attacks to aid accuracy, while others bombed from as high as 15,000 feet. The western U-Boot bunker had been marked on the target map with an X, and some crews witnessed a very large explosion followed by a column of black smoke, describing the target area as a mass of flames as they retreated to the west. S/L Tudor and crew were at 10,000 feet when their aircraft was hit by shrapnel from an exploding flak shell, which wounded the wireless operator in the leg, despite which, he was able to carry on, and a safe return was made at 03.10. Night-fighters were observed by the squadron's crews, but no engagements were reported. The town area bore the brunt of the attack on this night, and a long list was produced by local authorities of damaged buildings and disruption to utilities. The casualty figure of 125 dead and three hundred injured was probably the largest from a Bomber Command attack thus far in the war.

Coningsby was not involved in the operational activity on the 9th, when twenty-four Hampdens were detailed as part of an overall force of eighty aircraft to attack Berlin, while a single Manchester was prepared at Waddington to join eight other aircraft to target the shipbuilding yards at Vegesack, situated some eight miles downstream of the Weser to the north-west of Bremen city centre. Orders were received on some 5 Group stations on the 10th to prepare for a joint 4 and 5 Group effort against Düsseldorf that night involving fifty-three aircraft, for which twenty-nine Hampdens were detailed. The other operation on this night was another assault on Brest and its guest enemy warships, for which fifty-three aircraft also were made ready, including five Manchesters of 97 Squadron to represent 5 Group. 106 Squadron contributed seven Hampdens to the Düsseldorf endeavour, and they took off between 19.55 and 20.10 with S/L Nelms the senior pilot on duty. P/O Lakin and crew were back in the circuit a little more than an hour later after experiencing W/T failure, but the others pressed on to reach the southern edge of the Ruhr area, where, according to some, excellent conditions prevailed, while others insisted that industrial haze compromised the vertical visibility. S/L Nelms and crew described intense searchlight activity, but little flak, and they were among four from the squadron to bomb the target, P/O Paramore and crew specifying a glide approach to release their bombs from 10,000 feet. Five Hampdens failed to return, and two of them, both with experienced crews, were from 106 Squadron, the first time that two of its crews had been posted missing from a single operation. Each had the misfortune to be intercepted over Holland by Hptm Werner Streib of 1./NJG1 based at Venlo, and the first to fall to his guns was X3153, which crashed at 22.49 about eight miles north of Roermond. Sgt Osborne and one of his crew survived to be taken into captivity, but two others died in the wreckage. Twelve minutes later, X3148 came down near Weert some miles to the west of the first crash site, and Sgt West alone of his crew survived to join his squadron colleagues in enemy hands. By the end of the year Streib would have twenty-two kills to his credit, one more than the famed Helmut Lent, who operated from the "Wespennest" or wasp's nest at Leeuwarden in northern Holland, the town, incidentally, in which the famed so-called spy, "Mata Hari", had been born many years earlier. Meanwhile, at Brest, four bombs hit the under-repair Gneisenau on the starboard side of the forward superstructure, and, although only two detonated, seventy-two men were killed and ninety injured, sixteen of whom would not survive.

106 Squadron remained at home on the 12th, while a dozen Hampdens and six Manchesters were detailed to represent 5 Group in a force of sixty-six aircraft continuing the campaign against the enemy warships at Brest. A further fifteen Hampdens were detailed to participate in a raid with Wellingtons on Merignac aerodrome near Bordeaux, although, it is unlikely that the two elements were over the target at the same time. The Manchester's Rolls Royce Vulture engines were proving to be problematic, with overheating and component failures seriously affecting the squadrons' rate of serviceability. As a result, the first of a number of grounding orders was issued on the 13th, while investigations were carried out into the engine-bearing problem and modifications put in hand. This meant that no further operations would be undertaken by the type during what remained of the month. Seventeen Hampdens were made ready for mining duties in the Cinnamon garden off the port of La Rochelle that night, while their crews were being briefed to drop their wing-mounted bombs on a hotel south of Quiberon, which, presumably, was home to U-Boot personnel. 106 Squadron contributed seven of its own, which departed Coningsby in fine and clear conditions between 22.50 and 22.55 with S/L Nelms the senior pilot on duty, although he and his crew were back on the ground within thirty minutes after an engine failed. Cloud in the target area hampered identification of the dropping zone, and Sgt Topping failed to locate it, eventually jettisoning his mine into the sea. The force encountered searchlights and accurate flak from shore batteries and flak ships off the Ile-de-Re, and P/O Paramore's AD758 was hit while flying at 600 feet. The lower rear gunner, Sgt Sandom, was wounded, but continued to offer return fire to help the aircraft escape, and his actions were later said to be instrumental in its safe return. Sadly, despite receiving first-aid from the wireless operator, he died before Coningsby was reached. Sgt Howard and crew carried out their timed run from below 100 feet while under fire, but the rear gunner silenced the offending battery with a well-aimed burst of his own. Later, on the 14th, the awards of a DFC to P/O Wareing and a DFM to Sgt Furnell were announced, and these represented the first decorations to be bestowed upon active members of the squadron.

106 Squadron was not on the Order of Battle on the 15th, when Kiel was posted as the target for ninety-six aircraft, including nineteen Hampdens. The cloud at take-off dissipated over the North Sea, but returned to largely conceal ground features inland of the enemy coast. This created challenging conditions for crews attempting to establish pinpoints on their way across the Schleswig-Holstein peninsula, and many crews sought out alternative objectives for their bombs, while those reaching the target were unable to assess the outcome, and local reports would suggest an ineffective raid that had caused little damage.

Thirty minutes after midnight on the 16th, the crews of F/Ls Boylan and Altmann and Sgts Howard and Galloway departed Coningsby to plant mines in the Jellyfish garden off Brest. Conditions were described as excellent with bright moonlight, and all carried out their assigned tasks unopposed before returning safely home. Berlin was posted as the target for 118 aircraft on the 17th, thirty-nine of them Hampdens, of which seven belonged to 106 Squadron. This would be the first time for 106 Squadron over Germany's capital city, and it represented a momentous occasion in which every crew wanted to participate. The telephone exchange was one of two briefed aiming points, and the other, it is believed, was one of the main railway stations, and it was for the latter that the squadron crews were briefed. They departed Coningsby in the minutes either side of 20.30 with S/Ls Nelms and Tudor the senior pilots on duty, and accompanied by P/O Paramore and crew, who were bound for the Nectarine III garden off the eastern Frisians. They were routed out over Skegness and found themselves immediately in ten-tenths cloud at 12,000 feet until skirting the Dutch coastal region, where it began to disperse. S/L Nelms ran into heavy flak near Wilhelmshaven, and this, combined with poor visibility, persuaded him to abandon the attempt to reach the primary target and to seek out an alternative. He came upon the port of Cuxhaven, situated on the south-western bank of the Elbe estuary, and delivered his bombs there without observing the results. The others found clear skies over the border between southern Denmark and Germany, but haze blotted out ground detail as they made their way eastwards, where they ran into intense flak from the Baltic city of Lübeck. F/L Altmann and crew were defeated by the poor visibility and intense darkness and attacked Hannover as an alternative, leaving the remaining five crews to press on to Berlin, which they located without difficulty through haze, and bombed unopposed from around 11,000 to 12,000 feet. At debriefing, crews could only report having bombed in the general target area, blinded to an extent by searchlight glare, and a number observed fires. Having passed on what they knew to the Intelligence Section, they return to their billets to add the coveted target of Berlin to their logbooks. No valid assessment of the raid was possible, and any damage would have been slight. Meanwhile, P/O Paramore and crew had carried out their mining sortie off the Frisians, and dropped their wing bombs on the seaplane base on the island of Norderney. A total of eleven aircraft failed to return from the night's various operations, and this represented the highest loss to date in a single night. On the 19th, a number of crews carried out formation flying over Woodhall Spa and Horncastle in support of War Weapons Week.

While eleven Hampden crews were briefed to join fifty others to raid Cologne on the 20th, a further nine were detailed for mining duties in the Jellyfish garden off Brest. 106 Squadron supported the main event with seven Hampdens, which departed Coningsby between 23.55 and 00.10 with S/Ls Boylan and Altmann the senior pilots on duty. Neither was able to complete the operation, however, as first F/L Altmann and crew were forced to turn back with technical difficulties, and thick cloud prevented the crew of F/L Boylan from identifying the target, causing them to abandon their sortie. The crew of P/O Wareing was one of three from Coningsby to bomb the target, which they identified through gaps in the cloud from 10,000 feet, and the crews of Sgt Galloway and P/O Paramore also bombed as briefed, the former strafing an aerodrome near Aachen on the way home. Sgt Tilbury and crew also failed to locate the target through the thick cloud, and they dropped their bombs on an unidentified aerodrome as they made their way back towards the enemy coast. X2986 failed to return after crashing near Cologne, and there were no survivors from the crew of P/O Lakin.

Another assault by more than sixty aircraft, including ten Hampdens from Hemswell, was directed at Brest and its lodgers on the night of the 23/24th, and but most failed to identify the location of the vessels and bombed on approximate positions. In addition to the main event, fourteen Hampdens were assigned to gardening duties and were divided equally between Quiberon Bay, off the Biscay coast, and the Frisians. The Nectarine region encompassed the entire Frisian chain, and was divided into three gardens, Nectarine I from Texel to the eastern tip of Ameland, Nectarine II, from east of Ameland to Memmert, and Nectarine III, Juist to Wangerooge. The 106 Squadron element of seven was to represent 5 Group off Lorient (Artichoke), and departed Coningsby between 19.45 and 20.15 with F/L Altmann the senior pilot on duty. He and his crew were unable to locate the target in conditions of low cloud and intense darkness, but the others enjoyed greater success, and, after planting their vegetables, five of them delivered their wing bombs from low level onto buildings on the Quiberon Peninsula, south of the port.

106 Squadron remained at home on the night of the 24/25th, as ten Scampton crews set off for Kiel, six from Lindholme headed for the Daffodil garden in the southern straits of The Sound (Oresund) off Copenhagen, and three 44 Squadron freshmen joined three more from Lindholme for an attack on the docks and shipping at Le Havre. The Kiel raid was typical for the period, scattered and inconclusive, and demanded a follow-up attack twenty-four hours later by an initial force of sixty-two aircraft, ten of them Hampdens. 106 Squadron made ready six of its own, which departed Coningsby between 22.40 and 23.10 with S/L Nelms the senior pilot on duty. They encountered poor visibility and strong winds during the outward flight, and Sgt Tilbury and crew were forced to return early with an engine problem. S/L Nelms and crew failed to reach the target after the oxygen system failed in AD799, and they bombed the port of Emden as an alternative. F/L Boylan and crew became lost while searching for the target, and eventually abandoned the attempt and turned for home. Sgt Topping and crew were beaten by the visibility, and bombed an unidentified airfield on the Frisians on his way home, and only the crews of P/O Oliver and Sgt Galloway reached the primary target area to deliver their bombs.

Hamburg was a frequent destination throughout the war, and would receive its own mini campaign of six raids between the end of April and the middle of May. Twenty-eight Hampdens and twenty-two Wellingtons were prepared for an operation against it on the 26th, although, at this stage of the war, it is unlikely that they would have been scheduled to be over the target at the same time. The 106 Squadron crews of Sgts Howard and Wotherspoon and P/O Wareing departed Coningsby between 20.20 and 20.30, and soon encountered unfavourable weather conditions, characterized by strong winds and low cloud. The presence of ten-tenths cloud in the target area, with a base at around 6,000 feet, presented the usual challenges for aiming point identification, and this precluded any chance of delivering an accurate and effective attack. Sgt Howard opted for a glide approach, releasing his bombs on estimated position from 12,000 feet, while P/O Wareing and crew found the target area illuminated by a flare, which they presumed came from another aircraft, and bombed from 14,000 feet. Sgt Wotherspoon and crew commented on heavy flak from the Frisians on the way out, and, unable to see the target, they bombed a flak concentration in its vicinity. Most of the force bombed on estimated positions, observing detonations and a number of fires, while local sources estimated perhaps sixteen bomb loads and no major incidents.

Mannheim was the destination for seventy-one aircraft on the 29th, fourteen of them Hampdens, and this would prove to be final operation of the month for 106 Squadron. Seven of its Hampdens were made ready, and departed Coningsby between 20.45 and 21.05 with S/L Nelms the senior pilot on duty. Sgt Tilbury and crew were thwarted again by engine trouble, and were back on the ground within eighty minutes, leaving the others to press on to south-central Germany, guided, if they could see it, by the Rhine. Low ten-tenths cloud largely concealed the target, and it was the intense searchlight activity that confirmed its location. Bombing took place from between 7,000 and 12,000 feet in the face of surprisingly little flak, and it was possible to report only that bombs had been seen to burst in the vicinity of the target. The squadron operated twelve times during the month and dispatched eighty-four sorties for the loss of four aircraft and their crews and one gunner.

May 1941

Hamburg was to feature prominently during the first two weeks of May, and the first of five attacks on Germany's second city was posted on the 1st, only to be cancelled. It was reinstated on the following day, for which a force of ninety-five aircraft was made ready. The grounding order on the Manchester had been lifted, and three of the type representing 207 Squadron would join nineteen Hampdens as the 5 Group contribution. 106 Squadron was not involved in what was another inconclusive raid hampered by poor visibility, as a result of which, local sources mentioned thirteen large fires, but no significant damage. The squadron remained at home also on the following night, when 5 Group put up twenty-seven Hampdens and two Manchesters in an overall force of 101 aircraft bound for Cologne, while a predominantly Wellington force of thirty-three continued the assault on Brest and its lodgers. 106 Squadron appeared on the Order of Battle for the first time in the new month on the 4th, when detailing nine of twenty-one Hampdens for yet another attack on Brest, this time by an overall force of ninety-seven aircraft. The 5 Group ORB offered the thought that the warships must be crippled by now following repeated attacks, but effective camouflage and smoke screens ensured that the British authorities actually had no clear picture of the vessels' state of serviceability, and the raids would continue. The 106 Squadron crews departed Coningsby between 21.05 and 21.40 with S/L Tudor the senior pilot on duty, and arrived in the target area to encounter good weather conditions and visibility, which enabled all from Coningsby to identify the warships before carrying out an attack. The crews of S/L Tudor and Sgt Galloway claimed very near misses on the Scharnhorst which left large fires burning alongside her, and a number of direct hits were claimed by crews from other squadrons, but were not confirmed.

The teleprinters on 1, 3, 4 and 5 Group stations began churning out the orders of the day on the 5th, to reveal that Mannheim was to be the destination for a force of 141 aircraft, of which 5 Group's contribution amounted to thirty-three Hampdens and four Manchesters. 106 Squadron was not invited to take part in what developed into something of a lottery as crews struggled to establish their positions over the city and bombed largely on estimated positions. Although bursts and apparently large fires were observed by some, it was not possible to make a meaningful assessment of the results because of cloud and searchlight glare, and local sources would suggest that approximately twenty-five bomb loads had hit the city, causing only light damage. 115 aircraft were detailed for an attack on the Blohm & Voss shipyards in Hamburg on the 6th, an operation supported by 5 Group with twenty-seven Hampdens and four Manchesters. 106 Squadron made ready seven Hampdens, and sent them on their way to north-western Germany between 22.45 and 23.15 with S/L Nelms the senior pilot on duty and undertaking his final operation as the stand-in squadron commander. They all arrived in the target area to find ten-tenths cloud with an occasional break, which made pinpointing something of a challenge, and bombing took place either on e.t.a., or on the intense searchlight and flak activity. Five 106 Squadron crews were among eighty-one claiming to have positively identified and bombed the target in the face of intense opposition, and F/L Boylan and crew reported starting large fires, while Sgt Galloway saw his bombs burst between the docks and the Binnen-Alster Lake, a little to the north-west of the city centre and Altstadt districts.

On the 7th, W/C Bob Allen was posted in from his flight commander duties at 49 Squadron at Scampton to become the new commanding officer, allowing S/L Nelms to revert to his former role as A Flight commander. W/C Allen was to lay the foundations for later commanders to mould 106 Squadron into one of the finest units in the Command. He would not be required to preside over his first operation until the following day, as 106 Squadron was not called upon to provide aircraft and crews for the latest attempt on the warships at Brest. A force of eighty-nine aircraft was assembled, eighteen of them Hampdens, which was a reduced figure in the light of a forecast of adverse weather conditions in the 5 Group area for returning aircraft. In the event, the weather turned out to be more favourable than expected, particularly in the target area, where moonlight enabled some crews to identify the dry dock occupied by one of the vessels. On return, some crews reported bomb bursts in the docks area, while others were blinded by searchlight glare, and the claims of direct hits remained unconfirmed.

All 5 Group operational stations received orders on the following day, the 8th, to prepare aircraft for what would be a record-breaking night of activity involving 364 sorties. 188 aircraft were to attack Hamburg, 119 of them assigned to the Blohm & Voss shipyards in the Finkenwerder district to the west of the city centre, and sixty-nine to target the city itself, while 133 Whitleys and Wellingtons attended to the A.G. Weser U-Boot construction yards in Bremen. 5 Group contributed a record seventy-eight Hampdens and nine Manchesters to the Hamburg force, nine of the former representing 106 Squadron, their crews having been briefed to attack the shipyards. They departed Coningsby between 22.40 and 23.05 with S/Ls Nelms and Tudor the senior pilots on duty, but S/L Nelms was forced to turn back when his wireless operator became ill, and they were back on the ground just thirty-five minutes after leaving it. The others flew out over the Lincolnshire coast on course for Neumünster, intending to approach the target from the north, with conditions promising to offer a reasonable chance of identifying the aiming point. Sgt Wotherspoon was another to become indisposed before reaching the target, and he dropped his bombs on the northern end of the island of Sylt after turning for home. The others found the target without difficulty in good visibility, and described the defence as intense but inaccurate as they delivered their bombs from an average of 15,000 feet between 02.00 and 03.00. Bomb bursts were observed in the general area of the briefed aiming point and in the docks, and fifty fires were counted by one rear gunner, while Sgt Howard and crew claimed a direct hit on the aiming point with a 1,900 pounder, before being attacked by a night-fighter, which, ultimately, was evaded. Local sources confirmed that an accurate and effective raid had taken place, reporting eighty-three fires, thirty-eight of them large, ten apartment blocks demolished by a 4,000 pounder, and the highest death toll yet in a German city of 185 people.

During the course of the 9th, a force of 146 aircraft was assembled for that night's operation against the twin cities of Mannheim and Ludwigshafen, for which 5 Group would contribute twenty-four Hampdens and eleven Manchesters. The aiming point for the 5 Group element was the Badische Anilin & Soda-Fabrik (BASF) works in Ludwigshafen, which was part of the infamous I G Farben company, the largest manufacturer of chemicals and synthetic oil products in the world and major employer of slave workers. 106 Squadron made ready five Hampdens for the main event and another for the crew of Sgt Lockyer to take mining in the Nectarine III garden off the eastern Frisians. They departed Coningsby together between 22.25 and 22.35 with P/Os Oliver and Paramore the senior officers on duty and three Sgt pilots captaining the other Ludwigshafen-bound crews. They followed the same route as for the recent Mannheim operation, enjoying favourable conditions all the way into south-central Germany, where they encountered a little low cloud in the target area, which may well have been smoke drifting across the Rhine from Mannheim. Bombing took place from between 8,000 and 10,000 feet, mostly after a glide approach, and two crews claimed direct hits on their aiming points. Local reports would confirm that some useful industrial damage had been inflicted on both cities, and more than 3,500 people had been left homeless. While this operation was in progress, Sgt Lockyer and crew delivered their 1,500lb mine in the briefed location, and machine-gunned an enemy vessel off the island of Juist.

Hamburg was posted to face its fourth major operation of the month on the 10th, for which a force of 119 aircraft was assembled and the crews briefed to aim for shipyards, the Altona power station (Tiefstack) and the general city area. 5 Group put up thirty-five Hampdens and a 97 Squadron Manchester for the main operation, and six Manchesters for Berlin as part of a force of twenty-three aircraft. Conditions over Germany's Second City were described as perfect for an effective attack, returning crews offering enthusiastic reports about the outcome, and local sources confirmed that 128 fires had broken out, forty-seven of them classed as large, and extensive damage had resulted in the city centre.

Having sat out this operation, 106 Squadron's crews were fully rested and eager to find out what awaited them at briefing on the 11th. They learned that there would be no respite for Germany's Second City as plans were already in hand to send ninety-two aircraft back there, while eighty-one others, including thirty-one Hampdens and two Manchesters, sought out one of the Deutsche Schiff und Maschinenbau Aktien Gesellschaft shipyards in Bremen. Abbreviated to Deschimag, this had been formed in the mid-twenties as a co-operation of eight shipyards to compete with the Blohm & Voss and Bremer Vulkan yards. The largest was the A G Weser company, which, after six of the others had fallen by the wayside before the outbreak of war, was partnered only by the Seebeckwerft, now as part of the Krupp empire, after that organisation had been handed a controlling interest in 1941. Seven 106 Squadron Hampdens were made ready and took off between 22.10 and 22.30, led for the first time by W/C Allen. They met heavy opposition from the ground as they arrived in the target area, and W/C Allen and crew were coned by searchlights and subjected to a flak barrage. They made a straight and level run across the aiming point, and released their bombs from 10,000 feet without observing the results. In contrast, Sgt Galloway and crew released their bombs from 7,000 feet after a glide approach, and reported the position of a convoy spotted on the way home. Eagle-eyes in P/O Paramore's crew saw their incendiaries burst in the target area, and the high explosives on a foundry and engine shop, creating large fires. Sgt Lockyer and crew were unable to identify the target, and dropped their bombs on riverside buildings south of the target. Local reports confirmed that many bombs had fallen in the docks area, where a floating dock belonging to the A G Weser Company had been sunk. The main damage, however, was inflicted on the city, where housing was the principal victim. The Hamburg operation had also been effective, causing eighty-eight fires and damage mostly to residential property.

Mannheim and Ludwigshafen were posted again as the primary targets on the 12th, for which a force of 105 aircraft was divided 65/40 between the two cities, and would involve forty-one Hampdens and four Manchesters, most of the crews of which were briefed to employ the BASF plant in Ludwigshafen as the aiming point. They flew out across Belgium, and reached the target area to find thick haze obscuring ground features, and this combined with intense searchlight and flak activity to prevent most crews from identifying the aiming point. At least sixteen crews abandoned their attempt on the primary target and headed north to attack Cologne as an alternative, and local sources estimated that only around ten bomb loads had fallen within the primary target area, causing minor damage.

The weather precluded operations on the following two nights, during which period, news came through from the International Red Cross on the 14th concerning the fate of some of the crews failing to return during April. It confirmed the deaths of P/O Lakin and crew, and the survival in captivity of Sgts West and Osborne and one of Sgt Osborne's gunners. On the 15th, the northern city of Hannover was posted as the target for 101 aircraft, for which 5 Group detailed twenty-seven Hampdens, while a simultaneous raid on Berlin involved eight Manchesters and six Stirlings. The briefed aiming point for the latter was the main post office and telephone exchange, which, in reality, identified this as an area attack. A record twelve 106 Squadron Hampdens had been made ready for Hannover, but doubts about the weather caused the withdrawal of four less-experienced crews. S/Ls Boylan and Altmann were the senior pilots on duty as the squadron contingent got away from Coningsby between 22.15 and 22.30, only to lose the services of Sgt Wotherspoon and crew to oxygen system failure, and P/O Wareing and crew with engine trouble. F/L Boylan and crew missed their navigation point on the Dutch coast, and went on to bomb Emden as an alternative, while the others pressed on eastwards into northern Germany, where they were able to locate the target area, but were prevented by cloud from identifying the briefed aiming point. The crews had been instructed, somewhat optimistically, to aim for the main post office and telephone exchange, but bombs were dropped blind, and no results were observed. With this operation, Sgt Galloway completed two hundred hours of operational flying to finish his first tour, and was the first to achieve this milestone entirely in the service of 106 Squadron. S/L Tudor and F/O Price spent much of the afternoon of the 16th engaged in a search for the crew of a 97 Squadron Manchester, which was believed to have come down in the North Sea, but nothing was found, and two bodies washed ashore on the Danish coast sometime later confirmed its fate.

While 106 Squadron remained at home, 5 Group contributed twenty-four Hampdens to a force of ninety-three aircraft bound for Cologne on the night of the 16/17th, but the operation was ruined by adverse weather conditions. A force of ninety-five aircraft, including twenty-three Hampdens, was assembled to return to the same target twenty-four hours later, again without involvement by 106 Squadron and, indeed, Manchesters, after an order issued earlier in the day had forced the withdrawal of the type from operational activity, while intensive testing was carried out to identify and solve persistent problems, particularly with regard to the unreliable Rolls-Royce Vulture engines. 106 Squadron's P2099 experienced difficulties during a training flight in the afternoon, and stalled and crashed at 15.45, while trying to make an emergency landing at Uffington in the county of Rutland. P/O Harvey and two of his crew died in the wreckage, while the wireless operator sustained serious injuries. The Cologne operation went ahead that night, and the absence of a moon created extreme darkness, which, together with searchlight glare, thwarted the efforts of most crews to locate the aiming point. According to local sources, bombs were widely scattered across the city, resulting in some damage to housing and public and commercial buildings, mostly in districts south of the city centre.

When Kiel was posted as the target for seventy aircraft on the 18th, 5 Group responded with eighteen Hampdens, including a record twelve representing 106 Squadron. At briefings, the shipyards were designated as the aiming point, for which the 106 Squadron element departed Coningsby between 22.25 and 22.50 with F/L Altmann the senior pilot on duty. They flew out over the North Sea in unfavourable weather conditions, in which P/O Paramore and crew were unable to establish a pin-point on the enemy coast, and decided instead to make for Hamburg, where they dropped their bombs on the Blohm & Voss shipyards. Sgt Tilbury and crew suffered the failure of their oxygen system, and turned their attention upon a searchlight concentration on the island of Terschelling. The remaining ten Coningsby crews pressed on to the target area, where they met low cloud and haze, and delivered their bombs blindly through cloud and haze in the face of a spirited opposition.

The weather kept the Command on the ground during the ensuing four nights, while Blenheims carried out daylight "Circus" operations and shipping sweeps. On the 22nd, ten 44 Squadron crews at Waddington were put on stand-by for a possible operation against German surface raiders, which, although not named, were the battleship Bismarck and heavy cruiser Prinz Eugen. They had put to sea on operation "Rheinübung", which for Bismarck, would be its first offensive action, and were being shadowed by Coastal Command aircraft as they slipped out of Bergen, heading for the Denmark Straits between Greenland and Iceland. In the event, the Waddington crews were not required and were stood down. Orders were received on the 23rd to prepare for another attack on Cologne, for which a force of fifty-one aircraft included a 5 Group contribution of twenty-four Hampdens. 106 Squadron made ready a dozen of its own, and dispatched them from Coningsby between 23.15 and 23.30 with S/L Nelms the senior pilot on duty and first off the ground. They headed via corridor "G" for landfall over the Scheldt estuary, and encountered poor visibility as they crossed Belgium, some crews deciding early on that they would seek an alternative target. The 106 Squadron element reached the primary target area, where ten-tenths cloud largely obscured the ground, forcing ten of them to bomb on estimated positions from around 12,000 to 17,000 feet between 01.00 and 02.00, without being able to observe the results. Sgt Hadland and crew couldn't positively identify their position and flew north to drop their bombs on Düsseldorf as an alternative, while Sgt Clark and crew attacked Gilze-Rijen aerodrome in southern Holland. Local sources in Cologne reported only a few bombs falling within the city and causing damage to twenty-five houses.

5 Group operated alone on the 25th, committing forty-eight Hampdens to mine the approaches to Brest and St-Nazaire, (Jellyfish and Beech gardens), the former, in particular, anticipating the arrival of the

Bismarck, which, according to cyphers decoded at Bletchley Park, was racing for sanctuary with the Royal Navy snapping at its heels and determined to avenge the shocking sinking of HMS Hood on the 24th. In fact, the Bismarck's rudder would be crippled by a torpedo from a Fleet Air Arm Swordfish from the aircraft carrier, HMS Victorious, during the 26th, rendering the vessel unable to manoeuvre, and restricted to a top speed of ten knots. 5 Group ordered thirty-eight Hampdens to continue mining the approaches to Brest that night, the 106 Squadron ORB describing this operation as being indirectly part of the plan to avenge the Hood by destroying the battleship Bismarck. 106 Squadron made ready a new record of thirteen Hampdens, and sent them on their way from Coningsby between 22.10 and 23.05 with F/L Boylan the senior pilot on duty, but he and his crew returned almost immediately with technical problems. The others flew out via Chesil Beach on the Dorset coast, before crossing the Brest peninsula to attempt to pick up their pinpoints for the timed runs. Once again, the weather conditions were unhelpful, with a layer of five to eight-tenths cloud at between 1,000 and 8,000 feet dispensing hail and rain, despite which, all but three of the Coningsby crews located the garden, some assisted by shore-based searchlights after spending a considerable time searching. The vegetables were planted from around 400 to 1,000 feet in a ninety-minute slot to approximately 03.00, and all but one returned safely to make their reports. Returning low on fuel, P2083 crashed during an emergency landing at Wellesbourne Mountford in Warwickshire, killing the pilot, Sgt Forty, and seriously injuring his navigator. This was Sgt Forty's maiden operation as crew captain after completing the requisite number of sorties as second pilot, which, in a Hampden, meant performing the duties of navigator/bomb-aimer.

In the event, the pride of the Germany navy would never come within range of Brest. At first light on the 27th, multiple units of the Royal Navy closed in on the helpless ship, and, from 08.47, engaged her with guns and torpedoes until she slipped beneath the waves at 10.39. This left her consort, Prinz Eugen, at large, and the mining at Brest would continue over the succeeding nights in case she put in an appearance. The squadron operated on nine nights during the course of the month, and dispatched eighty-three sorties for the loss of two Hampdens on home soil, neither as the result of enemy action.

June 1941

The pattern of operations would remain largely the same during June, generally with small to medium-sized forces attacking three or more different targets simultaneously. Düsseldorf provided the objective for 150 aircraft for the first major operation of the month on the night of the 2/3rd, for which 106 Squadron contributed a dozen Hampdens. They took off from Coningsby between 22.45 and 23.10 with no senior pilots on duty, and, after exiting the English coast at Orfordness, most set course for Brussels, while a few headed directly for the southern Ruhr, all having to contend with far from ideal weather conditions. Sgt Lyon and crew lost their starboard engine while flying through a snowstorm, and were forced to abandon the sortie, jettison the bombs and return home. A layer of ten-tenths cloud stretched along the entire route at 2,000 feet, with broken medium cloud at 9,000 feet and another band at 17,000 feet, but this dispersed sufficiently to leave six to eight-tenths in the target area, through which glimpses of the Rhine provided an indication of the location of Düsseldorf. P/O Harwood and crew were unable to positively identify the target, and dropped their bombs on Duisburg at the western edge of the Ruhr as they headed for home. The remaining ten delivered their bombs on estimated positions through low cloud in the face of considerable searchlight and flak activity, Sgt Tilbury and crew having spotted the Rhine through a gap to provide some sense of their location. P/O Abbott lost the central panel of his windscreen to shrapnel, which added to the challenges that rendered it impossible to observe any results in the conditions other than the glow of a fire or two, but, at least, all returned home bringing with them a distinct lack of confidence that their efforts had borne fruit. In that regard they were correct, but what they were ignorant of, was the fact that the results of attacks during this month and July were being scrutinized, and the findings were to be published in a report.

Thereafter, 5 Group, and, in fact, most of the Command, was kept on the ground by an unprecedented period of adverse weather conditions during the best part of the moon period. Despite the inherent dangers of their job, the absence of operations was a source of monotony and massive frustration for crews, which was tempered to an extent at 106 Squadron on this occasion by its expansion through the addition of a third or C Flight, commanded by the newly promoted S/L Tommy Boylan. This would mean the squadron having an increased presence on operations, the first evidence of which would be made manifest on the night of the 11/12th. In the meantime, other squadrons were cheered by the news on the 10th that Brest would be the target that night for thirty-nine Hampdens in company with sixty-five Wellingtons and Whitleys, which would not have been over the target at the same time. The Scharnhorst and Gneisenau had been joined by Bismarck's former consort, Prinz Eugen, which had spent the previous two weeks evading British attempts to locate her and bestow upon her a similar fate to that of Bismarck. The defenders activated an effective smoke screen, which, together with skilful camouflage, obscured the target vessels, and, despite claims by some crews of direct hits, none was confirmed.

Düsseldorf and Duisburg were posted as the primary targets on the 11th, for which forces of ninety-eight and eighty aircraft respectively were made ready, the former to be targeted by 1 and 3 Groups and the latter by 4 and 5 Groups. 5 Group contributed thirty-five Hampdens, a new record of eighteen of them representing 106 Squadron, which also loaded an additional two with a mine each for the crews of Sgt Brownbill and P/O Baker to take to the Nectarine I garden off Terschelling in the western Frisians. The two elements departed Coningsby together between 22.45 and 23.20, with S/L Nelms the senior pilot on duty, and among other pilots making their operational debut was one of particular note. P/O David Maltby would soon be on his way across the tarmac to 97 Squadron, from which unit, in March 1943, he would be posted to become a founder member of 617 Squadron. He would take part in Operation Chastise, the epic attack on the Ruhr dams on the night of the 16/17th May, when his bomb would seal the fate of the Möhne Dam. Now, he was just setting out on his operational career, with thoughts on this night of doing the job to the best of his ability and returning his aircraft and crew safely home. They flew out over Skegness, climbing through five tenths ice-bearing cloud in a layer between 5,000 and 9,000 feet, and, once over enemy territory, found themselves in a race with a sheet of ten-tenths low cloud to reach the target first. Those ahead of the eastern edge of the front enjoyed the benefits of good visibility and bright moonlight to assist their map-reading, and found the target with ease by the fires already burning, while the others, beaten to the target by the cloud, would have to bomb on estimated positions. Sixteen of the 106 Squadron crews arrived to find the target partially obscured by cloud, and met with a spirited response from the defences in the form of heavy flak and searchlights. With accuracy out of the question, they could only deliver their bombs in the general vicinity of the city, P/O Maltby and crew reporting a bombing height of 15,000 feet, which was higher than the others, who were mostly at 11,000 or a little above. P/O Henderson and crew failed to identify the target, and dropped their bombs on the little town of Wipperfürth, situated on the southern fringe of the Ruhr south-east of Remscheid, and another attacked Essen as an alternative. Returning crews reported fires, and that the new 2,000 pounders exploded with a large orange flash. No information came out of Duisburg to provide a clue as to the outcome, but Cologne reported extensive damage to its main railway station, the docks area and 173 houses as a result of becoming the alternative target of choice for the Düsseldorf force. While this operation was in progress, the crews of P/O Baker and Sgt Brownbill, each of which was operating together as a crew for the first time, planted their vegetables as briefed, and returned safely.

The following night was devoted predominantly to attacks on railway yards at four locations in Germany to the east and north of the Ruhr and involved a total of 339 aircraft. 5 Group committed most of its available Hampden force, amounting to ninety-one aircraft, to the important hub at Soest, a town situated just to the north of the Möhne reservoir, while 1 and 3 Groups were handed those at nearby Hamm and at Osnabrück, some forty miles further north. 4 Group was to target the marshalling yards at Schwerte, south of Dortmund, and a small Halifax element was assigned to the so-called "Buna" works, a chemicals and synthetic rubber plant at Marl-Hüls on the north-eastern edge of the Ruhr. 106 Squadron made ready eighteen Hampdens for Soest, and they departed Coningsby between 23.10 and 23.50 with W/C Allen the senior pilot on duty for the first time, and S/Ls Boylan and Tudor also on the Order of Battle. They were routed out over Skegness, to proceed across the North Sea via corridor "B" and make landfall on the Dutch coast north of Rotterdam, during which they encountered large stretches of medium cloud extending from 5,000 to 12,000 feet. S/L Tudor and P/O Baker were forced to return early with technical failures, leaving the others to press on, but, in conditions of poor visibility, only six crews were able to locate the general area of the briefed target to deliver their bombs. Among them was that of S/L Boylan, who dropped their high explosives and incendiaries from 13,000 feet. Sgt Hadland and crew were at 8,000 feet, and observed their bombs bursting across the target, while P/O Robinson and his crew released theirs from 6,000 feet, and felt, as well as saw, the resulting explosions. W/C Allen and crew made four runs across the target at 5,000 feet, and watched two bombs burst on the tracks, and the crew of P/O Paramore also hit the marshalling yards, in their case from 1,000 feet. P/O Henderson and crew went lowest of all, down to 850 feet, and observed their bombs bursting along the tracks and the incendiaries start a fire. Of the other crews, four joined in the Wellington attack on nearby Hamm, where they experienced intense flak and searchlight activity, two bombed a railway junction at Wesel on the German side of the Rhine north of the Ruhr, and one each attacked Essen and Recklinghausen in the Ruhr and Gilze-Rijen aerodrome in southern Holland.

A major assault on the enemy warships at Brest was notified across 1, 3 and 5 Group stations on the 13th, and resulted in the assembling of a force of 110 aircraft, of which, thirty-seven were Hampdens. 106 Squadron did not participate, but prepared ten Hampdens on the 14th for a 5 Group effort that night by twenty-nine aircraft for the first of four raids on consecutive nights against Cologne, a city that would continue to be a popular destination throughout the month. F/L Altmann was the senior pilot on duty as they departed Coningsby between 23.20 and 23.30, but the crews of P/Os Oliver and Paramore and Sgt Haggar all returned early with technical difficulties. The others ran into ten-tenths low cloud with broken medium cloud up to 9,000 feet over the entire route, and not one crew was able to positively identify the target, which was probably one of the many marshalling yards in the city. The remaining seven Coningsby crews bombed on estimated positions from heights ranging from 11,000 to 20,000 feet, the latter that of P/O Henderson, guided largely by searchlight and flak activity, and all returned safely with little of value to pass on to the Intelligence Section.

Düsseldorf and Cologne were targeted on the night of the 15/16th, the first of seven occasions during the second half of the month on which the two cities would be attacked simultaneously. Forty-nine Wellingtons and forty-two Hampdens took off for the latter, the 106 Squadron element of sixteen departing Coningsby between 22.50 and 23.10 with S/L Nelms the senior pilot on duty. Sgt Lyon and crew were forced to turn back early with an overheating engine, leaving the remainder to press on in conditions of ten-tenths cloud, which persisted all the way to the target. Bombing took place from between 5,000 and 15,000 feet on estimated positions helped by the glow of searchlights and flak bursts, but most of it fell outside of the city. The only loss was the squadron's AD863, which disappeared without trace into the North Sea, taking with it the crew of P/O Dickie. While this operation was in progress P/O Walker and crew headed for the Frisians to lay a mine in company with three Hampdens from other units, but, finding the cloud base to be at only 300 feet, they brought their weapon home. In the late morning of the 16th, the crews of F/O Price and P/O Robinson took off to conduct a search for the missing Hampden, and the latter spent eight hours over the North Sea, for a time within sight of the Dutch coast, sadly to no avail.

It was Cologne and Düsseldorf again on the night of the 16/17th, when forty-three Hampdens and thirty-three Whitleys took off to return to the former, while fifty-seven Wellingtons were dispatched to the latter. 106 Squadron stayed at home on a night when thick ground haze created poor visibility, which prevented most crews from locating their respective targets, and the few bomb loads to find the mark caused only minor damage. At 11.55 on the 17th, W/C Allen took off in P2129 to carry out a bomb-load test, carrying two 2,000 pounders with a complete crew and full petrol tanks. He attained an altitude of 14,200 feet in one hour and forty minutes, and returned to declare that such a bomb load was practicable. That night, a force of forty-three Hampdens and thirty-three Whitleys took off for Cologne to continue the campaign against the Rhineland capital, while more than fifty Wellingtons targeted Düsseldorf. 106 Squadron dispatched a record nineteen Hampdens between 22.50 and 23.35 with S/L Tudor the senior pilot on duty, but he and the crews of P/O Baker and Sgt Haggar were compelled to return early because of technical problems. Weather conditions generally were good, but thick ground haze was present, and, although this did not hamper identification of the target area, it did prevent accurate bombing. Fifteen crews returned to Coningsby to report bombing from between 7,000 and 15,000 feet, some remarking on intense searchlight activity but little flak. P/O Wareing and crew carried out a glide attack and released their bombs from 12,000 feet, before being forced down by searchlights and flak to weave their way out of the target area at a lowly 4,000 feet. Sgt Bannister and crew were unable to reach Cologne in time, so attacked Eindhoven aerodrome in southern Holland as an alternative, causing a large fire to break out.

An unspecified aiming point in Bremen was posted as the target for a hundred aircraft on the 18th, for which 5 Group made a contribution of thirty-nine Hampdens, although, none representing 106 Squadron. Low cloud hindered attempts to locate the target, and returning crews reported a ring of dummy fires up to twenty miles outside of Bremen, and the employment also of dummy flares to draw the bombing away from the city. It was another inconclusive raid, typical of the period, and cost six aircraft and crews. The country was now basking in a spell of very hot weather, which began on the 19th, and would continue through the 23rd. 115 aircraft set off for Kiel on the 20th in search of the battleship Tirpitz, and among them were twenty-four Hampdens, which flew out over the Lincolnshire coast on course for landfall on the western coast of the Schleswig-Holstein peninsula. Ten-tenths cloud completely obscured the ground in the target area, preventing any hope of locating Tirpitz, and attention was turned instead upon the general area of the town.

It was not until the 21st that the Manchester was once more declared fit for operations after almost five weeks on the side lines. During the course of the day, a record number of eighteen was made ready to target the docks at Boulogne, and this figure included a contribution from 61 Squadron, which would be blooding the type for the first time. The night's operations would demonstrate the problems facing the Command, and would feature prominently in the forthcoming report on its performance. Sixty-eight aircraft set out for Cologne, while twenty-eight Hampdens and twenty-eight Whitleys turned their attention upon the marshalling yards at Düsseldorf, 106 Squadron supporting the latter with a new record of twenty aircraft led by S/L Nelms. The ORB recorded triumphantly all twenty aircraft getting away in a group-record time of fourteen and a half minutes, although the individual take-off times recorded in the log entries suggested at least twenty minutes. Sgt Clark and crew were forced to return early, but the others carried on to reach the target area after flying through the protective belt of searchlights and flak, and experienced difficulty in establishing their position, even the Rhine proving to be elusive in the hazy conditions. Fires provided the best reference, and bombing was carried out with the aid of flares, although, without observing the results. Some crews claimed to have identified the marshalling yards, while others were unable to pick out any ground detail at all. S/L Nelms and crew encountered fierce flak over the target, and were forced down to 2,500 feet to escape, before delivering their bombs from 3,000 feet and observing them to burst in the target area. Returning crews reported many fires, while local sources barely noticed that a raid had taken place and mentioned only two bomb loads falling and breaking windows. It was a similar story at Cologne, where none of the five hundred high explosives or five thousand incendiaries found the mark. P/O Herd and crew were compromised by engine problems and attempted to bomb the docks at Dunkerque, only for the load to fall short.

On the 22nd, the squadron was informed that it might be required to carry out daylight operations, and a training programme was immediately put into effect that included formation flying. That night, Bremen was the destination for twenty-five Hampdens in company with Wellingtons, and this operation was another abject failure. Kiel, Cologne and Düsseldorf were posted as the targets for modest forces on the following night, the last-mentioned for a 5 Group effort against railway yards involving thirty Hampdens and eleven Manchesters. After a brief period off the Order of Battle, 106 Squadron returned to the fray on the 24th to participate in an operation that night by twenty-five Hampdens and twenty-three Wellingtons against Kiel, where the naval dockyards in general and the Deutsche Werke shipyards in particular, were the objectives, while other elements of the Command continued their attempts to cause serious damage at Cologne and Düsseldorf, the last-mentioned the destination for the Manchester brigade. 106 Squadron committed fourteen Hampdens to the Kiel operation, which, in view of the likelihood of encountering enemy night-fighters in the favourable conditions, were to proceed much of the way to the target in formation. They took off in their boxes, two of four aircraft each and two of three, and all were airborne within eight-and-a-half minutes either side of 22.30, with S/L Boylan the senior pilot on duty. They exited the English coast near Skegness and set course for Rømø island on the western coast of South Jutland in accordance with the plan to fly to a predetermined map reference, before breaking up for the final approach to the target. From the west coast of Jutland, they flew eastwards to the Baltic to approach the target from the north, and, despite thick haze and intense searchlight and flak activity, eleven of the 106 Squadron element found it without major difficulty and bombed from between 7,000 and 14,000 feet in the face of intense light and heavy flak bursting at up to 13,000 feet. P/O Maltby and crew, who were operating with the squadron for the final time, suffered engine problems, and jettisoned their load into the sea before returning home. Sgt Lyon and crew were unable to locate the target, and, as an alternative, bombed the town of Kappeln, situated on the Schleswig-Holstein peninsula south-east of Flensburg. Sgt Tilbury and crew, likewise, were unable to find their aiming point, and dropped the bombs on a flak concentration. Sgt Wotherspoon and crew ran into a heavy flak barrage over Sylt, and were forced down to 1,000 feet to escape, before eventually reaching the target to bomb from 4,000 feet.

Yet again, Kiel, Cologne and Düsseldorf were selected as the targets on the 26th, and, on this occasion, it was for the important naval stronghold on the eastern side of the Schleswig-Holstein peninsula that eighteen Manchester crews were briefed, while thirty Hampden crews learned of their part in the operation against marshalling yards at Düsseldorf. The Manchester crews were told that they would have fifteen Stirlings and eight Halifaxes for company, although, not necessarily over the target at the same time, and the Hampden crews would share their target with 1 Group Wellingtons. On a night of cloud, snow, electrical storms and icing conditions up to 16,000 feet, many crews were persuaded to turn back or seek out alternative targets, and few of those bound for the Ruhr and the Rhineland reached their objective.

Continuing the maritime theme, the night of the 27/28th was devoted to Bremen and its northern district of Vegesack, where major ship-building yards were located. The Vegesack force consisted of twenty-eight Hampdens, of which a dozen were provided by 106 Squadron. They began taking off shortly after 23.00, and made their way to the target area in very unpleasant weather conditions, which included storms and icing. Nine aircraft delivered their bombs in the target area, some clearly identifying the shipyards in cloudy conditions, and others not. There were reports of large explosions and fires, and two claims of direct hits, in addition to which, a 2,000 pounder was seen to burst on or very close to the aiming point. The crews of P/O Walker and Sgt Purnell bombed the main city of Bremen after failing to locate their briefed targets, and F/L Sharp, the senior pilot on duty, bombed the Luftwaffe fighter aerodrome at Leeuwarden as a last resort. Crews returning from Bremen reported intense night-fighter activity, the first time that special mention had been made of this kind of defence. Fourteen aircraft failed to return home, a new record loss in a single night, and eleven of the casualties were Whitleys. While all of this was going on, Sgt Mooney was undertaking his first sortie as crew captain, and had been briefed to mine the waters of one of the Nectarine gardens off the Frisians. The night went well for the freshman crew, who returned safely to report some opposition from a flak ship, but a successful maiden operation.

Bremen was selected again to host an operation on the night of the 29/30th, for which a force of 106 aircraft was made ready, nine of thirty Hampdens provided by 106 Squadron, the number somewhat depleted because of the need to train crews for the forthcoming daylight operations mentioned earlier. The crews were briefed to aim for the Deschimag shipyards, and departed Coningsby between 23.10 and 23.20 with no senior pilots on duty, before crossing the Lincolnshire coast to encounter cloud over the North Sea. Those reaching the target area found it to be largely free of cloud, but ground haze created challenging conditions for navigation and target location on a night of otherwise fine weather and excellent horizontal visibility. Sgt Hadland and crew were attacked by an enemy night-fighter over Groningen in Holland while outbound, but AD925 made a safe return to Coningsby bearing the scars of battle and with its crew intact. Sgt Purnell and crew were also forced to return early with an engine problem in AD929, while Sgt Mooney and crew were unable to identify their aiming point, and dropped their bombs on warehouses on the west bank of the Weser, starting three large fires. Four crews positively identified and bombed the target, and, whether or not F/O Baker and crew did also is uncertain, as AD895 was dispatched by a night-fighter north-west of Hamburg, and there were no survivors. The latest grounding order on the Manchester was issued on the 30th, and the type's crews began to look with envy upon the trusty old Hampden. The squadron operated ten times during the month, dispatching 152 sorties for the loss of two aircraft and crews.

July 1941

Having been prominent during the final few days of June, it fell to Bremen to open the Command's July account on the night of the 2/3rd, while smaller forces targeted Cologne and Duisburg. The last-mentioned was an all-Hampden affair, for which 106 Squadron provided thirteen aircraft in an overall force of thirty-nine. They were briefed to aim for the marshalling yards and were given Cologne and Düsseldorf as alternative targets should weather conditions prove too challenging at the primary. They departed Coningsby between 23.00 and 23.10 with S/L Boylan the senior pilot on duty, and flew out over Skegness to make landfall via corridor "B" on the Den Helder peninsula, where they turned to the south-east to run across Holland and the Rhine to the target area. Sgt Brownbill and crew were forced to turn back because of an engine issue shortly after crossing the Dutch coast, leaving the rest to press on in fine weather with some cloud. On their arrival over the western Ruhr, they were greeted by seven-tenths cloud at 6,000 feet, with thick industrial haze lurking beneath, and this left the crews with no prospect of identifying the briefed aiming point. A total of eighteen crews would later claim to have bombed in the target area, and six of these were from 106 Squadron, including that of P/O Oliver, who bombed from 13,000 feet, and reported starting a large fire that was visible up to twenty minutes into the return flight. Sgt Bowering and crew delivered their bombs in a stick from west to east but saw no results, while Sgt Hadland and crew bombed from 12,500 feet and were prevented by searchlight glare from identifying their burst. They also described heavy and accurate flak over the target, a report echoed by Sgt Mooney and crew, who released their load from 10,000 feet. The crew of S/L Boylan found the town centre with a stick of bombs and commented on the searchlight activity, and F/L Stenner and crew also attacked Duisburg, but delivered their bombs across the northern district of Hamborn. The crews of F/O Harwood and P/O Herd went for the alternative of Cologne, while those of P/O Greenhalgh and Sgt Lockyer selected Düsseldorf. Two of the 106 Squadron element failed to return, AD862 falling victim over Belgium to the night-fighter of Lt Reinhold Knacke of II./NJG1 based at "Wespennest" Leeuwarden, the "wasps' nest". P/O Walker and two of his crew survived to be taken into captivity, but one of the gunners, Sgt Diggory, lost his life. AD873 crashed near Frechen on the western approaches to Cologne, and there were no survivors from the crew of F/L Sharp.

Scampton and Hemswell combined on the following night to send thirty-nine Hampdens to join Wellingtons in attacking shipyards at Bremen, while ninety Wellingtons and Whitleys attempted to hit the giant Krupp complex and railway installations at Essen.

Two nights later, it was the turn of French ports to host a visit from elements of the Command. Brest was targeted by more than eighty Wellingtons and Whitleys in an attempt to hit the resident enemy warships, while twenty-five Hampdens and twenty-two Wellingtons went for the U-Boot base at Lorient, where construction of the major new concrete structure was well under way on the Keroman peninsula. Five 106 Squadron crews were briefed for the latter, and they took off between 22.25 and 22.40 with F/L Stenner the senior pilot on duty, and they were followed into the air between 22.55 and 23.05 by six aircraft, whose crews had been instructed to make a nuisance of themselves over the Ruhr and Cologne. Those bound for France pointed their snouts to the south-west to begin the Channel crossing at Chesil Beach in Dorset. They benefitted from ideal weather conditions with an almost full moon shining down from a cloud-free south-western sky, and they were able to identify the Brittany coast from many miles away. They all reached the target area, where no U-Boots were evident, and the heavy flak was bursting at up to 18,000 feet as they aimed their bombs at the general dockyard from 8,000 to 16,000 feet between 01.50 and 02.30. For any of the force prepared to brave the light flak at lower levels, there lurked another danger in the form of barrage balloons tethered at between 4,000 and 8,000 feet. F/L Stenner and crew watched their bombs miss the U-Boot pens but burst across the docks, while F/O Harwood and crew saw three bomb bursts, which started fires, and commented on the lack of interference from the defences. The crew of P/O Oliver circled the target for twenty-five minutes before making their attack, and P/O Herd and crew claimed to have started two fires, one of them close to the power station. Sgt Hadland and crew mentioned only dropping their "bombs in the target area, visibility perfect, no opposition". Returning crews reported bomb bursts along the edge of the docks, in the dry dock adjacent to the Naval Fusiliers School, on the oiling jetty, naval barracks and a frigate, but there was no confirmation of specific damage.

The six Coningsby crews on a roving commission over the Ruhr fared less well, and only three of them returned home. Those of Sgts Daniels and Mooney attacked Cologne, while Sgt Lockyer and crew went for Hamborn, (Duisburg) and made three attacks in all, one on a railway junction north-east of Wesel, docks on the east side of the river north of Hamborn, and the southern end of a steel works in the town itself. These three crews made it back safely to Coningsby, but the arrival of the others was awaited in vain. Dortmund and Düsseldorf had been the objectives for them, and a message was received from P/O Greenhalgh and crew calling for assistance after their engines had failed on the way home. Nothing more was heard, and news eventually came through that L4185 had come down in the Thames Estuary with fatal consequences for the occupants. AD914 crashed in Holland without survivors from the crew of F/Sgt Bowering, and news also eventually came through that AD986 had come down in Germany to the east of Hamm, and Sgt Brownbill and his crew had also perished. These three losses represented the squadron's heaviest casualties thus far in a single night, and, perhaps, also demonstrated the futility of roving commission operations.

Coningsby, Waddington and Lindholme sat out a 5 Group attack on marshalling yards at Osnabrück on the night of the 5/6th, and then 106 Squadron made ready thirteen Hampdens on the 6th to contribute to a 5 Group force of eighty-eight of the type for the next assault on the German warships at Brest, which would also face twenty-one Wellingtons, although probably not simultaneously. Not all of the Coningsby Hampdens would take off with 106 Squadron crews on board, as some of the frustrated 97 Squadron and former 106 Squadron crews took the opportunity to "get some ops in". Six of the Hampdens were loaded for the first time with two 2,000 pounders each, while the remainder carried the standard load of 500 and 250 pounders, and all got away without incident between 22.15 and 23.05 with F/L Stenner the senior pilot on duty. The crews of Sgts Haggar and Wotherspoon were back on the ground after ninety minutes and two hours respectively because of engine issues, leaving the others to arrive in the target area in perfect weather conditions, with the usual intense searchlights and flak defence providing a barrier between them and the targets. Initially at least, the smoke generators were not active, allowing those arriving in the vanguard a clear run, but, for most from 106 Squadron, the smoke screen proved to be highly effective and completely obscured Scharnhorst and Gneisenau. The bombing was aimed at the general area of the docks, the crews of F/L Stenner and P/Os Harwood and Oliver observing their 2,000 pounders burst, before Harwood was caught in twenty-to-thirty searchlights. P/O Herd and crew also stumbled into searchlights and had to dive to 3,000 feet to evade them, all the time machine-gunning them. AD861 had been borrowed by Sgt Field and his crew from 97 Squadron, and ended up in Plymouth Sound after colliding with a balloon cable over the town on the way back. The pilot and observer survived, but both gunners lost their lives. In all, 5 Group delivered over three hundred high explosive, armour-piercing and semi-armour piercing bombs into the target area, and returning crews reported fires in the town centre, in the northern outskirts and near the seaplane base. A number also reported an aircraft being hit at around 3,000 feet and crashing into the sea in flames, and this was probably the single 5 Group casualty, a 144 Squadron Hampden. Despite the best efforts, the warships remained a threat as a "fleet in being", and the strategists at Bomber Command HQ continued to seek a solution.

Four main targets were posted on stations across the Command on the 7th, Cologne, Osnabrück and Münster for Wellingtons and or Whitleys, while forty Hampdens were to target the main station and marshalling yards in the town of Mönchengladbach on the south-western rim of the Ruhr. This last-mentioned operation was supported by a dozen 106 Squadron aircraft, some again containing crews from 97 Squadron. P/Os Oliver and Herd were the only officer pilots on duty as they departed Coningsby between 22.40 and 22.50, and, in accordance with the practice of the day, some squadrons adopted the northerly route, corridor "B" via Skegness and Enkhuizen, while others preferred corridor "G", Orfordness to the Scheldt estuary. Whichever, the outward flight took place under clear skies with a full moon to aid map-reading in coastal areas, until thick ground haze blotted out detail over land, and, ultimately, only five of the Coningsby crews would locate and attack the briefed target. Sgt Purnell and crew returned early with an engine problem, but the crews of Sgts Daniels, Mooney, Tilbury and Clark and P/O Oliver all identified the primary target and carried out an attack. Two crews selected Düsseldorf as an alternative, and two others Krefeld, while P/O Herd and crew failed to find Mönchengladbach, were driven off by flak at Düsseldorf, and finally achieved a near-miss on a steel works at Essen. AD735 was shot down over Holland by a night-fighter flown by Oblt Heinrich Griese of I./NJG/1, and Sgt Wotherspoon, who had recently been posted from 106 to 97 Squadron, survived to fall into enemy hands, while the other three crew members were killed. The attrition rate among the squadron's Hampdens was becoming alarming, with seven lost in the space of six nights from four operations, and that represented almost an entire flight.

5 Group was handed marshalling yards again on the 8th, when forty-five Hampdens were detailed at Scampton, Waddington and Lindholme to target the northern half of those at Hamm, situated just north of the Ruhr, while twenty-eight Whitleys attended to the southern half. A new Air Ministry directive issued on the 9th pointed to the German transportation system and the morale of the civilian population as the enemy's chief weaknesses, and a list of targets was drawn up accordingly, which took in the major railway centres ringing the Ruhr. These were to be attacked on moonlit nights, while the Rhine cities of Cologne, Düsseldorf and Duisburg would be easier to locate on dark nights. On dark nights in unfavourable weather conditions, the C-in-C, Sir Richard Peirse, was to send his forces to more distant objectives in northern, eastern and southern Germany. That night, thirty-nine Hampdens were detailed to join forces with Whitleys and Wellingtons for the first major raid of the war on Aachen, Germany's most westerly city perched on the frontiers of Holland and Belgium. 106 Squadron made ready seventeen of its own, while the crews were being briefed to use the Nazi Party HQ in the town centre as the aiming point. This signified the operation to be an area attack, at a time when it was still not openly admitted that such tactics were in use. They departed Coningsby in good weather conditions between 23.05 and 23.30 with F/L Stenner the senior pilot on duty, and he and his crew arrived over the target to find excellent visibility, which enabled them to make their attack from 14,000 feet, and observe the bombs to burst just east of the aiming point. Others carried out their attacks from much lower, and P/O Robinson and crew were among those, releasing their bombs from 5,000 feet before descending to 1,500 feet to strafe the town. Sgt Hadland and crew were intercepted by a Me110, which they evaded, but it threw off their navigation, and they ultimately bombed the Dutch town of Maastricht in error. P/O Hardy and crew were also attacked by a Me110, in their case north-east of Brussels, but return fire was seen to hit the enemy, and testimony from other crews during debriefing seemed to confirm its destruction. It was a successful operation, carried out in favourable conditions, and resulted in the destruction of and damage to many commercial properties and housing units, rendering almost 3,500 people homeless.

On the following night, 5 Group detailed thirty-two Hampdens to join ninety-eight Wellingtons in attacking a number of aiming points in Cologne. One of the 5 Group targets was the Klöckner-Humboldt mechanical engineering works in the Deutz district, situated on the East Bank of the Rhine in the city centre. They found the target largely hidden beneath eight-tenths cloud and thick haze extending up to 12,000 feet, which forced them to search for a pinpoint. Barely half of the force would claim to have bombed in the general target area, and local sources reported only a handful of bombs falling. 106 Squadron sat out this operation, and was at full strength to respond to orders on the 11th to prepare seventeen aircraft for that night's 5 Group raid by thirty-six Hampdens from Coningsby, Hemswell and Waddington against the main railway station in the naval port of Wilhelmshaven. The omens were good as they departed Coningsby between 23.10 and 23.30 in fine weather conditions with good visibility and S/L Nelms the senior pilot on duty undertaking his first operation for some time. They reached north-western Germany to find generally favourable conditions, but haze to inhibit the vertical visibility and S/L Nelms and crew bombed from 9,000 feet, observing four bursts, before gliding down to 800 feet to escape from the heavy flak. Their experiences were typical for the night, although some crews did not experience the same level of flak activity and all found it impossible to make an accurate assessment of the outcome. Four returning crews claimed direct hits on the aiming point, and the others reported bombing in the target area. Not unusually for the period, the crew claims did not tally with local reports, which suggested that most of the ordnance had fallen onto open ground and in the harbour.

Thirteen 106 Squadron crews were called to briefing on the 14th, to learn of that night's operation to the northern city of Hannover, where the railway station and main post office building were designated as the aiming points for a force of eighty-five aircraft, forty-four of them provided by 5 Group from Coningsby, Hemswell and Waddington. Based on past performances, the choice of aiming points was somewhat optimistic, and, in reality, disguised the actual intention to destroy the city centre. The 106

Squadron element departed Coningsby between 22.55 and 23.30 with S/L Boylan the senior pilot on duty, and performing the role of his observer was Sgt Mycock. There was no room for a second pilot in the single-seat fighter-style configuration of the Hampden cockpit, and freshman pilots gained experience as navigator/bomb-aimers for perhaps a dozen or more sorties before being appointed captain of their own crew. Sgt Mycock would eventually be posted to 97 Squadron and be selected to take part, with fatal consequences, in the audacious daylight attack by Lancasters on the M.A.N diesel engine works at Augsburg, deep in southern Germany, in April 1942. On this night, however, they headed for the Lincolnshire coast to begin the hour-long crossing of the North Sea, and, once at the other side, traversed northern Holland, before passing south of Bremen to reach the target. The crews of P/Os Herd and McGruer and Sgt Hadland flew out in formation as a continuation of the training that had been taking place in preparation for the imminent daylight operations, and their decision to do this was prompted by good weather conditions and clear visibility. The crews of Sgts Davies and Daniels returned early with technical problems, leaving the others to locate Hannover without difficulty, but unable to pinpoint the station through the haze. Some ground detail was revealed by the light of flares, and, as they ran in on the aiming point, S/L Boylan and crew found themselves held in searchlights for a short period and persistently fired upon. They delivered their bombs into the general built-up area, and the same scenario was experienced by the remaining crews, although two did claim near misses on the aiming point. Returning crews reported many fires, but few reports came out of Hannover, and it was not possible to establish the level of damage, if any.

Hamburg was posted as the target for 107 aircraft on the 16th, of which thirty-two Hampdens represented 5 Group. Coningsby and Waddington were not involved, and, in the event, poor visibility persuaded half of the force to seek out alternative targets, rendering the operation yet another disappointment. On the following day, the 17th, 44 Squadron's S/L Burton-Gyles, six aircrew and a maintenance party of ten proceeded to Boscombe Down to familiarise themselves with an Avro Lancaster, before returning with it to Waddington for evaluation trials. This was a momentous day for Bomber Command in general and 5 Group in particular, whose struggles with the Manchester had led to the development of the four-engine Lancaster, a type which would change the face of bombing, and, ultimately, contribute massively to victory.

That night, the weather intervened again, causing 5 Group to withdraw inexperienced crews from its contribution to a raid on the Gereon marshalling yards to the west of Cologne city centre. A dozen 106 Squadron crews attended briefing to learn that twenty-five Hampdens were to join fifty Wellingtons for the operation, and the Coningsby element took off between 22.55 and 23.10 with no senior pilots on duty. They flew out over Orfordness to follow corridor "G" to the Scheldt estuary and Brussels, but lost the services of Sgts Daniels and Ratcliffe and their crews, the former to an overheating starboard engine and the latter to intercom failure. However, the Ratcliffe crew did, at least, bomb Vlissingen aerodrome on the island of Walcheren in the Scheldt Estuary as they passed overhead on the way back. The others reached the target to encounter cloud and generally unfavourable conditions along with a hostile searchlight and flak defence, and bombed the general city area. Returning crews claimed many fires, while local sources would suggest that, perhaps, ten bomb loads had fallen within the city, causing little damage and no casualties.

5 Group issued orders to North Luffenham and Waddington on the 19th, to prepare for mining operations that night in the Eglantine and Yams gardens, respectively in the Elbe and Weser estuaries, which provided passage for shipping and U-Boots from the Hamburg and Bremen shipyards. 106 Squadron was not called upon on the 20th, when thirty-nine Hampdens were included in a force of 113 aircraft assembled to target marshalling yards in Cologne. Despite poor weather conditions of cloud and haze during the outward flight, all reached the target area to find seven to nine-tenths cloud with tops at 7,000

feet accompanied by haze. Glimpses of the Rhine provided an approximate reference, but there was no possibility of identifying the marshalling yards, and the bombing, carried out on estimated positions, produced little damage.

Frankfurt and Mannheim were named as the targets for a mini-campaign on three consecutive nights from the 21/22nd, and it would be the former's first taste of a major Bomber Command assault. Thirty-seven Wellingtons and thirty-four Hampdens were made ready, the latter at Coningsby, North Luffenham and Waddington, while thirty-six Wellingtons and eight Halifaxes were prepared to attack Mannheim city centre some forty-five miles to the south. At 5 Group briefings, crews were instructed to aim for the post-office and main telephone exchange building, which would guarantee damage in the city centre. F/O Harwood was the senior pilot on duty as twelve of the 106 Squadron element departed Coningsby in an eighteen-minute slot to 22.58, and P/O Hardy and crew brought up the rear some seventeen minutes later. P/O Haywood and crew were forced to return early with engine problems, but the others pressed on across France to reach the Frankfurt area, which they identified after locating the River Rhine and following it towards the south until picking up the River Main. They delivered their loads of either two 500, two 250 pounders and 120 x 4lb incendiaries or one 1,000 and two 500 pounders, through thick haze into the general city area from an average of 10,000 feet in the face of an accurate searchlight and flak defence, the glare from which largely concealed the results. A number of bursts were observed along with fires, but the local reports spoke of minor damage, and the city of Darmstadt, situated some ten miles to the south, sustained a greater level of destruction. On return, Sgt Curties and crew claimed a very near miss on the aiming point, and the debutant crews of Sgts Dashwood and Richardson found the general target area with their bombs. Sgt Lockyer and crew were unable to locate the city, but spotted a nearby aerodrome and saw three of their bombs burst on it. Despite confident claims, it seems that most of the bombs missed the target on this night, some falling on Darmstadt some fifteen miles away, but, at least, no aircraft were lost.

Twenty-four hours later, the squadron put up ten Hampdens as part of a mixed force of sixty-three aircraft for another crack at this south-central city. S/L Nelms and 97 Squadron's S/L "Flap" Sherwood were the senior pilots on duty as they began departing Coningsby at 22.40, but S/L Nelms couldn't coax sufficient altitude out of AE151, and, two hours into the outward flight decided to jettison the bomb load and turn for home. The others pressed on in very unfavourable weather conditions of thick cloud, rain and violent electrical storms, and, one by one, three others turned back. P/O Hayward and crew were among four to reach and bomb the target area on estimated positions through eight to ten-tenths cloud, with absolutely no prospect of identifying the briefed aiming point, the main post office and telephone exchange, and another inconclusive raid ensued. They came home on one engine after the starboard power plant failed while still an hour out from Coningsby. The crews of F/L Stenner, P/O Rodwell and Sgt Bannister were the others to reach Frankfurt to bomb blindly through the cloud, while P/O Oliver and crew attacked Mannheim as an alternative, and S/L Sherwood and crew dropped their bombs on what was believed to be Bonn. The final raid of the series on Frankfurt was an all-5 Group show involving thirty-two Hampdens from Scampton and Swinderby, the latter 50 Squadron's new home, while fifty Wellingtons tried their hand at Mannheim. They encountered a small amount of cloud, but thick haze blotted out ground detail, and bombing had to be carried out on estimated positions, a number of bursts offering some evidence that a few incendiaries and high-explosive bombs had fallen within the city.

The reason behind the formation-flying training that had been ongoing for a number of weeks was revealed to be an audacious attack by daylight on the German warships at Brest under the codename Operation Sunrise. Scheduled for the 24th, it was discovered at the last minute that Scharnhorst had slipped away to La Pallice, some two hundred miles further south, and this required an adjustment to the original complex plan of attack. The intention had been to send three 90 Squadron Fortress Is in to bomb from 30,000 feet to draw up enemy fighters, while 5 Group Hampdens performed a similar function at a less rarefied altitude under the umbrella of a Spitfire escort. While this distraction was in progress, it was hoped that Halifaxes and Wellington from 1, 3 and 4 Groups could sneak in unopposed to target the ships. Now that Scharnhorst had moved, it was decided to send the Halifax element to deal with her, while the rest of the original plan went ahead at Brest. 5 Group detailed six Hampdens each from Waddington, Coningsby and North Luffenham, and they had congregated at Coningsby on the previous day for the briefing. If successful, this would clearly be a prestigious operation to be involved in, even though highly dangerous, and one wonders if that played a part in the selection of exclusively officer pilots at a time when NCO pilots were the most numerous on other operations. It is noticeable that the six crews chosen had been absent from recent operations while formation training took place, so the selection process must have taken place when the operation was first devised back in June. The crews at final briefing for this first ever daylight operation for 106 Squadron were those of W/C Allen, F/L Altmann and P/Os Wareing, Robinson, Paramore and Henderson, and they took off in two vics of three at 10.40 and 10.45, before joining up to form a box of six, which was to remain together throughout the attack. The 5 Group formation proceeded to Predannack in three boxes with Coningsby leading, and collected the Spitfire escort provided by 10 Group over Cornwall. They were shepherded all the way to the target, which they reached at 14.15, seven minutes after the Fortresses had bombed. In the event, the flak and fighter opposition proved more fierce than anticipated, and the Hampdens found themselves in a hornets' nest of single and twin-engine fighters, which accounted for two of them and ten of the Wellingtons. In total, the Hampden element delivered fifty-nine 500lb bombs onto the target from 14,500 feet, but no hits were claimed, and, to its credit, the 106 Squadron box held firm despite the opposition, and all returned safely to Coningsby after six hours in the air. A number of hits on Gneisenau were claimed by the Wellington element, although not confirmed, but Scharnhorst did suffer significant damage at La Pallice, while inflicting heavy casualties on the attacking Halifaxes. Ultimately, she was forced to return to Brest to take advantage of the superior repair facilities on offer there.

Kiel was posted as the destination for thirty-four Wellingtons and thirty Hampdens that night, the latter on the stations at Coningsby, North Luffenham and Waddington. 106 Squadron contributed nine Hampdens with NCO crews to target the Deutsche Werke and Krupp Germania shipyards, and they took off between 22.10 and 22.25, before heading eastwards in favourable weather conditions that afforded visibility clear enough for ground features to be identified. They ran the gauntlet of an intense searchlight and flak barrage to reach the aiming point, where Sgt Lyon and crew bombed from 10,000 feet, and were on their way home when set upon by a Me110, which inflicted severe damage on AE123. The ORB credited the skill of the pilot as the main factor in the crew's safe return home. Sgt Haggar and crew bombed oil tanks south of the Kiel Canal, and were fired upon by a British convoy as they crossed the North Sea homebound. Sgt Curties and crew claimed hits on the main station, and other returning crews were also enthusiastic about the bomb bursts and the resulting fires, but in keeping with the performances of the times, very little damage actually resulted.

Orders were received at Scampton and Swinderby on the 25th to provide thirty Hampdens to join forces with twenty-five Whitleys for an attack on Hannover. The crews were briefed to aim for the main railway station and post office, which meant that it was to be an area raid to target the city centre. Whether or not they succeeded will never be known, as the crews themselves failed to observe the results and no local report was forthcoming. The teleprinters at Waddington and Coningsby spewed out the details of the forthcoming night's activities on the 27th, revealing them to relate to mining operations in the Artichoke garden off Lorient for the former and the Beech garden off St-Nazaire for the latter. Seventeen 106 Squadron crews had been briefed, but one had a slight incident on take-off and was scrubbed. The others became airborne between 21.35 and 22.15 in good weather conditions, and all but one experienced no difficulty in locating the garden area in excellent visibility. P/O McGruer and crew failed to find their drop zone and delivered the mine instead off La Pallice.

On the following night, the gardens were in the Baltic, Radish, Forget-me-not and Quince, (Kiel Harbour, Kiel Bay and the Fehmarn Belt), for which forty-two Hampdens were detailed on the stations at Scampton and Swinderby. Unfavourable weather conditions hampered attempts to identify pinpoints from which to time the runs, and only twenty-five vegetables were planted in the allotted locations, while another was dropped in an alternative garden. Following the spate of losses during the first week of the month, the squadron had come through the remainder unscathed. Sadly, the Reaper returned to the squadron on the 30th to claim the life of one of Sgt Lockyer's crew, Sgt Thurston, after AD970 stalled at low-level and crashed into the sea half a mile off Skegness pier during a training flight. A force of 116 aircraft was made ready to unleash on Cologne that night, 5 Group contributing forty-two Hampdens from North Luffenham and Waddington. Some crews ran into a severe electrical storm at the Belgian coast, and Aachen, situated close to the planned track to Cologne, proved to be a popular alternative target for crews recognising the futility of pressing on, and they based their attacks largely on searchlights and the flashes from flak batteries. Those reaching the primary target encountered nine to ten-tenths cloud at 4,000 feet, and not one made a positive identification of the city, local sources confirming that a few high explosive bombs and incendiaries had hit it, causing minor damage and no casualties. During the course of the month, the squadron carried out thirteen operations, twelve of them by night, and dispatched 159 sorties for the loss of seven aircraft and five crews.

August 1941

Multiple targets opened the August account on the night of the 2/3rd, when the Hampdens winged their way back to Kiel to attack the Deutsche Werke shipbuilding yards, while Hamburg and Berlin played host to other types. 106 Squadron contributed eighteen of the fifty Hampdens for Kiel, and they departed Coningsby between 22.15 and 22.30 with F/Ls Altmann and Stenner the senior pilots on duty, but lost the services of Sgt Dashwood and crew to an engine issue after reaching the enemy coast. The others found cloud and haze in the target area, and many were unable to positively identify the briefed aiming point, among them the crew of Sgt Ratcliffe, who carried out a long search before jettisoning their load. Seven Coningsby crews claimed direct hits, while nine others reported bombing in the target area and observing bomb bursts and many fires. A local source reported just one house hit within the town but made no mention of the outcome for the shipyards.

A busy night of operations on the 5/6th saw three separate forces set off for southern Germany, ninety-eight of them bound for Mannheim and Ludwigshafen, the twin cities facing each other on the east and west banks respectively of the Rhine. A further ninety-seven aircraft were to hit Karlsruhe located thirty miles to the south, and sixty-eight others Frankfurt a little over forty miles to the north. 106 Squadron supported the first-mentioned operation with eleven Hampdens, whose crews had been briefed to attack the main railway station at Ludwigshafen, while five other crews, those of P/Os Henderson, Paramore and Herd and Sgts Mooney and Hadland, were to attack the railway workshops at Karlsruhe. They departed Coningsby together between 22.20 and 22.30 with S/L Nelms the senior pilot on duty, and both elements routed out over Orfordness with orders to fly direct to their respective destinations after making landfall over the Scheldt. Sgt Ratcliffe and crew responded to a recall signal meant for another aircraft, and arrived back at Coningsby three hours later to learn of their error. Sgt Daniels and crew also aborted their sortie, when the intercom failed and left them unable to communicate with each other to co-ordinate their attack. The others flew the length of Belgium over cloud with a bright, full moon to light their way, but only three of the Ludwigshafen element, the crews of Sgts Richardson, Curties and Purnell, identified the aiming point and delivered their bombs, while five others, including S/L Nelms, went for Mannheim as an alternative. In contrast, all five of the Karlsruhe contingent located the target to find that the cloud extended over the top of it, and, whilst this prevented them from identifying the railway workshops, they were able to hit the town. Local reports revealed significant damage in Mannheim and the northern part of Ludwigshafen, and in the Rhine harbour and western districts of Karlsruhe. The sole Hampden loss from Mannheim was 106 Squadron's AE120, which suffered engine failure after being shot up by a night-fighter over Holland, and crashed onto a house, killing Sgt Knowles RNZAF and his crew, along with two people in the house. It was just their second operation.

It was decided to repeat the Mannheim and Karlsruhe operations on the following night, along with another to railway yards at Frankfurt. A 5 Group force of thirty-eight Hampdens from North-Luffenham and Swinderby was handed the Karlsruhe job, which was to be launched from North Luffenham in Rutland. The force encountered nine-tenths cloud over the target, which prevented the crews from identifying the railway workshops, and they mostly deposited their bombs and incendiaries on the town. Meanwhile, 5 Group dispatched twenty-one freshman crews from North Luffenham, Scampton and Waddington to bomb the docks and shipping at Calais, where they found eight to ten-tenths cloud in layers between 4,000 and 10,000 feet, which severely compromised target location and attempts to bomb.

The troublesome operational career of the Manchesters got under way again on the night of the 7/8th, when three from 207 Squadron and fifty-four Hampdens were made ready to join forces with forty-nine other aircraft to attack the mighty Krupp munitions complex in Essen. It is easy to think of Krupp as a giant factory, but the reality was vastly different. The Krupp organisation had been the largest manufacturer of weapons in Europe since before the Great War, and had a hand in all aspects of German war production from tanks to artillery and ship and U-Boot construction, and was given a controlling share in all major heavy engineering companies in Germany and the Occupied Countries. It also built manufacturing sites in other parts of Germany, many situated close to concentration camps, and employed vast numbers of forced workers in all of its factories. Once known as "Die Waffenschmiede des Reichs", the weapon-forge of the realm, its manufacturing sites in Essen included the Friedrich Krupp steelworks, the Friedrich Krupp locomotive and general engineering works, six coal mines and ten coke-oven plants, the Altenberg zinc works, the Presswerk plastics factory, and the Goldschmidt non-ferrous metals smelting plant, all situated either within or close to the four Borbeck districts, in a segment radiating out from near the city centre to the Rhein-Herne Canal on the north-western boundary on the banks of the Emscher River. The steel and engineering works alone employed in the region of eighty thousand people, and the company's sites covered an area of more than two thousand acres, of which three hundred acres were occupied by factories and workshops. All of that required massive rail and canal access in the form of marshalling yards and its own harbour, and energy from at least four nearby power stations.

106 Squadron made ready fourteen Hampdens, which got away from Coningsby in fine weather conditions and excellent visibility with S/Ls Boylan and Tudor the senior pilots on duty, supported by F/Ls Stenner and Altmann. The favourable weather conditions persisted all the way to the target, with good horizontal visibility, but the main problem, as always over the Ruhr, was the blanket of industrial haze, and, while some crews were able to establish their position by the Rhine, picking out individual buildings was a different matter. The density of Krupp buildings in the Borbeck districts should have guaranteed that some would be hit, if only the crews could pinpoint on that segment of the city. S/L Tudor and crew claimed a direct hit on the centre of the complex, that of F/L Altmann found the aiming point obscured by haze, while P/O Wareing and crew recorded it as being clearly seen. S/L Boylan and crew concurred with the latter assessment, releasing their bombs from 13,000 feet and observing them to burst in the target area, while P/O Herd and crew dropped their bombs, and then descended to ground level to strafe the searchlights. F/L Stenner and crew failed to locate the objective, and delivered their

bombs on Düsseldorf instead. Despite the claims of returning crews, only a few bomb loads fell in the city, and the destruction of a bakery was the most serious incident.

With another daylight operation in the planning stage, the crews of W/C Allen and P/O Oliver took part in practice formation flying on the 8th. At the same time, a force of fifty Hampdens from North Luffenham, Swinderby and Coningsby and four Whitleys was assembled to target the Deutsche Werke U-Boot construction yards at Kiel. A dozen 106 Squadron Hampdens departed Coningsby between 23.40 and 23.55 with no senior pilots on duty, and found themselves flying over ten-tenths cloud almost all the way to the target, where, as if by royal command, it dissipated to provide excellent visibility. Nine crews returned with confident claims of direct hits or near misses, and reported explosions and a number of large fires. Two other crews reported bombing the town, while that of Sgt Jeffers failed to locate the target at all, and bombed the town of Rendsburg on the Schleswig-Holstein peninsula as an alternative. The 5 Group ORB described this as a very successful operation, but, in truth, it once more failed to produce damage commensurate with the effort expended.

Awards were announced on the 9th to a number of those who had taken part in Operation Sunrise at Brest on the 24th of July. W/C Allen DFC received the DSO, and his observer, P/O Erly, the DFC. There was a DFC also for P/O Henderson, and a DFM for Sgt Overall, who was P/O Wareing's observer.

The daylight operations mentioned above were scheduled for the 12th, and turned out to be attacks on power stations at Knapsack and Quadrath near Cologne to be carried out by fifty-four Blenheims of 2 Group, while supporting and diversionary operations went ahead elsewhere. The purpose was to support the beleaguered Russians by persuading the Luftwaffe to withdraw fighters from the Russian front to protect economic targets in the west. The plan called for six Hampdens each from Waddington and Coningsby to target respectively Longueness aerodrome at St-Omer and Gosnay power station in north-eastern France, both under the protection of a fighter escort. This would be 106 Squadron's second daylight operation, and was likely to be extremely hazardous in view of its intention to attract enemy fighters. It was, in effect, a typical 2 Group "circus" operation, which involved the blatant use of RAF bombers as bait to bring enemy fighters into the gunsights of Spitfires and Hurricanes in a battle of attrition. As one might expect from a commanding officer of W/C Allen's calibre, he placed himself at the forefront, and led the 106 Squadron element away from Coningsby at 09.55. The other five crews were those of F/L Altmann and P/Os Oliver, Wareing, Paramore and Henderson, and again, there was a noticeable absence of NCO pilots. The target area was free of cloud, allowing the power station to be easily identified and bombed, and twenty-four 500 pounders and two 250 pounders went down to explode close to the aiming point. Although no enemy fighters appeared on the scene, anti-aircraft fire was accurate, and most of the Hampdens sustained shrapnel damage, but no crew casualties.

The night of the 12/13th was to be a busy one for the Command, and, throughout the day, aircraft were made ready for attacks on Berlin, Hannover, Magdeburg and Essen. 5 Group detailed thirteen Hampdens to join sixty-five Wellingtons for Hannover, and thirty-six to operate on their own at Magdeburg, while a force of seventy aircraft assigned to the Capital included nine Manchesters. Together with minor operations, the night's activities involved a total of 234 aircraft. Hannover lay on the route to both Magdeburg and Berlin, and the three forces would fly out together until reaching it, at which point the Berlin element would continue straight on for the 150 additional miles, while the Magdeburg element peeled off to the south-east with eighty miles still ahead of it. Fourteen 106 Squadron crews were briefed to target railway communications in Magdeburg and Hannover, but, at the last minute, eight sorties were scrubbed, and this left the crews of F/L Stenner and P/O Watts to depart Coningsby for Magdeburg at 21.10 and 21.15 respectively, and those of F/O Harwood, P/O Hayward and Sgts Mooney and Roberts to take off between 21.10 and 21.55 bound for Hannover. The crews of Sgt Mooney and P/O Watts misinterpreted a recall signal and abandoned their sorties, while F/L Stenner and crew failed to locate Magdeburg and bombed another town, believed to be Quackenbrück. F/O Harwood and crew were unable to locate Hannover, so continued on eastwards to Magdeburg, where they dropped their bombs just east of the target, and caused a terrific explosion. P/O Hayward and crew encountered ground haze, which made identification difficult, but dropped their bombs in the target area, and also witnessed a large explosion. The Roberts crew reported ten-tenths cloud throughout the trip, despite which, they identified Hannover and bombed the built-up area from 10,000 feet. Nothing of value was achieved at either target, but at least no Hampdens were lost. The policy of attacking multiple targets would continue, as would their lack of effectiveness, but the propaganda value to the morale of the civilian population was priceless at a time of gloomy news from all fronts. In fact, the impression that Bomber Command was laying waste to German industry was about to be shattered.

Orders were received across the Command on the 14th to prepare for operations that night against railway targets in three major cities in northern Germany to the north of the Harz mountains, Hannover the most westerly, Magdeburg the most easterly and Braunschweig (Brunswick) in-between. 5 Group detailed eighty-one Hampdens to operate alone against the main railway station in Braunschweig, while seven Manchester crews were briefed for Magdeburg as part of an overall force of fifty-two aircraft. Northern Germany was found to be concealed beneath a blanket of medium level cloud, and none of the participants in the night's events was able to determine precisely where their bombs fell. 106 Squadron was not involved, and would have a full complement of serviced aircraft and rested crews to offer when next called upon.

Railway objectives featured again on the 16th, when orders went out to stations across the Command to prepare for attacks on installations in the Ruhr cities of Düsseldorf and Duisburg, and Cologne to the south. Düsseldorf was to be a 5 Group show involving fifty-two Hampdens and six Manchesters, a record-equalling twenty of the former provided by 106 Squadron. They departed Coningsby between 22.05 and 22.40 with S/L Nelms the senior pilot on duty, and flew out via corridor "G" to make landfall over the Scheldt estuary, before arriving at the target to find generally fine conditions with medium cloud and the expected ground haze. S/L Nelms delivered his bombs from 14,000 feet, and saw them burst in what he believed to be the town centre, and he was one of fourteen to report attacking the primary target, most of the others on estimated positions from between 12,000 and 17,000 feet. Returning crews reported many fires at the primary target, some of them large, while a number reported bombing Essen as an alternative and Leeuwarden aerodrome as a last resort. Two crews failed to return, and, as events were to prove, these represented the first of a flurry of casualties to afflict the squadron in the second half of the month. AE134 crashed at 01.38 at Meijel, some ten miles north-east of Weert in southern Holland after an encounter with Oblt Wolfgang Thimmig of 1./NJG1, although not before P/O Robinson and his crew had managed to extricate themselves and float down into the waiting arms of their captors. Sadly, P/O Robinson would die later in the year while a prisoner. (Bomber Command Losses Vol 2 W R Chorley). AD756 was intercepted by Oblt Redlich of I./NJG1 over Belgium, and P/O Watts died with one of his usual crew in the crash at 02.44 near Gembloux. A P/O Grant had been given permission to join the crew to gain operational experience, and he also lost his life, while the two survivors were taken into captivity.

Waddington was not involved in the 5 Group operation on the 17th, for which thirty-nine Hampden crews were briefed to attack the main goods railway station in Bremen, while twenty 4 Group Whitleys targeted the city's Focke-Wulf aircraft factory at Hemelingen. It was another inconclusive attack in the face of extreme darkness and haze, and no results were observed by the 5 Group crews, while a number of those from 4 Group claimed hits on the aircraft factory.

The operations during June and July had been monitored in order to provide an assessment for the War Cabinet of the effectiveness of the strategic bombing campaign. The project was initiated by Churchill's chief scientific advisor, Professor Lindemann, otherwise known as Lord Cherwell, who handed the responsibility to David M Bensusan-Butt, a civil-servant assistant to Cherwell working in the War Cabinet Secretariat. What became known as The Butt Report was released on the 18th, and its disclosures sent shock waves reverberating around the Cabinet Room and the Air Ministry. Having studied around four thousand photographs taken during night operations, he concluded that only a small fraction of bombs had fallen within miles of their intended targets, and this was particularly evident in operations against the Ruhr, the very heartland of Germany's war production. This swept away at a stroke any notion, that the Command was reducing the enemy's capacity and will to continue the fight, and demonstrated the claims of the crews to be wildly optimistic. The revelation would also unjustly blight forever the period of tenure as Commander-in-Chief of Sir Richard Peirse, in whose defence it should be mentioned that the focus of operations changed frequently, the demands and expectations of his superiors were not realistic and the crews, though doing their best, were ill-equipped for the tasks required of them. In addition, the report provided the detractors with a bountiful supply of ammunition to back up their calls for the dissolution of an independent bomber force, and for the redistribution of its aircraft to the U-Boot campaign and to redress reversals in the Middle East.

While the report was being digested that evening, 5 Group sent forty-two Hampdens from North Luffenham and Coningsby to attack the West station at Cologne, while twenty Whitleys and Wellingtons targeted the main post office. The fourteen-strong 106 Squadron element departed Coningsby between 23.00 and 23.20 with P/Os Hardy, Herd, Oliver and Paramore the only commissioned pilots on duty. AD919 force-landed at 23.15 some ten miles north-west of Boston after an engine failed, and was written off, while the crew of Sgt Field emerged from its wreckage with nothing more than cuts and bruises. Sgt Mooney and crew were back in the circuit within an hour because of an engine issue, and Sgt Jefferis and crew, it is believed, had crossed the enemy coast before an overheating starboard engine persuaded them to turn back. The others reached the target area to find favourable conditions with clear skies and good horizontal visibility, and bombed through haze from 4,000 to 15,000 feet, observing many fires on the western side of the Rhine, and a few on the East Bank. P/O Oliver and crew observed three aircraft to fall in flames, at 01.05, 01.16 and 01.25, while Sgt Clark and crew were forced down to 300 feet to escape searchlights after bombing from 12,000 feet and found themselves about half a mile west of the Kalk marshalling yards. The claims of the crews were not supported by local sources, which spoke of nothing more than superficial damage, suggesting that a decoy fire site had attracted the main weight of bombs. With this, his thirty-first sortie, P/O Paramore completed two hundred operational hours and was declared to be tour-expired.

It was to be a similar story of failure on the following night, when forty-one Hampdens from Scampton and Waddington joined sixty-seven other aircraft to attempt to hit a railway junction in Kiel. They encountered unhelpful weather conditions in the target area in the form of nine to ten-tenths cloud with tops at around 8,000 feet and a base below 5,000 feet in places, and local sources reported that no bombs had fallen into the town.

A series of three operations against Mannheim began on the night of the 22/23rd, for which 5 Group provided forty-one Hampdens from Coningsby, Syerston and Waddington, which were to join forces with fifty-six Wellingtons. Three aiming points included the main railway station and marshalling yards, for which the nineteen 106 Squadron crews were briefed, and F/L Altmann was the senior pilot on duty as the squadron took off, apparently in sections, with six recorded as departing Coningsby at 21.00, three at 21.05 and five at 21.40, but it still took more than an hour to get them all away, with Sgt McGinley and crew last away at 22.05. They crossed the Belgian coast between Ostend and Dunkerque, and pressed on along the line of the Franco/Belgian frontier until crossing into Germany and reaching the target area by following the Rhine. They found the weather conditions to be favourable with only small amounts of medium cloud, but haze and darkness impaired the vertical visibility and prevented crews from identifying the briefed aiming point. F/L Altmann and crew bombed the town from 11,000 feet, and, on return, reported being unable to observe the bombs bursting because of intense searchlight activity. This was typical of the experiences of the other sixteen crews claiming to have attacked the primary target from between 10,500 and 15,000 feet, but all seemed adamant that their bombs had found the mark and were fairly precise in their assessment of where their bombs had fallen. P/O Herd and crew were unable to locate Mannheim, and dropped their bombs instead from 12,000 feet onto Karlsruhe, some twenty-five miles further south. AE246 suffered a port undercarriage collapse on landing, but Sgt Curties and crew extricated themselves none the worse for their experience. AE220 became the only loss of the night's activity, when it was shot down by flak over southern Germany with no survivors from the crew of P/O McGruer RNZAF, which included P/O Early DFC of the RCAF as second pilot/observer. Despite the confidence of crews that this had been a successful operation causing many fires, Mannheim authorities recorded just six high explosive bombs falling, and six houses sustaining damage.

It was left to Scampton to provide a dozen Hampdens to represent 5 Group at Düsseldorf on the 24th, when 4 Group Whitleys and Halifaxes completed the force of forty-four aircraft. Six additional Hampdens were assigned to searchlight suppression duties in the Wesel defensive belt, their task to attack with small bombs and guns any battery holding a bomber in its beams. This activity turned out to be more effective than the raid itself, and caused the beams either to become erratic or to be extinguished altogether. A 5 Group attack on Mannheim by thirty-eight Hampdens and seven Manchesters was briefed out on all stations on the 25th, when the main post office was specified euphemistically as the aiming point, rather than admitting it to be the city centre. 106 Squadron remained at home, while two 97 Squadron Manchesters represented Coningsby in what turned out to be another inconclusive affair.

A return to Cologne was posted on the 26th, for which a force of ninety-nine aircraft was assembled and included twenty-nine Hampdens and a single Manchester from Coningsby, Scampton and Syerston, while six other Hampdens were to carry out flak suppression sorties to the west of the city. 106 Squadron contributed thirteen Hampdens, which departed Coningsby between 22.00 and 23.05 with no senior officers on duty, and all crews briefed to attack a railway junction. On arrival, they found broken cloud that allowed them sight of the ground, and bombing took place from a variety of altitudes between 7,000 and 17,000 feet, most observing their bombs to fall onto the eastern bank of the river. Opposition was described as heavy and accurate, and P/O Hadland's AE151 was hit by flak, although not seriously damaged. Local reports confirmed that the main weight of the attack had hit the eastern side of the city, but most of it fell outside of the city limits. AE302 failed to return from this disappointing operation, and no trace was ever found of Sgt Wilkinson and his crew. While this operation was in progress, five other crews from the squadron were engaged in gardening duties in the Baltic. They had actually taken off before the Cologne contingent, and made their way to northern waters in fair conditions. P/O Oliver and crew were assigned to the Quince garden in Kiel Bay, where they delivered their mine accurately from 600 feet. During the course of the operation P/O Oliver reached two hundred hours operational flying, and had, therefore, completed his first tour, although starboard engine failure on the way home probably had his heart racing. P/O Henderson and crew were also successful in delivering their mine from 750 feet into the Hollyhock garden in the Travemünde area of Lübeck Bay, while Sgt Tilbury and crew planted theirs from 800 feet in Ringkøbing Fjord off the western coast of Jutland as an alternative. F/L Stenner was the senior pilot on duty among the gardeners, and he was at 12,000 feet on approach to his garden, believed to be Endive, when he opened his bomb doors and the mine fell out. AE301 was brought down by flak while mining in the Silverthorn II garden in the western Baltic off Aalborg, and just one of F/O Harwood's crew survived to be taken prisoner.

Orders arriving on the 27th revealed a return to Mannheim for ninety-one aircraft, including thirty-five Hampdens from North Luffenham, Waddington and Swinderby, whose crews were to attack the main railway station, while elements of 1, 3 and 4 Groups focused on other aiming points within the city. At the same time, seventeen Hampdens would be mining the waters of the Nectarine gardens around the Frisians. The bombing element found clear skies but extreme darkness and haze, and many were prevented by searchlight glare from identifying the aiming point, forcing them to bomb the built-up area generally. There was some optimism concerning the effectiveness of the raid, but local sources reported no significant damage.

The target for the night of the 28/29th was Duisburg, for which 5 Group put up thirty Hampdens and six Manchesters in an overall force of 118 aircraft, and six further Hampdens for searchlight suppression duties. 106 Squadron briefed fourteen crews for the main event to attack the marshalling yards or the built-up area generally, and those of P/O Hadland, P/O Herd and Sgt Lyon for a dangerous intruder role in the searchlight belt, to fly at low level and bomb and strafe any batteries they came upon. They took off together between 23.20 and 23.55 and made their way to their respective target areas in fine weather conditions with excellent visibility. F/L Stenner was the senior pilot on duty, and he could only report bombing on the estimated position of the target from 16,000 feet. Others were more certain of their position, the crew of P/O Henderson specifying the west end of the marshalling yards as their aiming point from 9,800 feet, although they did not observe the bombs bursting. On the way home they shot up a searchlight battery at Wesel from 1,000 feet. Sgt Dashwood and crew were among those briefed to attack the town centre, and they delivered their bombs on or near the aiming point from 12,000 feet, but were prevented by flak from observing them burst. P/O Hadland and crew carried out intruder duties between 01.40 and 02.15, during which they attacked searchlight batteries with bombs, incendiaries and guns from between 1,500 and 2,000 feet. P/O Herd and crew flew up and down the searchlight belt at altitudes ranging from 2,000 feet down to 100 feet, and observed all of their bombs bursting, one definitely hitting a blue (master) searchlight. AE193 had also been assigned to intruder duties, and ultimately ditched off the Frisian island of Texel. The experienced crew of Sgt Lyon was picked up by a Dutch trawler after four days adrift, but such was their state of exhaustion, that they felt unable to try to evade capture, and decided to surrender rather than put their rescuers at risk. Between them, the gunners in the crews of P/Os Hadland and Herd expended 8,756 rounds of ammunition. Despite the claims of accurate bombing, only a few loads fell within the city of Duisburg, and it is unlikely that significant damage resulted.

The final raid of the series against Mannheim was posted on Wellington stations on the 29th, while Frankfurt was notified as the destination for a 4 and 5 Group force of 143 aircraft. This would be the first time that this city had faced an attack by a hundred-plus aircraft, the crews of which had been briefed to use the inland docks as the aiming point. 5 Group would be contributing seventy-three Hampdens and three 207 Squadron Manchesters, 106 Squadron providing just three aircraft, captained by F/L Altmann, P/O Hayward and Sgt Purnell. They took off either side of 22.00, and adopted either the briefed route from Orfordness to Namur in Belgium, or a more direct outward track to the target from the English coast, which meant landfall over the Scheldt estuary and skirting northern Belgium to pass south of Cologne. Cloud lay over most of the route, and icing became a problem for some, but the 106 Squadron trio reached the target area, where seven to nine-tenths cloud prevented most of the force from identifying the planned aiming point. However, some crews were able to pick out the river and docks by running in from below 10,000 feet, and bombing was carried out on largely estimated positions. Sgt Purnell and crew identified Frankfurt, and believed their bombs to have slightly overshot the aiming point from 12,000 feet, while F/L Altmann and crew also positively identified the city, but lost sight of the docks on the run in to bomb at 9,000 feet, and believed that their load had fallen short. P/O Hayward and crew were unable to positively identify anything, and delivered their bombs on estimated position from 13,500 feet. This was the experience of most crews taking part, and local reports from Frankfurt described scattered and insignificant damage, and, certainly, nothing commensurate with the size of the force and the effort expended.

The night of the 31st would bring an attack on railway targets in Cologne involving a force of 103 aircraft, including thirty-nine Hampdens and six Manchesters, while a further five Manchesters were to perform a flak suppression role. The 106 Squadron elements of ten for the main event and five for gardening duties departed Coningsby together between 19.20 and 20.20 with P/Os Hadland, Hayward, Henderson and Herd the only officer pilots on duty, the three last-mentioned each assigned to horticultural activities along with the crews of Sgts Purnell and Roberts. They headed east from the Lincolnshire coast to cross the Schleswig-Holstein peninsula to gain access to the western Baltic, where the crews of Sgt Roberts and P/O Hayward were assigned to the Forget-me-not garden in Kiel Fjord, Sgt Purnell and crew to the Carrot garden in the Little Belt, P/O Henderson and crew to the Hollyhock garden in Lübeck Bay and P/O Herd and crew to Broccoli at the southern end of the Great Belt. All reached their respective gardens, where Sgt Roberts and crew delivered their mine accurately from 700 feet and observed the parachute to deploy and the store to strike the water. Sgt Purnell and crew dropped theirs also in the briefed location from 600 feet, while P/Os Henderson, Herd and Hayward were, likewise, all successful in planting their vegetables from 700 feet. Meanwhile, the bombing element had been routed out over southern Holland, and would have to run the gauntlet of searchlights and flak in the Roermond area, where the ground on this occasion was concealed by ten-tenths cloud with bright moonlight above to provide ideal conditions for night-fighters. P/O Hadland was the only officer pilot on duty for this operation, and he and his crew got away at 20.10, to encounter very unfavourable weather conditions in the target area. They were unable to locate the target in the dense cloud, and bombed on estimated position without observing any bursts. This was typical of the reports at debriefing, although some crews did see the glow of bursts beneath the cloud, and even the suggestion of a large fire after carrying out their attacks from 10,000 to 13,000 feet. The reality was, that damage in the city was slight, and the operation, like so many before it, was a failure. On return from the night's activities, many crews landed at North Luffenham and Waddington because of unfavourable conditions at Coningsby. During the course of the month the squadron operated on thirteen occasions by night and once by day, dispatching a total of 175 sorties for the loss of eight aircraft and seven crews.

September 1941

September would prove to be a less active month generally, but 5 Group was in action on the first night, when twenty Hampdens joined forces with Wellingtons to attack Cologne in what turned out to be favourable weather conditions. Despite this, few bombs found the mark, and the fires reported by returning crews were probably from decoy sites. Briefings took place across the Command on the 2nd for two operations to be carried out that night, both supported by 5 Group. The main operation would be conducted by 126 aircraft, including eleven Hampdens, against the inland docks at Frankfurt, while a force of forty-nine aircraft targeted the central railway station in Berlin, some 260 miles to the north-east. The bulk of the latter force, thirty-two Hampdens and four Manchesters, was provided by 5 Group, with a handful of 3 Group Stirlings and 4 Group Halifaxes in attendance. For the second night running, the services of 106 Squadron were not required, and there was, therefore, probably a ripple of excitement when thirteen crews were called to briefing on the 3rd, to be told they were to attack the enemy warships holed up at Brest, as they returned to the spotlight after a respite in recent weeks. A force of 140 aircraft was made ready, thirty Hampdens and two 207 Squadron Manchesters representing 5 Group, and the 106 Squadron element became safely airborne between 19.00 and 19.40, with P/Os Hadland and Loftus the only commissioned pilots on duty. They were around ninety minutes into the outward flight when a recall signal was sent, because of the risk that fog might provide lethal conditions for landing. All from Coningsby responded as did those from 1 and 4 Group, and, for whatever reason, landing times at Coningsby ranged from the first back at 21.55 to 01.00 in the case of Sgt Lockwood. In the event, 3 Group and four other aircraft that had failed to pick up the signal, carried on and bombed on estimated positions through a smoke screen.

It was not until the night of the 6/7th that the squadron had its chance to get at the enemy again, when a mixed force of eighty-six Wellingtons, Whitleys and Hampdens was sent to bomb the I G Farben-owned Chemische Werke synthetic rubber factory at Marl-Hüls, a town situated on the north-eastern rim of the Ruhr. The plant was known locally as the "Buna works", because of the Butadiene and Natrium (Sodium) chemicals employed in the manufacturing process of synthetic rubber for tyres. 106 Squadron provided all eighteen of the participating Hampdens, and they took off from Coningsby in what the summary section of the ORB claimed as a record six minutes, although the take-off times as recorded in the daily log ranged from 19.30 to 19.45. On arrival in the target area, the crews encountered good weather conditions and visibility, enhanced by brilliant moonlight, but also heavy flak and searchlights. Despite this, fourteen of them delivered their bombs from between 9,000 and 13,000 feet, mostly on estimated position over the centre of the target, and some bomb bursts were observed, but searchlight dazzle became a problem and prevented an accurate assessment of results. Sgt Mooney and crew spent an hour searching for the target, before bombing from 12,000 feet and observing three bursts. During the course of the sortie, Sgt Mooney notched up two hundred hours operational flying and, thereby, completed his first tour. P/O Hadland and crew found themselves in a spiral dive in AE151, which the pilot managed to correct, and they delivered their bombs from 8,000 feet over the centre of Hamborn. P/O Loftus and crew were among three others to fail to locate the primary target, and they bombed the town of Dorsten five miles to the west of it from 8,000 feet. Returning crews were adamant in their claims of a successful operation, and were dumbfounded when photographic-reconnaissance revealed the factory to be almost completely unscathed.

What would prove to be the month's largest operation was scheduled for twenty-four hours later, when Berlin was posted as the target for 197 aircraft, while the Deutsche Werke U-Boot yards and the town of Kiel would occupy a further fifty-one. 5 Group supported both operations, with eighteen Hampdens for the latter and forty-three Hampdens and four 207 Squadron Manchesters for the Capital, sixteen of the former provided by 106 Squadron. P/Os Hardy, Hayward and Herd were the commissioned pilots involved as they departed Coningsby between 21.20 and 22.05, and headed eastwards into excellent weather conditions and clear visibility. Since reaching cruising altitude, Sgt Jefferis had been contending with an inability to switch from a rich to an economical fuel mixture, which would leave him with insufficient reserves to complete the sortie. On approaching Germany's north-western coast, he selected the port of Cuxhaven as an alternative target, and the bombs were released from 15,000 feet, two of them to burst in the town. After traversing the Schleswig-Holstein peninsula, P/O Herd and crew realised that they were behind schedule and dropped their load in a stick from 11,000 feet across a row of about eight ships moored in Kiel harbour. AD760's heating system had failed three-quarters of an hour after take-off, but Sgt Roberts and crew pressed on until the cold became too intense to continue. They bombed Kiel Canal locks from 11,000 feet before returning home to land at 04.35 and get themselves thawed out, and P/O Hardy and crew also hit the town of Kiel from 14,000 feet after falling behind schedule. Sgt Dashwood and crew failed to locate the primary target, and selected Neuruppin, a town north-west of Berlin, as an alternative destination for their bombs, and observed six bursts in the town centre. Sgt Tilbury and crew were diverted from Berlin by heavy flak, and eventually bombed the coastal city of Lübeck from 8,000 feet as they headed home. Eight Coningsby participants arrived in the target area to find a continuation of the favourable conditions with no more than three-tenths cloud, which they exploited to carry out their attacks from between 8,000 and 14,000 feet, the crews of Sgts Healey and Daniel claiming direct hits on the briefed aiming point, the main post office, from 14,000 and 10,000 feet respectively. Sgt Richardson and crew found themselves caught in searchlights and flak at 12,000 feet, which persuaded them to dive for the ground until breaking free at 5,000 feet, but continued descending and were attacked then by a BF109, which they also shook off at 1,500 feet. They pulled out at 100 feet and evaded further attention by flying for ten to fifteen miles at 50 feet. 137 returning crews would claim to have reached and bombed the Capital, where a large fire was reported and local sources confirmed a significant amount of damage to industrial and residential property in districts to the north and east of the city centre. Fifteen aircraft failed to return, and the squadron was represented among them by AE299, which crashed near the north German coast with just the pilot, Sgt Curties, surviving to fall into enemy hands.

The first large Bomber Command attack on the city of Kassel was briefed to crews of all groups on the afternoon of the 8th, and would involve ninety-five aircraft, including twenty-seven Hampdens. Situated some eighty miles to the east of the Ruhr, the city was home among other major industrial concerns to the Henschel Company, the presence of whose numerous manufacturing sites dominated the city, and employed eight thousand workers in addition to a large number of slaves. Aside from building the Dornier Do17Z bomber under license, Henschel was the main producer of the Panzer III tank and the Tiger I and II, as well as narrow-gauge locomotives. There were to be two aiming points, for which the force was divided, sixty-eight aircraft assigned to the tank works, and twenty-seven to the locomotive workshops. Kassel lay beneath clear skies, the excellent visibility enhanced by bright moonlight, and returning crews reported at least a dozen fires among sheds in the locomotive works, with flames reaching a hundred feet and smoke rising through 5,000 feet. A particularly large conflagration was observed at the main railway station to the west of the aiming point, and the operation was concluded without loss. The enthusiasm of returning crews was dampened to an extent by reports from local sources that just two industrial concerns had sustained serious damage, and eleven houses had been destroyed, which was a poor return for the size of the force operating in favourable conditions.

106 Squadron had not been involved at Kassel, and had to wait until the 11th before receiving orders to prepare for an attack on the A G Neptun shipyards at Rostock, while the rest of the force targeted the nearby Heinkel factory and the town itself. A total force of fifty-six aircraft consisted of thirty-nine Hampdens and five 207 Squadron Manchesters from Coningsby, North Luffenham and Waddington, and a dozen Wellingtons. This was one of three Baltic coast targets for the night, the others, at Kiel and Warnemünde, having been assigned to Wellingtons and Whitleys respectively. Other operations on this night involved eight freshman crews to attack the docks and shipping at Boulogne, and twenty Hampdens mining off the Frisians, Heligoland and Warnemünde. Fifteen 106 Squadron Hampdens took off between 21.20 and 21.50 with no senior pilots on duty and headed eastwards into generally unfavourable weather conditions characterized by heavy cloud. Each was carrying a 1,000 and two 500 pounders, and made their way across southern Jutland to reach the western Baltic, where the cloud began to thin to eight-tenths by the time that the target area drew near, and ground features could be identified by some through a large gap at around 8,000 feet. There were no searchlights and only a small amount of light flak as they carried out their bombing runs from between 8,000 and 15,000 feet on estimated positions and observed a number of bursts and fires. Sgt Clarke and crew reported a large fire, which they estimated to be at or near the location of the Heinkel works, while Sgt Dashwood and crew were the only participants to specify aiming for the Neptun yards. Sgt Daniels and crew mistook Warnemünde for the primary target, and dropped their bombs there to add to those from the Whitley force for which it was the primary target. P/O Hardy and crew also bombed at Warnemünde, and observed three bursts through gaps in the cloud. An S.O.S. message was received from AE300 at 02.23, stating that an engine had cut, and placing the Hampden fifty miles from Sylt. The signal faded away within three minutes, and Sgt Bannister and crew

failed to return home. They had actually abandoned their stricken Hampden to its fate over Denmark, and arrived safely on the ground, where they found themselves in enemy hands within forty-eight hours. This was the second experienced crew to be lost in successive operations, and they would be missed.

Frankfurt's marshalling yards was posted as the main target for the night of the 12/13th, but the 5 Group contribution came from Waddington, Swinderby and Scampton, allowing the 106 Squadron crews to spend the evening in the local hostelries. The force encountered cloud over the sea and for most of the outward flight, until it thinned to some extent, but, as was usually the case, opinions varied as to the state of the conditions. The cloud density ranged between six and ten-tenths in the target area at around 6,000 feet, and some crews also mentioned moonlight filtering through gaps to provide a glimpse of the ground. The visibility was described as both good and poor with searchlight dazzle cited as a major impediment to aiming point identification. Returning crews reported large fires, and local sources confirmed that thirty-eight blazes had to be dealt with, and most of the damage had been in residential districts.

Fifteen 106 Squadron crews were called to briefing on the 13th, to learn that they were to take part in the next round in the eternal battle of Brest. Whether it was the status of the Scharnhorst and Gneisenau that brought the 106 Squadron's "big guns" out is uncertain, but the crews listed on the Order of Battle were headed by those of S/Ls Nelms and Boylan, along with the recently promoted F/L Henderson and P/Os Hardy, Hadland, Hayward and Loftus. It was already the 14th as they took off between 01.05 and 01.30 as part of an overall force of 147 aircraft, before arriving in the target area to find low cloud and the usual effective smoke screen. Bombing took place from between 10,000 and 17,000 feet on estimated positions, and the glow of bursts could be seen beneath the clouds.

Ten crews were back in the briefing room on the 15th, eight of them to learn that they were to participate in a heavy raid on Hamburg that night, while the other two were to carry out freshman sorties attacking the docks and shipping at Le Havre. The Hamburg element had the Blohm & Voss shipyards as its aiming point, and F/L Henderson was the senior pilot on duty as they departed Coningsby between 18.25 and 18.35 as part of an overall force of 169 aircraft. Twenty minutes later, the crews of P/O Wood and Sgt Newby set off on their maiden operations and headed for the south coast to begin the Channel crossing. On arrival at the Normandy coast, they carried out their bombing runs from 11,000 and 12,000 feet and observed two and three bursts respectively. Meanwhile, Sgt Lockwood's AD768 had developed engine trouble very early on, and he was forced to return after just thirty minutes in the air. Whatever the problem, it was put right quickly, and he and his crew set out again in the hope of reaching the target in time. In the event, they delivered their bombs from 10,000 feet on Wilhelmshaven, and returned safely home for the second time that night. Sgt Purnell's helmet microphone become unserviceable, putting him and his crew behind schedule, and it was decided to bomb Cuxhaven instead. Sgt Tilbury and crew also ran out of time, and they bombed Kiel as an alternative, observing two bursts within the town and the incendiaries to start a fire. A layer of ten-tenths stratus cloud at 5,000 feet hid the North Sea from view, but it had dispersed sufficiently to allow sight of the Elbe Estuary, from which point, the force would have to run the gauntlet of searchlights and flak all the way to the aiming points. The skies over the city were clear, but searchlight glare proved to be a serious impediment to aiming point identification. The four successful 106 Squadron crews bombed the primary target from between 9,000 and 15,000 feet, but found it difficult to assess the outcome and returned uncertain as to the results of their efforts. Some returning crews reported the glow of fires visible for eighty miles, and a post-raid analysis and local reports confirmed that Hamburg had sustained quite severe damage in various residential districts. Seven large fires had erupted, and more than fourteen hundred people had been bombed out of their homes, while a 4,000lb blockbuster had destroyed a block of flats in Wandsbek, killing sixty-six residents. Among the eight missing bombers from this raid were two Hampdens, one of which was AE232 from 106 Squadron. It fell victim to a night-fighter flown by Oblt Walter Barte of 1./NJG1, and crashed just south of Hamburg at 22.51. Sgt Richardson and both gunners survived to fall into enemy hands, but the Canadian observer lost his life. P4413 was flying on fumes as it approached Pocklington in Yorkshire after almost nine hours aloft, and the port engine cut out over the threshold, forcing P/O Loftus to pull off a crash-landing, which he accomplished with only minor injuries to the occupants.

The weather closed in at this point, and there would be no further operations for 106 Squadron for thirteen nights, and, in fact, for an entire week from the 21st to the 27th the poor weather conditions would prevent the Command from mounting any night operations. Just in time to beat the weather, orders were received at North Luffenham, Swinderby and Waddington on the 20th to prepare for operations that night against Berlin and Frankfurt, but there would be more than an element of chaos surrounding the Berlin endeavour, when the force of seventy-four aircraft was recalled because of deteriorating weather conditions. 5 Group had sent thirty-six Hampdens to forward bases at Horsham-St-Faith and Swanton Morley, but ten of these were cancelled when they could not be refuelled in time. The chaos continued as the crews made their way home to encounter challenging conditions of fog and mist, which resulted in diversion to a variety of stations in Lincolnshire and Yorkshire.

After eight days away from the operational scene because of the adverse weather conditions, 5 Group detailed forty-eight Hampdens from Coningsby, Scampton, Swinderby and Waddington on the 28th for an attack that night on the main railway station at Frankfurt. However, continuing bad weather at take-off time caused the withdrawal of the less experienced crews, and, together with accidents and incidents, this reduced the number to thirty Hampdens from Scampton, Coningsby and Waddington, while other small forces took off for Genoa and Emden. 106 Squadron supported the 5 Group endeavour with eleven Hampdens after the seven least experienced crews had been withdrawn, and the newly-promoted F/L Hayward was the senior pilot on duty as they departed Coningsby between 22.15 and 22.55. They headed across France over ten-tenths cloud, that thinned to an extent at the target to be replaced by thick haze, which may have been fog, and this conspired with rain and intense darkness to conceal the aiming point. Bombing was carried out on estimated positions from 10,000 to 14,000 feet based on flak and searchlight activity, and all from Coningsby made it safely home, although landing at a variety of stations from Manston in the south to Linton-on-Ouse in the north.

Coningsby was not called into action on the 29th, when the other 5 Group stations were instructed to prepare thirty-eight Hampdens and four Manchesters to join forty-seven other aircraft to attack the Hamburger Flugzeugbau aircraft factory, a subsidiary of the Blohm & Voss company manufacturing seaplanes at the Finkenwerde plant on the southern bank of the Elbe to the west of the city centre. A simultaneous attack by ten Hampdens was to be directed at the Admiral Scheer pocket battleship moored nearby. Conditions over Hamburg were hazy, which made identification something of a challenge, and accurate searchlight and flak activity added to the difficulties. There was also some moonlight, but it was insufficient to allow a positive identification of the aircraft factory, and bombs were estimated to have fallen up to four miles from the intended aiming point. A near-miss was claimed by a 44 Squadron crew on the warship, and it was left to local sources to confirm nine fires within the city, but no damage worthy of particular mention.

Hamburg was posted as the destination again on the last night of the month, this time for eighty-two aircraft again targeting the Blohm & Voss aircraft factory after the previous night's failure. 5 Group put up forty-eight Hampdens from Coningsby, Scampton, North Luffenham, Syerston and Swinderby, while sixteen freshman crews were briefed to bomb the docks and shipping at Cherbourg. Seven 106 Squadron crews were briefed for the main event, and P/O Hadland was the senior pilot on duty, supported by two recent additions to the squadron, P/Os Firth and Wood, while the remaining four crews were captained by stalwart NCO pilots. They took off between 17.45 and 18.05, and soon found themselves in icing conditions, which Sgt Newby and crew assumed was responsible for their Hampden's inability to maintain height. They turned back to land at 21.25, and were joined on the ground an hour and twenty minutes later by Sgt Jefferis and crew, who had been seventy-five miles from the Danish coast when severe icing forced them to turn back. Conditions over Hamburg for the others were fair, but cloud and haze prevented accurate bombing. Attacks were carried out from between 13,000 and 20,000 feet, but there was no assessment, and the local authorities later recorded ten fires. While this operation was in progress eight crews from the squadron joined others from 5 Group to carry out a low-level practice raid on a target in Yorkshire. During the course of the month the squadron operated on eight nights, dispatching 105 sorties, including those recalled from Brest, and losing four aircraft and three crews.

October 1941

The new month began for 106 Squadron with a call to arms for five crews, who were briefed on the 1st for an attack on marshalling yards at Karlsruhe that night. The numbers were small because eight other crews had been held in reserve for an unspecified special task. A total of forty-five aircraft took off, all but one of them Hampdens, the 106 Squadron element departing Coningsby between 18.20 and 18.30 led by S/Ls Nelms and Stenner, the latter now promoted to become B Flight commander. At 21.00 a recall signal was sent to the force because of the fear of fog developing at landing time, and the 106 Squadron crews were told to divert to North Luffenham. S/L Stenner was so close to the target by this time, that he decided to press on, and he bombed the west side of the town from 10,000 feet before returning safely. S/L Nelms and crew turned back as ordered, and they bombed the harbour at Calais before landing at Manston. P/O Wood and crew bombed an unidentified aerodrome twenty miles south of Lille, and landed at Wittering. P/O Hardy and crew had intended to drop their bombs on a Channel port, but found them all cloud-covered, and returned to West Malling with the bombs still on board. There was no sign of Sgt Newby and crew in AD768, and it turned out that they had travelled a mite further than necessary. They completely overflew England with dwindling fuel supplies, and were forced to abandon their transport as the tanks ran dry. Fortunately, they were over Ireland at the time, and the always hospitable Irish authorities transferred them to an internment camp for a period of rest and recuperation.

There were no operations for 5 Group and most other elements of the Command between the 2nd and 9th as the weather took a hand, and it was on the 10th, that Essen and Cologne were posted as the main targets. Sixty-nine aircraft were assigned to attack the latter, while thirty-five miles away to the north, an overall force of seventy-eight aircraft, containing a 5 Group contribution of forty-six Hampdens and ten Manchesters, was to target the Krupp complex. At the same time, an additional six Hampdens would be engaged in searchlight suppression duties in the Bocholt-Borken area on the northern approaches to the Ruhr. 106 Squadron made ready sixteen Hampdens, which departed Coningsby between 23.40 and 00.10 with F/Ls Henderson and Hayward the senior pilots on duty. It seemed that in 106 Squadron it helped if your name began with the letter H, Hayward, Harwood, Herd, Henderson, Hardy to name but a few. They set course via the Lincolnshire coast to cross Holland and approach the target from the north, passing through the searchlight belt as they made their way south to the central Ruhr, where five to ten-tenths cloud and haze created challenging conditions for target location. As already mentioned, the Krupp complex occupied many square miles in a north-western segment of the city, and some crews managed to locate it by following the River Ruhr and the canal system. Thirteen 106 Squadron crews reached Essen to encounter a fierce searchlight and flak defence, and many would return with shrapnel damage. P/O Loftus and crew bombed through haze from 10,000 feet on estimated position, and saw some bursts, but stumbled into the searchlight belt on the way home and were forced down to 800 feet. They decided to attack the searchlight batteries as they fought their way out over a thirty-minute period and extinguished a number of the six targeted by the gunners. Sgt Dashwood and crew bombed in the general target area from 11,000 feet, before also becoming ensnared in searchlights and hit by flak near the Zuider Zee. They escaped by flying across Holland and Belgium at 600 feet. Most crews bombed from between 9,000 and 13,000 feet, but Sgt Tilbury and crew came down to 6,000 feet, where they were able to observe two bursts and several fires. AE144 failed to return to Coningsby, and, eventually, news came through that it had crashed on the northern rim of the Ruhr, killing the recently-arrived P/O Gordon and his crew.

The first major night of operations in the month was notified across the Command on the 12th, when a number of targets were posted in northern and southern Germany and the Ruhr in-between, which would require the highest number of sorties yet in a single night. The largest effort, for which 152 aircraft were detailed from 1, 3 and 4 Groups, would be the first major assault of the war on the southern city of Nuremberg, the site of massive Nazi rallies during the thirties. The other targets were the Deutsche Schiff shipbuilding yards at Bremen, for which ninety-nine aircraft were detailed, including twenty-two Hampdens, and the "Buna" works at Marl-Hüls on the north-eastern rim of the Ruhr, which was to be a 5 Group show involving seventy-nine Hampdens and eleven Manchesters. The total number of sorties for the night was 373, which included eight Hampdens to repeat their intruder role in the searchlight belt in the Bocholt area. 106 Squadron dispatched a dozen Hampdens between 00.30 and 00.50 with S/L Boylan the senior pilot on duty, and began the North Sea crossing under clear skies and a half moon, setting a course for Enkhuizen on the eastern side of the Den Helder peninsula. They reached the Dutch coast to find nine to ten-tenths cloud at 7,000 to 10,000 feet, which extended all the way to the target and tested the crews' ability to establish their positions. The plan for the attack on the "Buna" works called for eight selected crews to go in slightly ahead of the main element to light up the target with their all-incendiary loads, but only three managed to fulfil their brief in the face of the cloud that extended down to 5,000 feet with very few gaps. S/L Boylan and crew were among five from 106 Squadron to bomb in the target area, without observing results, and the remainder bombed other Ruhr locations before returning safely home.

Thirty Hampdens and nine Manchesters eventually made their way to take-off from the 5 Group stations at Coningsby, Scampton, Swinderby, Syerston and Waddington in the early hours of the 14th, after a number had been withdrawn for technical reasons. The target for this 5 Group operation was the main railway station in Cologne, situated in the shadow of the cathedral on the West Bank of the Rhine. Twenty miles to the north, elements of 1 and 3 Groups would be attending to Düsseldorf, and the close proximity of the two operations would guarantee an intense searchlight and flak response. 106 Squadron made ready five Hampdens, which departed Coningsby between 00.45 and 01.00 with S/L Stenner the senior pilot on duty. They crossed the English coast at Orfordness, and headed for the Scheldt estuary in good weather conditions, which held firm all the way to Cologne, where haze and searchlight glare combined with accurate flak to render identification of the aiming point impossible. S/L Stenner and crew bombed from 13,000 feet, and watched their bombs burst across the centre of the town in the face of very strong opposition from the ground. Sgt Scatchard and crew, in contrast, reported little opposition and excellent visibility as they delivered their bombs into the city centre. The crews of Sgts McGinley and Cooke also reported bombing the centre of the target, both from 14,000 feet, but Sgt Jefferis and his crew were attacked by a Me110 while outbound in the Ostend area, and jettisoned their bombs in order to evade their pursuer. Local reports described only a few bombs finding the city, and many returning crews blamed searchlight glare for making identification difficult. While this operation was in progress, five others from the squadron were mining in the Forget-me-not garden in the Kiel Bay region, having preceded the bombing brigade into the air between 00.10 and 00.25. F/L Henderson was the senior pilot among these, and he and his crew made a number of attempts to plant the vegetable in the briefed location, but flak ships prevented them from doing so. They finally released it over the Carrot garden in the Little Belt between Fyn island and the Jutland coast before returning safely. The crews of P/O Loftus and Sgt Tilbury carried out successful sorties, while that of Sgt Lockyer was unable to locate the garden and dropped the mine in an alternative location, and the crew of Sgt Roberts returned early with wireless failure.

The month's largest effort was by 153 aircraft against Bremen on the night of the 20/21st, for which two aiming points were selected. The 5 Group element of eighty-two Hampdens and eight Manchesters included seventeen of the former representing 106 Squadron, whose crews had been briefed to bomb a railway junction. They departed Coningsby between 18.25 and 18.45 led by F/L Henderson, and flew out over the Lincolnshire coast to make landfall on the other side of the North Sea in the region of Texel. Those reaching the target area found intense darkness and ground haze that prevented them from clearly identifying the aiming point, and only thirteen delivered their bombs on estimated positions, guided largely by searchlight and flak activity from 9,000 to 15,000 feet. Of these, only Sgt Purnell and crew were confident that their bombs had fallen close to the briefed aiming point, while the crews of F/L Henderson, Sgt Dashwood and P/O Hardy found alternative destinations for their bombs in Bremerhaven, Cuxhaven and Hamburg respectively. Despite enthusiastic claims of fires by returning crews, the local sources described the attack as small. One of the two missing Hampdens was 106 Squadron's AD984, which crashed in northern Germany, taking the experienced crew of Sgt Lockwood RCAF to their deaths. Their squadron colleagues, Sgt Cooke and crew, made it back to Coningsby in AD746, after machine-gunning an aerodrome from 1,000 feet on the way home, but engine failure caused a stall and a landing crash, from which they walked away apparently unscathed.

The squadron sat out a return to Bremen on the following night, for which a force of 136 aircraft was assembled and the crews briefed to aim for the shipyards. They had to negotiate a bank of cloud that lay over the North Sea with a base at 5,000 and the tops somewhere around 15,000 feet, and reached the target area to find it covered by eight-tenths cumulus cloud with haze below. Again, most crews attacked from estimated positions, scattering bombs mostly in residential areas and causing minimal industrial damage. 106 Squadron remained at home on the night of the 22/23rd, when Mannheim was the target for a force of 123 aircraft, forty-five of them Hampdens. Thick cloud and icing conditions prevented an effective attack from taking place, and the local authorities reported a light raid.

The main operation on the night of the 23/24th was a two-wave attack on the Germania Werft and Deutsche Werke shipyards in Kiel, involving 114 aircraft, including thirty-eight Hampdens from Swinderby and Coningsby and six Manchesters from 97 Squadron. 106 Squadron detailed eighteen Hampdens and sent them on their way from Coningsby between 23.30 and 23.45 with F/L Henderson the senior pilot on duty and the Germania Werft yards as their aiming point. They crossed the western coast of the Schleswig-Holstein peninsula over ten-tenths cloud that denied them sight of the ground, and pushed on through pockets of flak to find the cloud diminishing to five to six-tenths over the primary objective. F/L Henderson and crew positively identified the Deutsche Werke yards rather than those to which they had been assigned, and dropped their bombs and incendiaries on them from 9,000 feet, while the remainder delivered theirs in the general target area or on the town from between 9,000 and 14,000 feet. Sgt Cooke and crew ran into searchlights, and were forced down to 2,000 feet before escaping, but then climbed back up to 7,000 feet to drop the bombs. A number of aircraft were held in a blue master-searchlight, but the flak proved to be less accurate and intense than anticipated. The two waves were widely separated, and it was the second one that gained some success by hitting the Deutsche Werke U-Boot yards.

Orders were received across the Command on the 24th to prepare for that night's operation against railway workshops and marshalling yards in Frankfurt-am-Main, which would involve a force of seventy aircraft. They ran into ten-tenths cloud at around 8,000 feet shortly after crossing the enemy coast, and this persisted all the way to the target, which was located by just a fraction of the crews taking part. The dismal failure of the operation was typical for the period, a situation that was heaping frustration and increasing pressure on C-in-C, AM Sir Richard Peirse.

Hamburg was posted as the target for 115 aircraft on the 26th, for which 5 Group contributed an unknown number of Hampdens and five 97 Squadron Manchesters, briefing the crews of the former to aim for the Blohm & Voss shipyards, and the latter for the main railway station. Eighteen Hampdens departed Coningsby between 17.50 and 18.20 with S/L Boylan the senior pilots on duty, but he and his crew were among three to return early, in their case after problems developed with the instrument panel, while the crews of Sgts Dashwood and Lipton both lost the use of their intercoms. Those reaching the target area found the city bathed in moonlight, but this was countered by searchlight glare, which made identification of ground detail difficult. F/L Henderson and crew bombed from 12,000 feet, but were unable to assess the result, while F/O Webber believed that they saw their bombs burst in the yards from 7,000 feet. In all, thirteen of the squadron's crews reported bombing in the docks or town area, and P/O Loftus and crew delivered theirs on the town of Rendsburg after failing to locate Hamburg. AE136 failed to return home after crashing midway between Hamburg and Bremen, and only the pilot, P/O Wood, survived, to be taken into captivity. AD785 crashed on the Whitby to Scarborough road at 02.15 following a mid-air explosion, and this resulted in the deaths of Sgt Smith and his crew.

Aerial reconnaissance had discovered a large fleet of enemy bombers assembled on the airfield at Schiphol near Amsterdam, and it was assumed that they were being prepared for a major attack on England. 5 Group was handed the task of preventing this and dispatched forty Hampdens and five Manchesters to carry out an attack. 106 Squadron provided eight aircraft, which departed Coningsby between 21.30 and 22.20 with S/Ls Nelms and Boylan the senior pilots on duty. They crossed the North Sea in unfavourable weather conditions, which persisted in the target area to blanket the ground beneath a layer of low cloud with tops at 4,000 feet and a base as low as 1,000 feet, and this made identification of the target almost impossible. S/L Nelms and crew made a long and careful search, but were unable to establish their position, while the crew of P/O Firth was more successful and delivered their bombs in a stick across the aerodrome without observing results. P/O Hardy and crew also managed to find it and dropped their bombs from 700 feet, leaving Sgt Jefferis and crew as the only others to claim success, after descending to 600 feet for their bombing run. X3021 failed to return having crashed into the sea off the Lincolnshire coast, and only the body of the pilot, Sgt Panting, was recovered.

A force of 123 aircraft was assembled on the 31st to be sent back to Hamburg for another crack at the Blohm & Voss shipyards. 5 Group called upon the services of Syerston, Coningsby and Swinderby to prepare forty-two Hampdens and five Manchesters, while a further eighteen Hampdens and a single Manchester were assigned to gardening duties in northern waters, in the Forget-me-not garden in Kiel Harbour and Nectarine II, off the central Frisians. Fifteen 106 Squadron Hampdens set out from Coningsby between 17.30 and 17.55, with F/Ls Hayward and Herd the senior pilots on duty, and headed out over the Lincolnshire coast to make landfall on the enemy coast to the north of the target. As frequently was the case, opinions differed as to the weather conditions, some crews describing good visibility, and even the presence of moonlight, while others reported up to ten-tenths cloud at between 5,000 and 8,000 feet, and great difficulty in identifying the briefed aiming point. However, all were in agreement about the intensity of the searchlight and flak defences, and all did their best to, at least, land their bombs within the city area. F/L Hayward and crew reported their bombs falling in the target area and starting a fire, and eleven other crews from the squadron claimed to have bombed in the area of the shipyards or the town. Three crews who failed to locate the primary target elected to cross the Schleswig-Holstein peninsula to the Baltic coast, where Sgt Brown's dropped their bombs on a convoy in Kiel Bay,

Sgt Picken's on Kiel itself and F/L Herd's from 8,000 feet onto the town of Eckernförde, located ten miles to the north-west. Only fifty-six crews, fewer than half of the original force, claimed to have reached the target to bomb, and local authorities reported that seven large fires were started. 106 Squadron operated on nine occasions during the month, and launched 119 sorties, one of which was the 1,000th. Seven aircraft were lost along with six crews, one of which was safe in internment.

November 1941

The autumn weather had done nothing to ease the path for the beleaguered Commander-in-Chief, who badly needed some successes following the Butt Report. It did not arrive with the first operation of the month, for which, preparations were put in hand on the 1st to send a force of 132 aircraft to attack harbour installations at Kiel. Thirty-two Hampdens were detailed from Scampton, North Luffenham and Waddington, while nine further Hampdens and two Manchesters conducted mining and anti-shipping sorties. Weather conditions were unfavourable in the extreme with severe icing, and only around half of the force reached the target area, where the residents heard the sound of aircraft in the vicinity, but observed no bombs falling in the town. Two nights later, 5 Group sent six Hampdens from North Luffenham, Scampton and Waddington to continue the anti-shipping patrols, and twenty-four others and four Manchesters for gardening duties in the Frisians and Kiel Bay. A further three crews from 50 Squadron were handed a "roving commission" to conduct individual sorties against targets of opportunity in north-western Germany with a load each of a single 2,000 pounder and two 250 pounders. The 5 Group ORB described these sorties as "sneakers".

November was to be a month of very little operational activity for 106 Squadron, which remained at home until the night of the 4/5th, when six of its Hampdens, described in the ORB as "pirates", were sent on anti-shipping patrols off the Frisians in search of enemy convoys. They departed Coningsby at 17.45, and the crew of the newly-promoted F/L Herd spotted two or perhaps three small vessels off Texel, (the 106 and 5 Group ORBs differ), which they proceeded to attack from 500 feet, but their four 500 and two 250 pounders overshot. The other five made no contact with the enemy, and all but one returned to Coningsby before midnight, leaving Sgt Cooke and crew to straggle back after 02.00. By this time, a further nine Hampdens had taken off to lay mines in the Forget-me-not garden in Kiel Bay, and also to attack targets of opportunity with their wing bombs. Sgt Roberts and crew successfully planted their mine in the correct position, before going for a ship with the bombs and missing. Undaunted, they went round again and machine-gunned the vessel. Sgt Dashwood dropped his bombs on the island of Nordstrand, but not on any specific structure, while P/O Hardy and crew swooped down to 800 feet to deliver theirs on Sylt. Sgt Healey and crew were unable to locate their briefed dropping zone, so planted their vegetable in one of the Nectarine gardens off the Frisians on the way home, and then attacked and failed to hit a motor vessel with the wing bombs. In all, seven of the squadron's crews were successful in their primary task, on a night when cloud made for unhelpful conditions.

On the 6th, sixteen 106 Squadron crews departed Coningsby for Skitten airfield at Wick in northern Scotland, which they were to use as a forward base for mining operations in the Onions garden in Oslo Harbour. This meant that the squadron would play only a minor role in the following night's record-breaking activities. No doubt still frustrated by his inability to deliver a telling blow on Germany during the extended period of unfavourable weather, and almost certainly eager to rescue the besmirched reputation of the Command after the damning Butt Report, Peirse planned a major night of operations for the night of the 7/8th. The main operation on this night was intended to be by more than two hundred aircraft against Berlin, and, despite a weather report that predicted thick cloud, storms and icing conditions, Peirse remained resolute in his decision to launch the attack. However, the doubts about the weather were sufficient to prompt the 5 Group A-O-C, AVM Slessor, to object to the plan, and he was allowed to withdraw his contribution, and send it instead to Cologne. The Berlin contingent ultimately amounted to 169 aircraft of 1, 3 and 4 Groups, while sixty-one Hampdens, including those containing the freshman crews of Sgts Moore and Power from 106 Squadron, and fourteen Manchesters made up the Cologne force, and fifty-three Wellingtons and two Stirlings from 1 and 3 Groups were prepared for Mannheim. In all 392 aircraft were to be active in the night's main and support operations, and this was a new record for a single night. It would turn out to be a record-breaking night for other reasons also for both the Command and 106 Squadron.

Seventy-three of the Berlin force reached the general area of the city, and bombs were scattered over a wide area. Some damage was caused, but only fourteen houses were classed as destroyed. In return for this meagre haul, twenty-one aircraft were lost, more than 12% of those dispatched, and the Mannheim force, which failed to find their target with a single bomb, lost seven Wellingtons. The 5 Group force did, at least, come away from Cologne unscathed, but had managed to destroy only two houses and damage fourteen others. 106 Squadron's Sgt Moore and crew of reported identifying the target and bombing from only 4,000 feet, a very creditable performance for a freshman crew, but Sgt Power and his crew returned early with an engine problem.

The minor operations also fared badly, with six aircraft missing from "rover" patrols over the Ruhr, and three from the 106 Squadron mining effort. F/Ls Henderson, Hayward and Herd were the senior pilots on duty as the thirteen Hampdens took off between 00.35 and 02.00 to fly slightly north of east for five hundred miles to reach their destination. F/L Haywood and crew returned early because of an engine issue, leaving the remainder to arrive in the target area to encounter severe icing conditions, which persuaded the crews of Sgts Lipton and Scatchard to abandon their sorties and return their mine and wing bombs to store. Six crews returned home to report planting their vegetable in or very near to the briefed location, while P/O Hardy and crew delivered theirs in Stavanger Fjord as an alternative. This left three crews unaccounted for, those of F/L Henderson DFC, F/L Herd DFC and P/O Firth in AD760, AD932 and P1290 respectively. F/L Herd and crew were heard calling for assistance seven hours and forty minutes after taking-off, and a fix put them at forty-eight miles from Wick, but nothing more was heard from them. The body of a gunner, Sgt Jones, eventually came ashore, but of the others, which included P/O McIver DFC of the RCAF, there was no trace. AD760 and P1290 were both picked off by flak in the target area, F/L Henderson and one other surviving from the former and falling into enemy hands. In the latter, P/O Firth and one other lost their lives, and the two survivors joined their squadron colleagues in captivity. It was a disastrous night for the Command, which registered a new record loss of thirty-seven aircraft, more than twice the previous highest at night. It was the final straw for the Air Ministry, and, on the 13th, Peirse was ordered to restrict further operations while the future of the Command was considered at the highest level, and he was summoned to a personal and uncomfortable meeting with Churchill to explain himself. With loud voices, particularly at the Admiralty, calling for the redeployment of bomber aircraft to combat U-Boots in the Atlantic and to redress reversals in the Middle East, the very existence of an independent bomber force now hung in the balance. The Peirse era at the helm of Bomber Command was effectively over, and he would be little more than a caretaker until leave his post in January.

In the meantime, on the 8th, 5 Group detailed twenty Hampdens for an attack on the Krupp complex in Essen in company with thirty-four other aircraft, and ten Hampdens and five Manchesters for freshman sorties over Dunkerque. Supporting the main event in a searchlight suppression role were six Hampdens, two belonging to 106 Squadron and containing the crews of Sgt Roberts and S/L Stenner. They departed Coningsby at 17.20 and 17.35 respectively bound for the Bocholt searchlight belt situated close to the Dutch frontier some twenty miles north of Duisburg. Before the drone of S/L Stenner's engines had receded, Sgt Power and crew lifted off the Coningsby grass field, before climbing out and heading south for an appointment with the docks and shipping at Dunkerque. They would enjoy a successful sortie, watching their bombs fall from 7,000 feet to burst among the docks and produce a great shower of sparks. Meanwhile, some two hundred miles to the north-east, S/L Stenner and crew were patrolling their beat at between 4,000 and 10,000 feet, dropping their bombs at intervals, while Sgt Roberts and crew chose 500 to 2,000 feet, bombing and machine-gunning as they went. Those attacking Essen claimed a number of large fires, but there was no confirmation from local sources and another indeterminate raid was chalked up.

Hamburg's Blohm & Voss shipyards were the target for which a force of seventy-one aircraft, including thirty Hampdens and six Manchesters, was made ready on the 9th. 106 Squadron did not take part in the operation, which, according to local sources, took place under clear skies and bright starlight, caused three large fires and bombed out almost four hundred people. A period of unfavourable weather kept most of the Command on the ground from then until mid-month, followed, thereafter, by relatively small-scale operations against German and French ports for the remainder of the month. The first of these were to be launched against Kiel and Emden on the night of the 15/16th, for which 106 Squadron made ready seventeen Hampdens, all but one for the former, only for deteriorating weather to persuade 5 Group to cancel its involvement an hour before take-off. The raid went ahead with Wellingtons, while forty-nine aircraft, including eleven Hampdens and six Manchesters, targeted the docks and shipping at Emden. 106 Squadron supported it with the single freshman crew of Sgt Hartgroves, who departed Coningsby at 17.30 and arrived over the target to find it hidden by cloud. They dropped their bombs on a flak and searchlight concentration and thought that they saw a red glow beneath the clouds.

There were no operations for 5 Group at all between the 16/17th and 22/23rd, before orders were received on all 5 Group stations on the 23rd to make ready fifty-one Hampdens and two Manchesters for an all-5 Group attack on the docks and U-Boots at Lorient, while 3 Group focused on Dunkerque. 106 Squadron sat out the operation, which took place in favourable weather conditions with little or no cloud and good visibility, and this resulted in most bomb loads falling within the confines of the target area. Three nights later, Emden was the objective for eighty Wellingtons and twenty Hampdens, fourteen of the latter provided by 49 Squadron at Scampton, while 106 Squadron put up the remaining six, all NCO-captained freshman crews, which departed Coningsby between 17.00 and 17.15 on another evening of poor weather conditions. Five of the 106 Squadron crews were among the fifty-five claiming to have bombed in the target area, all citing ten-tenths cloud as the reason for bombing on estimated positions based on dead-reckoning (DR) and evidence of flak. Sgt Moss and crew were missing from debriefing, and it would be a long time before news came through of their fate. AE317 had crashed into the sea off the Frisians, and only the body of a gunner eventually washed ashore for burial.

5 Group stations were alerted on the 27th to make ready for a raid that night on marshalling yards in Düsseldorf. Thirty-four Hampdens and six Manchesters were made ready, and they would be joined in the operation by forty-six Wellingtons and Stirlings representing 3 Group. 5 Group had actually cut sixteen Hampdens and two Manchesters from its original plan because of doubts about the weather, as a result of which, 106 Squadron did not take part. The southern Ruhr was found to be largely cloud-free, although some crews would report up to eight-tenths of the white stuff, but the usual blanket of industrial haze created poor vertical visibility, and, despite claims of large fires in the railway yards, local reports detailed only light damage, while, twenty miles to the south, Cologne recorded damage to 119 houses.

A major raid was planned for Hamburg on the last night of the month, for which a force of 181 aircraft was assembled, including forty-eight Hampdens and four Manchesters. The 5 Group crews had been briefed to aim for the Blohm & Voss shipyards, while other elements went for two other aiming points within the city. The fourteen 106 Squadron Hampdens departed Coningsby between 16.20 and 16.45 with F/L Hayward and the newly-promoted F/L Webber the senior pilots on duty. The weather, for a change, was excellent as they climbed away from Coningsby, but Sgt Dashwood became unwell two hours into his sortie and turned back. By that time Sgt Power and crew had already landed after aborting their sortie through a defective boost gauge. The 5 Group ORB recorded that the weather conditions over Hamburg were most favourable, with little or no cloud and bright moonlight, and the 106 Squadron ORB concurred, while the 50 Squadron ORB described much cloud and poor visibility that prevented all but one crew from identifying the shipyards. F/L Webber and crew dropped their bombs from 7,500 feet into the docks area, two miles east of the briefed aiming point, and saw no bursts. Sgt Scatchard and crew were at 16,000 feet when they released their bombs on what they believed to be the target, but also saw no results. Sgt Picken and crew bombed from 14,000 feet and thought they had scored a "near-miss", while the crew of Sgt Stoffer reckoned theirs was a direct hit from 6,500 feet, but again were unable to observe anything to back up the claim. As the final hour of November ticked away, a dozen 106 Squadron Hampdens were well into their return journey to Coningsby, Sgt Roberts no doubt buoyed up by the knowledge that he had now completed two hundred hours of operational flying, and could look forward to a rest. A flight sergeant wireless operator/gunner with a DFM flying on this night with F/L Hayward completed four hundred hours of operational flying during this operation, but, sadly, the hand-written entries in the squadron ORB are in a script so small that the name is unrecognisable. Thirteen aircraft failed to return, and this figure included 106 Squadron's P1228 and AT115 containing the crews of Sgts Moore and Rolfe respectively. Both were lost without trace, and, presumably, were swallowed up by the cold North Sea. 120 returning crews claimed to have reached and bombed the primary target, and left behind many fires, local reports confirming twenty-two, two of them large, and 2,500 people bombed out of their homes.

On his return, S/L Potts of 50 Squadron reported observing a new kind of shell, which exploded with great force and caused a violent disturbance of the surrounding air. Later in the war, other crews would begin to report "scarecrows", which, they were told, was a German shell designed to simulate the destruction of a bomber with a full bomb load, the purpose of which was to demoralize witnesses. Despite the insistence by many veterans that Scarecrows existed, they did not, and were, in realty, bombers exploding with a full bomb load on board. During the course of the month the squadron operated on seven nights and dispatched fifty-four sorties for the loss of six aircraft and crews.

December 1941

The dominant theme during December would be the continuing presence at Brest of Scharnhorst, Gneisenau and, sometimes, Prinz Eugen, and no less than fifteen operations of varying sizes would be mounted against the port and its guests during the month, some by daylight. The weather, mostly in the form of snow, kept the entire Command on the ground for the first six nights of the new month, and it was not until the 7th that a posted operation would actually go ahead. The target for a force of 130 aircraft was Aachen, Germany's most westerly city, perched on the frontiers with both Holland and Belgium. The briefed aiming point was the Nazi Party HQ, which had no special significance other than the fact that it was situated in the city centre, at a time when it was still not yet admitted publicly that population centres were being bombed. 5 Group detailed fifty Hampdens and a dozen Manchesters, six of the former provided by 106 Squadron, which departed Coningsby between 02.30 and 03.05 on the 8th, with P/Os Hardy and Loftus the senior pilots on duty. The night was characterized by wintry showers and low cloud as the Coningsby contingent climbed away and set course for the Scheldt estuary. The conditions improved during the journey south, but the cloud built up to nine to ten-tenths in the target area with tops at 15,000 feet. The crews of Sgts Brown and Healey and P/O Hardy all failed to identify the primary target, but each delivered their bombs onto the town without being able to observe anything below the cloud. P/O Loftus and crew abandoned their search and bombed Ostend from 5,000 feet on the way home. Sgt Dashwood and his crew bombed railway lines and saw bursts across them, and the crew of Sgt Cooke also attacked railway lines and lock gates. In all, only sixty-four crews claimed to have reached and bombed the general area, and local authorities reported a raid by an estimated sixteen aircraft with little damage. Meanwhile, numerous minor operations were taking place, including the first of the month against the enemy ships still sheltering in the port of Brest, carried out by a small force of Wellingtons and Stirlings.

Daylight operations were a matter of course for 2 Group squadrons, and some, known as "Circus", had the purpose of tempting enemy fighters into the air to face RAF Spitfires in a war of attrition. These were, however, very different from the unescorted daylight operations known as "moling", conducted by the other groups, which relied on cloud and surprise to protect the crews. Such operations were rarely, if ever, effective, and were frequently aborted over enemy territory if the cloud cover dissipated. Small numbers of 5 Group aircraft were detailed on successive days from the 10th to the 13th, with targets in Germany and Holland including shipping, airfields and anything else that presented itself, along with mining. On the morning of the 12th four 106 Squadron Hampdens stood ready for take-off in conditions which promised sufficient cloud to provide the necessary cover, and F/L Webber and crew were first away at 10.40, with, unquestionably, the toughest brief of the quartet. Their target was an oil refinery at Gelsenkirchen, at the eastern end of the Ruhr, and one has to question the sanity of senior officers in sending a single crew deep into enemy territory by daylight to attack a heavily defended target. Even if successful, the bombs from a single medium bomber could not create more than a nuisance, and certainly were not worth sacrificing the lives of four experienced and valuable young men.

S/L Nelms and crew took off five minutes after F/L Webber, and headed towards Oldenburg, a town to the west of Bremen, where they were to attack the marshalling yards, and they were followed immediately by F/L Hayward and crew, whose target was an oil refinery at Emmerich on the German side of the Rhine on the border with Holland. Five minutes later, Sgt Cooke and crew departed for a smelting works at Nordenham, a town across the bay from Wilhelmshaven. S/L Nelms and crew turned back when the cloud cover deserted them, and they landed at 13.05. F/L Hayward and crew attacked their objective with bombs and machine-gun fire from 300 feet, and claimed four direct hits followed by clouds of black smoke. Sgt Cooke and crew carried out two runs at 50 feet against a factory south of the one they were supposed to attack, scoring direct hits and causing terrific explosions. During their low-level dash for home across Germany, they strafed a ship in the Elbe, a train and a railway station, before arriving back at Coningsby at 15.50. The return of F/L Webber and his crew was awaited in vain, and news would be received at the end of the month, that AE391 had crashed at Osterfeld, a suburb of Oberhausen, well to the west of Gelsenkirchen, and all on board had been killed. It is not known whether they were outbound or homebound at the time.

106 Squadron remained at home thereafter until the night of the 15/16th, when providing two freshman crews for a small-scale operation to Ostend. Both P/Os Selfe and Horner were carrying out their first operations as crew captain as they departed Coningsby at 17.35 and 17.55 respectively, and good weather conditions and clear visibility helped them to complete their briefs successfully and return safely home. On the following night, after eleven crews had been briefed for an attack on Wilhelmshaven, the squadron's involvement was scrubbed at the last minute, and eight crews were sent instead to mine the waters of the Jellyfish garden off Brest, while two freshman crews bombed the docks at Dunkerque. The latter, in the shape of Sgt Bishop and P/O Hodgson and their crews took off first, at 17.30 and 17.50, but P/O Hodgson and crew were forced to turn back when their intercom failed. Sgt Bishop and crew pressed on, but were unable to locate the target in conditions of heavy cloud and brought their bombs home. S/L

Boylan and crew led the gardening contingent away at 18.15, and the others followed them into the air over the ensuing seventy-five minutes. Five were able to deposit their vegetables in precisely the correct position, but those of S/L Boylan, F/Sgt Jefferis and Sgt Power planted theirs within a quarter of a mile and two miles of the briefed locations.

Another unusual type of role for Hampdens was "intruding", which, fortunately, was not frequently undertaken. This differed from moling in being a roving commission to attack targets of opportunity rather than a specific objective. Shortly after noon on the 21st, six Hampdens each from 106 and 49 Squadrons took off for north-west Germany to find individual factory targets. Sgt Scatchard and crew were soon back on the ground with technical problems, and a reserve crew was sent up to replace them. S/L Stenner was the senior 106 Squadron pilot on duty, and his was one of five crews to abandon their sortie when the cloud disappeared. A recall signal was sent to Sgt Hartgroves, but it was not acknowledged, and AE151 failed to return. A German broadcast that evening announced that a British bomber had been shot down during the afternoon, and news eventually came through that it had crashed in Holland, and that the pilot and his two gunners had survived and were now in enemy hands.

Another major assault on Brest was notified across the Command on the 17th, for which a force of 121 aircraft was assembled, among them twenty-five Hampdens from Waddington, Scampton and Syerston. The attack took place in the face of extreme darkness, a smoke screen and intense searchlight and flak activity, and eighty returning crews claimed to have bombed in the approximate area of the target vessels.

The main target for the night of the 23/24th was Cologne, for which a force of almost seventy Wellingtons, Hampdens and Whitleys took off. They were unable to locate the target in conditions of complete cloud cover, and no bombs found the mark. 106 Squadron did not take part in this operation, but sent two freshman crews to join others from Swinderby, Syerston and Waddington in one of the Nectarine gardens off the Frisians. There was heavy rain and low cloud as the crews of Sgt Young and P/O Hodgson arrived in the target area, where the former were able to deliver their mine in the correct position, while the latter were beaten by the conditions and brought theirs back. Three Hampdens each from North Luffenham and Swinderby set off in daylight for Brest on Christmas Eve, but only one reached and bombed the target without observing the results. 83 Squadron sent six crews "moling", but all abandoned their sorties in the absence of sufficient cloud cover.

Early on the 27th, ten 50 Squadron Hampdens departed Wick to carry out their part in the audacious raid by commandos on the island of Vaagsö off the Norwegian coast. All objectives were achieved at minor cost to the ground forces and the operation was hailed as an outstanding success, but eight of twenty-nine Blenheims and Hampdens were lost. A major raid on marshalling yards in Düsseldorf was mounted that night, for which 5 Group contributed thirty Hampdens and seven Manchesters to an overall force of 132 aircraft. The only departure from Coningsby was of a single 97 Squadron Manchester, as 106 Squadron remained at home. Despite the claims of ninety-six crews to have bombed in the target area, a paltry thirty-two high-explosive bombs fell within the city along with a few incendiaries, and damage was described by local sources as very light.

The final operation of the year for the squadron took place on the night of the 28/29th, when two main targets were briefed, Wilhelmshaven for a force of eighty-six Wellingtons, and the "Buna works", otherwise known as the Chemische Werke synthetic rubber factory at Marl-Hüls for eighty-one Hampdens. This would be the third attempt to destroy the factory since September, but it should be remembered that it represented a precision target at a time when precision at night was beyond the capabilities of the available equipment. Fifteen Hampdens departed Coningsby from 18.00 onwards led by S/Ls Nelms and Stenner, and headed to what would be a moonlit target made even clearer by snow on the ground. The crews of F/L Hayward and P/O Horner both experienced engine failure and landed back at Coningsby around three hours after taking off, while Sgt Dashwood and crew, who had been assigned to fire-raising duties, did not arrive at the target in time, and in accordance with instructions, brought their bombs home. Sgt Power and crew were unable to locate the target and also returned their bombs to the store, leaving eleven crews to carry out an attack. Sgt Brown and crew scored a direct hit from 12,000 feet, and claimed that their bombs started a large fire, while Sgt Bishop and crew attacked from 4,500 feet and hit the south-west corner of the complex. S/L Stenner and crew reported one of their bombs exploding on the target and causing a vivid green flash followed by a fire. They were then attacked and damaged by a Me110, which was hit by return fire and possibly destroyed. At debriefing, Sgt Scatchard and crew claimed that the fires were visible from fifty miles into the return journey, and, once all had passed on their impressions at debriefing, the consensus was that the raid had been highly successful. The sad news came through on the 31st confirming that F/L Webber and his crew had lost their lives. During the course of the month the squadron operated on five nights and two days, launching forty-five sorties for the loss of two aircraft and crews.

1941 had been the squadron's first full year as an operational unit, and its experiences were similar to those of any other squadron in the group, and, indeed, in the Command. It had been a disappointing year for the Command, and despite the best efforts of the crews, one of under-achievement, with little to show in terms of an advance on the performance of 1940. The new generation of bombers, the Stirling, Halifax and Manchester, introduced into operational service early in the year, had each failed to meet the requirements expected of them, and had undergone long periods of grounding while essential modifications were carried out. 1942 would bring changes, chief among which were the arrival on the operational scene of the war-winning Lancaster, already in the hands of 44 (Rhodesia) Squadron, and a new Commander-in-Chief, who would know how to exploit it.

106 Squadron with Hampden September 1941

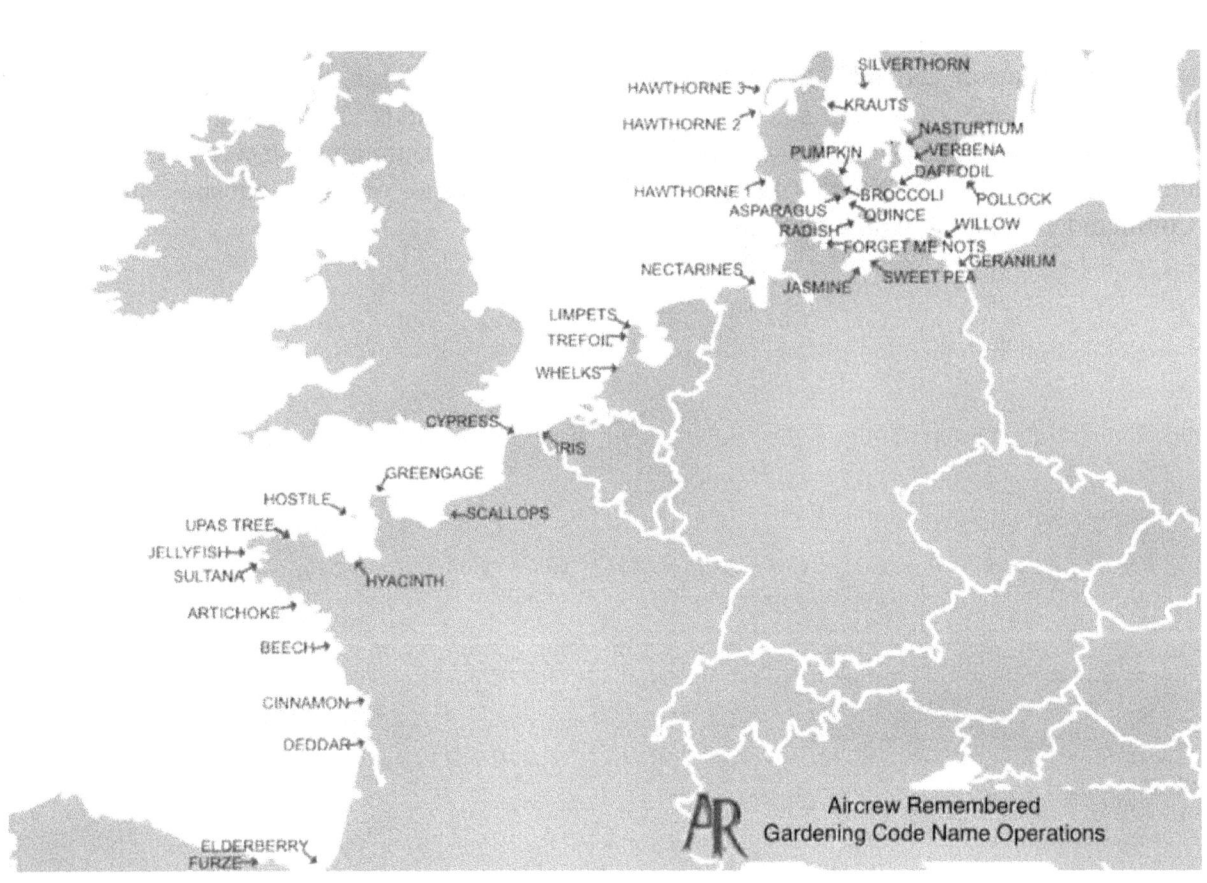

Mining 'Gardening' Areas (courtesy of Aircrew Remembered)

A Flak Barge
47,152 mines were laid offensively in enemy-controlled waters by aircraft of Bomber Command.

German Minesweeper of WWII

106 Squadron 1941. S/L Doran DFC and Ground Crew

106 Squadron Hampdens

*P/O A F McGruer
KIA 22nd August 1941*

*P/O J P Erly
KIA 22nd August 1941*

*Sgt Anthony Parker
KIA 30th November 1941*

P/O (later F/L) J Henderson at the control of a Hampden. (Simon Sanders).

Colleagues act as pall-bearers at the funeral of Sgt Edward Smith on 27th October 1941. Smith and his crew died when their Hampden exploded between Whitby and Scarborough on its return from Hamburg.

Hampden AD986 of 106 Squadron at Coningsby, Lincolnshire, June 1941. This aircraft was lost over Germany on the night of 4/5th July 1941. Crew of P/O L S Christman (RCAF), Sgt S Linley, Sgt S C Morse, Sgt A E Brownbill were all killed when the aircraft was shot down and crashed at Hervest, Dorsten, Germany.

*Hampden AD746 ZN-Z of 106 Squadron
Crashed at Coningsby when returning from Bremen 21st October 1941.*

German soldier manning a MG34 anti-aircraft gun in 1941.

Aircrew and ground staff examine some minor flak damage to a Hampden of 106 Squadron after returning from the daylight raid on the Gneisenau and Prinz Eugen at Brest, 24th July 1941.

The ventral rear gunner's position in a 106 Squadron Hampden at Coningsby, Lincolnshire, viewed from the starboard side. Operating the twin .303 Vickers K machine guns is F/L Chisholm, the Squadron Gunnery Officer.

P/O Brian Oliver, who was eventually to attain the rank of Squadron Leader. (Simon Sanders).

Roger Purnell and crew (Simon Sanders)

Pilot Sgt E.R.H. Lyon (Lee) in Hampden AE193 ZN-A of 106 Squadron.
Lost on combat operations on the night of 28/29th August 1941. Whilst returning from Duisburg, both the aircraft's engines cut out, and the crew were forced to ditch in the North Sea. After four days and nights at sea in the dinghy, they were rescued by a Dutch fishing boat. They were taken to Zoutcamp, Groningen. Suffering from exhaustion, the bomber crew decided to surrender, rather than jeopardise the lives of their Dutch saviours. Sgt R J K Woodroofe (Nav), Sgt G B Stanton (W.Op), Sgt G Luke (AG).

Cities of Germany

A salvo of bombs explodes on the hard standing at Schiphol airport, Amsterdam which was taken over by the Germans and bombed by 106 Squadron in September 1941. (not 106 Squadron)

*Air raid on Kiel in the night of 7/8th April 1941.
Stadtwerke's power station). Incendiary bomb burnt out the machine hall.*

German soldiers on quad-mounted 2cm flak.

P/O Robert Wareing

A vertical aerial photograph taken during a raid on Berlin on the night of 2/3rd September 1941. The broad wavy lines are the tracks of German searchlights and anti-aircraft fire. Vertical night aerial photograph taken during a raid on Berlin, showing bombs exploding in the vicinity of the central cattle-market and railway yard (middle right), east of the city centre. The broad wavy lines are the tracks of German searchlights and anti-aircraft fire can also be seen. Also illuminated by the flash-bomb in the lower half of the photograph are the Friedrichshain gardens and sports stadium, St Georgs Kirchhof and Balten Platz. 106 Squadron attacked Berlin five days later, but it is a typical representation.

Part of the Chemische Werke (Buna Works) at Marl-Hüls after allied bombing raids.

Photograph purporting to be W/C Patrick Polglase and Hampden P2083 were the first of the 106 Squadron contingent to arrive at Coningsby.

W/C Patrick Julyan Polglase   *(© Radley College)*

January 1942

As far as most crews were concerned, the New Year would look and feel exactly like the outgoing one, and, still under the restrictions of the November directive, the Command's activities reflected the continuing obsession with the German raiders at Brest, and a further eleven operations against the port would take place during January. The new year began for 106 Squadron with the dispatch of four NCO-captained Hampdens for daylight "sneaker" operations over north-western Germany on the 2nd in company with four others each from North Luffenham and Scampton. They took off in the late morning, but there were early signs of thinning cloud, and, after an hour's eastward progress, the crews of Sgts Scatchard, Lipton and Power turned back. Sgt Dashwood and crew pressed on until reaching the Frisian island of Schiermonikoog, where they were fired upon by a convoy and decided also to abandon what was clearly a futile sortie. While 44 (Rhodesia) Squadron watched from the side-lines as it continued its evolution to operational status with the Lancaster, 5 Group detailed a dozen Manchesters for a raid on St-Nazaire that night, and thirty-six Hampdens from Scampton, Swinderby and Syerston for gardening duties off the Biscay ports and the Frisians.

The exercise was repeated twenty-four hours later with smaller numbers, and, this time, 106 Squadron contributed five of ten Hampdens, whose crews were briefed to mine the waters in one of the Nectarine gardens off the Frisians. Sgt Dashwood and crew were first away at 16.20, and the others followed during the ensuing thirty minutes. They encountered heavy rain and low cloud in the target area, despite which, three crews managed to identify their garden location and plant their mines as briefed. By this time F/Sgt Jefferis and crew had returned home with an engine problem, and P/O Howard and crew were in trouble. A message was received, "S.O.S. landing in sea", and a fix plotted that located them some 130 miles off the English coast. Two crews conducted a sea-search on the 4th, but no trace of AT123 or its crew was ever found. Another "sneaker" operation was mounted on the 4th, which 106 Squadron supported with three Hampdens, captained by Sgts Power and Cooke and P/O Loftus, who departed Coningsby between 11.00 and 11.10. The crews of Sgts Power and Loftus ran out of cloud and turned back at 3° east, although there was sufficient of the white stuff for Sgt Power to dive into to evade a single engine enemy fighter. Sgt Cooke and crew, however, seemed to have a particular taste for this kind of operation, as demonstrated by their exploits in December, and they reached the town of Leer, on Germany's northern-most border with Holland. They delivered 250 pounders across the railway station and a junction from 300 feet, and tried but failed to bomb a train. During a further pass they machine-gunned trains and installations, and encountered some return fire for their cheek.

The campaign against Brest continued on the night of the 5/6th, when 5 Group contributed twenty-seven Hampdens and twelve Manchesters to an overall force of 154 aircraft, some briefed to aim for the Scharnhorst and Gneisenau, while the remainder concentrated on the naval docks. The 106 Squadron contingent of nine departed Coningsby very late, between 03.10 and 03.35 with P/Os Hodgson and Horner the only commissioned pilots on duty, and, like the other participants, they were thwarted by an effective smoke-screen and eight to ten-tenths cloud. They bombed on estimated positions from between 10,000 and 14,000 feet in the face of heavy flak, and despite claims of large fires by some returning crews, no accurate assessment of results could be made.

On the 6th, nineteen Hampdens from Scampton, Swinderby and Syerston were committed to "scuttle" sorties over northern Germany, which were roving commissions against targets of opportunity at specific locations that appeared to differ from "moling", only by relying on the cover of darkness rather than cloud. Brest was posted as the target for a force of 151 aircraft on the 8th, reconnaissance having revealed that Scharnhorst and Gneisenau had been joined by Prinz Eugen. 5 Group contributed thirty-seven

Hampdens and ten Manchesters from Bottesford, Coningsby, Scampton, Swinderby and Syerston for this attack, for which take-off was delayed until the early hours of the 9th. 106 Squadron remained at home as the force flew out over varying amounts of cloud, to establish their positions over the target by dead-reckoning (DR) and e.t.a. On arrival, they were met by seven to ten-tenths low cloud, with good visibility above and haze below, and some crews were able to identify the briefed aiming point through gaps in the cloud, aided by fires already burning.

A force of eighty-two aircraft was assembled for a return to Brest on the night of the 9/10th, for which 5 Group put up twenty-seven Hampdens and six Manchesters from Bottesford, Coningsby, North Luffenham and Scampton. W/C Allen took the lead of 106 Squadron on this night, departing Coningsby at a minute after midnight to be followed over the next twenty-nine minutes by the others. Sgt Dashwood and crew were back shortly before 04.00 with engine trouble, and landed at Boscombe Down. The weather in the target area continued to be unhelpful, but W/C Allen and crew described the visibility as good as they delivered their bombs onto the docks from 12,000 feet at around 02.40. The others reported nine to ten-tenths cloud obscuring the target area, and all bombed on approximate positions without observing any results. Returning crews mentioned quite heavy but inaccurate flak, but none of them was hit. It turned into another inconclusive raid, from which eleven Hampden crews brought their bombs home after failing to identify the target.

Thirty-four Hampdens and nine Manchesters were detailed by 5 Group on the 10th to contribute to an overall force of 124 aircraft bound for Wilhelmshaven that night for what turned out to be another wasted effort. They found the target area under three to five-tenths cloud at around 5,000 feet, which offered a fair chance for a change of actually identifying the aiming point, despite which, local reports suggested that few bombs found the mark, and damage was slight. The focus remained on north-western Germany for the next two operations, both of which were directed at Hamburg. While on a training flight on the morning of the 14th, AE292 span in and crashed four miles north-east of Boston, killing Sgt Lawton and the other occupant. That night, a force of ninety-five aircraft included a contribution from 5 Group of thirty-two Hampdens and eleven Manchesters, whose crews were briefed to attack the Blohm & Voss shipyards, situated on the Kuhwerder Island in the Finkenwerder district, opposite Sankt Pauli to the west of the city centre. Extreme darkness and thick ground haze created challenging conditions for aiming point identification, but crews could always rely on the searchlight and flak batteries lining the Elbe to guide them into the heart of the city. Large ground features like the Binnen and Aussen-Alster Lakes on the north-western edge of the centre were another good guide for non-precision bombing. At debriefing, half of the crews involved in this operation claimed to have bombed within the city, and local authorities confirmed seven large fires and damage to the Altona railway station, situated on the North Bank of the Elbe to the west of Sankt Pauli.

Hamburg was "on" again twenty-four hours later, for which a force of ninety-six aircraft was assembled, 5 Group's contribution amounting to twenty-seven Hampdens and ten Manchesters, including nine of the former belonging to 106 Squadron. They began taking off at 16.35, but X3131 crashed, happily, without injury to Sgt Power and his crew, but this slightly delayed the other departures. The remainder got away between 16.40 and 17.10, but the crews of P/O Loftus and Sgt Lipton were soon back in the circuit with engine problems. The others pressed on with S/L Stenner now the only commissioned pilot on duty, and had to negotiate large pillars of cumulonimbus cloud over the North Sea, which convinced half of the force of the futility of trying to reach the target. Of those continuing on, four were from 106 Squadron, and they found the target to be obscured by cloud, which persuaded Sgt Picken and crew to drop two 500lb bombs from estimated positions onto a searchlight concentration, but bring their incendiaries home, while Sgt Bishop and crew delivered two 500 pounders from 12,000 feet, and believed that they had fallen into the town area. The crews of Sgt Young and S/L Stenner reported similar experiences at debriefing and were among fifty-two crews claiming to have reached and bombed Hamburg without observing any results, and could only report that fires appeared to be taking hold as they turned away. Local sources reported thirty-six fires, only three of them large, but otherwise, no damage of significance. Four aircraft failed to return, among them P1341 of 106 Squadron, which crashed at the well-defended port of Esbjerg in south-western Denmark after being hit by flak. Happily, Sgt Dashwood RNZAF and his crew all survived, and were soon in enemy hands. Last to depart Coningsby on this night had been the crew of F/O Bareham, who lifted off the runway at 17.30 to carry out a freshman mining sortie in one of the Nectarine gardens off the Frisians. They avoided heavy flak by dropping down to 50 feet, before planting their vegetable into the briefed location and returning safely.

Two nights later, 5 Group dispatched twenty Hampdens and six Manchesters from Coningsby, North Luffenham and Scampton as part of an overall force of eighty-three aircraft bound once more for north-western Germany, this time to attack Bremen, but only eight crews reported reaching the city, and some of the others bombed at Hamburg instead. 106 Squadron was enjoying another six-night stand-down at the time and did not participate. It was during this period, on the 20th, that the squadron became the fifth in the Command to receive the Avro Manchester in preparation for its forthcoming conversion to the type. The ill-fated bomber was already in the process of being superseded by the Lancaster, which had just begun proving trials with 44 (Rhodesia) Squadron at Waddington, but would remain in service for a further six months until production numbers allowed 5 Group to fully convert. The Achilles Heel of the Manchester had been its Rolls Royce Vulture engines, which had not achieved expected performance levels, and frequently failed. The loss of one engine left a Manchester with the flying characteristics of a brick, and more of them fell victim to non-operational accidents than were lost to enemy action. L7390, L7398 and L7463 were shunted across the tarmac from 97 Squadron, and they would be joined on the 26th by L7474.

When Bremen was next posted as the target on the 21st, 5 Group detailed eleven Hampdens from Coningsby and Syerston as part of an overall force of fifty-four aircraft. The six 106 Squadron participants took off between 16.45 and 17.15 with P/O Selfe the senior pilot on duty on an intensely cold night, which would severely curtail the squadron's efforts. Sgt Scatchard and crew were one of only two from the squadron to reach the target, which they found to be free of cloud. The visibility was excellent, and they were preparing to bomb when ensnared by a cone of some thirty searchlights. Sgt Scatchard pushed the nose of the Hampden down, and they broke free at 3,000 feet, from which altitude they delivered the bombs into the town. Sgt Stoffer and crew also described conditions over the target as cloud-free, and they dropped their bombs from 12,000 feet before returning home in temperatures of minus forty-one degrees at 17,000 feet. Three other crews abandoned their sorties after the heating system in their aircraft broke down, exposing them to temperatures of around minus fifteen degrees Celcius at 7,500 feet. The general pattern of failure continued as only half of the crews involved reported reaching the target area, and the operation cost the squadron the crew of Sgt Deere. His body was found in the wreckage of AE123 near Zwolle in Holland, but his three crew mates survived to be taken into captivity. Throughout the month, freshman crews had been cutting their teeth by attacking the port of Emden, and 106 Squadron's involvement on this night was by the crew of Sgt Sporny, he a member of the Polish Air Force, who were carrying out their maiden sortie. The weather was good, but the target was obscured by mist, making it difficult to pinpoint ground detail, in spite of which, in a typical display of Polish determination, the bombs were delivered and seen to burst in the target area.

The first foray into inland Germany for a month took place on the night of the 22/23rd, when the garrison city of Münster was posted as the destination for forty-seven aircraft, of which twenty-two Hampdens and six Manchesters from Bottesford and Swinderby represented 5 Group with orders to attack the main railway station. 106 Squadron, meanwhile, sent two Hampdens with freshman NCO crews to mine the waters around the Frisians. Sgt Kent and crew took off at 17.30, and returned at 21.20 to report finding fair weather and no cloud in the garden area, and locating the drop zone without difficulty to plant the vegetable in the correct position. Sgt Ellis and crew had taken off at 17.35, never to be seen again, and it has to be assumed that AT146 went into the North Sea. Overnight it began to snow heavily, and this continued for a number of days, rendering Coningsby unserviceable and incapable of launching any aircraft. This situation persisted until the 27th, although the other 5 Group stations were able to continue operating and contributed thirty-five Hampdens and fifteen Manchesters to a raid on Brest on the 25/26th and eighteen Hampdens for Hannover on the 26/27th. 5 Group dispatched thirty-four Hampdens and eight Manchesters to attack the cruisers at Brest on the night of the 27/28th, when most of the force reached the target and bombed, although no crews were able to identify the ships, and haze prevented any assessment of results.

A force of fifty-five Wellingtons and twenty-nine Hampdens was made ready on the 28th to send back to Münster that night, and, this time, 106 Squadron supported the operation with ten Hampdens. F/L Bareham was the senior pilot on duty as the squadron contingent departed Coningsby between 17.55 and 18.10 on another intensely cold night, and headed into the most appalling conditions of ten-tenths snow and ice-bearing cloud and blizzards, which stretched all the way into Germany, and, undoubtedly, contributed to the unfolding tragedy. They arrived in the target area to find ten-tenths cloud, which led to just four aircraft bombing on estimated positions, and not a single bomb found the mark. One Wellington and four Hampdens failed to return, and it was a disastrous night for 106 Squadron, to which all four of the latter belonged. Sgt Sporny and his crew were killed when P4398 crashed near Düsseldorf, and there were no survivors also among the crew of P/O Selfe. They had successfully crash-landed AT122 in a forest about seven miles north-west of Winterswijk in Holland, and, possibly badly injured, had remained with the aircraft only to freeze to death during the night. An S.O.S signal was received from AT121 at 21.22 reporting "one engine failed", and a fix located it in the general area of the Zuider Zee. Nothing more was heard, until news eventually filtered through that the Hampden had been homebound when it crashed into a house in Den Helder, at the tip of the peninsula pointing towards Texel. F/L Bareham and his observer survived, and they were taken into captivity. Gunner, Sgt Snelling, had baled out over the sea, and in such weather conditions he would have succumbed to the cold within minutes. His body eventually came ashore nine months later on the island of Amrum off the western coast of the Schleswig-Holstein peninsula. Finally, X3058 was successfully ditched off East Anglia on the homeward flight by Sgt Brown, and all four members of the crew managed to get into the dinghy. Rescue by lifeboat did not occur until sixteen hours later, by which time three had frozen to death, and only Sgt Brown was still alive.

While this operation was in progress, P/O Paget and crew took off at 19.50 to undertake their first freshman operation together, which was against the docks and shipping at Boulogne in company with forty-seven other aircraft. They found the target easily in fair but hazy conditions, and, from 12,000 feet, observed their bombs to burst across the docks. There would be no further operations in the month for 106 Squadron, and this night had brought its worst reversal of the war to date, raising the month's losses to eight aircraft from seven night and two daylight operations, during which sixty-five sorties had been launched. 5 Group still had business to attend to, however, and sent forty-one Hampdens and eleven Manchesters back to Brest on the 31st in company with twenty other aircraft. It became another inconclusive operation that cost two Hampdens and three Manchesters, the latter all from 61 Squadron. February was about to bring major changes, both for the squadron and the Command as a whole, although one wonders how the crews at 106 Squadron greeted the prospect of going to war in the Manchester, the reputation of which was well-known within 5 Group.

February 1942

As it turned out, the squadron's brief association with the type would produce a record of serviceability second to none, but, after a year in service, many of the type's more minor niggles had been dealt with and crews had forewarning of its idiosyncrasies. That still lay in the future, and during the working up period, operations continued with the trusty, but now obsolete Hampden. Snow kept 106 Squadron on the ground for the first five nights of the new month, and the first operation to which it contributed took place in daylight on the 6th, when 5 Group sent thirty-three Hampdens and thirteen Manchesters to mine the waters in the Nectarine I garden off the western Frisians. 106 Squadron supported the effort with five aircraft, which took off between 10.55 and 11.20 led by F/L Hayward, and made their way across the North Sea concealed by low cloud. The drop zone, off the island of Terschelling, was easily located, mostly by an approach from the south via Vlieland, some finding cloud to mask their runs and others not. Those finding cloud cover were able to make timed runs to their briefed release points, while the remainder planted their vegetables as close as possible in known sea-lanes. The crews of Sgts Scatchard, Picken and Stoffer and P/O Loftus all successfully delivered their mines into the correct locations after carrying out timed runs from an established pinpoint, but the attempt by F/L Hayward and crew to let theirs go from 1,500 feet failed because of a fault in the bomb release mechanism.

The daylight gardening operation in the Frisians was repeated on the following day employing thirty-two Hampdens, when the target area on this occasion was further north, in the Nectarine III garden off the island of Wangerooge in the Waddensee, where cloud was very thin and provided little cover. They attracted some moderately accurate heavy flak from the western end of the island, and German fighters were seen to be operating, and were probably responsible for the loss of three Hampdens. 5 Group was not called into action again until the 10th, when nineteen Hampdens and a handful of Manchesters were assigned to attack the main railway station in Bremen. It became another shambolic operation, carried out by a few crews through complete cloud cover, while most attacked alternative targets, jettisoned their bombs or returned them to store. Orders were received at Bottesford, Coningsby and Swinderby on the 11th to prepare a dozen Hampdens and six Manchesters between them for an operation that night against a railway station at Mannheim. They were part of an overall force of forty-nine aircraft, six of them provided by 106 Squadron. They departed Coningsby between 18.00 and 18.20 with P/O Horner the senior pilot on duty, and had been given a new route over Belgium in an attempt to avoid the searchlight belt. AE425 lost its port engine at forty feet as it took off, and it struggled the couple of miles to Woodhall Spa before crashing at Kirkstead, fortunately without injury to the crew of P/O Horner. *(The account in the squadron ORB is entirely different, and reports P/O Horner reaching and bombing the target, while Sgt Scatchard returned early with engine trouble and landed three-and-three-quarter hours after take-off.)* The remainder found the target blanketed in snow, but under clear, starlit skies, and bombed from between 11,000 and 14,000 feet before returning safely home, although not to Coningsby. This was the night on which the final sorties were mounted in the long-running saga involving Brest and its lodgers. Eighteen Wellingtons took part, and as they turned back towards the English coast, the weather conditions were fairly benign, a situation which would alter to the enemy's advantage before long.

As the sound of their engines receded into the eastern cloud-filled skies, Vice-Admiral Otto Cilliax, the Brest Group commander, whose flag was on Scharnhorst, put Operation Cerberus into action at 21.14, and Scharnhorst, Gneisenau and Prinz Eugen slipping anchor, before heading into the English Channel under an escort of destroyers and E-Boats. It was an audacious bid for freedom, covered by bad weather, widespread jamming and meticulously planned support by the Kriegsmarine and the Luftwaffe, all of which had been rehearsed extensively during January. The planning, and a little good fortune, allowed the fleet to make undetected progress until spotted off Le Touquet by two Spitfires piloted by G/C Victor

Beamish, the commanding officer of Kenley, and W/C Finlay Boyd, both of whom maintained radio silence, and did not report their find until landing at 10.42 on the morning of the 12th.

The British authorities had prepared a plan in advance for precisely this eventuality, under the codename, Operation Fuller, and, in anticipation of an imminent breakout, had put aircraft on stand-by since early in the month. Despite that, the authorities were still caught by surprise, and, once the enemy fleet had been spotted in the late morning, frantic efforts were made to get Coastal and Bomber Command aircraft away, but only 5 Group was standing by at four hours readiness. It was 13.30 hours before the first sorties were launched, and the 5 Group stations worked frantically to get sixty-four Hampdens and fifteen Manchesters into the air. They were part of the largest commitment of aircraft by daylight in the war to date, amounting to 242 sorties, and were given a search area off the Hague, where rainstorms and squally conditions compounded the difficulties and prevented most crews from locating the enemy fleet. 106 Squadron contributed four Hampdens to the operation, the crews of S/Ls Stenner and Nelms and Sgt Cooke, taking off between 14.45 and 15.00, and that of P/O Paget at 16.35, before heading east-south-east through cloud that ranged in density from five to ten-tenths at between 500 and 4,000 feet. The last-mentioned returned with engine and intercom problems, while S/L Nelms ran out of cloud cover and decided to abandon his sortie. Sgt Cooke and crew found cloud at 700 feet and visibility at a thousand yards, and they, too, returned home after searching in vain for forty-five minutes. S/L Stenner and crew found the enemy after breaking cloud, and were fired upon by a destroyer, before carrying out an attack on Scharnhorst in a shallow dive from 4,000 down to 1,300 feet, but the bombs overshot. Despite the heroic effort and sacrifice of the Bomber Command, Coastal Command and Fleet Air Arm crews, the enemy fleet made good its escape into open sea, although, its own trials and tribulations were not yet over. Scharnhorst struck a mine in the late afternoon and began to fall back, and, at 19.55, a magnetic mine detonated close enough to Gneisenau, when off Teschelling, to open a small hole in the starboard side, and, temporarily, slow her progress also. Later still, at 21.34, when passing through the same stretch of water, Scharnhorst hit another mine which stopped both engines and damaged steering and fire control. The vessel got under way again at 22.23 using its starboard engines and making twelve knots, while carrying an additional one thousand tons of seawater. The day's activities were not yet over for 5 Group, and the crews of twelve Hampdens and nine Manchesters were briefed to lay mines in the Nectarines garden off the Frisians through which the enemy fleet would have to pass to reach safety.

Gneisenau and Prinz Eugen reached the Elbe Estuary at 07.00 on the 13th, and tied up at Brunsbüttel North Locks at 09.30, while Scharnhorst arrived at Wilhelmshaven at 10.00 with three months-worth of damage to repair. The mines had been laid almost certainly by 5 Group Hampdens over the preceding nights, and demonstrated the remarkable effectiveness of this war-long campaign. The entire episode, which became known as "The Channel Dash", was a major embarrassment to the government and the nation, but, worse still, cost the Command a further fifteen aircraft and crews on top of all of those sacrificed to this endeavour over the past eleven months. 5 Group alone posted missing nine Hampdens and crews, all lost in the North Sea, six of them without trace. On a positive note, this annoying and distracting itch had been scratched for the last time, and the Command could now concentrate its forces against the strategic targets for which it was best suited.

A new Air Ministry directive, issued on the 14th, was to change the emphasis of bomber operations from that point until the end of the war. Lengthy consideration having been given to the Butt Report and the future of an independent bomber force, the new policy authorized the blatant area bombing of Germany's industrial towns and cities in a direct assault on the morale of the civilian population, particularly its workers. This had, of course, been going on since the summer of 1940, but no longer would there be the pretence of claiming to be attacking industrial and military targets. Waiting in the wings, in fact, at this very moment, four days into his voyage from the United States in the armed merchantman, Alcantara, was a new leader, a man well-known to 5 Group, who would not only pursue this policy with a will, but also possessed the self-belief, arrogance and stubbornness to fight his corner against all-comers on behalf of his beleaguered Bomber Command.

That night, a force of ninety-eight aircraft took off to employ the main post office and railway station as the aiming points for an area attack on Mannheim, to which 5 Group contributed twenty-five Hampdens and nine Manchesters. Crews were guided to the city by the searchlight and flak activity, and encountered four to ten-tenths cloud at between 2,000 and 12,000 feet, with fair visibility above and ground haze below. Such weather conditions proved to be unhelpful, and, despite the claims of sixty-seven crews to have bombed the city, local reports spoke of two buildings destroyed and fifteen damaged. 5 Group detailed thirty-seven Hampdens and twelve Manchesters on the 16th to carry out gardening duties in the Nectarine I garden off Terschelling and Nectarine III garden, encompassing the east Frisian islands of Wangerooge, Juist and Borkum. 106 Squadron provided two freshman crews, those of Sgt O'Hare and P/O Aytoun, who took off forty-five minutes apart from 17.30 and encountered ten-tenths cloud with a base below 1,000 feet, poor visibility and icing conditions, which prevented either from fulfilling their brief.

The first mention of the squadron training in Manchesters appeared in the ORB on the 17th, and that night the Command carried out a "scuttle" or roving commission operation over Germany, which did not involve 106 Squadron. The night of the 21/22nd brought more of the same, and this time six 106 Squadron Hampdens were among the twenty detailed for targets of opportunity between Cologne and Koblenz to the south-east. The plan had been to raid Mannheim, but this was changed at the last minute. The newly-commissioned P/Os Picken and Stoffer were the senior pilots on duty as the 106 Squadron element got away from Coningsby at 18.30, and headed towards enemy territory in decent weather conditions. Sgt Cooke and crew found Cologne in good visibility and free of cloud, and released their bombs from 9,000 feet, observing them to burst in the northern part of the town. P/O Stoffer and crew also described excellent visibility and no cloud, and reported dropping a thousand pounder on Neuweid, a town a little to the north of Koblenz, and another at a second location at Bendorf. Both were direct hits, in response to which they were fired upon and hit, but not seriously. Sgt Kent and crew bombed Siegen, a town some forty miles east of Cologne, from 10,000 feet, and, later, a flak concentration as they made their way home through the searchlight belt near Maastricht, and were also was hit by flak for their pains. P/O Picken and crew returned early with wireless failure, while the crew of Sgt Power lost their heating system, in spite of which, they pushed on for a time, but, ultimately, were beaten by the intense cold and turned back. P4414 failed to return with the crew of Sgt Bishop, and no trace of the aircraft and crew was ever found, leading to the conclusion that it found a final resting place in the North Sea.

Air Chief Marshal Sir Arthur Harris took up his post as the new Commander-in-Chief of Bomber Command on the 22nd. He was a man well-known to 5 Group, having served as its A-O-C until November 1940, when he became second deputy to Sir Charles Portal, the Chief-of-the-Air-Staff. Harris arrived at the helm with firm ideas already in place on how to win the war by bombing alone, a pre-war theory, which no commander had yet had an opportunity to put into practice. It was obvious to him, that the small-scale raids on multiple targets favoured by his predecessor, served only to dilute the effort, and that such pin-prick attacks could not hurt Germany's war effort. He recognized the need to overwhelm the defences and emergency services, by pushing the maximum number of aircraft across the aiming point in the shortest possible time, and this would signal the birth of the bomber stream, and an end to the former practice, whereby squadrons or even crews determined for themselves the details of their sorties. He knew also that urban areas are most efficiently destroyed by fire, rather than blast, and it would not be long before the bomb loads carried in his aircraft reflected this thinking. It was a policy of the bludgeon over the scalpel, but the war to date had demonstrated that precision bombing was a dream still awaiting the scientific means to achieve it. In the meantime, while he developed his ideas, he would continue with the fairly small-scale attacks on German ports favoured by his predecessor, and, later on the evening of his appointment, he sent thirty-one Wellingtons and nineteen Hampdens to Wilhelmshaven to attack the floating dock likely to be employed during repairs to Scharnhorst. Sadly, the target area was covered by dense cloud and the bombing that took place on estimated positions missed the aiming point altogether.

On the night of the 23/24th, 5 Group detailed twenty-three Hampdens for gardening duties in the Rosemary and Yams regions in the Heligoland Bight and Schillig Roads respectively, 106 Squadron dividing its six crews equally between them. The usual suspects were involved, the crews of Sgts Scatchard and Kent and P/O Stoffer assigned to Rosemary, and those of Sgts Cooke, Power and P/O Pickens to Yams, and they departed Coningsby together between 01.50 and 02.06. Sgt Scatchard and crew found no cloud but poor visibility, and pinpointed on Westerhever on the western side of the Schleswig-Holstein peninsula, before making a run from there and dropping the mine on dead-reckoning in the approximate briefed position. P/O Stoffer and crew followed suit, and believed their mine also to be placed accurately. P4323 was shot down by naval flak in the target area and crashed on Sylt, killing Sgt Kent and his crew, who would have the sad distinction of being the last to be posted missing by the squadron in a Hampden. Two of the remaining crews pinpointed on the Danish coast before dropping their mines on e.t.a, while P/O Picken and crew were unable to locate their drop zone, and, returning via the Dutch Frisians, observed flak and searchlights off Terschelling, and planted their vegetable there in the Nectarine I garden. At 18.10 that evening, the crews of Sgt Hurd and P/O Gallacher took off to carry out freshman mining sorties in the Nectarine II garden off the Frisians. The former pinpointed on Schiermonikoog before planting their mine in the correct location in good visibility, and the latter likewise reported a successful and uneventful trip.

5 Group detailed a dozen Manchesters on the 25th for the first of three operations on consecutive nights targeting the Gneisenau under repair at Kiel, while eighteen Hampdens and a Manchester took care of gardening duties in the Nectarines I and II, Yams and Rosemary gardens. The accommodation ship, Monte Sarmiento, was hit in Kiel harbour and destroyed by fire at a cost of around 120 lives. Scampton and North-Luffenham dispatched ten Hampdens between them on the 26th to join Wellingtons and Halifaxes in targeting the floating dock at Kiel, and the operation, which took place under clear skies, threw up one of the war's great ironies. A high explosive bomb struck the bows of Gneisenau, now supposedly in a safe haven after enduring eleven months of constant bombardment at Brest, and, not only did it kill 116 of her crew, it also ended her sea-going career for good. Her main armament was removed for use in coastal defence, and she was towed to Gdynia, where she remained unrepaired for the rest of the war. 106 Squadron was not involved in this success, but sent a single freshman crew, that of P/O Cockbain, to mine the waters off the Frisians. Unfortunately, they experienced engine problems while outbound, and decided to abandon the sortie. The British authorities were unaware of the success on this night, and sent another raid of sixty-eight aircraft back to Kiel on the 27th, which included eighteen Hampdens and seventeen Manchesters. They encountered bright moonlight above the ten-tenths cloud in the target area, but poor visibility below, which offered no chance of identifying the floating dock, and most bombed the general area of the town, guided by the flashes of searchlights and flak.

Among other operations on this night was one by six 106 Squadron Hampdens against the Scharnhorst, which was under repair at Wilhelmshaven. They departed Coningsby between 18.10 and 18.45 with S/L Nelms the senior pilot on duty, but lost the services of Sgt Power and crew to wireless failure after around two hours. P/O Gallacher and crew ran into severe icing conditions and must have been close to the target when their problems were compounded by persistent harassment from night-fighters, which persuaded them to jettison their bombs and also turn for home. The remainder arrived over

Wilhelmshaven in entirely the wrong weather conditions for any realistic chance of success, with complete cloud cover topping out at 12,000 feet, and although there was bright moonlight above the cloud, that was of benefit only to night-fighters. S/L Nelms and crew bombed on e.t.a., aiming at a flak concentration from 10,000 feet, and Sgt Young and crew dropped their load onto the town and observed four bursts. Sgt Hurd and crew bombed a flak concentration from 17,000 feet and saw six bursts, and there was a similar report from the crew of Sgt O'Hara. This was the squadron's final operation of the month, during the course of which it had undertaken operations on seven nights and two days and dispatched thirty-eight sorties for the loss of three aircraft and crews.

March 1942

Adverse weather conditions welcomed in the new month and kept the bomber force on the ground on the 1st. It was the same on the 2nd, by the end of which, 106 Squadron had become the sole residents of Coningsby, after 97 Squadron completed its move to Woodhall Spa, a new station about three miles away to the north-west. It was the 3rd, before orders were received across the Command to prepare for an operation, which, in its bold conception, was a clear indication of what was to come. Bomber Command's evolution to war-winning capability was to be long, arduous and gradual, but the first signs of a new hand on the tiller came early on in Harris's reign with this meticulously planned attack on the Renault lorry factory, which was located in a loop of the River Seine in the district of Billancourt to the south-west of central Paris. The plant was capable of producing 18,000 lorries per year, which was a massive boon to the German war effort, and the attempt to destroy it came in response to an Air Ministry request. The operation would be conducted in three waves, led by experienced crews, and would involve extensive use of flares to provide illumination. In the face of what was expected to be scant defence, crews were also encouraged to attack from as low a level as practicable, both for the sake of accuracy, and in an attempt to avoid civilian casualties. In time, such operations would be led by Gee-equipped aircraft, but the 3 Group squadrons already employing the device were forbidden from taking part on this occasion, lest one be lost over enemy territory and its secrets revealed. A force of 235 aircraft was assembled, a new record for a single target, and among them were forty-eight Hampdens and twenty-six Manchesters representing 5 Group. 106 Squadron briefed seven crews, who departed Coningsby in a six-minute slot from 18.15 with F/L Hayward the senior pilot on duty on an evening of fine weather, which would persist throughout the operation.

They arrived in the target area a little under three hours later to find bright moonlight, which enabled them to follow the course of the Seine to the factory, which was easily identified in the light from flares and already burgeoning fires. P/O Stoffer and crew carried out their attack from 2,200 feet at 21.07, the same time recorded by Sgt Cooke and crew from three hundred feet higher. The crew of the newly promoted F/Sgt Scatchard delivered their bombs from 2,000 feet at 21.10, and watched them burst across the target and cause a large explosion. P/O Picken and crew reached Paris at 21.00, but hung around until dropping their load from 3,000 feet at 21.28. They also released bundles of nickels (leaflets) over the city, a standard procedure throughout the war, as did F/L Hayward and crew, who observed their bombs falling onto the diesel engine repair shops. This left the crews of Sgt Young and F/Sgt Brown to complete the squadron's part in the raid from 2,700 and 3,000 feet respectively, and they were among 223 returning crews to report successful sorties, many describing the factory buildings as well alight as they turned away. Post-raid reconnaissance confirmed the operation to have been an outstanding success for the loss of just one aircraft. 40% of the factory's buildings had been destroyed, and production was halted for four weeks, costing the Germans around 2,300 lorries, although, sadly, not all of the bombs had fallen precisely where intended. Inevitably, adjacent workers' housing had been hit by stray bombs, killing 367 French civilians and severely injuring 341 others, some of whom would not survive. At the time, this was more than twice the heaviest death toll inflicted on a German target. It was somewhat paradoxical, that, as a champion of area bombing, Harris should gain his first major victory by way of a precision target.

While the above operation was in progress, some 330 miles to the north, four Lancasters were taxiing to the runway at Waddington under the eyes of the 5 Group A-O-C, AVM Slessor, each carrying four mines for delivery to the Yams and Rosemary gardens in the Schillig Roads and Heligoland Bight areas respectively off north-western Germany. They encountered favourable weather conditions with no low cloud, and planted their vegetables into the allotted positions from 600 and 700 feet before returning home safely to make their reports. It was a low key beginning for an aircraft type that would be dominant among bombers, and contribute more than any other to the destruction of Germany and the winning of the war.

It rained all day on the 4th, and snowed all day on the 5th, and it was the 7th before Coningsby could be declared serviceable for flying. Orders came through from 5 Group to make ready seventeen Hampdens for mining duties in the Artichoke garden, in the approaches to the port of Lorient, an operation not recorded in the 5 Group ORB, but 106 Squadron was not invited to take part, and, instead, detailed two freshman crews to support a small-scale attack on the U-Boot base at St-Nazaire. It was the graveyard shift for the crews of F/Sgt Duff and P/O Cockbain, as they took off at 01.30 and 01.45 respectively, and both were back in time for a late breakfast after successfully bombing the docks in excellent weather conditions.

Essen was to feature prominently in Harris's future plans, and a series of raids was planned against this massively important industrial powerhouse of a city, beginning on the 8th with the first of three on consecutive nights. A force of 211 aircraft was assembled during the course of the 8th, of which thirty-seven Hampdens and twenty-two Manchesters were to represent 5 Group. The leading aircraft, belonging to 3 Group, would be those equipped with the new Gee navigation device, which carried the great hope that it could solve the problem of blind target locating. 106 Squadron briefed the crews of P/Os Churcher and Aytoun and Sgt O'Hara and sent them on their way between 01.05 and 01.10 on another night of good weather, and the force did, indeed, benefit from Gee to reach the general area of the target. Once there, however, the ever-present industrial haze hanging over the Ruhr like a blanket, prevented the crews from picking out ground detail, although P/O Churcher and crew were confident that they were over Essen when releasing their bombs from 15,000 feet. Sgt O'Hara and crew attacked from a similar height, and thought that their bombs had fallen into the suburbs, while P/O Aytoun and crew had to spend ten minutes fending off a Ju88 before also hitting the outskirts of the city on the northern side. Local sources reported a light raid with little damage, and Bomber Command recorded eight failures to return.

The Krupp complex was briefed out twenty-four hours later as one of two aiming points at Essen, and a force of 187 aircraft made ready, which included a 5 Group contribution of fifteen Hampdens and ten Manchesters. This figure had originally been higher, but adverse weather conditions, technical difficulties and one unidentified Manchester becoming bogged down on the way to take-off at Bottesford, reduced the numbers significantly. 106 Squadron put up just two Hampdens, captained by F/Sgt Duff and Sgt Young, which departed Coningsby at 20.20 before heading for the Dutch coast, from where some crews claimed to be able to see the flares over Essen, thus confirming that the horizontal visibility was reasonable, while vertical visibility at the target would be compromised by industrial haze. It is believed that the Coningsby duo had been briefed to aim for the city's main square, but this was better interpreted as ordering them to continue the assault on the morale of the civilian population, particularly its work force, in line with the February 14th Directive. Searchlight glare prevented an identification of the aiming point by the two 106 Squadron participants, who released their single 1,900 and four 250 pounders each from 11,000 and 13,000 feet and watched them burst across the built-up area. The rest of the force scattered their bombs over twenty-four other Ruhr towns and cities, with Hamborn and Duisburg the chief beneficiaries, and the Essen authorities reported the destruction of two buildings, with seventy-two others damaged.

For the third night running Harris tried again at Essen on the 10th, for which a force of 126 aircraft was made ready, almost half of them provided by 5 Group. Forty-three Hampdens, thirteen Manchesters and, for the first time over Germany, two Lancasters, took to the air, the four 106 Squadron crews of P/Os Cockbain, Churcher and Aytoun and Sgt O'Hara departing Coningsby between 19.20 and 19.30. Surprisingly, this was the first time that the squadron had operated on four consecutive nights. P/O Aytoun and crew had an engine fail, while the crew of P/O Churcher lost their heating and oxygen systems, and both were compelled to return early. This 50% failure rate was reflected in the force as a whole, and only half reached the target, where bombing was again scattered and ineffective at a cost of four aircraft. Neither 106 Squadron crew was able to positively identify the aiming point and delivered their bombs from around 12,000 feet onto the general area of the city. Both returned safely, and when Sgt O'Hara and crew touched down at 00.30 in AT160, they closed the chapter on 106 Squadron's Hampden era.

The squadron adjutant took great pains to record the operational statistics of the Hampden in 106 Squadron service, and, according to his calculations, the squadron had operated on 136 nights and eight days, launching 1,230 sorties, and accumulating 7,018 hours of operational flying time. Over eight hundred tons of bombs and incendiaries had been delivered, along with 180 mines, in return for the loss of fifty-five aircraft, a loss rate of 4.4% of those dispatched.

The squadron would not be required to operate now for nine nights as it prepared to go to war in Manchesters. During this period, just two major operations were carried out by the Command, the first of them against the Deutsche Werke U-Boot construction yards at Kiel, which was the target for a force of sixty-eight Wellingtons on the night of the 12/13th, while forty Wellingtons and Whitleys, probably crewed by freshmen, attended to Emden. 5 Group was also active, committing twenty-six Hampdens and a lone Manchester to gardening duties in the Yams, Hawthorn and Rosemary regions off Germany's North Sea coast. The Kiel raid was relatively successful and caused damage to two U-Boot yards and the naval dockyard. While the above was in progress, 106 Squadron suffered its first Manchester incident, which involved L7474 and the crew of Sgt Carter. An attempt to land resulted in a bounce and a "go-around", during which it was discovered that the port undercarriage unit could not be locked down. The windscreen was also glazed over by ice, and, probably after a consultation with the ground, the decision was taken that the crew should abandon the Manchester and put their trust in the parachute-packing section. They parted company with L7474 in the vicinity of Horncastle at 23.45, and drifted down over rural Lincolnshire, leaving the Manchester to its inevitable fate, which was realised in a crash at Winceby, a few miles to the north-east of Coningsby.

During the course of the 13th, a force of 135 aircraft of six different types was assembled for an assault on Cologne, which the crews were able to identify through the partial cover of three to five-tenths cloud at between 8,000 and 12,000 feet. They had to run the gauntlet of intense searchlight and flak to reach the aiming point, where flares provided adequate illumination, and an effective attack ensued. A post-raid assessment revealed that some useful industrial damage had resulted, mainly in the Nippes district, to the north of the city centre, west of the river, which was also the location of a major marshalling yard with railway workshops. In addition to this, 1,500 houses had been hit in what proved to be the first genuinely successful Gee-led raid. Thereafter, only very minor operational activity took place until the final third of the month, and it was during this time that 106 Squadron welcomed a new commanding officer and went to war in Manchesters for the first time.

On the 20th, W/C Bob Allen departed the squadron at the end of a very successful tour as commanding officer, and he left behind him a spirit of efficiency and confidence, that future commanders would build upon. His successor was acting W/C Guy Gibson, whose finest hour lay more than twelve months hence, but who would use his time at 106 Squadron to enhance not only his own reputation, but also that of the squadron. Having completed a tour of operations with 83 Squadron during the first year of war, Gibson had managed to obtain a posting to 29 Squadron as a Beaufighter night-fighter pilot, rather than be screened from operations altogether. While at 83 Squadron he had developed a reputation for "line-shooting", but he had impressed Harris, his A-O-C at 5 Group, with his desire to get at the enemy at every opportunity. During his time on night-fighters, Gibson had failed to match the success of those who would become legendary in the role, like Cunningham and Braham, and this was a source of disappointment and frustration for him. However, before leaving Bomber Command, he had extracted from Harris the promise of a return to bombers in the future, and he had set out to redeem that pledge once Harris returned to England. Harris had recommended to AVM Slessor, the A-O-C of 5 Group, that 207 Squadron would be a suitable first command for Gibson, to replace W/C Fothergill, who was not given to leading his men from the front, and, in Harris's eyes, did not provide the necessary inspiration. However, the decision was left to Slessor, and it was through the main gate at Coningsby that Gibson swept on the day of Allen's departure.

Immediately, Gibson threw himself into his new role and set about improving standards of efficiency in all areas of 106 Squadron, and he would manage to drag out of the troubled Manchester an operational serviceability that other squadrons had been unable to achieve. It has to be said, of course, that, after twelve months in the front line, many of the serviceability problems had been ironed out, and only three months remained before the type was relegated to non-operational duties. By no means would Gibson be universally popular, and he admitted to an inability to relate to "other ranks", or to those whose jobs did not require them to put their lives at risk. Having spent his earliest years in India with authority over the native servants, he had a rigid view of class, and exercised it constantly during his service life. To those aircrew officers who managed to find a place in his inner circle, he was an inspirational leader, and he collected around him pilots with potential, who, under his tutelage, would achieve reputations in their own right.

As events turned out, Gibson's arrival coincided with the squadron's first operational foray in Manchesters. Seven crews had been briefed on the 19th for a daylight mining operation in one of the Nectarine gardens off the Frisians, but it was scrubbed and rescheduled for the following day. During the period of stand-down, many new faces had arrived at Coningsby to fill the vacancies created by the seven-man crew required by the Manchester. Among the new arrivals were a number of pilots who would become mainstays of the squadron, like P/O Whamond, who came in from 97 Squadron and found himself on the Order of Battle for this maiden operation. Beside him in R5839, and flying as second pilot, was P/O John Hopgood, who would become a member of Gibson's inner circle and follow him to greater things a year hence. They took off between 14.35 and 15.00 and headed into very unfavourable weather conditions and a low cloud base, and soon lost the services of P/O Whamond and crew after their Manchester suffered a hydraulics system failure. They were forced to return early, and the problem led to a crash on landing, from which the crew walked away unhurt. P/O Worswick and crew abandoned their sortie after encountering cloud at 200 feet and deciding that it would be impossible to locate the garden, and the crew of W/O Young followed suit after carrying out a long search. F/Sgt Appleyard and his crew encountered identical conditions, but located the drop zone and delivered the mines in the correct position, as did the crew of W/O Merralls. The crews of F/Sgt Brown and P/O Loftus found cloud at sea level, and released their four mines on e.t.a after failing to find a pinpoint from which to carry out a timed run.

On the 23rd, 5 Group detailed twelve Hampdens and two Manchesters for mining duties in the Artichoke garden off the port of Lorient, and this was repeated twenty-four hours later by twenty-three Hampdens three Manchesters and two Lancasters. In his classic book, Enemy Coast Ahead, Gibson recounted an event, which he claimed took place on the day of his arrival, but was actually on the 24th. It involved the former 106 Squadron C Flight commander, S/L "Tommy" Boylan, who was now with 97 Squadron, and had landed his Lancaster at Coningsby during the morning. Gibson must have looked with envy at the grace and power of the new bomber, which had been born out of the failure of the Manchester. He knew it was only a matter of time before he and his crews got their hands on them, but it must have been hugely frustrating to have to wait. Gibson was watching that afternoon as Boylan began his take-off run for the short hop to Woodhall Spa and knew instinctively that something was wrong. This was confirmed when the Lancaster failed to unstick and careered out of control to collide with a crane near the bomb dump. Some time later, Boylan appeared in the officers' mess, where he ordered a pint, and downed it with the steadiest of hands, or so the story goes. Later that evening, the crews of P/Os Picken and Whamond, with P/Os Churcher and Hopgood respectively acting as second pilots, joined a 3 and 5 Group mining operation off Lorient, from which a 44 (Rhodesia) Squadron Lancaster became the first of the type to go missing. Both 106 Squadron crews easily identified their garden area in excellent visibility, and delivered four mines each into the correct locations before returning safely.

Harris resumed his campaign against Essen on the night of the 25/26th, when sending the largest force yet to a single target of 254 aircraft. 5 Group played its part by contributing twenty Manchesters, nine Hampdens and seven Lancasters, four of the Manchesters representing 106 Squadron. They departed Coningsby between 19.55 and 20.10, having been preceded into the air at 19.25 by the crew of F/Sgt Cooke, who were bound for the Artichoke garden off Lorient, but would be thwarted by hydraulics leaks in the front and rear turrets and forced to turn back. F/L Dunlop-Mackenzie was the senior pilot on duty among the bombing quartet, each of whom was sitting either on six 1,000 pounders or a cookie and four 500 pounders. They crossed the enemy coast untroubled by the defences and approached the target through clear skies and good visibility, but found thick industrial haze to frustrate all attempts to identify Essen. P/O Worswick and crew dropped their bombs from 11,500 feet, but were unable to observe the results, while W/O Merralls and his crew were aided by the light of flares, and saw their bombs burst in the town. They reported heavy flak and returned with slight damage to their aircraft. W/O Young and crew bombed from 15,000 feet and observed a large burst in the town, and they also described the flak as heavy, but inaccurate. A total of 181 crews reported bombing in the target area, some even claiming hits on the Krupp complex, when, in fact, only a handful of bombs had fallen within the city, the majority, according to local sources, having been drawn away by a decoy fire site at Rheinberg some eighteen miles away. A post-raid analysis suggested that some of the Wellington-laid flares had burned at 18,000 feet, which was of no benefit in terms of ground illumination, and, the promise of Gee demonstrated in the recent attack on Cologne had not been repeated. It was a bad night for 5 Group, which posted missing six aircraft, two-thirds of the overall casualty figure, and among them were five of the twenty Manchesters dispatched, a loss rate for the type of 25%. The operation brought about the inevitable loss to 106 Squadron of its first Manchester, L7390, which had been shot down into the ice-covered Ijsselmeer at 22.28 by a night-fighter flown by the ace, Oblt Ludwig Becker of 6./NJG2, and there were no survivors from the crew of F/L Dunlop-Mackenzie.

On the following night, a force of 115 Wellingtons and Stirlings returned to Essen, while 5 Group detailed thirty Hampdens and fifteen Manchesters to conduct mining operations in the Yam, Nectarine and Deodar gardens. The main event would result in another failure at a cost of almost 10% of those dispatched, and Harris was left wondering how he might overcome the problem of target identification over a blacked-out, often cloud-covered, hostile city nestling under a blanket of industrial haze. Meanwhile, the five 106 Squadron participants in the gardening activities departed Coningsby between 18.55 and 19.05, the crews of P/Os Loftus and Whamond and F/Sgt Appleyard bound for the Deodar garden in the Gironde estuary on the Biscay coast, while F/Sgt Cooke and P/O Stoffer and their crews headed east to the Jade Bay and Weser estuary region of north-western Germany. The former had a long outward flight ahead of them to reach the gateway to the highly important port of Bordeaux, where the banks of the estuary contained a number of oil processing and storage facilities at Pauillac, Blaye and Bec-d'Ambes, and the waterway provided access to the Atlantic for the U-Boots sheltering in the concrete pens in Bordeaux itself. P/O Loftus and crew described the weather as good at first but deteriorating, and they jettisoned their mines after failing to locate the target area. While trying to land at Exeter, they overshot the runway in R5841, but no casualties were incurred and the Manchester was soon back in harness. P/O Whamond's L7391 was damaged by light flak on the way out, and he and his crew deposited the mines in an alternative location, while F/Sgt Appleyard and crew described an uneventful trip, during which they successfully delivered their mines as briefed. The crews of F/Sgt Blake and P/O Stoffer experienced no problems in northern waters, and each planted four mines in the required location before returning safely.

Despite Harris's frustrations with the failures at Essen, he was certain of one thing. If he could provide his crews with easily identifiable pinpoints on the ground, they would be able to put their bombs where intended, as had been the case at the Renault factory at Billancourt at the start of the month. The immediate answer to the problem was to target a city close to a coastline, to provide clear and unmistakeable pinpoints. Accordingly, on the night of the 28/29th, Harris dispatched a force of 234 aircraft to Lübeck, an historic Hanseatic (free trade) city at the western end of Germany's Baltic coast. The operation was to be conducted along the same lines as that against the Renault factory, which meant three waves, led by experienced crews in Gee-equipped aircraft. The target was actually beyond the range of Gee, but it would provide a useful navigation tool for as long as reception lasted. The defences were expected to be light, and this would enable crews to bomb from as low as 2,000 feet in conditions of bright moonlight. The layout of the city with narrow streets and half-timbered buildings in the Altstadt would be ideal for a fire-raising attack, and the predominantly incendiary bomb loads carried by the force reflected this intention. 106 Squadron detailed five crews, captained by F/Sgts Appleyard and Cooke, W/Os Young and Merralls and P/O Worswick, and they took off from Coningsby between 21.40 and 22.00, each carrying high-explosives bombs in the form either of six 1,000 pounders or a cookie and four 500 pounders. They flew out in excellent conditions, which enabled them to map-read their way across the Schleswig-Holstein peninsula, and, on arrival at the target, they found the city already burning furiously, which hampered to a degree their ability to pick out the briefed aiming point. The 106 Squadron crews delivered their payloads from between 4,000 and 12,000 feet in perfect conditions of bright moonlight, and, as F/Sgt Appleyard and crew were already at low level after bombing, they shot up searchlights on their way out of the target area. The outcome for Lübeck was precisely as Harris had intended, and left an estimated 30% of the city's built-up area in ruins. This represented the first major success for the area bombing policy and provided a demonstration of what was in store for the residents of Germany's towns and cities. There was an outcry following this unexpected attack on Lübeck, which was a city of culture and a vital port for the Red Cross and had not expected to be attacked. An agreement was struck that ensured its future protection from bombing, and this was largely adhered to.

On the following night, the squadron dispatched three Manchesters between 19.20 and 19.30 to lay mines in one of the Nectarine gardens off the Frisians, and those of P/O Stoffer and Sgt Carter experienced no difficulty in identifying the target area in good conditions, and planting their vegetables as required. F/Sgt Dimond and his crew failed to return in L7394, and no trace of the Manchester and its crew was ever found. During the course of the month the squadron operated ten times by night and once by day, launching a total of eighteen Hampden sorties and twenty-seven by Manchesters for the loss of two of the latter.

April 1942

April would prove to be the busiest month of the war yet for 106 Squadron, and the new month began for 5 Group with operations on the 1st in company with Wellingtons, although not operating together. Twenty-two Hampden crews were briefed to take part in a raid on the docks area and shipping at Le Havre, while fourteen others were to be sent to carry out low-level attacks on railway targets in north-western Germany in the Meppen and Lingen region situated close to the frontier with Holland. Eleven Manchester crews from 61 and 106 Squadron were briefed to return to the Deodar garden at the mouth of the Gironde, for which the five 106 squadron participants departed Coningsby at intervals between 18.20 and 19.15. One of them, not listed in the ORB as taking part, turned back with hydraulics failure, while S/L Stenner and crew lost their starboard engine while over France, and had little choice but to return. According to the squadron ORB, they brought their mines home, which was a very courageous act considering the perils of flying a Manchester on one engine. The crews of F/Sgt Cooke and W/Os Merralls and Young found the garden area with ease in fine weather and excellent visibility, although a strong wind was found to be troublesome. All delivered their four mines each into the correct locations and returned safely home after being airborne for up to nine-and-a-quarter hours. It turned into a disastrous night for 3 Group, whose railway targets were at Hanau and Lohr to the east of Frankfurt, from which five out of twelve 57 Squadron Wellingtons failed to return and seven of fourteen belonging to 214 Squadron. This caused a rethink by those responsible for planning operations, despite which, a similar disaster awaited 5 Group in December.

Minor operations occupied the Command as a whole for the first four nights, until Harris launched the first major operation of the new month against Cologne on the night of the 5/6th. A new record force of 263 aircraft was assembled, which included a 5 Group contribution of forty-four Hampdens and eleven Manchesters. The aiming point was the Klöckner-Humboldt engineering works in the Deutz district on the East Bank of the Rhine in the city centre, which manufactured a wide range of commercial and military vehicles and artillery pieces. 106 Squadron supported the operation with four Manchesters, which departed Coningsby between 00.55 and 01.10 with S/L Stenner once more the senior pilot on duty. They flew to the target in ten-tenths cloud, but gaps appeared as they closed on the city, and over the target, bright moonlight penetrated the nine-tenths cloud to glint off an S-bend in the Rhine to the south of the city centre. This assisted crews in establishing their positions for the bombing runs, and all four from Coningsby delivered their loads from between 10,000 and 12,000 feet in the face of heavy and accurate flak. Despite the advantages, and the claims of 211 crews to have hit the target area, bombing photos revealed that the nearest bombs to the aiming point had fallen five miles away and the attack had been spread right across the built-up area with no concentration. Ninety houses were destroyed or seriously damaged, but nothing of industrial significance was hit.

Harris turned his attention back upon Essen on the night of the 6/7th for the first of three raids on the city in the space of six nights. 5 Group contributed eighteen Hampdens and ten Manchesters to the force of 157 aircraft, with just two of the latter provided by 106 Squadron. The crews of W/O Young and F/Sgt Cooke took off at 00.30 and 00.40 respectively, and flew towards the Ruhr in complete cloud cover on a night of bad weather. They bombed the approximate location of the target on e.t.a from 16,000 and 11,000 feet, again in the face of a hostile defence, and W/O Young's R5840 was damaged by flak. Only a third of the overall force battled the stormy conditions to reach the cloud-covered target, which escaped with minor damage at a cost to the Command of five aircraft, three of them belonging to 5 Group.

Hamburg was posted as the target on the 8th, and yet another record force, this time of 272 aircraft, was made ready. 5 Group stepped up with thirty-two Hampdens and thirteen Manchesters assigned to the Blohm & Voss shipyards located in the Finkenwerder district to the west of the city centre, while the Lancasters and nine further Hampdens were to attack aiming point C, which was not otherwise identified. 106 Squadron made ready five Manchesters, which departed Coningsby between 22.10 and 22.30 with no senior pilots on duty and P/O Churcher flying as second pilot to P/O Picken and P/O Hopgood with P/O Whamond. It was one of those not infrequent nights on which a towering bank of cumulonimbus cloud built up over the North Sea to act as Hamburg's gatekeeper, forcing the bombers to pass through electrical storms and icing conditions to reach their destination. P/O Loftus and crew found their Manchester struggling to make height, and pressed on for a time, before ultimately admitting defeat and jettisoning the bombs as they turned for home. F/Sgt Brown and crew were an estimated twenty minutes from Heligoland when their aircraft iced-up severely and began rapidly to lose height. They also jettisoned their bomb load and turned back, leaving P/Os Picken, Whamond and W/O Young to press on towards Germany's Second City, which none of them was able to positively identify, and bombs were delivered on estimated positions from between 11,000 and 14,000 feet. Despite the claims of 188 crews that they had attacked the target, local sources confirmed that very few bomb loads had fallen within the built-up area, and damage was not significant.

Four 106 Squadron Manchesters were among the forty-three Hampdens, ten Manchesters and eight Lancasters provided by 5 group in an overall force of 254 bound for Essen late on the 10th. It was to be a "Shaker" operation, the codename given to the dropping of target illuminator flares by 3 Group aircraft employing Gee as a rudimentary form of pathfinding. P/O Loftus and crew were the last of the Coningsby element to leave the ground at 22.45, only to return seventy-six minutes later because of W/T failure. The crews of F/Sgt Brown and P/Os Picken and Whamond had taken off a few minutes before Loftus, and had been briefed to expect clear conditions in the target area, but what they actually encountered was a layer of eight-tenths cloud across the central Ruhr at between 5,000 and 8,000 feet. The approach to the target was described by some crews as "hot", with scores of searchlights from all sides working in conjunction with light and heavy flak. The cloud prevented identification of the target, and bombs were delivered on dead reckoning (DR) through heavy and accurate flak, and P/O Picken and crew returned to Coningsby in a Manchester displaying the scars of battle. On their return, the crew of P/O Whamond reported being coned in searchlights for forty-five minutes on the way home, but escaped damage. It was F/Sgt Brown and crew who experience the most torrid time, after taking a serious flak hit, which appeared to be terminal for L7461. The pilot lost control and ordered his crew to bale out, while he fought to give them time to do so. His efforts were successful and he rescued the situation, but, before he could rescind the bale-out order, the navigator and wireless operator had already jumped. F/Sgt Brown coaxed the Manchester back to English air space, and pulled off a crash-landing at Martlesham Heath near Ipswich, without casualty to the occupants. At debriefing, crews reported some bomb bursts and the glow of fires beneath the cloud, but little information of use to the Intelligence Section. It had been yet another scattered and ineffective attack, which, according to local sources, had destroyed a dozen houses.

Orders were received across the Command on the 12th to prepare another large force to return to Essen that night, and 251 aircraft were made ready accordingly, 5 Group responding with thirty-one Hampdens and nine Manchesters. 106 Squadron made ready five Manchesters for the main event and a sixth for S/L Nelms, who would be undertaking his first Manchester sortie, a nickelling (leaflet) trip to Lille in north-eastern France. They took off together between 22.10 and 22.40, and it wasn't long before P/O

Whamond became aware of excessive fuel consumption and an inability to maintain height, which persuaded him to turn back a little over an hour into the outward flight. It was a clear and starlit night over the Ruhr, but ground haze hampered identification, and only P/O Picken and crew were able to bomb in the general target area in the face of intense flak and searchlight activity. W/O Merralls and crew failed to locate the aiming point, and dropped their bombs on a flak concentration south-east of the target, while the crews of P/Os Loftus and Worswick chose Koblenz as an alternative target, the latter after their oxygen system had failed. The Loftus crew dropped their load from 12,000 feet and observed bomb bursts in the built-up area, and were not, therefore, among the 173 crews claiming to have bombed the primary target. Meanwhile, S/L Nelms and crew had delivered 120 bundles of what Harris described as "toilet paper" from 12,000 feet, having had to gauge the wind strength and direction to ensure that the propaganda reached the inhabitants of Lille. Local sources in Essen confirmed that a number of bombs had hit buildings in the Krupp district, but generally, the level of destruction had fallen woefully short of what might be expected from such a large force. Eight operations had now been directed at Essen since the first one in early March, and 1,555 sorties had been launched for the loss of sixty-four aircraft, one more than the number of civilians killed.

The night of the 13/14th was one of minor operations, during which 106 Squadron committed five Manchesters to mining sorties in the Rosemary garden in Heligoland Bay, four of them with pilots undertaking their first Manchester operations as crew captain. F/L Robertson, who, like Whamond, was a Rhodesian, had arrived at 106 Squadron on the same day as Gibson, and he and his crew were first to leave the ground at 20.35 along with P/O Hopgood and crew. They were followed into the air five minutes later by the crews of F/Sgt Appleyard and Sgt Hurd, and, finally, at 21.00, by that of Sgt Young. The weather off Germany's north-western coast was good, and the visibility excellent, but despite this and an extensive search, Sgt Hurd and crew were unable to locate a suitable pinpoint for a timed run to the drop zone and brought their four mines home. The others all located their respective gardens without difficulty and planted their vegetables in the correct positions.

Dortmund was posted as the target for a force of 208 aircraft on the 14th, by far the largest effort against this industrial giant situated at the eastern end of the Ruhr. The 5 Group contribution of thirty-four Hampdens and four Manchesters included just two Manchesters from 106 Squadron, containing the crews of P/Os Worswick and Whamond. They departed Coningsby at 22.40 and 22.45 respectively, and headed into clear skies over the Ruhr, where the usual thick blanket of ground haze prevented an accurate identification of the aiming point. P/O Worswick and crew located the general built-up area and saw their bombs burst in the southern part of the town, and then strayed well off track during the homebound journey, running critically short of fuel as they approached the south coast with the intention of landing at Lee-on-Solent naval air station. The tanks ran dry a mile short, and, after eight hours and forty minutes aloft, P/O Worswick carried out a successful ditching in the Solent, from which he and his crew emerged unscathed. Sadly, it would be a temporary reprieve for this crew. Meanwhile, P/O Whamond and crew had not been able to pinpoint the primary target, and had dropped their bombs onto an alternative built-up area somewhere in the Ruhr, before returning safely home. Despite the claims of 132 crews that they had attacked Dortmund, the operation had gone the way of the others directed at targets in this region in inflicting only minor damage over a forty-mile stretch.

Harris tried again twenty-four hours later, with a force this time of 152 aircraft, which included nineteen Hampdens and seven Manchesters. 106 Squadron contributed five Manchesters, which departed Coningsby either side of midnight with S/L Nelms the senior pilot on duty, and flew into ten-tenths cloud, heavy rain and severe icing conditions, which inevitably took their toll. S/L Nelms and crew were unable to locate the target, or even maintain height, and jettisoned their load as they turned for home. F/Sgt Brown and crew searched long and hard for a pinpoint, but ultimately gave up and also dumped their bombs "safe". F/Sgt Appleyard and crew reported cloud from 14,000 feet down to 2,500 feet, and they, too, abandoned their sortie, but returned the bombs to store. Sgt Young and crew dropped their bombs on a flak concentration, which they believed to be near Cologne, and only W/O Merralls and crew were able to convince themselves that they were in the correct general area when releasing their bombs through the clouds from 9,000 feet onto the western edge of the target. Eighty-eight returning crews claimed to have bombed the primary target, where, according to local sources, one house was destroyed and thirteen seriously damaged.

Minor operations occupied the night of the 16/17th, for which 5 Group contributed ten Hampdens and two Manchesters for gardening duties in the Deodar garden in the Gironde Estuary, and five Hampdens and two Manchesters for nickelling activities over Lille in north-eastern France. The two gardening Manchesters belonged to 106 Squadron, and departed Coningsby at 20.50 with the crews of P/O Picken and the newly commissioned P/O Scatchard on board and an outward flight of three hundred miles ahead of them. The weather was fine as they crossed the Channel, and, apart from a little inaccurate flak at the French coast, P/O Picken and crew enjoyed an uneventful trip, during which they located the garden in good visibility and delivered four mines accurately. L7485 did not return to Coningsby, and the eventual recovery of the remains of the pilot and four members of his crew on the French coast confirmed that the Manchester had gone down in the English Channel. This was an experienced crew, and their presence in the squadron and Coningsby community would be missed.

If the Germans had not yet had a close-up view of a Lancaster, they now had seven smouldering wrecks to pick over following the epic and audacious daylight raid by six aircraft each of 44 and 97 Squadrons on the M.A.N diesel engine factory at Augsburg during the afternoon of the 17th. S/L Nettleton and crew, who had led the 44 (Rhodesia) Squadron element, were the only ones from Waddington to make it back to England, and Nettleton was awarded the Victoria Cross. While Operation Margin was in progress, 173 aircraft were being prepared for an operation that night against Hamburg, for which 5 Group contributed five Manchesters. For a record sixth night in a row, 106 Squadron found itself called into action, and made ready two of the Manchesters for the crews of P/Os Hopgood and Stoffer. They departed Coningsby at 23.00, each carrying what the ORB described as fourteen 250lb oil bombs, which were similar to those employed by the Luftwaffe as incendiary devices during the Blitz. Both aircraft arrived over the city at 12,000 feet in a cloudless sky with good visibility, and watched their bombs burst in the town area. Over a hundred other crews claimed to have bombed the city, and it was, in view of the recent run of total failures, a modestly successful raid, which started thirty-three large fires if nothing else.

Following a rare night off, the squadron was instructed to make ready three Manchesters to contribute to a 5 Group force of twenty-five Hampdens, ten Manchesters and two Lancasters joining thirteen other aircraft to mine the waters of the Nectarine gardens around the Frisians. The crews of S/L Nelms, F/Sgt Appleyard and Sgt Hurd had been assigned to Nectarine I, and were airborne by 21.00, but the last-mentioned were thwarted by very poor visibility and were unable to locate the garden. S/L Nelms and crew described the night as very dark as they carried out a timed run from Terschelling to deliver their four mines into the correct position, and the crew of F/Sgt Appleyard followed suit after the rear gunner had shot out searchlights on Terschelling.

It was a month into his tour before Gibson felt himself to be fully converted to the Manchester, but wasted no time once he was ready. His first Manchester operation was carried out in L7418 on the night of the 22/23rd, when the squadron put up six aircraft to lay mines in northern waters, the crews of Gibson and S/L Stenner in the Radish garden in the Baltic's Fehmarn Belt, and those of F/L Robertson, P/O Worswick and the newly commissioned P/O Cooke and Sgt Young in Quince in the Kiel Bay area of the

Great Belt. They took off from Coningsby between 20.20 and 20.25 in good weather conditions with a half moon and clear visibility. S/L Stenner and crew experienced a mechanical failure, and decided to shorten the trip by dropping their mines in the Hawthorn garden off Esbjerg on Denmark's western coast. Sgt Young's port engine began to give cause for concern, and he and his crew also chose the Hawthorn garden as a suitable alternative location for their vegetables, as did P/O Worswick and crew, who failed to locate their briefed drop zone. Gibson and crew used Fehmarn island as a pinpoint for their run to the garden, and delivered their four mines into the correct position. F/L Robertson and crew found a pinpoint on the Danish coast from which to carry out a successful run, and P/O Cooke and crew also experienced no difficulty in fulfilling their brief.

The first attempt to employ Gee as a blind bombing aid took place on the night of the 22/23rd, when Cologne was the target for a 3 Group force of sixty-four Wellingtons and five Stirlings. Fewer than 20% of the bomb loads fell into the city, and some landed up to ten miles away, proving that Gee was capable of guiding a force to a general area, but lacked the precision necessary to deliver a telling blow on an urban target. While this operation was in progress, 5 Group dispatched twenty-two Hampdens and a dozen Manchesters on gardening duties on both sides of the Schleswig-Holstein peninsula in Forget-me-not (Kiel Harbour), Quince (Kiel Bay), Radish (Fehmarn Belt) and Rosemary (Heligoland Bight). They encountered clear skies and good visibility over the western Baltic and pinpointed on the southern tip of Denmark's Langeland Island and on the German mainland north-east of Kiel, before making their timed runs and dropping their mines into the briefed locations.

In an attempt to repeat the success of Lübeck, Harris launched a series of four raids on consecutive nights against Rostock, another Baltic port, beginning on the 23/24th. An added incentive was the presence on the southern outskirts of the town of the Heinkel aircraft factory, to which the 5 Group element of eleven Hampdens, six Manchesters and a single Lancaster were assigned, while 143 aircraft from the other groups targeted the town. 106 Squadron's six participants departed Coningsby between 21.50 and 22.00 with S/L Nelms the senior pilot on duty, and flew out at what, for the time, was low-level for a night raid, and approached the target at between 4,000 and 5,000 feet in moonlit, cloudless conditions which afforded excellent visibility. S/L Nelms and crew were able to identify the runway and factory buildings, and watched their six 1,000 pounders burst across the target, as did P/O Hopgood and crew from 4,500 feet. F/Sgt Appleyard and crew did not observe the results of their efforts as they took violent evasive action to avoid the light flak, which damaged the aircraft slightly. The crews of W/O Young and Sgt Hurd reported similar experiences, and these five crews returned home confident that they had inflicted massive damage on the factory. L7463 had developed an overheating engine, which eventually erupted into flames over southern Denmark, upon which, P/O Stoffer ordered his crew to take to their parachutes. They reached the ground safely to be taken prisoner, but P/O Stoffer was still on board when the Manchester broke up at low level and crashed at 03.20 near Tinglev. In the classic book, Enemy Coast Ahead, Gibson related being in the operations room on that night, watching a pretty WAAF climb the step ladder to write landing times on the large wall-mounted operations board. She turned out to be Mary Stoffer, and, according to his account, Gibson ended up driving the distraught young woman home at the end of her shift.

The ORB described the enormous damage inflicted upon the factory, and when the reconnaissance photos were eventually posted on the squadron notice board some days later, the participating crews were incredulous to discover that it had escaped damage. The attack on the town had also been disappointing, and had fallen between two and six miles from the Altstadt aiming point. Five 106 Squadron Manchesters were detailed to accompany 120 other aircraft in a return to Rostock on the night of the 24/25th, ninety-one assigned to the town and thirty-four from 5 Group, including four Lancasters from the newly-converted 207 Squadron at Bottesford, to the factory. The 106 Squadron ORB listed only the crews of P/O Cooke, F/L Robertson and W/O Young as taking off at 21.55 and 22.00, and stated in the summary section that two other crews returned early with engine problems. On another night of excellent weather conditions and visibility, the crews experienced no problems in identifying the target, and, in fact, were drawn on from many miles away by the fires left burning by the spearhead. Bright moonlight illuminated the Warnow River running south from the coast to the heart of the town, and provided excellent visibility for the low-level attacks. The town seemed to be ablaze as they crossed over it to reach the Heinkel factory, which most attacked on existing fires, while trying to evade the attentions of the many searchlights co-operating with light flak. The three Coningsby crews delivered their bombs from between 5,000 and 6,000 feet, apparently observing them to burst among the factory buildings, and the consensus among returning 5 Group crews was that the Heinkel factory and adjacent aerodrome had been hit by many bombs and were left burning. The 106 Squadron ORB triumphantly announced that the damage appeared to be as extensive as that inflicted on the previous night, but this was before the bombing photos of the first raid had reached squadron level. While post-raid reconnaissance did, indeed, reveal extensive damage within the town, the factory buildings were found to be still intact, demonstrating that the impressions gained by crews in the heat of battle could be somewhat unreliable.

On the following night, W/C Gibson put his own name at the top of the list of five 106 Squadron crews detailed for a return to the Heinkel factory at Rostock as part of a 5 Group element of eighteen Hampdens, Manchesters and Lancasters. They departed Coningsby between 21.55 and 22.30 on yet another night of clear conditions and bright moonlight, but F/Sgt Young and crew were forced to turn back when L7276 refused to run on the weak mixture necessary to make the fuel last. Gibson and crew carried out a level run at 4,500 feet at an indicated air speed of 220 mph, and, although certain that they had found the mark, thick smoke prevented a detailed assessment of the results. P/O Cockbain and crew, who had Whamond flying as second pilot, also found the target obscured by smoke as they attacked from 5,000 feet, and they were uncertain as to the precise fall of their 1,000 pounders, as were the crews of Sgt Hurd and F/Sgt Heddon, who were too busy taking evasive action to observe where they landed. At debriefing, all expressed confidence in the accuracy of their work, and, this time, the bombing photos confirmed that the factory had sustained heavy damage, as had the town. The fourth raid by 109 aircraft included a 5 Group contribution of nineteen Hampdens, nine Manchesters and a single Lancaster, five of the Manchesters representing 106 Squadron. The crews of P/Os Cooke, Worswick and Picken and F/Sgts Browne and Young got away from Coningsby between 22.05 and 22.40, but L7457 developed intercom problems, and F/Sgt Browne turned back. The force of a little over a hundred aircraft was divided between the town and the factory with the 5 Group element assigned to the latter, and arrived over Germany's Baltic coast to find moonlight, excellent visibility and existing fires to aid target location. P/O Picken and crew were caught in searchlights and subjected to intense flak that forced them to take violent evasive action and jettison their bombs. P/O Worswick and crew were attacked by a Ju88 after bombing, but successfully evaded it without sustaining damage. Both sections of the attack achieved accuracy, and by the end of the four-raid series 1,765 buildings had been destroyed, and more than five hundred seriously damaged. This amounted to an estimated 60% of the town's built-up area reduced to ruins. It was also the first time that the word "Terrorangriff", or terror raid, appeared in German reports.

5 Group sat out an effective attack on Cologne on the night of the 27/28th, when fifteen hundred houses and nine industrial premises were damaged to some extent. The first Lancaster to be taken on charge by 106 Squadron was L7569, which arrived from 44 (Rhodesia) Squadron on the 28th, and this made the squadron the fifth in the Command to receive the type. That night, 5 Group contributed ten Hampdens to an operation at Kiel, during which, damage was inflicted upon the important shipyards, the Deutsche Werke and the Krupp-owned Germania Werft. At the same time, five 106 Squadron Manchesters were conducting mining sorties in the Forget-me-not and Wallflower gardens in Kiel Harbour, Quince in Kiel Bay and Radish in the Fehmarn Belt. The crews of recently promoted F/O Cockbain, W/O Merralls,

F/Sgt Young and Sgt Hurd had taken off between 22.35 and 22.45, leaving F/O Loftus and his crew on the ground until 00.10. The last-mentioned turned back early on because of W/T failure, and on landing at Coningsby, found F/O Cockbain and crew had beaten them by ten minutes, also having been thwarted by a W/T issue. This meant that the Wallflower and Radish gardens would not be topped up on this night, but the crews of W/O Merralls and F/Sgt Young found the Forget-me-not garden basking in moonlight, and planted their four vegetables each into the briefed locations, as did Sgt Hurd and crew in the Quince garden. While 106 Squadron remained at home on the following night, other elements of 5 Group took part in an unsuccessful attack on the Gnome & Rhone aero engine factory at Gennevilliers in Paris. Although it escaped damage, other industrial concerns in the nearby Port-de-Paris were hit. During the course of the month the squadron operated on eighteen nights, and dispatched forty-four sorties for the loss of three Manchesters and two crews.

May 1942

The weather kept the Command on the ground on the night of the 1/2nd, but it had relented sufficiently on the following day for ninety-six aircraft from 3 and 5 Groups to be detailed for mining operations that night from the Biscay coast in the south-west to the Baltic in the north-east. 5 Group provided twenty-one Lancasters, eight Manchesters and twelve Hampdens for gardening and nine Manchesters for nickelling duties in the Rennes area of north-western France. 106 Squadron made ready eight Manchesters, while briefing their crews for the Forget-me-not and Wallflower gardens in Kiel Harbour. To get eight Manchesters off the ground for a single operation was not only a new record for the squadron, it was also something of a feat, the type's serviceability record generally precluding any possibility of achieving a maximum effort. This night's performance was very much to the credit of Gibson, and a sense of satisfaction no doubt accompanied their departure from Coningsby between 22.20 and 22.30. P/O Aytoun and crew experienced an engine issue while outbound, and opted to drop their four 1,500lb parachute mines into the Hawthorn garden off Esbjerg on Denmark's western coast. The others reached their respective target areas to find clear skies and good visibility, despite which, F/O Loftus and crew failed to locate their target area and also selected the Hawthorn garden as an alternative on the way home. The crews of P/Os Cockbain, Cooke and Picken and F/Sgt Appleby planted their vegetables in the required locations, and returned safely, leaving the crews of F/Sgts Hurd and Young unaccounted for and the only two missing from the night's activities. L7399 crashed some nine miles west of Haderslev in eastern Jutland, killing F/Sgt Young and all but a gunner and the wireless operator, who fell into enemy hands. They were soon joined in captivity by F/Sgt Hurd and his crew, whose R5840 had been brought down by flak to crash on or close to the German island of Pelworm in the Waddensee.

On the following night, a forecast of unfavourable weather persuaded Harris to send a modest force of eighty aircraft, including five Hampdens, to Hamburg. Fifty-four of them reached the target area to bomb through cloud, and despite the odds stacked against them, they produced a remarkably effective raid that started over fifty large fires and bombed out more than sixteen hundred people. The first of a series of three operations on consecutive nights against Stuttgart was posted on the 4th, and a force of 121 aircraft assembled, of which fourteen Lancasters and nineteen Hampdens were provided by 5 Group. The Lancaster crews were briefed to attack military barracks, while the Hampden element was assigned to the Robert Bosch electrical component factory located just south of Zuffenhausen on the northern outskirts of the city. At the end of their five-hundred-mile outward flight, with a rising moon to light the way, the crews found all of their good intentions thwarted by ten-tenths cloud at around 6,000 feet over the series of deep valleys occupied by the sprawling city. It proved impossible to pick out ground features by which to establish a position, and the bombing was carried out on DR and evidence of flak. The flak emanated from a clever "defended" decoy fire site at Laufen, some fifteen miles north of the city, which attracted many bomb loads and helped to protect the Bosch factory from damage. 5 Group's Manchesters had not been invited to take part, and, instead, 106 Squadron sent five crews to lay mines in the Rosemary garden off the island of Sylt on Schleswig-Holstein's western coast. They departed Coningsby between 21.15 and 21.30 with W/C Gibson the senior pilot on duty in L7378, and the recently promoted F/Os Whamond and Hopgood and P/Os Aytoun and Cockbain in his wake. They arrived in the target area to find some cloud but good visibility, and all were able to deliver their four mines each into the briefed locations. In addition to these sorties, P/O Duff and crew had departed Coningsby at 21.55 to drop leaflets (nickels) on Amiens, but a faulty compass forced them to abandon their sortie after two hours and return home.

5 Group contributed four 97 Squadron Lancasters to a force of seventy-seven aircraft detailed to return to Stuttgart on the following night, and they again bombed the town rather than the Bosch factory to which they had been assigned. Despite clear skies, ground detail was obscured by haze, and no bombs fell in the city. The nickelling of Amiens was rescheduled for the night of the 6/7th, and, this time, the crews of P/Os Churcher and Duff took off at 22.15 and 22.20 respectively, carrying between them 320 bundles of reading matter to boost the morale of the residents. They benefitted from excellent weather conditions, and, apart from inaccurate flak in the Dunkerque area, performed their postman duties as briefed and without incident. The main event on this night was the third of the series on Stuttgart, which involved ninety-seven aircraft, including ten Hampdens and ten Lancasters representing 5 Group. The force flew out across Belgium, and, after an outward flight lasting almost three hours, reached the target area to find largely clear skies, but haze compromising the vertical visibility and making target identification difficult. Most picked out a built-up area on e.t.a., backed up by evidence of searchlights, flak and burning incendiaries from other aircraft, and scattered their bombs over a wide area. The operation was another massively ineffective affair, which again failed to land a single bomb in Stuttgart, but did hit 150 buildings in Heilbronn, a large town situated five miles from the Lauffen decoy site and twenty miles from Stuttgart. The only positive note was the loss of just ten aircraft from 295 sorties over the three operations.

The crews of P/Os Aytoun and Picken, W/O Young and F/Sgt Appleyard were called to briefing on the 7th to learn that they would be undertaking horticultural duties in the Rosemary garden off the island of Sylt that night. They departed Coningsby between 23.55 and 00.05, but lost the services of P/O Aytoun and crew to starboard engine failure twenty minutes after crossing the English coast. The others reached their respective target areas in clear conditions and good visibility, and used the islands of Sylt and Pellworm as pinpoints from which to make their timed runs.

The recent successes at Lübeck and Rostock may have encouraged the posting of another Baltic coast target on the 8th, this time, Warnemünde, situated on the West Bank of the estuary ten miles north of Rostock. The docks were the site of U-Boot crew training, and also supplied German forces on the Russian front, but, equally important was the Heinkel aircraft factory, the destruction of which was handed to 5 Group. An initial force of more than two hundred aircraft was detailed, among which 5 Group put up twenty-one Lancasters, nine Manchesters and nineteen Hampdens, the last-mentioned representing the two Canadian squadrons, 408 and 420, the only units still equipped with the type. An elaborate plan called for a three-phase operation, beginning at zero hour with eighteen aircraft delivering high-explosives in a five-minute slot, followed by phase two, which involved 104 aircraft attacking with GP bombs, and phase three, six 44 (Rhodesia) Squadron Lancasters and a dozen aircraft from other groups targeting the Heinkel factory at low level to ensure its destruction. As this was ongoing, sixty-two 1 Group crews were to drop incendiaries, while others carried out low-level attacks on searchlight and flak batteries. In the event, 193 aircraft took off, which would reduce slightly the aircraft available for each phase.

The 106 Squadron contingent of six Manchesters departed Coningsby between 21.50 and 22.05 with W/C Gibson the senior pilot on duty and flying in R5770, with the newly promoted F/L Whamond, F/L Robertson, F/O Hopgood, P/O Cockbain and W/O Merralls in support. P/O Cockbain and crew turned back with an electrical fault before reaching enemy territory, and F/L Whamond had to nurse his port engine to get as far as the Danish coast, before also abandoning his sortie. As the others reached the eastern coast of Jutland, a veritable forest of searchlights could be seen seventy miles away at the target, where they arrived to find clear skies and excellent visibility and an intense flak response. A huge concentration of searchlights had been laid horizontally to dazzle approaching aircraft, but Gibson was able to carry out a straight-and-level run, and believed his bombs had fallen across the target. The crews of Robertson and Hopgood went in at 2,000 feet, and also believed that they had hit the aiming point, although they were unable to make an accurate assessment because of the need to take evasive action. W/O Merralls and crew adopted a glide approach, delivering their bombs from 4,500 feet and observing them to burst across the buildings of the factory. The operation was actually something of a disaster, which cost nineteen aircraft, including four Lancasters from 44 (Rhodesia) Squadron, one of which contained its newly appointed commanding officer. There was not even any confirmation of a successful outcome to compensate for the losses and the disappointment.

Thereafter, 106 Squadron stayed at home for a week, during which time the crews continued with the ground-based part of their conversion training on Lancasters. The Command, too, remained largely dormant, and most of the small-scale operations that did take place were devoted to mining. Hopgood's rapid rise through the ranks continued, as he now became a flight lieutenant, and this was a sure sign of his popularity with Gibson and his acceptance into the inner circle. Hopgood, W/O Young and F/Sgt Appleyard departed Coningsby between 23.35 and 23.40 on the 16th, bound for the Rosemary garden off Sylt, where they pinpointed on Pellworm island in ideal conditions, and ran to the drop zone to release their four mines each at ten-second intervals. On the 19th, Sgt McHardy and crew took off in L7418 to carry out a navigation exercise over the route Base-Aberystwyth-Land's End-Hurn-Base, and were last seen off the Pembrokeshire coast. They failed to arrive back, and it is assumed that the Manchester crashed somewhere in the Irish Sea. Also, on this day, the first flight took place of a 106 Squadron Lancaster, but the ORB omitted to reveal the identity of either the crew or the aircraft.

Mannheim was posted as the primary target for that night, and a force of 193 aircraft made ready, which included a 5 Group contribution of fifteen Hampdens, thirteen Lancasters and four Manchesters. 106 Squadron contributed a single Manchester containing the crew of P/O Cockbain, who departed Coningsby at 22.45, and had reached the Belgian coast when the oxygen system failed and the mid-upper gunner passed out. The cause of the problem could not be located, and the sortie had to be abandoned. In keeping with the performances of the period, most of the bombs missed Mannheim and fell into open country, and the operation was a failure. Meanwhile, the crews of P/Os Duff and Churcher, who were still considered to be freshmen, had taken off at 23.20 to join an attack on the docks and shipping in the port of St-Nazaire. The latter found the target under clear skies but shrouded in mist and well-defended, and delivered their bombs from 7,000 feet, observing them to burst in the target area. P/O Duff and crew were unable to locate the aiming point despite searching, but selected a pinpoint and dropped their bombs on e.t.a on a flak concentration. Back home, it was discovered that they had produced an outstanding photograph of their twelve 500 pounders bursting in a stick across the inland docks at Nantes, some miles to the east of the intended target.

There now followed another lull in major operations as Harris prepared for his master stroke. At the time of his appointment as C-in-C, the figure of four thousand bombers had been bandied around as the number required to wrap up the war. Whilst there was not the slightest chance of procuring them, Harris, with a dark cloud still hanging over the existence of an independent bomber force, needed to ensure that those earmarked for him were not spirited away to what he considered to be less-deserving causes. The Command had not yet achieved sufficient success to silence the detractors, and the Admiralty was still calling for bomber aircraft to be diverted to the U-Boot campaign, while others demanded support for the North Africa campaign. Harris was in need of a major victory, and, perhaps, a dose of symbolism to make his point, and, out of this was born the Thousand Plan, Operation Millennium, the launching of a thousand aircraft in one night against a major German city, for which Hamburg had been pencilled in. One small fly in the ointment was the fact that Harris didn't have a thousand frontline aircraft to call upon, and required the support of other Commands to make up the numbers. This was forthcoming from Coastal and Flying Training Commands, and, in the case of the former, a letter to Harris on the 22nd promised 250 aircraft. However, following an intervention from the Admiralty, the offer was withdrawn, and most of the Flying Training Command aircraft were found to be not up to the task, leaving the Millennium force well short of the magic figure. Undaunted, Harris, or more probably his able deputy, AM Sir Robert Saundby, scraped together every airframe capable of controlled flight, or something resembling it, and pulled in the screened crews from their instructional duties. He also pressed into service aircraft and crews from within the Command's own training establishment, 91 Group. Come the night, not only would the thousand mark be achieved, it would be comfortably surpassed.

During the final week of the month, the arrival on bomber stations from Yorkshire to East Anglia of a motley collection of aircraft from training units gave rise to much speculation among crews and ground staff alike, but, as usual, only the NAAFI staff and the local civilians knew what was really afoot. 106 Squadron began high-level training in Lancasters on the 25th, the day on which orders were received across the Command to stand by for a "special effort", to restrict flying so as not to impair serviceability and to recall all crews from leave. On the 26th, Gibson undertook his first flight in a Lancaster, with B Flight commander, S/L Stenner, alongside him to assist in his conversion. Within days, however, Gibson had fallen ill, although the precise nature of his indisposition has never been established. He would spend a frustrating two weeks in Rauceby Hospital and three more convalescing, and would miss the impending series of massive operations under the Thousand Plan. Gibson hated to miss out on any innovation, and the forthcoming Operation Millennium would be the largest employment to date of the bomber stream, the tactic that would become standard practice for the remainder of the war.

The most pressing remaining question was the weather, and, as the days ticked by inexorably towards the end of May, this was showing no signs of complying. Harris was aware of the genuine danger, that the giant force might draw attention to itself, and thereby compromise security, and the point was fast approaching when the operation would have to take place or be abandoned for the time being. Harris released some of the pressure by sanctioning operations on the night of the 29/30th, for which the Gnome & Rhone aero-engine and Goodrich tyre factories at Gennevilliers in Paris were the main targets for a force of seventy-seven aircraft, including a contribution from 5 Group of fourteen Lancasters and three Hampdens. The operation failed to cause anything other than minor damage to the factories, but thirty-eight houses were destroyed and a further forty-nine knocked about to some extent and there were civilian fatalities.

It was in an atmosphere of frustration and hopeful expectation, that "morning prayers" began at Harris's High Wycombe HQ on the 30th, with all eyes turned upon the civilian chief meteorological adviser, Magnus Spence. After careful deliberation, he was able to give a qualified assurance of clear skies over the Rhineland, while north-western Germany and Hamburg would be concealed under buckets of cloud. Thus, did the fickle fates decree that Cologne would bear the dubious honour of hosting the first one thousand bomber raid in history. At briefings, crews were told that the enormous force was to be pushed across the aiming point in just ninety minutes at a rate of twelve aircraft per minute. This was unprecedented and gave rise to the question of collisions as hundreds of aircraft funnelled towards the aiming point. The answer, according to the experts, was to observe timings and flight levels, and they calculated also that just two aircraft would collide over the target. It is said that a wag in every briefing room asked, "do they know which two?"

The lull in operations had allowed 106 Squadron sufficient time to work up on its Lancasters, and this epic occasion would provide a fitting operational baptism. The operation was to conform to the now established pattern of three waves, with the genuine heavy bombers bringing up the rear. 5 Group had seventy-three Lancasters, forty-six Manchesters and thirty-four Hampdens bombed up and ready to go, and, at Coningsby, five Manchesters and eleven Lancasters, two of the latter borrowed from 97 Squadron, awaited the arrival of their crews, who had been briefed to attack aiming point Y, which bordered the western and southern extremities of the city centre on the West Bank. Among the new arrivals at Coningsby during the month had been S/L John "Dim" Wooldridge, one of the great characters to grace Bomber Command. He had been posted in from 207 Squadron at Bottesford, shortly to succeed S/L Stenner as B Flight commander, and Millennium was to be his maiden operation with 106 Squadron. He and S/Ls Robertson and Stenner were the senior pilots on duty on this momentous occasion, while the other participating Lancaster crews were those of F/Ls Hopgood and Whamond, P/Os Picken, Cooke, Worswick and Healey, and W/Os Young and Merralls, while the Manchester crews were those of P/Os Aytoun, Cockbain, Duff and Churcher and F/Sgt Appleyard. Two of the spare Manchesters were lent to 50 Squadron, one of them, as events turned out, being involved in the award of a posthumous Victoria Cross.

The first away of an eventual 1047 assorted aircraft either side of 23.00 were the Wellingtons, Hampdens and Whitleys of the training units along with the front-line Wellingtons equipped with Gee. Some of the older training hacks were long past their best, and would take somewhat reluctantly to the air, lifted more, perhaps, by the enthusiasm of their crews than by the power of their engines. A number of these, unable to climb to a respectable height, would fall easy prey to the defences, or just drop out of the sky through mechanical breakdown. The 106 Squadron Manchesters departed Coningsby between 23.05 and 23.20 as part of the second wave, leaving the Lancasters to follow in their wake between 23.50 and 00.15. It was to be a disappointing night for F/L Hopgood and crew, whose intercom failed shortly after take-off, and despite desperate attempts to rectify the problem, their efforts were in vain and they were forced to return home. The remainder pressed on in good weather conditions, making landfall over the Scheldt estuary on a direct course to the target, and found the Cologne area to be precisely as predicted by Magnus Spence, clear of cloud and under bright moonlight. Bombing by the Coningsby crews took place from as low as 7,500 feet by F/Sgt Appleyard and crew and as high as 15,000 feet by the crew of F/L Whamond, while S/L Wooldridge and crew attacked from 12,000 feet at 01.45, and watched their bombs fall among already-burning buildings. All returned safely home via a reciprocal route a little to the south of the outward track, and W/O Merralls and crew were the last to land at Coningsby at 05.50.

Returning crews described a city on fire from end to end, and never-before-witnessed scenes, while post-raid reconnaissance confirmed that the operation had, by any standards, been an outstanding success, and had destroyed more than 3,300 buildings, while inflicting serious damage to two thousand others. Although the loss of forty-one aircraft represented a new record high, the conditions had favoured both attackers and defenders alike, and, in the context of the scale of success and the numbers dispatched, it could not be considered an inordinately high figure. 5 Group registered the loss of four Manchesters, one Lancaster and one Hampden, but it was the training units that sustained the greatest losses amounting to twenty-one aircraft. Two of the Manchesters borrowed by 50 Squadron, L7301 and L7456, were among the casualties, the former crashing in Belgium after sustaining severe flak damage over Cologne. The pilot, F/O Manser, sacrificed his life to allow his six crew colleagues to parachute to safety, and all but one evaded capture, their testimony on return to England leading to the award to Manser of a posthumous VC. An interesting postscript to this incident involved P/O Horsley, the wireless operator/gunner in Manser's crew. He eventually re-mustered as a pilot, and joined 617 Squadron with a crew of his own in November 1944. During the course of the month the squadron operated on seven nights, and dispatched forty-nine sorties, thirty-seven by Manchesters and eleven by Lancasters, and registered the operational loss of two Manchesters and their crews, two others in 50 Squadron hands and one during training.

June 1942

While the Millennium force remained assembled, Harris wanted to exploit its potential again immediately, and was no doubt excited about the prospect of visiting upon the old enemy of Essen a similar ordeal to that just experienced by Cologne. A force of 956 aircraft was the best that could be achieved during the 1st, 5 Group managing seventy-three Lancasters, thirty-three Manchesters and twenty-six Hampdens. The operation would be conducted in similar fashion to that on Cologne, with experienced crews in 3 Group Wellingtons leading the way with an abundance of flares for illumination. 106 Squadron's adjutant had, at last, got his hands on a typewriter, and the infinitesimally small and difficult-to-decipher handwriting was banished from the Form 541 for good, but not yet from the Form 540. He recorded that the squadron made ready nine Lancasters and six Manchesters, the former loaded with a cookie and eight SBCs of incendiaries each, and the latter with all-incendiary loads, and it was the twin-engine brigade that departed Coningsby first, between 23.05 and 23.55, to be followed by the Lancasters immediately afterwards between 23.55 and 00.45. S/L Robertson had now been installed as the successor to S/L Nelms as commander of A Flight, and he and S/L Wooldridge were the senior pilots on duty. The crews had been briefed to employ the sprawl of the Krupp-dominated Borbeck sector as the aiming point, and flew out under favourable weather conditions that promised the possibility of actually being able to identify ground detail. However, on arrival in the target area they encountered a layer of five to ten-tenths cloud at 4,000 to 6,000 feet, which combined with industrial haze and smoke drifting over from Cologne to muddy the vertical visibility. Bombing took place largely on TR (Gee) supported by occasional visual references on waterways, although it was the glow of a large fire, believed to be in the city, that attracted S/L Robertson's load, which was observed to burst but could not be plotted. F/L Whamond and crew climbed above the cloud to bomb from 16,000 feet on what was estimated to be Essen, while S/L Wooldridge and his crew bombed on a Gee-fix from 13,000 feet, and claimed to see bomb bursts in the western part of the target. Others delivered their loads on e.t.a, and all but one returned to report having little clue as to what had gone on beneath the clouds.

Absent from debriefing was the crew of P/O Worswick, who had been called back from leave to take part in the Thousand raids. R5844, which actually belonged to the Conversion Flight, came down in a suburb of Essen after being hit by flak. There were no survivors from this experienced crew, and this was the first of many Lancasters to be lost in 106 Squadron service in the remaining three years of war. P/O Worswick held a DFC, and his navigator and bomb-aimer, W/O Robson and P/O Bake respectively, were holders of the DFM. It will be recalled that this crew had survived the ditching in the Solent in mid-April, and their loss would be felt by the Coningsby community. Two nights earlier, Worswick's wireless operator had been P/O Bob Hutchison, who would find himself a respected member of Gibson's "Chastise" crew a year hence. Sadly, the scale of the failure of this operation was equal to the scale of success at Cologne, as the usual problems of target location prevented the majority of the force from finding the city. Bombs were scattered all over the Ruhr, with only eleven houses classified as destroyed in Essen, and this scant reward was in return for the loss of thirty-one aircraft.

A follow-up raid was planned for twenty-four hours later, and a much-reduced force of 197 aircraft made ready, with 5 Group providing twenty-seven Lancasters and a dozen Hampdens, although none representing 106 Squadron. It was a night of cloudless skies over the Ruhr, with the usual industrial haze and a low moon providing some illumination. Most crews would describe the visibility as good, and reported being further aided by flares, which highlighted the Rhine over to the west. Those 5 Group crews with Gee at their disposal confirmed their positions over what they believed to be the Krupp district aiming point, and delivered their cookies and incendiaries from up to 18,000 feet either side of 01.30. Despite the apparent confidence of the crews that they had attacked Essen, local authorities reported just three high explosive bombs and three hundred incendiaries falling in the city to cause only minor damage. Such was the density of the Ruhr, with overlapping town and city boundaries, it was difficult not to hit something urban, but concentration was the key to success, and the scattering of bombs over a wide area was never going to achieve a knock-out blow. Harris was stubborn and would keep trying, but it would be a further nine months before the means were to hand to make a genuine impact.

For the next operation, on the 3rd, Harris turned his attention upon Bremen, which, along with Essen and Emden, would share the Command's attention for the remainder of the month. A force of 170 aircraft was made ready for the first major attack on the port since the previous October, of which 5 group provided fifteen Lancasters, nine Hampdens and six Manchesters. 106 Squadron supported the operation with the freshman crews of Sgts Brinkhurst and Jones, both pilots captaining their crews for the first time, and they departed Coningsby at 23.10 to act as fire-raisers with bomb loads of 1,260 x 4lb incendiaries. Those reaching the primary target found clear skies with ground haze to mar the vertical visibility, through which the 106 Squadron pair delivered their incendiaries from 10,000 and 9,000 feet respectively, and observed them to ignite. Most returning crews were less than enthusiastic about the probable outcome, but in fact, this was the most destructive raid to date on this target. Damage was visited upon residential and industrial buildings, and there were hits on U-Boot construction yards, an aircraft factory and the harbour. The freshman crew of Sgt Crowfoot had been detailed to take part in this operation, but their Manchester had become unserviceable at the last minute. Their chance came twenty-four hours later, when they took off at 22.30 to deliver the contents of twelve SBCs, each containing thirty-six bundles of reading matter for the residents of Amiens and its surrounds. They positioned themselves twenty-two miles east of the city and released one bundle every thirty seconds before returning safely after a gentle round-trip of four hours.

On the 5th, the squadron was ordered to stand down from operations in order to devote all of its energy to the conversion programme. That night, 180 aircraft were prepared for the next intended assault on Essen, for which 5 Group put up thirteen Lancasters and eleven Hampdens. The force flew out over Belgium, and some identified a bend in the River Ruhr to the south-east of the target, while others relied on a TR-fix, flares or evidence of searchlight and flak concentrations to establish their positions in conditions of poor vertical visibility. Local sources again confirmed an ineffective and wasteful raid, which caused only minor damage in Essen at a cost of twelve aircraft and crews. The first of four attacks during the month on the naval port of Emden was posted on the 6th, and a force of 233 aircraft made ready, 5 Group contributing twenty Lancasters, fifteen Hampdens and seven Manchesters. The skies over the coast of north-western Germany were found to be clear of cloud and the visibility was good, which enabled those dropping flares to illuminate the docks area for the bomb-aimers of the main force. Smoke was rising through 8,000 feet as they retreated, and the glow from the port remained visible for up to eighty miles into the return journey. Photographic-reconnaissance and local reports confirmed that the raid had been responsible for the destruction of some three hundred houses, with a further two hundred severely damaged, in return for the loss of nine aircraft.

The Command entered a period of gardening and minor operations, thereafter, punctuated by two further attacks on Essen. The first of these, by an initial force of 170 aircraft, took place on the night of the 8/9th, and was supported by 5 Group with thirteen Lancasters and nine Hampdens. It was another disappointing and widely scattered raid, which caused only minor housing damage. On the 10th, S/L John Wooldridge was appointed to command 106 Squadron's B Flight. Wooldridge was an enigmatic character with great creative abilities as an author and composer, and he preferred to spend his nights off indulging in these pastimes, rather than carouse in the mess bar or local watering holes. As such, he was the kind of person that Gibson found difficult to fathom and of which he was faintly suspicious. Wooldridge was a good organiser, was popular with the crews, and sported a luxuriant "wizard prang" moustache in the finest traditions of the heroic aviator. Perhaps of greatest importance was the fact that he was a seasoned campaigner, having served with 44 and 61 Squadrons during 1940, and had completed forty-one operations by that autumn. Within a year he was back on operations at 61 Squadron, before the brief spell with 207 Squadron preceding his arrival at 106. He would never be invited into Gibson's inner circle, and would certainly have declined the opportunity, had it been offered. There would always be a degree of strain between the two men, and one suspects that Wooldridge had the upper hand and employed his superior intellect to unsettle Gibson. On the 15th, perhaps, as a break from the intensity of conversion training, but mostly to provide a morale-boost for the workforce, a party of twenty-eight pilots from Coningsby visited the Rolls Royce factory at Derby, where the Merlin engine was being built.

After spending four nights on the ground because of adverse weather conditions, the Command stirred itself on the 16th at Harris's behest to have another crack at Essen, for which 106 aircraft were made ready, 5 Group contributing fifteen Lancasters. All crews had been briefed to employ TR to locate the target and bomb blindly based on that, which, under the conditions of up to eight-tenths cloud on a moonless night with visibility down to three miles, was the best that could be expected. It emerged at debriefing that only sixteen crews claimed to have bombed the primary target, while fifty-six others had found alternatives, mostly the city of Bonn. This concluded a series of five raids on Essen in sixteen nights, during which 1,607 sorties had been dispatched and eighty-four aircraft lost. The city had sustained no industrial damage, and a few wrecked houses was all that Bomber Command had to show for the massive effort expended.

Having hosted an effective attack earlier in the month, Emden became the focus for three raids in the space of four nights, beginning on the 19th, for which a force of 194 aircraft was assembled with nine Lancasters and eleven Hampdens representing 5 Group. The crews had been briefed to switch to Osnabrück, eighty miles to the south, if the weather conditions over the coastal region became troublesome, and part of the flare force did, indeed, initiate an attack on Osnabrück by twenty-nine aircraft, leaving 131 others to claim that they had bombed the primary target. Despite the numbers, the Emden authorities reported only a handful of high-explosive bombs falling and a few hundred incendiaries. 185 aircraft were made ready to return to the port on the following night, twenty-four Lancasters and a dozen Hampdens provided by 5 Group. They reached the target area at around 01.00 to be greeted by five to eight tenths cloud and generally poor visibility. The docks were the briefed aiming point and the town the alternative, and positions were established by TR-fix and glimpses of the coastline. It was another inconclusive raid, and local sources confirmed that only a proportion of the force had located the target, and around a hundred houses had been damaged. A force of 227 aircraft took off late on the 22nd for the third raid of the series on Emden, for which 5 Group contributed eleven Lancasters and eight Hampdens. Most crews established their approach to the target by identifying the coastline and confirming it via a TR-fix backed up by flak and fires, before running in on the aiming point in good visibility under moonlight. Some returning crews had been able to distinguish between genuine and decoy fires, but the latter succeeded in drawing off many loads, and those finding the target destroyed fifty houses and damaged a hundred more.

The time had now arrived for the final deployment of the Thousand Force, and, indeed, the Manchester in operational service. A force of 960 aircraft was assembled on the 25th, made up of ten types, including Blenheims, Bostons and Mosquitos from 2 Group, with 5 Group providing ninety-six Lancasters, twenty-six Hampdens and twenty Manchesters. It was an indication of the failure of the Manchester, that the aircraft it had been intended to replace, the Hampden, would continue to serve 5 Group in small numbers until mid-September. To the above numbers were added five aircraft from Army Co-operation Command and 102 Hudsons and Wellingtons from Coastal Command, which had been ordered by Churchill himself to take part, although, its contribution was to be deemed a separate operation. However, the 1,067 aircraft from all sources would represent a larger combined force than that sent to Cologne at the end of May. 106 Squadron's contribution amounted to seventeen Lancasters and two Manchesters, and would have been a record-equalling twenty aircraft had one Manchester not become unserviceable at the last minute.

The 106 Squadron departure from Coningsby began with the Manchesters containing the crews of Sgts Crowfoot and Jones at 23.25 and 23.30 respectively, and continued with the Lancaster element between 23.40 and 00.15 with S/Ls Robertson and Wooldridge once more the senior pilots on duty. Flying as second pilot to S/L Robertson was P/O Cooper, another who would join 617 Squadron, although after Operation Chastise. Sadly, he was destined to lose his life in April 1944 during a Cheshire-led operation to Munich. After climbing out, the individual squadrons headed for the Lincolnshire coast between Skegness and Mablethorpe and began to form into a stream as they made their way across the North Sea. Their briefed aiming point was the Focke-Wulf aircraft factory in the south-eastern district of Hemelingen on the East Bank of the Weser, which F/L Hopgood and crew would not reach, after losing both starboard engines shortly after crossing the Dutch coast. The others pressed on, and, above the ten-tenths cloud that persisted all the way from the English coast to the target area, the sky was extremely bright, courtesy of a full moon and the Northern Lights. A band of nine to ten-tenths cloud lay over Bremen at between 3,000 and 5,000 feet, completely obscuring ground detail, which precluded any chance of picking up the Focke-Wulf aircraft factory, and positions were established by TR-fix, the glow of fires on the ground and the volume of flak coming up through the cloud. S/L Robertson and crew bombed on e.t.a., which happened to be over a flak concentration, but they was not able to determine the outcome, while Bill Whamond and crew came down to 8,000 feet to bomb on DR, and observed bursts beneath the clouds and the start of a fire. In contrast, P/O Churcher and crew let their bombs go from 15,000 feet, aimed at the glow of a large fire, and P/O "Wimpy" Wellington, who was undertaking his first operation as a Lancaster captain, dropped his from 12,000 feet, and was certain that they fell in Bremen. Sgt Jones and crew recorded the lowest bombing height of 7,000 feet, where their Manchester must have been in danger from the hardware falling from above. Happily, they dodged the lot, and were one of three crews last back with a landing time of 05.50. Sgt Jones' wireless operator on this night was the previously-mentioned Bob Hutchison, who was one of those dogged characters that suffered from air-sickness. He would "throw up" into his RAF-issue "spewbag", and then get on with his job without fuss or complaint.

Returning crews could only estimate that they had hit the city, and reported several areas of fire, but none of the 696 crews claiming to have attacked the primary target had any real clue as to the outcome. Local sources confirmed a number of hits on the Focke-Wulf aircraft factory and some shipyards, along with the destruction of 572 houses, and damage to more than six thousand others, mostly in southern and eastern districts, but estimated the size of the bomber force to be around eighty. The level of success fell well short of that achieved at Cologne, but surpassed by far the failure at Essen, albeit at a new record loss of forty-eight aircraft, which represented 5% of those dispatched. The O.T.Us of 91 Group suffered the highest casualty rate of 11.6%, largely because they were employing tired, old Whitleys, Wellingtons and Hampdens, which were not up to the task, while 5 Group lost one Lancaster and one Manchester. 106 Squadron came through unscathed having delivered a new 5 Group record of fifty-four tons of bombs. The 26th brought a well-deserved DSO for S/L Stenner to add to his DFC, and was reward for his great courage, skill and devotion to duty during his second tour of operations, and for his leadership while serving as a flight commander with 106 Squadron.

The first of a number of follow-up operations against Bremen was mounted on the night of the 27/28th, and involved 144 aircraft, including twenty-four Lancasters from 5 Group. Weather conditions were very much as those of two nights earlier, with ten-tenths cloud up to around 4,000 feet and decreasing amounts thereafter as high as 15,000 feet. The sky above as bright as day under a large moon, even though the Northern Lights, on this occasion, were masked by high cloud. Most located the target area by TR-fix, and crews could only estimate that they were over the target. Local reports confirmed hits on the previously damaged Atlas Werke shipyard and the Korff refinery, but further details were scant and of little value.

On the following night, the squadron sent seven Lancasters with freshman crews to lay mines in the Deodar garden in the Gironde estuary. They departed Coningsby between 22.45 and 23.00, and all reached the target area under cloudless skies and in bright moonlight to establish their positions without difficulty and deliver five mines each into their briefed locations before returning safely home.

It was Bremen again on the 29th, for which a force of 253 aircraft was assembled, including 108 Wellingtons, while 5 Group contributed sixty-four Lancasters, 3 Group forty-seven Stirlings and 4 Group thirty-four Halifaxes, and this was the first time that four-engine aircraft represented more than 50% of the overall numbers on a major operation. 106 Squadron loaded seven Lancasters with a cookie and incendiaries and launched them into the air between 23.45 and 00.05 with S/L Wooldridge the senior pilot on duty. Accompanying Wooldridge as second pilot was P/O David Shannon, a twenty-year-old Australian, who had a glittering operational career ahead of him and would become a member of Gibson's inner circle. They flew out over Skegness aiming for Haarlem, and crossed the North Sea over six to ten-tenths cloud at between 3,000 and 5,000 feet, with excellent visibility above. Arriving in the target area, they encountered around seven to ten-tenths cloud in layers up to 16,000 feet, with large gaps that afforded some a glimpse of the ground. S/L Wooldridge and crew bombed from 10,000 feet, and were chased out of the target area by two enemy night-fighters, which they shook off. Even from 15,000 feet, F/Sgt Appleyard and crew were able to observe the flash of their bombs, which, they believed, had fallen within the built-up area of the city. Returning crews had little of use to pass on to the Intelligence Section, but local sources spoke of extensive damage to the Focke-Wulf factory, the A G Weser U-Boot construction yard and three other important war-industry premises, along with the local gas works and some limited destruction of housing. The squadron operated on six nights during the month and dispatched forty-five Lancaster sorties and nine by Manchesters for the loss of a single Lancaster and crew.

July 1942

The campaign against Bremen would span the turn of the month, but 106 Squadron's first task in July was to send a single Lancaster to northern waters on the night of the 1/2nd to lay mines in the Nasturtium garden at the northern end of Oresund (The Sound), situated between Denmark's Sjælland island and Sweden. Sgt Crowfoot and crew took off at 21.55 with five vegetables in the bomb bay and P/O Cooper flying as second pilot, and they carried out their brief in excellent weather conditions before returning home safely after a round trip of five hours and forty minutes. The campaign against Bremen continued on the 2nd, with the preparation of a force of 325 aircraft, more than half of which were Wellingtons. 5 Group squadrons contributed fifty-three Lancasters and twenty-eight Hampdens, five of the former provided by 106 Squadron and departing Coningsby between 23.55 and 00.05, each loaded with a cookie and eight SBCs containing 720 x 4lb incendiaries. They crossed the North Sea to make landfall on the Dutch coast near The Hague, before reaching north-western Germany to find favourable weather conditions, with excellent visibility, no low cloud, high cirrus at around 22,000 feet, and only a little haze to spoil the view below. Positions were established by TR-fix confirmed by a visual check, but searchlight glare created great difficulty for the bomb-aimers trying to identify the Focke-Wulf aircraft factory aiming point, and most would settle for estimating the point of release of their bombs. The 106 Squadron crews, each with a pilot officer as captain, carried out their attacks from 13,500 to 17,000 feet, during which, P/O Grein's R5864 was hit by flak that knocked out both port engines. This left the crew with a tense return flight on two engines, which they complete to land a full forty minutes after the last of the others had returned. A large fire was reported on the aerodrome attached to the Focke-Wulf factory, and another at Delmenhorst to the south-west, and the consensus was of an effective operation. Local reports spoke of a thousand houses damaged, along with four small industrial premises, while three cranes and seven ships were hit in the port, one of the vessels sinking and becoming a danger to navigation. The likelihood is, however, that much of the effort was wasted beyond the city's southern boundary.

Gibson had now returned from his sick leave, and re-acquainted himself with the Lancaster in a familiarization flight with Hopgood on the 4th. The remainder of the first half of the month would be low-key, with mining operations occupying much of the night-time activity. A five-night respite for most squadrons ended on the 8th, when a force of 285 aircraft was assembled to return to north-western Germany to attack the naval port of Wilhelmshaven. This operation gave W/C Gibson the opportunity to go to war in a Lancaster for the first time, and having assisted in Gibson's conversion, the young Australian, P/O David Shannon, accompanied him as second pilot. Unlike many, and typical of the irreverent Antipodean attitude to authority, Shannon was not fazed by Gibson's martinet tendencies, and, once a member of the inner circle, a bond of genuine friendship would develop between the two, and Shannon's allegiance to his leader would remain steadfast throughout his life. On this night they were on board R5681, one of ten 106 Squadron Lancasters involved and loaded with a 4,000lb cookie, and six 500 and two 250 pounders for use against the Kriegsmarinewerft ship and U-Boot construction yards. They departed Coningsby between 23.55 and 00.15 and headed for the Lincolnshire coast, only to find that the squadron's usual high level of serviceability had deserted it. Sgt Cassels and crew turned back after just forty miles with wireless failure, while the crews of Sgt Crowfoot and P/O Churcher both suffered engine failure early on, and were forced also to abandon their sorties. The others pressed on across the North Sea to find the target only partially protected by around three-tenths thin cloud at 10,000 feet and by haze at low level. This made it almost impossible for most to identify ground detail, including the docks and shipyards aiming points, and positions were established on e.t.a., and by TR-fix, some backed up through a visual check assisted by the use of flares. S/L Robertson and crew bombed from 12,500 feet, but were too busy taking evasive action to observe the result, while Gibson saw his bombs fall into the docks area from 12,000 feet, but could not confirm that they hit the U-Boot yards. Hopgood and crew bombed on a Gee-fix, but did not observe the results, and the others attacked from between 10,000 and 17,000 feet either side of 01.45 in the face of a fairly heavy flak response thrown up by the defenders. There was evidence of dummy fires, which, inevitably, would lure away some bomb loads, and this was confirmed by post-raid reconnaissance, which revealed that much of the bombing had missed the town to the west. Local sources reported some damage in Wilhelmshaven, but, in truth, it was a disappointing attack that brought to an end a five-week loss-free period for 106 Squadron. A night-fighter sent R5861 crashing into the sea about twenty miles off the North Frisian island of Ameland, and there were no survivors from the crew of P/O Brodrick.

The first daylight foray deep into enemy territory by Lancasters, the previously mentioned raid on the M.A.N diesel engine factory at Augsburg in April, had cost seven of the twelve aircraft dispatched, and Harris, never an enthusiast of such operations, particularly at low level, had not been eager to repeat the exercise. Despite this, he sanctioned a similar plan by 5 Group for an attack on the Kaiserliche Werft and Schichau Werft U-Boot construction yards in the distant port of Danzig on the 11th. The forty-four Lancasters of 61, 83, 97, 106 and 207 Squadrons were to fly out in formation at low level, before splitting up to cross Denmark independently. Having reached the Baltic, they were to make their own way to the target by following its coastline, climbing to normal bombing height by the time that they arrived at dusk. The attack was to be carried out in the fading light, to allow a withdrawal to take place under the cover of darkness, and the 1,700-mile round-trip would be the longest yet attempted by the Command. The distance dictated that fuel took priority over bombs, and each of the nine 106 Squadron Lancasters would have just four 1,000 pounders in its bomb bay.

They departed Coningsby in three sections of three in a six-minute slot from 17.00 with W/C Gibson and S/L Robertson the senior pilots on duty, and Shannon once again acting as Gibson's second pilot. They headed for landfall on the west coast of Jutland, but ran into an unanticipated band of ten-tenths ice-bearing cloud over the North Sea, which extending from 14,000 feet almost to sea-level. This ruined the plan, as aircraft not only lost contact with each other, but some crews were forced by ice-accretion to abandon their sorties and turn back. The break-up of the formation would have a detrimental effect on the raid and cause some crews to arrive late, when darkness had already settled over the area to create challenging conditions for aiming point identification. Hopgood's run of bad luck continued with a fuel-flow problem, which had become so acute by the time he crossed the Danish coast, that he was forced to turn back. P/O Cockbain's Lancaster developed generator problems while he was outbound over the sea, and he also turned back. After breaking formation, P/O Aytoun and crew remained at low level for the remainder of the outward flight, and attacked the target from 3,500 feet at 22.07, claiming a direct hit with their four 1,000lb RDX bombs. Some crews found it difficult to identify Danzig in the darkness, while others located it but could not pick out the aiming point, and Gibson and crew were among these. They attacked an eight-hundred ton ship at Gdynia, and watched the nearest bomb fall twenty yards away. P/O Churcher and crew reached the target at 22.20, and released the bombs from 5,000 feet, F/Sgt Appleyard and crew turned up three minutes later to bomb from 4,000 feet, and S/L Robertson and crew were the last to arrive, locating the target at 22.45, and bombing from 3,500 feet. The others all searched long and hard, but were defeated by diminishing fuel reserves and the weather, and were forced to give up and return home. In all, twenty-four crews reported bombing either the ship-building wharfs or the town, and two Lancasters were lost to flak in the target area.

Harris turned his attention back upon the Ruhr two nights later, when launching the first of a series of five operations over a four-week period against the heavily industrialized city of Duisburg situated on the East Bank of the Rhine on the north-western edge of the Ruhr. A force of 194 aircraft was assembled during the afternoon of the 13th, 5 Group represented by thirteen Lancasters belonging to 97 and 106 Squadrons at Coningsby. 106 Squadron loaded its seven Lancasters with five 2,000 pounders each, and sent them on their way between 00.25 and 00.40 with F/L Hopgood the senior pilot on duty. For once, Hopgood's Lancaster held together during the outward flight, undertaken in unhelpful weather conditions, and he and his crew reached the target to find seven-tenths cloud with a base at around 5,000 feet, through which they bombed on a TR-fix (Gee) from 14,000 feet. R5638 was hit by flak and seriously damaged over the well-defended target and the flight engineer wounded, but W/O Merralls completed the bombing run, and brought the aircraft and crew home on three engines. The others from the squadron carried out their attacks from between 10,000 and 14,000 feet, and all admitted to bombing on e.t.a or TR-fix after failing to positively identify the target. Local sources confirmed a scattered raid that achieved only a very modest amount of housing damage. The following night was devoted to mining and nickelling operations, and 106 Squadron dispatched the lone freshman crew of Sgt Jones on their maiden sortie at 23.00 bound for the city of Amiens in north-eastern France. Taking into account the wind speed and direction on a night of fine weather conditions, they positioned themselves some eighteen miles west of Amiens before releasing 216 bundles.

The 17th brought the award of a DFM to F/Sgt Appleyard and his navigator, F/Sgt Darvill, for their excellent work during the Danzig operation. The next operation for W/C Gibson and crew was supposed to be a small-scale "moling" attack on Essen on the 18th, for which they and the crews of S/L Wooldridge, P/O Picken and W/O Merralls took off from Coningsby between 13.00 and 13.30 to follow in the wake of six others each from 83 and 44 Squadrons, which had taken off earlier. It was described in the 5 Group ORB as a "Porpoise" operation, with the objective as "Stoat C". After messages were received from the 44 Squadron aircraft of lack of cloud, and also a signal from an 83 Squadron crew stating they had a badly injured mid-upper gunner, a recall signal was sent to the 106 Squadron element. Gibson turned back when near Flushing, at the mouth of the Scheldt, and it was on this occasion that he spotted a Lancaster a mile ahead, which he caught up for mutual protection. It was then that he noticed his favourite Lancaster, R5681, O-Orange, being piloted by S/L Wooldridge, who had led Gibson to believe that it was unserviceable, and, therefore, unavailable to him. Wooldridge was five miles north of Walcheren when he picked up the recall signal, and it was just rank bad luck that Gibson happened to see him. He landed at Mildenhall, and one wonders if that was, in part, to delay the inevitable confrontation with Gibson. W/O Merralls and crew were outbound over Holland when called back, and they aimed their bombs at a ship in the Oosterschelde, only for them to overshoot. They were then attacked simultaneously by a BF109 and an FW190, which inflicted slight damage on the Lancaster, while the gunners shot down the BF109 and damaged the FW190. Gibson sought out his B Flight commander afterwards, and one can imagine an explosive encounter taking place behind closed doors. To his credit, Gibson speaks of "Dim" Wooldridge in glowing terms in Enemy Coast Ahead, extolling his skill and courage as a bomber pilot, his popularity and standing in the squadron, and his organisational ability, particularly with regard to crew training. However, he also referred to Wooldridge's underhand tactics to get what he wanted, like borrowing Gibson's car without permission, and arranging postings-in of people he wanted around him.

An all-four-engine force of ninety-nine aircraft took off late on the 19th to bomb the Vulcan U-Boot yards at Vegesack, in Bremen. 106 Squadron sent four Lancasters, which took off between 23.59 and 00.10 with F/L Bill Whamond the senior pilot on duty, and each carrying fourteen SBCs containing ninety 4lb incendiaries. Just like the rest of the force, they were unable to identify the target visually because of complete cloud cover, and the back-up plan, to use Gee, resulted in the attack missing the town altogether. P/O "Taffy" Williams and crew picked up a pinpoint on the River Weser, and that enabled them to make a timed-run, but they were too busy evading the heavy flak to notice any results. P/O Picken and crew were also experiencing a torrid time as they passed through the flak barrage during the bombing run at 12,000 feet, and it was a battle-scarred R5700 that was first to land at base at 04.25. Flying with the crew as second pilot was P/O Carlyle RCAF, who was at the controls of R5576 on the 21st, when it took off on a practice bombing exercise. As the Lancaster climbed away, the port-inner engine cut, and witnesses watched it stall at 200 feet, before crashing to the ground near the airfield, killing all ten occupants. There were three other members of the RCAF in the crew and one belonging to the RAAF, and the three passengers were all members of the ground crew.

A force of 291 aircraft was assembled on the 21st for the second raid of the series on Duisburg, and this number included twenty-nine Lancasters and seventeen Hampdens representing 5 Group. 106 Squadron was not involved, but dispatched the crew of F/Sgt Church at 00.50 on a nickelling trip to Lille, which had to be abandoned after both generators failed during the outward flight. It was a moonless night, and, despite clear skies over the western Ruhr, those engaged in the main event were hindered by the extreme darkness and the usual industrial haze, the effects of which, it was hoped, would be negated by flares dropped from the leading aircraft by TR. However, these proved to be not entirely accurate, and some illuminated an area of open country on the West Bank of the Rhine. Those crews reaching the target returned with enthusiastic claims of many fires, but photographic evidence revealed that a proportion of the bombing had fallen to the west of the Rhine and short of the city. However, local reports confirmed extensive damage in residential districts, with ninety-four apartment buildings destroyed and 256 seriously damaged, and there was also mention of damage to the Thyssen steel works and to two other important war-industry factories.

A reduced force of 215 aircraft was made ready to continue the assault on Duisburg on the 23rd, and forty-five of these were Lancasters, five of them representing 106 Squadron. They took off from Coningsby between 01.00 and 01.40 with F/L Hopgood the senior pilot on duty, and each carrying a cookie, six 500 and six 250 pounders. They encountered seven to ten-tenths cloud in the target area with tops as high as 12,000 feet in places, and a large gap appeared that afforded some crews a sight of the ground. Despite that, for many, there was little chance of locating the briefed aiming point, which was probably the Thyssen steel works. The Gee-based (TR) flares were again scattered and largely ineffective, leaving most crews to carry out their attacks on their own TR-fix. Hopgood and crew found sufficient breaks in the cloud to pick up a number of pinpoints to keep them on track, but it was necessary to use a TR-fix to put them over the target, where they delivered their load from 12,000 feet. Taffy Williams and Ginger Crowfoot used TR fixes confirmed by the glow of fires, the former flying in Gibson's R5681, which he brought home full of shrapnel holes. P/O Butterworth and crew reported bombing from 16,000 feet on TR, and complained of being fired upon by a British convoy off Skegness. Returning crews were confident that they had hit the city's built-up area, many claiming to have identified specific ground features, and the outcome of the raid was revealed to be similar to the previous one, with residential property sustaining the bulk of the damage. Even so, the outcome was another disappointment and not commensurate with the effort expended.

The fourth raid on Duisburg was posted on the 25th, for which the largest force yet of the series was assembled. Among the 313 aircraft were 177 Wellingtons and fourteen Hampdens, with the four-engine types making up the numbers. The thirty-three Lancasters included just three representing 106 Squadron, each of which was loaded with fourteen SBCs containing ninety 4lb incendiaries. Seventy-five minutes before the departure of the crews of F/Sgts Appleyard and Jones and Sgt Cassels between 00.10 and 00.15, F/Sgt Church and crew had set off the for the long round-trip to the Deodar garden in the Gironde estuary. They did not return, and news eventually came through that R5608 had crashed somewhere near St-Nazaire, and that only the pilot and one gunner had survived to fall into enemy hands. Meanwhile, F/Sgt Appleyard DFM and crew were heading south towards The Wash, when R5683 blew up and fell in pieces onto a mud bank at Butterwick, some four miles east-north-east of Boston. There were no survivors, and only two of the occupants could be identified. The others pushed on to find around seven-tenths cloud at 7,000 feet over the target, with fair visibility, which enabled a visual confirmation of the TR-based approach, but not the briefed aiming point D. The extensive and distinctive Ruhrort inland docks complex provided a solid reference point to bomb the built-up area generally for those unable to identify the briefed aiming point, and bomb bursts and fires were reported by returning crews. Opposition was described as not heavy, but there was a night-fighter presence, and the crew of Sgt Cassels was chased out of the target area, but escaped undamaged. It was left to local sources to confirm further damage to residential property, but less extensive than in the two previous attacks.

A maximum effort was planned on the 26th for the annual last-week-of-July attack on Germany's Second City, Hamburg, and 404 aircraft answered the call, among them seventy-seven Lancasters and thirty-three Hampdens. 106 Squadron made ready nine Lancasters, which departed Coningsby between 22.55 and 23.35 with W/C Gibson in his beloved, and now repaired, R5681, and S/L Robertson the other senior pilot on duty. They flew out over the Lincolnshire coast, and continued on an easterly heading across the North Sea, where they were forced to negotiate the frequently-met conditions on this route of towering cumulonimbus cloud, electrical storms and severe icing. The skies over the target were clear, however, and the visibility excellent, which allowed the crews to confirm their positions by visual reference, with the docks area standing out particularly clearly in the bright moonlight. Gibson, who had Shannon with him as second pilot, bombed from 14,000 feet, and watched his cookie, six 500 and six 250 pounders explode south-west of the aiming point, and cause further fires in the already-burning shipyards lining the Elbe. Hopgood and crew dropped their bomb load from 11,000 feet into the old city, where they were observed to start new fires. The crews of "Taffy" Williams and "Johnny" Coates were each sitting on fourteen SBCs of 4lb incendiaries, while those of "Bill" Whamond, "Ginger" Crowfoot, "Wimpy" Wellington and P/O Crowe all had high-explosive loads beneath their feet, which all but P/O Wellington used to good effect. R5749 was caught in a heavy flak barrage during the bombing run, and sustained extensive damage as a result, a difficulty exacerbated by the fact that the electrical circuits of the bomb-release gear had been severed, preventing the bombs from being jettisoned to save weight. If this were not enough to contend with, three members of the crew had been wounded, and, while homebound, still weighed down by a full bomb load, they were attacked by a night-fighter, which the gunners drove off. P/O Wellington brought the Lancaster home on three engines, and praised his crew for their outstanding work. On return to Coningsby, the crews were enthusiastic about their part in the operation, and reported carrying out their attacks from between 11,000 and 15,000 feet. The outcome was a rare major success for the period, which caused widespread damage in residential districts and started eight hundred fires, more than five hundred of them classed as large. It was not a one-sided affair, however, and twenty-nine aircraft failed to return, among them 106 Squadron's R5748, which fell to the guns of a night-fighter flown by Lt Lothar Linke of II./NJG1. It crashed near Drachten in northern Holland at 02.05, killing S/L Robertson and three of his crew, while the navigator and both gunners survived to fall into enemy hands.

Another maximum effort was called for on the 28th, and a force well in excess of four hundred aircraft was assembled for the return to Hamburg that night, 256 of them provided by 3 Group and the operational training units. In the event, these would take off alone, after the weather conditions over the 1, 4 and 5 Group stations prompted the withdrawal of their contributions to the operation, and, as conditions worsened over the North Sea, the O.T.U aircraft were recalled. Many of the 3 Group crews turned back also, and only sixty-eight would claim to have attacked the primary target, where fifteen large fires and forty smaller ones were reported. This modicum of success was gained at the high cost of twenty-five aircraft, 15% of those dispatched, and four O.T.U Wellingtons also failed to return, while a fifth, a Whitley, ditched, and its crew was picked up safely.

106 Squadron had not been involved on that night, but made ready three Lancasters for an attack on Saarbrücken, a new target for 106 Squadron. This major industrial and coal-producing Saarland Capital city, located right on the frontier with France south-east of Luxembourg, had been targeted before, but never by a force as large as the 290-strong one assembled during the 29th. Sgts Crowfoot and Cassels and their crews departed Coningsby at 23.50, to be followed fifteen minutes later by the crew of P/O Crowe. They had been briefed to attack aiming point C, and, in the expected absence of a strong searchlight and flak defence, the intention was to attack from a lower level than customary for the period.

Each carried a cookie along with six 500 and four 250 pounders, and completed the sea crossing to make landfall on the French coast, before following the frontier with Belgium and entering Germany south of Luxembourg. At the target, they encountered a layer of four to eight-tenths low cloud at between 2,000 and 9,000 feet, below which the visibility was good, and this enabled crews to confirm their TR positions by visual references on ground features like the River Saar. Weather conditions were not particularly favourable, and the crews met with a 7,000-foot cloud base in the target area, which required them to descend to 5,000 feet to obtain a view of the ground. P/O Crowe and crew made three runs across the target to confirm that they were, indeed, over the primary target, and delivered their bombs from 4,000 feet, observing them to burst across the built-up area. The defenders responded with intense light flak, and R5780 collected a number of holes. "Ginger" Crowfoot's report was almost a carbon copy, but Sgt Cassels and crew experienced a much more action-packed operation. They bombed the target from 4,400 feet, and on return, reported being attacked by night-fighters on five separate occasions. Two were shaken off by evasive action, two were driven off by the gunners, and one was shot down in flames and seen to impact the ground, and all of this was accomplished without sustaining any damage. The operation was highly successful, and caused the destruction of almost four hundred buildings, mostly in central and north-western districts.

The month ended with a major assault on the Ruhr city of Düsseldorf, for which a force of 630 aircraft was assembled, the numbers bolstered by a large contribution from the training units. 5 Group offered 113 Lancasters, the first time that the one hundred-figure had been reached, and they would be accompanied by twenty-four Hampdens belonging to the two Canadian squadrons, 408 and 420. 106 Squadron had been dispatching single figures of late, but managed a new record of twenty-one Lancasters on this night, led by W/C Gibson in R5681. S/L "Dim" Wooldridge and crew were first to take off at 00.15, and "Bunny" Grein brought up the rear with his crew an hour later. All were carrying a cookie, some with small calibre high-explosive bombs and others with incendiaries, but W/O Merralls and crew had the squadron's first 8,000 pounder in their bomb bay. Sgt Cassels and crew began to experience engine trouble shortly after taking off, but pushed on until seventy miles from the target, where they gave up and brought their bombs home. The others pressed on via the Scheldt estuary to the southern Ruhr, where bright moonlight, clear skies and good visibility enabled them to confirm their TR-fixed positions visually by an S-bend in the River Rhine. P/O Aytoun was five minutes from the target when his starboard-outer engine cut, and sent the heavily-laden Lancaster temporarily out of control. Once back on an even keel, it was discovered that the front and rear turrets were out of action, and it was decided to head for home and bomb Mönchengladbach on the way.

Gibson and crew arrived over the target to find it already well alight, and added to the destruction in the city centre by dropping into a cookie and twelve 500 and 250 pounder GP bombs. Gibson recorded his speed while over enemy territory as 230 mph. The remaining 106 Squadron participants carried out their attacks from between 9,000 and 16,000 feet in the face of an intense and accurate searchlight and flak defence. Sgt Lace and crew were leaving the target when an engine failed, to be followed by another before the Dutch coast was reached. The entire North Sea crossing was carried out on two engines, but these began to falter over England, and the crew, who had been prepared for the bale-out order for some time, took to their parachutes, leaving the pilot, and second pilot, Sgt Brinkhurst, to bring the crippled Lancaster to a safe landing at Docking in Norfolk. At debriefing, most crews expressed confidence in the quality of their work, some commenting on a column of black smoke rising through 10,000 feet as they turned away. More than nine hundred tons of bombs were dropped, some wasted in open country, but the remainder had been scattered across all parts of the city and the neighbouring city of Neuss on the opposite bank of the Rhine. Local sources confirmed the destruction of 453 buildings, with varying degrees of damage to fifteen thousand more, and sixty-seven large fires had to be dealt with. The success came at the cost of twenty-nine aircraft, of which five Hampdens and two Lancasters belonged to 5

Group, including 106 Squadron's R5604, which crashed north-west of Cologne with fatal consequences for the experienced crew of W/O Merralls DFM. The squadron created a new record on this night by delivering sixty-three tons of bombs, which exceeded the fifty-five tons dropped during the Thousand Bomber raid on Bremen a month earlier. The O.T.U.s were again hit disproportionately hard, losing fifteen of their number, and one wonders if the wisdom of employing aircraft from the training units was called into question after this operation. These losses were on top of more than sixty others resulting from participation in the three Thousand Bomber raids. During the course of the month the squadron carried out fourteen operations on twelve nights and dispatched eighty-four sorties for the loss of five Lancasters. The 239.7 tons of bombs delivered represented a new record for the squadron, and surpassed the efforts of all other 5 Group squadrons.

August 1942

August was to be a busy month for the Command, and by the time operations began for 106 Squadron, it would average better than one operation every two nights. The squadron typewriter was now made available for the Form 540 as well as for the Form 541, and all of the entries became clear and legible! There was a soggy start to the new month as rain washed out flying at Coningsby until the 3rd, and it was the same for 5 group as a whole until orders were received at Swinderby and Woodhall Spa on that day to prepare small numbers of Lancasters for mining duties in the Forget-me-not and Radish gardens, respectively Kiel Harbour and the Fehmarn Belt in the western Baltic. On the following night, 5 Group contributed a handful of Lancasters and Hampdens for mining duties around the Frisians and off the Biscay coast, in which two 106 Squadron Lancasters were supposed to take part. In the event, one was scrubbed after becoming unserviceable at the last minute, and Sgt Smith, flying as crew captain for the first time, took off with his crew at 01.50 bound for one of the Nectarine gardens off the Frisians. They located the drop zone without difficulty beneath a cloud base at 1,000 feet, and delivered all five mines into the correct location. It was the same fare on the following night for the crews of P/O Cooper and Sgt Lace, who departed Coningsby at 01.45, also for a Nectarine garden, and fulfilled their briefs unopposed from beneath a cloud-laden sky.

420 Squadron vacated Waddington on the 6th on transfer to 4 Group, where it would convert to Wellingtons, and, on the 7th, 9 Squadron would arrive from 3 Group to begin conversion to the Lancaster as the replacement for 83 Squadron, which was about to leave 5 Group for pastures new.

The spate of post-midnight take-offs continued on the night of the 6/7th, when the fifth and final raid was mounted in the current series against Duisburg. 5 Group's contribution amounted to forty-seven Lancasters and ten Hampdens, which were part of an overall force of 216 aircraft. Eight of the Lancasters were provided by 106 Squadron, and they departed Coningsby between 01.00 and 01.20 with S/L "Dim" Wooldridge the senior pilot on duty and each carrying a cookie, some with ten SBCs of 4lb incendiaries and others with a mix of 500 and 250 pounders. S/L Wooldridge lost both starboard engines while outbound, and had to jettison the bombs in order to maintain control and get back home, while "Taffy" Williams and crew had to turn back with a fuel system issue and TR failure. W4102 became uncontrollable shortly after take-off through an aileron malfunction, but, to their credit, P/O Butterworth and crew pressed on to complete the entire operation on "George" (automatic pilot). Those reaching the target encountered cloud reported at anything between zero and ten-tenths with tops at 10,000 feet and barrage balloons tethered as high as 12,000 feet. Positions had to be established by TR-fix confirmed by visual reference aided by fires, flak and flares, and the bombs were delivered by the Coningsby crews from 11,000 to 21,000 feet (P/O Butterworth) without their fall being plotted. According to local reports, eighteen buildings were destroyed and sixty-six seriously damaged at a cost to the Command of five aircraft. It was another unsatisfactory operation, and the statistics of the past three weeks made discouraging reading for Harris. He had committed 1,229 sorties over the five Duisburg operations, of which forty-three had failed to return in exchange for the destruction of 212 houses, serious damage to 741 others and significant industrial damage resulting from just one raid.

On the night of the 8th, the squadron was notified of a return to mining duties that night, to be carried out in one of the seven Silverthorn gardens in the Kattegat and the Forget-me-not garden in Kiel Harbour. The crews of W/C Gibson, S/L Wooldridge, P/O Wellington and Sgt Cassels were assigned to the former, and those of F/O Churcher, P/Os Butterworth, Coates and Grein to the latter, and they departed Coningsby between 22.30 and 23.55, the ORB making the point that this must be a very important operation, otherwise the appalling weather conditions would have caused a scrub. For once, Gibson had a flight engineer, Sgt Russell, rather than Dave Shannon beside him in the cockpit. P/Os Butterworth and Coates were unable to locate their target areas despite searching long and hard, and both abandoned their sorties. Despite the rain, mist and low cloud, the others all found pinpoints from which to make a timed run, Gibson and crew releasing their five vegetables at twenty-second intervals.

The garrison city of Osnabrück was posted as the target on the 9th, and a force of 192 aircraft assembled accordingly, 5 Group contributing forty-two Lancasters, just three of them made ready by 106 Squadron. The crews of Sgts Lace and Smith and the recently promoted F/O Aytoun departed Coningsby between 00.30 and 00.45, each sitting on a cookie, six 500 pounders and two of 250lbs, and headed for the Lincolnshire coast at Skegness. Thirty-five minutes later, Sgt Hamilton and crew took off on their freshman sortie to deliver mines to one of the Nectarine gardens off the Frisians, which they would complete without incident. There were clear skies over the Münsterland region of Germany to the north of the Ruhr, but haze contributed to the poor visibility that awaited the approaching bombers. They all found that they were unable to establish their positions by TR after it was jammed by the enemy on crossing the Dutch coast. Flares were dropped to illuminate the area, and some crews picked out railway lines and the River Hase, but it was mainly the fires, searchlights and flak that pointed the way to the aiming point. Bombing was carried out by the 106 Squadron crews from between 9,000 and 13,000 feet, and some observed the burst of their cookie. The resulting fires remained visible for eighty to a hundred miles into the return flight, and TR functioned again once the Dutch coast had been crossed homebound. Local sources confirmed an effective raid, which destroyed 206 houses and a military building, and damaged a number of industrial premises along with four thousand other buildings, mostly lightly.

The night of the 10/11th was devoted to mining operations in northern waters, and would occupy fifty-two aircraft, including a contribution from 5 Group of seventeen Lancasters, including three representing 106 Squadron. The crews of W/C Gibson, S/L Wooldridge and P/O Coates all got away at 21.15, and proceeded to the Asparagus garden in the Great Belt between the Danish main islands of Fyn and Sjælland. It was a night of extreme darkness, particularly below the 700-foot cloud base, despite which, Gibson and crew identified Helskov Point from which to carry out their DR run, and accurately delivered five mines into the briefed location. S/L Wooldridge and crew were also successful in delivering four mines, but P/O Coates was unable to locate his garden, and jettisoned his mines "safe".

The main operation on the night of the 11/12th was the first of two on consecutive nights against the city of Mainz, situated to the south-west of Frankfurt-am-Main, for which 154 aircraft were made ready. The number included a contribution from 5 Group of thirty-three Lancasters, including eight representing 106 Squadron, for what would be the first large-scale raid on this target and another to add to the squadron's already impressive list. The 106 Squadron element departed Coningsby between 22.50 and 23.30 with F/Os Aytoun and Churcher the senior pilots on duty, four of the Lancasters with four 2,000 pounders in the bomb bay and the remainder with a cookie and up to a dozen SBCs of incendiaries. After successive sorties as second pilot to "Dim" Wooldridge, P/O Cooper returned to the pilot's seat for this operation, which would be taking place on a night of favourable weather conditions. The three to five-tenths cloud during the outward flight had largely cleared by the time the target was reached, and F/O Churcher and crew bombed from 7,000 feet by the light of flares, observing their bombs to burst on a large building, possibly a factory, and start a fire. Apart from P/O Coates and crew, who attacked from 8,000 feet, the others bombed from between 13,000 and 15,000 feet, and all but one returned to report a successful outcome. Absent from debriefing were P/O "Bunny" Grein and crew, whose W4109 had crashed about six miles south-south-west of Koblenz without survivors. The raid was highly successful, and caused major destruction in the central districts, where many historic and cultural buildings were damaged or destroyed. In the excellent tome, Bomber Command War Diaries by Martin Middlebrook and Chris Everitt, the losses from this operation are put at six aircraft, but the actual number failing to return was fourteen, while four others were lost in crashes at home.

The ordeal was not yet over for Mainz, which was posted as the primary target again on the following day, and a force of 138 aircraft made ready, to which 5 Group contributed thirty-three Lancasters and ten Hampdens. This time, 106 Squadron prepared seven Lancasters, which departed Coningsby between 22.50 and 23.15 with W/C Gibson and S/L Wooldridge the senior pilots on duty. A number of names that would become familiar as future "Dambusters" were appearing in the ORB at this time. Sgt Tony Burcher has already been mentioned, and flew on this night with the crew of Sgt Cassels, while Sgt George Chalmers had recently flown with Sgt Smith, also as mid-upper gunner. On this night, Sgt Charles Brennan was beside Dim Wooldridge in the cockpit of W4118 as flight engineer, and, like Burcher, he would go to the dams in Hopgood's crew. They all reached the target area, where they found eight to ten-tenths cloud at between 3,000 and 12,000 feet and generally poor visibility, although Gibson and crew assessed the cloud base to be at 6,000 feet, and dropped beneath it, where they found a pinpoint on an island in the Rhine. The bomb-aimer, F/Sgt Crozier, delivered the load of four 2,000 pounders with the target in his sights, but intense light flak had Gibson diving for the ground, before he was unable to plot their fall. "Wimpy" Wellington and his crew caught sight of the target through one of the few gaps in the cloud, and they bombed from 16,000 feet, a full 10,000 feet higher than Gibson. S/L Wooldridge and crew searched for forty-five minutes, by which time the cloud base had ascended to 7,000 feet, and they bombed from there, as did a number of others. F/O Aytoun and crew were unable to identify the target, and dropped their bombs on e.t.a from 17,000 feet before returning safely along with the others. Post-raid reconnaissance and local reports confirmed further heavy damage in central and industrial areas, where the main railway station was also a casualty, and, according to Bomber Command estimates, 135 acres had been destroyed over the two nights.

A new era for Bomber Command began on the 15th, with the formation of the Path Finder Force, and the arrival of the four founder-member heavy squadrons on their stations in Huntingdonshire and Cambridgeshire. 83 Squadron moved into Wyton, the Path Finder HQ, as the 5 Group representative operating Lancasters, and it would be the responsibility of 5 Group's front-line units to provide a steady supply of their most promising crews. The other founder members were 35 Squadron, which took up residence at Graveley with Halifaxes to represent 4 Group, while 156 Squadron retained its Wellingtons for the time-being at Warboys, drawing fresh crews from 1 Group, and 3 Group would be represented by the Stirling-equipped 7 Squadron at Oakington. In addition to the above, 109 Squadron was posted in to Wyton, where it would spend the next six months developing the Oboe blind-bombing device and marrying it to the Mosquito under the command of W/C Hal Bufton. The new force would occupy 3 Group stations, falling nominally under 3 Group administrative control and receiving its orders through that group, which was commanded by AVM Baldwin, whose tenure, which had lasted since just before the outbreak of war, was shortly to come to an end.

A "Path Finder" force was the brainchild of the former 10 Squadron commanding officer, G/C Sid Bufton, Hal's brother, and now Director of Bomber Operations at the Air Ministry. He had used his best crews at 10 Squadron to find targets by the light of flares and attract other crews by firing off a coloured Verey light, and, it could be said, that the concept of target-finding and marking had been born at 10 Squadron. Once at the Air Ministry, Bufton promoted his ideas with vigour, and gained support among the other staff officers, culminating with the idea being put to Harris soon after his enthronement as Bomber Command C-in-C. Harris rejected the principle of establishing an elite target-finding and marking force, a view shared by the other group commanders with the exception of 4 Group's AVM Roddy Carr. However, once overruled by higher authority, Harris gave it his unstinting support, and his choice of the former 10 Squadron commanding officer, and still somewhat junior, G/C Don Bennett, as its commander, was both controversial and inspired, and ruffled more than a few feathers among more senior officers. Australian, Bennett, was among the most experienced aviators in the RAF, a pilot and a Master Navigator of unparalleled experience, with many thousands of hours to his credit. He also had the recent and relevant experience as a bomber pilot through his commands of 77 and 10 Squadrons, and had demonstrated his strong character when evading capture and returning from Norway after being shot down while attacking the Tirpitz in April. Despite his reserve, total lack of humour and his impatience with those whose brains operated on a lower plane than his, he would inspire in his men great affection and loyalty, along with an enormous pride in wearing the Path Finder badge, once having qualified to do so. He would forge the new force into a highly effective weapon, although this would not immediately be apparent.

There is some confusion surrounding 5 Group operations on the night of the 15/16th, the group ORB recording no operations because of the weather conditions, while the 44, 50 and 207 Squadron ORBs recorded, three, four and four of their Lancasters respectively operating from Waddington and Swinderby against Düsseldorf, along with nine others from 106 Squadron at Coningsby in an overall force of 131 aircraft. The 106 Squadron element took off between 00.20 and 00.55 with F/L Hopgood the senior pilot on duty and Sgt Brennan beside him as flight engineer, and all reached the target area to encounter six to nine-tenths cloud at 10,000 feet and poor to modest visibility. On a very dark night, they established their positions either by TR-fix confirmed by a visual confirmation on the River Rhine, as in the case of P/O Wellington and crew, or simply relied on e.t.a., and carried out their attacks from between 9,000 and 16,000 feet in the face of an intense flak barrage. Hopgood was coned by searchlights, but managed to avoid damage, while "Ginger" Crowfoot's W4118 brought home severe scars of battle and P/O Butterworth's R5673 a hole in the fuselage, but they, at least, came home. R5678 failed to do so after crashing in the target area, and there were no survivors from the popular crew of P/O "Johnny" Coates RAAF. (Bomber Command Losses records Coates in the rank of flying officer). At debriefing, some crews reported bomb bursts and flashes, while others saw nothing, and the abiding impression was of a scattered attack, a fact confirmed by local reports from Düsseldorf and its neighbour across the Rhine, Neuss, which described a light raid and no damage of note.

Orders were received on some 5 Group stations on the 16th to prepare for gardening expeditions that night involving a total of fifty-six aircraft off the Frisians and in the Baltic, despite the fact that the 5 Group ORB again denied any operational activity by its squadrons. Six Lancasters each were made ready by 106 and 207 Squadrons to mine the Willows, Geranium and Spinach gardens, located respectively off the Baltic ports of Sassnitz on the island of Rügen, Swinemünde, further east along the coast, and off the port of Gdynia in Danzig Bay (Gdansk), which, at the time, was part of Germany, rather than Poland as it is today. They had a very long night ahead of them, and the crews of F/L Hopgood, P/O Williams and Sgt Crowfoot faced a round-trip of some seventeen hundred miles as they departed Coningsby for the Spinach garden between 20.30 and 20.45 to begin the four-and-a-half hour outward flight. With 250 fewer miles to travel to reach their Willows destination, the crews of P/Os Wellington and Butterworth and Sgt Cassels took off between 22.15 and 22.30, but both sections would have to deal with the intense darkness. The weather conditions, however, were very different, with clear skies and haze to the east, and electrical storms and ten-tenths cloud down to 600 feet further west. Visibility was good enough for the Gdynia trio to pick up pinpoints on the distinctive coastline, and each successfully laid their three mines as briefed. Of the others, P/O Wellington and crew failed to locate their drop zone and abandoned the attempt, while P/O Butterworth and his crew were grateful to the enemy for throwing up sufficient numbers of flares to light up their part of the coast and give them a pinpoint from which to make a DR run. Sgt Cassels and crew dropped a flare float, which enabled them, likewise, to complete a successful operation.

Harris had hoped to employ the fledgling Path Finder Force immediately at Osnabrück on the night of the 17/18th, but the squadron commanders felt that they were unready, and the operation went ahead in standard fashion in the absence of a 106 Squadron contribution. It was, therefore, on the following night, the 18th, that the Path Finder Force took to the air in anger for the first time, when contributing thirty-one aircraft to an overall force of 118, of which twenty Lancasters and sixteen Hampdens were provided by 5 Group. 106 Squadron loaded nine of its own with five 1,900lb bombs and dispatched them from Coningsby between 21.10 and 21.30 with F/L Hopgood the senior pilot on duty and bound for the naval port of Flensburg, situated on the eastern coast of the Schleswig-Holstein peninsula close to the border with Denmark. The U-Boot pens in particular and the town generally were the briefed aiming points, and had been selected as worthwhile and easy-to-locate targets, but the planners had not factored in an incorrect wind forecast, which pushed the bomber stream north of the intended track and over southern Denmark. The Path Finders failed to notice, and, haze further hindered attempts to identify ground features, as a result of which, they illuminated an area of similar coastal terrain up to twenty-five miles north of the frontier with Denmark. Six of the 106 Squadron element believed that they had pinpointed on the Flensburger Fjord, but no bombs fell on the intended target, and some of those released by the 106 Squadron crews from between 5,000 and 10,000 feet hit the towns of Abenra and Sønderborg. It was an inauspicious operational debut of a force, which, in time, would become a highly efficient, successful and vital component in Bomber Command's armoury.

It would be almost a week before the next Path Finder-led operation took place, and in the meantime, 106 Squadron committed six Lancasters on the 20th to gardening activities in the eastern Baltic, in the Spinach, Privet and Tangerine gardens in Danzig Bay. P/O Williams and crew were assigned to the privet garden off Danzig, Sgt Lace, P/O Crowe and F/O Aytoun and their crews to Spinach, off Gdynia, and the crews of F/L Whamond and W/O Young to Tangerine, off the port of Pillau, now Baltiysk, some fifty-five miles beyond Gdynia. They set off from Coningsby at 20.20 for what, for the last-mentioned duo, would be a nine-hour round trip, but P/O Crowe and crew experienced navigational difficulties, and delivered two mines further west than intended, off Sassnitz, and a third in the Pollock garden, west of Bornholm Island off southern Sweden. The Whamond crew enjoyed an uneventful sortie on a dark night with good visibility, and delivered four mines after finding a strong coastal pinpoint on Alkiefer Haken, which no longer appears on a map. They spotted a convoy, and reported its position by W/T, before returning safely to land at 05.20, exactly nine hours after taking off. Sgt Lace and crew suffered the excruciating frustration of arriving in the target area only to find that the bomb doors would not open, and they had to bring their stores home. P/O Williams and crew pinpointed on Hel Point for their DR run, and planted four vegetables without interference. The remaining two crews also fulfilled their briefs, and returned safely from uneventful sorties.

Frankfurt was selected on the 24th to host the second Path Finder-led operation, for which a force of 226 aircraft was assembled. 5 Group contributed forty-seven Lancasters, seven of them made ready at Coningsby after eight others had been scrubbed because of doubts about the weather. They took off between 21.20 and 21.40 with F/Ls Hopgood and Whamond the senior pilots on duty, each crew sitting on four 2,000 and a single 1,000 pounder, and headed out across The Wash on course for the Belgian coast. The target area was found to be covered by five to nine-tenths cloud at between 7,000 and 9,000 feet, with ground haze adding to the difficulties experienced by the Path Finders in locating the aiming point. A number of crews managed to pick up a pinpoint on the Rhine, while Hopgood and crew glimpsed Koblenz through the cloud and the navigator plotted the remainder of the route accordingly. They bombed the target from 10,000 feet, and as they turned away, were approached by a night-fighter, which was evaded. Shortly afterwards, an FW190 attacked, and was shot down by the rear gunner, Sgt Hobson, whose claim was confirmed later. The other 106 Squadron crews bombed from between 12,000 and 14,000 feet, having located the target themselves by ground features, timed runs and existing fires rather than by the guidance of the Path Finders. Opinions at debriefing would be mixed, some satisfied with the results and others not. Certainly, a number of fires had been observed across the built-up area, but no detailed assessment was possible, and no mention was made of the Path Finder contribution, which, at this early stage of its development, restricted crews to identifying and then illuminating the target. Sixteen aircraft failed to return, 7.1% of those dispatched, and among them were five Path Finders and 106 Squadron's R5684, which crashed into the sea off the Belgian coast. W/O Young DFM had earned his decoration while serving on Hampdens with 144 Squadron in 1941, and he perished along with all but his mid-upper gunner, who was taken into captivity. Local sources confirmed some damage within the city, and seventeen large fires, but much of the bombing had fallen into open country and village communities to the north and west.

The squadron took part in two operations on the night of the 27/28th, the first of which involved three Lancasters captained by W/C Gibson and F/Ls Whamond and Hopgood, who were to join up with six from 97 Squadron for a special operation against the new German aircraft carrier, Graf Zeppelin, which was believed to be ready for sea-going trials out of Gdynia. This would explain the focus on the region, which had led to the recent mining sorties in the Spinach, Privet and Tangerine gardens. Built in the Deutsche Werke yards at Kiel, the carrier had been launched in December 1938, but her fitting-out was delayed by other priorities, and she would never leave the Baltic or see completion. This was, of course, not known as the trio departed Coningsby between 19.55 and 20.00 for the long trip out, each Lancasters carrying a single 5,500lb Capital Ship Bomb, designed for use against large warships, and it was believed that a single direct hit would be enough to do the job. Also freshly installed was the new Stabilized Automatic Bomb Sight (SABS), which had been undergoing trials at Coningsby, and was the closest thing yet to a computerised sighting system. Two specialist bomb-aimers conversant with SABS had been drafted in for the operation, S/L Richardson and W/O Naylor from the Armament School at Manby, and they would fly with Gibson and Hopgood respectively, while the squadron's own Sgt McNair was with the Whamond crew. A long relationship would develop between S/L Richardson and 5 group, and he would become almost a fixture during extensive work with 617 Squadron at Woodhall Spa in 1944, where his enthusiasm for the topic of bombing would see him christened "Talking Bomb". They arrived in the target area to find nine-tenths cloud that made it impossible to locate the warships, and despite making a dozen runs across the docks, Gibson and crew were forced to bomb from 8,000 feet on the estimated whereabouts of the hulk of the Gneisenau. Whamond and crew occasionally caught a glimpse of the docks through gaps in the cloud, but after thirty minutes of searching they, too, bombed the docks from 8,500 feet. Hopgood and crew, in contrast, identified the docks easily, but saw no ships, and bombed from 10,000 feet on a hunch as to where the Graf Zeppelin might be. They witnessed a large explosion, and returned home safely with the others without a clue as to the outcome of their ten-hour sortie.

While this operation was in progress, the third Path Finder-led operation was being carried out at Kassel, the home, as already mentioned, to three Henschel aircraft and tank factories and other important war-industry concerns, as well as being the HQ for the military's Wehrkreis IX, and the site of a subcamp of the Dachau concentration camp, which supplied slave labour to the factories. A force of 306 aircraft had been assembled, of which seventy-five Lancasters and a dozen Hampdens were provided by 5 Group, thirteen of the former made ready at Coningsby. They took off between 20.50 and 21.30 with S/L Wooldridge the senior pilot on duty and carrying bomb loads of either five 2,000 pounders or a cookie and twelve SBCs of incendiaries. They flew out under bright moonlight, and P/O Wellington and crew had reached enemy territory when the failure of their TR9 set and a hydraulics issue ended their interest in proceedings. The crews of Sgt Cassels and F/Sgt Jones were forced north of track by strong defensive activity west of Münster, the latter held in searchlights and bombarded by flak for forty-five minutes and becoming hopelessly lost. They bombed an unidentified built-up area as they headed for home, as did the Cassels crew from 5,000 feet in the face of a spirited flak response. F/O Aytoun and crew lost their port-outer engine and were unable to maintain height, and this persuaded them to seek an alternative built-up area to attack, which, although unidentified at the time, they believed was Paderborn, situated some forty miles north-west of Kassel. The remaining nine 106 Squadron crews continued on to the target, where they were greeted by minimal cloud and good visibility, with only ground haze between them and the aiming point. The Path Finder flares assisted greatly in enabling the crews to pick out ground detail, like a bend in the River Fulda and lakes to the south-west, and the Coningsby crews took advantage to deliver their payloads from 8,000 to 13,000 feet. Sgt Lace and crew released their load of five 2,000 pounders from 10,500 feet, and were then attacked by a Ju88 at the Dutch coast on the way home. After a brief engagement, during which the Lancaster sustained slight damage, the enemy fighter was claimed as probably destroyed. Perhaps this was the same Ju88 that had tried to attack P/O Butterworth and crew also off the Dutch coast, but had been shaken off by skilful evasive action. "Ginger" Crowfoot and crew returned on three engines after R5680 had been badly damaged by flak, but they also brought back a splendid photograph of the target. Local reports confirmed the effectiveness of the raid, which was spread across the city and destroyed 144 buildings, while causing serious damage to more than three hundred others. Among those afflicted to some extent were all three Henschel factories and a number of military establishments, and the fire services had to deal with seventy-three large blazes. However, the success was gained at the high cost of thirty-one aircraft, 10% of those dispatched, and twenty-one of them were Wellingtons, of which fifteen belonged to 1 Group.

A force of 159 aircraft was assembled on the 28th to send to the city of Nuremberg, deep in southern Germany, and the scene of massive Nazi Party rallies during and after Hitler's rise to power during the thirties. The Path Finders were to employ target indicators (TIs) for the first time in adapted 250lb bomb casings. 5 Group detailed sixty-three Lancasters, while also contributing seventeen Hampdens to a simultaneous raid on Saarbrücken by a force of 113 "oddments", which included 4 Group Halifaxes and new crews from other groups, but no Path Finders. 106 Squadron had detailed ten Lancasters, but some of those damaged twenty-four hours earlier could not be made ready in time, and only six presented themselves for departure from Coningsby between 21.10 and 21.25. F/O Aytoun was the senior pilot on duty for this operation, and like the other participants, he and his crew had been ordered to bomb from as low as possible. They set off on the six-hundred-mile outward leg across France, and Sgt Lace and crew had penetrated as far as the Frankfurt area when L5574 was badly damaged by a night-fighter, which knocked out the rear turret and wounded its occupant. A fire that broke out in the fuselage was extinguished by the mid-upper gunner, who sustained burns as a result, and the squadron's single 8,000 pounder was dropped on Darmstadt after they turned for home. The others found southern Germany to be beneath clear skies, which combined with a four-fifths moon to aid a visual identification of the city and enable the Path Finder element to exploit the conditions, and deliver the TIs with great accuracy. Some of the main force crews pinpointed on the autobahns leading into the city, and, with the TIs in their bomb sights from 12,000 and 13,000 feet, the Coningsby crews emptied their bomb bays of their four 2,000 pounders or cookie and twelve SBCs of 30lb incendiaries. Many bursts and fires were observed, and the lingering glow behind them for seventy miles as they retreated to the west left no doubt in their minds that they had hit the target. Local reports suggested that about a third of the force had landed bombs within the city, causing damage to the Altstadt, but that others had wasted their effort on communities up to ten miles to the north, and this was confirmed by photo-reconnaissance. Twenty-three aircraft failed to return, 14.5% of the force, and the Wellingtons were hit particularly hard again, losing a third of their number. During the course of the month the squadron took part in fifteen operations, dispatching one hundred sorties for the loss of three Lancasters and crews.

September 1942

The first half of the new month would distinguish itself through an unprecedented series of effective operations, although, it would begin ignominiously for the Path Finder Force, when posting a "black" on the night of the 1/2nd by marking the wrong town. The city of Saarbrücken had been briefed out to 231 crews, of which sixty-nine represented 5 Group, sixty-two to fly Lancasters and seven in Hampdens, a type with just two more weeks of front-line service ahead of it. 106 Squadron briefed eleven crews while their aircraft had a variety of bomb loads winched into their cavernous 33-foot-long bomb bays. W/C Gibson and crew would be sitting on a single 8,000 pounder, while the Cooper and Williams crews had the same weight beneath their feet, but in the form of four 2,000 pounders. The others carried a cookie and ten SBCs of 4lb incendiaries or a dozen of 30lbs, and all got away safely from Coningsby between 23.30 and 00.10, and reached south-western Germany to find the target under clear skies with good visibility. They established their positions by TR, confirmed by visual identification of the River Saar and Path Finder flares, and Bill Whamond and crew carried out their attack from 7,000 feet, while their squadron colleagues ran in at varying heights up to 14,500. They observed bomb bursts in the town centre and many large fires, Gibson's 8,000 pounder causing a particularly enormous explosion. It was only later that the truth emerged, that the Path Finders had not marked Saarbrücken, but the non-industrial town of Saarlouis, situated thirteen miles to the north-west. Much to the chagrin of its inhabitants, and those in surrounding communities, the main force bombing had been unusually accurate and concentrated, and heavy damage had been inflicted. Gibson placed the blame for the error squarely on the shoulders of the Path Finders, who had "misled" the main force crews. Hopgood and crew were the only ones to claim to have bombed Saarbrücken, which they found on e.t.a., and by the light of flares, but local reports suggested that no hardware at all fell in the intended target city.

This could have been an ill-omen for the month's efforts, but, in fact, the Command now embarked on the unprecedented run of effective operations mentioned above. It began at Karlsruhe on the night of the 2/3rd, for which a force of two hundred aircraft was made ready, the 4 Group Halifax brigade having now returned to operations following intensive training to restore confidence in the type after a period of above average losses and a series of design-flaw accidents. 5 Group put up sixty Lancasters and five Hampdens, of which eight of the former were provided by 106 Squadron, and they departed Coningsby between 23.15 and 23.35 with F/O Aytoun the senior pilot on duty. The crews of P/O Cooper and Sgt Crowfoot were carrying four 2,000 pounders each, while the others were loaded with the standard cargo of a 4,000lb cookie and ten or twelve SBCs of incendiaries. They made landfall on the Belgian coast and reached the target area to find Karlsruhe under clear skies and basking in moonlight, its ground features naked to the eyes of the bomb-aimers high above. The autobahn and the Rhine and its docks stood out clearly as a guide to the aiming point, and all but one of the 106 Squadron crews bombed from between 10,000 and 13,000 feet in the face of little opposition, while Sgt Lace and his crew came down to 7,000 feet. All returned safely to describe the town as appearing to be swallowed by a sea of flames, before becoming obscured by smoke, and most brought back photographs of their bomb bursts within two miles of the aiming point. Other returning crews reported as many as two hundred fires, the glow from which remained visible for a hundred miles into the homeward journey. Post-raid reconnaissance confirmed much residential and some industrial damage, and local reports mentioned seventy-three fatalities.

When Bremen was posted as the target on the 4th, 5 Group responded with a contribution of forty-six Lancasters in an overall force of 251 aircraft. Crews were told at briefing that the Path Finders would be rolling out a new three-phase technique of illumination, visual marking and backing-up, which, if successful, would form the basis of Path Finder operations for the remainder of the war. At the head of the bomber stream, illuminator crews would light up the target area with white flares, so that visual marker crews could identify and mark the aiming point with TIs, while backers-up, spread through the force, kept the aiming point marked for the duration of the raid. 106 Squadron made ready thirteen Lancasters, loading them with a cookie and ten or twelve SBCs of incendiaries, and sent them on their way between 00.20 and 00.35 with S/L Wooldridge the senior pilot on duty, and beside him in the cockpit the recently-arrived S/L Howell, who had been posted in to replace the missing A Flight commander, S/L Robertson. On his first operation as crew captain was P/O David Shannon, but his wireless failed during the outward flight, and he and his crew were forced to return early. The others reached the target area to find cloudless skies and good visibility, although ground haze and smoke created challenging conditions for target identification. According to the 5 Group ORB, ten of the Coningsby crews had been briefed to attack the city, while three others were among a contingent of twenty-four assigned to the Focke-Wulf aircraft factory located in the Hemelingen district on the East Bank of the Weser south-east of the city centre. The 106 Squadron ORB, on the other hand, recorded that all had been briefed to attack the factory. Although the city was identified with ease, haze, smoke and fires prevented the factory from standing out, and bombing photographs would show that most missed the mark. Hopgood eventually bombed the docks from 15,000 feet, a little higher than his squadron colleagues, who chose altitudes of 11,000 to 13,000 feet from which to deliver their loads of a cookie and SBCs or five 1,900 pounders. Bill Whamond's bomb bursts were plotted to be more than three miles from the aiming point, and this was about average. The attack took place in the face of an intense and accurate flak response, which continued as the crews retreated towards the Frisian island of Norderney. Debriefing reports of fires in the central districts were confirmed by local sources, which listed 460 dwelling houses, six large/medium industrial premises and fifteen small ones destroyed, and a further fourteen hundred buildings seriously damaged. For the second operation running, 106 Squadron brought back more target area photos than any other squadron in the Command, and was not represented among the twelve missing aircraft, although Whamond had an engine fail, and brought his crew home on three.

Operations on the night of the 6/7th began for 106 Squadron with the departure shortly before 01.00 of the crews of P/Os Shannon and Downer on freshman mining sorties in the Rosemary garden area off the western coast of Schleswig-Holstein. The Shannon crew found the target area without difficulty, and delivered six mines into the correct location after pinpointing on the island of Pellworm and making a timed run. The Downer crew lost the use of their intercom shortly after take-off, but, to their credit, pressed on to reach the target area and delivered the mines into what was hoped to be the correct position, but which was plotted later to be just north of Pellworm. Meanwhile, back at Coningsby, seven Lancasters had taken off between 01.10 and 01.29 bound for the western-Ruhr city of Duisburg as part of a force of 207 aircraft, which included fifty-four Lancasters and four Hampdens representing 5 Group. F/L Whamond was the senior pilot on duty, but lost an engine early on, and was back on the ground at 03.40, leaving the others to find clear skies over the target with thick ground haze. "Ginger" Crowfoot and crew picked out the River Rhine and a railway bridge as they approached, and, after confirming these pinpoints with a TR fix, dropped their cookie and SBCs from 12,500 feet, observing them to burst in a built-up area, before bringing back a splendid photograph of the docks. The others attacked from between 11,000 and 15,000 feet before returning to describe what appeared to be a successful outcome, achieved in the face of the usual hostile defence. A number of Lancasters were handed back to their ground crews to have the shrapnel damage patched up. The destruction of 114 buildings, while not large, did represent something of a victory at this target, and was reported by the local authorities to be the heaviest raid to date.

There had been no pattern to the choice of targets thus far in the month, southern and north-western Germany and the Ruhr all featuring during the busy first week, and Frankfurt in south-central Germany was posted as the latest target on the 8th, for which a force of 249 aircraft was assembled. 5 Group contributed sixty-two Lancasters and nine Hampdens, the eleven participants from 106 Squadron departing Coningsby between 20.55 and 21.20 with F/O Aytoun the senior pilot on duty. Sgt Hamilton and crew were two hours into the flight out when the oxygen system failed, leaving them with no choice but to turn back. The predicted fine weather did not materialize, and cloud and ground haze made it difficult to pick up navigational pinpoints. Most crews identified the target area by rivers and other ground features illuminated by Path Finder flares, but the scene generally was one of chaos, in which some crews reported clear skies and good visibility, while others reported up to eight-tenths cloud at 2,000 feet and poor to moderate visibility. Another factor was the intensity of the searchlight and flak activity, which should, perhaps, have helped to guide the Path Finders to the aiming point, but, surprisingly, they failed to locate the city. Path Finder flares were in evidence, but scattered over a wide area, and it was clear that they were by no means certain of their position in relation to Frankfurt. F/Sgt Jones and crew carried out three runs across the target to be sure, before releasing their 8,000 pounder from 10,000 feet on an estimated position. Sgt Lace's bomb-aimer had the aiming point in his bombsight as he dropped the cookie and twelve SBCs from 11,500 feet, but the bombing photo would be plotted at Laubenheim, many miles to the south-west. This was Shannon's first bombing operation as crew captain, and he and his crew identified the target by flares, bridges over the river and e.t.a, commenting on the abundance of searchlights but little flak. According to local reports, only a handful of bomb loads hit the intended target, and this halted the run of successes thus far in the month. The majority of bombs appeared to have fallen to the south-west of Frankfurt as far as Rüsselsheim, fifteen miles away. The Rüsselsheim authorities confirmed damage to the Opel tank works and a Michelin tyre factory, which compensated in small measure for the failure to hit the primary target.

The squadron had just four Lancasters operating on the following night, as part of a thirty-four-strong force of minelayers operating off Denmark's eastern coast. Sgts Phair, Brinkhurst and Tucker and P/O White took off at 23.30, and all found their respective gardens in the Kraut and Silverthorn areas, before planting four vegetables each as briefed. The Path Finder Force was constantly evolving in tactics and equipment and had a new weapon in its armoury for the next operation, which was to be against the Ruhr city of Düsseldorf on the 10th. The "Pink Pansy", which weighed in at 2,800lbs, was the latest attempt to produce a genuine target indicator, and used converted 4,000lb cookie casings. A force of 479 aircraft included a contribution from the training units of 91, 92 and 93 Groups, and eighty-one Lancasters and eight Hampdens from 5 Group, thirteen of the former provided by 106 Squadron. They departed Coningsby between 20.40 and 21.05 with S/L Wooldridge the senior pilot on duty and S/L Howell hitching a lift on this occasion with Bill Whamond to act as his second pilot. Sgt Tucker and crew were the last to lift off, but R5559 clipped the boundary fence with an undercarriage leg, and returned two-and-a-half hours later after jettisoning the bombs into the sea and burning off some fuel. The crews of P/Os Downer and Wellington also came back early with technical problems, leaving the others to reach the target area in conditions described by the Whamond crew as clear with slight ground haze. By the time that he and his crew had divested themselves of their cookie and incendiaries from 15,000 feet, the city was already burning, and they were unable to distinguish the blast of the bombs. Back at base, their bombing photo would be plotted to a mile-and-a-half from the aiming point. S/L Wooldridge and crew attacked from 14,000 feet on a straight run across the target, and believed that they had slightly undershot the aiming point. The bombing photo would reveal it to be about two miles short, but the US Army Air

Corps major, who was on board to "see for himself", was apparently impressed. Sgt Hamilton and crew were thrown off course by taking violent evasive action, and, unable to relocate the target, dropped their cookie and SBCs on Mönchengladbach as they headed home. The others from the squadron fulfilled their briefs from 9,000 to 13,000 feet, and were confident as they flew home, that their efforts had been worthwhile. The operation was, indeed, highly successful, creating widespread damage throughout the city, and destroying nine hundred houses, although at a cost of thirty-three aircraft, over 7% of the force, sixteen of them from the training units. Among the missing was 106 Squadron's R5638, which crashed into the target with no survivors from the experienced crew of Sgt Smith RAAF.

Fourteen 106 Squadron crews attended briefing on the 13th to learn that Bremen was to be their target for that night, and for the second time during the month. A force of 446 aircraft was assembled, again bolstered by aircraft and crews from the training groups, and there was a contribution from 5 Group of ninety-eight Lancasters and seven Hampdens. The Coningsby crews took off between 23.15 and 23.40 with W/C Gibson the senior pilot on duty in W4127, which he had borrowed from the Conversion Flight, and S/L Howell undertaking his first sortie as crew captain since his arrival. F/L Whamond and crew were sitting on a single 8,000 pounder, while the rest had the standard load of a cookie and a dozen SBCs beneath their feet.

P/O Butterworth lost both starboard engines and was back within two hours, to be followed by Sgt Cassels and crew with a rigging problem some time afterwards. The others crossed the Dutch/German frontier over eight-tenths cloud and were unanimous in their descriptions of the conditions in the target area, clear with thick ground haze, and Gibson, Whamond and Wellington commented on the intensity and accuracy of the flak, Whamond with just cause. As R5573 was on its bombing run at 12,000 feet, a flak shell exploded nearby, wounding the bomb-aimer, Sgt Humphreys. The bomb was jettisoned "live", its burst unobserved, and the Lancaster came home safely to Coningsby, where Whamond praised the performance of his crew in difficult circumstances. The bombing photo plotted the bomb some two miles short of the aiming point. S/L Howell picked up the river as his pinpoint, and bombed from 13,000 feet, without being able to observe a burst. His bombing photo showed it to have fallen a little over two miles from the aiming point in a semi-built-up area. The others from the squadron carried out their attacks from between 9,000 and 14,000 feet, and Hopgood's bombing photo showed his load bursting at Uphusen, some eight miles south-east of Bremen. Overall, the operation was a major success, which inflicted damage considerably in excess of that caused by the Thousand raid in June. Over eight hundred houses were destroyed, and substantial damage was caused to war-industry factories. Twenty-one aircraft failed to return, and the training units took another beating, with eleven missing and four others crashing at home.

The end of the Hampden era arrived on the following night, when the naval port of Wilhelmshaven was posted as the target for 202 aircraft. Sixty-two Lancasters and four Hampdens were made ready on 5 Group stations, the latter representing 408 (Goose) Squadron RCAF at Balderton, which, within days, would transfer to 4 Group to convert to Halifaxes. 106 Squadron made ready nine Lancasters and dispatched them from Coningsby between 20.15 and 20.30 with S/L Howell the senior pilot on duty. The ORB recorded that one crew returned early because of an engine issue, while the Form 541 stated that P/O Wellington and crew picked up what they interpreted as a recall signal when twenty minutes from the target, and turned back. The others arrived to find clear skies over the coastal region of Jade Bay, with extreme darkness and ground haze to impede vertical visibility, but the waterline and the docks had provided an adequate pinpoint for the Path Finders to establish their position and mark accurately. The Coningsby crews carried out their attacks from between 8,000 and 14,000 feet, mostly after picking out ground detail by the light of the Path Finder flares, and four crews had their impressions confirmed by bombing photographs. It had been difficult to distinguish individual bomb bursts, but the consensus was of a successful outcome. There were reports of an enormous explosion, believed to be from an ammunition dump, which lit up the ground for five seconds and emitted flames a hundred feet into the air along with a cloud of smoke that rose to several thousand feet. Local sources confirmed that this had been the port's most destructive raid to date and caused much damage in the town centre and in residential districts.

After such a run of successes, Harris had to have another go at Essen, and a force of 369 aircraft was assembled on the 16th, which again called upon the training units to supply aircraft and crews. Ninety-three Lancasters represented 5 Group, eleven of them made ready by 106 Squadron at Coningsby, and they took off between 20.15 and 20.35 with S/L Howell the senior pilot on duty and briefed to aim for the Krupp complex. It is believed that they headed south to cross the Channel and make landfall over the Belgian/French coast in order to approach the target from the south through the Cologne-Düsseldorf corridor. W4179 had reached Aachen when brought down to crash in a monastery garden in the north-eastern suburb of Soers, and there were no survivors from the crew of S/L Howell. The others reached the target area to encounter between three and eight-tenths cloud, but generally good visibility despite the industrial haze, which could be penetrated sufficiently for some ground detail to be identified visually by the light of Path Finder flares. Even so, the overlapping boundaries of the Ruhr towns and cities made it difficult to establish positions with absolute certainty, and not a single 106 Squadron crew was able to positively identify Essen, let alone the Borbeck districts containing the Krupp manufacturing plants. All dropped their bombs on e.t.a., or TR-fixes, and would find from the evidence of their bombing photos, that they had been over Bochum, Oberhausen or some other built-up expanse. Some of the Path Finder flares were estimated to have fallen some twenty miles to the east of Essen, which would have put them over Dortmund and Hagen. Crews were unanimous in their descriptions of heavy and accurate flak, and P/O Crowe commented that it was particularly active over the French coast. He and his crew bombed on e.t.a., and the bomb bursts were plotted later to be almost eight miles from the aiming point. Sgt Hamilton and crew saw a built-up area on e.t.a., which they bombed from 15,000 feet, while observing a number of aircraft going down. Hopgood and crew pinpointed on a canal to the north of the town, and bombed ninety seconds after e.t.a., their bombing photo showing only cloud with numerous fire tracks. Sgt Stamp and crew returned on three engines having watched many aircraft go down over the target. Photo-reconnaissance revealed, that despite scattered bombing, the city had received its most destructive attack to date, which created over a hundred large and medium fires. The Krupp works had been hit by fifteen high explosive bombs and a crashing bomber with incendiaries on board, and housing had suffered heavily, whilst the towns of Bochum and Wuppertal also sustained substantial damage. On the debit side, the Command paid the massive price of thirty-nine missing aircraft, 10% of those dispatched, and nineteen of them from the training units. This was the final time in the year that they would be asked to support major operations. Three empty dispersals at Coningsby on the morning of the 17th told of a particularly bad night for 106 Squadron. In addition to the loss of S/L Howell and crew outbound, R5681 had crashed over twenty miles to the east of Essen, between Datteln and Oer-Erkenschwick on the way home, while W4178 found the sea off the Dutch coast near Egmond, and there was not a single survivor from the crews of P/O "Taffy" Williams and P/O Downer respectively.

Despite the tragedies, if any period in Bomber Command's accession to effectiveness could be identified as the turning point, then, perhaps these two weeks in September 1942 was it. It can be no coincidence, that the Path Finder Force was emerging from its hesitant start, as the crews got to grips with the complexities of their demanding role, and new tactics and aids were being brought to bear against the enemy. It would be no overnight transformation, and failures would still outnumber victories for some time to come, but the encouraging signs were there, that all of the elements of technical and tactical advance were coming together, and, with other technological wizardry in the pipeline, it boded ill for Germany's industrial towns and cities.

Extensive mining operations occupied 115 aircraft on the night of the 18/19th, 5 Group supporting the effort with forty-nine Lancasters, six of them representing 106 Squadron and assigned to the Privet garden. F/L Whamond was the senior pilot on duty as they took off from Coningsby in a ten-minute slot from 19.10, each carrying three 1,570lb mines, with, ahead of them, a 1,700-mile round trip to Danzig Bay in what is now Poland. The crews used the mouth of the River Vistula as a pinpoint from which to make a timed run, and, in clear conditions and good visibility, five planted their vegetables in the required location, before returning home to report some flak activity from coastal batteries, but more particularly from flak ships. R5899 fell victim to the defences when at around 800 feet, and following a successful ditching off the Danzig coast, broke in two. Sgt Stamp and four of his crew were rescued and became PoWs, but both gunners failed to survive.

Munich was posted as one of two targets on the 19th, and would involve sixty-one 5 Group Lancasters, seven Lancasters from 83 Squadron of the Path Finders and twenty-one Stirlings, including some representing 7 Squadron, also of the Path Finders. A simultaneous operation by 118 aircraft of 1, 3 and 4 Groups would target Saarbrücken, also with Path Finder support, and the two forces were to follow a common route as far as Saarbrücken, leaving the 5 Group element a further 220 miles to travel to reach the Bavarian Capital, the birthplace of Nazism and a city of cultural and industrial significance. 106 Squadron made ready six Lancasters for what would be a new destination on its burgeoning target list, and they departed Coningsby between 20.00 and 20.10 with F/L Hopgood the senior pilot on duty. Each had six thousand pounds of ordnance in their bomb bay, consisting either of three 2,000 pounders or a cookie and six SBCs of incendiaries. They flew out across France, entering southern Germany near Strasbourg to be greeted by clear skies and good visibility, which enabled them to identify the lakes to the south-west of the city. Most crews adopted a time-and-distance run from Lake Constance to bring them to the aiming point, which had been well-illuminated by Path Finder flares, and the Coningsby crews released their loads from an unusually low altitude of between 7,500 and 9,000 feet shortly before midnight. Bomb bursts were observed in the city centre, along with a large explosion to the north and numerous fires, including a large one to the south-west, and 40% of returning crews would claim to have bombed within three miles of the city centre. Saarbrücken was reported to be well-alight by crews passing by on the way home, and the Path Finders were complimented on their performance at debriefings. Fewer than half of the participating crews reported bombing within three miles of the target, and bombing photos revealed that the main weight of the attack had fallen into western, southern and eastern suburbs of Munich. Saarbrücken had largely escaped damage after the bombing became widely scattered. All returned safely to Coningsby after round-trips lasting between seven hours fifty minutes and nine hours thirty, and, at debriefing, Hopgood described the opposition as intense at times, and reported an encounter with a Ju88, which his gunners drove off and claimed as damaged.

The squadron was notified on the 23rd, that it would be operating that night against the Baltic coastal town and Hansastadt (ancient free trade city) of Wismar and the nearby Dornier aircraft factory, and would be part of an all-5 Group affair involving eighty-three Lancasters. Thirteen Lancasters were loaded at Coningsby with either six 1,000 pounders with an eleven-second delay fuse, or fourteen SBCs of 4lb or 30lb incendiaries, before taking off between 22.30 and 22.50 with W/C Gibson and S/L Wooldridge the senior pilots on duty and Bill Whamond, John Hopgood and Dave Shannon also on the Order of Battle. Two-thirds of the force were assigned to the town, situated some thirty miles east of Lübeck, while a third, including the 106 Squadron element, were to target the factory. They headed for the North Sea, and ran into icing conditions and a violent electrical storm when around a hundred miles short of Denmark's western coast, which caused many crews to turn back. In all, twenty-one crews abandoned their sorties for one reason or another, and this represented 25% of those dispatched. Those reaching the target found ten-tenths cloud with tops at 8,000 feet and a base at 800 feet, with intense and accurate searchlight and flak activity awaiting any crews brave enough to venture so low. Despite that,

Gibson and Sgt Phair described the visibility as good, and each bomb-aimer had the factory in their bomb sights as they released their loads. Gibson and crew let their fourteen SBCs of 30lb incendiaries go at 2,000 feet, while the Phair crew delivered their six 1,000 pounders from a little higher, and saw them burst in a built-up area. Light flak was intense, and the Phair crew would return on three engines. F/L Whamond and crew picked up a number of pinpoints during the final leg to the target, which enabled them to make their run on the factory at 1,000 feet, and they were certain that the 1,000lb RDX bombs had scored direct hits or near misses. S/L Wooldridge and crew had arrived early, and while circling the target waiting for the attack to begin, their starboard-outer engine burst into flames. The Lancaster, W4118, became temporarily uncontrollable, and the all-incendiary load had to be dumped. Hopgood bombed from 2,000 feet, and descended to 500 feet to clear the target area, allowing his rear gunner to shoot out a searchlight. P/O Cooper and crew couldn't find the target, but made a timed run at 1,500 feet, and delivered the 1,000 pounders without seeing any results. P/O White and crew found ten-tenths cloud at 1,000 feet, so delivered their SBCs into the town from 800 feet, and picked up considerable light flak damage for their pains. Numerous fires were claimed, including a large one in or near the factory, and local reports confirmed that some housing and eight industrial buildings had sustained severe damage.

During the course of the month the squadron operated on thirteen nights and launched 128 sorties for the loss of five aircraft and their crews. A major programme of airfield development was under way at this time to lay concrete runways to support the increasing weight of heavy bombers and their loads. All grass fields had to be upgraded, and it was now the turn of Coningsby. The final three days of September were occupied by 106 Squadron's move to Syerston, an airfield nestling alongside the A46 in Nottinghamshire, midway between Leicester and Lincoln. The station had opened on the 1st of December 1940 under 1 Group control, and it was only on the departure of the two Polish Wellington squadrons that it was transferred to 5 Group and was occupied by 408 Squadron RCAF. The Canadians moved out in December to allow concrete runways to be laid, and the station was reopened in the first week of May 1942 with 61 Squadron as its first and still current residents. S/L Hill was posted in towards the end of the month to fulfil the role of A Flight commander following the loss of S/L Howell, but his time with the squadron would also be brief.

October 1942

Despite the move, 106 Squadron was on the Order of Battle on the 1st, for that night's return to Wismar, for which a force of seventy-eight Lancasters was prepared, thirteen of them by 106 Squadron at Syerston. The plan called for three-quarters of the force to attack the town, with the main square as the aiming point, while the remainder targeted the Dornier aircraft factory. F/L Hopgood was the senior pilot on duty and first away at 18.05, to be followed by the others in a forty-minute slot. The crew of P/O Butterworth misinterpreted a recall signal and came home early to find P/O Cooper and crew already on the ground, after experiencing an engine issue. The others pressed on for what would be a round-trip of some eleven hundred miles in unfavourable weather conditions, which included varying amounts of cloud with a base at 5,000 feet, and ground haze blotting out pinpoints. They crossed Jutland seemingly without incident, arriving in the target area to encounter three to ten-tenths cloud with a base at between 1,500 and 7,000 feet. Poor visibility over the town was caused by heavy ground haze and an effective smoke screen, which combined with intense searchlight glare to blot out identifying features. Brief glimpses of the coastline provided a scant reference by which to establish position, but Hopgood and crew couldn't get a fix on the target, and ultimately dropped their all-incendiary load on what they believed to be Warnemünde, some 125 miles along the coast to the north-east. P/O Healey and crew actually caught a glimpse of the town on e.t.a., and dropped their mixed high explosives and incendiary load from 5,000 feet, while P/O Cassels and crew were immediately coned by searchlights and forced down to 2,500 feet, at which point the bombs were jettisoned "live" into the town. Shannon and crew dropped their load on estimated position, and caught sight of an aerodrome and runways, which, their bombing photo revealed to be near the Heinkel works, also at Warnemünde. Wimpy Wellington had all four engines cut out during the return flight, but they restarted before any of the crew had time to respond to the bale-out order. Post-raid analyses suggested that bombing was scattered, and it was unlikely that any telling damage had been inflicted.

The Ruhr city of Krefeld was posted as the target for a force of 188 aircraft on the 2nd, for which 5 Group contributed twenty-four Lancasters from Waddington, Coningsby and Syerston, while the rest of 5 Group stood down. 106 Squadron contributed five Lancasters, each of which had a cookie and ten SBCs of 4lb incendiaries winched into their bomb bays before departing Syerston between 18.50 and 19.00 with F/L Whamond the senior pilot on duty. His wireless operator apparently picked up what he interpreted as a recall signal, and they returned to base, whereupon, probably not yet accustomed to the lie of the land after the move from Coningsby, they inadvertently joined the circuit at nearby Newton, a former 1 Group station on the A46 a few miles south-west of Syerston, which was no longer in use as an operational bomber airfield. F/L Whamond made his approach in the belief that he was about to land at Syerston, and was caught out by the shorter runway, which he overshot. W4238 crashed into a defence post at 21.25, and caught fire after the crew had scrambled away to safety. The Lancaster was burnt-out, but happily, no injuries were reported. The Path Finder spearhead reached the western edge of the Ruhr to encounter dense industrial haze, which thwarted their best efforts to provide a reference for those following behind. The main force crews were not able to positively identify the target through the haze and mist, and the three 106 Squadron crews bombed ineffectively on e.t.a., and TR-fix from between 12,500 and 14,500 feet. W4768 failed to return after being brought down by flak near Bochum, and P/O Butterworth and his navigator, P/O Osmond, died in the wreckage. The rest of the crew fell into enemy hands, the wireless operator, Sgt Pitchford, with a fractured skull, to which he would succumb four days hence.

All heavy groups were alerted on the 5th to an operation that night against the city of Aachen, for which a force of 257 aircraft was put together, 5 Group detailing sixty-nine Lancasters, ten of them belonging to 106 Squadron. They departed Syerston between 18.50 and 19.15 with F/L Hopgood the senior pilot on duty and each carrying a cookie and a dozen SBCs of 4lb incendiaries. An hour after its departure, W4102 was back over Nottinghamshire with a failed engine, and its bomb load still on board. Had the Lancaster reached the coast, the ordnance would have been jettisoned, but a crash-landing was successfully accomplished at Langar, another neighbouring station on the Leicestershire/Nottinghamshire boundary. The Lancaster caught fire, but Sgt Lace and his crew escaped unhurt, and were well away from the scene before the cookie exploded and ripped the aircraft apart. Their colleagues, meanwhile, continued south over Essex towards the Channel, flying in ice-bearing cloud most of the way, and the stormy weather extended inland from the French coast, which encouraged some of the force to descend for the rest of the journey to the target. They encountered up to nine-tenths cloud in the target area with a base at 12,000 feet, and most of the 106 Squadron crews established their positions by the Path Finder flares confirmed by a TR-fix and bombed from beneath the cloud or from above it on e.t.a. Local sources reported that the southern district of Burtscheid had suffered quite extensive damage to housing and industry, and five large fires had required attention. Even so, they estimated the attack to have involved only around ten aircraft. Some bombs fell seventeen miles away onto the small Dutch town of Lutterade, and this would have annoying but minor consequences for the trials of the Oboe blind-bombing device in late December.

Osnabrück was posted as the target on the 6th, for which 237 aircraft were made ready, including fifty-nine Lancasters of 5 Group, five of them belonging to 106 Squadron. No senior pilots were called into action as the crews of P/Os Wellington, Curtin, Crowfoot and Cassels and Sgt Phair departed Syerston between 19.15 and 19.40 and headed for the Münsterland region of Germany immediately north of the Ruhr. The aiming point for the 5 Group element was the marshalling yards, for which the Lancasters had been loaded with a cookie each and twelve SBCs of incendiaries. The Path Finders dropped flares over Makkum in Holland and the Dümmer See to the north-east of the target as route markers, and these proved to be very effective in guiding the main force in, although, inevitably, some bomb loads were released early during the twenty-mile leg between the Dümmer See and the town. Four to eight-tenths cloud lay over the target at 8,000 feet, and provided challenging conditions for accurate bombing, although opinions varied as to the quality of the visibility. The 106 Squadron crews carried out their attacks from between 10,000 and 12,000 feet, and much of the effort fell into the central and southern districts. Returning crews described many fires and a glow visible by some from the Dutch coast homebound, and most had confidence in the effectiveness of the raid. According to local reports, 149 houses and six industrial buildings were destroyed, 530 houses seriously damaged and more than 2,700 others slightly afflicted.

Most of the following week was devoted exclusively to mining operations, and there would be little activity for 5 Group squadrons other than a series of formation flying exercises, the first one, on the 9th, involving six 106 Squadron aircraft. On the 10th, twelve aircraft took part in a low-level formation practice lasting five hours, and this was repeated on the 11th, when part of the route took them over the sea on course for southern Scotland, and then Northern Ireland, North Wales, Upper Heyford and back to base. Clearly something was afoot at 5 Group, which the crews would not be told about until briefing.

5 Group launched another shot at Wismar and the Dornier aircraft factory on the night of the 12/13th, for which a force of fifty-nine Lancasters was made ready, ten of them representing 106 Squadron. They departed Syerston between 17.35 and 18.05 with F/L Whamond the senior pilot on duty, but soon lost the services of P/O Healey and crew, who arrived back in the circuit an hour later with their port-outer engine streaming oil. P/O Cassels and crew had almost reached the Danish coast when their starboard-outer engine failed, and they were forced to turn back also. Difficult weather conditions over the sea prevented many from establishing a pinpoint on the enemy coast and forced them to navigate by DR. The town lay under six to ten-tenths cloud in a band between 1,000 and 7,000 feet, and the lack of pinpoints forced some crews to search for up to thirty minutes before bombing on estimated positions. F/Sgt Jones and crew tried a square search that lasted forty-five minutes, but saw nothing, and eventually dropped their fourteen SBCs of 30lb incendiaries from 6,200 feet on the approximate position of Wismar. "Ginger" Crowfoot and crew caught a glimpse of the estuary and timed their run from there, bombing from 6,000 feet on what they hoped was the town. David Shannon and crew searched long and hard, and even came down to 500 feet, but found nothing and abandoned their sortie. Sgt Phair and crew spotted aerodrome runways, which they bombed from 6,000 feet, and were the only ones from the squadron to get close to the aiming point. The conditions led inevitably to a scattered and probably ineffective attack, despite which, some returning crews from other squadrons reported that the factory had been left burning furiously and the flames had remained visible for seventy miles into the homeward journey.

The naval port of Kiel was posted as the target for a force of 288 aircraft on the 13th, for which 5 Group weighed in with sixty-nine Lancasters, eight of them provided by 106 Squadron, each loaded with a cookie and 4lb or 30lb incendiaries. They departed Syerston between 18.30 and 19.00 with S/L Hill the senior pilot on duty for the first time, and reached the target area to find almost clear skies and good horizontal visibility, but haze and an effective smoke screen and a heavy and accurate response from the flak batteries. Red and white Path Finder flares marked out the Selenter Lake, some ten miles to the east, from where Hopgood and crew carried out a DR run to bomb visually from 12,000 feet by the light of the Path Finder flares deployed over the town itself. These had revealed the built-up area, which the other 106 Squadron crews bombed from a uniform 12,000 feet, with the exception of Sgt Hamilton and crew, who chose a slightly more lofty 14,000 feet. Probably half of the crews were deceived by a decoy fire site, which lured their bomb loads into open country, but the rest hit the town and caused an appropriate amount of damage, particularly in the Elmschenhagen suburb some miles to the south-east. Returning crews reported a much-reduced searchlight and flak defence, and, conscious that defensive measures attracted attention, this was a tactic employed occasionally and effectively by the Luftwaffe, which was responsible for flak and searchlight defence.

A force of 289 aircraft was assembled on the 15th to send against Cologne, which had been left in peace for a considerable time, and the operation was supported by sixty-two Lancasters of 5 Group from Coningsby, Scampton, Syerston and Waddington. 106 Squadron made ready eleven of its own, and sent them on their way from Syerston between 19.00 and 19.30 with W/C Gibson and S/L Hill the senior pilots on duty. They headed for the Scheldt estuary, some experiencing severe icing over the sea, but the conditions improved as they made their way across northern Belgium, only to be eased off track by inaccurately forecast winds, which, together with a layer of ten-tenths cloud, prevented the Path Finders from establishing their positions. The Path Finder flares were scattered, and a large, effective decoy fire site conspired with the conditions to attract the main force away from the target. Many crews pinpointed on the river, and made timed runs, and believed their bombs had fallen into the city, and some did return with photos showing built-up areas. Gibson and crew identified bridges over the Rhine, and dropped their bombs from 10,000 feet, watching them burst on the eastern bank. They described the opposition as heavy, and their aircraft picked up some damage. The other squadron participants to make it home reported bombing from between 10,000 and 12,300 feet, while Hopgood and crew beat off three attacks by a Ju88 on the way home, and claimed it as damaged. Sadly, not all of the squadron participants were destined to return, and for the second time in the space of a month, daylight revealed three empty 106 Squadron dispersal pans. W4195 was on its way home over Holland when intercepted by a night-fighter, and it crashed at 22.45 about eight miles south-west of Arnhem. P/O White RCAF and three of his crew, including two other Canadians, managed to bale out and they fell into enemy hands. W4771 was also on the way home, and was at 17,000 feet between the target and Mönchengladbach when hit by flak, which killed the wireless operator and rear gunner. Four others managed to escape from the Lancaster, probably because P/O "Ginger" Crowfoot DFC remained at the controls to give them time. His body was found in the wreckage with those of his wireless operator and rear gunner, and the survivors were all taken into captivity. S/L Hill DFC and his crew all died when W4302 crashed somewhere in the area between the southern Ruhr and Cologne. F/L Whamond became the temporary successor to S/L Hill as A Flight commander, until a permanent appointment could be arranged.

On the 17th, the purpose behind the formation-flying training that had been causing speculation for more than a week, was revealed to crews in 5 Group briefing rooms. They learned that Operation Robinson was a daylight attack on the Schneider armaments works at Le Creusot, deep in eastern France, and the nearby Montchanin transformer station, which provided its power. Often referred to as the French "Krupp", the company belonged to the Schneider family, which had donated the famous aviation trophy bearing its name. The Schneider Trophy was initially a prize to encourage technical advances in civil aviation, but, eventually, became a speed contest for float and seaplanes competed for biannually by Britain, France, Italy and the USA. It was a massively prestigious and popular spectator event that drew crowds of up to 200,000 people. Britain claimed it outright after three consecutive wins culminating in 1931, when the revolutionary Supermarine S6B triumphed in the hands of 44 Squadron's first wartime commanding officer, W/C Boothman. Ninety-four Lancasters were to take part in the operation, which required an outward flight at low level by daylight, the attack at dusk, and a return under the cover of darkness. It was a bold plan to commit such a large force, which would be difficult to conceal, and it was only six months since the Augsburg disaster had claimed seven out of twelve Lancasters.

The plan called for eighty-eight aircraft to bomb the factory complex from as low as practicable, led by W/C Len Slee of 49 Squadron, while six others, two each from 106, 61 and 97 Squadrons, led by W/C Gibson, went for the power station in a line-astern attack. The full 106 Squadron contribution amounted to ten crews, flying out in two formations of three and one of four. They would join up with the rest of the force over Upper Heyford, before heading for Land's End at below 1,000 feet, and, once over the sea, aim for a point just south of the Ile d'Yeu to cross the French coast midway between St Nazaire and La Rochelle at around 100 feet. Shortly before the sea crossing began, Coastal Command Whitleys would carry out a sweep to force enemy U-Boots beneath the surface and prevent them from spotting the force and transmitting a warning. The 106 Squadron element took off between 11.55 and 12.15, and there were no early returns. For most, the three-hundred-mile low-level dash across France would be relatively uneventful, but bird strikes became a constant threat, causing injuries as they smashed Perspex, while others became ingested in engines. F/O Silcock of 44 Squadron complained that the lead section was too low, which placed upon him an exhausting physical strain as he wrestled with slipstream turbulence, and others commented on bunching-up and occasional congestion, despite which, this middle leg terminated successfully at the predetermined point some forty-five miles from the target. It was at this juncture that the main force broke up to form into a fan and climb to a bombing height of between 4,500 and 7,000 feet. The target was reached at dusk under clear skies and in good visibility, and crews were able to follow a railway line directly to the heart of the factory complex. P/O Crowe and crew delivered their five 1,000 pounders from 3,400 feet, the crews of Sgt Lace and P/O Shannon from 7,000 feet, and others from between 5,500 and 7,500 feet, but all claimed to have watched them burst among the factory buildings. A few miles to the south-east, Gibson and crew went in at 500 feet to attack the power station, while Hopgood and crew chose 150 feet, and picked up some damage from the blast of their own bombs. A 61 Squadron Lancaster in Gibson's formation was so low that it crashed into a building, and was the operation's only casualty. The return across France under cover of darkness was accomplished without incident, and the returnees landed at Syerston between 21.40 and 22.40 after a very long round-trip. At debriefing on all stations, it was unanimously agreed that the target had been utterly devastated, and the success prompted a message from the A-O-C 5 Group, AVM Coryton, who added to his own congratulations with similar sentiments from the Secretary of State for Air, Sir Archibald Sinclair. Unfortunately, it would be discovered later, that the damage had been less severe than first thought, and much of the bombing had fallen short onto the workers' housing estate. Production had soon returned to normal, and it would be necessary to mount another raid against the plant eight months hence.

A new campaign, against Italian cities in support of land operations in North Africa under Operation Torch began on the night of the 22/23rd against the city-port of Genoa and the naval dockyard, where part of the Italian fleet was sheltering. It was the eve of the opening of the Battle of Alamein, which, after twelve days' fighting, would see Montgomery push Rommel's forces all the way back to Tunisia and out of the war. Ten 5 Group squadrons mustered between them 101 Lancasters, while 83 Squadron of the Path Finders contributed eleven more to take care of target marking. 106 Squadron provided a dozen Lancasters for its first operation to Italy, and they departed Syerston between 17.30 and 18.05 with W/C Gibson the senior pilot on duty. P/O Crowe and crew experienced engine trouble, while it was the failure of Sgt Brinkhurst's oxygen system that precluding any chance of either being able to cross the Alps, and they were forced to turn back. The remainder pushed on in perfect moonlight conditions, excited to confront for the first time the glistening wall of rock, on the far side of which lay Italy, where the clear air and perfect visibility was a joy to behold after contending with the industrial haze at German targets. The Path Finder flares could be seen by approaching main force crews from sixty miles away, and, on arriving over the city, they found the flak defence to be wildly inaccurate, while a smoke screen proved ineffective as the wind blew it straight out to sea. The crews were able to establish their positions visually on the layout of the docks and the city, Gibson and crew releasing their two 1,000 pounders and seven SBCs of 4lb incendiaries from 10,000 feet. Their bombing photo would plot the bomb bursts to a mile-and-a-half from the aiming point. The others bombed from between 9,000 and 12,300 feet, and all returned safely to report a highly successful operation. The effectiveness of the attack was confirmed by photo-reconnaissance, which revealed substantial damage in central and eastern districts, achieved, because of the need for fuel over bombs, with just 180 tons of high-explosives and incendiaries, and, remarkably, without loss.

Twenty-four hours later, a force made up of elements from 3 and 4 Groups and the Path Finder Force attempted to follow up at Genoa, but, in cloudy conditions, attacked in error the town of Savona, thirty miles to the west. Eighty-eight 5 Group crews attended briefings on the morning of the 24th to learn that they would be undertaking the first daylight crossing of the Alps to attack the city of Milan, which was home to many war-industry factories, including the Isotta Fraschini luxury car works, which had been converted to military vehicle and aero engine manufacture, the Pirelli rubber works, Alfa Romeo, the Caproni aircraft plant, the Breda locomotive, armaments and aircraft works and the Innocenti machinery and vehicle factory. This would require an even longer flight over fighter-defended territory than the Le Creusot operation of a week earlier, but it was forecast, that cloud would protect them for most of the way. 106 Squadron made ready eleven Lancasters, which departed Syerston between 12.20 and 12.40 again led by Gibson in W4118, who had with him his regular all-officer crew, other than the NCO flight engineer. His wireless operator was P/O "Bob" Hutchison, who, contrary to the impression given by the 1955 motion picture "The Dambusters" starring Richard Todd, would be the only one to remain as one of Gibson's Dams crew. The flight engineer on this occasion was Sgt Guy Pegler, who would also go to the Dams, but as a member of Burpee's crew, and would not return. They headed for Selsey Bill, from where they were to cross the Channel at very low level with the rest of the loose formation under a Spitfire escort. Crews had been briefed to expect the cloud of a warm front awaiting them at the Normandy coast, but, to their discomfort, they saw that it had formed further inland, and they had to run the gauntlet of anti-aircraft fire as they raced over the clifftops with three hours to go before even reaching the Alps. After flying inland for a few minutes under clear skies, P/O Wellington decided to turn back, leaving the remainder to press on towards a bank of cloud that could be seen in the distance, and to which they climbed as rapidly as possible. Thereafter, the crews had to plot their own individual course, until rendezvousing over Lake Annecy, some sixty miles short of the target. From there they formed a loose formation and lost height, until reaching the target to find eight to nine-tenths cloud with a base at 3,000 feet, but sufficient gaps through which to establish their positions visually. The marshalling yards, a seaplane base and an aerodrome were among ground features identified as the 106 Squadron crews established their positions, Gibson and crew coming down to 4,000 feet to obtain their bearings and identifying the railway station, before climbing back to 6,000 feet to bomb through a break in the cloud. Bill Whamond and crew had found plenty of cloud cover at first, and when that dissipated, they dropped down to 50 feet, before climbing back up to 15,000 feet on approach to the target. They reduced height to 7,000 feet, and saw the city through a break in the cloud, whereupon they delivered their fourteen SBCs of 30lb incendiaries and watched them burst among large buildings. Before returning home, they circled for a time taking photographs. Sgt Brinkhurst and crew formated on four other Lancasters over the Alps, and arrived over the target at 8,000 feet, before diving to 4,500 feet to make their attack, bringing home a sequence of nineteen excellent photographs of the city. The others from the squadron delivered their high-explosive and incendiary payloads from 3,000 to 7,000 feet, and, bearing in mind that the safe height to avoid the blast from a 4,000lb cookie was 4,000 feet, it demonstrated the disregard for their personal safety in order to get the job done, particularly by those descending to a few hundred feet to strafe factories and other targets of opportunity. The sun was setting ahead of them as they crossed the Alps homebound, and France passed beneath them unseen in darkness, with enemy night-fighters waiting over the coastal region as the returning bombers passed through. At debriefing, crews were enthusiastic about the effectiveness of the raid, which had cost three Lancasters, each of them shot down into the Channel homebound. Post-raid reconnaissance revealed that the 135 tons of bombs had caused extensive damage to housing, public buildings and a number of war-industry factories, including the Caproni aircraft works, and had also seriously affected railway communications between Italy and Germany. Local reports confirmed a figure of 441 houses destroyed or seriously damaged along with nine public buildings.

This proved to be the final operation of the month for 106 Squadron as minor operations held sway for the final week. During the course of the month the squadron had operated on eight nights and two days, dispatching a total of ninety-five sorties for the loss of five Lancasters and four crews. S/L Wooldridge was posted from the squadron at the end of the month following the completion of his tour. His tally of operational sorties now stood at seventy-three, fourteen of which had been undertaken with 106 Squadron. He was posted to the tri-Service Petroleum Warfare Department in London, where his academic skills could be put to good use in various scientific projects. In March 1943, he would return to operations as the commanding officer of 105 Squadron, a 2 Group Mosquito unit engaged in daring low-level daylight operations over Germany. He would undertake a further twenty-four operations during a three-month tour of duty, before returning to desk duties, and would survive the war as the proud holder of a DSO, DFC & Bar and DFM. In 1948, he married the actress Margaretta Scott, best known later for her role as Mrs Pomfrey in television's All Creatures Great and Small, and continued to write and compose. He wrote the screenplay and composed the score for a number of productions, most notably the 1953 motion picture, Appointment in London, which depicted a Lancaster squadron at war and starred Dirk Bogarde as W/C Mason, the squadron commander. He also composed the incidental music for other films, including Angels One-Five and Fame Is The Spur. His plays were staged in London theatres and his career was blossoming until it was cut short tragically in 1958 at the age of thirty-nine as the result of a motoring accident. His widow continued to attend 105 and 106 Squadron reunions for the remainder of her life, and his actress daughter, Susan Wooldridge, appears frequently in television dramas.

November 1942

Once 83 Squadron had departed 5 Group to take up its duties with the Path Finders, 106 Squadron had found itself at the top of the 5 Group bombing ladder. As a result, its growing reputation invited the kind of attention that would see it selected for any special tasks that presented themselves. One of these had been to deliver the first Capital Ship Bomb at Gdynia at the end of August. With the continuing offensive against Italian targets, which would remain the main focus of attention for the rest of the year, the squadron would also drop the first 8,000lb HC (high capacity) bomb in anger on Italy. Gibson always led from the front, particularly when there was a difficult operation, or when it was in some way innovative, and he was also ever ready to experiment. As an example, back in the Manchester days, he had been the first to have photo-flash cameras fitted to every aircraft to enable him to assess and improve bombing accuracy, at a time when such matters were only in the discussion stage at HQ.

There would be no operations for the majority of the Command during the first week of the new month, largely as a result of the weather, and 106 Squadron was put on stand-by twice, only to be stood-down as the operations were cancelled. The first operation to actually take place was posted on the 6th, when Genoa was revealed at briefings to be the target for fifty-seven Lancasters of 5 Group and fifteen belonging to 83 Squadron of the Path Finder Force. 106 Squadron made ready six aircraft, which would be led for the first time by the twenty-nine-year-old S/L John Searby, who had been posted in on the 1st of the month to succeed S/L Wooldridge as B Flight commander. He had joined the RAF in 1929 as a

"Halton Brat" engineering apprentice, before becoming a sergeant pilot in the mid-thirties, and his post before joining 106 Squadron had been as Group Navigation Officer at 2 Group. The 106 Squadron element departed Syerston between 21.10 and 21.50, and as S/L Searby lifted W4771 off the ground at 21.40, he was embarking on his first ever operational sortie. Sgt McDonald and crew returned early with hydraulics failure, but the others pressed on to reach the target after an uneventful outward flight of four hours in favourable weather conditions. The excellent visibility, along with accurate Path Finder flares, enabled them to locate the aiming point visually after identifying ground features like the breakwater, harbour and town, and S/L Searby and crew were able to pick out ground detail with ease, before delivering their load of ten SBCs of 4lb incendiaries from 10,000 feet and observing them to ignite just west of the aiming point. The others from the squadron carried out their attacks from within a few hundred feet of each other at 10,000 feet either side of 02.00. Fires of increasing intensity were concentrated in the docks area, and a number of ships appeared to be burning in the harbour, one 44 Squadron pilot counting a total of 116 fires across the city. Crews at the tail end of the stream found the effectiveness of the attack laid out before them, and described a colossal fire on a hill near the city centre. The glow from the burning city remained visible from the Alps and Nice, some eighty miles away, but, as no local report emerged, the full extent of the damage could not be assessed.

The Italian campaign was a welcome break from the nightly grind to Germany, with its hostile and well organised defences. In comparison, and in the context of the period, Italy was considered to be a soft touch, illustrated by the painting of an ice cream cone rather than a bomb symbol on the side of the fuselage to signify an operation. A follow-up raid on Genoa was posted on 3, 4 and 5 Group stations on the 7th, and a force of 175 aircraft assembled, which included Halifaxes, Stirlings and a handful of Wellingtons to join eighty-one Lancasters of 5 Group. 106 Squadron put up eight Lancasters, which were loaded with either two 1,000 pounders and six SBS or ten SBCs and departed Syerston between 17.25 and 17.40 with W/C Gibson the senior pilot on duty in W4118. There was a maiden operation on this night for F/Sgt Lewis Burpee RCAF, known as John, who would follow Gibson to Scampton as a founder member of 617 Squadron. Two members of his Dams crew, flight engineer, Guy Pegler, and rear gunner, Joe Brady, were with him for their 106 Squadron baptism, but, frustratingly on this occasion, R5677 was not performing at its best, and lost an engine soon after crossing the French coast, before suffering TR failure. The final straw came with the incapacitation by illness of the navigator, and the sortie was abandoned. The bomber stream crossed France at 12,000 feet without incident, until climbing in the Dijon area to 17,000 feet as they approached the foothills of the Alps. It was here that some ran into extreme icing conditions, which would force them to jettison their loads and turn back, while those able to press on experienced the same ideal conditions as on the previous night, particularly on the far side of the Alps, and were able to make a visual identification of the coastline, harbour and aiming point in the light of the punctual and accurately delivered Path Finder flares. A smoke screen failed to shield the city, and the flak defence seemed to give up once the bombing began, although light flak from rooftops continued to fire, even if inaccurately. Gibson and crew were able to pick out the detail of the town and docks area, and dropped their two 1,000 pounders and six SBCs from 9,500 feet, observing them to burst slightly to the east of the aiming point. Sgt Hamilton and crew were on their bombing run at 9,500 feet, when an explosion occurred in the Lancaster, which they assumed had been caused by flak. The captain ordered the bombs to be jettisoned, only to discover that the noise had been caused by the TR set blowing up. The others from the squadron carried out their attacks from 8,500 to 10,000 feet, and, on return, reported bombs exploding in the built-up area causing numerous fires. Many crews brought home an aiming point photograph to add to those from reconnaissance flights, which confirmed the operation to have been highly successful.

The campaigns against Italy and Germany would have to run side-by-side for the time being, and, in a break from Italy, Hamburg was posted as the target on the 9th. No mention was made by the "met boys" during briefing of strong winds and ice-bearing cloud of the type that often lay in wait across the bombers' path to Germany's Second City. The four heavy groups put together a force of 213 aircraft, of which, sixty-seven Lancasters were provided by 5 Group, nine of them by 106 Squadron. They were loaded with a cookie and nine SBCs of incendiaries each, before departing Syerston between 17.40 and 18.00 with the newly promoted F/O Shannon the senior pilot on duty, but lost the services of F/Sgt Hamilton and crew to an engine issue within an hour. The others negotiated the storm clouds, and 133 crews would claim on their return that they had bombed the primary target. They had found it to be completely hidden by ten-tenths cloud with tops at 16,000 feet, which forced them to bomb on e.t.a., in the absence of Path Finder flares, but in the presence of heavy flak, particularly from naval guns, the shells from which were detonating above the bombing height. Sgt Brinkhurst and crew dived beneath the 5,000-foot cloud base to bomb, and from that lowly vantage point, watched their bombs burst across part of the city. The others from the squadron attacked on estimated positions and e.t.a., from between 9,500 and 16,000 feet and saw nothing of the outcome. A strong wind from the north almost certainly pushed the bombing south of the intended aiming point, and this seemed to be confirmed by local reports, that many bombs had fallen into the River Elbe or into open country, and only three large fires had required attention. Fifteen aircraft failed to return, five of them belonging to 5 Group, but there were no empty dispersal pans at Syerston. Later, on the 10th, awards were announced to a number of 106 Squadron personnel as a result of the recent daylight operations to France and Italy. Gibson received a DSO, P/O Healey was awarded a DFC to add to his DFM, as was P/O Pennington, the navigator in F/O Aytoun's crew, and F/Sgt Crosier, Sgt Smith's bomb-aimer, earned a DFM. F/O Aytoun had finished his first tour in September, and would return to the operational scene with the recently formed 619 Squadron in July. He was, by then, a flight lieutenant, and, in November 1943, he would rise to acting squadron leader rank and assume the role of flight commander. In February 1944, he would be reunited with S/L Whamond, who joined 619 Squadron as the other flight commander, and both would survive their operational careers.

Mine-laying would occupy the ensuing two nights, and 5 Group detailed a dozen Lancasters on the 10th to send that night to the Biscay coast to the Elderberry and Furze gardens, located respectively off Bayonne and a dozen miles further south at St-Jean-de-Luz, right down on the border between France and Spain. 106 Squadron remained at home until the 13th, when orders were received at Syerston to prepare ten aircraft for an operation that night against Genoa as part of a 5 Group effort involving sixty-one Lancasters, which would act as the main force for a Path Finder element comprising six Lancasters of 83 Squadron and nine Stirlings of 7 Squadron from Oakington. Nineteen of the 5 Group element, including those from 106 Squadron, were to attack the Ansaldo engineering works, which could be viewed as the Italian "Krupp", while the remainder had their own aiming point in the town. The Ansaldo company owned a number of manufacturing sites in the city, including a shipyard and factories producing armoured vehicles and aircraft, at which the company employed some thirty-five thousand people. The 106 Squadron element took off between 17.45 and 18.15 with S/L Searby the senior pilot on duty, and, there were no early returns as they made their way via Selsey Bill across the Channel and France in favourable conditions to find clear skies with just a little ground haze at the target. The bomb-aimers were able to pick out the aiming point with ease, and the five 1,000 pounders rained down from each Lancaster from between 8,500 and 11,000 feet to fall across and around the target. Many excellent bombing photographs were brought back, three of which featured the aiming point, while others were plotted within a few hundred yards. Sgt Phair and crew were among those to bring home an aiming point photo, which they secured while on three engines, after one had failed while they awaited their turn to bomb. A second engine cut out shortly afterwards, and they endured a long and tense homeward flight during which, everything moveable was thrown overboard to save weight. There must have been intense relief when the Coastal Command aerodrome at Thorney Island near Portsmouth appeared on the horizon as the first available place to land after ten hours and forty-five minutes aloft. Some returning crews reported the glow of fires to be visible for 130 miles into the return flight, and confidence was high that the loss-free raid had been successful. Some also commented that the searchlight and flak defence had been "beefed up" since the previous raid, obviously with the drafting in of German crews.

Two days later, a force of seventy-eight aircraft was made ready to continue the assault on Genoa, and twenty-one of twenty-seven Lancasters were provided by 5 Group. 106 Squadron stayed on the ground, while those taking part enjoyed an uneventful outward flight across France, and the ten-tenths cloud to the south of the Alps stopped just short of the target to provide clear skies and moonlight. The Path Finders performed well to illuminate the aiming point, allowing it to be identified visually for a force largely untroubled by the defences. Six large fires were observed in the built-up area, and the glow was still visible from up to a hundred miles into the return journey.

The squadron sent two Lancasters to join others for mining operations in the Kattegat Channel between Denmark and Sweden on the night of the 16/17th, and this gave F/Sgt Burpee the opportunity to complete his first sortie as crew captain, having had to abort an earlier attempt. He and Sgt McDonald took off at 17.00 on a clear but hazy evening bound for Silverthorn IV, and Burpee and crew made a timed run from Anholt Island to deliver their four mines into the correct location. Sgt McDonald and crew searched long and hard, but failed to find their garden, and brought the mines back. On the following night, P/Os Cassels and Curtin and F/Sgt Hamilton set off either side of 18.00 for the long trek to the waters of the Spinach garden off Gdynia in Danzig Bay. All reached the target area to find a cloud base hovering at around 3,000 feet, and each established a pinpoint from which to carry out a timed run to the release point, where the three mines were delivered at ten-second intervals.

Operational orders arriving on 5 Group and Path Finder stations on the 18th revealed that attention had shifted from Genoa to the northern powerhouse of Turin, which was home to Fiat's Lingotto and Mirafiori car plants, the Lancia motor works, the Arsenale army munitions factory, the Nebioli foundry, the SNIA chemicals and textiles production sites and plants belonging to the Westinghouse company. The force of seventy-seven aircraft had originally been significantly larger, but forty-two 5 Group Lancasters had been withdrawn because of doubts about the weather over their stations. 106 Squadron contributed eight of the twenty-five-strong 5 Group effort, and loaded them with either a single 1,000 pounder and thirteen SBCs, or four 1,000 pounders and three SBCs, while briefing the crews to employ the Fiat factories, located some three miles south-west of the city centre, as their aiming point. They departed Syerston between 17.55 and 18.15 with W/C Gibson and S/L Searby the senior pilots on duty, and arrived at the target some three-and-a-half hours later to find clear skies that left the city naked to the eyes of the bomb-aimers. The main force crews benefitted from another excellent performance by the Path Finders, who ensured that the aiming point was illuminated and marked out as they ran in. The 106 Squadron crews carried out their bombing runs from between 8,500 and 10,000 feet, some observing the burst of their own bombs and others not, but many fires were raging in the city centre as they climbed towards the west to re-cross the Alps. After making his attack, Searby circled in the target area to watch others bomb, and confirmed that the factory was hit a number of times. All returned safely with reports of a highly successful attack, and the crews of Searby, Shannon and Sgt Lace brought back aiming point photos, while the others were plotted within two miles. Photo-reconnaissance confirmed that the city centre and Fiat works had sustained significant damage.

Following the recent run of relatively small-scale operations to Italy, the 20th brought a return to Turin with greater numbers, amounting this time to 232 aircraft, of which seventy-eight Lancasters were provided by 5 Group. 106 Squadron made ready ten of its own, and dispatched them from Syerston between 18.10 and 18.45, with S/L Searby the senior pilot on duty. The crews of Sgts Freeman and Price were forced back early with technical malfunctions, leaving the others to negotiate the almost four-hour-long, seven-hundred-mile outward leg. P/O Cooper lost an engine before reaching the Alps, but he hauled R5750 and its load of a cookie and five SBCs over the snow-covered peaks and carried on. Those arriving at the front end of the attack were able to establish their position by following the autostrada and identifying ground features in the light of flares, but, by the time that the majority of the Syerston crews arrived over the city, smoke was already drifting across it, and ground features appeared only fleetingly, creating challenging conditions for target identification. Ground haze added to the difficulties, but, even so, by running in at low to medium level, some crews were able to identify the Fiat factory visually, and deliver the bombs with some degree of accuracy. Sgt Brinkhurst and crew caught a glimpse of the target through a break in the smoke, and it was definitely in the bombsight as the load fell away from 10,000 feet. P/O Curtin and crew also picked out the factory from 8,000 feet, and saw their bombs fall on the edge of it. F/Sgt Hamilton and crew delivered their attack from 7,600 feet, and thought that their bombs burst about half-a-mile short of the factory, but probably hit the adjacent aerodrome. As the force headed back towards the Alps, it left behind massive fires raging in the city centre, with smoke rising already through 6,000 feet. A post-raid analysis based on bombing photos confirmed the confidence of the crews and revealed many fires in the city centre and evidence that the Fiat works had sustained an unspecified degree of damage.

Sixty-four 5 Group crews attended briefings on the 22nd, to learn that their destination that night was to be Stuttgart as part of an overall force of 222 aircraft. 106 Squadron made ready four Lancasters, for what would be the squadron's first visit to this industrial southern city, which was the centre of Germany's automotive industry with factories belonging to Porsche, Daimler and Mercedes-Benz, in addition to a major Robert Bosch electronics plant and two others belonging to the infamous I G Farben chemicals giant. First attacked by the RAF in August 1940, Stuttgart is located in a series of valleys and often covered by cloud, which, sometimes, rendered it difficult to find. The 106 Squadron quartet consisting of the crews of S/L Searby, F/O Shannon, F/Sgt Burpee and Sgt Lace departed Syerston between 18.40 and 18.51, and, after an outward flight of three hours and fifteen minutes, the first of the main force crews were confronted by seven to ten-tenths cloud at around 6,000 feet and Path Finder flares illuminating the target area to enable them to make a visual identification of the aiming point. The 106 Squadron crews carried out their attacks from 10,000 to 11,000 feet either on e.t.a., or on green marker flares, but saw little of the results, and S/L Searby and Sgt Lace flew home across France at 100 feet. A post-raid analysis revealed that a thin layer of cloud and ground haze had prevented the Path Finders from identifying the aiming point, and much of the bombing had fallen onto south-western and southern districts and outlying communities up to five miles from the city centre. Local reports confirmed that a modest eighty-eight houses had been destroyed and more than three hundred others seriously damaged, and described two bombers attacking the city centre at low level and causing extensive damage to the main railway station. 106 Squadron was not represented among the ten failures to return, three of which belonged to 5 Group.

Aircraft actually became airborne for operations on the 26th and 27th, only to be recalled immediately on receipt of a cancellation order. Instructions came through to all heavy groups on the 28th to prepare aircraft and crews for operations that night against Turin, and, during the course of the day, a force of 228 aircraft was made ready, ninety-one of the Lancasters on 5 Group stations. 1 Group was in the process of converting from Wellingtons to Lancasters, and 101, 103 and 460 Squadrons had begun to operate the type in the past week. 106 Squadron contributed thirteen Lancasters, including R5551, R5573 and R5574, each of which had a single 8,000 pounder winched into its bomb bay, so that W/C Gibson, F/L Whamond and P/O Healey and their crews respectively could introduce the weapon to the Italians. The other Lancasters were carrying all-incendiary loads as they departed Syerston between 18.35 and 19.10, Gibson accompanied by Major Mulloch, the 5 Group Flak Liaison Officer, as an observer. P/O Healey was unable to retract his undercarriage, and, frustratingly, had to dump the 8,000 pounder in the sea before returning home. Sgt Hayward and crew lost one of their port engines over the Alps, and, unable to maintain height, jettisoned their load and turned back. Over France, they were attacked first by four enemy fighters, and then fifteen, which they evaded, and later by a FW190, which was seen to burst into flames after a long burst of fire from the rear turret. Meanwhile, the others had reached the target, where they found clear skies and good visibility, enabling Gibson's bomb-aimer, F/Sgt Lewis, to pick out a suitable destination for the blockbuster and release it from 8,000 feet. He watched it explode in the centre of the city, and Gibson then circled for thirty minutes taking cine-film of the attack. Whamond's 8,000 pounder fell just north of the city centre, leaving a large red mushroom with black smoke rising from it. The remaining 106 Squadron crews carried out their attacks from between 6,000 and 10,000 feet, and Sgt McDonald and crew brought back a bombing photo showing the Fiat works, and most others were plotted within two miles of the aiming point. All from Syerston returned safely, thus sealing a loss-free month for 106 Squadron, its first since January 1941, during the course of which ten operations had been carried out generating seventy-three sorties.

December 1942

The weather at the start of the new month restricted operations, and an unsuccessful raid on Frankfurt involving 112 aircraft on the 2nd did not include a contribution from 5 Group. Squadrons were warned of operations daily between the 2nd and 5th, but each was cancelled, and it was the 6th before an operation was posted at Syerston that would actually go ahead. 106 Squadron detailed eight Lancasters, while their crews were informed at briefing that Mannheim was to be their target in company with sixty-two other Lancasters of 5 Group in an overall force of 272 aircraft. A further three 106 Squadron freshman crews were to join a handful of others for mining duties in one of the Nectarine gardens off the Frisians. Take-offs were accomplished safely, firstly by the gardening brigade of Sgts Markland, Page and Irvine by 17.00, and then by the bombers between 17.20 and 17.40, with S/L Searby the senior pilot on duty and last away. Four crews had a cookie and incendiaries beneath their feet, while four were sitting on all-incendiary loads. Sgt Phair and crew had an engine burst into flames shortly after take-off, and the failure of the propeller to feather forced them to turn back. The others pressed on in increasingly unfavourable weather conditions, and the target was found to be covered by ten-tenths cloud at between 4,000 and 12,000 feet, which prevented the Path Finders from establishing their position, and only a few flares were released. S/L Searby and crew dropped their fourteen SBCs on e.t.a., on flak concentrations from 8,500 feet, and the other crews described similar experiences on return. Bombing took place from between 6,000 and 10,000 feet, without any chance of assessing the results, and local reports confirmed the ineffectiveness of the attack. The gardeners fared much better, and all three located their drop zones and delivered four mines into the required locations.

On the following night, 5 Group called for nine crews to carry out gardening duties in the Elderberry and Furze gardens off the south-western coast of France. They found up to three-tenths cloud and good visibility in the target area off Bayonne, and lights from the notoriously poor blackout at Biarritz to provide a solid reference. Lights were blazing in Spain, and a steel works at Bilboa appeared to be in full production.

Notification was received on 5 Group stations on the 8th that Turin was to be the target for that night, in an operation to be conducted by a 5 Group main force of ninety-eight Lancasters, supported by thirty-five Path Finder aircraft of all types. 106 Squadron briefed eleven crews while their Lancasters and those of 61 Squadron were being made ready out on the dispersals. Gibson and station commander, G/C "Gus" Walker, were watching proceedings from the control tower, and saw some incendiaries fall from the bomb bay of a 61 Squadron Lancaster, which was in danger of catching fire. Walker jumped into his car and raced across the airfield to warn everyone to get clear, and then ran towards the aircraft, hoping to be able to rake the burning incendiaries from underneath and prevent the detonation of the cookie. Sadly, it went off when he was yards away, and a piece of shrapnel took off his right arm below the elbow. The diminutive Walker was a bulldog of a man, and would return to duty with a prosthetic arm two months to the day later, spending the rest of the war in 4 Group, where he assumed legendary status.

Sgts Page and Irvine were taking part in their first bombing operation, and, according to the ORB, took off well in advance of the others, shortly before 17.00, and perhaps this was to enable them to carry out a fully loaded air-test before setting out for the target. The others followed between 17.25 and 17.55, with S/L Searby the senior pilot on duty. Sgt McDonald's rear gunner became ill, probably as a result of oxygen feed issues, and the sortie had to be abandoned, and F/O Curtin and crew lost their starboard-outer engine before reaching enemy territory. The remainder pushed on in excellent weather conditions, and all reached the eastern side of the Alps to find clear skies and good visibility, and the city visible to the south as they approached the final turning point. Swinging towards the start of their bombing run, over to port to the east of the city, a large bend in the River Po provided a strong reference, which enabled the Path Finders to identify the aiming point and mark it out with two arcs of flares. P/O Cooper and crew bombed from 6,000 feet, and watched their cookie and SBCs burst near a bridge a thousand yards from the aiming point. Rather than heading straight for home to celebrate the completion of their first tour of operations, P/O Cooper and crew hung around for eighteen minutes to watch the show unfolding beneath them. Sgt Irvine and crew bombed from 7,000 feet, and brought back a photo covering the aiming point, while Sgt Peter Page's photo, taken from 5,800 feet, showed an area 2,000 yards away. The other 106 Squadron participants carried out their attacks from between 6,000 and 9,000 feet, and observed the city to be well-alight, while other crews reported one massive explosion a mile-and-a-half to the south-west. Those arriving when the attack was already well underway reported smoke drifting across the aiming point, and counted thirty to forty sizeable fires burning across the city. A huge pall of smoke was rising through 8,000 feet as the force retreated towards the Alps, and the fires would still be burning when the next bomber force arrived twenty-four hours later. The attack caused extensive damage in both industrial and residential districts, and the fires were still visible a hundred miles into the return flight.

Orders came through on the 9th to prepare for another assault on Turin that night, and eight 106 Squadron crews attended the briefing at Syerston to learn that they would be part of a 5 Group effort of eighty-two Lancasters in an overall force of 227 aircraft. They took off between 16.50 and 17.35 with F/O Curtin the only commissioned pilot on duty, but matters began to go awry soon afterwards, when Burpee's generators became unserviceable, and, although he and his crew pressed on for a couple of hours until crossing the French coast, it was clear that they could not traverse the Alps and they turned back. Sgt Freeman became ill, almost certainly because of oxygen starvation, and was forced to hand control of the Lancaster to flight engineer, Sgt Young, who brought it back from France until his pilot had recovered sufficiently to carry out the landing. Sgt Irvine and crew were concerned about not reaching the target in time, possibly after being led astray by a faulty compass, and they were the third crew to land back at base between 21.30 and 22.00. Peter Page and crew, meanwhile, were well into the outward flight when both port engines cut, and they eventually struggled home on two to land at 01.20, a mere thirty minutes ahead of the first to return from the target. The others had enjoyed an uneventful outward flight and had been guided the final few miles to the target by the fires still burning from the previous night. This, however, proved to be a double-edged sword, as the smoke hanging over the city created challenging conditions for the Path Finders, who failed to deliver as strong a performance this time. The raid was spread out over more than thirty minutes, during which, the four 106 Squadron crews dropped their bombs from between 5,550 and 8,000 feet. They observed them to burst in built-up areas of the city and add to the fires to produce even larger volumes of smoke that obscured much of the ground from those arriving at the tail end of proceedings. Returning crews reported explosions and fires, but the consensus was of a less effective raid than that of the previous night.

The majority of the 106 Squadron crews would now enjoy ten nights off, and, therefore, missed the third raid on Turin, which was posted on the 11th, and for which a reduced force of eighty-two aircraft was drawn from 1 and 4 Groups and the Path Finders. They had to fight their way through severe icing conditions over France, and more than half of the force turned back before reaching the Alps. Those completing their sorties failed to inflict more than the slightest damage on the city, in what proved to be the final raid of this first Italian campaign. Despite participating in ten of the operations to Italy since the 22nd of October, 106 Squadron had lost no crews. Sixty-eight aircraft were sent mining on the night of the 14/15th, but the twenty-three 5 Group Lancaster crews assigned to one of the Nectarine gardens, including those of 106 Squadron's F/L E L Hayward, who had just returned to the squadron to begin a second tour, and Sgt Anderson, were recalled after an hour because of concerns about the weather for their return. This would have been Anderson's first sortie as crew captain, but he would now have to wait a further six nights.

5 Group detailed twenty-seven Lancasters to target eight small German towns on the night of the 17/18th, seventeen for what was referred to in the 5 Group ORB as "Batter", against Soltau, some forty miles east of Bremen, and Neustadt-am-Rübenberge and Nienburg, located between Bremen to the north-west and Hannover to the south-east. A further ten Lancasters were assigned to "moling" sorties over five other towns in north-western Germany including, Cloppenburg, Diepholz and Quakenbrück, and one wonders, if, in the cold light of the following dawn, anyone in raid planning recalled the disaster that had afflicted 57 and 214 Squadrons of 3 Group as a result of similar operations on the first night of April. 106 Squadron was fortunate not to be involved in the ill-conceived venture, which took place in unhelpful weather conditions and cost nine Lancasters, while six Stirlings and two Wellingtons were lost raiding the Opel works at Fallersleben, further to the east. Thus, a total of seventeen aircraft and crews had been sacrificed on this night for little or no gain.

Apart from isolated "moling" daylight operations, the Ruhr had been left in peace since Krefeld at the start of October, while attention had been focussed on Italian targets. Now, on the 20th, Duisburg was posted as the target, and this would mask another operation of great significance for the Command that was taking place at the same time over Holland. Although, in the event, not all would proceed according to plan at the latter, it would be a mere blip in the development of the Oboe blind-bombing device. A force of 232 aircraft was assembled for the main event, of which seventy-five were Lancasters of 5 Group, a dozen of them representing 106 Squadron. They departed Syerston between 17.40 and 18.05, with F/Os Cooke, Shannon, Healey and Curtin the senior pilots on duty. F/O Cooke DFC, DFM had just returned for his second tour, and although the ORB recorded his rank as flying officer, it is believed that he was an acting flight lieutenant. Sgt Anderson was also on the Order of Battle, hoping to complete his first sortie as crew captain. The operation began tragically with a collision between two Lancaster from Waddington as they climbed out over the station, and both plunged to the ground to crash on Canwick Road, Bracebridge Heath, two miles south of Lincoln, killing all fourteen occupants. The others from 9 and 44 Squadrons and those from 49 and 57 Squadrons from Scampton would have observed the incident, and were probably in sombre mood as they pressed on across the North Sea. Mercifully, the 106 Squadron crews had passed well to the south of Lincoln on their passage to the North Sea, and were spared sight of this stark reminder that bomber station circuits could be lethal. Sgt Hayward (not to be confused with F/L Hayward) and his crew turned back with engine trouble, but the remainder pushed on to make landfall on the Dutch coast near Haarlem, some having to negotiate a patch of icing conditions before reaching the Ruhr. Those arriving over the target encountered some cloud with a base at 16,000 feet, through which bright moonlight beamed to help to diffuse the industrial haze, and this allowed the crews to pick up ground features like the Rhine, its bridges and the massive Ruhrort inland docks complex. Bombing by the 106 Squadron crews took place from between 9,500 and 15,000 feet, but most were not able to distinguish their bomb bursts. One aiming point photo was brought back by Sgt Markland and crew, along with others up to two-and-a-half miles away, and all returning crews were confident of a successful outcome. Twelve aircraft failed to make it home, and among them was 106 Squadron's R5697, which crashed about nine miles north-east of Amsterdam on the way home at 20.42, killing Sgt Anderson and his crew.

Meanwhile, unnoticed by those engaged in the main event, six 109 Squadron Oboe-equipped Mosquitos were targeting a power station at Lutterade in Holland, in a test to gauge the device's margin of error, believing the target to be free of bomb craters so as not to impair the data. Unfortunately, three of the Mosquitos suffered Oboe failure, and went on to bomb Duisburg instead, leaving W/C Hal Bufton and two other crews to deliver the bombs. What they hadn't bargained for was a whole carpet of bomb craters left over from the attack on Aachen, seventeen miles away, in October, and it proved impossible to identify those aimed by Oboe. The calibration tests would continue, however, and, come the spring, Oboe would be ready to unleash with devastating results against the Ruhr.

Orders were received on the following day to prepared for an operation that night against Munich, deep in southern Germany, and a force of 137 aircraft from 1, 5 and 8 Groups was duly assembled. As already mentioned, 1 Group had begun converting to Lancasters during the autumn, and would contribute in small numbers on this night, but eighty-two of the 119 of the type made available for this operation were provided by 5 Group, and some by 83 Squadron of the Path Finder Force. 106 Squadron briefed ten crews, while their aircraft were being loaded with either four 1,000 pounders and four SBCs of 4lb incendiaries or thirteen SBCs. They departed Syerston between 16.45 and 17.25 with S/L Searby the senior pilot on duty, but lost the services of Sgt Page and crew early on to an issue with the starboard-outer engine. The others continued on their three-and-a-half-hour outward journey across France under clear skies, only to find the target concealed beneath ten-tenths cloud with tops at a lowly 2,000 to 5000 feet. The Path Finders illuminated the Ammersee to the south-west of the city, and crews carried out a time-and-distance run from there to the aiming point, where the 106 Squadron crews bombed blind from 8,000 and 13,000 feet. Sgt Price and crew adopted a direct course from Munich to the Belgian coast, passing over Stuttgart on the way at 500 feet and shooting out two searchlights. At debriefing, crews reported accurate flak and a strong night-fighter presence, and numerous flashes below the cloud together with the glow of fires, but, it is likely, that a decoy site was operating, as any plottable bombing photos revealed open country. Twelve aircraft failed to return, six of them belonging to 5 Group, and two to 106 Squadron. R5574 went down at Beaufort-en-Argonne in north-eastern France, close to the Belgian frontier, almost certainly on the way home, and only the navigator, P/O Moore, survived from the crew of F/L Cooke DFC DFM to be taken into captivity. It was just the second operation of their second tour, and the wireless operator, F/Sgt Louch, and mid-upper gunner, P/O Goodwin, were also holders of the coveted DFM. (*F/L Cooke's twin brother, Sgt Harold Cooke, had also lost his life in a 10 O.T.U Whitley during the final Thousand Bomber operation against Bremen in June.*) R5914 was shot down at 23.55 by a night-fighter, while homebound over Belgium, and four men escaped by parachute to be taken prisoner. Their survival was largely due to the gallantry of the pilot, Sgt Brinkhurst, who freed the jammed forward hatch before returning to the controls to hold the aircraft steady. Testimony from the survivors after the war led to the award to their gallant pilot of a posthumous DFM.

This was the final operation of a month severely hampered by bad weather. Planned operations were cancelled on sixteen occasions, and another had been subject to a recall. During the course of the month the squadron took part in six bombing and one mining operation, and launched fifty-four sorties for the loss of three aircraft and crews.

The fourth wartime Christmas was celebrated in traditional style across the Command, and operational activity ceased until the 29th, when fourteen 5 Group Lancasters were made ready for mining duties off France's Biscay coast. On New Year's Eve, eight Path Finder Lancasters accompanied two Oboe Mosquitos to Düsseldorf to conduct another calibration trial, and these small-scale operations would dominate the first two weeks of 1943. In comparison with 1941, it had been a successful year for the Command, characterized by improving serviceability, the accession to operational status of the Lancaster, and the coming together of new tactics and technology. As the New Year beckoned, a great responsibility lay on the nine operational Lancaster squadrons of 5 Group to carry the war to the enemy. There was no question that the Stirling and Mk II and V Halifaxes were inferior aircraft, and their limited availability and restricted bomb-carrying capacity meant that the Command still had to rely very much on the trusty but aging Wellington to make up the numbers if the defences were to be overwhelmed. That said, the advent of Oboe and the ground-mapping radar, H2S, would greatly enhance the Command's ability to deliver a telling blow, and 1943 would see the balance of power shift massively in the Command's favour. The days of treading water were over.

Crew of 106 Squadron Lancaster R5914. Shot down on a Munich raid on the 21/22nd December 1942 by a night-fighter. Those who died: F/Sgt John Brinkhurst F/Sgt Trevor Mellors and Sgt Victor Greenwood. Sgt N J Elsom, F/Sgt J A Shepherd RNZAF, F/Sgt S F Leedham and Sgt C Ward became PoWs.

Sgt Goodings, F/Sgt Leedham, Sgt Elsom Sgt Brinkhurst (DFM)

PEOPLE OF ROSTOCK FLEE FROM THE FURY OF THE R.A.F.

Heinkel Works Wrecked: Town in Ruins

WHAT PHOTOGRAPHS REVEAL

800 Tons of Bombs Dropped in Four Successive Nights

Rostock, Royal Air Force target for four nights in succession, is a heap of smouldering ruins, crushed by nearly 800 tons of British bombs. Its population is fleeing in panic. Its war production has ceased.

Yorkshire Post 27th April 1942

Rostock after the four successive nights of bombing April 1942.

106 Squadron P/O W N Whamond's Manchester Crew. March/April 1942.
L-R: W/O E C McClelland RCAF (Nav), F/Sgt B E Sutton (MUG), T Kiell (W.Op), F/Sgt R Clarke (RG), A Parsons (FE & BA)

106 Squadron F/O Derek Page's Crew
L-R: John Rowe, Ron Hence, Archie Steele, Gerry Green, Derek Page, Ernie Woodhouse

Aircrew Training - Bridlington 1942

F/L John Vernon Hopgood.
Later joined 617 Squadron and was killed
on the Dams Raid.

P/O Antony Burcher, rear gunner in 106
Squadron, later in 617 Squadron.
PoW 17th May 1943

Renault Works at Billancourt 4th March 1942

P/O J R Cassels and P/O E White with new Lancaster W4178

F/O A.G. Williams who became S/L in 617 Squadron in late 1944 (Tirpitz)

S/L John Searby, W/C Guy Gibson, S/L Peter Ward-Hunt

Lancaster R5900 ZN-X 'Admiral Airgoosk' 20 Operations. P/O J R Cassels aircraft. December 1942.

From 1942-43, 106 Squadron named some of their Lancasters 'Admiral' -

Admiral Von Gremlin W4195 (ZN - R)	Admiral Prune W4118 (ZN - Y)
Admiral Prune II ED593 (ZN - Y)	Admiral Fighting Cock R5684 (ZN - P)
Admiral Airgoosk R5900 (ZN - X)	Admiral Chattanooga R5677 (ZN - A)
Admiral Foo Bang V R5573 (ZN - B)	Admiral Dumbo (ZN - T)
Admiral Shyte Awk II (ZN - Z)	Admiral Shyte Awk II
Admiral Pegasus	Admiral Fire Brand

106 Squadron 'Admiral' nose art   (Clive Smith)

A rather muddy Coningsby

Above and below: December 1942.
Lancaster R5900 ZN-X 'Admiral Airgoosk' 20 Operations. P/O J R Cassels' aircraft.

St Nazaire U-Boot Pens bombed 1942

Lancaster of 5 Group, flying at low-level over the French countryside on the evening of 17th October 1942, en route to attack the Schneider engineering factory at Le Creusot, France. The nearest aircraft, R5497 'OF-Z', of 97 Squadron is being flown by F/O James Bunt RCAF and crew, who were shot down and killed on an operation in the same aircraft exactly two months later. The film was shot by the navigator of the Lancaster flown by the Commanding Officer of 106 Squadron W/C Guy Gibson, who was to command 617 Squadron the following year.

A Lancaster of 106 Squadron flies at low level over the sea on the daylight raid to Schneider factories in Le Creusot, France on 17th October 1942.

17th October 1942. Daylight raid to Schneider factories in Le Creusot, France.

Daylight raid on Le Creusot works by 94 Lancasters of 5 Group on 17th October 1942.
Photo taken by P/O Ruskell from W/C Guy Gibson's aircraft at 50 feet over the Bay of Biscay, outward bound.
Aircraft is Lancaster R5900 ZN-X of 106 Squadron. Crew – P/O J R Cassels, Sgt Horsfall, F/Sgt J A Woollard,
Sgt Eastwood, Sgt Wakerley, Sgt A F Burcher, Sgt D Robin.

106 Squadron officers.
John Hopgood third from right, Gray Healy third from left and Brian Oliver second from right and David Shannon centre.

106 Squadron Lancaster W4118 ZN-Y and Manchester L7434 at Syerston November 1942 being loaded with sea mines

Guy Gibson's dog, 'Nigger', at Coningsby with Lancaster R5676 ZN-E, in May 1942

W/C Guy Gibson VC, DSO & Bar, DFC & Bar

G/C Augustus Walker GCB, CBE, DSO, DFC, AFC

W/C Guy Gibson, taken while he was Commanding Officer of 106 Squadron at RAF Syerston. G/C Augustus Walker, CO of RAF Syerston, W/C Richard Coad, the CO of 61 Squadron, which was also based at Syerston.

W/C Guy Gibson talking to Brian Oliver.

106 crews at Coningsby gathering for an operation.

F/L David Shannon
Later joined 617 Squadron

S/L A H Crowe
Completed two tours with 106 Squadron

106 Squadron ground and flying crews at raid briefing August 1942

David Shannon and crew in front of 106 Squadron Lancaster

Rear Gunner P/O Robert Chase (P/O Downer's Crew), was one of twenty one members of the Squadron who failed to return from Essen raid on 16/17th September 1942. All lost their lives.

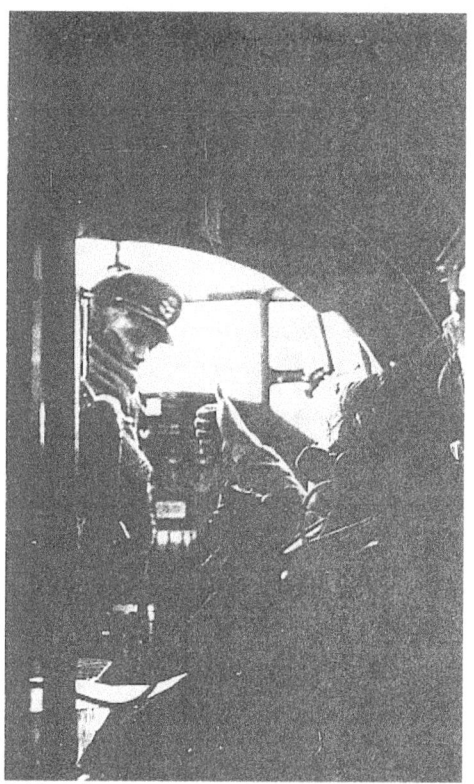

*P/O John Cooper at the controls 1942
A member of 617 Squadron - 1944*

W/C Guy Gibson, S/L John Wooldridge, F/L John Hopgood.

Famous picture of 106 Squadron after the 1000 bomber raid on Cologne 30/31st May 1942
Never one to be camera-shy, W/C Guy Gibson poses happily with crews who have just returned from the first 'Thousand Bomber' raid, on Cologne. In the background can be seen two Avro Manchesters, five of which had taken part in Operation Millennium, along with nine Lancasters from the Squadron.

W/C Gibson left with Brian Oliver on right

Gibson with Don Curtin and David Shannon

W/C Guy Gibson and crew
Guy Gibson and his crew. From left: unnamed; Hutch' Hutchinson; Gibson; Frank Russell; Brian Oliver and Johnny Wickins. Gibson carried a stick because of gout (Simon Sanders).

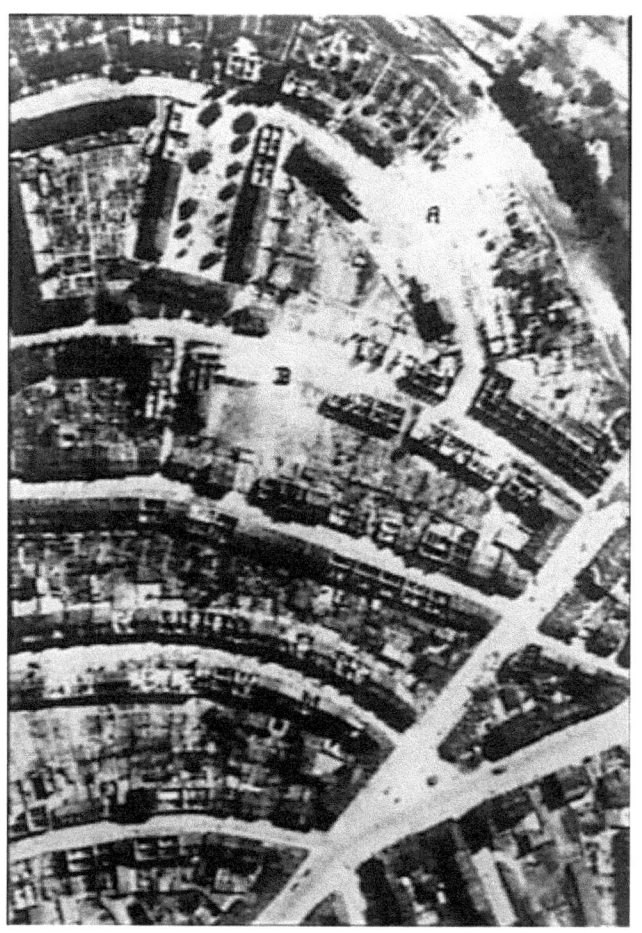

Saarbrücken, Germany.
29/30th July 1942.

Two 4,000lb high capacity blast bombs explode on a residential area in an attack during the night of 29/30th July. Two points of impact can be seen clearly marked "a" and "b" in the photograph. (Crown copyright)

Good friends David Shannon and Don Curtin

P/O H M Stoffer
Killed on the 24th April 1942 on Rostock raid. The engine of Manchester L7463 overheated and burst into flames. The rest of the crew baled out and were taken into captivity.

W/C Robert Swinton Allen DSO, DFC*
Led the Squadron on their first daylight raid on the Gneisenau, while in dry dock in Brest.

106 Squadron
F/L Lewis Burpee (third from right) and crew returning from a night raid on Berlin.

Sgt Joseph Cooper
KIA 27th July 1942

Sgt Reginald Anderson
KIA 24th February 1942

Allied air attack Flensburg 1942.

The Fiat factory, Turin. Pictured in 1928 with the race track on the roof.

106 Squadron Hampdens at RAF Coningsby

P/O John MacLeod
KIA 16th September 1942

F/Sgt Terence Clark RNZAF
KIA 16th September 1942

Lancaster R5700 being flown by Avro test pilot Harry 'Sam' Brown over Woodford 6th July 1942.

Capt H.A 'Sam' Brown OBE was Avro's chief test pilot and made all the first flights of prototype aircraft for Avro from the Tutor in 1929 to the Lincoln in 1944.

Lancaster R5700 6th July 1942

106 Squadron Lancaster R5700 ZN-G after raid on Essen 13/14th January 1943

Lancaster R5700 top damage after Essen 13/14th of January 1943 belly landing

Gdynia Harbour. Bombed 1942.

S/L John De Lacy Wooldridge, DSO, DFC & Bar, DFM

Wife actress Margaretta Scott (Mrs Pumfrey in original 'All Creatures Great and Small)

Lancaster R5684 "ZN-P" and named "Admiral Fighting Cock" of 106 Squadron. Took off from Coningsby 24th August 1942. Failed to return from a raid on Frankfurt. Sighted at 02:22 crashing into the North Sea off Belgium, cause not known. Crew: Pilot W/O R.F.H. Young DFM, Sgt. J. Canniff, F/O. C.F. Isaacs, Sgt. E. Collingwood, Sgt. N.F. Johnson, P/O. S. Rosenberg, Sgt. S.J. Livingstone (PoW).

Brest bombed 5/6th January 1942.

Aerial photo taken during the 13/14th November 1942 raid on Genoa.

An air raid on Genoa, Italy, in late 1942

Bombing of Turin 18/19th November 1942

A Tiger I tank is loaded onto a special rail car at the Henschel plant in Kassel.

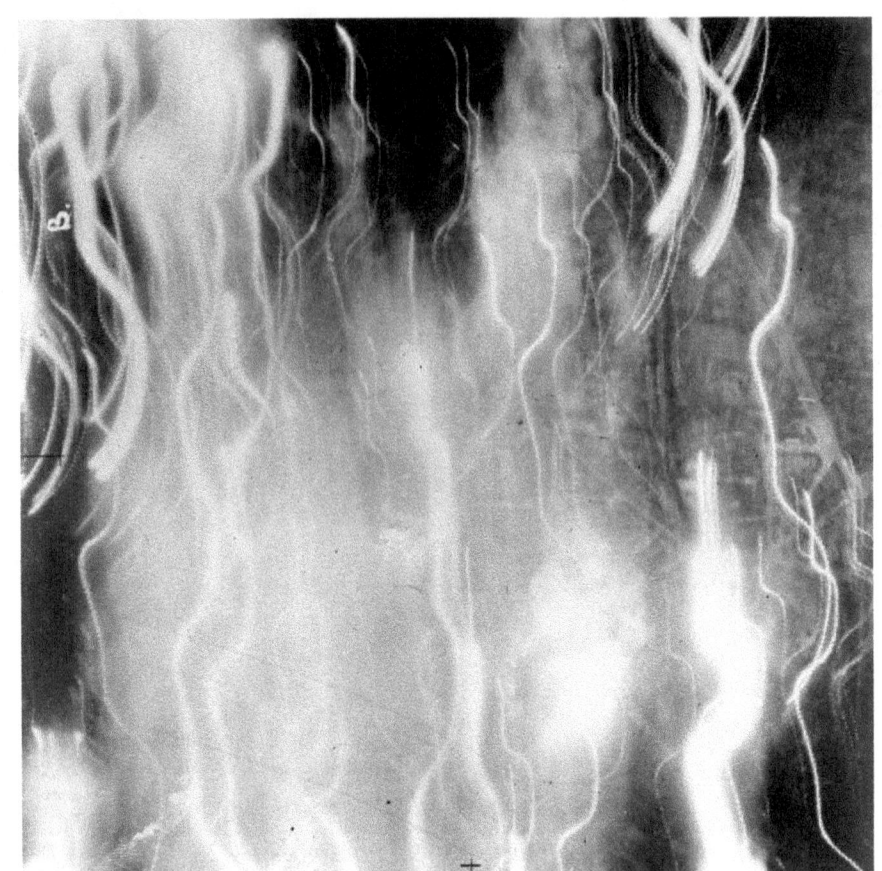

Vertical aerial photograph taken over the centre of Dusseldorf at 11 pm on 10th September 1942, at the height of the major night raid by 479 aircraft of Bomber Command including 106 Squadron. Most of the area photographed is covered with widespread incendiary fires, from which flame and smoke are rising to obscure the target.

Guy Gibson, David Shannon, Don Curtin and colleagues.

Scharnhorst

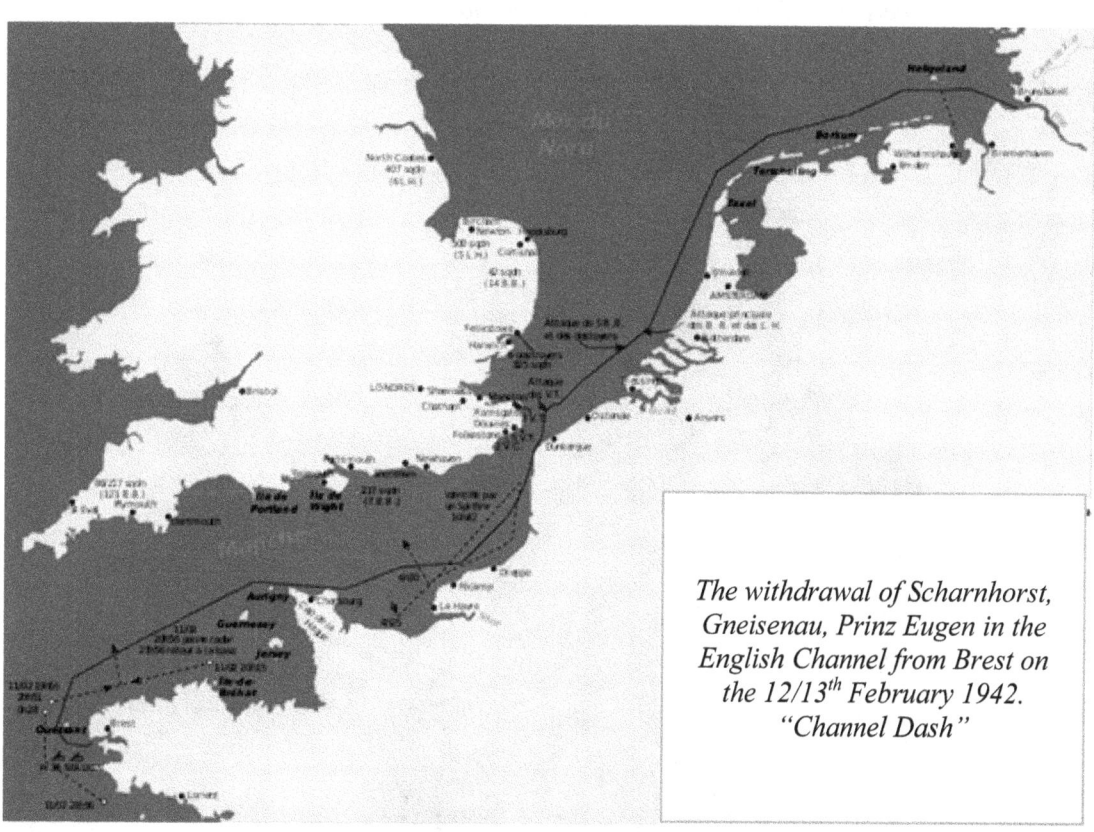

The withdrawal of Scharnhorst, Gneisenau, Prinz Eugen in the English Channel from Brest on the 12/13th February 1942. "Channel Dash"

Key:
B.B: Bristol Beauforts L.H: Lockheed Hudson Sqdn: Squadron
V.T: Torpedo Boat B.B: Bristol Beaufort V.C: Motor Gun Boat
RAF Patrols ----------▶-----
Route followed by the German Flotilla. ───────▶
Royal Navy Submarine Patrols

Gneisenau after her second bow alteration in 1942.

Scharnhorst and Prinz Eugen, along with Gneisenau, broke the British sea blockade in what was known as the 'Channel Dash'. The three German capital ships successfully survived a marine and air onslaught by British forces; air casualties exceeded those on board the ships.

106 Squadron aircrew in front of a Manchester. Second from left is P/O Ronnie Churcher

F/O Cockbain completed his first tour with 106 Squadron before going on to complete a second with 44 Squadron, where he achieved the rank of Squadron Leader. Posted to Ferry Command, S/L Cockbain was flying a Short Stirling EH 988 on a flight from RAF Syerston on 14th January 1945. After take-off the aircraft suffered an engine fire. S/L. Cockbain attempted to land at Hucknall, Nottinghamshire, but was killed when the aircraft crashed. (Simon Sanders)

Sgt Geoff Lace and crew (Simon Sanders)

A well-publicised and iconic photo shows crews returning to Syerston after the Genoa raid on 22/ 23rd October 1942.

Ansaldo Shipyards Genoa, bombed by 106 Squadron 13/14th November 1942

F/O Whamond's Lancaster R5677 'Admiral Chattanooga' carried out 29 operations.

L-R: W/O E C McLelland RCAF,
F/Sgt R Clarke, F/Sgt H Hanson,
Sgt J L Cunningham, Sgt H Humphries
F/L W N Whamond

Lancaster 5677 ZN-A
F/Sgt H Hanson, Sgt J L Cunningham
W/O E C McClelland, F/L W N Whamond, F/Sgt B E Sutton
F/Sgt R Clarke, Sgt H Humphries

Lancaster W4238 wrecked 2nd October 1942 at Newton when F/O W N Whamond landed in bad visibility after being recalled from a Krefeld operation.

January 1943

The year began with the official formation on New Year's Day of the Canadian 6 Group, and the handing over to it of the former 4 Group stations in North Yorkshire on which its squadrons had been lodging. Eventually, all Canadian squadrons would find a home in the group, which was financed by Canada and controlled by Harris, but, initially, there were eight founder members, including 408 and 420 Squadron, which had left 5 Group during the autumn. Further south, a continuation of the Oboe trials would occupy the first two weeks, during which 109 Squadron marked for small forces of 1 and 5 Group Lancasters at Essen on seven occasions and Duisburg once. For the first time, the cloud cover and ever-present blanket of industrial haze would have no bearing on the outcome of the raid as reliance on e.t.a., DR and Gee was cast aside in favour of Oboe, at least, that is, at targets within the device's range. Until the advent of mobile transmitter stations late in the war, Oboe would be restricted by the curvature of the earth and the altitude at which Mosquitos could fly, but this meant that the entire Ruhr lay within range of Harris's bombers. That said, the success of a raid would still rely on the ability of the Path Finders to back up the initial Oboe markers and maintain a supply of target indicators on the aiming point.

It was for the first of these forays against Essen on the 3rd, that 5 Group detailed nineteen Lancasters, including five belonging to 106 Squadron, and, while each of their Lancasters was having a cookie and ten SBCs of 4lb incendiaries winched into position, the tannoys at Syerston summoned the crews of F/Os Curtin and Wellington, P/O Lace and F/Sgts Burpee and Phair to the briefing room. They took off in a six-minute slot from 17.20, but lost the services of F/Sgt Phair and crew after the failure of their TR1335 (Gee) early on. The others arrived over the target two hours and twenty-five minutes later to find little cloud and good visibility, and observed the Path Finder warning flares igniting at various points short of the target, and red and green flares identifying the aiming point over the Krupp complex in the Borbeck districts. The 106 Squadron quartet attacked from 19,700 to 20,000 feet between 19.46 and 19.48, observing some bursts, but not their precise location, and, on return, commented on the masses of searchlights in operation. Flak was bursting well above 20,000 feet, and P/O Lace and crew handed W4156 back to the ground crew to have a few patches applied. Post-raid reconnaissance revealed some damage in the centre of Essen, and this suggested that Oboe might, perhaps, indeed, provide the answer to hitting Ruhr targets. If nothing else, much valuable information was gleaned from this second "live" trial of Oboe.

5 Group was not invited to take part in the next foray against the Krupp complex at Essen, which involved four Oboe Mosquitos and twenty-nine Lancasters of 1 Group on the night of the 4/5th. 5 Group was back in the saddle on the 7th, when a force of nineteen of its Lancasters actually took off after four from 106 Squadron plus a reserve had been withdrawn because of technical failures at the last minute. It was left to the newly promoted F/L Don Curtin and his crew to represent the squadron, departing Syerston at 03.15 on the 8th to reach the target over ten-tenths cloud with tops at 12,000 feet. The concealment of the target was unimportant, as its location was identified by the Oboe-laid parachute flares, upon which they delivered their cookie and ten SBCs from 20,000 feet at 06.08 in the face of heavy opposition. They were unable to assess the results of their efforts, in what was a relatively ineffective raid, but it was all part of the process of gaining experience while honing a new cutting-edge weapon.

Orders were received on the 8th for 106 Squadron to make ready six Lancasters to continue the Oboe trials that night, this time at Duisburg, as part of a force of thirty-eight Lancasters and three Mosquitos. This was the day on which the Path Finder Force was granted group status as 8 Group, and the stations it occupied were transferred from 3 Group. For the purpose of this book, the titles Path Finders and 8 Group are interchangeable. It was unusual for 106 Squadron to suffer serviceability difficulties, but for the second night running, the gremlins struck to significantly impact its contribution to the operation. The Lancasters had departed Syerston between 16.30 and 17.05 with F/O Wellington the senior pilot on duty, but, between 19.30 and 19.55, the crews of F/Sgt Burpee, Sgt McDonald and Sgt Hayward returned to Syerston with engine failures and P/O Lace and crew with an unserviceable TR1335 set. This left just the crews of F/Sgt Phair and F/O Wellington to represent the squadron over the western Ruhr, which they approached in clear horizontal visibility at around 20,000 feet above a layer of ten-tenths cloud ten thousand feet below them. They focused purely on the Path Finders' red and green parachute flares to establish the position of the target, and let their bomb loads go in the face of intense and accurate flak, F/O Wellington and crew from 18,000 feet at 19.22 and the Phair crew from 20,500 feet a minute later. No assessment of the results was possible, and flashes beneath the cloud might have been from bombs or flak batteries. However, this was what Oboe was all about, the ability to bomb blind, secure in the knowledge that the genius of electronic warfare had provided an unerring guide to within a few hundred yards of an aiming point.

While this operation was in progress, six other crews from the squadron were among seventy-three undertaking mining duties in northern waters, four in the Sweet-pea garden in the Mecklenburg Bay between Rostock and the southern Danish islands in the Baltic, and two in the Nectarine III garden off the eastern Frisians. They had taken off after the bombing element, between 18.45 and 19.05, and the crews of Sgts Marsh and Thompson had located their pinpoint on Baltrum island within two hours in conditions of seven to nine-tenths cloud at 1,800 to 3,000 feet. Each delivered four mines into the briefed locations at ten-second intervals and were back home before 23.30. The crews of Sgts Page, Price and Markland and F/L Hayward had an additional two hundred miles to travel to reach their garden, where they found ten-tenths cloud with a base at 1,000 feet. Three of them pinpointed on the southern shore of Møn island before carrying out their timed runs to the drop zone, but Sgt Markland and crew were defeated by very poor visibility and abandoned the attempt after an extensive search.

The squadron detailed five Lancasters for Essen on the 9th, as the numbers involved in the trials became progressively larger. On this night, two Oboe Mosquitos were to mark for fifty Lancasters, the 106 Squadron quintet taking off between 16.40 and 17.00 with F/O Wellington the only commissioned pilot on duty. Sgt McDonald and crew experienced a starboard-outer engine issue that prevented R5665 from maintaining height, and they were back on the ground before two hours had elapsed, leaving their colleagues to find the target area clear of cloud, but blanketed by considerable haze. Some ground detail was identified, but three of the 106 Squadron crews relied on the accuracy of the Path Finder flares, and delivered their loads from 18,000 to 20,000 feet between 19.22 and 19.30. F/O Wellington and crew saw the flares late, and bombed visually onto a built-up area that they believed to be Essen. They described the flak defences as heavy, and returned with a number of holes in their Lancaster as proof. Sgt Thompson and crew bombed on the release-point marker flares, and brought back a photo revealing roads, a railway and open country, which was plotted to be thirteen miles from the Krupp works. There was still much work to do to perfect the system.

On the 10th, the squadron welcomed to its bosom Major Richard Dimbleby, the acclaimed BBC war correspondent, who was to stay for a number of days in order to fulfil a "special" assignment. Seventy-two Lancasters of 1 and 5 Groups were made ready for Essen on the 11th, and among them were nine representing 106 Squadron, which departed Syerston between 16.30 and 17.10 led by W/C Gibson in LM303 for what would prove to be the largest raid of the series. The newly promoted F/L Wellington and his crew turned back with engine failure after around ninety minutes, and they were followed by F/Sgt Burpee and crew, whose rear turret became unserviceable. Finally, F/L Hayward and crew were forced to abandon their sortie after W4265 proved unable to climb satisfactorily, and this left six aircraft to represent the squadron at the target, which was concealed beneath ten-tenths cloud at 15,000 feet. The

Path Finders employed skymarker flares, which tended to drift across the target at the behest of the wind, and, on this night, they employed red and green warning flares and white flares as aiming point indicators. Gibson and crew bombed from 20,000 feet at 19.35 in the face of heavy flak, and came away with a feeling that it had not been a successful attack. P/O Lace and crew did not see the white flares, but bombed at 19.34 from 21,500 feet on release of the second warning flares. The other 106 Squadron crews also failed to see the aiming point markers and let their cookie and twelve SBCs each go over the general target area from between 20,000 and 21,500 feet between 19.32 and 19.36, all within the allotted six-minute window allowed. This was the final operation of P/O Lace's first tour, during which he had earned a DFM and Bar, and he returned safely with his crew to celebrate. Sgt Phair and crew echoed Gibson's doubts about the effectiveness of the operation, and this was the consensus at debriefing.

It was similar fare for seven crews on the following night who were to be part of a Lancaster force of fifty-five with four Oboe Mosquitos to carry out the marking. It was actually well into the 13th before they finally departed Syerston, between 02.30 and 02.45, with F/Ls Hayward and Wellington the senior pilots on duty, and, for the second operation in a row, F/Sgt Burpee and crew returned early, after the bomb-aimer inadvertently jettisoned the entire bomb load while testing the bomb doors off the English coast. One can imagine the tongue-lashing that Gibson would deliver during the obligatory interview, and, the next time that the Burpee crew took off in anger, it would be with a replacement bomb-aimer. The others reached the target area to find ten-tenths cloud with tops at 15,000 feet, and all observed the release-point marker flares before bombing from 19,000 to 20,000 feet between 06.18 and 06.23 within the four-and-a-half-minute allotted window. At debriefing, they made particular mention of the heavy flak, and their inability to assess the results of their efforts. An analysis revealed that the operation had failed largely because the Oboe equipment in the lead Mosquito had become unserviceable, and the three other Mosquitos had arrived late, resulting in sparse and inadequate marking.

The final operation of the current series was posted on the 13th, when 106 Squadron put up eight Lancasters as part of a main force of sixty-six and three Oboe Mosquitos. They departed Syerston between 16.25 and 16.40, just seven hours after the last had landed from the previous raid, and this time, S/L Searby was the senior pilot on duty, and David Shannon was back on the Order of Battle, now in the rank of flight lieutenant. F/L Curtin and crew returned early after their mid-upper turret failed, but the remainder pressed on to the target, where S/L Searby reported eight-tenths cloud at 10,000 feet. He and his crew saw the release-point marker flares, and dropped their cookie and twelve SBCs of 4lb incendiaries from 20,000 feet at 19.31. They were unable to comment on the outcome, but did describe heavy flak and searchlight activity, and returned with some damage to W4118. The others also saw the marker flares, with the exception of Shannon and crew, who ended up bombing on estimated position. Sgt Reed and crew carried out a three-minute timed run after seeing the warning flares, and believed their attack to be successful. On leaving the target they were attacked by a FW190, which raked R5700 from tail to nose, and then made a second attack from nose to tail. The mid-upper gunner, Sgt Hood, was killed, the rear gunner, Sgt Twinn, wounded, and the Lancaster was severely damaged. Sgt Reed coaxed it back to England, where a forced landing was made at Hardwicke in Norfolk without further casualties. Problems had again afflicted the Oboe element, with two Mosquitos returning early and the flares from a third failing to ignite above the clouds, but despite this, many bombs did fall within the city, where fifty-two buildings were destroyed. This operation brought to an end a loss-free period for the squadron, which had lasted since just before Christmas. R5680 was shot down by a night-fighter on the way out over Holland, and crashed near Apeldoorn, killing the crew of F/L Healey DFC, DFM. This was a highly experienced and popular crew, which included navigator, F/O Pennington DFC, and bomb-aimer P/O Crosier DFM RCAF, and their presence would be missed. W4261 crashed near Düsseldorf, almost certainly after bombing, and there were no survivors either from the crew of F/Sgt Phair RCAF, who were also highly experienced and valued within the squadron and Syerston communities.

A new Air Ministry directive was issued on the 14th, which authorized the area bombing of the French ports providing a home for U-Boots with concrete bunkers and support facilities. A list was drawn up accordingly, headed by Lorient, and included St-Nazaire, Brest and La Pallice. As mentioned earlier, between February 1941 and January 1942, the Germans had built three giant concrete structures K1, K2 and K3 on the southernmost point of Lorient's Keroman Peninsula. They were capable of housing and servicing thirty U-Boots and providing accommodation for their crews, and were impregnable to the bombs available to Bomber Command at the time. The purpose of this new campaign, therefore, was to render the town and port uninhabitable, and block or sever all road and rail communications to them. The first of the series of nine attacks on the port over the ensuing four weeks took place that very night at the hands of a force of 122 aircraft in the absence of 5 Group, and, despite accurate marking by the Path Finder element, the main force bombing was scattered and destroyed a modest 120 buildings.

5 Group's involvement with Lorient would come in February, and, in the meantime, Harris planned two operations against the "Big City", Berlin, beginning on the 16th, for which a force of 201 aircraft was made ready. This would be the first raid on Germany's capital for fourteen months, and would bring with it the first use of custom-designed target indicators. The main force would be made up predominantly of 5 Group Lancasters, with others from 1 Group, while eleven 35 Squadron Halifaxes would be included in the Path Finder element. This was the kind of operation that Gibson liked to be involved in, and he was the senior pilot on duty as the thirteen-strong 106 Squadron element departed Syerston between 16.00 and 16.35, he and his crew in R5611 with an 8,000 pounder under their feet and BBC journalist, Major Richard Dimbleby on board to record his impressions for a broadcast to the nation. *(Bomber Command War Diaries records Dimbleby's flight as taking place on the following night, which is in error, as Gibson did not participate in that operation. This is an error that I have perpetuated in my many squadron histories.)* This was the first operation for S/L McDougall, who had been posted in as the new A Flight commander following the loss of S/L Hill back in October, and S/L Searby was also on the Order of Battle. After crossing the Lincolnshire coast, the bomber stream headed for Mandø Island off the west coast of Jutland, from where the route would take it across southern Jutland to the western Baltic, to follow the coastline eastwards until reaching Swinemünde, from where they would swing to the south for the run on the target. Inevitably, aircraft turned back early with a variety of technical reasons, among them those from 106 Squadron containing the crews of Sgts Irvine and Reed and F/L Hayward, but the remainder reached Berlin, which was beyond the range of any electronic navigation and blind bombing device. Bright moonlight illuminated the six-tenths cloud laying over the region at 10,000 feet, through which the built-up area could be seen clearly. Gibson and crew made three runs across the target before dropping their 8,000 pounder from 18,000 feet, and, on return, commented on the haze that made pinpointing difficult. Some crews caught sight of red marker flares, while others bombed on estimated positions mostly from 19,000 and 20,000 feet, Shannon and crew after carrying out a timed run from the Müggelsee situated some ten miles to the south-east of the city centre. All from 106 Squadron were left feeling disappointed with their efforts, despite some observing black smoke rising through 5,000 feet as they turned away. The general failure of the raid was confirmed by local sources, but, one notable scalp was the ten-thousand-seater Deutschlandhalle, the largest covered venue in Europe, which was hosting the annual circus as the bombers approached, and was efficiently emptied of audience, performers and animals with only minor injuries to a few people. Shortly afterwards, incendiaries set fire to the building and reduced it to ruins. Remarkably, only a single Lancaster failed to return from this operation, but the balance would be redressed somewhat twenty-four hours later.

170 Lancasters and seventeen Halifaxes were made ready on 1, 4, 5 and 8 Group stations for the return to Berlin that night, the nine of the former representing 106 Squadron departing Syerston between 16.00 and 16.40 with F/Ls Curtin, Hayward and Wellington the senior pilots on duty, the first-two-mentioned

carrying an 8,000 pounder each, as was the crew of Sgt Markland.. They would follow the same route as for twenty-four hours earlier, and had a three-and-a-half hour outward flight ahead of them, stalked constantly by night-fighters once they reached western Denmark. Sgt Irvine and crew lost their port-outer engine shortly after crossing the English coast, but demonstrated great fortitude by continuing on to traverse southern Jutland, until the starboard-inner engine also failed, and they dumped their bombs in the Baltic as they turned for home. The others reached the target area to be greeted by eight to ten-tenths cloud with tops at between 10,000 and 14,000 feet, through which it was possible for most to pick out the Müggelsee to the south-east of the Capital, from where a timed run was carried out to the target. Some crews failed to see any flares, which was understandable as the Path Finders arrived thirty-seven minutes late, and so bombed on e.t.a., or DR. Some did benefit later from target marking, which, sadly, was once more concentrated over the southern fringes of the city rather than over its centre. The 106 Squadron crews carried out their attacks from 18,500 to 22,000 feet, and F/L Wellington and crew witnessed the flash as their blockbuster detonated and brought back a bombing photo showing the Daimler-Benz, Fritz Werner (munitions) and Siemens factories situated some six miles west of the aiming point. Remarkably, some other crews found little or no cloud, and that of F/L Hayward pinpointed on two lakes north of the city, before circling for thirty minutes to confirm their position. F/L Curtin and crew found the target by the light of the Path Finder flares, and their 8,000 pounder caused a mighty explosion, which was caught by the camera and illuminated suburbs. Sgt Markland and crew claimed the 22,000-foot bombing height, and observed the flash of their 8,000 pounder bursting, but little else. They were hit by flak over Kiel, probably on the way out, and later on were attacked twice by a Ju88, probably on the way home. It was driven off by the gunners during the first attack, and shot down in flames during the second, after which, the gunners shot up a searchlight battery at Flensburg. Sgt Reed and crew were becoming accustomed to eventful sorties, and, on this night, R5900, "Admiral Air Goosk", was hit by flak, which damaged the hydraulics. It was necessary to "pull the bottle" to get the wheels down for landing, but they collapsed on touch-down, and the Lancaster was written-off, happily without crew casualties. Little was seen of the results of the bombing, and local reports confirmed that the operation had not been successful, and no significant damage had occurred. The disappointment was compounded by the loss of twenty-two bombers, 11.8% of those dispatched, and many of these disappeared without trace in the Baltic or North Sea.

A force of seventy-nine Lancasters and three Mosquitos was detailed to resume the Oboe trials programme at Essen on the 21st, for which 106 Squadron briefed five NCO-captained crews and dispatched them from Syerston between 16.50 and 17.10. On the way out, F/Sgt Hayward and crew were attacked by a FW190 and later by a BF110, both of which were thrown off by skilful flying and crew co-operation. During the violent manoeuvres, however, the dinghy came loose from its stowage, and fouled the elevator, making control difficult. As a result, the bombs had to be jettisoned and the sortie abandoned. They arrived back in the Syerston circuit at the same time as F/Sgt Burpee and crew, whose W4842 had been hit by flak at 18,000 feet during the bombing run and damaged in many places. When a fire broke out in the bomb bay, Burpee had ordered the load to be jettisoned, and this left just three crews to carry out their attacks. There was a question as to the cloud conditions, some reporting clear skies and others ten-tenths cloud at 15,000 feet, neither of which would have mattered if the Oboe marking had worked and been visible to all. In the event, the entire Ruhr was concealed beneath thick industrial haze, which proved to be impenetrable, and condensation trails forming at 18,000 feet advertised the location of the bombers to the German defences. As far as Sgt Irvine and crew were concerned, there were no Path Finder markers to point the way, and they released their load from 21,000 feet on estimated position, while those of Sgts Glaholme and Reed found flares to aim at from 22,000 and 20,000 feet respectively. Four Lancasters failed to return, and the outcome of the raid remained undetermined.

The Oboe trials programme moved to Düsseldorf on the 23rd, the huge industrial city situated some fifteen miles south-south-east of Essen. 1, 5 and 8 Groups assembled a force of eighty Lancasters and three Mosquitos, of which the eight Lancasters belonging to 106 Squadron were loaded at Syerston with a cookie each and a dozen SBCs of incendiaries. They were again all captained by NCO pilots, and got away from Syerston between 16.50 and 17.30 before climbing out and heading towards the North Sea. Sgt Markland and crew had just crossed the enemy coast when they were attacked by a night-fighter, which they were unable to shake off. During the evasive action they shed a lot of height, and, ultimately, decided that there was insufficient time to climb back up to bombing altitude to complete the operation. F/Sgt Hayward and crew must have been close to their destination when W4256 lost the use of its rear turret through hydraulics failure, and they also returned without fulfilling their brief. The others arrived over the target to find complete cloud cover, with tops ranging from 14,000 up to 20,000 feet, and the crews of Sgts Irvine and Price circled to await the appearance of the release-point flares. The Irvine crew dropped their cookie and SBCs from 20,000 feet at 19.52, and saw the flash of the impact through the clouds. The Price crew released their load eight minutes later, but observed nothing. The crews of F/Sgt Burpee and Sgts McGregor and Glaholme bombed on the warning flares from 19,000 and 20,000 feet between 19.52 and 19.54, and they also were unable to comment on the outcome. Lorient had faced another assault on this night with a token Lancaster presence in a force of 121 aircraft, which inflicted further heavy damage.

The 26th brought notification of decorations for squadron members, a Bar to his DFC for F/L Curtin, a DFC for W/C Gibson's wireless operator, P/O Bob Hutchison, and a DFM each to Sgts Greep and Parry, mid-upper and rear gunners respectively in Sgt Markland's crew. The fourth raid in the series against Lorient took place on the night of the 26/27th at the hands of an initial force of 157 aircraft, which attacked in poor weather conditions.

Düsseldorf was selected again as the primary target on the 27th, when the evolution of Path Finder techniques took another step forward. Thus far, skymarking had been the means by which targets were marked, coloured or white parachute flares igniting at altitude and drifting down over, or, in strong winds, across the target area. This night was to bring the first employment of ground marking, coloured target indicators, fused to burst and cascade just above the ground and be visible through thin or partial cloud cover and industrial haze to provide a much more reliable and constant, non-shifting focal point. However, skymarking would remain an indispensable part of target marking techniques on nights of heavy cloud, or to use in combination with ground markers. From this night onwards, Path Finder heavy aircraft would back-up the Mosquito-laid Oboe markers, to ensure that the aiming point remained marked throughout the operation. A heavy force of 124 Lancasters and thirty-three Halifaxes was made ready on 1, 4, 5 and 8 Group stations, 106 Squadron providing a dozen of the Lancasters, which departed Syerston between 17.30 and 18.00 with S/L Searby the senior pilot on duty. There were no early returns as they made their way to a landfall over the Scheldt over ten-tenths cloud, which persisted all the way to the southern Ruhr, until thinning to five to ten-tenths at between 10,000 and 15,000 feet, through which the red and green TIs could be seen burning on the aiming point. S/L Searby and crew saw two red TIs and one green, and bombed the second red at 20.00 from 20,000 feet, without being able to observe any bursts, but they would bring back an excellent photograph of the clouds. Just as their cookie and twelve SBCs were leaving the bomb bay, some twenty-five miles to the west, R5637 was crashing about four miles south-west of Roermond in Holland, killing Sgt Marsh RNZAF and his crew. (*A monument has since been erected on the crash site.*) The other 106 Squadron crews carried out their part in the proceedings from 14,000 to 20,000 feet between 20.00 and 20.16, and returned safely, impressed by the potential of ground marking, and confident that they had hit the aiming point. This was confirmed by local reports, which spoke of widespread destruction in southern districts amounting to 456 houses, ten industrial premises and nine public buildings destroyed or seriously damaged, and many others affected to a lesser extent.

Seventy-five aircraft of 1, 4 and 6 Groups carried out the fifth attack of the series on Lorient in unfavourable weather conditions on the night of the 29/30th, and delivered scattered bombing. Another new blind-bombing device, the ground-mapping H2S radar, was to be employed operationally for the first time at Hamburg on the 30th, for which a force of 135 Lancasters of 1, 5 and 8 Groups would be joined by thirteen H2S-equipped Path Finder Stirlings and Halifaxes of 7 and 35 Squadrons respectively. The H2S equipment was housed in a cupola aft of the bomb bay, and projected an image of the terrain onto a cathode-ray tube in the navigator's compartment. It was the job of the operator to interpret what he was seeing, and guide the pilot to the aiming point, but this was no easy task, particularly with the Mk I set, and it proved difficult to distinguish particular ground features in the jumble of images presented to him. It would take much practice and experience to master the device, but, in time, and once the Mk III set became available, it would become an indispensable tool, which, ultimately, would become standard equipment for main force as well as Path Finder aircraft. 106 Squadron made ready fifteen Lancasters, loading each with a cookie and incendiaries, and sent them on their way from Syerston between 23.40 and 00.20 with S/L McDougall the senior pilot on duty. As if to compensate for the excellent serviceability enjoyed during the previous operation, this night brought a high number of early returns amounting to a third of the 106 Squadron effort. S/L McDougall and crew lost the use of their rear turret almost immediately, and the crew of Sgt McGregor turned back with the same problem. Sgt Reed's engines behaved erratically, preventing him from maintaining height, while Sgt McDonald's oxygen system failed, as did Sgt Burton's TR1335 (Gee) equipment, and they too came home early. As mentioned frequently before, north-western Germany had a "gatekeeper" in the form of weather fronts, which, on this night, contained severe icing conditions and electrical storms for the bombers to negotiate as they made their way across the North Sea. The bomber stream shed further aircraft during this stage of the outward flight, but no more from 106 Squadron, whose crews arrived over Germany's Second City to encounter between zero and ten-tenths cloud, according to which crew report one reads, with tops at between 6,000 and 15,000 feet. F/L Curtin's bomb-aimer had the green TI in his sights as he let the cookie and SBCs go from 17,000 feet at 03.06, followed two minutes later by F/L Hayward's load from a thousand feet higher, and they would comment on return that the only incident in an otherwise uneventful trip was excessive static, which temporarily blinded the whole crew and slightly burned the wireless operator. They others from the squadron bombed on flares or TIs from 16,000 to 21,000 feet between 02.56 and 03.15, and observed the reflections of explosions in the cloud, which led to a consensus that the operation had been effective. On return, P/O Edmunds and crew searched in vain for Syerston in very poor visibility, and, with fuel running low, the crew was ordered to jump. Most had done so when the navigator reported his parachute to be unserviceable, and while searching for a suitable forced-landing site, the 4 Group station at Burn presented itself, and a safe landing was carried out. Local sources partially confirmed an effective operation, mentioning seventy-one large fires, but much of the bombing fell either into the Elbe or into marshland outside of the city. This would have been disappointing to the raid planners, as Hamburg, with the nearby coastline and wide River Elbe, was an ideal target for H2S, and should have been easy to identify on the cathode-ray tubes. Among five missing Lancasters was 106 Squadron's W4826, which crashed at 03.20 into the railway station at Imsum, a northern suburb of Bremerhaven, killing Sgt Johnson and his crew.

During the course of the month the squadron notched up its 2,000th sortie and carried out thirteen operations, generating 109 sorties for the loss of five aircraft and four crews.

February 1943

It was a time of honing and refining for Bomber Command, in preparation for the launching of a major campaign a month hence, and the new month opened with the posting of Cologne as the target for an experimental operation on the 2nd, in which two marking methods were to be employed. Situated just to the south of the Ruhr, the Rhineland's capital city was within range of Oboe Mosquitos, and these were to be supplemented by Path Finder aircraft relying on H2S. A force of 159 heavies included seventy-four 5 Group Lancasters, eight of them provided by 106 Squadron, while two Path Finder Mosquitos of 109 Squadron carried the Oboe markers. The 106 Squadron element departed Syerston between 17.45 and 18.05 with F/O Edmunds the only commissioned pilot on duty, although a F/L Burnside was flying as second pilot to Sgt Renshaw. They flew out through severe cold, which caused many guns to freeze solid, and made landfall over the Scheldt before closing on the target to find a layer of two to five tenths thin cloud up to 8,000 feet and patches of white stuff above. This afforded good vertical visibility and a clear sight of the red and green skymarkers, even from some distance on approach to the bombing run. There was some debate as to the accuracy and concentration of the markers, which a few crews from other squadrons would report as five to ten miles to the north-west of the city, while others described them as scattered. Sgt Reed and crew must have been on their bombing run when ED409 fell suddenly out of control, leading the pilot to think they had been hit by flak. In the confusion he ordered the bombs to be jettisoned, and the sortie was abandoned. Most of the 106 Squadron crews picked up the red and green TIs burning on the ground, and had them in the bombsight as they delivered their cookies and incendiaries from 13,000 to 19,000 feet between 21.01 and 21.19. Only F/O Edmunds and Sgt McGregor saw the burst of their cookies, and they returned safely with the others to report a seemingly successful attack. Debriefing threw up reports of many scattered fires, the glow from which could be seen from a hundred miles into the return journey, and local sources confirmed bombs falling all over the city, but nowhere with concentration. Damage was, consequently, not commensurate with the size of the force, the effort expended and the cost of five aircraft and crews, among them three belonging to 5 Group.

Hamburg was posted as the target on the 3rd, for which a force of 263 aircraft was made ready, unusually, with Halifaxes representing the most populous type followed by Stirlings. 5 Group contributed forty of the sixty-two Lancasters, six of them belonging to 106 Squadron, and they departed Syerston between 17.55 and 18.15 with F/L Haywood the senior pilot on duty. Fifteen of the 5 Group crews turned back on encountering the towering cloud and severe icing conditions common to this route over the North Sea, and most of them cited frozen guns. The freshman crew of Sgt Renshaw had been entrusted with W4118, Admiral Prune I, a Lancaster frequently used by Gibson and Searby, and, after deciding that they would not reach the target within the allotted time, possibly after straying off course, they abandoned their sortie to face the wrath of their squadron commander, who was particularly intolerant towards non-officer types. The others arrived in the target area to find nine to ten-tenths cloud, which they estimated topped out at between 7,000 and 8,000 feet, while 207 Squadron crews reported the cloud to be at 17,000 to 20,000 feet. Scattered red and green Path Finder H2S-laid skymarker flares were in the bomb sights as the 106 Squadron crews settled into their runs at 17,500 to 19,000 feet to deliver their cookie and twelve SBCs each between 21.03 and 21.11. Sgt Irvine and crew reported a brilliant red colour beneath the clouds that lasted for ten seconds, and all were aware of fires, but none could assess their own work. Returning crews suspected an ineffective raid, and this was confirmed by local reports, which mentioned forty-five large fires but no concentration or significant damage, a disappointing outcome that cost the Command sixteen aircraft. The losses by type made interesting reading, and would reflect the trend for the remainder of the year, with the Stirlings suffering the highest numerical and percentage casualties, followed by the Halifaxes and Wellingtons, with the Lancasters clearly at the top of the food chain. Sgt Reed and crew, who had crashed on landing after the Berlin raid two weeks earlier, and had rarely experienced an uneventful sortie, failed to return from this operation. Clearly, they had used up their ration of luck, and all died when W4770 crashed somewhere near Hannover on the way home.

A return to Italy was posted on the 4th with Turin the destination for a force of 188 aircraft, while 128 others, mostly Wellingtons, were prepared to continue the assault on Lorient, 5 Group contributing forty-eight Lancasters to the former and eight with freshman crews to the latter. 106 Squadron waved off six Lancasters between 18.05 and 18.20, led by F/Ls Hayward, Curtin and Shannon, with W4118 on this night in the hands of Sgt Thompson and crew. Their aiming points were Fiat's Lingotto and Mirafiore factories in the south of the city, which Sgt Hayward and crew would not reach with their 8,000 pounder, after their rear turret became unserviceable on the way out. The others pressed on via the familiar route across France to cross the Alps in cloud at 21,000 feet, before finding conditions on the Italian side much improved, with clear skies and excellent visibility that facilitated a visual confirmation of the accuracy of the Path Finder TIs. An estimated one hundred searchlights were active, and the flak defence had also been "beefed-up", but was still inaccurate and in keeping with expectations at an Italian target. F/L Shannon and crew were on their bombing run when W4156 was hit in the bomb bay by flak, which set the all-incendiary load on fire and required it to be jettisoned immediately. The crew then had the satisfaction of watching the individual incendiaries fall into a wooded area just short of the city, which was subsequently engulfed by a raging fire that swept towards the suburbs. Red TIs were much in evidence in the city centre as the crews of F/Ls Curtin and Hayward found the target easily, the former delivering their 8,000 pounder from 11,000 feet, and the latter fourteen SBCs from 12,500 feet, and their bombing photos would plot their fall at 1¾ miles and 3,000 yards respectively from the aiming point. Sgt McGregor and crew bombed from 15,000 feet at 21.51, and their bomb would later be plotted at 5,000 yards from the aiming point. A message was received from W4118 at 22.30 stating that an engine had failed, and that height was rapidly being lost. A fix placed the Lancaster near Dijon in France, and although the timing suggests that it was homebound at the time, it seems, according to survivor testimony, that it was, in fact, still outbound. It emerged later that both port engines had failed, and Sgt Thompson RCAF was forced to crash-land on a hill at Valsonne, a little over twenty miles north-west of Lyons. Four of the eight men on board lost their lives, but Thompson and three others joined the growing roll-call of Bomber Command airmen on extended leave in Germany. The operation was highly successful, and local sources confirmed later that serious and widespread damage had resulted at a cost to the Command of three Lancasters.

The seventh raid in the series on Lorient was posted on the 7th, and would be by far the largest to date, employing 323 aircraft, of which forty-three of eighty Lancasters were provided by 5 Group. It was to be conducted in two waves, an hour apart, and it was for the second wave that 106 Squadron made ready four Lancasters for the freshman crews of F/O Edmunds and Sgts Glaholme, McGregor and Renshaw, and sent them on their way from Syerston between 18.55 and 19.20. The first wave crews had arrived in the target area to find clear skies and ideal bombing conditions, which they exploited after making a visual identification of the aiming point confirmed by Path Finder TIs. They left behind them a glow in the sky visible from the English coast, acting as a beacon to draw on the second wave, which arrived at the target to find it ablaze and ground detail obliterated by smoke. F/O Edmunds and crew spent five minutes looking for a place to bomb, and eventually let their cookie and SBCs go at 21.35, watching them burst within a ring of fires, before bringing back an aiming point photo.

After a busy first week of the month the majority of the Command enjoyed a few nights at home courtesy of unfavourable weather conditions, which caused operations to be cancelled on the 8th, 9th and 10th. Before the penultimate raid took place on Lorient, attention was switched to the important naval port of Wilhelmshaven, situated on the north-western coast of Jade Bay, some sixty miles to the west of

Hamburg. A force of 177 aircraft was put together on the 11th, of which 129 were Lancasters, sixty-eight of them representing 5 Group. Eight Lancasters were made ready by 106 Squadron at Syerston, while their crews attended briefing to be told that they would be bombing blind through ten-tenths cloud. They took off between 17.15 and 17.35 with F/O Picken the senior pilot on duty after his return to the squadron to begin a second tour. They climbed out into heavy cloud, with F/Sgt Burpee and crew in W4156, the Lancaster Shannon had brought back in a damaged state from Turin on the 5th. They were approaching the German coast when the rear turret became unserviceable and forced them to turn back, and, fifty minutes after they landed, Sgt Markland and crew touched down. An aileron problem had struck them during the climb-out over the station, and, to their credit, they set course with the intention of continuing the sortie, only for the malfunction to become more acute and force them to throw in the towel. The others reached the target area to find the forecast ten-tenths cloud with tops at around 10,000 feet, and the least reliable marking method, H2S skymarking, in progress. On the credit side, at a smaller, more compact urban target, like Wilhelmshaven, it was easier to interpret the images on the cathode-ray screens, and, on this night, great accuracy was achieved. F/O Picken's bomb-aimer had the red and green marker flares in his bombsight as the cookie and twelve SBCs went down from 16,000 feet at 20.07, and they saw the flash of their impact about twenty seconds later. Sgt McDonald and crew didn't see the burst of their bombs from 19,500 feet at 20.08, but two minutes later they, and most of the other crews, witnessed a giant explosion that lit up the sky like day for many seconds and left a glow that lingered for ten minutes. What they had seen was the destruction of the Mariensiel naval ammunition dump located in the south of the town, which blew itself into oblivion, devastating 120 acres of the naval dockyard and built-up area. The three remaining 106 Squadron crews carried out their attacks from 13,000 to 17,000 feet between 20.03 and 20.08, but found it impossible to assess what was happening on the ground. Only three Lancasters failed to return, and among them was 106 Squadron's LM303, which was shot down at 20.44 by a night-fighter off Borkum on the way home, killing F/Sgt Hayward RCAF and his crew. This was the first successful operation for blind-bombing by H2S skymarking.

It was back to Lorient for eleven 106 Squadron crews on the 13th, who learned at briefing that they were to be part of a force of 466 aircraft, the largest yet sent to the port, for what would be a two-phase attack. 5 Group contributed 103 Lancasters, and those representing 106 Squadron departed Syerston between 18.40 and 18.55 led by S/L Searby, and, for once, there were no early returns. They were part of the first wave, which flew south to begin the Channel crossing in the area of Exmouth, and found the target in good visibility under clear skies with a half moon and accurately marked by the Path Finders. The town was already well alight when F/O Picken and crew bombed from 12,000 feet, but smoke obscured the impact, and the other crews were similarly unable to plot the fall of their bombs after delivering their attacks from 9,500 to 14,000 feet. F/O Picken and S/L Searby brought back aiming point photos from what was a highly effective attack, which delivered more than a thousand tons of bombs onto the already rubble-strewn port. As they headed out to sea, Sgt Irvine and crew spotted something in the water, which, after they descended to 100 feet, turned out to be a dinghy containing five men waving torches. They reported the position of the dinghy, and continued on their way, leaving behind them massive fires across the town and around the U-Boot pens on the Keroman peninsula, and smoke drifting across the area.

Orders came through from 5 Group on the 14th to make ready for a return to Italy that night for a crack this time at Milan. A force of 142 Lancasters of 1, 5 and 8 Groups was assembled to carry out the attack, while 243 Halifaxes, Stirlings and Wellingtons were made ready to try their hand at Cologne. Among the eighty-nine 5 Group Lancasters were eleven representing 106 Squadron, which took off from Syerston between 18.20 and 18.45 with W/C Gibson and S/L Searby the senior pilots on duty, the commanding officer accompanied in W4842 by F/L Morrison as second pilot and a Sgt Cartwright, who would be operating the movie camera. Sgt Glaholme and crew lost the use of their compass during the passage across France, and were forced to turn back, leaving the others to press on to the target area, which most reached after a trouble-free outward flight. They were guided to the aiming point by green and red Path Finder route-marker flares, and were able to identify the aiming point visually in excellent conditions. S/L Searby and crew attacked from 12,000 feet at 22.38, and saw the impact of their all-incendiary bomb load, while the others from the squadron ran in at 10,000 to 12,500 feet between 22.37 and 22.44, some delivering a cookie and incendiaries. Gibson stooged around for twenty minutes after bombing, while his camera operator shot a movie, and he brought back a bombing photo plotted at a mile-and-a-half from the aiming point. Most loads were observed to hit the city, and many fires were reported, the glow from which remained visible for at least a hundred miles into the return journey. The crews of S/L Searby, P/O Edmunds, Sgt McDonald, F/L Hayward, Sgt Markland and Sgt Price were others to bring back an aiming point photo, which was a record in 5 Group, and prompted a message of congratulations from the A-O-C, AVM Coryton. The operation was hailed as a success, although no local report was forthcoming to confirm or deny.

The final raid of the series on Lorient was posted on the 16th, for which another large force was made ready, this time of 377 aircraft. Of seventy-five Lancasters offered by 5 Group, eight were made ready by 106 Squadron at Syerston, and took off between 18.15 and 18.45 with F/O Edmunds and P/O Brodrick the only commissioned pilots on duty. All reached the target, where they were among the earlier arrivals at the target and found clear conditions aided by an almost full moon, which enabled them to deliver their cookies and SBCs of incendiaries onto red TIs burning on the Keroman peninsula from 9,500 to 12,000 feet between 20.47 and 20.53. The majority of the force dropped incendiaries into the town, which, after nine attacks, 1,926 sorties and four thousand tons of bombs, was now a desolate and deserted ruin. The crews of F/Sgt Burpee, P/O Brodrick and Sgt Markland brought back aiming point photos to add to the squadron's album. Later, on the 17th, it was announced that P/O Cassels had been awarded a DFC, and his navigator, F/Sgt Woollard, a DFM.

Preparations were put in hand on the 18th to make ready 195 aircraft for the second of four raids on Wilhelmshaven during the month. 5 Group contributed seventy-nine Lancasters, including nine belonging to 106 Squadron, which departed Syerston between 18.00 and 18.20 with F/L Hayward and the newly-promoted F/L Picken the senior pilots on duty. Each Lancaster had a cookie and twelve SBCs in its bomb bay, and all of this weaponry reached the target area, which was identified visually in excellent conditions. F/L Picken and crew located the target both visually and by a red TI, and the TI was in the bombsight as they attacked from 14,000 feet and observed bursts in a built-up area. F/Sgt Burpee and crew were seven thousand feet higher when they let their load go, too high to observe the results, but the bombing photo would reveal fires, roads, canals and fields covering an area five miles from the aiming point. The other crews also claimed to have had the target indicators in their sights as they released their bombs from 13,000 to 17,000 feet either side of 20.30, and all but one returned home to pass on their impressions of bomb bursts and fires that left them confident in the effectiveness of their efforts. The return to Syerston of R5750 was awaited in vain, and it would be confirmed later that the Lancaster had crashed into the North Sea in the general target area, killing the experienced and popular crew of Sgt Markland RNZAF. Five bodies were recovered by the Germans on the 21st, and the others eventually came ashore for burial. It will be recalled that both gunners had been awarded a DFM following an operation to Berlin in the previous month. An analysis of the raid would reveal that most of the effort had fallen to the west of the town into open country, and Path Finder claims of accurate marking were found to be mistaken. Local sources did admit to a number of bombs hitting the town, but they caused no serious damage or casualties. The outcome was a major disappointment, which confirmed that all was still not well with regard to target identification and marking beyond the range of Oboe.

Twenty-four hours later, a force of 338 aircraft set off to return to Wilhelmshaven, with Wellingtons and Halifaxes accounting for 230 of the number and Stirlings and Lancasters the rest. 5 Group dispatched thirty-three Lancasters, but did not call upon the services of 106 Squadron. Once again, excellent conditions prevailed, with visibility that enabled crews to identify the coastline and line themselves up on the target, which was being marked by green TIs. Bomb bursts and fires were observed in the docks area and the town, and left the crews with the impression that another successful raid had taken place. However, bombing photos would tell a different story, and revealed that the Path Finder marking had fallen to the north of the built-up area, partly through reliance upon outdated maps, which would now be replaced. Of the twelve missing aircraft five were Stirlings and represented 8.9% of those dispatched, thus confirming the type's vulnerability compared with the Lancaster and Halifax. The four missing Lancasters represented a 7.7% loss rate, while no Halifaxes failed to return, but this would prove to be a blip. During the course of the year, the food chain would become established with Lancasters firmly at the top, Halifaxes in the middle and Stirlings at the bottom, when all types operated together.

An all-Lancaster main force from 1 and 5 Groups was made ready on the 21st to attack the city of Bremen, with Path Finder Lancasters, Halifaxes and Stirlings to provide the marking in an overall force of 143 aircraft. Seventy-four of the Lancasters were put up by 5 Group, and the nine representing 106 Squadron departed Syerston between 18.10 and 18.20 with S/L Searby the senior pilot on duty. The squadron's recent excellent record of serviceability continued on this night, and all reached the target area after attempting to follow scattered route-marker flares. They had been briefed to expect complete cloud cover and to bomb blind on a combination of skymarker flares and TIs, and were greeted by ten-tenths cloud at 3,000 feet. Above, the red and green flares were drifting down, also in a somewhat scattered manner and up to nine minutes late to join the TIs dimly visible burning on the ground. The crews faced intense opposition as they made their bombing runs at 14,000 to 18,000 feet, and all except that of Sgt Renshaw dropped their bombs within seconds of each other at 20.52, leaving them the last from the squadron to let their load go some six minutes later. A considerable glow from beneath the clouds suggested a successful outcome, and that was the belief as they were diverted to the 6 Group station of Topcliffe on return because of fog at Syerston. In the event, bombing photos depicted only cloud, and no local report was available to provide details of damage.

115 aircraft of 6 and 8 Groups concluded the current series of raids on Wilhelmshaven on the night of the 24/25th, with indeterminate results, and the port would now be left in peace until October 1944. A major operation against Nuremberg was posted on stations across the Command on the 25th, and 5 Group responded with a maximum effort of 101 Lancasters, thirteen of them made ready by 106 Squadron at Syerston. They took off between 19.00 and 19.20 with W/C Gibson the senior pilot on duty, and each Lancaster carrying a cookie and SBCs of 4lb or 30lb incendiaries. They all made it to the target area, which they found to be under cloudless skies, and had to wait for the Path Finder element to turn up, some sixteen to twenty minutes after the raid was due to begin. It was "squeaky bum" time while orbiting over a target, because no crew wanted to stooge around among hundreds of others and face the very real risk of collision. The Path Finders dropped marker flares on the approach, and the 5 Group crews carried out a time-and-distance run to the aiming point, which was marked by red and green TIs. The 106 Squadron element bombed from 12,000 to 17,000 feet between 23.22 and 23.32, and all of the indications, including what looked like an oil-depot exploding, suggested a concentrated attack, which fell predominantly in northern and western districts. This was confirmed by local reports, which mentioned damage to three hundred buildings, but also revealed that bombs had fallen onto other communities and open country up to seven miles to the north. Only nine aircraft failed to return on this occasion, but the squadron lost an experienced and popular crew, that of the American, F/L Don Curtin DFC & Bar, a New Yorker, who had enlisted in the RCAF to get into the war. He and his crew, which included S/L McGrath RNVR, who was on attachment from HMS Daedalus, were just three operations

short of completing their first tour, and died in the wreckage of W4886, after it crashed eight miles north of the target.

When Cologne was posted as the target on the 26th, 5 Group responded with ninety Lancasters, ten of which were made ready by 106 Squadron at Syerston as part of an overall force of 427 aircraft. They took off between 18.35 and 18.45 with W/C Gibson the senior pilot on duty, flying in ED649 on the twenty-eighth and penultimate sortie since becoming the squadron's commanding officer eleven months earlier. It was also his seventieth bomber operation in all, on top of the ninety-nine sorties he had accumulated as a night-fighter pilot with 29 Squadron between his two bomber tours. There were no early returns as the excellent run of perfect serviceability continued, and all reached the much-bombed city in favourable conditions, which included vertical visibility good enough for some bomb-aimers to pick out the Rhine bridges. It seems from some comments from other squadrons that a proportion of the force bombed before the Path Finders had a chance to mark, but, once the red and green TIs were seen on the ground, F/Sgt Burpee and crew were among the first to bomb, delivering their cookie and SBCs from 17,500 feet at 21.15. Gibson made a fast (220 i.a.s.), straight run at 16,000 feet, and the bombs were dropped at 21.21 in the face of heavy and accurate flak. They were seen to burst near the aiming point, and Gibson assessed at this stage that a concentrated raid was taking place. S/L Searby and crew had an additional ten m.p.h on Gibson, as they raced across the city at 17,000 feet and saw the flash of their cookie's impact, and the others from the squadron carried out their attacks from 13,000 to 18,500 feet between 21.16 and 21.28. Fires were reported in the city centre, as were decoys to the west of the city, and bombing photos showed fire tracks and smoke that suggested an effective raid. In fact, a large proportion of the effort had fallen to the south-west of the city, and perhaps, only a quarter had landed in the built-up area, causing much damage to housing, minor industry and public buildings at a cost to the bomber force of ten aircraft.

The night of the 27/28th was devoted to mining operations around the Frisians, for which the squadron contributed the freshman crews of F/O Wesley and Sgts Munro, Abel and Britton. They departed Syerston between 18.30 and 18.45 bound for the Nectarine III garden, and each pinpointed on the eastern end of Juist or established their position by Gee-fix, before conducting a timed run to the drop zone. They delivered six 1,570 mines each at eight or nine-second intervals into the correct location from around 1,000 feet, and described their experiences as "uneventful", "uninteresting", "satisfactory" and "successful".

Having dealt with Lorient under the January Directive, attention now turned upon St-Nazaire, situated further south along the Biscay coast. The force of 437 aircraft assembled on the 28th included a contribution from 5 Group of eighty-nine Lancasters, of which ten represented 106 Squadron. They departed Syerston between 18.05 and 18.30 with S/L Searby the senior pilot on duty, and there was a first bombing operation for F/O Wesley and crew. All reached the target area to find clear skies and good visibility, with only a little ground haze and smoke to contend with. S/L Searby picked out the docks clearly, and his bomb-aimer had the red and green TIs in his bombsight as he let the cookie and SBCs go from 14,000 feet at 21.17. The others from the squadron also bombed on the TIs from 8,500 to 14,400 feet between 21.14 and 21.31, and it was clear from the many explosions and at least forty fires burning in the docks that the port was undergoing an ordeal of destruction. All returning crews commented on the town being consumed by a conflagration, and Sgt Renshaw and crew reported still being able to see the glow from 5,000 feet as they approached Start Point on the Devon coast. The crews were correct in their belief that the operation had been an outstanding success, and reconnaissance revealed that the marking had been concentrated and the bombing accurate, leaving an estimated 60% of the town's built-up area in ruins.

During the course of the month the squadron operated on fourteen occasions and dispatched 117 sorties for the loss of five Lancasters and crews.

March 1943

March would bring with it the opening rounds of the Ruhr campaign, the first for which the Command was adequately equipped and genuinely prepared, with a predominantly four-engine bomber force to carry an increasing weight of bombs and Oboe to provide accuracy. 106 Squadron welcomed a new A Flight commander, who would be a major influence on those taking part. S/L Peter Ward-Hunt had been born on Gibraltar in 1916, and was a man of small stature, but enormous personality, and someone who had gained operational experience since the very beginning of strategic bombing in May 1940. His operational career began with 49 Squadron at Scampton, where he was a contemporary of Gibson who was serving on the station at the same time with 83 Squadron. At the end of a tour of thirty-two operations, Ward-Hunt was awarded a DFC, and, after a period of screening, he joined 207 Squadron to fly Manchesters, taking part in the attack on the Renault lorry factory in Paris, and later, while an instructor, he flew a training unit Manchester on the first thousand bomber raid on Cologne. His style was to lead from the front, and his opportunity to do so at 106 Squadron came with the first major operation of the new month.

Before the Ruhr offensive began, the crews would have to negotiate operations to Germany's Capital and Second Cities, and it was the "Big City" itself, Berlin, that opened the month's account on the 1st. A force of 302 aircraft was assembled, made up of 156 Lancasters, eighty-six Halifaxes and sixty Stirlings, 5 Group putting up a maximum effort of ninety-eight Lancasters, of which a dozen represented 106 Squadron. They departed Syerston between 18.25 and 18.50 with S/Ls Searby and Ward-Hunt the senior pilots on duty on a night of good weather conditions, and headed for the rendezvous point over the North Sea, from where they would set course for the target. Sgt Glaholm and crew were well into the outward flight and over enemy territory when their compass let them down and compelled them to turn around. The target was found to be under clear skies with only haze to impair the vertical visibility, however, reliant upon H2S, the Path Finder navigators experienced great difficulty in establishing their positions based on the images on their cathode-ray tubes over such a massive urban sprawl. This made it impossible to establish a concentration of TIs around the intended aiming point, and, even though the target was easily identified both visually and by markers, the high-flying crews were presented with a variety of choices. S/L Ward-Hunt's bomb-aimer had red markers in his bomb sight as he delivered the cookie and twelve SBCs from 17,000 feet at 22.12, and although he did not observe the detonation, he saw several large fires and brought back a bombing photo showing a built-up area plotted at five thousand yards from the aiming point. S/L Searby and crew bombed from 20,000 feet at 22.13, and described large areas of the city on fire, while the others from the squadron attacked from 15,000 to 19,000 feet on red and green TIs between 22.10 and 22.35, and many fires were reported, the glow from which, according to some, could be seen from two hundred miles away on the return flight. A post-raid analysis based on bombing photos revealed the attack to have been spread over an area of a hundred square miles, with the main weight falling into south-western districts. However, because of the increasing bomb tonnage now being carried, more damage was inflicted on the city than on any previous raid. 875 buildings, mostly houses, were destroyed, and twenty factories seriously damaged, along with railway workshops in the Tempelhof district. Seventeen aircraft failed to return, five of them Lancasters belonging to 5 Group.

A force of 417 aircraft was assembled to send against Hamburg on the 3rd, and eighty-nine of 149 Lancasters were provided by 5 Group, ten of them by 106 Squadron at Syerston, where each had a cookie and twelve SBCs of incendiaries winched into its cavernous thirty-three-foot-long bomb bay. They took off between 18.30 and 18.50 with F/Ls Hayward and Picken the senior pilots on duty, and, other than F/O Wesley, the remaining crew captains were of sergeant rank. All negotiated the North Sea crossing, enjoying favourable weather conditions for the entire flight, and, from clear skies, some crews pinpointed on the River Elbe, confirming their positions by the Path Finder red and green target indicators, which most had in their bombsights as they delivered their cookies and SBCs from 16,000 to 18,000 feet between 21.27 and 21.40. Numerous fires were observed in the docks area along with black smoke rising to meet the bombers as they turned away, but the crews of F/Ls Hayward and Picken both commented on the fact that most of the bombing appeared to be falling to the west of the aiming point. Back home, their observations were proved to be correct when bombing photos were plotted, and the small town of Wedel, thirteen miles downstream on the northern bank of the Elbe, was revealed to have borne the brunt of the attack, after some H2S operators had misinterpreted the images on their cathode-ray tubes. Some bombs did fall within Hamburg itself, however, and the city's fire-fighters had to deal with a hundred conflagrations before lending their assistance to their neighbour. At debriefing, crews reported the glow of fires still visible up to a hundred miles into the return flight, but absent at Syerston was 106 Squadron's R5731, which had crashed near Hohenaspe on the Schleswig-Holstein peninsula, north-west of Hamburg. There were no survivors among the crew of F/O Wesley RCAF, who had only recently begun their first tour of operations.

The decks were now cleared for the opening of the Ruhr offensive, which, over the ensuing months, would change the face of bombing and provide for the enemy an indication of the burgeoning power of the Command. This was a momentous occasion, a culmination of all that had gone before during three and a half years of Bomber Command operations. The backs-to-the-wall desperation of 1940, the tentative almost token offensives of 1941, the treading water and gradual metamorphosis under Harris in 1942, when failures still far outnumbered successes, had all been leading to this night, from which point would begin the calculated and systematic dismantling of Germany's industrial and population centres. The only shining light during these dark years had been the quality and spirit of the aircrew, and this had never faltered. It would begin on the 5th at Essen, Harris's nemesis thus far and the home of the giant armaments-producing Krupp complex occupying the Borbeck districts, which fanned out from the city centre to the north-western boundary. For the first time since the war began, the Command would have at its disposal a device which would negate the industrial haze that had protected this city and its neighbours, Duisburg, Dortmund and Düsseldorf, frustrating Harris and rendering ineffective thousands of bomber sorties. The magnificent pioneering work on Oboe by W/C Hal Bufton and his crews at 109 Squadron was about to bear fruit in spectacular fashion, and, with a margin of error of four to six hundred yards, it no longer mattered that the ground was hidden from the crews. It mattered only that the high-flying Oboe Mosquitos reached the target with functioning Oboe equipment, and, if they did, the cities of Germany's arsenal would suffer destruction on an unprecedented scale.

A force of 442 aircraft included ninety-seven Lancasters representing 5 Group, 106 Squadron contributing a dozen of them, which departed Syerston between 18.30 and 18.45 with S/Ls Searby and Ward-Hunt the senior pilots on duty. Sgt Munro and crew were recorded as taking off at 19.17, possibly having been delayed by a technical issue, and they returned after three hours with an unserviceable rear turret, not the first time that W4156 had manifested that particular fault. They were among an unusually high number of early returns, although, only seven from the ranks of 5 Group, which, together with those bombing alternative targets, would reduce the size of the force reaching Essen and bombing as briefed to 362 aircraft. 5 Group favoured a time-and-distance approach to the aiming point, and the 106 Squadron crews employed the Path Finders' yellow route markers over the town of Dorsten as the initial reference point. The five serviceable Mosquitos marked the centre of the city to perfection, and the Path Finder heavy brigade backed up on time up to maintain the aiming point. The main force arrived in three waves, with the Lancaster element coming in last, and the result would be the most accurate and destructive attack of the war to date on this formerly elusive city. S/L Ward-Hunt and crew described hazy conditions and a thin layer of cloud over the target as they ran in to bomb on a red marker from 18,000 feet at 21.18. They were unable to see the impact of the bombs, but reported concentrated fires, one very large explosion, and many searchlights accompanied by heavy flak. S/L Searby and crew bombed from 20,000 feet at 21.20, and echoed the comments of S/L Ward-Hunt, adding that the glow from the burning city was visible at the Dutch coast. The others from the squadron exploited the good visibility to bomb through the industrial haze onto red and green TIs from 16,000 to 20,000 feet between 21.18 and 21.23. The overwhelming impression was of a concentrated attack, which left many fires burning, and a glow in the sky reported by some to be visible from the North Sea homebound.

At debriefing, crews reported terrific explosions among fires, which lit up the sky, and a pall of smoke hanging above the dull, red centre of the conflagration. Missing from debriefing was the crew of F/L Picken DFC, who had all been killed when W4918 crashed in the general target area. It was the sixth operation of Rhodesian Bill Picken's second tour, and he was considered to be one of the squadron's outstanding captains. There is a degree of uncertainty concerning the precise location of the Lancaster's crash, Bill Chorley, in his superb and indispensable Bomber Command Losses series, placing it to the north of Düsseldorf at 21.15. This location, south of Essen, would suggest that they were on the way home when the end came, but the time is a fraction too early for that to be the case. Another source claims the Lancaster came down onto farmland at Bönninghardt, north of the Ruhr and west of Dorsten, with its bombs still on board, and this would harmonize better with the timing. The explosion of the cookie apparently killed the farmer, Herr Schlootz, and four members of his family, and only a six-month-old baby girl survived. Post-raid reconnaissance revealed 160 acres of devastation and damage to fifty-three buildings within the Krupp district, and the success of the operation was confirmed by local reports of 3,018 houses destroyed and more than two thousand others seriously damaged. The operation cost the Command an acceptable fourteen aircraft, and it was a most encouraging start to what would become a five-month-long offensive.

It would be a further week before round two of the Ruhr offensive was mounted, and, in the meantime, Harris turned his attention upon southern Germany, beginning with Nuremberg on the 8th. A force of 338 aircraft included 105 Lancasters from 5 Group, of which a dozen representing 106 Squadron departed Syerston between 19.10 and 19.25 with S/Ls Searby and Ward-Hunt the senior pilots on duty, and each crew sitting on a cookie and assorted incendiaries. There were no 106 Squadron crews among the eight 5 Group early returns as they made their way across France on a clear and moonless night, and they followed yellow route markers to the target, where they encountered clear skies but ground haze and extreme darkness. This seemed to impede the Path Finders' ability to locate the city centre blind by H2S, and the main force crews experienced the same difficulty in identifying ground detail, allowing themselves to be guided to the aiming point by a few red and green TIs, which appeared to lack concentration and soon burned out. The usual difficulties with H2S interpretation led to the marking spreading along the line of approach up to ten miles short of the city boundaries. S/L Ward-Hunt and crew made out some ground detail and homed in on green target indicators, which they bombed from 20,000 feet at 23.36. They saw one very large blaze in the east of the city, and several scattered fires, and returned home to report an uneventful trip. F/L Edmunds and crew brought back a bombing photo plotted at 3,000 yards from the aiming point, while the Burpee crew saw their bombs burst near the aiming point, and they were among a number to report two distinct concentrations of fire. The bombing photo of P/O Brodrick's crew was plotted at 1¾ miles from the aiming point, and they claimed that the glow of fires remained visible for 120 miles into the homeward flight. The other 106 Squadron participants carried out their attacks from 14,000 to 18,000 feet between 23.30 and 23.43, and gained an initial impression of a scattered raid, but a greater concentration of fires began to developthe , and the glow from these was reported by some to be visible for two hundred miles into the return journey. Local reports confirmed the marking and bombing to have undershot, half of it falling outside of the city boundaries, while the rest destroyed six hundred buildings and damaged fourteen hundred others, including a number of important war-industry factories, among them those of the M.A.N. (Machinenfabrik Augsburg Nürnberg) and Siemens companies.

On the following day, preparations were put in hand to return to southern Germany to attack the city of Munich, situated deep in the Bavarian mountains of south-eastern Germany, a round-trip of more than 1,200 miles. A force of 264 aircraft included eighty-one Lancasters of 5 Group, of which eight belonging to 106 Squadron were loaded with a cookie each and SBCs of incendiaries, while a ninth had an 8,000 pounder in the bomb bay. They took off between 20.10 and 20.30, with S/Ls Searby and Ward-Hunt the senior pilots on duty, but the latter became indisposed before reaching the French coast and abandoned the sortie. Sgt Burton and crew were over enemy territory when their rear turret became unserviceable, and they, also, were compelled to turn back. The others reached the target area, where clear skies and good visibility prevailed, and the Path Finder green and white TIs could be seen falling within the built-up area. They carried out "time-and-distance" runs from the Ammersee, west-south-west of the city centre, F/L Edmunds and crew locating the target by Path Finder flares, and were also able to pick out ground detail. They bombed from 16,500 feet at 00.17, and would bring back a photo plotted at 4½ miles from the aiming point. They described a good concentration of bombing, and reported one particularly large orange explosion in a south-western district on the track from the Ammersee. This was noted also by the other crews, who carried out their attacks from 14,000 to 18,000 feet between 00.20 and 00.27, and their photos would be similarly plotted at three thousand yards and more from the aiming point. Another huge explosion at 00.25 lit up the sky for twenty seconds and illuminated an area of ground with a ten-mile radius, described by some as the largest they had experienced, and one more particularly large one occurred at 00.43. Fires were taking hold and sending a large pall of smoke rising above the city as the bomber force withdrew to the west, and a 44 Squadron crew counted eighteen blazes in or close to the city centre. A relatively modest eight aircraft failed to return, and only two of these were from 5 Group. A post-raid analysis concluded that a strong wind had pushed the attack into the western half of the city, where 291 buildings had been destroyed and 660 severely damaged. The aero-engine assembly shop at the B.M.W factory was put out of action for six weeks, and many other industrial concerns also lost vital production.

The 10th brought news of decorations for a number of squadron personnel, including some who had been members of Gibson's crew. There was a Bar to his DFC for F/L Oliver, a DFC for F/Ls Wellington, Scrivener and Drew and F/Os Burnside, Ruskell and Wickens, and DFMs for F/Sgt Kennedy and Sgts Robin, Evans and Herbert. There were no major operations that night, but thirty-five Lancasters and Stirlings were sent on wide-ranging gardening sorties from the French coast to the Baltic. 106 Squadron selected four crews who hadn't operated over the previous two nights, those of F/Sgt Burpee and Sgts Renshaw, Price and Yackman, and dispatched them between 18.20 and 18.45, the first three-named to the Baltic to mine the waters in the Pollock garden, off the Island of Bornholm, east of Denmark and south of Sweden, and the last-mentioned to the Deodars garden in the Gironde estuary. Those heading east flew out over eight-tenths cloud, which gave way to clear skies in the garden area, and all of them located Rönne as the pinpoint from which to make their timed runs and successfully deliver five 1,570lb mines each at twelve-second intervals. Sgt Yackman and crew, who were undertaking their first sortie together, encountered thick haze off the Biscay coast, and despite an extensive search, failed to locate a pinpoint and brought their stores home.

The trio of operations to destinations in southern Germany concluded with the highly industrial city of Stuttgart, for which a force of 314 aircraft was assembled on the 11th, 5 Group contributing ninety-six of

152 Lancasters. Ten of these were made ready by 106 Squadron at Syerston, where take-off was accomplished safely between 19.45 and 20.20 with W/C Gibson the senior pilot on duty and last away, having been preceded among others by S/Ls Searby and Ward-Hunt. Having been with the squadron for twelve months, Gibson must have known his time was up, and he probably recognised that this would be his final operation before being posted. He had a second pilot on board, F/O Walter Thompson, a Canadian, who had arrived that very day from a conversion unit, and who, after the war, would recount his experiences in a book entitled Lancaster to Berlin. They had a three-and-a-half-hour flight ahead of them, which was made more difficult for Gibson and crew after ED649 was hit by flak at the French coast and lost most of the power from the starboard-outer engine. A lesser man might have turned back at that stage with more than three hundred miles still to cover before even reaching the target, but Gibson continued on, mostly at 4,000 feet, before climbing to 12,000 feet for the bombing run. Sgt Burton and crew lost their W/T shortly after take-off, and did abandon their sortie. The others pressed on across France to the target, where visibility was found to be excellent as the main force element arrived late to observe Path Finder TIs already burning out on the ground. Gibson and crew delivered their cookie and twelve SBCs at 23.20, and watched them burst near a concentration of fires, and S/L Ward-Hunt and crew bombed TIs two minutes later, but from considerably higher, 18,500 feet, and observed their bombs bursting. S/L Searby and crew noted a large concentration of fires well to the north-west of the aiming point, and this was probably the result of the defenders employing dummy target indicators for the first time to lure the attack away from the city. In this endeavour they were largely successful, although, to the bomb-aimers high above, the green TIs appeared to be legitimate, and were bombed by the remaining 106 Squadron crews from 14,000 to 17,500 feet between 23.19 and 23.40. Most of the effort was wasted in open country, but the south-western suburbs of Vaihingen and Kaltental were hit and 118 buildings, mostly houses, were destroyed. It was a disappointing outcome, which cost eleven aircraft, only one of which was from 5 Group. Gibson and crew arrived home safely along with the squadron's other participants, and brought back a bombing photo plotted at four miles from the aiming point. Gibson now had the happy prospect of well-earned leave with his wife Eve in Cornwall, but it would be a few more days before his future was revealed to him.

Round two of the Ruhr campaign was posted on the 12th, when 457 crews learned at briefing that Essen was once more to be their destination, and ninety-five of them would be in 5 Group Lancasters. Syerston, as usual on any day of an operation, was a hive of activity, with riggers and fitters crawling over Lancasters, preparing them for an air-test to prove their fitness to take part. That established it was the turn of the armourers to fill the bomb bays and replenish the racks with fresh belts of .303 ammunition, before the tankers arrived to top up the fuel to the required level. On this evening, thirteen 106 Squadron Lancasters snaked their way to the runway threshold, before taking off safely between 18.55 and 19.15 with S/Ls Searby and Ward-Hunt the senior pilots on duty. They all reached the target having been briefed to aim for the Krupp complex, and found it well marked by red and green Path Finder TIs, with only smoke to mar the visibility. S/L Ward-Hunt's bomb-aimer had a green TI in his bombsight as he delivered the cookie and SBCs from 22,000 feet and watched them explode in a concentration of fires. The crew also observed one large explosion, as did a number of others including that of Sgt Irvine, who were at 18,000 feet as they made their bombing run on a red TI at 21.35. They were approaching the release point, when the Lancaster was coned by searchlights, dazzling every member of the crew and persuading the bomb-aimer to jettison the load "live", it was believed, still within the target area. P/O Brodrick and crew were at 14,000 feet as they bombed, and must have been at risk of being hit by the hardware falling from above. They, like many others, brought back a photo of fire tracks, and reported a great concentration of fires and two large explosions, both comments backed up by the crew of F/L Hayward. The 106 Squadron crews had delivered their attacks from a variety of altitudes between the 14,000 and 22,000 feet already mentioned, in a fifteen-minute slot to 21.42, and it was clear that the bombing had been accurate and mostly concentrated around the Oboe-laid TIs. Post-raid analysis confirmed that the initial Oboe marking by Mosquitos had fallen across the Krupp complex, and the subsequent bombing had produced 30% more damage than the attack of a week earlier. Five hundred houses were also destroyed, but a proportion of the bombing still managed to find its way into nearby towns, and F/Sgt Burpee's bombing photo was plotted at three miles from the aiming point. He and his crew commented on the ferocity of the defences and abundance of searchlights, and it had been a relatively expensive night for the Command, which registered the loss of twenty-three aircraft. Essen invariably claimed a 106 Squadron aircraft, and true to form, R5749, "Admiral Filha da Puta", failed to return after being torn apart by flak over the target. F/Sgt McDonald RAAF and five of his crew were killed, and only the Australian bomb-aimer, F/Sgt Lindsay, escaped with his life after falling through the smashed Perspex nose. He landed right in the centre of the Krupp district and soon found himself in captivity.

A welcome lull in operations now lay ahead for the crews as fog rolled across the bomber counties of eastern England. Minor operations would hold sway for the next week and a half, and Sgt Price and crew were sent mining in the Privet garden off distant Danzig on the night after Essen. Conditions were good until just before the garden was reached, when ten-tenths cloud was encountered with a base at 100 feet. Sgt Price opted to head for the secondary target area of Silverthorn in the Kattegat Channel, and here they successfully delivered four mines before returning safely after a round-trip of more than nine hours.

To his surprise, Gibson found himself posted to 5 Group HQ at St Vincents in Grantham on the 14th, and believed, initially, that he was to assist in the writing of a book. On the 15th, Harris met with the recently appointed A-O-C 5 Group, AVM Sir Ralph Cochrane, formerly the 3 Group A-O-C, to tell him to form a special squadron under Gibson to train for an attack on the Ruhr Dams. On the 18th, Gibson met with Cochrane, initially to establish his willingness to cancel his leave and take on one more operation. On the following day he was recalled to Cochrane's office, where he met base commander, G/C Whitworth, and was told to form a new squadron at Whitworth's main base at Scampton. Given a degree of autonomy in selecting his crews, Gibson naturally called upon a number of those with whom he had shared part of the past twelve months. Hopgood, having completed his tour back in October, was an automatic choice, as was Shannon, who by this time, was about to begin training as a Path Finder, and had barely had time to unpack at Wyton when Gibson's call came through. Canadian P/O Lewis "John" Burpee and crew also departed 106 Squadron and found their way to Scampton to join the new unit. Other current and former sons of the squadron would also answer the call to Scampton, and thereby gain a unique place in RAF Bomber Command history.

S/L Searby, who was very much a protégé of Gibson, was promoted on the 15th to step into his shoes as the squadron's new commanding officer. Although his time in office would be relatively brief as a result of his burgeoning reputation and career, he would continue to provide the outstanding leadership that had been a hallmark of the squadron since the earliest days. His promotion allowed F/L Hayward to step up one rank and take over as B Flight commander. A much-refreshed bomber force returned to operations on the night of the 22/23rd, when St-Nazaire and its U-Boot facilities were the target for an initial force of 357 aircraft. 106 Squadron detailed fourteen Lancasters, all but one of which would be carrying a new record load of eleven 1,000 pounders, one of them fitted with a delay fuse of between six and 144 hours. The odd man out was Sgt Munro's aircraft, which had an 8,000 pounder in its bomb bay. S/Ls Ward-Hunt and Hayward were the senior pilots on duty, and the former carried a passenger in the person of the new Syerston station commander, G/C Odbert. The squadron's association with the Fleet Air Arm continued on this night with Lt Jess and Sub Lt Lee DSO flying as bomb-aimers. Lt Muttrie was already serving with the squadron, currently as a member of F/O Brodrick's crew. They took off in a thirty-minute slot from 19.00, and made their way south towards Portland Bill in excellent conditions with clear skies and just a little haze. The number of aircraft converging on the target was reduced by the recall of the majority of the Stirling element, and P/O Browne was also forced to turn back after losing two engines. He, ultimately, carried out a skilful landing on the remaining two at Downham Market. At the target, red and green Path Finder TIs confirmed the location of the aiming point, and the 106 Squadron element carried out their attacks from 10,000 to 15,000 feet between 21.36 and 21.56. F/L Edmunds and crew made four bombing runs to ensure accuracy, while S/L Ward-Hunt took a long run-up at 11,000 feet after easily identifying the aiming point, and, according to his bombing photo, he missed it by four miles. P/O Thompson was flying as crew captain for the first time, and he described an uneventful trip, which ended with a diversion to the O.T.U station at Wellesbourne-Mountford in Warwickshire because of fog at Syerston. F/Sgt Page and crew reported one particularly large explosion, which they believed to be of an oil-storage facility, and then found themselves diverted on return to Desford in Page's home county of Leicestershire. The crews of F/O Brodrick and Sgt McGregor each brought back an aiming point photograph, which showed the target to have been well-plastered. In all, 283 crews claimed to have bombed the target as briefed, and just one Lancaster failed to return.

Duisburg was selected as the host for the third operation of the Ruhr offensive, for which a force of 455 aircraft was assembled on the 26th, 5 group contributing ninety-four of the Lancasters. 106 Squadron made ready eleven, loading two of them with an 8,000 pounder and the remainder with a cookie and twelve SBCs. They departed Syerston between 18.20 and 18.40 with S/L Ward-Hunt the senior pilot on duty, having learned at briefing that marking would be by "Musical Wanganui", the code for Oboe skymarking, to be carried out by nine Mosquitos of 109 Squadron. Sgt Abel and crew lost the use of their W/T before reaching the enemy coast and turned back, leaving the others to press on to the target area, where, as forecast, they found ten-tenths cloud with tops at between 10,000 and 20,000 feet and good visibility above. Under current standard circumstances, the cloud would not have been a problem, but one of the Oboe Mosquitos ditched in the North Sea and five turned back with equipment malfunctions. The remaining three were unable to provide adequate skymarking, and the parachute flares visible in the distance to the approaching bombers quickly fell out of sight, and most crews bombed on timed runs. The 106 Squadron crews attacked from 17,000 to 22,000 feet between 21.43 and 21.55, and a large explosion was witnessed at 21.53. According to local sources, the raid was scattered and ineffective, causing only minor damage, and cost a modest six aircraft, none of which belonged to 5 Group.

Orders were received on stations across the Command on the 27th to prepare for a trip to the "Big City" that night, and a force of 396 aircraft was duly assembled, which included 111 Lancasters from 5 Group. A dozen of these were made ready by 106 Squadron at Syerston, and took off between 19.40 and 19.50 with F/O Brodrick the senior pilot on duty, before heading for the rendezvous point over the North Sea. F/Sgt Page's Lancaster developed supercharger problems two hours out, and he was forced to turn back, while the others pushed on to approach the city from the south-west. The Path Finders again relied upon H2S to locate the city-centre aiming point, but, the sheer size of Berlin thwarted the attempts of the operators to establish their positions accurately, and this resulted in the marking of two areas at least five miles short of where they should have been. Crews reported three-tenths cloud at 13,000 feet and five tenths stratus at 19,000 feet with moderate to good visibility, and those from 106 Squadron dropped their cookies and incendiaries or 8,000 pounders on red and green TIs from 17,000 to 20,000 feet between 23.04 and 23.20. From bombing altitude, the attack appeared to be effective, but local reports confirmed that the main weight of bombs had fallen between seven and seventeen miles short of the target, with the main concentration around eleven miles from the centre, where, by good fortune alone, a secret store of valuable electronic equipment was hit and severely damaged.

There would be a chance to rectify the failure two nights hence, but, in the meantime, St-Nazaire would face its third heavy assault under the January Directive, for which a force of 323 aircraft was made ready on the 28th. 5 Group detailed twenty-one freshman crews, those of Sgts Howells and Robbins representing 106 Squadron and departing Syerston shortly after 20.00. The latter abandoned their sortie for an undisclosed reason, while the former arrived in the target area in clear skies and good visibility below 14,000 feet, and identified the coastline visually, before bombing on red and green TIs from 12,000 feet at 22.24. They observed the cookie to burst near the aiming point among fires, and, on return, expressed themselves as satisfied with their part in what post-raid reconnaissance confirmed had been an accurate and effective raid.

On the following day, a force of 329 aircraft was assembled for the return to Berlin, for which 106 Squadron made ready a dozen of the 106 Lancasters provided by 5 Group. They departed Syerston between 21.00 and 21.35 with S/L Hayward the senior pilot on duty on a night of difficult weather conditions, which included severe icing. For the second operation running F/Sgt Page and crew turned back early, this time with pneumatic system failure, while Sgts Irvine and Yackman fell victim to the icing conditions and were unable to maintain height. They were among an alarming eighteen 5 Group crews to abandon their sorties for a variety of causes, leaving the remainder to follow the route over the Baltic and reach Berlin behind schedule because of inaccurately forecast winds. The Path Finders provided route markers north of the target, and some crews pinpointed on them, while others focused on the cascading TIs over what was believed to be the city centre, seemingly unaware that the entire focus of the raid had been misplaced. Visibility was described by most as good, which enabled them to identify the target visually, aided by red TIs burning on the ground, and bombing was carried out by the 106 Squadron crews from 17,500 to 21,000 feet between 01.02 and 01.16. The freshman crew of Sgt Robbins had a red target indicator in their bombsight as they delivered their cookie from 21,000 feet at 01.16 at the tail-end of the 106 Squadron effort, and saw the flash of its impact. They described the whole of Berlin as "patterned" with fires running in all directions. The other crews echoed the impression of many fires and an effective attack, but, in fact, the Path Finders had delivered the markers well to the south of the planned aiming point, and the subsequent bombing had turned over a lot of earth in open country. This was confirmed later, when bombing photos revealed that most of the effort had fallen into open country south of the city, a disappointment compounded by the loss of twenty-one aircraft. A bitter blow for the squadron came with the failure to return of S/L Hayward DFC and crew, who were all killed when ED596 "Himself King" was shot down on the way home by Lt August Geigner of III./NJG1. The Lancaster crashed at 04.29 near Lichtenvoorde in Holland, a few miles from the frontier with Germany. S/L Hayward was just two sorties short of completing his second tour of operations, both of which had been served with 106 Squadron. Among his crew were navigator F/O Young DFC, wireless operator P/O Mantle DFM & Bar and mid-upper gunner F/Sgt Pryor DFM, and all would be mourned by the squadron and station communities.

During the course of the month the squadron established three new records, to whit, 350 tons of bombs and mines delivered over fourteen nights of operations, 134 sorties dispatched, and 834 hours of operational flying, all for the loss of four aircraft and their crews.

April 1943

April was to be the least rewarding month of the Ruhr campaign, largely because of the number of operations directed at targets outside of the region, and, therefore, beyond the range of Oboe. As Bomber Command was about to be released from its obligation to attack the French ports, small-scale operations took place against St-Nazaire and Lorient on the night of the 2/3rd, and 106 Squadron supported the latter with two Lancasters, with Sgts Ridd and Rosner flying as crew captains for the first time. They took off either side of 21.00, and the latter had just crossed the Brittany coast at Paimpol when intercom problems forced them to turn back. Sgt Ridd and crew arrived at the target to encounter thin cloud and smoke haze, and bombed on red TIs from 13,000 feet at 23.20 without observing the results. Meanwhile, Sgt Robbins and crew had been sent to the Deodars garden in the Gironde estuary, where, after making a timed run from the Ile de Cordouan, they delivered six mines into the briefed location.

The Lancaster and Halifax stations received orders on the 3rd to prepare for an operation against Essen that night, for which the Krupp works was designated as the aiming point. They responded with forces of 225 and 113 aircraft respectively, 5 Group contributing 123 of the Lancasters, and this would be the first time that more than two hundred of the type had operated together. 106 Squadron loaded a dozen of its fourteen participating aircraft with a cookie and twelve SBCs of incendiaries each, and two with an 8,000 pounder, before dispatching them from Syerston between 19.00 and 19.30 with the newly promoted F/L Brodrick the senior pilot on duty. Sgt Yackman and crew lost their starboard-outer engine while over the North Sea, and returned their bombs to store. Their colleagues crossed the Dutch coast near Haarlem and uncomfortably close to the Amsterdam defences, which opened fire in greeting. The force had been routed in north of the Ruhr, and red route-marker flares identified the final turning point at Dorsten, from where the stream headed due south for the final twelve miles to the target, where almost clear skies prevailed. There had been uncertainty among the meteorological section forecasters as to the likely weather conditions, and the Path Finders had prepared both sky and ground marking plans, which would lead to a degree of confusion among the main force crews. The 106 Squadron crews arrived between 22.01 and 22.10, and bombed on red and green release point flares from 17,000 to 20,000 feet, before observing the TIs on the ground. All but one returned to report a concentrated attack with many large fires emitting large volumes of smoke. The glow from the burning city was still visible to some from the Dutch coast homebound, and the consensus was of a successful raid. This was confirmed by bombing photographs and local reports, which spoke of widespread destruction in central and western districts, where 635 buildings had been reduced to rubble and many more seriously damaged. The searchlight and flak defence had been intense, and it became an expensive night for the Command, which registered the loss of a dozen Halifaxes and nine Lancasters. This represented 6% of those dispatched, but it was the respective loss rates of the types that was most telling, with the Halifaxes suffering 10.62% compared with 4% for the Lancasters. 106 Squadron's ED542 crashed near Haltern, just north of the Ruhr, killing Sgt Ridd and his crew, who were operating together for just the second time, and this demonstrated the particular vulnerability of freshman during their first half-dozen sorties.

The largest non-1,000 force to date of 577 aircraft was made ready on the 4th for an attack that night on the naval port of Kiel, for which 5 Group put up 112 Lancasters, fourteen of them representing 106 Squadron. They departed Syerston between 20.35 and 20.50 with W/C Searby the senior pilot on duty, and the new B Flight commander, S/L Young, flying as second pilot with F/L Brodrick and crew, and there was a first operation as crew captain for F/O Stephens. All reached the target area, where they were guided towards the aiming point by yellow route marker flares released by the Path Finder heavy brigade either side of 23.00. On arrival, Kiel was found to be concealed beneath ten-tenths cloud with tops at 8,000 feet with good visibility above, and red and green skymarkers were drifting across the target at speed before being swallowed up. The cookies and incendiaries were released mostly on the glow of fires from 16,500 to 18,000 feet between 23.23 and 23.46, but it was not possible to assess the outcome. As bombing photos revealed only cloud, it was left to a post-raid analysis to conclude that decoy fires were operating, and probably lured away a proportion of the effort, while the strong wind caused the markers to drift and lead the remainder astray, resulting in most of the bombs missing the target altogether. According to local reports, only eleven houses were destroyed, and this was a major disappointment in view of the size of the force involved.

The Ruhr offensive continued at Duisburg on the 8th, for which a mixed force of 379 Lancasters, Wellingtons, Halifaxes and Stirlings was assembled as the heavy element, while ten Oboe Mosquitos would provide the initial marking. 5 Group was responsible for eighty-four of the Lancasters, seven of them belonging to 106 Squadron, which also made ready three Lancasters for the crews of F/L Browne and Sgts Abel and Yackman to take mining in the Elderberry garden off Bayonne, just a dozen or so miles north of the Franco-Spanish frontier. They departed Syerston together between 20.30 and 21.05 with F/L Brodrick the senior pilot on duty among the Ruhr-bound contingent and the standard Ruhr payload of a cookie and assorted 4lb and 30lb incendiaries in the bomb bays. The bomber stream began to shed aircraft after meeting icing conditions over the sea, but it was an unserviceable rear turret that forced Sgt Burton and crew to turn back, while F/Sgt Page and crew were defeated by compass trouble. The remainder reached the western Ruhr to encounter ten-tenths cloud with tops in places as high as 20,000 feet, conditions which completely nullified the Path Finders' attempts to mark either the route or the target, and the bombing had to be carried out on e.t.a., some crews embarking on a time-and-distance run from as far away as the Dutch coast as the last visual reference. Sgt Munro and crew bombed from 18,000 feet at 23.45 on e.t.a., from their last Gee fix, and the crews of F/L Brodrick and Sgt Glaholm did exactly the same after seeing no flares or markers. F/L Edmunds and crew emptied the contents of their bomb bay from 20,000 feet on dead reckoning at 23.37, and all came home with a feeling of disappointment and expectation of failure and nothing of value to pass on to the Intelligence Section at debriefing. Local reports confirmed a widely scattered raid, which hit at least fifteen other Ruhr locations and destroyed just forty buildings in Duisburg. Among nineteen missing aircraft was W4156, which crashed in the target area, killing P/O Irvine and his crew, who were now well into their first tour and would be missed. Meanwhile, the gardeners had located Cape Higuer beneath eight-tenths cloud, observing the lights of San Sebastian across the frontier, and delivered their mines at three-second intervals from beneath the 1,500-foot cloud base. They returned safely from totally uneventful sorties, which kept them airborne for between nine hours and five minutes and ten hours and twenty-five minutes.

Not content with the outcome at Duisburg, Harris ordered another raid twenty-four hours later, only this time, employing a much-reduced force of 104 Lancasters and five Mosquitos. 5 Group detailed seventy Lancasters, of which six represented 106 Squadron, and departed Syerston between 20.20 and 20.30 with F/Ls Brodrick and Edmunds the senior pilots on duty, and S/L Young again accompanying the former as second pilot. There were no early returns, and they were guided to the target by red route-marker flares, and then red and green skymarkers over the aiming point, which was hidden by ten-tenths cloud with tops at 5,000 to 15,000 feet. F/L Edmunds and crew were approaching the aiming point at 20,000 feet, when attacked by an enemy night-fighter, which forced them to take evasive action, during which the cookie and SBCs were jettisoned. A second pass by the enemy resulted in damage to both aircraft, but the encounter ended inconclusively after the night-fighter disappeared. F/L Brodrick's bomb-aimer had a green marker in his bombsight when he delivered his load from 19,000 feet at 23.07, while F/Sgt Page and crew made a timed run from a red flare, and bombed from 20,000 feet a minute later. The others attacked from 20,000 and 21,000 feet between 23.07 and 23.11 observing indications of fires, but nothing of value, and it was left to local sources to confirm another highly scattered raid, which spread bombs over a wide area of the Ruhr and destroyed only fifty houses in Duisburg.

Frankfurt was posted as the destination for 502 aircraft on the 10th, on a night when Wellingtons would represent the most populous type, demonstrating that this trusty old warhorse still had an important part to play in Bomber Command operations. 5 Group provided sixty-six of 136 Lancasters, five of them representing 106 Squadron, and they departed Syerston between 23.35 and 23.55, four carrying the standard bomb load for city-busting of a cookie and twelve SBCs of 4lb incendiaries, while F/O Thompson and crew had an 8,000 pounder beneath their feet. They adopted the usual route for south-central Germany across France with, on this night, ten-tenths cloud beneath them, and reached the target area shortly before 03.00 to find heavy cloud again preventing any view of the ground. The 5 Group element carried out time-and-distance runs of around seven minutes from green route marker flares, four of those from 106 Squadron to deliver their loads on green skymarkers, from 16,000 feet between 02.56 and 03.03, while Sgt Reid and crew chose an altitude of 19,000 at 03.01. There was a hint of an explosion and fires beneath the cloud, but, in truth, returning crews had no idea where their bombs had fallen, and bombing photos would reveal nothing. Local sources suggested that a few bomb loads had fallen into the southern suburbs, but that most of the bombing had missed the city altogether.

The three 106 Squadron crews of F/L Browne, F/Sgt Page and Sgt Burton supported a mining operation in the Bay of Biscay on the night of the 11/12th, departing Syerston either side of 20.40 for what would be an eight-hour round-trip. They found excellent conditions including bright moonlight in the Furze and Elderberry garden areas, respectively off St-Jean-de-Luz and Bayonne, and experienced no difficulty in picking up pinpoints from which to make a timed run. The crews of F/L Browne and F/Sgt Page found ground features all along the French coast, and the former selected San Sebastian on the Basque coast as their reference, before heading north to deliver five mines into Elderberry at three-second intervals. The latter pinpointed on the confluence of the Rivers Nive and Adour off Bayonne and headed south to drop their stores into the same garden. Sgt Burton and crew arrived over the Furze drop zone, only to be frustrated by the failure of the bomb doors to open, and they had to bring their mines home.

Lancaster stations were notified on the 13th of a change of scenery for the next operation, which was to involve 208 aircraft and be directed against the docks and warships at berth at La Spezia on Italy's northern coast some forty miles south-east of Genoa. 5 Group detailed 124 of the Lancasters, with the remainder provided by 1 and 8 Groups, the latter also sending three Halifaxes as part of the marker force. 106 Squadron loaded a dozen of its aircraft with either six 1,000 pounders or four, together with SBCs of incendiaries, and sent them on their way between 20.00 and 20.20 with F/Ls Brodrick and Edmunds the senior pilots on duty. The station commander, G/C Odbert, hitched a ride with the latter and S/L Young with the former, and two other aircraft carried a second pilot. They headed south, forming into a stream as they passed Reading on their way to the Sussex coast to begin the Channel crossing. There were no early returns among the 106 Squadron contingent, and it was approaching 02.00 when they arrived over the Italian coast to find almost cloudless skies and only haze and smoke to mar the vertical visibility. An engine issue had prevented F/Sgt Page and crew from climbing to the briefed bombing height, and they had continued on to the target at low level, eventually reaching it at 4,700 feet. They had the docks in the bombsight, and watched the 1,000 pounders burst across them before turning for home. The engines continued to behave erratically, however, and it was decided unwise to try to attempt to reach England. The alternative option was to make for North Africa, and, after pinpointing on Corsica, the Lancaster eventually reached Maison Blanche, where a safe landing was made at 06.20. The other squadron participants established their positions by visual reference of ground detail, such as rivers and the docks, confirmed by Path Finder flares, and bombed from between 6,500 and 12,000 feet between 01.42 and 02.10, contributing to the severe damage inflicted upon the docks. Three large vessels tied together east of the outer harbour were seen to be on fire, and the naval oil stores were targeted by some aircraft. By the later stages of the raid, many fires had added to the smoke obscuring the town, and a number of large explosions encouraged the crews' belief that a successful operation had taken place, which, ultimately, would be confirmed. Two aircraft from other squadrons landed on recently captured airfields in North Africa, and were the first to do so before so-called "shuttle-raids" became a feature of operations to the Mediterranean region.

The busy round of non-Ruhr operations continued at Stuttgart, for which a force of 462 aircraft was made ready on the 14th, 5 Group detailing fifty-seven Lancasters, seven of them made ready by 106

Squadron and each loaded with a cookie and twelve SBCs of incendiaries. They departed Syerston between 21.50 and 22.00 with F/L Brodrick the senior pilot on duty with S/L Latimer DFC on board, who had been posted in to succeed the now departed S/L Ward-Hunt as A Flight commander. Some crews ran into icing conditions over Northern France, among them F/L Browne and crew, who found themselves unable to continue and abandoned their sortie. The others approached the city from the northeast to find an absence of cloud, but haze, aggravated by smoke rising through 8,000 feet, made ground detail indistinct. The aiming point was established by the green and red Path Finder TIs, but, it seems that not all of the Path Finder backers-up pressed on to the city centre aiming point, but re-marked the first target indicators they came upon, which encouraged a creep-back along the line of approach. F/O Thompson and crew were able to pick out ground detail before bombing from 16,000 feet at 01.29, and, after descending to low level, shot up a train and an aerodrome and brought back a bombing photo plotted at two miles from the aiming point. Sgt Munro's bomb-aimer had factory buildings in his bombsight as he released his load from 17,000 feet three minutes later, and they were the only 106 Squadron crew to bring back an aiming point photo. The crews of Sgt Burton and P/O Rosner carried out their attacks from 17,000 feet at 01.27 and 01.32 respectively, while Sgt Reid and crew arrived later than the others after being coned by searchlights, and by the time they bombed at 01.43, no target markers were visible. Few crews were able to make out the impact of their own bombs, and noted only a concentration of fires and considerable amounts of smoke. Post-raid reconnaissance revealed that the Path Finders had, indeed, marked the centre of the city, but the "creep-back" had resulted in much of the bombing falling short. Creep-back was a feature of many large raids, and was caused by crews bombing the first fires they came upon, rather than pushing through to the planned aiming point. It could work for or against the effectiveness of the attack, and, on this night, worked in the Command's favour by falling across the industrial district of Bad-Canstatt, before spreading further back along the line of approach onto the residential suburbs of Münster and Mühlhausen. It was here that the majority of the 393 buildings were destroyed and more than nine hundred others severely damaged. The squadron's ED752 failed to return with the crew of F/L Brodrick after crashing in France on the way home. Hit by flak over the target, the Lancaster had lost altitude and was down to 100 feet when passing over Amiens, where it was raked by machine-gun fire and set ablaze. Too low for a bale-out, F/L Brodrick attempted a forced-landing at Sauvillers-Mongival at 03.30, and five of the eight occupants were killed, including S/L Latimer DFC. F/L Brodrick, his bomb-aimer, Lt Muttrie RNVR and rear gunner, Sgt Jones, survived as guests of the Reich, and this was another highly experienced and popular crew whose presence would be missed at Syerston.

S/L Jerrard Latimer had been born with the surname Jefferies in Warwickshire in 1916, and was educated at Warwick School. Shortly after his twentieth birthday, he joined the RAF on a short service commission and his first posting was to 17 Squadron, a Hurricane unit at Kenley, in August 1937. He shot down his first enemy aircraft over Holland on the 11th of May 1940, and, a week later, arrived in France on posting to 85 Squadron as a flight commander in the rank of acting flight lieutenant. Two days later he claimed a BF109 as a "probable", before the squadron was withdrawn to Debden on the 22nd. A further posting in July took him as a flight commander to 310 Squadron, which was forming with Czech pilots at Duxford, and, during the Battle of Britain, he claimed two Me110s, a He111 and a Do17, and shared in the destruction of three other Do17s. His DFC was gazetted on the 1st of October 1940, and this was followed by the Czech Military Cross in December. He was appointed to command the squadron in January 1941, and, having married, changed his name by deed poll to Latimer on the 1st of March. He continued to lead 310 Squadron until the end of June 1941, and, in July, formed and commanded 1455 Flight, a Turbinlite Havoc unit, with which he remained until early 1942. Thereafter, until arriving at 106 Squadron, probably fresh from Lancaster conversion training, his career was undocumented.

Two major operations were planned for the 16th, the main one employing 327 Lancasters and Halifaxes to target the Skoda armaments factory at distant Pilsen in Czechoslovakia, while a force of 271 aircraft, consisting predominantly of Wellingtons and Stirlings, created a large-scale diversion at Mannheim some 240 miles to the west. 197 Lancasters and 130 Halifaxes were detailed for Pilsen, of which 102 of the former were provided by 5 Group. The plan of attack called for the Path Finders to drop route markers at the final turning point, seven miles from the target, which the crews were to then locate visually in the anticipated bright moonlight, and bomb from as low a level as practicable. It was a complicated plan that invited confusion and failure, and the outcome would question the quality of some of the briefings. 106 Squadron made ready fourteen Lancasters, loading them with either a cookie and two 1,000 pounders or all-incendiary loads, before dispatching them from Syerston between 21.00 and 21.20 with S/L Young the senior pilot on duty for the first time and ahead of them a round-trip of some 1,500 miles and nine hours duration.

They had been told to cross the fighter belt at around 1,500 feet, before climbing to a minimum bombing height of 6,000 feet. P/O Rosner and crew were forced to jettison their bomb load and turn back early after ED649 began to judder uncontrollably, but the others pushed on in excellent conditions, becoming somewhat spread out, but arrived in the target area to find the forecast favourable weather conditions, with a layer of eight-tenths cloud at between 8,000 and 15,000 feet, below which, visibility was good and ground features could be made out clearly. The briefings should have made clear that the bombing was to be carried out visually from below the cloud base after making a timed run from the turning-point, which had been marked by TIs. However, many 5 Group crews reported bombing from 7,000 to 10,000 feet visually and on TIs between 01.42 and 01.55, proving that they had failed to understand and comply with the instructions at briefing, and had bombed the turning point, which happened to be an asylum at Dobrany, situated some seven miles to the south-west. The 106 Squadron crews carried out their attacks from 5,000 to 10,000 feet between 01.44 and 02.12, and, on return, some expressed doubts about the accuracy of the raid. Alarm bells should have rung at debriefing when returning crews began to describe bombing on target indicators, which were, in fact, the route markers, and Sgt Reid and crew admitted to a conviction at the time that they had bombed a dummy target, which others were attacking also. Their bombing photo was plotted at 6½ miles from the Skoda factory, and others from the squadron were plotted at seven miles. S/L Young made three runs across the asylum at 5,000 feet before bombing on green target indicators, but he was unable to determine any results. The attack was a dismal failure, compounded by the loss of thirty-six aircraft, split evenly between the two types, and this amounted to a massive 11% of those dispatched. The Mannheim force also suffered heavy casualties amounting to eighteen aircraft, and the combined figure of fifty-four failures-to-return represented the heaviest loss to date in a single night.

A return to the docks at La Spezia was notified to the Lancaster squadrons of 1, 5 and 8 Groups on the 18th, and 8 Group would also contribute five Halifaxes to the overall force of 178 aircraft. The eighty-nine 5 Group Lancasters included thirteen representing 106 Squadron, which departed Syerston between 20.40 and 21.05 with S/L Young the senior pilot on duty. Nine were carrying six 1,000 pounders, two had been loaded with fourteen SBCs of 4lb incendiaries, while the crews of S/L Young and Sgt Munro were sitting on a 5,500lb capital ship bomb. They all negotiated the outward flight across France and the Alps, and arrived in the target area after an outward flight of some four-and-a-half hours to find excellent conditions, but an effective smoke screen blotting out most of the dockyard. They had again become spread out during the flight to the target, and bombing times would range from 01.42 to 02.12. The aiming point was identified visually after a timed run from Palmaria Island to the south, and confirmed by red Path Finder TIs. S/L Young and crew made two runs across the aiming point, picking out the battleships at berth and bombing from 8,000 feet at 01.53 without observing the results, but managed to capture an image of the aiming point. The crews of F/O Thompson, Sgt Robbins and Sgt Howell were the others to bring back an aiming point photo after bombing from 9,000 feet at 01.42, 01.51 and 02.12 respectively. Sgt Munro and crew found the dockyard completely obscured, but made a visual identification of the town and island before carrying out a timed run of sixty-six seconds, and bombing from 8,000 feet also at 01.53 to produce a bomb-plot at 1¼ miles from the aiming point. Sgt Abel and crew reported a large explosion at 01.54, which they took to be an ammunition dump going up. The fires were becoming concentrated as the force set course for home, completely satisfied with their night's work. Photographic reconnaissance revealed that the marking and bombing had missed the dockyards to the north-west, but had caused extensive damage to the railway station and public buildings in the town centre.

Later, on the 19th, awards were announced to a number of squadron members. There was a DFC for W/C Searby and also for F/O Margach, F/L Edmund's bomb-aimer, and P/O Lewis. F/Sgt Leavesley received a Bar to his DFM, and there was a DFM also for Sgt Burcher.

Orders were received on the 20th to prepare for another long-range operation that night, this one against the port of Stettin, situated 640 miles away as the crow flies at the midpoint of Germany's wartime Baltic coast. 5 Group contributed ninety-one Lancasters to the force of 339 aircraft, thirteen of them belonging to 106 Squadron, for which this was a new target, and whose crews learned at briefing that the route would take the bomber stream across the North Sea to a point north of Esbjerg on the Danish coast, before traversing Jutland to then head south-east towards the target. The distance was similar to that for Pilsen, but the mighty Lancaster was still able to lift a cookie and twelve SBCs of 4lb or 30lb incendiaries and carry them all the way. The 106 Squadron element departed Syerston between 21.15 and 21.40 with F/L Browne the senior pilot on duty, and set course for Denmark, which they were to cross at around 5,000 feet in an attempt to avoid night fighters. There were targets, like Duisburg for example, that seemed to enjoy something of a charmed life, and managed to dodge the worst ravages of a Bomber Command attack, but Stettin was not among them, perhaps because of its location near an easily identifiable coastline. On this night, clear skies and good visibility paved the way for the Path Finders to deliver a perfect marking performance, and the 106 Squadron element arrived to find the city basking in moonlight after most had carried out a timed run from a lake on the north-western approaches. The city was laid out before them with the river, built-up area and the docks clearly defined, and the aiming point marked by green TIs. F/O Thompson and crew delivered their load from 14,000 feet at 01.13 in the face of intense flak, evaded a night-fighter over the target, and then came down low to shoot up three trawlers off the Danish coast. F/O Stephens and crew were coned in searchlights during the bombing run, and forced to break off and go on to bomb visually in a Lancaster badly holed by shrapnel. Sgt Munro and crew were the odd-man-out with an 8,000 pounder on board, which failed to release on the first pass across the target. The others carried out their attacks from 12,000 to 14,000 feet between 01.10 and 01.26, and, on return, reported fires raging across the built-up area and the glow from the burning port-city visible for ninety miles into the return journey. F/O Thompson and crew arrived home with a Lancaster showing significant shrapnel damage, and a rear gunner with a leg wound, and it is not known whether this resulted from flak over the target or from one of the many uncharted light flak batteries and flak ships dotted along the Danish coast. It was thirty-six hours before a reconnaissance aircraft captured photographs of the still-burning city, and these revealed an area of one hundred acres of devastation across the centre. Local reports confirmed that thirteen industrial premises and 380 houses had been destroyed at a cost to the Command of twenty-one aircraft, four of them 5 Group Lancasters.

On the 22nd, F/Sgt Page and crew returned from North Africa, having been pressed into service as a taxi driver to transport Field Marshal Wavell and Air Marshal Sir Richard Peirse to Gibraltar, where they picked up a number of staff officers requiring a lift back to the UK. Minor operations occupied the following five nights, until orders on the 26th signalled a return to the Ruhr and Duisburg, for which a large force of 561 aircraft was assembled. The numbers were bolstered by the inclusion of 135 Wellingtons, while 215 Lancasters represented the largest contribution by type. 5 Group was responsible for 105 of them, and 106 Squadron thirteen, which departed Syerston between 23.15 and 00.05 with F/Ls Browne and Edmunds the senior pilots on duty. They set course for the Dutch coast near Alkmaar for the northern approach to the Ruhr, but lost the services of the freshman crew of Sgt Brown to oxygen system failure. The others reached the target area after approaching from the north-east, finding largely clear skies and good visibility, and were guided to the aiming point by red and green TIs. The target was well alight by the time the 106 Squadron crews bombed from 18,000 to 20,000 feet between 02.18 and 02.46 in the face of a hostile searchlight and flak defence. Sgt Yackman and crew were coned by at least thirty searchlights during the bombing run, forcing them to jettison their cookie and twelve SBCs in order to escape. A large orange explosion was witnessed to the east of the aiming point at 02.34, but fires had not gained a hold by the time that the force withdrew, although black smoke was rising through 7,000 feet. Returning crews commented on the volume of fire around the aiming point, and they were confident that this was the most successful raid yet on the city. F/L Edmunds and Sgt Burton brought back aiming point photos as proof of their efforts, and there was, perhaps, a degree of disappointment when post-raid reconnaissance revealed that the attack had fallen short of the city centre and had been focussed around the north-eastern districts under the line of approach. This spared Duisburg yet again from the full weight of a Bomber Command heavy raid, but, even so, local reports confirmed the destruction of more than three hundred buildings, which represented something of a telling blow upon this target. Seventeen aircraft failed to return, but only one of these was from 5 Group.

The largest mining effort of the war to date was mounted on the night of the 27/28th, when 160 crews were briefed to plant their vegetables in the sea lanes off the Biscay and Brittany ports and the Frisians. 106 Squadron contributed four Lancasters, three for Nectarine I and one for Nectarine III, and the crews of Sgts Abel, Howell and Yackman, and F/L Browne took off between 01.20 and 01.30, each carrying six mines. They encountered poor weather conditions in the target area and eight-tenths cloud with a base at 600 feet, and three of them made a timed run after gaining a Gee-fix to the North of Terschelling, while Sgt Howell pinpointed on Juist. All successfully carried out their assigned tasks and returned safely from uneventful sorties. Twenty-four hours later, a new record was set when 207 aircraft were sent mining in northern waters. The six 106 Squadron participants were all captained by NCO pilots, with the crews of Sgts Glaholm and Munro briefed for the Hollyhock garden off Travemunde on the German coast near Lübeck, Sgt Brown for Silverthorn III off the eastern coast of Jutland, Sgts Reid and Robbins for Verbena off Copenhagen and F/Sgt Foulsham for Daffodil, the southern end of The Sound (Oresund) off Saltholm island. They departed Syerston in a five-minute slot from 20.30, and all reached their target areas to pinpoint respectively on Pelzerhaken, Kullen, Saltholm and Falsterbo Odde, contributing to a record number of 593 mines laid. Although the 106 Squadron crews all returned safely, the operation cost twenty-two aircraft, the most ever sacrificed to a gardening operation, and these were largely the victims of light flak while seeking their target areas at low level.

Essen was posted as the target on the 30th, as attention swung once more towards the Ruhr, and would remain upon it almost exclusively now until well into July. A force of 305 aircraft included 101 Lancasters of 5 Group, of which thirteen belonging to 106 Squadron were loaded with a cookie and twelve SBCs each at Syerston and dispatched between 23.55 and 00.15 with F/Ls Browne and Edmunds the senior pilots on duty. A layer of ice-bearing cloud lay across the bomber stream's path over the North Sea, which most crews negotiated to reach the target, where they were greeted, as forecast, by ten-tenths cloud with tops in places as high as 21,000 feet. Red and green Oboe-laid Wanganui flares (skymarkers) identified the aiming point, and F/L Edmunds and crew were among those to carry out a time-and-distance run from green tracking markers to bomb from 20,000 feet at 03.10. The others from the squadron attacked from 18,000 to 21,000 feet between 03.00 and 03.10 in the face of an intense flak barrage, and all had some kind of flare in the bomb sight, or, at least the glow of one, as they released their loads. Returning crews reported the glow of fires beneath the cloud and a number of large explosions, but it was impossible to determine whether or not concentration had been achieved, particularly as bombing photos showed only cloud. Post-raid reconnaissance and local reports confirmed a lack of concentration and the liberal distribution of bombs onto ten other Ruhr locations, particularly Bottrop to the north, but 189 buildings were destroyed and 237 severely damaged in Essen, and, importantly, Krupp sites sustained further damage. The Essen jinx struck 106 Squadron again, when accounting for Sgt Abel and his crew, who were all killed when ED451 crashed north-east of Dorsten. This town, on the northern fringe of the Ruhr, was often used as a route marker for the final run-in, and it seems likely, therefore, that this experienced crew was still outbound at the time of its demise.

This was the squadron's most successful month since becoming equipped with Lancasters a year earlier. During the course of the month the squadron operated on sixteen nights, dispatching a total of 150 sorties and delivering a record bomb tonnage for the loss of four aircraft and crews.

May 1943

May would bring a return to winning ways, with a number of outstanding successes and new records as the Ruhr offensive expanded its horizons to include targets other than Essen and Duisburg. The first of these "new" targets was Dortmund, which had been attacked many times before, but not on the scale that it was about to face on the 4th, when a force of 596 aircraft was assembled, which represented the largest non-1,000 effort to date. 5 Group made available 125 Lancasters, of which fifteen were prepared by 106 Squadron at Syerston and loaded with either a cookie and twelve SBCs or an 8,000 pounder, before taking off between 21.45 and 22.10 with W/C Searby the senior pilot on duty. The crews of F/Sgt Foulsham and Sgt Howell were back home by 01.00 after experiencing engine and oxygen supply issues respectively, leaving the others to push on across Holland to enter Germany to the north of the Ruhr and make their way to the eastern end, where they found clear skies, good visibility and only industrial and smoke haze to spoil the vertical view. Yellow Path Finder tracking skymarkers were used as the starting point for a timed run to the target, while the defences responded with many searchlight cones and intense heavy flak, which would require of some crews extensive evasive action after bombing if they were to vacate the target area intact. The initial Path Finder marking was accurately placed around the city centre, but some of the backing-up fell short, and a decoy site was also successful in luring away a proportion of the bombing. The 106 Squadron crews had become dispersed throughout the bomber stream, and some would contribute to the early stages of the attack, while others arrived much later. The crew of the newly-commissioned P/O Glaholm described perfect weather conditions as they made a timed run from a yellow route marker, and the bomb-aimer had a green target indicator in the bombsight as he released the 8,000 pounder from 19,000 feet at 01.03. They would bring back a bombing photo plotted at two miles west-north-west of the aiming point and described searchlights concentrated in one solid mass over the target accompanied by heavy predicted flak. It was a full thirty minutes later when W/C Searby and crew bombed from 23,000 feet, and their photo would show only fire tracks. In between, the other 106 Squadron participants bombed on red and green TIs from 18,000 to 21,000 feet between 01.04 and 01.33, among them, Sgt Robertson and crew, who were operating with the squadron for the first time. They had dumped their SBCs into the North Sea after the port-outer and starboard-inner engines gave cause for concern, but continued on to bomb on a Gee-fix at 01.20. The two faltering engines failed on the way home, and by the time that they crossed the English coast, the two healthy engines were overheating. To add to their problems, they found an air raid in progress, and landed at the first station they could find, which turned out to be Docking in Norfolk. Returning crews reported many sizeable explosions, including a particularly large on at 01.12, which may have been the one reported by a 50 Squadron crew, who described flames erupting to a height of 2,000 feet and burning for ten seconds. Others reported developing fires, the glow from which could be seen, according to some, from 150 miles into the return flight. Post-raid reconnaissance revealed that approximately half of the force had bombed within three miles of the aiming point, and had destroyed 1,218 buildings and seriously damaged more than two thousand others. Local reports confirmed a death toll of 693 people, which was a record from a Bomber Command attack. It was not a one-sided affair, however, and the loss of thirty-one aircraft was a foretaste of what was in store for the bomber crews operating over "Happy Valley" for what remained of the campaign.

W/C Searby's brief spell of command came to an end on the 9th, when he was posted to 8 Group to command 83 Squadron, whose previous commander, W/C Gillman, had been lost on the Dortmund operation. W/C Searby had undertaken twenty-six sorties with 106 Squadron, and he would go on to gain fame as the Master Bomber for the operation against Germany's rocket research and development centre at Peenemünde in August. Later on, he would be appointed station commander at Warboys and then Upwood. His successor as commanding officer of 106 Squadron was W/C Edmund "Ronnie" Baxter, who was posted in from 50 Squadron, where he had been gaining operational experience in preparation for a squadron commander post. He was an officer under whom the squadron would continue to display its efficiency and esprit de corps. Baxter had learned to fly at Cambridge in the early thirties before joining the RAF, and was already an experienced pilot in the rank of squadron leader when posted to Bomber Command to serve at 1 Group HQ in early 1942. In May of that year, he moved on to 24 O.T.U in the rank of acting wing commander and served also in the BAT Flight at Abingdon. By the time he reached 1660 Conversion Unit at Swinderby on the 22nd of February 1943, he had more than 950 hours in his logbook. After conversion on a Halifax, he undertook Lancaster training, and arrived at Skellingthorpe on attachment to 50 Squadron on the 2nd of April with 993 hours to his credit. His first operation was undertaken as second pilot to S/L Birch with Essen as the target on the following night.

There were no operations after Dortmund, and the lull took the Command through to the 12th, when Duisburg was posted as the target for a heavy force of 562 aircraft with ten Oboe Mosquitos to take care of the initial marking. 5 Group was responsible for 119 of the 238 Lancasters, and they would be accompanied by 142 Halifaxes, 112 Wellingtons and seventy Stirlings. Fourteen 106 Squadron Lancasters departed Syerston between 23.35 and 00.25 with F/Ls Browne, Edmunds and Hartley the senior pilots on duty. The newly-commissioned P/O Page and his crew turned back early after a gunner reported sick, but the remainder carried on guided by yellow tracking flares, and found ideal bombing conditions with no cloud and good visibility, which helped the Path Finders to mark with great accuracy and focus. The main force crews were able to identify ground features despite the usual hostile response from flak and searchlights, but pushed through to bomb on the concentration of red and green ground markers. P/O Rosner and crew found themselves in the vanguard of the main force element, and were the first from the squadron to deliver their load, a single 8,000 pounder, at 02.02. They were unable to assess the results of their work, but the fires were just starting as they turned away from the target. F/L Browne and crew were among five from the squadron carrying ten 1,000 pounders, which they dropped from 20,000 feet at 02.11, and as they headed for home, witnessed a huge explosion at 02.16. P/O McGregor and crew were the others with an 8,000 pounder on board, and they confirmed the above-mentioned explosion, and brought back an aiming point photo. The others from the squadron, mostly carrying the standard city-busting bomb load of a cookie and twelve SBCs, delivered their attacks on red and green TIs from 18,000 to 20,000 feet between 02.03 and 02.32, and contributed to the first genuinely successful operation against this elusive target. By the time that Sgt Brown and crew wheeled away from the scene, the city centre was a mass of flames. Returning crews were enthusiastic in their descriptions of a large explosion at 02.30 and streets outlined by fire, and some claimed the raid to be the most devastating they had yet witnessed. Their impressions were confirmed by photo-reconnaissance, which revealed extensive damage in the city centre and the Ruhrort Rhine docks complex, the largest inland port in Germany. Local sources recorded 1,596 buildings totally destroyed and reported the Thyssen steelworks to have been hit, while dozens of barges and ships were sunk or damaged. However, many crews were absent from debriefing at stations across the Command, and it soon became clear that the success had been gained at a cost of thirty-four aircraft. The loss rates by type again made interesting reading and confirmed the established food chain, the Lancasters sustaining a 4.2% loss, compared with 8.9% for Wellingtons, 7.1% for Stirlings and 6.3% for Halifaxes. Such was the level of destruction that Duisburg would now be left in peace for a year.

On the following night, the squadron contributed fifteen aircraft to a 5 Group force of 124 Lancasters, which, with thirty-two other Lancasters and twelve Halifaxes from 8 Group, would attempt to rectify the recent failure at the Skoda armaments works at Pilsen. A simultaneous raid on the Ruhr city of Bochum was planned, and would involve 442 aircraft from the other groups, and, perhaps, split the defences. The 106 Squadron element departed Syerston between 21.20 and 21.35 with S/L Young the senior pilot on duty and a 650-mile outward flight ahead of them, which, unusually, would take them north of the Ruhr rather than along the Franco-Belgian frontier and across south-central Germany. S/L Young's rear turret became unserviceable before reaching the Dutch coast and he was forced to turn back, while the crews of P/O Stephens and Sgt Davidson were others with technical problems that prevented them from continuing. This left F/Ls Browne, Edmunds and Hartley now the senior pilots on duty, and the last-mentioned was shot up by flak as he and his crew flew over Münster. Despite the damage, they kept going and arrived in the target area four hours after take-off to find clear skies and good visibility, but with ground haze and a smokescreen to impair the vertical visibility. The Path Finders dropped yellow and white track markers, and red TIs with a fairly good concentration that would have been perfectly adequate over a built-up area, but, at a precision target like the Skoda works, they were too scattered to be effective. The Hartley crew bombed on a red TI from 11,500 feet at 01.26, and saw their 8,000 pounder burst in a built-up area, which their bombing photo would reveal to be two miles north of the aiming point. F/L Edmunds and crew watched their cookie and ten 500 pounders burst alongside the TIs, which their bombing photo would reveal to be three miles west-north-west of the target. F/L Browne and crew bombed the centre of the TIs from 10,000 feet at 01.23, and the point of impact would be plotted at 2¼ miles from the aiming point. The others from the squadron delivered their attacks from 9,500 to 12,000 feet between 01.15 and 01.26, and all but one returned to base to offer the opinion, that, if the TIs had been on the target, the operation had been successful. Sadly, they were found to have missed the factory complex, and most of the bombs had fallen into open country to the north. Some compensation was gained at Bochum, where almost four hundred buildings were destroyed and seven hundred seriously damaged at a cost of twenty-four aircraft, and these were added to the nine Lancasters missing from Pilsen. Among the latter was 106 Squadron's R5611, which was shot down by a night-fighter flown by Hptm Herbert Lütje of III./NJG1 while outbound over Holland, and crashed three miles north of Oldenzaal at 23.42, with no survivors from the crew of Sgt Howell.

There followed a nine-night rest from operations for the heavy brigade, and it was during this period, on the night of the 16/17th, that W/C Gibson assured his place in history, by leading the epic Operation Chastise against the Möhne, Eder and Sorpe Dams. There was good news in the form of a Victoria Cross for Gibson and a DFC for Shannon, but sadness at the loss of former 106 Squadron stalwarts, F/L Hopgood, who was shot down over the Möhne, and Burpee and his crew, who crashed onto the Luftwaffe aerodrome at Gilze-Rijen. It was ironic that the newly-commissioned P/O Burpee had heard of the award of a DFM on the very day that he flew to the Dams. The long lay-off for the squadrons had allowed time for an expansion programme to take place, which would substantially boost the numbers of aircraft available for operations from this point on.

By the time that the next major operation was launched on the 23rd, many of the main force squadrons had added a third or C Flight, which, in most cases, would eventually be hived off to form the nucleus of a brand-new squadron. The giant force of 826 aircraft was the largest non-1,000 force to date, and surpassed the previous record set three weeks earlier by a clear 230 aircraft. The number of available Lancasters had leapt by eighty-eight, Halifaxes by forty-eight, Stirlings by forty, and Wellingtons by forty-one, and their destination for the second time in the month was to be Dortmund. The entire Command was rested and replenished, and ready to resume the Ruhr offensive, and activity on all participating stations was hectic. 5 Group detailed a record 154 Lancasters, and sixteen of them were made ready by 106 Squadron at Syerston, where they were loaded with either the standard Ruhr load of a cookie and twelve SBCs of incendiaries or a single 8,000 pounder. They took off between 21.50 and 22.20 with W/C Baxter the senior pilot on duty for the first time and P/O Crowe DFC and crew back to start a second tour. It was to be a night of poor serviceability for the squadron resulting in five early returns, the first two of which occurred as the Lancasters climbed out over the station as the crews of P/O Page and Sgts Munro and Robbins each suffered the failure of an engine. W/C Baxter and crew were some forty miles out from the Lincolnshire coast when they lost their port-outer engine, while Sgt Davidson and crew had reached the midpoint of the North Sea crossing, when, unaccountably, they gained the impression that their 8,000 pounder had been released prematurely. There must have been red faces after they landed to find the bomb still aboard. The others reached the target area to find clear skies but considerable industrial haze, which, before the advent of Oboe, would have rendered the attack a lottery, but, now, the thirteen Path Finder Mosquitos marked the centre of the city accurately, for their colleagues of the heavy brigade to back-up to maintain the aiming point with red and green TIs. These could be seen by the main force crews from twenty miles away on approach, as could the yellow track markers assisting the early 5 Group arrivals for their time-and-distance runs, among them F/L Edmunds. His bomb-aimer had a red TI in his bombsight as he let the cookie and SBCs go from 20,000 feet at 01.03, but he was not able to distinguish the bursts. The fires were beginning to take hold as they turned away, and then they had to spend a minute shaking off a cone of twenty-five searchlights that had ensnared them. The other squadron crews attacked from 18,000 to 21,800 feet between 01.05 and 01.42, aiming largely at the clusters of red and green TIs, and many explosions and fires were observed, which were merging into a large area of conflagration with thick columns of black smoke rising up through 18,000 feet as the bomber force retreated. Returning crews reported fierce night-fighter activity over the target and on the way home, and this was reflected in the high casualty rate of thirty-eight aircraft, the largest loss of the campaign to date. Almost half of these were Halifaxes and eight were Lancasters, 5 Group posting missing just four crews. Post-raid reconnaissance revealed the operation to have been an outstanding success, which had hit mainly central, northern and eastern districts, where almost two thousand buildings had been destroyed, and some important war industry factories had suffered severe damage and loss of production. The scale of the success was such, that, like Duisburg, this city would remain unmolested by the heavy brigade for a year.

The Ruhr offensive continued with the posting of Düsseldorf as the target on the 25th, for which a force of 759 aircraft was assembled. 5 Group contributed 139 Lancasters, fifteen of them representing 106 Squadron, which departed Syerston between 23.05 and 23.40 with S/L Young the senior pilot on duty. The serviceability gremlins intervened again to bring three crews back early, and, for the second operation running, S/L Young was thwarted by the failure of a turret, this time the mid-upper, while F/O McGregor lost his air speed indicator (a.s.i.), and P/O Yackman most of his instruments. Some crews crossing the Dutch coast were able to observe feverish activity at the target some one hundred miles and thirty minutes flying time away, and arrived there to find the weather conditions less favourable than of late with up to eight-tenths cloud, and a profusion of condensation trails further reducing visibility. The target lay beneath two layers of thin cloud, and the generally poor visibility impacted the Path Finders' ability to back up the Mosquito-laid TIs to the extent that two red TIs were seen to be thirty miles apart.

There were also decoy markers and dummy fire sites operating, which succeeded in causing confusion and prevented a concentration of bombing. The 5 Group crews carried out time-and-distant runs from yellow track markers, before identifying the target visually and by red and green TIs. The 106 Squadron contingent delivered their attacks from between 16,000 and 20,000 feet over a period of forty-two minutes from 01.43, but only F/O Stephens and crew saw the impact of their own bomb. W4242 was attacked by an unidentified enemy fighter, which illuminated the Lancaster with a searchlight, something to which F/O Crowe's mid-upper gunner, Sgt Christie, took exception, and fired a burst which knocked bits off the offender, and sent it down in flames to be claimed as destroyed. Post-raid reconnaissance and local reports confirmed that the raid had failed to achieve concentration, and had developed into an "old-style" scattering of bombs across a wide area, leading to the destruction in Düsseldorf of fewer than a hundred buildings. Twenty-seven aircraft failed to return, five of them belonging to 5 Group, and among them was the one containing 207 Squadron's commanding officer, W/C Parselle.

Harris was not yet done with Essen, and the fifth visitation by the bomber force during the campaign was notified to stations on the 27th, and 518 aircraft made ready. 5 Group put up 133 Lancasters, thirteen of them representing 106 Squadron, which departed Syerston between 21.50 and 22.40 with S/L Young the senior pilot on duty and determined to complete a sortie. There was one early return, and for once it wasn't S/L Young, but F/O Crowe and crew, who had problems with three engines. The others reached the target to be greeted by the forecast six to eight-tenths cloud with tops at 12,000 feet, and had tracking flares to guide them on their time-and-distance run through the forest of searchlight cones and intense and accurate flak. Over the aiming point, Wanganui skymarkers gently descended into the cloud tops, leaving a glow within, while above at 22,000 feet, P/O Yackman and crew were doing their best to avoid the flak. In that regard they were not entirely successful, as the ground crew discovered when they received a badly-holed Lancaster back into their care. In contrast, Sgt Whyatt was on his first operation as crew captain, and he and his crew bombed the target from 20,000 feet at 01.17, before returning safely home to describe the trip as uneventful. The other 106 Squadron crews bombed on white flares and red parachute markers with green stars from 18,000 to 21,000 feet between 00.17 and 01.22, and all but one returned home to make their reports. The Essen jinx struck again, as, among the twenty-three missing aircraft was the squadron's W4842, "Fema Dora", containing the crew of Sgt Robbins. It was learned later from the International Red Cross that they had made an emergency landing on Dutch soil, and all had survived to become PoWs. Post-raid reconnaissance revealed that much of the bombing had fallen short, but 488 buildings had been destroyed, mostly in central and northern districts, and ten nearby towns reported themselves to be victims of collateral damage.

A force of 719 aircraft, including a 5 Group contribution of 129 Lancasters, was assembled on the 29th, to pitch against a new Ruhr target, the conurbation known as Wuppertal, perched on the southern rim of the Ruhr Valley east of Düsseldorf. It consisted of the towns of Barmen and Elberfeld, which were built on the proceeds of rich coal deposits. The aiming point for this night's attack was the Barmen half at the eastern end, for which the 106 Squadron element of eleven Lancasters departed Syerston between 22.20 and 22.45 with S/L Young the senior pilot on duty. There were no early returns among the 106 Squadron contingent, and all negotiated the southern approach to the Ruhr, running the gauntlet of searchlights and flak in the Cologne and Düsseldorf corridor. They were greeted by clear skies over the southern Ruhr, with the usual industrial haze extending up to 10,000 feet, but the yellow tracking flares clearly identified the final turning-point, and, first, concentrated green and then red TIs marked out the aiming point. The 106 Squadron crews carried out their attacks with cookies and incendiaries and a single 8,000 pounder from 18,000 to 21,000 feet between 00.58 and 01.37, and it was clear to all that something extraordinary was taking place as the built-up area beneath them became a sea of explosions and flames with smoke rising very quickly through 15,000 feet. Post-raid reconnaissance revealed this to be the most awesomely destructive raid of the campaign thus far, which devastated by fire a thousand acres, or around 80% of the built-up area, and destroyed almost four thousand houses, five of the six largest factories and more than two hundred other industrial buildings. The shocked and now homeless residents may have been cheered to know that thirty-three aircraft had been brought down, and that more than 220 of their tormentors would not be returning to their homes either. Among the seven missing Lancasters was 106 Squadron's R5677, "Admiral Chattanooga", which had crashed in the target area, killing Sgt Whyatt and his crew, who were undertaking just their second operation together. It would be some time before the human cost could be established at Barmen, but it is now accepted that 3,400 people lost their lives during this savage Saturday night.

This was the final operation of the month, during the course of which the squadron had operated on just seven occasions, dispatching ninety-nine sorties for the loss of three aircraft and crews.

June 1943

There were no major operations at the start of June because of the moon period, and, although 5 Group stations were alerted on most of the first ten days, no operations actually took place. This kept the Path Finder and main force crews kicking their heels on the ground, although, from a positive perspective, this allowed the squadrons time to refresh and replenish, and to ease the new crews into their maiden tour. It was the 11th, when Düsseldorf was briefed out to 783 crews, of which 326 were members of Lancaster squadrons, 162 of them in 5 Group and fifteen of them belonging to 106 Squadron. The armourers winched a cookie, four 500 pounders and a dozen SBCs into eleven of the Lancasters, and an 8,000 pounder and eight SBCs into the others, and they were sent on their way from Syerston between 22.20 and 23.25 with W/C Baxter and S/L Young the senior pilots on duty, the crew of P/O Burton on the final sortie of their first tour and Sgt Bristow and crew on their first. S/L Williamson had recently been posted in to take over as A Flight commander, and he was flying as second pilot with F/L Edmunds. They climbed into heavy cloud, which towered over the North Sea to 24,000 feet and contained static and electrical storms, but this thinned as the target hove into sight to leave just small amounts at 2,000, 5,000 and 10,000 feet, dependent upon their time of arrival on final approach to the target. Those in the vanguard of the main force were drawn on by yellow tracking flares from 01.05, and red skymarkers with green stars at 01.16, while those a little further back in the bomber stream were guided by red and green skymarkers. They carried out their time-and-distance runs to the aiming point five minutes away in bright moonlight, noting that fires were beginning to build and join together. The Paramatta ground markers did not seem to appear until these crews were turning away, but they were clearly visible to those in the rear-guard, who described a sea of flames covering a massive area, and columns of smoke rising through 21,000 feet. The 106 Squadron effort was spread throughout the duration of the raid, and attacks were delivered from 18,000 to 20,000 feet. F/L Hartley and crew were the first from the squadron to bomb, at 01.28, and they described the target burning furiously, and knew already that this was a successful attack. P/O Burton and crew took a photograph of the docks as they bombed at 01.32, before heading home to celebrate the end of their tour, while W/C Baxter and crew saw red markers cascading ahead of them, and released their load at 01.33 only to lose sight of their impact in the cauldron below. Sgt Brown and crew were the last squadron participants over the target, and they bombed from a lowly 14,500 feet at 02.19, before also returning safely home to describe their sortie as "interesting", having been unable to climb beyond 16,000 feet. All returned home to pass on their impressions to the Intelligence Section at debriefing, but, not all squadrons had fared so well, and, when all aircraft had been accounted for, thirty-eight were found to be missing, a figure that equalled the heaviest loss of the offensive to date. To put this figure into context, it represented the equivalent of two standard squadrons plus reserves wiped out in a single operation. Post-raid reconnaissance revealed an area of fire across central districts measuring eight by five kilometres, and local reports confirmed 8,882 individual fire incidents. More than seventy war-industry factories suffered a complete or partial loss of production, 140,000 people were bombed out of their homes and 1,292 lost their lives. Had it not been for an errant Oboe marker attracting a proportion of the bombing onto open country some fourteen miles to the north-east, the destruction would have been greater.

Bochum would face its second heavy visitation of the campaign on the 12th, and a force of 503 aircraft was made ready for the purpose. 5 Group contributed 165 Lancasters, of which sixteen were provided by 106 Squadron and departed Syerston between 22.10 and 22.45 with S/Ls Williamson and Young the senior pilots on duty, but lost the services of F/L Browne, P/O Munro and Sgt Barker and their crews to engine failures, the last-mentioned undertaking their maiden sortie. The bomber stream passed over central Holland and entered Germany to the west of Münster, before turning south for a direct run on Bochum, situated between Essen to the west and Dortmund to the east. It is believed that night-fighters were waiting over Dutch airspace and the frontier region, and a number of bombers fell victim at this stage of the operation. According to the superb book, the Bomber Command War Diaries, by Martin Middlebrook and Chris Everitt, Bochum was completely covered by ten-tenths cloud, but, according to many 5 Group crew reports, they encountered three to six-tenths patchy cloud, and many described almost clear skies and good visibility. The 5 Group crews carried out time-and-distance runs from yellow tracking markers, and had green or red TIs in the bombsights as they let their loads go from 17,000 to 23,000 feet between 01.15 and 01.50. F/L Hartley and crew were experiencing stability problems as they approached the target, and jettisoned four SBCs of incendiaries to avoid stalling. They bombed from 17,000 feet at 01.23 with little manoeuvrability available to the pilot, but he negotiated the return home to land at Wittering. Returning crews offered similar reports of scattered bombing early on, becoming concentrated later, with many large fires taking hold and at least one very large explosion. Heavy predicted flak was accurate up to 20,000 feet and beyond, but defence was described by some as not up to usual Ruhr standard. The glow from the burning city remained visible for a hundred miles into the return flight, and photo-reconnaissance revealed 130 acres of devastation. This was backed up by local reports that 449 buildings had been destroyed and more than nine hundred severely damaged at a cost to the Command of twenty-four aircraft, at least nine of which had fallen victim to night-fighters. Later, on the 13th, awards were announced to a number of squadron personnel, and among the recipients of the DFM were P/Os Glaholm and McGregor.

Following a night's rest, the Ruhr offensive continued at Oberhausen, a major centre of oil production situated between Duisburg to the west and Essen to the east. An all-Lancaster heavy force numbering 197 aircraft contained 108 provided by 5 Group, of which thirteen represented 106 Squadron. They departed Syerston between 22.20 and 22.50 with S/L Williamson the senior pilot on duty, and set course for the Scheldt estuary to bypass Antwerp on their way to the Belgian/German frontier. However, it wasn't long before some of them turned back with technical difficulties, F/L Crowe and crew thwarted by a failed port-inner engine, F/O Hoboken and crew with frozen guns, while P/O Robertson and crew lost their rear turret to a hydraulics failure. F/L Edmunds and crew located the target by means of Path Finder route markers, but, as they passed by Duisburg, they were coned for three minutes in searchlights, and it became necessary to jettison the bomb load in order to escape. Sgt Brown and crew experienced a torrid time after being attacked three times by a Ju88 while on approach to the target. Both combatants sustained damage, and the Lancaster's rear gunner was slightly wounded, but the Ju88 was seen to dive down with black smoke pouring from it, and was claimed as damaged. The others reached the target area to find three to ten-tenths cloud with tops in places at 18,000 feet bathed in very bright moonlight, with tracking flares drifting above from which to make time-and-distance runs. The 106 Squadron crews aimed at reds with green stars and white skymarkers, delivering their attacks from 18,000 to 20,500 feet between 01.22 and 01.37 in the face of intense heavy flak, which continued to chase them out of the target area into the guns of night-fighters. Between them, they accounted for seventeen Lancasters, 8.4%

of the force, and there were two empty dispersals on the 106 Squadron side of Syerston, the first multiple loss to afflict the squadron since the middle of January. Veteran R5551, which had a bulged bomb bay to accommodate an 8,000 pounder, and had been the first Lancaster to carry one over the Alps, fell victim to a night-fighter over Holland, and crashed near Arnhem, killing P/O Brown RCAF and six others of the eight men on board, the sole survivor falling into enemy hands. ED649 crashed in the target area, and the crew, captained by the forty-year-old F/O Oates, who were only a couple of operations into their tour, all lost their lives. Local reports confirmed that the Wanganui flares had been right over the city centre, where 267 buildings had been destroyed and 584 seriously damaged.

While the above operation was in progress, five crews carried out a special night exercise, the significance of which would be apparent a few days hence. On the 16th, 1, 5 and 8 Group stations were notified that Cologne was to be the target for that night, for which a force of 202 Lancasters and ten Halifaxes was made ready. They learned at briefings that there would be no Oboe Mosquitos on hand to mark the target, as that role was to be undertaken by the Path Finder Halifax element and six Lancasters employing H2S. 5 Group detailed eighty Lancasters, of which ten representing 106 Squadron were loaded with the usual mix of high explosives and incendiaries and dispatched between 22.10 and 22.40 with S/L Williamson the senior pilot on duty. Sgt Davidson and crew returned early with intercom failure, and P/O Robertson and crew were attacked by a Ju88 soon after crossing the enemy coast. The combat lasted eight minutes, during which, both aircraft sustained damage and the bomb load was jettisoned. The Path Finders were late on target, and problems with some of the H2S sets led to sparse and scattered marking with solid white flares and reds with green stars. The main force crews found the target under six to ten-tenths cloud, and were provided with green tracking flares from which to carry out their time-and-distance run to the aiming point. S/L Williamson and crew delivered their mixed load of a cookie, four 500 pounders and 30lb and 4lb incendiaries from 22,000 feet at 01.02, but saw no results. They observed a large red glow beneath the clouds and scattered fires, but they were more occupied by a frozen gun in the rear turret, severe icing conditions and condensation trails, the last-mentioned advertising the bomber's presence to enemy night-fighters. They would arrive home safely, but describe their experience as "altogether an uncomfortable trip". The other 106 Squadron crews bombed from 19,500 to 21,000 between 01.07 and 01.14, and a number witnessed a large orange explosion at 01.08, although, generally, they were unable to assess the outcome. The impression was that a proportion of the bombing had been concentrated where intended, but that some crews had been lured away by dummy markers. Local sources suggestions that only around a hundred aircraft had been involved, tended to support this view. Residential districts bore the brunt of the raid, and 401 houses were destroyed, with 13,000 others sustaining damage to some extent, mostly lightly, while sixteen industrial premises and nine railway stations were hit, along with public and utility buildings. Fourteen aircraft failed to return, five of them belonging to 5 Group squadrons.

The recent successes in the Ruhr had been aided by the sheer size of the urban areas below, which all but guaranteed that the bombs would hit something useful, even after smoke had obscured the aiming point TIs. It was a different matter at a small or precision target, however, which would rapidly be enveloped in smoke from the first bombs before the rest of the attacking force had a chance to draw a bead on the aiming point. When, on the 20th, therefore, an attack was mounted under the codename Operation Bellicose against the production site of the Würzburg radar sets, which the enemy was employing very successfully to warn of and intercept Bomber Command raids, a plan was already in place to combat the problem by adopting the oft-used and still-under-development 5 Group time-and-distance method. Briefings actually took place on the day before, when crews learned that the factory was housed in the old Zeppelin sheds at Friedrichshafen, situated on the shore of Lake Constance (Bodensee) on the frontier with Switzerland, and represented a very small target. The plan was to use a designated "Master of Ceremonies" to direct the bombing, much in the manner of Gibson at the Dams, and the officer chosen was the highly experienced G/C Len Slee, the former 49 Squadron commanding officer, with the popular W/C Cosme Gomm, commanding officer of 467 Squadron RAAF, as his deputy. (*Gomm's career was eerily similar to that of Gibson, in that both were born overseas, Gibson in India and Gomm in Argentina, and both slotted a tour on night-fighters between bomber tours.*) 5 Group was to provide the main force element of fifty-six Lancasters, five of them from 106 Squadron, with four others from 8 Group's 97 Squadron to provide the marking for the selected crews at the head of the stream. The plan called for the Channel to be crossed at a standard altitude, before descending gradually to 10,000 feet by the time that Orleans was reached, and, thereafter, to fly at between 2,500 and 3,000 feet all the way to the Rhine. After crossing the Rhine near Strasbourg, they were to climb to their briefed bombing height of between 5,000 and 10,000 feet for the rendezvous over the north-western shore of Lake Constance, and then circle until receiving the start signal.

The 106 Squadron quintet consisted of S/L Young, F/Ls Browne and Hartley and P/Os Reid and Yackman, and they took off in a five-minute slot from 21.45 to join up with the rest of the force. All would make it to the target on a rare night when not a single aircraft from the entire force turned back, despite encountering electrical storms and having to adjust the briefed course. That said, G/C Slee lost an engine over France, and was forced to drop back into the formation and hand over the lead to W/C Gomm, who, on arrival at the target under clear skies and in bright moonlight, became concerned about the hostility of the searchlight and light flak defences. In order to reduce the very real risk of heavy casualties, he decided to add five thousand feet to the bombing height, where, unknown to him, the wind was stronger and would push the bombing towards the north-east. The Path Finder element also had little time to climb to the new height, and this caused a slight delay in the opening of the attack. The first TI fell wide of the aiming point, but the second one was assessed by W/C Gomm to be accurate, upon which he called in the first crews, whose high explosives and incendiaries created the expected smoke and obscured the target. He decided that another TI on the aiming point might still provide a reference for some crews, but the Path Finders were driven off by the searchlights and light flak and abandoned the attempt. The skies were clear and the visibility good as the first wave crews aimed their bombs at the TIs in accordance with Gomm's instructions. S/L Young's bomb-aimer released his cookie and seven 500 pounders from 13,000 feet at 02.48, and watched them burst in the target area. He described very accurate bombing, observing one stick to burst right across the aiming point, and the other crews echoed his remarks. The Path Finders then dropped flares along the shore of Lake Constance, to enable the remaining crews to begin their time-and-distance runs from a pre-determined landmark, fly across the lake to the opposite shore, pick up another landmark 2,000 yards from the target, and continue at a constant speed for the requisite number of seconds to cover the distance to bomb release. The remaining 106 Squadron crews aimed at cascading green TIs from 11,500 to 14,500 feet between 02.50 and 03.00, and the impression was that most of their bombs had straddled the aiming point, some scoring direct hits. Reconnaissance revealed that about 10% of the bombs had hit the factory, causing extensive damage, and other nearby industrial buildings were also afflicted. No aircraft were lost, and the force avoided the night-fighters waiting for their return over France by flying on to bases in North Africa. The 106 Squadron crews landed at Maison Blanche in what was the first of what became known as "shuttle" operations.

While these crews were absent from England, a hectic round of four major operations to the Ruhr in the space of five nights began at Krefeld on the 21st, for which a force of 705 aircraft was assembled. 5 Group contributed ninety-two Lancasters, of which ten represented 106 Squadron, and departed Syerston between 23.00 and 23.35 with F/Ls Edmunds and Crowe the senior pilots on duty. There were no early returns, and all reached the target, situated a short distance to the south-west of Duisburg, and on the opposite side of the Rhine. Conditions in the target area were ideal, with small amounts of thin cloud between 6,000 and 10,000 feet and bright moonlight from a half-moon, which would benefit attacker and defender alike. The Path Finders delivered a near-perfect marking performance, red TIs falling in concentrated fashion to clearly identify the city centre aiming point for the main force crews. The 106 Squadron crews carried out their attacks from 18,500 to 20,200 feet between 01.33 and 02.19, and described a sea of red fire giving off masses of smoke, with one particular jet-black column rising through 18,000 feet as they turned away. All were convinced of the success of the operation, and one crew likened it to the Wuppertal-Barmen raid. There was no hint of troublesome flak or night-fighters, and yet, forty-four aircraft failed to return, the heaviest casualties of the campaign to date, and many of these were lost to the Nachtjagd. Remarkably, only three 5 Group Lancasters were among the missing, while 35 Squadron of the Path Finder Force lost six of its nineteen Halifaxes. Three-quarters of the bombing photos were plotted within three miles of the aiming point, and the 2,306 tons of bombs wiped out by fire an estimated 47% of the built-up area. 5,517 houses were destroyed, the largest number to date at a single target, and more than a thousand people lost their lives.

The medium-sized town of Mülheim-an-der-Ruhr, a close neighbour of Duisburg, Oberhausen and Essen, was most associated with steel production, and also had an important and vibrant docks area. It lies around a dozen miles to the north-east of Krefeld, and it was here that the red ribbon terminated on the target maps at briefings across the Command on the 22nd. A force of 557 aircraft was prepared, of which ninety of the Lancasters were provided by 5 Group, eleven of them representing 106 Squadron, and they departed Syerston between 22.20 and 23.10 with W/C Baxter the senior pilot on duty. As they headed out across the North Sea towards the Dutch coast, they lost the services of Sgt Leonard and crew to engine problems. The others arrived at the target to find small amounts of cumulostratus cloud at between 5,000 and 10,000 feet, with red and green TIs clearly visible and defining the aiming point. The 106 Squadron crews were spread throughout the stream, that of F/L Crowe bombing from 18,500 feet at 01.18, and noting that bombs were falling all around the markers, indicating that the attack was concentrated and accurate. Sgt Barker and crew arrived at the tail end of the raid with their 8,000 pounder, and found a red target indicator to aim at, thus demonstrating the effectiveness of the Path Finder backers-up, who continued to maintain the aiming point. The blockbuster went down from 18,000 feet at 01.56, and added to the destruction that was evident from the many fires. The others bombed from 18,000 to 20,500 feet between 01.20 and 01.53, and witnessed the development of a concentrated area of fire, which was visible from the Dutch coast homebound. Returning crews commented on the intense searchlight and flak response, and the number of night-fighters, and reported that Krefeld was still burning from the night before. Local reports confirmed that the town had suffered severe damage, particularly in the northern districts, where 1,135 houses had been destroyed and more than 12,000 others damaged to some extent. Some two acres of the Vereinigte Stahlwerke A G complex was in ruins, four other factories associated with steel production were damaged and the railway station was obliterated. The road and telephone communications to Oberhausen had been cut, preventing any passage out of the town other than on foot. In fact, some of the bombing had spilled into the eastern districts of Oberhausen, which was linked to Mülheim for air-raid purposes. It was another expensive night for the Command, however, which registered the loss of thirty-five aircraft, with the Halifaxes and Stirlings representing two-thirds of them, and suffering a respective loss rate of 7.7% and 11.8%.

While the Path Finder and main force units were enjoying a night off on the 23rd and girding their loins for the next round of the Ruhr offensive, fifty of the 5 Group Lancasters that had landed in North Africa following the Friedrichshafen raid, took off with two 97 Squadron Path Finder aircraft to bomb the docks at La Spezia on the way home to England. The 106 Squadron crews of S/L Young, F/Ls Browne and Hartley and P/Os Reid and Yackman took off from Maison Blanche in Algeria between 19.30 and 20.05, and arrived in the target area to find clear skies but hazy conditions made worse by a smoke-screen. There appeared to be a degree of confusion in getting the raid started, but a lucky hit on an oil storage facility resulted in a large explosion at 23.41 just as the main force was running-in, and most crews were able to identify the target visually and by red, green and white Path Finder flares. P/O Reid and crew were the first from the squadron to arrive, and decided not to hang around in case the smoke blotted out the target. They carried out a timed run from the headland, and delivered their 1,000 and 500 pounders at 23.57 from 9,500 feet. F/L Hartley and crew were instructed to bomb five hundred yards north of the oil fire, and complied at 00.05 from 12,500 feet. S/L Young and crew received no instructions, and let their load go at 00.06 from 11,000 feet, while the crew of F/L Browne circled at 12,000 feet for forty-five minutes before being ordered to bomb at 00.07. P/O Yackman and crew heard no instruction, and, after circling for thirty minutes, bombed of their own accord from 10,000 feet at 00.22. All returned safely after nine hours aloft, and, at debriefing, moaned about the length of time it had taken for the raid to develop, and the poor communications with the raid controller. The authorities seemed happy to claim the destruction of the oil depot and an armaments store, and declared the operation to be a success.

Having destroyed the Barmen half of Wuppertal at the end of May in one of the most devastating attacks to date, it was time to visit the same catastrophe upon the western half, Elberfeld, for which a force of 630 aircraft was made ready on the 24th. 5 Group managed to support the operation with 103 Lancasters, thirteen of which were provided by 106 Squadron, and they departed Syerston between 22.20 and 22.55 with S/L Williamson the senior pilot on duty. He and his crew flew to the target in five-tenths cloud, which had cleared by the time they arrived shortly before 01.30. The Ruhr defensive ring forced the crews to run the gauntlet of flak well before any individual town or city was reached, and there was a myth that a gap existed between Mönchengladbach and Cologne when a southerly route was in use as on this night. Sgt Davidson and crew were driven off course by intense flak and huge searchlight concentrations, and bombed Düsseldorf as an alternative, while Sgt Leonard and crew were attacked by a night-fighter south-south-west of Düsseldorf, and jettisoned their bombs during a successful evasion. The others ran the usual gauntlet of searchlights and flak from the Cologne and Düsseldorf defence zones, the enemy aided by the formation of condensation trails at between 18,000 and 21,000 feet to advertise the presence of the bomber stream. There seemed to be fewer guns firing at them over the target, where small amounts of cloud with tops at 17,000 feet were insufficient to obscure the ground. The 5 Group crews carried out time-and-distant runs from yellow tracking flares until observing cascading red and green TIs, S/L Williamson and crew watching a red one at 01.32, before bombing on it from 19,000 feet two minutes later. The others from the squadron delivered their standard war loads from 13,500 to 19,100 feet between 01.01 and 01.40, those arriving at the tail end of the attack, when the built-up area was well-alight, describing thick columns of smoke already passing through 19,000 feet and the glow of fires visible from the Dutch coast. Post-raid reconnaissance revealed another massively concentrated and accurate attack, which had reduced to rubble an estimated 90% of Elberfeld's built-up area, including three thousand houses and 171 industrial premises. It had also severely damaged 2,500 houses and dozens of important factory buildings, and the fact that more buildings had been destroyed than damaged, provided a telling commentary on the conditions on the ground. The number of fatalities stood at around eighteen hundred, and some of the survivors might have been cheered to know that thirty-four bombers, containing 240 of their tormentors, would not be returning to England that night. Remarkably, only two of these belonged to 5 Group. The combined loss over these three consecutive Ruhr operations was 113 aircraft and crews, which represented almost two percentage points above what was considered to be sustainable. 106 Squadron posted no crews missing from these operations, but the balance was about to be redressed.

114 Lancasters were made ready on 5 Group stations on the 25th as part of an overall force of 473 aircraft, which were to attack the Ruhr city of Gelsenkirchen, the first major attack on this target since 1941, when it had been a regular destination under the Oil Directive. At briefings, crews were instructed to focus on the Nordstern synthetic oil plant (Gelsenberg A G), which was one of two Bergius-process manufacturers of high-grade petroleum products, particularly aviation fuel, the other being the

Hydrierwerke-Scholven A G hydrogenation plant situated in the north-western suburb of Buer. 8 Group was to provide seven Oboe Mosquitos plus two in reserve to drop route markers and skymark the aiming point, and two to bomb after the main force, but none of its heavy aircraft was to be involved. At Syerston, fourteen 106 Squadron Lancasters were loaded either with a cookie, four 500 pounders and mix of 4lb and 30lb incendiaries or an 8,000 pounder and incendiaries, and took off between 22.30 and 23.00 with S/L Young the senior pilot on duty. The spearhead of the main force arrived before the Path Finders, and, while circling, P/O Rosner's aircraft was hit by flak, which knocked out the oxygen system. He and his crew turned for home, bombing what they believed to be Essen on the way, leaving the others with a blanket of ten-tenths stratus between them and the target, with tops at 10,000 to 15,000 feet. This would not have been a problem for Oboe, had five of the twelve participating Mosquitos not suffered equipment failures, causing the tracking flares to be late and drop in the wrong sequence in a somewhat scattered manner at a time when the crews were contending with an intense flak barrage. Searchlights illuminated the cloud as those from 106 Squadron bombed on red flares with green stars from 17,000 to 20,000 feet between 01.21 and 01.53. A large explosion was witnessed at 01.43, and the glow from the target was visible from the Dutch coast, to which the returning bombers were chased by a large deployment of enemy night-fighters. Post-raid reconnaissance and local reports confirmed that the operation had failed to achieve accuracy and concentration, and, in an echo of the past, bombs had been sprayed all over the Ruhr, leaving Gelsenkirchen largely untouched. Thirty aircraft were missing, and, this time, eight of them were from 5 Group, four alone from 106 Squadron, equalling its worst reversal of the war to date. R5572 crashed in central Holland, and produced the only survivor from among the four crews. The fact that it was the pilot, Sgt Davidson RCAF, who escaped with his life, suggests that the Lancaster may have broken up in the air and thrown him clear. W4256 crashed in northern Holland with the crew of Sgt White, while EE125 was lost without trace with the crew of the B Flight commander S/L Young, and presumably found the sea. W4367 was hit at the Dutch coast and came down in the Ijsselmeer, taking with it the crew of P/O Peter Page. After the war, the land was reclaimed, and the actual crash site is now in the village of Dronten, north-north-east of Harderwijk. Peter came from the village of Gilmorton, a few miles from the Leicestershire town of Lutterworth, where he attended the grammar school and where, a few years earlier, Frank Whittle had formed Power Jets Ltd and built his first jet engine. Peter had married Joan Heaton on the 27th of June 1942, and, therefore, died one day short of their first wedding anniversary, two weeks after which, his daughter was born. His widow would not remarry, and, in 2002, she officiated at the naming of Page Close in honour of her late husband. She passed away some years later.

A series of three operations against Cologne would span the turn of the month, and began on the night of the 28/29th, when 608 aircraft took off in the late evening to deliver what would be the Rhineland Capital's greatest ordeal of the war to date. 5 Group contributed 131 Lancasters, the 106 Squadron element of thirteen departing Syerston between 22.45 and 23.20 with F/Ls Browne, Crowe and Hartley the senior pilots on duty, F/L Crowe now having stepped up temporarily to fill the vacancy of B Flight commander following the loss of S/L Young. The services of Sgt Charters and crew were lost to a rear turret issue when they had been outbound for an hour, but the remainder pressed on to the target area, where they encountered ten-tenths cloud below them at 8,000 to 10,000 feet, with good visibility above. The main force crews were unaware that five of the Oboe Mosquitos had turned back and a sixth was unable to drop its skymarkers, leaving just six to do so, and these were behind schedule by seven minutes and could manage only intermittent flares. The omens for a successful attack were not good, particularly as skymarking was the least reliable method because of drift. F/L Crowe and crew were among the first from the squadron to reach the city, having struggled with an engine problem that prevented them from climbing as high as they would have liked. They bombed at 01.50 from 16,000 feet before observing the first TIs go down, and made their way home in cloud at 4,000 feet. The others from the squadron arrived to find tracking flares and then red flares with green stars over the target, which F/L Hartley's bomb-aimer had in his bombsight as he delivered the load from 19,500 feet at 01.50. He saw no results, but witnessed a large explosion two minutes later. F/L Browne's port-outer engine started to give trouble soon after take-off, and eventually had to be feathered. Just as he opened the bomb doors to run across the target, a night-fighter attacked, and the bomb load was jettisoned over Euskirchen, south-west of the target, during evasive action. The others carried out their attacks from 18,500 to 20,000 feet between 01.48 and 02.17, and deduced from the glow beneath the clouds and the presence of smoke rising through them that they had contributed to a successful operation. This was confirmed by post-raid reconnaissance and local reports, which provided details of forty-three industrial buildings and 6,374 others completely destroyed, and a further fifteen thousand sustaining damage to some extent. The death toll was put at 4,377, the greatest by far from a Bomber Command attack, and 230,000 others had lost their homes for varying periods. By recent standards, the figure of twenty-five missing aircraft could be considered moderate, but that was no consolation to the individual stations with an empty dispersal.

This was the last of eleven operations conducted by the squadron during the month, which generated 125 sorties for the loss of six Lancasters and their crews.

July 1943

106 Squadron began the new month with a mining operation on the night of the 1/2nd, involving three new crews, for whom it would be their maiden operation together. The target area was one of the Nectarine gardens off the Frisians, for which the crews of F/Sgt Hendry, P/O Hayley and F/O Harvey departed Syerston either side of 22.30. Each employed Gee to locate their drop zone, where they delivered a total of eighteen mines at six-second intervals from 2,500 to 4,000 feet between 00.07 and 00.14.

The rest of the squadron was not called upon until the 3rd, when thirteen Lancasters were detailed as part of 5 Group's contribution of 141 to the 653-strong force assembled for the second of the raids on Cologne. They departed Syerston between 22.15 and 23.15 with S/L Williamson the senior pilot on duty, and all would complete the outward flight in favourable conditions, the spearhead of the squadron contingent arriving within sight of the target shortly after 01.00. Ten Oboe Mosquitos were to drop green flares four-and-a-half miles from the target as a preliminary warning, and red, green and white flares and red TIs on the aiming point. On this night, that was on the East Bank of the Rhine in the industrial Deutz district, where the Klöckner-Humboldt-Deutz works manufactured aero-engines and heavy and tracked vehicles for the Wehrmacht, and was served by the nearby Kalk and Gremberg marshalling yards. Fires had already taken hold when F/L Hartley and crew, the point of the 106 Squadron spear, bombed from 20,800 feet at 01.18, a minute ahead of the crew of F/L Browne and two ahead of F/Sgt Foulsham's, and both Hartley and Browne would bring back an aiming point photo. The others found the target to be clearly visible under two to three-tenths cloud at 8,000 feet, and protected by many searchlight cones and a moderate flak defence. Green tracking flares guided the first wave crews to the aiming point, which the Path Finders marked with red skymarkers with green stars and red and green ground markers, achieving great accuracy and concentration, while later crews were drawn on for the final one hundred miles by the sight of the city already burning fiercely. The remaining 106 Squadron crews bombed on red TIs from 18,400 to 20,000 feet between 01.10 and 01.56, and reported the city to be a mass of flames, the glow from which remained visible for 170 miles into the return journey.

Some crews commented on the presence of day fighters over the target, and this was clear evidence of a new tactic being employed by the Luftwaffe. The newly formed JG300 was operating for the first time, employing the Wilde Sau (Wild Boar) tactics, which was the brainchild of former bomber pilot, Major

Hans-Joachim (Hajo) Herrmann. The unit had been formed in June with borrowed standard BF109 and FW190 single-engine day fighters to operate directly over a target, seeking out bombers silhouetted against the fires and TIs. On this night, the unit would claim twelve victories, but would have to share them with the flak batteries, which claimed them also. Unaccustomed to being pursued by fighters over a target, it would take time for the bomber crews to work out what was happening, and, until they did, friendly fire would often be blamed for damage incurred by unseen causes. Post-raid reconnaissance and local reports confirmed another stunningly accurate and concentrated attack, in which twenty industrial premises and 2,200 houses had been destroyed, and 72,000 people bombed out of their homes at a cost to the Command of thirty aircraft.

The series against Cologne would be completed on the 8th by an all-Lancaster heavy force of 282 aircraft drawn from 1, 5 and 8 Groups, with six Oboe Mosquitos to carry out the initial marking. 5 Group provided 151 Lancasters, of which fourteen were made ready by 106 Squadron at Syerston, and took off between 22.10 and 22.35 with F/Ls Browne and Crowe the senior pilots on duty. F/Sgt Bristow and crew had only recently embarked on their first tour, and they took off in ED360 at 22.25, before heading for the east coast. It was not long before an engine fire developed, which forced them to turn for home, and the Lancaster made it as far as the Cambridgeshire Fens before crashing about five miles north-west of Wisbech at 01.40 with a 4,000 pounder still on board. The flight engineer and bomb-aimer were the only survivors after the cookie went up and totally destroyed the Lancaster along with all trace of F/Sgt Bristow and his wireless operator, Sgt Worthington, who are commemorated on the Runnymede Memorial. F/Sgt Brown and crew lost their port-inner engine early on, and also had to abandon their sortie. Their squadron colleagues flew through the tops of towering cumulonimbus as they made their way to the target, where ten-tenths cloud at around 10,000 feet concealed the ground from view. F/L Crowe and crew arrived to find no markers, and bombed on e.t.a., from 20,000 feet at 01.10, confident in their position because of a Gee-fix obtained by the navigator, also named Crowe, just before. Tracking flares guided the rest of the main force crews to the aiming point, but the release-point flares were late, and some crews bombed on e.t.a., before they were deployed. The remaining 106 Squadron crews carried out their attacks from 19,500 to 23,000 feet between 01.13 and 01.30 in the face of an intense flak barrage, and a very large orange explosion was witnessed by some at 01.23. The operation cost a remarkably low figure of just seven aircraft, five of them belonging to 5 Group and two to 106 Squadron. R5573, "Admiral Foo Bang III", fell victim to a night-fighter over Belgium on the way home, and crashed at 01.30 north-north-east of Liege. There were no survivors from the crew of Sgt McLean, who were on their first operation together. ED720 exploded over Cambrai in France while homebound, again as the result of an encounter with a night-fighter, and only one man survived as a PoW from the eight-man crew of American 1Lt Rosner, the squadron veteran, who had recently transferred to the USAAF from the RCAF. Post-raid reconnaissance and local sources revealed another highly successful operation, which had caused extensive damage in north-western and south-western districts, where nineteen industrial premises and 2,381 houses had been destroyed. When the dust had settled over Cologne, the local authorities catalogued the destruction as a result of the three raids of more than eleven thousand buildings, and a death toll of almost 5,500 people, with a further 350,000 rendered homeless.

The Ruhr campaign was winding down by the time that Gelsenkirchen was posted across Lancaster and Halifax stations as the target on the 9th, for which a heavy force of 408 aircraft was made ready supported by ten Oboe Mosquitos. Eleven 106 Squadron Lancasters were among the 112 representing 5 Group, and they departed Syerston between 22.30 and 23.10 with F/L Browne the senior pilot on duty. They made their way to the target above ten-tenths cloud, which stretched over the Ruhr at around 16,000 feet and topped out in places at 20,000 feet. The Path Finder skymarkers were several minutes late, partly as a result of a 50% failure rate of the Oboe equipment, while a sixth Mosquito dropped its markers ten miles to the north. The 106 Squadron crews timed their runs from red and green tracking flares, and P/O

Robertson and crew were the first to deliver their payload, at 01.14 from 21,000 feet, and the crews of F/L Browne and F/Sgt Brown followed up a minute later. None was able to see the results of their efforts, but a glow beneath the clouds encouraged them to be optimistic about the success of the attack. The others from the squadron were over the aiming point between 01.16 and 01.41 delivering their bombs from 19,000 to 21,000 feet onto the Wanganui markers as they drifted into the cloud. Some explosions were reflected in the cloud, one particularly large one at 01.40 lighting up the area like day. However, the impression gained by those taking part was that the raid had fallen short of the recent outstanding successes, and this was confirmed by local reports. To those on the ground, it appeared that the attack had been intended for Bochum and Wattenscheid, which received more bombs than Gelsenkirchen, although the Scholven-Buer hydrogenation plant was among ten industrial sites hit, and limited damage occurred in southern districts. Flak was intense and a number of 106 Squadron Lancasters sustained damage, but all returned home to fight another day.

Although two more operations to the region would be launched late in the month, Harris was already planning his next attempt to shorten the war by bombing and was buoyed by the success of the spring offensive. He could look back on the past four and a half months with genuine satisfaction at the performance of his squadrons, and, as a champion of technological innovation, take particular pride in the performance of Oboe, which had been the decisive factor. Although losses had been grievously high, and the Ruhr's reputation as "Happy Valley" well earned, its most important towns and cities had suffered catastrophic destruction. In Britain, the aircraft factories had more than kept pace with the rate of attrition, while the training units both at home and overseas were pouring eager new crews into the fray to fill the gaps. With confidence high in the ability of his Command to destroy almost any target at will, Harris prepared for his next major campaign, the erasure from the map of a prominent German city in a short, sharp series of maximum effort raids to be launched during the final week of the month.

In the meantime, 1, 5 and 8 Groups were alerted to prepare for a trip to Italy to attack the city of Turin, for which 295 Lancasters were made ready on the 12th. 5 Group put up 130 aircraft, thirteen of them representing 106 Squadron, and they departed Syerston between 22.15 and 22.30 with twenty-four-year-old S/L Philip Brandon-Trye the senior pilot on duty for the first time since his arrival from 207 Squadron on the 1st. He had been serving as a deputy flight commander in the rank of flight lieutenant, and was promoted to acting squadron leader rank to enable him to succeed S/L Young as B Flight commander. There were no early returns, despite having to negotiate poor weather conditions over France, which included violent electrical storms and severe icing, and, after his a.s.i. froze up, F/L Crowe attempted to climb above the cloud to find warmer air. Unable to break through, he tried three times to fly round the high cumulonimbus cloud, but was thwarted each time, and, accepting that he had insufficient altitude to safely cross the Alps, he reluctantly ordered the bombs to be jettisoned and turned back. The others reached the target shortly before 02.00 to be greeted by clear skies and good visibility, and defences up to their usual poor standard, characterised by ineffective searchlights and inaccurate light flak rising to 15,000 feet. Crews were able to identify ground detail and clearly see the Path Finder markers outlining the aiming point, and the 106 Squadron participants bombed from 15,000 to 20,000 feet between 01.46 and 02.20, observing a column of black smoke rising through 12,000 feet as they withdrew. The return route involved a low-level circumnavigation of the Brest peninsula, and many of the thirteen missing Lancasters disappeared without trace into the sea after running into enemy night-fighters in this area. 5 Group posted missing one of its heroes, W/C Nettleton of 44 (Rhodesia) Squadron, who had worn the VC since the epic daylight raid on the M.A.N factory at Augsburg in April 1942. Also missing was 106 Squadron's DV181, from which an indistinct wireless message was received at 06.30 stating, "We are being attacked by enemy f"…... The broadcast was cut off at that point, and it seems certain that P/O Hayley and his crew suffered the same fate as Nettleton, and disappeared into the sea off the French coast. Photo-reconnaissance revealed that both crews had contributed to an accurate attack, that fell predominantly to the north of the city centre, and produced the highest death toll to date at this target of 792 people.

On the 14th, awards were announced to a number of 106 Squadron members, including F/L Edmunds, who received a DFC and F/L Oliver, whose DFM was probably in recognition of his time serving in Gibson's crew while an NCO. There was also a DFM for the now tour-expired P/O Burton. On the 15th, the squadron bade farewell to S/L Williamson, who was posted to Dunholme Lodge to fill the vacancy at 44 (Rhodesia) Squadron created by the loss of W/C Nettleton. This allowed S/L Brandon-Trye to step into his shoes as A Flight commander, rather than replace S/L Young as B Flight commander and provided the opportunity for F/L Crowe to become the permanent successor to the latter, for which he would shortly be promoted to acting squadron leader rank. During a lull in major operations during the mid-month period, 5 Group targeted a number of electricity transformer stations in northern Italy, in an attempt to disrupt electricity supplies to railways ferrying troops and supplies to the battle in Sicily. 617 Squadron carried out its first operation since the Dams on the night of the 15/16th against transformer stations near Bologna and Genoa, and similar targets at Cislago and Bologna were selected for eighteen Lancasters from 5 Group on the following night. 106 Squadron contributed three aircraft to Bologna, captained by F/L Crowe and P/Os Munro and Yackman, who departed Syerston at 22.15, and each made a number of runs across the target at around 2,500 feet, releasing a few of their fourteen 500 pounders each time. The bombs were seen to straddle the aiming point, and the crews followed up with machine gun fire. There were no losses, and the three 106 Squadron crews landed safely at Blida in Algeria after a ten-hour trip.

Tragedy struck on the afternoon of the 18th, when a number of senior officers attended a gunnery course demonstration run by 1485 Bombing and Gunnery Flight at Fulbeck. G/C Odbert, the Irish station commander at Syerston, and 106 Squadron's S/L Brandon-Trye, were among those invited to witness the "5 Group corkscrew" evasive manoeuvre, and it was decided that they should do this at first hand rather than from the ground. The students, who had been intended to fly on this fighter affiliation exercise were dismissed, and the four officers climbed aboard the Wellington to join the pilot, W/O Heard, and the gunnery instructor, Sgt Breslin. The fighter was a Miles Martinet, piloted by F/O Jordan, and, as he made his approach to simulate an attack, and while still two hundred yards behind the Wellington, he watched its starboard wing break off outboard of the engine. It immediately went into a dive, and crashed near Appleby in Lincolnshire, killing all on board.

Hamburg, had been a regular target for the Command throughout the war to date, and had been attacked, amongst other occasions, during the final week of July in 1940, 1941 and 1942. It had been spared by the weather from hosting the first "One Thousand" bomber raid at the end of May 1942, but Harris now identified it as the ideal candidate for destruction under Operation Gomorrah, the intention of which was to cause the maximum impact to the enemy's morale in a short, sharp campaign, employing ten thousand tons of bombs. Hamburg's political status was second only to Berlin, and its value to the war effort in terms of ship and U-Boot construction and other war production was undeniable. However, it suited Harris's criteria also in other respects, its location close to a coastline to aid navigation and make it accessible from the North Sea without the need to spend time over hostile territory, and its relatively short distance from the bomber stations, which allowed a force to approach and retreat during the few hours of darkness afforded by mid-summer. Finally, lying beyond the range of Oboe, which had proved so decisive at the Ruhr, Hamburg had the wide River Elbe to provide a solid H2S signature for the navigators high above.

The bell for round one sounded on the 24th, when orders went out across the Command for a maximum effort against Germany's Second City, for which a force of 791 aircraft was assembled, 143 of the

Lancasters provided by 5 Group, and fourteen of these by 106 Squadron. The crews would be aided by the first operational use of "window", tinfoil-backed strips of paper of precise length, which, when released in bundles into the airstream at a predetermined point, would drift down slowly in vast clouds to swamp the enemy night-fighter, searchlight and gun-laying radar with false returns and render it blind. The device had actually been available for a year, but its use had been vetoed in case the enemy copied it for use against Britain. It was not realized that Germany had, in fact, already developed its own version called Düppel, which it had withheld for the same reason. The 106 Squadron element departed Syerston between 22.15 and 23.00 with W/C Baxter the senior pilot on duty, and, after climbing out over the station, headed for the North Sea to rendezvous with the rest of the bomber stream. At a predetermined point shortly before sighting the enemy coast, the force began to dispense "window", beginning shortly after 00.30, and the effects appeared to be immediate as few fighters rose to meet the approaching bombers. A number of aircraft were shot down over the sea during the outward flight, two of them 103 Squadron Lancasters, but these were off course, and outside of the protection of the bomber stream, and may well have been returning early with technical difficulties.

The efficacy of "window" was made more apparent in the target area, where the crews noticed an absence of the usually efficient co-ordination between the searchlights and flak batteries, and defence appeared random and sporadic. This offered the Path Finders the opportunity to mark the target by visual reference and H2S virtually unmolested, and, although the red and green TIs were a little misplaced and scattered, they landed in sufficient numbers close to the city centre to provide the main force crews with ample opportunity to deliver a massive blow. They were guided in by yellow tracking flares and red and green skymarkers, and those from 106 Squadron reaching the target early on were able to identify ground detail and observe the Path Finder TIs cascading. F/O Hoboken and crew bombed first at 01.03 from 19,000 feet, and a number of other crews from the squadron followed up from 18,000 to 20,000 feet during the ensuing seven minutes. By the time that W/C Baxter and crew arrived to bomb at 01.37, there was a concentration of fires and smoke rising to 16,000 feet. F/O Harvey and crew were the last of the squadron participants over the target, and attacked from 23,000 feet at 01.42, before joining the others in a safe return, by which time the column of smoke was rising through 20,000 feet. Post-raid reconnaissance revealed that a six-mile-long creep-back had developed, which cut a swathe of destruction from the city centre along the line of approach, out across the north-western districts, and into open country, where a proportion of the bombing had been wasted. In fact, less than half of the force had bombed within three miles of the city centre during the fifty-minute-long raid, in which 2,284 tons of bombs had been delivered, but, despite that, the city had suffered a telling blow, and fifteen hundred of its inhabitants lay dead. For the Command, it was an encouraging start to the campaign, particularly in the light of just twelve missing aircraft, for which "window" was largely responsible.

While this operation was in progress, the shuttle force that included F/L Crowe and P/O Munro, returned from North Africa, having bombed the docks at Leghorn on the way from 18,000 and 15,000 feet respectively. F/L Crowe lost an engine during the attack, and made the entire return journey from the target on three. A 61 Squadron crew brought back P/O Yackman's Lancaster with two members of his crew, while the others remained at Blida suffering from some form of sickness.

On the following night, and in the expectation that Hamburg would be covered by smoke, Harris switched his force to Essen, where he could take advantage of the body blow dealt to the enemy defensive system by Window. A force of 705 aircraft included 136 Lancasters of 5 Group, the seventeen belonging to 106 Squadron departing Syerston between 22.00 and 22.25 with F/Ls Browne, Hartley and Stephens the senior pilots on duty. There were seventeen early returns from the 5 Group contingent, and among these were the crews of F/Os Hoboken and Harvey because of rear turret and a.s.i failures respectively. The others arrived in the target area to find conditions ranging from clear to three-tenths thin cloud at up to 15,000 feet, and there was a general consensus that searchlights were ineffective and flak not as heavy as might be expected at this target. F/Sgt Foulsham and crew were the first from the squadron to arrive, drawn on by yellow tracking flares and observing red TIs cascade at 00.26, which they bombed four minutes later from 19,700 feet. There was already a concentration of fires, and this would be clearly visible on their aiming point photograph. The remaining 106 Squadron crews continued to pass over the target and bomb for a further forty minutes at altitudes ranging from 18,000 to 21,000 feet, and for once, the Essen jinx did not claim a 106 Squadron crew. Returning crews reported concentrated fires around the aiming point in a one-and-a-half-square-mile area of the city, two large, red explosions at 00.36 and 00.39, and a column of smoke rising through 20,000 feet as they withdrew to the west. Post-raid reconnaissance confirmed the raid to be another outstanding success against this important war materials producing city, with more than 2,800 houses destroyed, while the complex of Krupp manufacturing sites suffered its heaviest damage of the war to date. Twenty-six aircraft failed to return, and just two of them were from 5 Group.

After a night's rest, a force of 787 aircraft was made ready for round two of Operation Gomorrah, for which 106 Squadron bombed-up and fuelled eighteen Lancasters as part of 5 Group's contribution of 155. They departed Syerston between 22.20 and 23.00 with F/Ls Crowe, Hartley and Stephens the senior pilots on duty, but lost the services of the Crowe crew immediately after ED819's starboard-inner engine cut at just 100 feet and caught fire. The fire was extinguished with difficulty, and F/L Crowe made two complete circuits of the airfield before landing in the dark with a full fuel and bomb load on board. The weight of the aircraft had been 62,000lbs, a full 9,000lbs above the safe landing weight. F/O Hoboken and crew turned back early for the second operation running for an undisclosed reason, and the freshman crew of Sgt Large and crew were also unable to complete their sortie because of rear-turret failure. The remainder pushed on towards Hansastadt Hamburg, crossing the coast over the Schleswig-Holstein peninsula to the north, none of them having any concept of the events that were to follow their arrival.

A previously unknown and terrible phenomenon was about to present itself to the world and introduce a new word "firestorm" into the English language. A number of factors would conspire on this night to seal the fate of this great city and its hapless inhabitants in an orgy of destruction quite unprecedented in air warfare. An uncharacteristically hot and dry spell of weather had left the city a tinderbox, and the spark to ignite it came with the Path Finders' H2S-laid red and green TIs, which fell with almost total concentration some two miles to the east of the intended city-centre aiming point, and into the densely populated working-class residential districts of Hamm, Hammerbrook and Borgfeld. To compound this, the main force, which had been drawn on to the target by yellow release-point flares, bombed with rare precision and almost no creep-back, and deposited much of its 2,300 tons of bombs into this relatively compact area. None of this was evident to the crews high above, who were focused on delivering their bombs onto the Path Finder markers, obtaining a photo and then getting the hell out of the target area as quickly as possible. F/L Hartley and crew found the visibility to be poor as they watched TIs cascade at 00.55 and bombed four minutes later from 19,000 feet. They remained on course until the photo-flash confirmed a picture, which would be plotted later at four miles east-north-east of the aiming point, as was that of F/L Browne and crew. The other 106 Squadron crews carried out their attacks from 17,800 to 21,500 feet between 01.01 and 01.39, and observed many explosions and a sea of flames developing below. Those bombing towards the later stages of the raid observed a pall of smoke rising through 20,000 feet, and the glow of fires was reported to remain visible for up to two hundred miles into the return journey.

On the ground, individual fires began to join together to form one giant conflagration, which sucked in oxygen from surrounding areas at hurricane speeds to feed its voracious appetite. Trees were uprooted and flung bodily into the inferno, along with debris and people, and temperatures at the seat of the flames exceeded one thousand degrees Celcius. The defences were overwhelmed, and the fire service unable to pass through the rubble-strewn streets to gain access to the worst-affected areas. Even had they done so, they could not have entered the firestorm area, and, only after all of the combustible material had been consumed, did the flames subside. By this time, there was no-one alive to rescue, and an estimated forty thousand people died on this one night alone. A mass exodus from the city, which would ultimately exceed one million people, began on the following morning, and this undoubtedly saved many from the ravages of the next raid, which would come two nights later. Seventeen aircraft failed to return, reflecting the enemy's developing response to the advantage gained by the Command through "window". No gain was ever permanent, and the balance of power would continue to shift from one side to the other for the next year. For a change, it was the Lancaster brigade that sustained the highest numerical casualties on this night of eleven, six of them belonging to 5 Group. Among them were two from 106 Squadron, ED303, "Flag Day", which crashed in the target area with the crew of Sgt McLeod, who were all killed on just their second operation together, and ED708, which was shot down into the North Sea by a night-fighter on the way home, taking with it the crew of F/Sgt Charters, who were on their eighth operation.

Bomber Command's heavy brigade stayed at home on the following night, while four Mosquitos carried out a nuisance raid on Hamburg, to ensure that the residents' sleep was disturbed. A force of 777 aircraft was put together to continue Hamburg's torment on the 29th, and, this time, 5 Group contributed 148 Lancasters, of which sixteen would represent 106 Squadron. They departed Syerston between 22.10 and 22.50 with W/C Baxter the senior pilot on duty, and lost the services of Sgt Reid and crew to starboard-inner engine failure within an hour. The others continued on to reach the target, which they found under clear skies and protected only by slight ground haze. The plan was to approach from due north to hit the northern and north-eastern districts, which, thus far, had escaped serious damage, but the Path Finders strayed two miles to the east of the intended track, and dropped their markers just to the south of the already devastated firestorm area. W/C Baxter and crew arrived to find no cloud, but considerable smoke at 14,000 feet from the previous attack, and bombed on green TIs at 00.57 from 19,800 feet. They were some ten minutes behind the earliest 106 Squadron arrivals, and squadron aircraft would continue to pass over the target at heights ranging from 17,500 to 22,500 feet until the crews of F/Os Cole and Harvey delivered their loads at 01.25. F/O Harvey and crew reported smoke rising through 17,000 feet, the glow of fires again visible from two hundred miles away, and were among those commenting that the flak and searchlight activity had increased since the surprisingly muted effort of the previous raid. A four-mile creep-back rescued the situation for the Command, by spreading along the line of approach into the residential districts of Wandsbek and Barmbek, and parts of Uhlenhorst and Winterhude. It was another massive blow against this proud city, but, as the defenders began to recover from the effects of Window, so the bomber losses began to creep up, and twenty-eight aircraft failed to return home on this night, five of them from 5 Group.

Before the final round of Operation Gomorrah took place, the curtain on the Ruhr offensive was brought down finally with a raid on the town of Remscheid, situated on the southern edge of the region, about six miles south of Wuppertal, where the main industries were mechanical engineering and tool-making. Up until this point, only twenty-six people had lost their lives in this town as a result of stray bombs, but it was now to face a modest force of 273 aircraft consisting of roughly equal numbers of Lancasters, Halifaxes and Stirlings with nine Oboe Mosquitos to mark out the aiming point. 5 Group put up thirty-nine Lancasters, four of which represented 106 Squadron and took off from Syerston between 22.00 and 22.15 bearing aloft the crews of F/Os Claridge, Hoboken and Wodehouse and P/O Reid. They all reached the target area to find clear skies and good visibility, and bombed on red TIs from 18,000 to 19,000 feet between 01.02 and 01.11, observing the burst of many cookies and a pall of smoke rising through 5,000 feet. Three set off for the return flight with a red glow in the sky behind them, that remained visible as they crossed the enemy coast homebound and gave promise of another Ruhr town left devastated. R5665 fell victim to a night-fighter near the target shortly after bombing, and P/O Reid RCAF, who, it is believed, was American, stayed with the aircraft while his crew parachuted into captivity, and sacrificed his life. The bomb-aimer, P/O Gold RCAF, discovered that his parachute had been burned, and decided to jump to his death from 18,000 feet rather than die in the fire or the crash. Remarkably, he regained consciousness on the ground, and found he had suffered only a dislocated shoulder and knee. The sad news was received from 44 Squadron at Dunholme Lodge that W/C Williamson and crew had failed to return from this, their first operation since his appointment as commanding officer just two weeks earlier, and none had survived. It would be left to a post-war bombing survey to establish that a mere 871 tons of bombs had laid waste to around 83% of Remscheid's built-up area, destroying 107 industrial buildings and 3,117 houses and killing more than a thousand people. Three months war production was lost, and the town's industry never recovered fully. In all, fifteen aircraft failed to return, and the Stirling brigade suffered 10% casualties.

During the course of the month the squadron was involved in twelve operations, including the two "shuttle" raids, and dispatched 128 sorties for the loss of six aircraft and crews.

August 1943

The new month began for 106 Squadron with a training accident on the afternoon of the 1st involving veteran Lancaster R5614. Sgt Fred Mifflin touched down heavily, and opened up the throttles to go round again, just as a cross wind caused him to lose control, and the aircraft ended up in the overshoot area off the runway, where it was destroyed by fire. The entire crew managed to escape, but all sustained injuries to some degree. Sadly, Mifflin would be one of the casualties on a bad night for the squadron nine months hence.

Briefings for the final act of Operation Gomorrah took place on the 2nd, and a force of 740 aircraft was made ready, 128 of the Lancasters provided by 5 Group. 106 Squadron detailed ten Lancasters, which took off from Syerston between 23.20 and 00.20 with no pilots on duty above flying officer rank. The weather conditions were good initially, until 7 degrees East, where a towering bank of ice-bearing cumulonimbus cloud was encountered, which could not be circumnavigated, and stretched upwards to 20,000 feet and beyond. Upon entering it, aircraft were thrown around by violent electrical storms, and it was a hugely terrifying experience beyond anything that most crews had ever experienced, with enormous flashes of lightning, thunder, electrical discharges and instruments behaving erratically. F/Sgt Barker found his rudder was sticking, and in turning to bypass a particularly evil area of storm, it jammed and sent the Lancaster into a diving turn to port. The bomb load was jettisoned, along with some of the fuel, and the sortie was abandoned. F/O Wodehouse and crew reached the German coast before the conditions defeated them, while the crew of F/Sgt Foulsham got as far as the target area, where they found the aircraft threatened by lightning, pounded by hail stones and ringed by static. The engines began to misbehave, and two had to be feathered, whereupon the bombs were jettisoned and the sortie abandoned. The remainder battled through the conditions to reach the target area, which was concealed beneath seven to ten-tenths cloud with tops reported at 25,000 feet, and, while some caught a glimpse of the Elbe and isolated yellow and green Path Finder flares, the majority bombed on e.t.a., and on the glow of fires beneath the cloud and the smoke rising through it. Somehow, F/Sgt Hendry and crew saw a concentration of green markers on the ground from 19,000 feet, and bombed these, while P/O Whetter and his crew picked up red route markers, but saw nothing over the target, and bombed on e.t.a., from 17,800 feet at 02.44. ED358 was attacked by a night-fighter after bombing from 17,000 feet, and had a large hole in a wing to show for it, but F/O Poore and crew came home without further incident. The other 106 Squadron crews carried out their attacks from 16,700 to 19,000 feet before returning to report unanimously an unsuccessful operation, described by some from other units as "pure hell". Little fresh damage occurred in Hamburg as bombs were sprayed over an area of a hundred miles, the main weight perhaps falling on the little town of Elmshorn, some twelve miles to the north-west, but that was of little consequence in view of what had gone before. The Command suffered the relatively heavy loss of thirty aircraft, and some of these had fallen victim to the weather conditions. During the course of the four raids of Operation Gomorrah, the squadron despatched fifty-eight sorties of which fifty-one bombed as briefed and two Lancasters failed to return. *(The Battle of Hamburg. Martin Middlebrook)*.

Italy was now teetering on the brink of capitulation, and Bomber Command was invited to help nudge it over the edge in a mini campaign mounted during August. It began with elements of 1, 5 and 8 Groups assembling a total of 197 Lancasters to attack Genoa, Milan and Turin on the 7th, and, with preparations already in hand for, perhaps, the most important operation of the war to date to be launched in ten days' time, the Turin raid was to be used to test the merits of employing a raid controller, or Master of Ceremonies, in the manner of W/C Gibson during Operation Chastise. The man selected for the job was the former 106 Squadron commanding officer, Group Captain John Searby, currently serving as commanding officer of 83 Squadron of the Path Finders. The Master Bomber technique, involving voice control by VHF, would require him to remain over the target for the duration of the operation, exposed throughout to the defences. He would assess the accuracy of the markers, and advise the main force as to which to aim for, and, once the attack was well under way, he would exhort and encourage the crews to press through with their bombing run and not drop short. As far as G/C Searby was concerned, this was simply a new tactic to improve bombing accuracy, and he would have no concept of the wider implications of his role in future operations. 5 Group contributed thirty Lancasters to the Genoa force and fifty to Milan, 106 Squadron supporting the latter with ten Lancasters, which departed Syerston between 20.50 and 21.10, again with no senior pilots on duty. The target was located without difficulty in good weather conditions, and the 106 Squadron crews carried out their attacks from 16,700 to 19,000 feet between 01.15 and 01.24, the crews of F/O Ham and Sgt Trill bringing back aiming point photos. DV196 was shot down by a night-fighter on the way home and crashed some twenty miles south-west of Dijon in eastern France. F/O Wodhouse and his bomb-aimer were killed, but five of the crew survived, and four of them ultimately evaded capture. Although the Master Bomber experiment at Turin was not entirely successful, experience was gained which would prove useful for the forthcoming Operation Hydra.

The rest of the heavy brigade remained inactive until the 9th, when a force of 457 Lancasters and Halifaxes was made ready for an operation that night against Mannheim. 106 Squadron prepared a dozen Lancasters as part of a 5 Group contribution of 143, and they departed Syerston between 22.50 and 23.15, before climbing out and heading for the rendezvous point over Reading on their way to the Channel coast at Beachy Head. P/O Robertson was back for a second tour, and had flown on the previous operation as a second pilot to F/Sgt Harris. There were no early returns, and they made landfall near Boulogne and adopted a direct course across Belgium to the target, where they were greeted by a layer of five-tenths broken cloud at 4,000 feet and eight-tenths at 10,000 feet. Despite this, the visibility was fair, and the yellow skymarkers and green TIs were sufficient to provide a reference for the bomb-aimers. The 106 Squadron participants carried out their attacks from 15,400 to 20,000 feet between 01.36 and 01.58, and returned home to report a number of very large fires but a generally scattered raid. In fact, according to local reports, 1,316 buildings had been destroyed, forty-two industrial concerns had lost production, locomotives and rolling stock had sustained damage in the marshalling yards and more than fifteen hundred fires of varying sizes had required attention. Six Halifaxes and three Lancasters failed to return, two of the latter belonging to 5 Group.

Nuremberg was posted as the target on the 10th, for which a force of 653 aircraft was assembled, 128 of the Lancasters provided by 5 Group. 106 Squadron briefed twelve crews while their Lancasters were being loaded with a cookie and SBCs of 4lb and 30lb incendiaries and sufficient fuel and reserves for the 1,300-mile round-trip. Take-off was safely accomplished between 21.30 and 22.15 with W/C Baxter the senior pilot on duty, and, after climbing out and forming up, they set course for Beachy Head on the Sussex coast to follow a route similar to that of the previous night. There were no early returns to deplete the squadron's effort, and all arrived in the target area, where conditions also reflected those of twenty-four hours earlier with eight to ten-tenths cloud at 12,000 feet. The Path Finders had prepared a ground-marking plan, and there were no release-point flares to draw the head of the main force on, but W/C Baxter's bomb-aimer had green ones in his bombsight as he emptied the bomb bay from 19,100 feet at 01.05, and he could make out the glow of fires. They may have been the same TIs that F/O Ham's bomb-aimer picked out from seven hundred feet lower at exactly the same time, and he saw several explosions as well as the fires. F/Sgt Hendry and crew arrived thirty-six minutes later to find the target by means of Path Finder flares, but saw no TIs on the ground, and bombed on e.t.a., from 18,000 feet. They were one of nine crews to return safely to Syerston from what was generally described as a quiet trip. P/O Perry and crew related an attack by a Ju88 on the run-in to bomb, but the rear gunner, Sgt Groombridge, claimed to have shot it down. The absentee at debriefing was the crew of the newly commissioned P/O Harris RAAF, whose DV195 had crashed into a north-western suburb, about four miles from the city centre, possibly after colliding with a 619 Squadron Lancaster, and all on board lost their lives. The other 106 Squadron crews reported bombing from 18,000 to 19,500 feet between 01.06 and 01.41, and returned safely to report a good concentration of fires, the glow from which remained visible for 150 miles into the return journey. Post-raid reconnaissance and local reports confirmed that the city had sustained much housing and industrial damage in mostly central and southern districts, and a death toll of 577 people was evidence of the intensity of the bombing.

During the course of the 12th, two forces were prepared for a return to Italy that night, one of 504 Lancasters and Halifaxes to attack Milan, and the other of 152 Stirlings, Halifaxes and Lancasters to target Turin. 5 Group contributed 130 Lancasters to the former, 106 Squadron supporting the endeavour with eleven Lancasters, which departed Syerston between 21.20 and 21.50 in the absence of a senior pilot. The route took the bomber stream via Selsey Bill to Cabourg on the Normandy coast, and then south-east in a straight leg across central France to the northern tip of Lake Bourget, to cross the Alps and skirt southern Switzerland before the final run-in on the target. This represented a round-trip of some sixteen hundred miles, which all from 106 Squadron would complete. They arrived at the target shortly after 01.00 under clear skies with just ground mist to spoil the view, and bombed visually or on yellow flares and green TIs from 17,800 to 20,000 feet between 01.15 and 01.38, observing large fires surrounding the aiming point in the city centre, and a thick column of black smoke rising through 20,000 feet as they turned away. The glow in the sky remained visible for 150 miles into the return flight, and crews were confident of success. The crews of P/O Whetter, F/Sgt Barker and Sgt Trill brought back aiming point photos, and local reports, though short on detail, confirmed that four important war-industry factories had sustained serious damage during August, and most of it probably occurred on this night, as did the majority of the 1,174 fatalities in the city in 1943.

Milan would face two further attacks before the Command's interest in Italy ceased for good, and the first of these was posted on the 14th, for which 1, 5 and 8 Groups put together a force of 140 Lancasters. Fifty-nine of them represented 5 Group, with 106 Squadron providing six, which took off between 21.15 and 21.25 with F/O Claridge the most senior pilot on duty. They all reached the target under clear skies and in good visibility aided by a brilliant moon and Path Finder route markers. The Path Finder target marking with green TIs was accurate and concentrated, and was exploited by the main force crews, those representing 106 Squadron attacking from 14,000 to 17,600 feet between 01.19 and 01.27. Many fires were seen to take hold as the force turned away, and the glow remained visible for a considerable distance into the return flight. The crews of Sgt Trill and F/Sgts Callan and Hay returned with aiming point photos from another successful and uneventful operation.

There was to be no respite for Milan as a force of 199 Lancasters was made ready later on the 15th for a return that night for what would be the last time over Italy for main force Lancasters. 106 Squadron provided eight of the eighty-five 5 Group Lancasters, and they took off from Syerston between 20.20 and 20.40 with Syerston's new station commander, G/C Hodder, flying as second pilot with P/O Robertson, and, also undertaking his first sortie with the squadron as second pilot to F/Sgt Barker was S/L Howroyd, who had been posted in on the 19th of July to replace S/L Brandon-Trye, who, it will be recalled, had been lost in the same accident as G/C Hodder's predecessor. All reached the target to find clear skies, and the Path Finders guided them in with green flares over lake Bourget. Haze and smoke hung over the city from the previous night to spoil to an extent the vertical visibility, but the Path Finders marked the city-centre aiming point with green TIs, and these were bombed to good effect by all of the 106 Squadron crews from 15,000 to 18,000 feet between 00.11 and 00.21. Enemy night-fighters were waiting over France to catch the bombers as they returned home, and, among the seven missing aircraft was that of 467 Squadron's popular commanding officer, W/C Gomm DSO, DFC, who died with all but one of his crew. The consensus of returning crews was of a concentrated attack, but no local report was forthcoming to confirm or deny. P/O Robertson and crew impressed their new station commander by bringing back an aiming point photo, as did P/O Perry and crew. Later that day, the award of a DFC was announced to F/L Hartley and to P/O Crowe, the navigator in the crew of his namesake, F/L Crowe.

The final raid of the war on an Italian city was carried out by 154 aircraft of 3 and 8 Groups against Turin on the following night. A successful raid was claimed at the modest cost of four aircraft, but many of the participating Stirlings were diverted on return, and did not reach their home stations in time to be made ready for the night's highly important operation, for which a maximum effort had been planned. This would deplete the available number of Stirlings by sixty, and heap an even greater responsibility upon the rest of the force to complete the job.

Since the very beginning of the war, intelligence had suggested that Germany was researching into and developing rocket technology, and, although scant regard was given to the reports, photographic reconnaissance had confirmed the existence of an establishment at Peenemünde at the northern tip of the island of Usedom on the Baltic coast. The activities there were monitored through Ultra intercepts and surreptitious reconnaissance flights, and the V-1, known to the photographic interpreters at Medmenham because of its wingspan as the "Peenemünde 20", was captured on a photograph. The brilliant scientist, Dr R V Jones, had been able to gain vital information concerning the V-1's range, which would ultimately be used to feed disinformation to the enemy, largely through the double agent "Zigzag", otherwise known as Eddie Chapman. Unfortunately, Churchill's chief scientific adviser, Professor Lindemann, or Lord Cherwell as he became, steadfastly refused to give credence to the existence and feasibility of rocket weapons, and held stubbornly to his viewpoint even when presented with a photograph of a V-2 on a trailer, taken by a PRU Mosquito in June 1943. It required the combined urgings of Duncan Sandys and Dr Jones to persuade Churchill of the urgency to act, and Operation Hydra was planned for the first available opportunity, which occurred on the night of the 17/18th. Earlier in the day, the USAAF 8th Air Force had carried out its first deep-penetration raids into Germany to attack ball-bearing production at Schweinfurt and the Messerschmidt aircraft plant at Regensburg, and, to the shock of its leaders, had learned the harsh lesson that unescorted daylight raids in 1943 were not viable. The folks at home would not be told that sixty B17s had failed to return. It was vital that the Peenemünde installation be destroyed, ideally, at the first attempt, and a force of 596 aircraft and crews answered the call. 5 Group contributed 117 of the 324 Lancasters, with Dunholme Lodge making ready thirteen, and the rest of the force was comprised of 218 Halifaxes and fifty-four Stirlings.

The operation had been meticulously planned to account for the three vital components of Peenemünde, the housing estate, where the scientific and technical staff lived, the factory buildings and the experimental site. Each was assigned to a specific wave of aircraft, which would attack from medium level, with the Path Finders bearing the huge responsibility of shifting the point of aim accordingly. After last minute alterations, 3 and 4 Groups were given the first mentioned, 1 Group the second, and 5 and 6 Groups the third. The whole operation was to be overseen by a Master of Ceremonies (referred to hereafter as Master Bomber), and the officer selected for this hazardous and demanding role was G/C Searby, whose role was to direct the marking and bombing by VHF, and to encourage the crews to press on to the aiming point, a task requiring him to remain in the target area and within range of the defences throughout the attack. In an attempt to protect the bombers from the attentions of enemy night-fighters for as long as possible, eight Mosquitos of 139 Squadron were to carry out a spoof raid on Berlin, led by the highly experienced G/C Len Slee. In the expectation of encountering drifting smoke as the last wave on target, the 5 Group crews were instructed to employ their oft-used time-and-distance approach to the aiming point, and had practiced this over a stretch of coast near the Wainfleet bombing range at the mouth of the Wash in Lincolnshire, progressively cutting the margin of error from one thousand to three hundred yards.

The 106 Squadron element of nine departed Syerston between 21.15 and 21.35 with W/C Baxter the senior pilot on duty on a night when many squadron commanders elected to fly, in some cases, with fatal consequences. There were no early returns to deplete the squadron's impact, and the overall early-return rate was lower than normal, suggesting that crews had taken to heart the importance of the operation. The various groups made their way individually to a rendezvous point some ninety minutes flying time or three hundred miles from the English coast and sixty miles from Denmark's western coast, where they formed into a stream. Darkness had fallen as they crossed the North Sea, and, twenty miles short of landfall over the southern tip of Fanø island, south of Esbjerg, windowing began, in order to simulate a standard raid on a northern or north-eastern city. Southern Denmark was traversed by the Lancaster brigade at 18,000 feet, twice the altitude required for the attack, but, worryingly, in a band of cloudless sky under a bright moon. They adopted an east-south-easterly course and began to shed altitude gradually during the 240-mile run to the target a little over an hour away, and, at the rear of the stream, the 5 Group crews focussed on the island of Rügen, the ideal starting point for their timed run to Peenemünde, which lay some fifteen miles beyond to the south-east.

There was an early problem for G/C Searby to solve when the initial marking of the housing estate went awry, and some target indicators fell onto the forced workers camp at Trassenheide, more than a mile south of the intended aiming point. Many of the 3 and 4 Group bombs fell here, inflicting grievous casualties on friendly foreign nationals, who were trapped inside their wooden barracks. Once rectified, however, the attack proceeded according to plan, and a number of important members of the technical staff were killed. The 1 Group second-wave crews encountered strong crosswinds over the narrow section of the island where the construction sheds were located, but this phase of the operation largely achieved its aims, and they were on their way home before the night-fighters arrived from Berlin, having been attracted by the glow of fires well to the north. On arrival at Rügen, the 5 Group crews began their timed run, and reached the experimental site to encounter the expected smoke, and bomb on green TIs in accordance with the instructions of the Master Bomber. W/C Baxter and crew were directed by G/C Searby to a cluster of green TIs, which they bombed from 7,000 feet at 00.49, at the same time and altitude of F/L Hartley and crew, who, later, would comment on the lack of flak but evidence of many night-fighters. They and the 6 Group Halifaxes and Lancasters then ran into the night-fighters, which proceeded to take a heavy toll of bombers, both in the skies over the target, and on the route home towards Denmark. They were employing their "Schräge Musik" (jazz music) upward-firing cannons for the first time, and these would prove to be lethal to Bomber Command aircraft over the ensuing eight months. Somehow, the 106 Squadron crews avoided contact, and all returned safely, F/O Ham and crew to report observing at least two bombers falling in flames. The other 106 Squadron crews reported attacking from 6,400 to 8,500 feet between 00.45 and 00.58, and those of P/O Yackman and Sgt Storer were among many from the raid to bring home an aiming point photo. Twenty-nine of the forty missing aircraft came from this third wave, seventeen of them belonging to 5 Group and twelve to 6 Group, which represented a loss rate for the Canadians of 19.7%. The performance of the Master Bomber and the Path Finder Force received praise, and post-raid reconnaissance revealed the raid to have been sufficiently effective to delay the V-2 development programme by a number of weeks, and, ultimately, to force the manufacture of secret weapons underground. The flight testing of the V-2 was eventually withdrawn eastwards into Poland, beyond the range of Harris's bombers, and, thus Peenemünde had been nullified as a threat and would not be targeted again.

Before the next campaign began, the Ruhr city of Leverkusen was posted on the 22nd as the target for a heavy force of 449 Lancasters and Halifaxes with 8 Group Oboe-Mosquitos to provide the initial marking. Situated on the Rhine with Düsseldorf fifteen miles to the north and Cologne seven miles to the south, it was home to a factory belonging to the infamous Interessengemeinschaft Farben chemicals company, better known as I G Farben. Formed in 1925 with the merger of BASF, Bayer and Hoechst, like the Krupp empire in the engineering sector, it had been given a controlling interest in every company engaged in the development and production of synthetic oil and chemicals, and employed slave labour at all of its factories across Germany, including 30,000 from the Auschwitz concentration camp, where it had built a plant. One of the company's subsidiaries manufactured the Zyklon B gas used during the Holocaust to murder millions of Jewish victims. 106 Squadron briefed its eleven crews to aim for the I G Farben plant, while loading each of their Lancasters with a cookie and incendiaries as part of a 5 Group contribution of 108, and they departed Syerston between 20.45 and 21.15 with the A Flight commander, S/L Howroyd, the senior pilot on duty for the first time. After climbing out, they headed for the Belgian coast at Knokke, to follow a well-worn route to the southern Ruhr, which would require them to pass through the searchlight and flak belt near Cologne. All of the others made it safely through the narrow searchlight and flak corridor to reach the target, where ten-tenths cloud topped out at up to 22,000 feet. The conditions forced the use of skymarkers, the least accurate method of target marking, but Oboe-equipment failures forced most crews to bomb on e.t.a., in the absence of markers, until the glow of fires came to their aid as the raid developed, although a small number of crews spotted green TIs on the ground and S/L Howroyd's bomb-aimer had these in his bombsight as he released his load from 19,000 feet at 00.20. He saw the glow of fires beneath the clouds, and a number of other crews reported large explosions, but, in reality, no one had a clue where their bombs had fallen. F/O Cole and crew had a very close encounter with another Lancaster, and P/O Forsyth was attacked four times by a night-fighter, but evaded each time. Bombing was carried out by the remaining 106 Squadron crews in the face of intense flak from 19,000 to 20,000 feet between 00.09 and 00.30, and the glow of fires and the flash of explosions was initially the only confirmation of something happening under the cloud, until a column of smoke was observed to be rising through 12,000 feet. Local reports would reveal that up to a dozen neighbouring towns had been hit, Düsseldorf suffering the destruction of 132 buildings. A modest five aircraft failed to return, and among them was 106 Squadron's JA871, which crashed near Düsseldorf, killing F/O Kain RCAF and his crew, who had only recently embarked on their first tour. An analysis blamed the cloud and a partial failure of the Oboe signal for the scattered attack, which missed the I G Farben factory.

Harris had long believed that the key to ultimate victory lay in the destruction of Berlin, the seat of the Nazi government and the symbol of its power. On the 23rd, orders were received on stations across the Command to prepare for a maximum effort that night against Germany's capital city, which had not been visited by the heavy brigade since the end of March. The crews, of course, could not know that this was to be the first of an eventual nineteen raids on the "Big City", in a campaign which, with an autumn break, would drag on until the following spring. It was a campaign that would test the resolve of the crews to the absolute limit, whilst also sealing the fate of the Stirlings and the Mk II and V Halifaxes as front-line bombers. There are varying opinions concerning the true start date of what became known as the Berlin offensive or the Battle of Berlin, some commentators believing these first three operations in August and September to be the start, while others point to the sixteen raids from mid-November. However, there was little doubt in Bomber Command circles that this was it, a fact demonstrated by the comments in numerous squadron ORBs, which speak of the "long-awaiting Berlin campaign" and similar sentiments. There would be a Master Bomber on hand for this operation, and the officer chosen was Canadian W/C "Johnny" Fauquier, the tough, grizzled and popular onetime bush pilot and frequent brawler, who was enjoying his second spell as the commanding officer of 405 (Vancouver) Squadron, now of the Path Finders, and formerly of 4 Group. The route had been planned to take the bomber stream to a rendezvous point over the North Sea, before crossing the Dutch coast near Haarlem and setting a course to pass between Bremen and Hannover to bypass the southern rim of Berlin. The intention was then to turn back to approach the city from the south-east, and, after bombing, to pass out over the Baltic coast and make for the Schleswig-Holstein peninsula. Finally, seventeen Mosquitos were to precede the Path Finder and main force elements to drop route markers at key points in an attempt to keep the bomber stream on track.

A force of 727 aircraft was assembled, of which 124 Lancasters represented 5 Group, and, as the days shortened towards autumn, so the take-off times became earlier, the thirteen 106 Squadron participants departing Syerston between 20.10 and 20.35 with the newly promoted B Flight commander, S/L Crowe, the senior pilot on duty and undertaking his first operation of the month. The route was to take the bomber stream across the North Sea to make landfall near the known gap in the defences at Egmond, before traversing northern Holland to enter Germany between Meppen to the north and Osnabrück to the south, and pass to the south of Hannover to reach a position south-east of Berlin, before turning sharply to adopt a north-westerly course across the city centre. Those reaching the target area found clear skies and moonlight, but the Path Finders were unable to identify the aiming point in the centre of the city, a result of the inherent difficulties of interpreting the H2S images over such a massive urban sprawl, and marked the southern outskirts instead. Many main force crews then cut the corner to approach the city from the south-west rather than south-east, and this would result in the wastage of many bomb loads in open country and on outlying communities. S/L Crowe and crew located the target by means of red and green TIs and visual identification of a built-up area, and bombed from 19,000 feet at 23.51, before bringing back a photo plotted at 3½ miles south-west of the aiming point. The crews of P/O Robertson and F/O Poore were the last from the squadron to bomb at 00.20, the latter directed to three green TIs by the Master Bomber, whose contribution they described as "very helpful". P/O Robertson commented on the lack of flak but abundance of night-fighters, and he observed a number of combats. In between, the remaining 106 Squadron crews carried out their attacks from 17,500 to 19,000 feet between 23.50 and 00.18, and observed a good concentration of fires as they turned away from the target, by which time smoke had drifted up to 15,000 feet. On the way home over Denmark, the crews of F/Os Cole and Harvey were each attacked by a Ju88, which their gunners shot down after short combats. Returning crews reported large explosions and many fires, the glow from which was visible for at least 140 miles, but, curiously, only a few crews commented on hearing the Master Bomber, and finding his instructions helpful. A new record of fifty-six aircraft failed to return, twenty-three Halifaxes, seventeen Lancasters and sixteen Stirlings, representing a percentage loss rate respectively of 9.1, 5.1 and 12.9, which perfectly reflected the food chain when all three types operated together. Berlin experienced a scattered raid, but, because of the numbers attacking, extensive damage was caused, a little in or near the centre, but mostly in south-western residential districts and industrialized areas a little further east. 2,611 buildings were reported to have been destroyed or seriously damaged, and the death toll of 854 people was surprisingly high, caused largely, perhaps, by a failure to heed the alarms and go to the assigned shelters.

Orders were received on the 27th to prepare for an operation that night against Nuremberg, for which a force of 674 aircraft ultimately lined up for take-off in mid-evening. 5 Group contributed 140 Lancasters, the fifteen representing 106 Squadron departing Syerston between 20.40 and 21.20 with S/L Howroyd the senior pilot on duty. There was a first operation for Canadian F/Sgt Don Cheney and his crew, who had arrived on the squadron on the day of the Peenmünde operation, and who, like their colleagues, F/O Poore and crew, were destined one day to join 617 Squadron. After climbing out in favourable conditions, they headed for the French coast, and, once there, followed the line of the frontier with Belgium until crossing into Germany south of Luxembourg on course for the target, where clear skies and intense darkness prevailed. The Path Finders had been briefed to check their H2S equipment by dropping a 1,000 pounder on Heilbronn, and some crews complied, while others, it seems, experienced technical difficulties. The initial marking was accurate, but a creep-back developed, which the backers-up and the Master Bomber could not correct, in part, because of communications problems, and this resulted in many bomb loads falling into open country, while others hit Nuremberg's south-eastern and eastern districts. F/L Hartley was on his fiftieth operation, and the final one of his second tour, and he and his crew were among the early arrivals over the target, delivering their cookie and incendiaries at 00.31, and observing many large fires. In contrast, P/O Roper and crew were another on their first operation, and they bombed at 00.47, also noting a good concentration of fires already burning. S/L Howroyd was among the last from the squadron to arrive in the target area, and his bomb-aimer focused on the centre of three cascading green TIs from 21,000 feet at 01.02. The others from the squadron delivered their attacks on green TIs from 18,500 to 21,000 feet between 00.30 and 01.08. Crews generally gained an impression of a fairly concentrated and accurate attack, which produced many fires, and described searchlights and night-fighters as numerous. When the 106 Squadron bombing photos were plotted, they were seen to be between 1½ and five miles south-south-east of the aiming point, and this confirmed that much of the bombing had been wasted on open country. Thirty-three aircraft failed to return, eleven of each type, which again revealed the vulnerability of the Stirlings and Halifaxes when operating alongside Lancasters. The loss rate on this night was 3.1% for the Lancaster, 5% for the Halifax and 10.6% for the Stirlings.

The twin towns of Mönchengladbach and Rheydt were posted as the targets for a two-phase operation on the 30th, and it would be the first major attack for both of them. Situated some ten miles west of the centre of Düsseldorf in the south-western Ruhr, they would face an initial force of 660 aircraft of four types, in what, for the crews, was a short-penetration trip across the Dutch frontier, which would be a welcome change from the recent long slogs to eastern and southern Germany. The plan called for the first wave to hit Mönchengladbach, before a two-minute pause in the bombing allowed the Path Finders to head south to mark Rheydt. 106 Squadron made ready fifteen Lancasters as part of a 5 Group contribution of 138, and their crews, none of which was captained by a pilot above flying officer rank, were divided between the first and second waves, which was reflected by the take-off times between 23.10 and 00.30. F/O Roper and crew lost their port-inner engine while outbound, thus ending the recent run of excellent serviceability, but the others reached the target to find good visibility above the seven to ten-tenths cloud at 8,000 feet. A near-perfect display of target-marking by Oboe delivered red and green flares to draw on the main force to bomb with scarcely any creep-back, and the 106 Squadron element carried out their bombing runs from 18,000 to 19,300 feet between 01.57 and 02.42. By the time that F/O Poore and crew turned up at 02.50 after a navigational error had delayed them, there were no markers to aim at, so they chose the centre of three fires, and let their cookie, four 1,000 pounders and 964 incendiaries go from 19,000 feet at 02.54. On return, they reported many fires, the glow from which could be seen from the Dutch coast homebound, and photo-reconnaissance confirmed a highly accurate and concentrated attack, which destroyed more than 2,300 buildings in the two towns, 171 of them of an industrial nature, along with 869 residential properties. Twenty-five aircraft failed to return, and Halifaxes narrowly sustained the highest numerical casualties.

The month ended with preparations for the second of the Berlin operations on the night of the 31st, for which 622 aircraft were made ready, more than half of them Lancasters, and 129 of these were provided by 5 Group. 106 Squadron loaded fourteen of its own with a cookie each and SBCs of 4lb and 30lb incendiaries, and dispatched them between 20.05 and 20.55 with no senior pilots on duty. The route on this night took the bomber stream on an east-south-easterly heading across Texel to a position between Hannover and Leipzig, before turning to pass to the south-east of Berlin and approach the city-centre aiming point on a north-westerly track. The return leg would involve a south-westerly course to a position south of Cologne for an exit over the French coast, but, despite the attempts to outwit the enemy night-fighter controller, he would be able to predict to some extent where to concentrate his fighters. F/O Roper and crew took off late, and realised that they would be alone over the target if they continued, and P/O Yackman and crew also returned early after their port-outer engine gave trouble. The remainder pressed on, and, for the first time, would report the use by the Germans of "fighter flares" to mark out the path of the bombers to and from the target. F/Sgt Hendry RNZAF and crew had crossed the Dutch/German frontier at 18,000 feet when intercepted by a night-fighter shortly afterwards. ED409 crashed near Bramsche on the northern side of the Mittelland Canal, killing the pilot and three others and delivering the three survivors into enemy hands. The Path Finders encountered five to six-tenths cloud in the target area, and this combined with H2S equipment failure and a spirited night-fighter response to cause the markers to be dropped well to the south of the planned aiming point. The main force crews became involved in an extensive creep-back, which would stretch some thirty miles into open country and outlying communities. P/O Whetter and crew were probably the first from the squadron to make an attack, having been guided to the target by route markers and red and green TIs. They bombed from 19,000 feet at 23.38, and described the defences as heavy and accurate. F/O Ham and crew were on their bombing run when JB146 was hit by flak and sustained crippling damage, which included ruptured fuel tanks, and the pilot and wireless operator received serious wounds. They turned for home, streaming fuel, and made it back to a crash-landing on Romney Marshes in Kent at 03.00. F/O Ham's heroics had saved five members of the crew, but he and wireless operator, Sgt Weight, succumbed to their injuries before help came. Meanwhile, the majority of the squadron's aircraft had arrived over the city in a fifteen-minute slot either side of midnight, and bombed from between 17,500 and 20,000 feet, largely untroubled by the defences. One exception was DV229, which lost its hydraulics system to flak, but was skilfully force-landed at home by P/O Storer, without causing any crew casualties or further damage. Returning crews reported many fires over a wide area, some noting that two groups of green TIs were ten miles apart and attracting attention from the main force. The outcome of the raid was a major disappointment, brought about by woefully short marking and a pronounced creep-back, and resulted in the destruction of just eighty-five houses, a figure in no way commensurate with the effort expended and the loss of forty-seven heavy bombers. The percentage loss rates made alarming reading at Bomber Command HQ, the Lancasters with an acceptable and sustainable 3%, the Halifaxes with 11.3% and the Stirlings with 16%.

During the course of the month 106 Squadron operated on thirteen occasions, launching 144 sorties for the loss of five Lancasters and four complete crews.

September 1943

Probably as a result of the heavy losses recently incurred by the Halifaxes and Stirlings, an all-Lancaster force was to conclude the current series of operations against the "Big City". 316 aircraft were made ready on the 3rd, of which 121 were provided by 5 Group, including eleven by 106 Squadron, which departed Syerston between 19.50 and 20.15 with S/L Howroyd the senior pilot on duty. After rendezvousing over the North Sea, the bomber stream crossed the Dutch coast over the Den Helder peninsula, and adopted a direct course of 350 miles, which took them north of Hannover to Brandenburg, some thirty-five miles short of the target. Long, straight legs were rarely employed because of the risk of interception by the Luftwaffe, but the forecast heavy cloud with tops at 18,000 feet accompanied the stream all the way from the Dutch coast to the target area, and helped to keep the enemy at bay. The Path Finders had been briefed to use H2S to navigate their way via the region's lakes to the city centre aiming point, but the cloud miraculously dispersed in time to leave clear skies and allow them to drop ground-marking TIs rather than the less reliable skymarkers. The first TIs fell right over the aiming point, before others crept back for between two and five miles along the line of approach from the west. Fortunately, the backers up maintained the marking as the main force Lancasters came in in a single wave, and, although much of the bombing fell short of the city centre, most of it landed within the city boundaries, principally into the largely residential districts of Tiergarten, Wedding, Moabit and Charlottenburg, and the industrial Siemensstadt, where much useful damage occurred and caused loss of war production. The 5 Group crews carried out a time-and-distance run from yellow track markers and bombed on red and green TIs, those from 106 Squadron from 14,000 to 20,700 feet between 23.27 and 23.39. P/O Large and crew bombed from 20,000 just to starboard of a cluster of green TIs at 23.36, and reported seeing the glow of fires from 150 miles into the return journey. Don Cheney and crew were down at 14,000 feet when they bombed at 23.27, and described a big concentration of fires along with heavy and accurate flak and many searchlights. They had an engine fail over the target, and undertook the long flight home on three. S/L Howroyd and crew had just bombed from 20,000 feet at 23.37, when JA893 was attacked by a night-fighter and a fierce combat ensued, during which the enemy aircraft was shot down and the Lancaster severely damaged. The bomb-aimer, P/O Saxby, was fatally wounded, while the rear gunner, Sgt McKenzie, sustained serious wounds, and he was still alive as the Lancaster was ditched 150 miles off the English coast. His colleagues managed to get him into the dinghy, leaving the body of P/O Saxby behind, and, within hours, a Hudson of 279 Squadron had dropped a lifeboat and a naval launch completed the rescue, but, sadly, not before Sgt McKenzie had succumbed to his wounds. They five survivors were put ashore at Immingham on the north Lincolnshire coast at 05.45, for what would be but a temporary reprieve for four of them. Meanwhile at the target, many fires were observed, which appeared to be merging as the bombers turned towards the north for a return route that would intentionally violate Swedish airspace. Four Mosquitos laid spoof route marker flares well away from the actual track to mislead the night-fighters, but, in the absence of the poorer performing Halifaxes and Stirlings, twenty-two Lancasters failed to return, almost 7% of those dispatched. 106 Squadron's ED385 crashed into woods when east-north-east of Hannover on the way home, and F/O Roper RAAF died with his crew.

Whether by design, or as a result of the loss of 125 aircraft, Berlin was now shelved for the next ten weeks, while Harris sought other suitable targets, of which there were many. He would shortly begin a four-raid series against Hannover stretching over a four-week period, but, first, he focused on southern Germany, beginning on the 5th with the twin cities of Mannheim and Ludwigshafen, which face each other from the East and West Banks respectively of the Rhine. The plan was to exploit the creep-back phenomenon that attended most large operations, by approaching the target from the west, and marking the eastern half of Mannheim, with the expectation that the bombing would spread back along the line of approach across western Mannheim and into Ludwigshafen. A force of 605 aircraft was assembled, which included 108 Lancasters of 5 Group, the 106 Squadron ORB stating, " No replacements being forthcoming to build up our depleted resources, the squadron could offer only eight aircraft for tonight's raid". The next sentence read, "The night proved disastrous". The armourers loaded them with a cookie each and a variety of incendiaries before they departed Syerston between 19.40 and 20.20 with no senior pilots on duty and station commander, G/C Hodder, flying as a passenger with P/O Robertson and crew. After climbing out, they set course for Beachy Head and the Channel crossing and lost F/Sgt Hart and crew to engine failure within an hour and F/Sgt Turnor and crew a few minutes later because of an unserviceable rear turret. The others made it all the way in favourable weather conditions to find clear skies over the target, where the Path Finders performed at their absolute best. P/O Trill and crew were the first from the squadron to arrive, and the bomb-aimer focused on a cluster of five cascading green TIs before releasing the contents of the bomb bay from 18,700 feet at 23.05. The accuracy of their attack would be confirmed by an aiming point photo, something for which they were gaining a reputation. P/O Forsyth and crew were just two minutes behind and a thousand feet higher, and saw nothing of the fall of their bombs, while Sgt Mifflin and crew bombed another cluster of greens from 20,000 feet five minutes later, and their detonations would be plotted at three miles from the aiming point. Sgt Gibbs and crew arrived much later on, and bombed at 23.38, by which time they was able to describe, "a very fine concentration of fires". Those arriving towards the later stages of the raid were drawn on by the burgeoning fires fifty miles ahead, and a number of large, red explosions were observed at 23.12, 23.23 and 23.27, the last of which was followed by a purplish-red mushroom of fire. Searchlights were numerous, but the flak negligible, and it was the abundance of night-fighters that posed the greatest risk to life and limb. Black smoke was rising through 15,000 feet as the bombers withdrew to the west, and the glow from the burning cities was visible for 150 miles into the return journey, which thirty-four aircraft would fail to complete. Thirteen Lancasters, an equal number of Halifaxes and eight Stirlings were missing, and the percentage loss rates continued to tell the same story. Seven 5 Group Lancasters failed to return, two of them belonging to 106 Squadron, W4922 having crashed in or on the banks of the Rhine at Ludwigshafen, killing F/Sgt Taylor RAAF and his crew. DV182 was attacked by a night-fighter, the first burst of fire from which killed the pilot, P/O Robertson, and mortally wounded his flight engineer, Sgt Cunliffe. A fire broke out as the Lancaster went down, and only the bomb-aimer, F/O Willatt, was able to escape from the Lancaster before it crashed north-west of Karlsruhe killing the remaining occupants, including Syerston's station commander, G/C Hodder. Local reports confirmed that both Mannheim and Ludwigshafen had suffered catastrophic destruction, with almost two thousand fires in the latter alone, 986 of them classed as large. Mannheim's reporting system broke down completely, and little detail emerged of this raid, although it would recover in time for the next assault in less than three weeks' time.

Munich was posted as the target on the 6th, for which 106 Squadron made ready seven Lancasters as part of the ninety-two-strong 5 Group element in an overall force of 257 Lancasters and 147 Halifaxes, the Stirling brigade made conspicuous by its absence. They departed Syerston between 19.50 and 20.10 with no senior pilots on duty, each carrying a similar bomb load and adopting the same route as for the previous night. As they closed on the Bavarian capital city with cloud beneath them that varied between five and nine-tenths, they picked up the Path Finder flares over the Ammersee, located twenty-one miles away to the south-west, which was the starting point for the time-and-distance run. It is believed that 106 Squadron's ED819 was on this leg, approaching the target to bomb, when it crashed fewer than ten miles from the centre of Munich, killing P/O Large and his crew. Some ground features, like the River Isar, could be identified, and the red, yellow and green TIs were in evidence as the remaining 106 Squadron crews delivered their attacks from 19,000 to 21,000 feet between 23.34 and 23.50. A large number of fires was observed to be grouped around the markers, but an accurate assessment was not possible, and local reports would suggest that the attack had been scattered across southern and western districts. The searchlights were ineffective because of the cloud, but large numbers of night-fighters were again active, and sixteen aircraft failed to return, thirteen of them Halifaxes, a percentage loss rate of 8.8, compared with 1.2 for the Lancasters.

Fog settled over the bomber stations of Lincolnshire to keep the squadrons on the ground, and when fine weather returned from the 14th, there was no immediate call to arms for most. 5 Group largely left the war to the other groups, during which period attacks were carried out against coastal batteries at Le Portel near Boulogne under Operation Starkey, and industrial and railway targets, also in France. Only 617 and 619 Squadrons were in action on behalf of 5 Group, first on the night of the 15/16th, when the former sent eight Lancasters to attack the raised earthen banks of the Dortmund-Ems Canal at a point south of the twin aqueduct section near Ladbergen, and five of them failed to return. Among those lost was the former 106 Squadron member, F/L Bob Hutchison, who had flown to the Dams as Gibson's wireless operator and had been performing that role in the crew of Gibson's successor, W/C Holden. On the following night, small elements from the two squadrons combined to attack the Antheor viaduct in southern France.

It was not until the commencement of the series of raids on Hannover that 5 Group, as a whole, was roused from its slumber. The irony of such long layoffs was that airmen, despite occupying the most dangerous jobs in the fighting services, grew listless and bored when left to kick their heels, attend lectures and take part in PT, and, no doubt, cheered when the tannoys called them to briefing on the 22nd. They learned that they were to be part of a force of 711 aircraft to attack the ancient city of Hannover, situated in northern Germany midway between the Dutch frontier and Berlin. They were told that it was home to much war industry, including the Accumulatoren-Fabrik A G, manufacturers of lead acid batteries for U-Boots and torpedos, the Continental tyre and rubber factory at Limmer, the Deurag-Nerag synthetic oil refinery at Misburg, the VLW (Volkswagen) metalworks, and the Maschinenfabrik Niedersachsen Hannover and Hanomag factories, which were producing guns and tracked vehicles. and it was also the location of seven Nazi concentration camps, although, this was not known at the time among the Allies. According to Martin Middlebrook and Chris Everitt in Bomber Command War Diaries, the first two operations produced concentrated bombing, but mostly outside of the target, while only the third one succeeded in causing extensive damage, which, if the figures are to be believed, seem to be massively out of proportion. The author contends that the reports of the crews after the first two operations suggest strongly that the damage to Hannover was accumulative over the first three raids and did not result from just one, as will be explained in the following narrative. The telling feature is, perhaps, that no reports came out of Hannover to corroborate the testimony of the crews on the first two raids, although post-raid reconnaissance by the RAF after the second one did show that some of the bombing had fallen into open country, and the Path Finders did admit to at least one poor performance.

Thirteen Lancasters were made ready by 106 Squadron, and they departed Syerston between 18.40 and 19.10 with W/C Baxter the senior pilot on duty, before climbing out and joining up with the other 135 participants from 5 Group for the 430-mile outward leg. The route took the bomber stream out over the north German coast, where some aircraft came within range of the Emden flak defences. P/O Barker's ED420 was hit and the rear turret rendered unserviceable, persuading him to abandon the sortie and drop the cookie and incendiaries on Emden from 20,000 feet at 21.25. Having negotiated this region, the others made their way across the Schleswig-Holstein peninsula, and completed the two-and-a-half-hour outward flight to arrive in the target area and find good weather conditions, but stronger-than-forecast winds pushing the marking and bombing towards the south-east. The 106 Squadron crews carried out their bombing runs from 16,000 to 21,000 feet between 21.25 and 21.49, aiming at red and green TIs and dodging the intense searchlights and heavy flak, which was bursting at around 18,000 feet. W/C Baxter and crew bombed a concentration of seven green TIs from 21,000 feet at 21.33. and reported being attacked by a single-engine fighter, which the gunners drove off. F/O Harvey and crew were attacked by a Ju88 while on the bombing run, and their bombs were dropped unsighted. F/O Poore brought back an aiming point photo, while, for once, P/O Trill's showed only fire tracks, but all crews returned with reports of many fires and a highly successful attack. Some returning crews observed a line of fires developing from west to east, with smoke rising through 14,000 feet, while others claimed that fires ran from the aiming point in a north-north-westerly direction across the city. F/O Cooper and crew were on their first operation together, and they, too, commented on the fires covering a large area, and all were unanimous, that the raid had been highly successful, and that the glow of fires was still visible from the Dutch coast, a distance of two hundred miles. Twenty-six aircraft failed to return, twelve of them Halifaxes, which, again, sustained the highest numerical losses, and, this time, at 5.3%, even exceeded the loss rate of the Stirling.

Let us now examine the claim that the main weight of bombs fell two to five miles south-south-east from the city centre, and that the operation largely failed. Firstly, two to five miles in any city means that the bombing fell within the boundaries, and, therefore, within the built-up area. Secondly, the majority of crews, if not all, reported a highly successful raid with fires right across the city, smoke rising to 14,000 feet as they left the scene and the glow visible from the Dutch coast. It is true that crews were very frequently mistaken in their belief that an attack had been successful, but the evidence on this occasion would seem to confirm their testimony. Decoy fire-sites do not produce a glow visible from a distance of two hundred miles, or sufficient volumes of smoke to reach bombing height during the short duration of a raid, and be dense enough to be visible at night.

On the 23rd, and for the second time in the month, Mannheim was posted as the target, and would face a force, which, at take-off, numbered 628 aircraft, 139 of them 5 Group Lancasters. Fifteen of these were made ready by 106 Squadron, and departed Syerston between 18.45 and 19.15 with S/Ls Crowe and Howroyd the senior pilots on duty. There were no early returns to deplete the squadron's presence at the target, and the bomber stream pushed on across France and into southern Germany, where they encountered largely clear skies and good visibility. At the head of the stream, the Path Finders had dropped red, green and yellow TIs accurately and with concentration into the northern districts, which had not been hit so severely during the previous operation. This allowed the main force crews a clear opportunity to deliver a telling blow, those representing 106 Squadron carrying out their attacks from 17,800 to 21,000 feet between 21.47 and 22.13. The latter time was that of P/O Gibbs and crew, who reported many fires and a pall of smoke rising into the air. The later bombing had spilled over into the northern fringe of Ludwigshafen and out into the nearby towns of Oppau and Frankenthal, where much damage resulted. Returning crews reported that smoke had reached around 6,000 feet as they turned away, and that the glow of fires remained visible for 150 miles into the return journey. Thirty-two crews were absent from debriefing, and, this time, eighteen of them were in Lancasters, compared with seven each for the Halifaxes and Stirlings. This provided a somewhat topsy-turvy and unusual loss-rate of 5.7%, 3.6% and 6% respectively. Post-raid reconnaissance and local reports revealed that 927 houses and twenty industrial premises had been destroyed in Mannheim, and that the I G Farben factory in Ludwigshafen had sustained serious damage, while two thousand fires had to be dealt with in the two cities and more than thirty thousand people were rendered homeless. It proved to be an expensive success for the Command, however, after thirty-two aircraft failed to return, among them 106 Squadron's DV271, which crashed near Neuleiningen, some fifteen miles to the north-west of Mannheim, and only the bomb-aimer, P/O Heatherington, escaped with his life from the crew of P/O Trill.

Hannover was posted as the target again on the 27th, and a force of 678 aircraft made ready. 106 Squadron answered the call with fourteen Lancasters in a 5 Group contribution of 141, and they departed Syerston between 19.10 and 19.50 with S/L Howroyd the senior pilot on duty. A number of new crews, those of

F/O Lee and F/L Ginder, were undertaking their first operation with the squadron, while F/L Poore was on his first since being promoted. They climbed out through ice-bearing cloud, and it may have been this that persuaded the crews of F/O Cooper and P/O Storer to return early with turret malfunctions, probably frozen guns, which was a major cause of "boomerangs" on this night. The others pressed on in the wake of the Path Finders, who were unaware that the weather forecasts on which their performance would be based, were incorrect. The result of that would be to push the marking some five miles from the city centre towards the north of the city, but, at least, the weather improved markedly over Germany to present the crews with clear skies at the target. P/O Barker and crew arrived in the first wave after identifying a lake north-west of the city, and bombed from 20,000 feet at 22.00, reporting that fires were just starting as they turned away. P/O Holbourn and crew were attacked by an FW190 at 19,000 feet over the target, and claimed it as damaged, The other 106 Squadron crews carried out their attacks with cookies and incendiaries from 18,600 to 21,300 feet between 22.00 and 22.22, and observed many fires with smoke rising to 15,000 feet. The Syerston crews returned to appalling weather conditions, but managed to get down safely, and P/O Hanavan and crew brought back an aiming point photo. At debriefings across the Command, crews again reported the glow of fires visible from the Dutch coast, and confidence in the success of the operation was unanimous, giving lie to the claim that little damage resulted. Post-raid photos did reveal many bomb craters in open country, but the fire and smoke evidence did not support decoy fire-sites, and no local report was forthcoming to shed further light. The loss of thirty-eight aircraft was probably something of a shock, but, at least, common sense returned to the statistics to re-establish the status-quo after the topsy-turvy outcome of the Mannheim raid. Seventeen Halifaxes, ten Lancasters, ten Stirlings and one Wellington failed to return, giving loss-rates for the four-engine types of 9% for the Stirling, 7.3% for the Halifax and 3.2% for the Lancaster.

The month ended with an operation to Bochum in the central Ruhr on the 29th, for which 106 Squadron made ready thirteen Lancasters in a 5 Group effort of 111, and they were part of an overall heavy force of 343 aircraft. Before they departed Syerston, the crews of F/O Hoboken and F/L Claridge took off at 18.00 for the long round trip to lay mines in the Privet garden off the port of Danzig. They were followed into the air by the bombing brigade between 18.15 and 18.30 with F/L Ginder the senior pilot on duty, but soon lost the services of P/O Hay and crew to rear turret failure. The others proceeded to the target via the northern tip of Texel, kept on track by two route-marker flares at 20,000 feet, and, after a two-and-a-half-hour outward flight, established their positions visually. The Path Finders marked the aiming point with green TIs, and the bombing was carried out by the 106 Squadron crews from 18,000 to 21,000 feet between 20.46 and 21.08 in the face of a strong searchlight and moderate flak defence. Some returning crews described the target as a mass of flames, with smoke rising rapidly to meet them, while local reports confirmed the destruction of 527 houses, with 742 others seriously damaged. Meanwhile, the gardening duo had reached their destination to find favourable conditions, and had delivered five mines each at 5½-second intervals into the briefed locations, before landing safely after ten hours and ten hours forty minutes aloft.

During the course of the month the squadron operated on seven occasions, dispatching eighty-three sorties for the loss of five aircraft and four complete crews. The ORB mentioned also that the squadron had been operational for three years by this point, and had dispatched 3,050 sorties since the 9th of September 1940.

October 1943

The start of October was a busy time for the Lancaster squadrons, which would be called upon to participate in six major operations in the first eight nights. The month's account was opened on the 1st at Hagen, a relatively small town at the eastern end of the Ruhr, south of Dortmund, which was associated mostly with steel and coal. A moderately-sized heavy force of 243 Lancasters was drawn from 1, 5 and 8 Groups, 5 Group contributing 125 aircraft, fifteen of them representing 106 Squadron, and they were loaded with a cookie and SBCs of incendiaries before departing Syerston between 18.10 and 18.50 with W/C Baxter the senior pilot on duty. They flew out over Skegness aiming for Egmond on the Dutch coast, to then skirt the northern edge of the Ruhr as far as Werl, to the north of the now famous Möhne reservoir, from where they would turn sharply to the south-west to run in on the target. They arrived to find ten-tenths cloud with tops at 8,000 feet and red and green Oboe-laid skymarkers to aim at, and all of the 106 Squadron crews carried out their attacks from 17,200 to 21,000 feet between 20.59 and 21.08. They returned safely to report a column of black smoke rising through the clouds, a large bluish-green explosion at 21.03, the glow of fires beneath the cloud, and an effective Path Finder performance. Only two Lancasters failed to return, in exchange for which, the raid produced the usual housing damage, and local sources confirmed the destruction of forty-six industrial firms, among them a manufacturer of accumulator batteries for U-Boots, and this would have an impact on U-Boot production.

1, 5 and 8 Groups detailed 294 Lancasters on the 2nd, and called their crews to briefings to learn that Munich was to be their target for that night. 5 Group contributed 113 Lancasters, thirteen of them representing 106 Squadron, and they were to adopt the time-and-distance method of bombing. At Syerston the armourers toiled to load a cookie and SBCs of incendiaries into each aircraft, before they took off between 18.30 and 19.10 with S/L Howroyd the senior pilot on duty and all other pilots of commissioned rank. This was rare for 106 Squadron, which, for whatever reason, and more than any other squadron in 5 Group, had been top-heavy with NCO crew captains, most of whom, it seems had now been commissioned. F/O Forsyth and crew turned back before reaching the enemy coast because of starboard-outer engine failure, leaving the others to make landfall in the Dunkerque region, before traversing France to enter Germany south of Strasbourg. They reached the target area after an outward flight of some three-and-a-half hours, and encountered cloud over the Wörthsee, situated some fifteen miles west-south-west of the centre of Munich, which was the starting point for the time-and-distance run. The skies over the city were clear of cloud, but the marking was scattered and led to most of the early bombing falling into southern and south-eastern districts. The 5 Group crews were unable to establish a firm fix on the Wörthsee, and this would lead to a creep-back of up to fifteen miles along the line of approach. The 106 Squadron crews bombed on red and green TIs from 19,000 to 21,000 feet between 22.36 and 22.44, and P/O Hanavan and crew brought back an aiming point photo, while that taken by F/O Cole and crew was plotted at five-and-a-half miles away. At least, for the 106 Squadron crews, it proved to be another quiet trip, while eight Lancasters were lost, six of them representing 5 Group. Returning crews suggested that the raid appeared to be concentrated on the eastern side of the city, and local authorities reported that 339 buildings had been destroyed.

Kassel, as already established, was an industrial city located some eighty miles to the east of the Ruhr and a little beyond the now famous Edersee, where the repairs to the dam were nearing completion. A local sub-camp of the Dachau concentration camp provided slave labour for this and for the city's factories, including the Henschel tank and aircraft works. It would receive two visits from the Command during the month, the first on the 3rd, for which a force of 547 aircraft was assembled consisting of 223 Halifaxes, 204 Lancasters and 113 Stirlings. 5 Group supported the operation with ninety-two Lancasters, of which nine were made ready by 106 Squadron, before they departed Syerston between 18.25 and 18.46 with no senior pilots on duty. There were no early returns as they made their way eastwards via the northern tip of Texel, and all reached the target area to find largely clear skies but thick ground haze. The Path Finder H2S "blind" markers overshot the planned aiming point, and, because of the haze and, possibly, decoy markers, the backers-up, whose job was to confirm the accuracy of the TIs by visual means, were unable to correct the error. The 106 Squadron crews identified the target visually and by green TIs, and bombed from 18,000 to 21,000 feet between 21.17 and 21.36, reporting on their return what appeared to be a good concentration of fires and a pall of smoke rising to meet them. In fact, the main weight of the attack had fallen onto the western suburbs, where the Henschel aircraft and tank factories and the Fieseler aircraft plant were hit, but a stray bomb load had also detonated an ammunition dump at Ihringshausen, situated close to the north-eastern suburb of Wolfsanger, which was left devastated by the blast. P/O Holbourn and crew brought back an aiming point photo. Twenty-four aircraft failed to return, fourteen Halifaxes, six Stirlings and four Lancasters, which gave a loss-rate of 6.3%, 3.2% and 2.9% respectively.

The busy schedule of operations was to continue at Frankfurt on the 4th, for which a force of 406 aircraft was made ready. The American confidence in the ability of its forces to deliver daylight attacks on military and war production targets in Germany had been shaken by the high loss rates, which were not sustainable. Since the first Hannover raid, a small number of 8th Air Force B17s had been flirting with night raids alongside their RAF colleagues, and this night would bring their final involvement. 5 Group detailed ninety-five Lancasters, of which eleven represented 106 Squadron, and they departed Syerston between 18.15 and 18.45 with S/L Howroyd the senior pilot on duty. They had to follow a somewhat circuitous route, which departed England over the Sussex coast and tracked across Belgium as if heading for southern Germany, before swinging to the north-east and passing to the west of Frankfurt for the final run-in of around eighty miles. This added significantly to the mileage, but avoided the flak hotspots from the Dutch coast and north of the Ruhr. The crews of P/Os Holbourn and Lee returned early because of turret and engine failure respectively, while F/O Latham and crew, who were on their first operation together, lost their port-inner engine soon after take-off, but elected to carry on. The bomber stream reached the target after a four-hour outward flight, although an hour of that was generally accounted for in climbing-out and gaining height before setting course. Frankfurt was found to be clear of cloud, and the Path Finders produced a masterful marking performance to leave the city at the mercy of the main force. All but one of the 106 Squadron crews bombed on red and green TIs from 18,500 to 20,000 feet between 21.35 and 21.52, and witnessed a highly-concentrated attack taking place that left the eastern half of the city and the docks area a sea of flames. A large red explosion was observed at 21.37, which threw flames up to 3,000 feet, and smoke was rising through 8,000 feet as the bombers turned away, some crews reporting the glow from the burning city to be visible for 120 miles into the homeward leg. F/O Latham and crew had been late arriving on their three good engines, by which time, there were no markers to aim at and they had been unable to climb above 14,500 feet. They bombed a concentration of fires from that altitude before turning for home, and were picked up by an enemy night-fighter, which the gunners drove off, and they arrived home last at 02.00, having undertaken almost the entire round trip on three engines. The success was gained at the modest cost of ten aircraft, half of which were Halifaxes.

The busy first week of the month concluded with an operation against Stuttgart, for which a force of 343 Lancasters was drawn from 1, 3, 5, 6 and 8 Groups on the 7th. A new weapon in the Command's armoury was introduced for the first time in numbers on this night with the participation of a night-fighter-communications-jamming device called "Jostle". It required a specialist operator in addition to the standard crew of seven, who, though not necessarily a German speaker, could recognise the language, and, on hearing it, jam the signals on up to three frequencies by broadcasting engine noise over them. At 101 Squadron the device was referred to as ABC or Airborne Cigar, and, once proved to be effective, ABC Lancasters would be spread throughout the bomber stream at ninety-second intervals for all major operations, whether or not 1 Group was otherwise involved. The Lancaster would also carry a full bomb load reduced by 1,000lbs to compensate for the weight of the equipment and its operator. 5 Group put up 128 Lancasters, of which fourteen were made ready by 106 Squadron, and they departed Syerston between 20.15 and 20.55 with F/Ls Claridge and Poore the senior pilots on duty. The route crossed

London, and some crews from other squadrons would complain later that they had been coned in searchlights been subjected to heavy anti-aircraft fire. P/O Richards and crew lost the use of their rear turret and turned back before reaching enemy territory, leaving the others to continue on under clear skies, until the cloud began to build up fifty miles from the target, and was at ten-tenths with tops at 10,000 feet over the city. The Path Finders employed H2S and established two areas of marking, which led to bombs falling in many parts of the city from the centre to the south-west. The 106 Squadron crews bombed from 18,000 to 21,500 feet between 00.11 and 00.23, before returning safely to report their impressions of a scattered attack, which cost a remarkably modest four aircraft. Whether or not the presence of the radio-countermeasures Lancasters was responsible, or a Mosquito diversion at Munich, but it was a promising start, and would lead, ultimately, to the formation of a dedicated RCM group, 100 Group, in November. Despite the doubts about the effectiveness of the raid, it had caused substantial damage to the city, with 344 buildings destroyed and more than four thousand damaged to some extent.

The third raid of the series on Hannover was posted on the 8th, and a force of 504 aircraft duly assembled. 5 Group contributed eighty-four Lancasters, eight of them made ready by 106 Squadron, which sent them on their way from Syerston between 22.40 and 23.10 with S/L Howroyd the senior pilot on duty. After climbing out, they set course for the northern tip of Texel, but the crews of P/Os Gibbs and Richards turned back with engine failures before reaching the enemy coast, leaving their colleagues to press on and arrive at their destination shortly after 01.30. They were greeted by largely clear skies and red and green TIs marking out the city-centre aiming point, and bombed from 19,000 to 21,000 feet between 01.34 and 01.39. Having arrived in the early stages of the attack, they saw fires just beginning to take hold, and it became clear as they retreated westwards, that the fires were developing into a serious conflagration, but, curiously, despite the claim by some commentators that this was the one successful raid of the series, there was no mention of the glow being visible from a considerable distance, as had been the case with the first two operations. This time a local report did emerge, which described heavy damage in all districts except for those in the west, with a large area of fire engulfing the central districts. A total of 3,932 buildings was destroyed, and thirty thousand others damaged to some extent, with a death toll of 1,200 people. These statistics seem somewhat excessive for a single operation by fewer than five hundred aircraft, particularly in the absence of the kind of crew reports common to the first two raids, and this adds weight to the author's contention, that the damage was accumulative over the three operations. Some returning crews commented on the success of the diversionary raid on Bremen, which seemed to some to have diluted the defences. Even so, twenty-seven aircraft failed to return, and it emerged later that 106 Squadron's W4242 had crashed on approach to the target, about twenty-five miles to the north-west, and P/O Hay and his crew had been killed. S/L Howroyd and crew, some of whom had survived a ditching on return from Berlin a month previously, were in DV272, which crashed about seven miles south-west of the city, probably after bombing, and only the bomb-aimer, P/O Cromb RCAF, survived to fall into enemy hands.

The Path Finder and main force squadrons would effectively stand down now for a period of ten days, while 8 Group's Mosquitos squadrons took the war to Germany, and this provided the crews with nine nights to catch up on sleep and visit the local hostelries. 106 Squadron had been informed of an impending move from Syerston to a new home named after nearby Metheringham, an airfield still under construction, hewn out of the farmland at Martin Moor, a few miles west of Woodhall Spa, and it was bereft of the permanent buildings and comfortable accommodation so treasured by its soon-to-arrive occupants. An advance party left for Metheringham in mid-month to begin the process, and they found conditions to be very basic, having to endure a cold and miserable existence, sleeping wherever they could find a convenient spot, mostly in the cookhouse and the messes. On the 15th, the award of a DFC was announced to P/O Yackman, and a DFM to F/Sgt Foulsham.

The crews were, no doubt, relieved when the lull in operations came to an end on the 18th with a call on Lancaster stations to attend briefings. The wall map revealed Hannover as the target for the fourth and last time in this series, and the crews learned that this was to be an all-Lancaster affair involving 360 aircraft. 5 Group provided 143 of them, thirteen made ready by 106 Squadron, and they departed Syerston between 17.10 and 17.45 with F/L Ginder the senior pilot on duty and P/O Anderson and crew undertaking their maiden operation. They made landfall over Texel, and continued on an easterly track across Holland aiming for Cloppenburg, and thence Nienburg and Celle, before turning to the south-west to run in on the target close to the Deurag-Nerag synthetic oil plant at Misburg. They remained unmolested by the defences until encountering a nest of night-fighters on crossing the frontier into Germany, and at least thirteen aircraft were brought down during the ensuing forty-five minutes that encompassed the approach and withdrawal phases. A layer of eight to ten-tenths cloud hung over Hannover with tops at 12,000 to 15,000 feet, and these conditions made it difficult for the Path Finders to establish the aiming point. It resulted in them dropping both sky and ground markers, both of which lacked concentration, and this would lead to a scattering of the effort. The 106 Squadron crews bombed on red and green TIs or on release-point flares from 19,500 to 21,000 feet between 20.16 and 20.23, and most found the defences to be light to moderate but not troublesome. This was not the case for R5609, which underwent a torrid time, beginning with an attack by a Me110 during the bombing run, during which the Lancaster sustained severe damage, as did the rear gunner, and was then hit by flak. The bombs were jettisoned, before a Ju88 tried its luck and was beaten off, and there was a final encounter with a flak shell before they vacated the target area, battered and bruised. P/O Richards brought the Lancaster home to a safe landing, and both enemy aircraft were claimed as damaged. Other crews witnessed a colossal explosion at around 20.19, but the strong night-fighter presence dissuaded most from hanging around to assess the outcome further, and the impression of those returning was of a scattered attack. It was established later that most of the bombs had fallen into open country, a disappointment compounded by the loss of eighteen Lancasters. The four raids on Hannover had cost the Command 110 aircraft from 2,253 sorties, a loss rate of 4.9%, but much of the city now lay in ruins and would receive no further attention for a year, when the oil offensive and the close proximity of the Misburg synthetic oil plant to the east, would keep the region in the firing line.

The first major attack of the war on the eastern city of Leipzig was planned for the 20th, and an all-Lancaster force of 358 aircraft representing 1, 5, 6 and 8 Groups assembled. 5 Group was responsible for 140 Lancasters, and 106 Squadron thirteen, which took off from Syerston between 17.00 and 17.30 with the new A Flight commander, S/L Dunn, the senior pilot on duty and first away. The station commander, G/C Pleasance, joined the crew of P/O Perry, and, perhaps, wished he had chosen another night for a jaunt after atrocious weather conditions were encountered outbound, with a towering front of ice and electrical storm-bearing cumulonimbus east of Hannover extending to 25,000 feet, and this persuaded many crews to turn back as engines began to falter and ice-accretion destroyed lift. P/O Anderson had all of his instruments fail when he and his crew were around ninety minutes out, and they were the first to land back at 20.15. The crew of P/O Mifflin lost their intercom soon after take-off, but continued on to Holland, where they bombed Bergen-Alkmaar airfield before turning back and touching down an hour later. P/O Perry and crew lost both inner engines three hours into the flight, when they were twenty-five miles east of Magdeburg and already struggling to maintain height through severe icing, and they also came back. The others pushed on through the front to reach the target after a three-and-a-half-hour outward flight, to then encounter seven to ten-tenths cloud with tops as high as 14,000 feet. The Path Finders had been unable in the conditions to establish and mark the aiming point, leaving crews to bomb on e.t.a., on fires glimpsed through the cloud or on scattered skymarkers, the 106 Squadron attacking from 14,500 to 22,000 feet between 21.06 and 21.13. Sixteen Lancasters failed to return, and those crews that did make it home were unable to offer any useful details at debriefing. F/O Jardine and crew had been the first from the squadron to reach the target area, and they bombed from

22,000 feet at 21.06 on the glow of fires reflected in the clouds, without seeing any route or target markers. They returned to describe it as a long, tedious trip, which achieved doubtful results. The crews of P/O Callan and F/O Latham were a minute behind, and the latter did see a yellow TI and two "Wanganui" flares (skymarkers), and bombed the second flare from 14,500 feet. As on a previous occasion, F/O Latham had been forced to feather an engine while outbound, and carried out most of the operation on three. On approach to the target, S/L Dunn's bomb-aimer believed he saw a red target indicator, and they headed in that direction to bomb from 20,000 feet at 21.12. That proved to be the only suspicion of Path Finder activity seen by this crew, and they returned with a pessimistic assessment of the likely results. F/L Boyle had a similar story to tell of the absence of route markers and target flares, and they bombed on estimated position at 21.13. ED358 failed to arrive back with the others, and news eventually came through that it had crashed in northern Germany, with no survivors from the crew of P/O Hanavan, which included an additional air-bomber.

The final major operation of the month was the second one against Kassel, for which preparations were put in hand on the 22nd. A force of 569 aircraft ultimately stood ready to take off in the early evening, 133 of them 5 Group Lancasters, fourteen provided by 106 Squadron. All were airborne from Syerston between 17.50 and 18.25 with F/L Boyle the senior pilot on duty, but F/O Harvey had his a.s.i and altimeter ice up shortly after take-off, and pressed on in the hope that it would rectify itself. When this had not happened by the time he and his crew had reached the Scheldt estuary, it was decided to turn back, and the bombs were dropped on a flak battery on the island of Schouwen. P/O Barker and crew also came home early after suffering supercharger problems. The others pressed on across Belgium in continuing unfavourable weather conditions, which miraculously improved in the target area to leave clear skies between the bombers and the target, but ten-tenths cloud above them at 24,000 feet. At the opening of the raid, the H2S "blind" markers overshot the city-centre aiming point, leaving the success of the operation reliant upon the visual marker crews backing up, and they did not disappoint. The red and green TIs were concentrated right on the aiming point, and the main force followed up with accurate and concentrated bombing with scarcely any creep-back. The 106 Squadron crews carried out their attacks from 18,000 to 21,000 feet between 21.05 and 21.19, and observed the fires just beginning to take hold as they turned away. P/O Callan's DV274 was hit by flak during the bombing run, and ED593 was attacked by a night-fighter on the way home and severely damaged. Six members of the crew, including the pilot, F/O Hoboken, were wounded, the rear gunner seriously, and, after being driven off once, the fighter returned and inflicted further damage, before it was finally evaded. The pilot skilfully brought the crippled Lancaster back to Syerston, where the weather conditions had deteriorated, and a safe landing was deemed impossible. F/O Hoboken ultimately pulled off a masterful landing at nearby Coleby Grange, and there were no further crew injuries to report.

It was after the sound of their engines had receded that the fires joined together to engulf Kassel in what, in some areas, developed into a firestorm, though not one as fierce as that experienced in Hamburg. The shell-shocked inhabitants emerged from their shelters to find their city devastated and unrecognizable, and, once 3,600 fires had been dealt with, it would be established eventually that more than 4,300 apartment blocks containing 53,000 dwelling units had been destroyed or damaged, representing 63% of the city's living accommodation. This rendered up to 120,000 people homeless, and in excess of six thousand others dead. 155 industrial buildings had also been destroyed or severely damaged, along with numerous schools, hospitals, churches and public buildings. The massively successful operation was achieved at a high cost of forty-three bombers, which represented 7.6% of those dispatched, and twenty-five of them were Halifaxes.

Beginning on the 23rd, stores and equipment began to move eastwards from Syerston to Metheringham, and this would continue for the next two weeks. During the course of the month the squadron operated on eight nights, dispatching 109 sorties for the loss of three aircraft and crews.

November 1943

November brought with it the long, dark, cloudy nights which enabled Harris to return to his main theme, the destruction of Germany's capital city. The next four months would bring the bloodiest, hardest fought air battles between Bomber Command and the Luftwaffe Nachtjagd, and test the hard-pressed crews to the limit of their endurance. In a minute to Churchill on the 3rd, Harris stated, that with the participation of the American 8th Air Force, he could "wreck Berlin from end to end". He estimated that the campaign would cost the two forces between four and five hundred aircraft, but that it would cost Germany the war. This would remove the need for the kind of bloody, expensive and protracted land campaign, which he had personally witnessed during the Great War, and had prompted him to "get into the air" at the earliest opportunity. It should be remembered that this was the first time in the history of air warfare, that the means had existed to prove the theory, that an enemy could be defeated by bombing alone. It is only in the light of more recent experiences, that we have learned of the need, in a conventional conflict at least, to occupy the enemy's territory to secure submission. The Americans, however, were committed to victory on land, where film cameras could capture the glory, and would not accompany Harris to Berlin.

Düsseldorf was selected to open the month's operational account that very night, and, no doubt, while the Prime Minister was digesting Harris's epistle, a force of 589 Lancasters and Halifaxes was being prepared for action. 5 Group's contribution amounted to 147 Lancasters, of which the sixteen representing 106 Squadron lined up for take-off at Syerston at 17.00, and all got away safely over the ensuing forty minutes with S/L Dunn the senior pilot on duty, and each aircraft bearing aloft 5½ tons of bombs in the form of a cookie and SBCs of 4lb and 30lb incendiaries. This would amount to 88 tons of bombs carried by 106 Squadron alone. There were no early returns as they joined the bomber stream over the North Sea, and approached the south-western Ruhr after flying out via the Scheldt estuary to cross Belgium and pass through the concentration of fifty to sixty searchlights in the Mönchengladbach-Cologne corridor, some fifteen miles from the target. Small patches of cloud below them at 12,000 feet were drifting across the target along with smoke from the early fires, despite which, the visibility remained generally good, and the Path Finders employed both sky and ground markers to good effect to identify the aiming point in the city centre. Searchlights at the target were plentiful, but the flak was described by most as slight and not troublesome, and the 106 Squadron crews bombed on red and green TIs and skymarkers from 20,000 to 22,000 feet between 19.43 and 20.02. Fires were observed to be developing on both sides of the Rhine with black smoke rising through 6,000 feet as they turned away, and P/O Perry and crew captured an aiming point photo. Eighteen aircraft failed to return, and, unusually, eleven were Lancasters and only seven Halifaxes. It was on this night, that 61 Squadron's F/L Bill Reid earned the award of a Victoria Cross for pressing on to bomb the target after his Lancaster, LM360, had been severely damaged, and a number of his crew either killed or wounded. Post-raid reconnaissance revealed that central and southern districts had sustained widespread damage to industry and housing, but no report came out of Düsseldorf to provide detail. This was the final operation with the squadron for Don Cheney and crew, who found themselves posted to the newly-formed 630 Squadron at East Kirkby. They would eventually be invited to join 617 Squadron, and, in August 1944, would fail to return from a daylight attack with Tallboys on the U-Boot pens at Brest. Cheney and three others would survive, three evading capture, while one was temporarily held by the Germans, and all four would return to the UK within weeks.

The following week passed by without operations, and on the 5th, an advance party of five officers and sixty-one NCOs and airmen moved to Metheringham to prepare the way for the remainder of the squadron. The squadron was warned on the 7th to be prepared for the aircraft and main party to move on the 8th, followed by the farewell party on the 9th and the completion of the whole process on the 10th. However, plans were changed when operations were scheduled on the nights of the 8th and 9th, only to be cancelled at the last minute. The aircraft were then expected to fly to Metheringham on the 10th, but another operation was called and the squadron was told to prepare instead for that. They would be part of a 5 and 8 Group force of 313 Lancasters sent to destroy railway yards at Modane, situated in the foothills of the Alps in south-eastern France. 5 Group supported the operation with 136 Lancasters, of which fourteen representing 106 Squadron departed Syerston for the last time in anger between 20.30 and 21.10 with F/L Claridge the senior pilot on duty. Ahead of them lay an outward flight of more than 650 miles, which took them over the south coast at Selsey Bill on course for landfall on the Normandy coast at Cabourg. The 106 Squadron contingent completed the outward leg in around four-and-a-quarter hours to be rewarded by the presence of a full moon shining brightly from a cloudless sky. They pinpointed on Lake Bissorte, from where they carried out a time-and-distance run to the target, which they identified visually and by red and green TIs. F/O Cooper and crew were the first from the squadron to deliver their nine 1,000 pounders a few seconds before 01.00, aimed at the centre of six red TIs from 16,700 feet, and the rest of the squadron followed up from 15,000 to 17,000 feet between 01.00 and 01.10. The attack seemed to be concentrated around the markers, and fires appeared to be taking hold, while a large explosion was observed at 01.13. Returning crews were fairly confident in the quality of their night's efforts, and the crews of P/O Perry and F/O Cooper were represented among the two hundred bombing photos revealing extensive damage to track and installations within one mile of the aiming point. Remarkably, not a single aircraft had been lost.

On return from this nine-hour round trip the 106 Squadron contingent had landed back at Syerston, before flying over to Metheringham later in the day. The first training and familiarisation flights took place on the following day, and on the 13th, W/C Baxter took S/L Dunn's crew on a fifty-minute inspection from the air and to test the airfield approach equipment after a number of complaints from crews. Among awards announced on the 14th was a DFC for the now tour-expired F/L Stephens. A lull in operations after Modane allowed a brief settling-in period at their new home, and an opportunity for the squadron to swap its Lancasters for a new batch equipped with H2S. These were ready for action on the 18th, the day that would herald the resumption of Harris's war against Germany's capital city.

Undaunted by the American response to his invitation to join the Berlin party, Harris would go alone, and the rocky road to the Capital was re-joined by a 440-strong all-Lancaster heavy force on the night of the 18/19th, while a predominantly Halifax and Stirling contingent of 395 aircraft acted as a diversion by raiding Mannheim and Ludwigshafen three hundred miles to the south-west. The Berlin-bound crews would benefit from four Mosquitos dropping dummy fighter flares, while other Mosquitos carried out a spoof raid on Frankfurt to protect the Mannheim force. The two forces would cross the enemy coast simultaneously some 250 miles apart to confuse the enemy night-fighter controllers, and the route chosen for the Berlin brigade was via the Frisian island of Texel to a point north of Hannover, and thence to the target to pass over the centre on an east-north-easterly heading. After bombing they would return south of Berlin and Cologne, before crossing central Belgium to gain the English Channel via the French coast. An innovation for this operation was a shortening of the bomber stream to reduce the time over the target to sixteen minutes. When the first Thousand Bomber raid had taken place in May 1942, with an unprecedented twelve aircraft per minute crossing the aiming point, there was considered to be a high risk of collisions. The number had since been increased to sixteen per minute, with large raids lasting up to forty-five minutes, but, on this night, twenty-seven aircraft per minute were to pass over the aiming point.

Thirteen 106 Squadron Lancasters were loaded with a cookie and incendiaries, and departed Metheringham for the first time between 17.10 and 17.35 with W/C Baxter the senior pilot on duty and first off the ground. They made for the Lincolnshire coast and a direct route to the target passing to the north of Hannover to attack Berlin from west to east. A blanket of cloud covered the whole of northern Germany, and crews were grateful for the red spotfire route marker dropped by the Path Finders northeast of Hannover, which confirmed that they were on track. The horizontal visibility was good, despite the absence of a moon, but the vertical view was blocked by the cloud that persisted all the way to the target with tops at 6,000 feet. The cloud was illuminated by searchlights as the head of the bomber stream closed on the target, and the H2S-delivered skymarkers remained in view for a considerable time before disappearing into the cloud tops. The 106 Squadron crews all reached Berlin, and aimed at the red and green skymarkers from between 20,000 and 25,000 feet in a ten-minute slot from 21.00. They were unable to assess the results of their efforts, but the general opinion was that the bombing had been scattered. The Berlin defences were not troublesome, but F/O Forsyth and crew ran into heavy and accurate flak on the way home, which knocked out an engine. P/O Gibbs' mid-upper gunner, Sgt Smith, passed out and sustained severe frostbite after his oxygen tube broke, and, at debriefing, it was claimed that they had undertaken the return journey at the unheard-of altitude of 29,000 feet with an unserviceable rear turret, before eventually landing safely at Tangmere on the south coast. Local sources confirmed that there had been no concentration and confirmed the destruction of 169 houses and a number of industrial units, with many more damaged to some extent. The diversion at Mannheim was deemed to have been successful in its purpose, and caused some useful industrial damage, most seriously to the Daimler-Benz motor factory, which suffered a 90% loss of production for an unknown period. In addition to this, more than three hundred buildings were destroyed at a cost of twenty-three aircraft, while the losses from Berlin were encouragingly low at just nine.

The Lancasters stayed at home on the 19th, while 3, 4, 6 and 8 Groups combined to put 170 Halifaxes, eighty-six Stirlings and 10 Mosquitos into the air for a raid on the Ruhr city of Leverkusen, home to an I G Farben plant. They were greeted in the target area by ten-tenths cloud and an absence of marking, which was caused by equipment failure among the Oboe Mosquitos. A few green TIs were spotted some five to ten miles to the north-west of the target during the approach, but the crews were left to establish their positions on the basis of their own H2S, which, over a region as densely built-up as the Ruhr, was a challenge. As a result, the operation was a complete failure, which sprayed bombs over twenty-seven towns in the region, mostly to the north of Leverkusen.

Harris called for a maximum effort on Berlin on the 22nd, and 764 aircraft were made available, of which sixteen of 5 Group's 166 Lancasters were provided by 106 Squadron. They departed Metheringham between 16.40 and 17.30 with S/L Crowe the senior pilot on duty and operating for the first time since September. After climbing out, they adopted an outward route similar to that employed by the all-Lancaster force four nights earlier, which took them from Texel to a point north-west of Hannover, where a slight dogleg to port put them on a due-easterly heading directly to the target. Unlike the previous raid, however, rather than the circuitous return south of Cologne and out over the French coast, they would come home via a reciprocal route. This was based on a forecast of low cloud and fog over Germany, which would inhibit the night-fighter effort, while broken, medium-level cloud over Berlin would facilitate ground marking. An additional bonus was the availability to the Path Finders of five new H2S Mk III sets, while a new record of thirty-four aircraft per minute passing over the aiming point would be achieved by abandoning the long-standing practice of allocating aircraft types to specific waves. On this night, aircraft of all types would be spread through the bomber stream, and this was bad news for the

Stirlings, which, by the very nature of their design, would be below the Lancaster and Halifax elements, and in danger of being hit by friendly bombs.

JB566 was hit by flak shortly after crossing the Dutch/German frontier, and the resulting engine fire persuaded P/O Garnett and crew to jettison their load and turn for home. P/O Gibbs and crew were only a few miles further into Germany, north of the Mittelland Canal east of the little town of Bramsche, when a petrol tank seal issue forced the curtailment of their sortie, and F/O Harvey and crew were the third to turn back after their navigation equipment failed. The others pressed on to discover that the meteorological forecast had been inaccurate, and that Berlin was hidden under a blanket of ten-tenths cloud with tops at around 12,000 feet. This meant that ground marking would be largely ineffective, and that the least reliable Wanganui (skymarking) method would have to be employed. Crews ran into intense predicted flak and a mass of searchlights as they began their bombing runs, and those from 106 Squadron aimed at red and green TIs and release-point flares from 18,000 to 23,000 feet between 20.05 and 20.27. The glow of fires was observed beneath the clouds, as was a very large detonation that lit up the sky at 20.10, and those still in the target area at 20.22 witnessed a second massive explosion. The impression was of a successful operation, but an assessment through the clouds was impossible. Post-raid reconnaissance and local reports confirmed that this attack on Berlin had been the most effective of the war to date, and had caused a swathe of destruction from the city centre through the western residential districts of Tiergarten and Charlottenburg as far as the suburb town of Spandau. A number of firestorm areas were reported, and the catalogue of destruction included three thousand houses and twenty-three industrial premises. Many thousands more sustained varying degrees of damage, costing 175,000 people their homes and an estimated two thousand their lives, and, by daylight on the 23rd, the smoke had risen to almost 19,000 feet.

Twenty-six aircraft failed to return, eleven of them Lancasters, ten Halifaxes, and five Stirlings, which amounted to a loss-rate among the types respectively of 2.3%, 4.2% and 10.0%. This proved to be the final straw for Harris as far as the Stirling was concerned, which, because of its short wing design, was restricted to a low service ceiling, and by the configuration of its bomb bay to small calibre bombs. Unlike the Lancaster and Halifax, it lacked development potential, and was immediately withdrawn from future operations over Germany. It would still have an important role to play on secondary duties, however, bombing over occupied territory, mining, and, in 1944, it would replace the Halifax to become the aircraft of choice for the two SOE squadrons, 138 and 161, at Tempsford. Many of those released from Bomber Command service would find their way to 38 Group, where they would give valuable service in support of the SOE, and as transports and glider-tugs for airborne landings.

Most of the squadron's participants had been diverted on return from Berlin because of bad weather at home, and by the time they arrived back at Metheringham, orders had already come through for a return to Berlin that night. This placed an insurmountable burden upon the ground crews and armourers to get a full complement of aircraft ready in time, and, despite their Herculean efforts, only six could be offered as part of the all-Lancaster heavy force of 365 aircraft, 130 of which belonging to 5 Group. On the 1 Group station at Ludford Magna, armourers were unable to load all nineteen 101 Squadron Lancasters with the intended weight of bombs, and sent them off 2,000lb short. The Metheringham sextet took off between 17.05 and 17.30 with F/L Ginder the senior pilot on duty, and rendezvoused with the rest of the bomber stream over the North Sea before adopting the now familiar route across northern Holland and Germany. The German night fighter controller correctly guessed Berlin to be the destination, but the recently-introduced Sahme Sau (tame boar) running commentary system was compromised by spurious instructions broadcast from England, ordering night-fighters to land because of fog over their bases. It produced a theatre of comedy as each side claimed to be the legitimate one, but, even so, night-fighters would still play their part in bringing down twenty Lancasters. For the second operation running F/O

Harvey and crew were forced to return early, after severe icing prevented them from climbing above 12,000 feet. They were among eighteen 5 Group early returns out of forty-six from the force as a whole, a massive 12% of those dispatched, which was a further indication of the strain of back-to-back long-range operations. Another was the dumping of bombs over the North Sea by crews intending to push on to the target, but wanting to gain more height. It involved largely those from 1 Group, who were shedding their cookies in protest at their A-O-C's policy of loading each Lancaster to its maximum all-up weight at the expense of altitude. The slogan "H-E-I-G-H-T spells safety" could be found on the walls of most bomber station briefing rooms at the time. Guided by the glow of fires still burning through the clouds, the Path Finders easily located the target, and the main force crews had plenty of red and green target indicators to aim at. The 106 Squadron crews bombed from 19,000 to 21,000 feet between 20.01 and 20.14, and, on return, described a column of smoke reaching 20,000 feet, and the glow of fires visible again from the Hannover area some 150 miles from the target. They had contributed to another accurate raid, which destroyed a further two thousand houses along with industrial buildings, and led to more than fourteen hundred people losing their lives at a cost to the Command of twenty Lancasters. These two operations would prove to be the most successful of the entire campaign.

Before the next assault on the "Big City", Frankfurt was subjected to a scattered but moderately successful raid on the night of the 25/26th, but this did not include main force Lancasters. 106 Squadron had now operated for five weeks without having to post missing any crews, but this was about to change. For the fourth time in nine nights Berlin was selected on the 26th as the target, this time for an all-Lancaster heavy force of 443 aircraft, of which 161 were provided by 5 Group, eighteen of them representing 106 Squadron. The planners decided it was necessary to make the target less predictable, and laid on a simultaneous diversionary operation on Stuttgart by a Halifax main force, along with a more complex route. The plan called for both forces to exit England over Beachy Head before making for the French coast, and then adopt an easterly course across Belgium to a point north-east of Frankfurt, where the two forces would diverge, one due south, and the other to the north-east. The bombing run at Berlin would be roughly west to east across the city, with a 180° turn and a direct flight back between Hannover and Bremen to exit the Dutch coast near Egmond.

The Metheringham contingent took off between 17.00 and 17.35 with F/Ls Boyle and Ginder the senior pilots on duty, and joined up with the bomber stream over the North Sea. An indication of the beneficial effects of the three-day lay-off was a 44% reduction in early returns by 5 Group crews compared with the previous Berlin raid. While outbound, ED873 developed a surging starboard-outer engine, which prevented the Lancaster from climbing and persuaded P/O Neil and crew to turn back when at the midpoint of the Channel crossing. The bomb load was jettisoned, and a return to Metheringham on three engines ended with an overshot landing and a crash near the airfield, fortunately, with only an injury to the rear gunner. JB592 crashed in Germany north-east of Frankfurt on the way to the target, and F/O van Hoboken DFC, was killed with his crew. At thirty-two years of age, Brussels-born Jaques van Hoboken was considerably older than most of his contemporaries, and was well into his first tour of operations. His presence and that of his crew would be greatly missed by the squadron. P/O Hinckley and crew were probably in the same general area, when the navigator reported sick, and an attack was made on Koblenz as an alternative. Berlin was found to be under clear skies, despite which, the Path Finders overshot the city centre aiming point by six or seven miles, and marked an area well to the north-west, which happened to contain many war-industry factories. The 106 Squadron crews bombed on red and green TIs from 20,000 and 23,000 feet between 21.18 and 21.27, and returned to pass on their impressions to the Intelligence Section at debriefing. F/O Harvey and crew observed the bombing to be concentrated around the markers, and, while running across the target at 22,000 feet, flak caused slight damage to the bomb doors, and a Ju88 was seen diving over the target with a trail of black smoke behind it. They also watched a Path Finder Lancaster being shot down at 21.15, before bombing three minutes later, and returning home safely. P/O Pezaro and crew had only recently joined the squadron, and they described the target area as a mass of flames, with smoke rising up to 10,000 feet, while F/O Forsyth and crew saw an explosion at 21.18, which caused a building to disintegrate. P/O Mifflin and crew had remained at 23,000 feet during the outward leg, and they commented on the number of bomb loads being jettisoned by aircraft below them, an observation backed up by F/O Cole and crew, who specified "outside the searchlight belt" as the location of most of this activity, which was again carried out by 1 Group crews. On other stations, returning crews spoke of a mass of fires and thick smoke rising to 15,000 feet, and it was learned later that thirty-eight war-industry factories had been destroyed in the Siemensstadt and Tegel districts and many others damaged. Weather conditions at home caused major diversions, and 6 Group stations had to deal with landing the majority of returning aircraft, commendably achieving this feat with only one collision. In the absence of the poorer performing Halifaxes and Stirlings, the Lancasters suffered a 6.2% loss rate amounting to twenty-eight aircraft. This was the final operation of a month in which 106 Squadron had operated on six occasions, dispatching eighty-three sorties for the failure to return of a single Lancaster and the loss of a second one at home.

December 1943

Berlin would continue to be the dominant theme during December, and, as November had ended, so December would begin. A heavy force of 443 aircraft stood ready to take off in the late afternoon of the 2nd, all but fifteen of them Lancasters, after the main Halifax element had been withdrawn because of fog over their Yorkshire stations. 5 Group contributed 145 Lancasters, of which sixteen belonged to 106 Squadron and departed Metheringham between 16.40 and 17.05 with F/Ls Claridge and Ginder the senior pilots on duty. After climbing out, they headed for the Lincolnshire coast to rendezvous over the North Sea with the rest of the force for a straight-in-straight-out route across Holland and northern Germany with no feints or diversions. First, however, the crews had to negotiate a towering front of ice-bearing cloud over the North Sea, which would contribute to a 10% rate of early returns. 106 Squadron's P/O Richards and crew cited icing as the cause of their "boomerang", although it would be more than six hours after taking off before they returned, suggesting that their problems occurred later in the flight out. The others pushed through the challenging conditions, and made it to the target area, although mostly south of track after variable winds had thrown them off course and dispersed the bomber stream. They also had to contend with large numbers of enemy night-fighters that would harass the bombers all the way to the target, after the controller had been able correctly to predict it. Inaccurately forecast winds led to the bomber stream becoming spread out, and this would impact upon the accuracy of the attack. The Path Finders were employing H2S to establish their position at Stendal, but had strayed some fifteen miles south of track and mistakenly used the town of Genthin as their reference for the run-in. F/O Jardine and crew got as far as Brandenburg, on Berlin's western approaches, having contended with the absence of an intercom since early on, and now, hampered by a frozen windscreen that the pilot could not see through, it was decided to bomb Brandenburg and head for home. The main force crews found good visibility, and were drawn to the aiming point by release-point flares, and encountered a thin layer of two to three-tenths cloud at around 5,000 feet, but up to nine-tenths between 10,000 and 12,000 feet, which the searchlights were able to pierce and through which the TIs could be seen burning on the ground. They bombed on skymarkers and red and green TIs, and, where possible, ground detail like burning streets, those from 106 Squadron from 18,000 to 21,500 feet between 20.19 and 20.32. They reported scattered fires and a number of large explosions, and some claimed the glow to be visible from 120 miles into the homeward leg. P/O Mifflin's JB612 was attacked and severely damaged by a night-fighter over the target after bombing, and was then hit by heavy flak, requiring them to complete the whole return journey on three engines. Bombing photographs suggested that the raid was only partially successful, causing useful damage in industrial districts in the west and east, but scattering the main weight of bombs over the southern districts and outlying communities to the south. It was a bad night for the bomber force, which lost forty aircraft, mostly in the target area and on the way home. At debriefing some reported persistent, accurate flak, while others saw little or none, but a number of references were made to night-fighter activity and the use of rocket projectiles, which seemed to have a range of about one mile. Having used up their ration of luck a week earlier, P/O Neil and his crew were killed, when ED874 was brought down to crash about ten miles north-east of the centre of Berlin. The sixty-seven tons of bombs dropped by the squadron on this night was the best in 5 Group.

Having been spared by the weather from experiencing an effective visitation from the Command in October, and exploiting the enemy expectation that Berlin would be the target again, Leipzig found itself at the end of the red tape on briefing-room wall-maps from County Durham to Cambridgeshire on the 3rd. A force of 527 aircraft was made ready, which included 103 Lancasters of 5 Group, thirteen of them belonging to 106 Squadron, and they departed Metheringham between 00.01 and 00.25 with S/L Dunn the senior pilot on duty. The bomber stream headed for Berlin as a feint, passing north of Hannover and Braunschweig with ten-tenths cloud beneath it and an hour's journey to Leipzig still ahead. Then, as it turned towards the south-east, the Mosquito element continued on to carry out a diversion at the Capital. Night-fighters had already infiltrated the stream at the Dutch coast, but the feint had the desired effect, and few night-fighters were encountered in the target area, where two layers of ten-tenths cloud prevailed with tops at around 7,000 and 15,000 feet. The Path Finders marked by H2S with green skymarkers, and the 106 Squadron crews bombed on these from 20,000 to 23,000 feet between 03.58 and 04.11, observing explosions and a strong glow beneath the clouds. The emergence through the cloud tops of black smoke suggested that an accurate and concentrated attack had taken place, and the smoke and glow remained visible for 150 miles into the return journey south-east towards the French frontier. Had many aircraft not then strayed into the Frankfurt defence zone, the losses may have been fewer, but twenty-four aircraft failed to return, fifteen of them Halifaxes. Local reports confirmed this as a highly successful operation, which had hit residential and industrial areas, and was the most destructive raid visited upon this eastern city during the war. Sadly, for the Command, it would take its revenge in time. For the second night running, 106 Squadron topped the bomb-tonnage ladder for 5 Group with fifty-seven tons.

Thereafter, fog descended upon the bomber stations of Lincolnshire, and, when it lifted, the moon period allowed minor operations to carry the Command through to mid-month, during which period the opportunity was taken to train crews on the use of H2S. Among awards announced to 106 Squadron personnel on the 11th was a DFC for P/O Barker. When the crews next attended briefing, on the 16th, they discovered the red tape on the wall map once again terminated at Berlin, for the sixth time since the resumption of the campaign, and learned that an all-Lancaster main force and Path Finder heavy brigade of 483 aircraft was to be accompanied by ten Mosquitos and adopt a direct route to the target. The concession to diversionary measures was incorporated into the return flight, which would take the retreating bomber stream in a north-westerly direction to the Baltic, to gain the North Sea by way of southern Denmark. 5 Group put up 165 Lancasters, 106 Squadron contributing fifteen, which departed Metheringham between 16.20 and 16.50 with F/Ls Boyle, Claridge, Ginder and Harvey the senior pilots on duty. They were to cross the Dutch coast in the region of Castricum-aan-Zee, and then head due east all the way to the target with no deviations. A three-quarter moon would rise during the long return leg, but it was hoped that the very early take-off and the expectation of fog to keep the enemy night-fighters on the ground would reduce the risk of interception. Night-fighters were sent to meet the bomber stream at the Dutch coast, and it was shortly after crossing into Germany that 106 Squadron's JB638 crashed at Achmer on the northern bank of the Mittelland Canal, and P/O Storer and his crew were killed. The others pressed on to find Berlin obscured by ten-tenths cloud with tops at around 5,000 feet, but identifiable by means of red and green skymarkers, and the crews of F/L Harvey and F/O Cole were the first from 106 Squadron to arrive and aim for them from 21,000 feet at 20.01. The others from the squadron followed up from 19,500 to 22,000 feet over the next nine minutes, and only F/O Forsyth and crew reported trouble from the defences in the form of a Ju88, which the gunners drove off and claimed as damaged. The return flight over Denmark passed largely without major incident, but the greatest difficulties awaited the 1, 6 and 8 Group crews as they arrived home to find their airfields covered by a blanket of dense fog. With little reserves of fuel, the tired crews began a frantic search to find somewhere to land, stumbling blindly through the murk to catch a glimpse of the ground. For many, this proved fatal, while others gave up any hope of landing, and abandoned their aircraft. 5 Group had been lucky to have clear conditions to land, while the 1 Group squadrons in the northern half of Lincolnshire had suffered grievously, and it was only later on the 17th that the fog began to roll in across Metheringham. Twenty-nine Lancasters and a mine-laying Stirling were lost in these most tragic circumstances, and more than 150 airmen were killed when so close to home and safety. To this number was added the twenty-five Lancasters failing to return from the raid itself, many of which were accounted for by night-fighters over Holland and Germany while outbound. At debriefing, some crews reported the glow of fires, while others saw nothing through the cloud, and it was a local report that confirmed a moderately effective raid, which had fallen principally onto central and eastern districts, where housing suffered most.

A three-day stand-down allowed the crews to recover from the Berlin operation, and it was the 20th when all stations were notified of an operation that night to Frankfurt, for which a force of 390 Lancasters and 257 Halifaxes was assembled. 5 Group made ready 168 Lancasters, of which seventeen were to be provided by 106 Squadron. W/C Baxter put himself on the Order of Battle, and there were maiden operations for the crews of P/O Dickerson and P/O Leggett. They were led away by the commanding officer at 17.00, and all were safely airborne by 17.25, climbing out above the station before heading for the coast at Southwold and the rendezvous with the rest of the bomber stream on the way across the North Sea to the Scheldt estuary. While the main operation was in progress, forty-four Lancasters and ten Mosquitos of 1 and 8 Groups were to carry out a diversion at Mannheim, some forty miles to the south. The intention was to keep the enemy guessing as to the final destination, Stuttgart, Munich, Mannheim or Frankfurt in the south, or Kassel, Hannover or Berlin to the north, and, if not deceiving the enemy entirely, the ploy might dilute the strength of the night-fighter numbers brought to bear. After making landfall, the bombers passed north of Antwerp and flew the length of Belgium to the German frontier north of Luxembourg, perhaps unaware that the German night-fighter controller had picked up transmissions from the bomber stream as soon as it left the English coast, and was able to track it all the way to the target and vector his fighters into position. Many combats took place during the outward flight, and the diversion failed to draw fighters away from the main action. The problems continued at the primary target, where the forecast clear skies failed to materialize, and the crews were greeted by four to nine-tenths cloud at between 5,000 and 10,000 feet. This allowed some of them to pick out ground features, while others fixed their positions by H2S, if so equipped, and, if not, simply waited for TIs on e.t.a. The Path Finders had prepared a ground-marking plan in expectation of good vertical visibility, and dropped red, green and yellow TIs, while the Germans lit a decoy fire-site five miles to the south-east of the city. W/C Baxter and crew found five-tenths cloud over the target, but good visibility, and aimed their bombs at two green target indicators from 20,000 feet at 19.43. They observed a good concentration of fires and smoke rising through the cloud tops, and were complimentary about the route. That last comment was echoed by P/O Holbourn and crew, who described the trip as "devoid of incident". The other 106 Squadron crews bombed from 20,000 to 22,000 feet between 19.42 and 19.52, and all returned safely, many of them commenting on the abundance of night-fighters, but only F/O Jardine and crew had to fight one off. Some crews described the marking as late and erratic, while most thought the attack to be scattered in the early stages, becoming more concentrated as it progressed, and many commented on the new cookies detonating with a brighter flash than the old ones. Any success was achieved largely as the result of the creep-back from the decoy site falling across the suburbs of

Offenbach and Sachsenhausen, situated on the southern bank of the River Main, and the glow remained visible to some for 150 miles into the return flight. 466 houses were destroyed and more than nineteen hundred seriously damaged, despite which, the operation fell well short of its aims, and the loss of forty-one aircraft was a high price to pay. The Halifaxes suffered heavily, losing twenty-seven of their number, a loss-rate of 10.5%, compared with the Lancaster's 3.6%. 106 Squadron delivered ninety-two tons of bombs, including five minol cookies, and this exceeded all other 5 Group squadrons by a clear thirteen tons. *(Minol was an explosive substance developed for use in mines, but was a useful supplement to TNT and RDX when they were in short supply.)*

Just two more operations remained before the year ended, and both were to be directed against Germany's capital city. The first was posted on the 23rd, and would involve an all-Lancaster heavy force with seven Halifaxes among the Path Finder element, and eight Mosquitos to provide a diversion. The 130 Lancasters of 5 Group included ten representing 106 Squadron, a figure which would have been higher had not the eleventh in line become bogged down off the perimeter track, preventing itself and four others from taking part. They departed Metheringham between 23.59 and 00.35 with S/L Dunn the senior pilot on duty, each loaded with a cookie and mix of 4lb and 30lb incendiaries. The route to the target was somewhat circuitous, and took the bomber stream in a south-easterly direction to the Scheldt estuary, before hugging the Belgian/Dutch frontier to cross into Germany south of Aachen, as if threatening Frankfurt. When a point was reached south of Leipzig, the route turned sharply towards the north and Berlin, while the Mosquito feint threatened Leipzig as the target. After bombing, the crews were to continue to the north, before turning sharply west for the direct route home across Holland. The vanguard of the bomber stream reached the target to find it enveloped in up to eight-tenths cloud between 5,000 and 10,000 feet, which might not have been critical had the Path Finders not suffered an unusually high failure rate of their H2S equipment. This resulted in scattered and sparse sky-marking, but S/L Dunn and crew found release-point flares and cascading green TIs to aim at, and delivered their minol cookie and incendiaries from 20,000 feet at 04.04. F/Sgt Milne and crew were only a few sorties into their first tour, and as an NCO pilot, he was a very rare animal indeed in a squadron that had, for some time, been populated exclusively by officer pilots. They confirmed the Dunn crew's observation of two good fires, and commented on the presence of night-fighters, but reported no contact with them. The other 106 Squadron crews found red and green skymarker flares at which to aim their bombs from 20,000 to 22,000 feet between 04.07 and 04.17, and observed well-concentrated fires and at least four large explosions, one described as being orange and red and lasting for thirty seconds. A relatively modest sixteen Lancasters failed to return, and only F/O Leggett and crew had an actual encounter with night-fighters, having to evade three separate attacks. A local report named the south-eastern suburbs of Köpenick and Treptow as the ones to sustain the most damage, with 287 houses and other buildings suffering complete destruction.

Christmas passed for the fifth time in relative peace before the "Big City" was posted as the target again on the 29th, for what, for the Lancaster operators, would be the first of three raids on it in five nights spanning the turn of the year. A force of 712 aircraft included 163 Lancasters of 5 Group, of which sixteen belonged to 106 Squadron, and they departed Metheringham between 16.20 and 17.05 with S/L Crowe the senior pilot on duty. It was from this juncture that the intolerable strain on the crews of successive long-range flights in difficult weather conditions would begin to become manifest in some squadrons through the rate of early returns, which on this night reached forty-five or 6.3%. The bomber stream was routed out over the Dutch Frisian islands pointing directly for Leipzig, and, having reached a point just to the north of that city, was to turn to the north towards Berlin, while Mosquitos carried out spoof raids on Leipzig and Magdeburg. 106 Squadron was among the 5 Group units exempt from early returns, and its crews reached the target area to find ten-tenths cloud with tops at anywhere between 7,000 and 18,000 feet. Red and green Path Finder release-point flares could be seen hanging over the city, upon which they aimed their bombs from 20,000 to 22,000 feet between 20.09 and 20.26. At debriefing, the Metheringham crews largely reported what they believed had been a fairly successful and relatively uneventful operation, but when F/O Leggett and the survivors of his crew got back to Metheringham, they had a different story to tell. The route home had been via a point south of Bremen, to exit the enemy coast over the Frisians, but it seems that veteran Lancaster, ED593, was perhaps a little north of track and strayed too close to Bremen. It was hit by flak, and, the crew believed, rocket projectiles, and was severely damaged. Worse, the flight engineer, Sgt Braid, was killed, and the wireless operator, P/O Worthy, wounded, and they had to nurse the struggling Lancaster back to England on two engines, before landing at Coltishall in Norfolk without further mishap. Generally, crews reported a considerable red glow beneath the clouds, which remained visible for a hundred miles and gave the impression of a concentrated and successful assault, but this was not entirely borne out by local reports, which revealed that the main weight of the raid had fallen onto southern and south-eastern districts, and, also, into outlying communities to the east. 388 buildings had been destroyed, although none of significance, and ten thousand people had been bombed out of their homes. Eleven Lancasters and nine Halifaxes failed to return, a loss-rate of 2.4% for the former and 3.5% for the latter.

During the course of the month 106 Squadron operated on six nights, dispatching eighty-seven sorties for the loss of two aircraft and crews. Of particular pride was the fact that it topped the 5 Group bomb tonnage ladder on four of those six occasions. It had been a testing end to a year which had brought major successes and advances in tactics, but it had also been a year of high losses, particularly among the Stirling and Halifax squadrons. While Window had been an instant success, it had also caused the Luftwaffe to rethink and reorganise, and the night-fighter force which emerged from the ruins of the old system, was a leaner, more efficient and altogether more lethal beast than that of before. As far as the crews of Bomber Command were concerned, the New Year offered the same fare as the old one, and few would view that with relish.

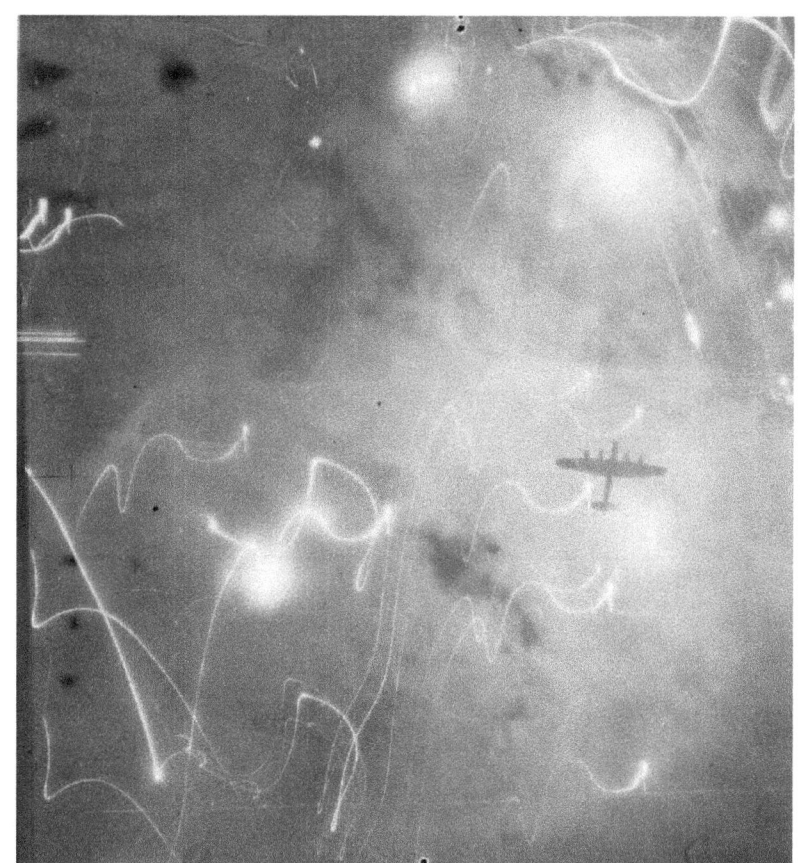

An Avro Lancaster of 1 Group, Bomber Command, silhouetted against flares, smoke and explosions during the attack on Hamburg, Germany, by aircraft of 1, 5 and 8 Groups on the night of 30/31st January 1943. This raid was the first occasion on which H2S centimetric radar was used by the Path Finder aircraft to navigate the force to the target. The pilot of the photographing aircraft Lancaster ZN-Y of 106 Squadron, based at Syerston was F/L D J Shannon .

St Joseph's Church, Kiel, bombed on the 4/5th April 1943 raid.

P/O A Urquhart

Lost on the 30th March 1943 on a Berlin raid. Lancaster ED596 was shot down by a night fighter. All crew killed: Pilot S/L E L Hayward DFC, Sgt G W F Baker, F/L J O Young DFC, P/O A Urquhart, P/O E H Mantle DFM+, Sgt D Brown, P/O G V Pryor DFM.

Lancaster W4118 'Admiral Prune' crashed on Turin raid 4/5th February 1943.
Those killed – Sgt N H Johnstone, F/Sgt F L Darlington RCAF, F/O G R Powell, Sgt W E Baker. PoWs – Sgt D L Thompson RCAF, Sgt R P Sutton, Sgt J Picken, Sgt P Ward

F/O George Roland Powell KIA

106 Squadron Lancaster W4242 ZN-G 'Admiral Filha Da Puta' (Son of a Bitch)
Pilot F/L 'Wimpy' Wellington. Aircraft posted missing 8/9th October 1943 during raid on Hannover with the loss of P/O Hay's Crew.

Jack Clark (MUG to Ted Robbins)   *George Calvert*

Sgt Calvert   *Les Carpenter*   *W/O Edward Robbins*

HMS Minesweeper "Rotterdam" which picked up Sgt Robbins and crew on 21ˢᵗ February 1943. He then joined 106 Squadron March 1943. On his 16th operation, he ditched off Holland in Lancaster W4842 on an operation to Essen on 27ᵗʰ May, 1943. All became PoW's.

Famous picture of 106 Squadron, taken in March 1943. The dog strategically sitting next to Guy Gibson is Diny belonged to S/L Eric Hayward who was to lose his life two operations short of completing his second tour.

106 Squadron send-off May 1943

Maintenance in the open air at Syerston 1943

Group of 106 Squadron in 1943. Rear: Third from right - P/O Clifford Stephens pilot
Front Row: Desmond Richards electrician and chairman 106 Squadron association

F/O Douglas Jordan and colleagues.

F/O Alan Horobin killed 9th October 1943 in S/L Howroyd's crew on Hannover operation

S/L Jerrard Latimer DFC killed 15th April 1943 on a Stuttgart sortie on which he was an observer.

Lancaster JB663 ZN-A. Completed 111 operations.

Dinghy drill at Syerston in Lancaster R5611 and the wreckage of the same Lancaster, shot down at Rossum, Holland, on 13th May 1943.

Broadcaster Richard Dimbleby joined W/C Gibson for a bombing raid on Berlin on 16th January 1943. (Photograph not 106 Squadron operation.)

Sgt S Abel   *Sgt J G Alderson*   *Sgt D Brown*   *Sgt C M Harrower*
All killed 1st May 1943

Ground Crew, Ground Crew, Sgt Harrower, Ground Crew, P/O Plaskett, Ground Crew, Sgt Barber

Crew of Lancaster ED451. Sgt Brown, P/O Plaskett, PO Nono, Sgt Alderson, Sgt Abel (Pilot), Sgt Harrower, Sgt Barber. All killed on 1st May 1943 on Essen raid.

*Second from left - F/Sgt Charters, extreme right - Sgt Eric Jordan.
Others believed to be crew of Lancaster ED708*

F/Sgt John Charters   Sgt Charters and W/OII Thomas Roche

All crew of Lancaster ED708 lost without trace on Hamburg operation 28th July 1943 and commemorated on the Runneymede Memorial to the Missing.

F/Sgt John Charters   W/OII Thomas Roche

Sgt E G McLeod (Pilot)   *Sgt F L Backhouse*   *Sgt I G Armet*

Sgt V R Jacob   *P/O D A Campbell*
All crew of Lancaster ED303 lost without trace on Hamburg operation 28th July 1943 and commemorated on the Runneymede Memorial to the Missing. Sgt Backhouse was from Chile.

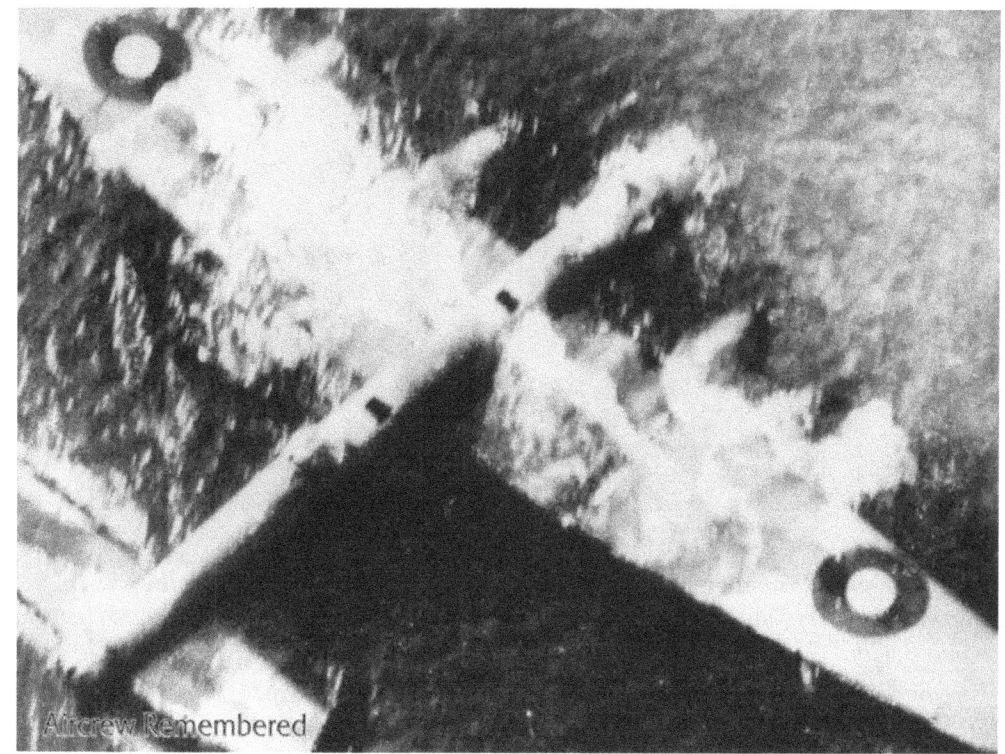

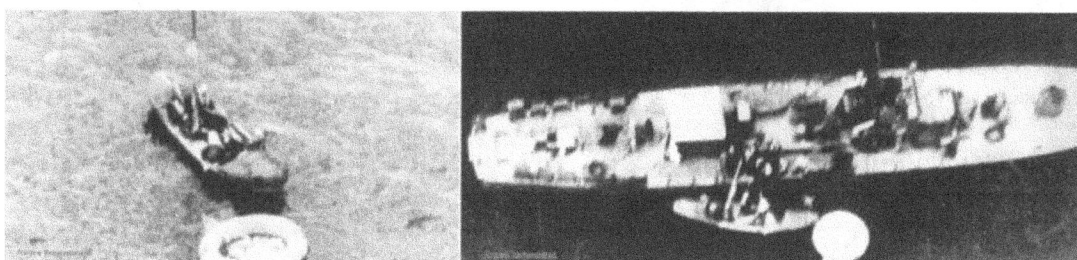

106 Squadron Lancaster JA893. Badly shot about by a night-fighter and, subsequently ditched in the North Sea. F/O Thomas Saxby and Sgt Leslie McKenzie died.

106 Squadron Ground Crew

Sgt Ernest Cannon   *W/OII Kenneth Wellwood*

Both killed along with the rest of the crew in Lancaster ED385 when it crashed into a wooded area near Hannover on the way to bomb Berlin. Crew: F/O Leslie Walter Roper (Pilot), Sgt Kenneth Ernest Bright, Sgt Ernest Albert Cannon (RCAF), Sgt Andrew Steel Carscadden, Sgt Harry Fisher, W/O II Kenneth Douglas Wellwood (RCAF), Sgt Ronald Clifford Woolnough

1Lt Eugene L Rosner (US)   *F/Sgt Hiram Davies*   *P/O Walter Thompson March 1943*
KIA 9th July 1943   *KIA 25th June 1943*   *106 Squadron later 83 Squadron*

106 Squadron Lancaster

F/Sgt Kenneth McLean (Pilot)   Sgt Samuel Leigh   F/Sgt Donald McLeod

Sgt Reginald Muir   Sgt Ronald Barratt   F/Sgt Leslie Johnson   Sgt Edward Hannell

All killed on the 9th July 1943

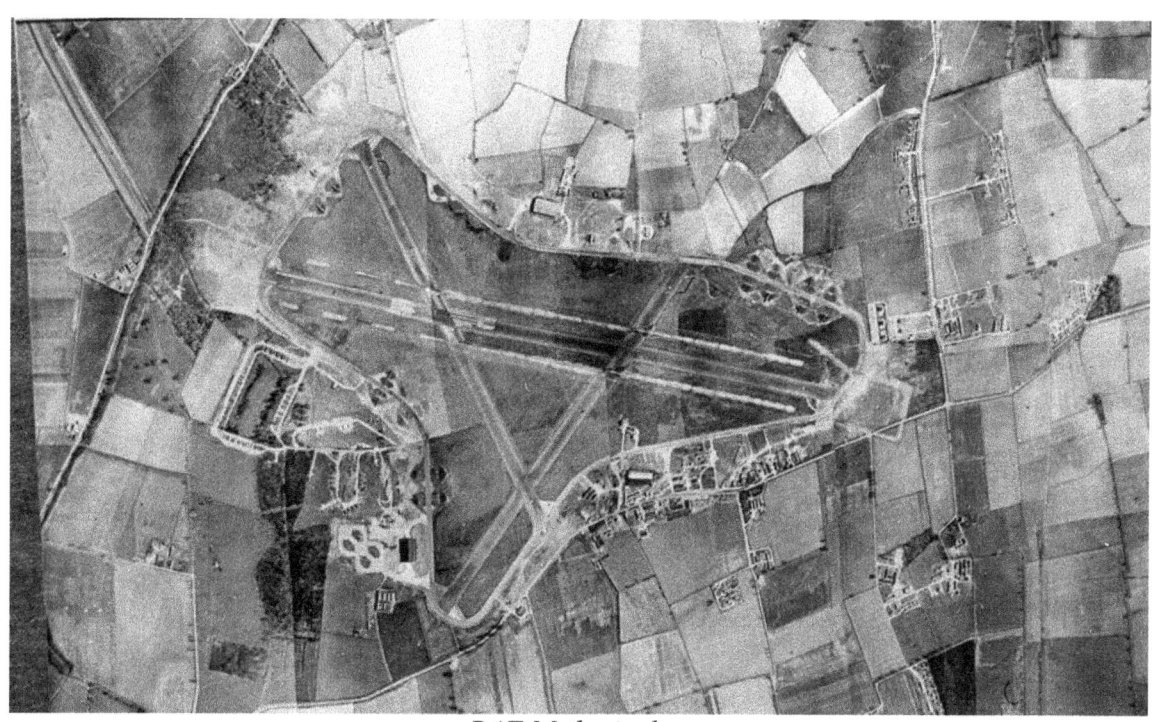

RAF Metheringham

Above and below: Wreckage of Lancaster R5573 in Liège, Belgium.

106 Squadron Lancaster R5665 ZN-D loading oxygen.

Sgt Browell   Sgt Dean   Sgt Smith   Sgt Bennett   Sgt MacGregor   Sgt Robertson

P/O Kenneth Reid RCAF   *Sgt Victor Askey (PoW)*

Pilot of Lancaster R5665 killed 31st July 1943 on Remscheid raid. Remaining crew, including Sgt Askey, were all taken into captivity.

Part of a. RAF reconnaissance photograph taken over Remscheid following the raid on 31st July 1943. showing the very heavy damage sustained by the steel works of Bergische Stahlindustrie

106 Squadron Lancaster ZN-S

W/C Baxter and crew in earlier days, with a Wellington

W/C R E Baxter and crew
Back L-R: Murphy, J Coulton, A Thursby, L G Berry.
Front L-R: R Moore, R E Baxter, Horobin

G/C R E Baxter

F/O C.E Runge and crew

What remains of Metheringham Control tower

RAF Metheringham Mess Staff

Lancaster ED593

A 'Cookie' is loaded onto a 106 Squadron Lancaster at Syerston prior to delivery to Stuttgart. The bomb, weighing either 4,000 or 8,000 lbs, was devastating as an 'area weapon' and was used extensively against industrial targets inside Germany (Crown Copyright).

Armourers prepare to load 1,000-lb MC bombs into the bomb-bay of a 106 Squadron Lancaster at Metheringham, Lincolnshire, for a major night raid on Frankfurt, Germany. The chalk markings on the bombs indicate that each has been fused with a No. 43 air-armed nose pistol, the safety pins of which can be seen hanging from the nose rotor. These will be removed shortly before the crew board the aircraft.

F/O Burroughs' crew. Undated but location believed to be RAF Metheringham. F/O M R Burroughs, pilot (seated, centre); F/O O G Owen, bomb aimer (seated left) and F/Sgt T E Gray, flight engineer (standing second left). The remaining crew members, all sergeants, are D P Brown, navigator; R J Goddard, WOP; C T Bradley, MUG and J A Ormerod, RG. F/O Burroughs joined 106 Sqn in April 1945, survived the war and was transferred away from 106 Squadron in January 1946.

FIDO in operation at Graveley

On the 19th November 1943, FIDO was used for the first time at RAF Graveley, to enable four 35 Sqn aircraft to land when the airfield was covered by fog. Installed at Metheringham in 1944.

St Nazaire 28th February 1943. (Source: Quarterly Review)

Krupps, Essen. Target of many operations of Bomber Command throughout the war.

Vertical photographic-reconnaissance aerial taken over the docks at La Spezia, Italy, showing destroyed sheds, storehouses and workshops in an area of the naval dockyard north-east of Bassin I (lower centre), as a result of the raid by aircraft of Bomber Command on the night of 18/19th April 1943. Damage has also been inflicted on buildings of the San Vito works (top left).

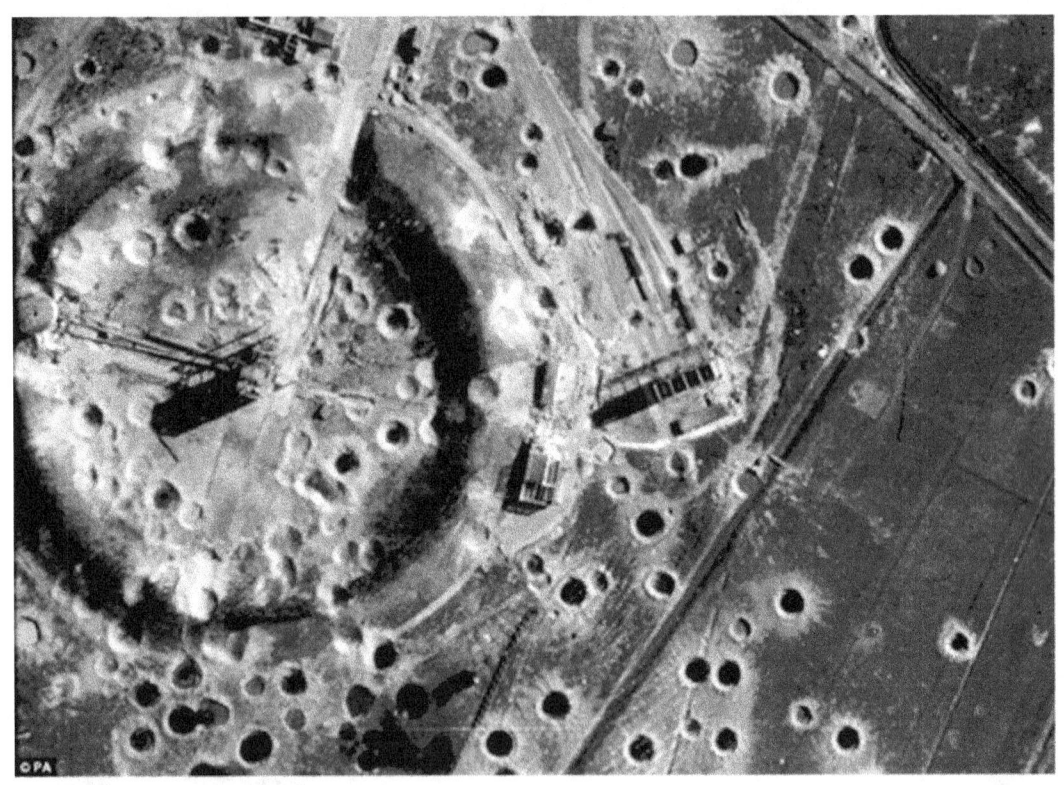

Peenemünde raid 17th August 1943

Factories destroyed in Milan.

S/L John Searby at the controls of a 106 Squadron Lancaster. The photograph is taken from the entrance to the bomb aimer's compartment.

Arriving as a Squadron Leader, John Searby was to command 106 Squadron for two months in 1943.

Crew of P/O Clifford Stephens October 1943

German 88 mm flak gun in action against Allied bombers.

F/L L Burpee, later 617 Squadron pilot Lost on Dams Raid.

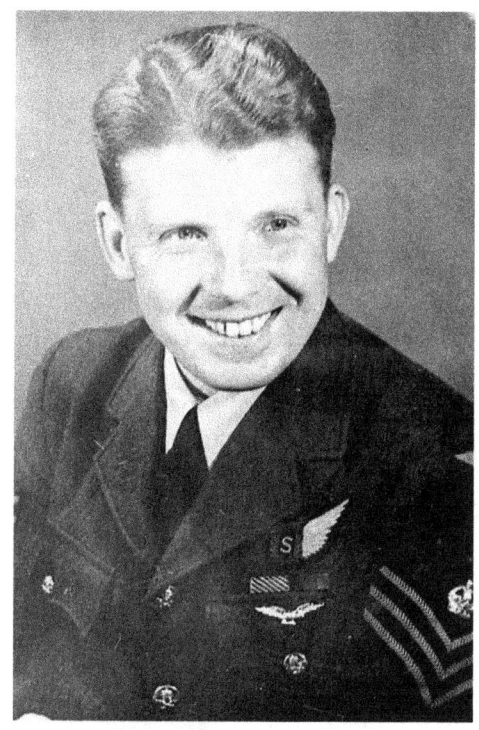

F/Sgt Andy Wilkes W/Op in crew of P/O W R Thompson

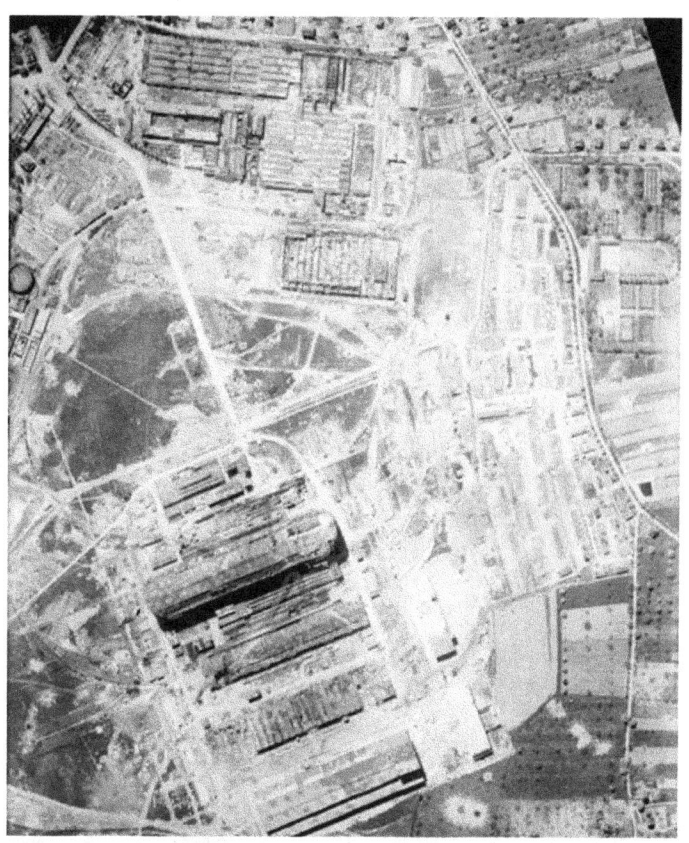

Friedrichshafen, Germany. Wurzburg Radar Works

106 Squadron Syerston - F/Sgt Foulsham Crew
Standing: E J Foulsham RAAF, Keenan. Centre: Bright, Hayward. Front: Black, Yeomans, Coxon

Moonlit 106 Squadron Lancasters

January 1944

The change of year was not destined to effect a change in the emphasis of operations, and this was, no doubt, a disappointment, not only to the hard-pressed crews of Bomber Command, but also to the beleaguered residents of Germany's capital city. Proud of their status as Berliners first and Germans second, they were a hardy breed, and, just like their counterparts in London during the Blitz of 1940, they would bear their trials with fortitude and humour, and would not buckle under the constant assault from above. "You may break our walls but not out hearts", proclaimed banners in the streets, and the most popular song of the day, Nach jedem Dezember kommt immer ein Mai, After every December there's always a May, was played endlessly over the airwaves, its sentiments hinting at a change in fortunes with the onset of spring. The winter of 1943/44 was an inauspicious period for new crews to embark upon their first tour of operations. It had been standard practise to ease a new crew into operations with freshman trips to French coastal targets or leafleting over Occupied Europe, but now a maiden operation could mean Berlin, and some crews would make this hazardous journey a dozen times or more during their tour. Harris allowed the Berliners little time to enjoy New Year, and, as New Year's Day dawned, plans were already in hand to continue the onslaught. Before it ended, the first of 421 Lancasters, 161 representing 5 Group, would be taking off and heading eastwards to arrive over the city as the clock showed 03.00 hours on the 2nd.

Take-off had actually been delayed because of doubts over the weather, and this meant that insufficient hours of daylight remained to allow the planned outward route over Denmark and the Baltic. Instead, the bomber stream would adopt the previously used almost direct route across Holland and northern Germany, but return, as originally planned, more circuitously, passing east of Leipzig, before racing across Germany between the Ruhr and Frankfurt and traversing Belgium to reach the Channel near the French port of Boulogne. 106 Squadron's fifteen participants departed Metheringham between 23.59 and 00.35 with S/L Dunn the senior pilot on duty, and each carrying a cookie and mix of 4lb and 30lb incendiaries. The bomber stream formed up over the North Sea and crossed the Dutch coast at Egmond, before passing over the northern tip of the Ijsselmeer and heading on an almost direct route to the Capital. The bomber stream was gradually depleted by twenty-nine early returns, none of them belonging to 106 Squadron, as a strong tail wind drove the individual aircraft along the four-hundred-mile leg from the Dutch coast to Berlin in under two hours without the crews once catching a glimpse of the ground through the dense cloud. 106 Squadron's JB642 did not make it all the way, after crashing near the town of Hoya on the River Weser between Bremen to the north-west and Hannover to the south-east, and only the rear gunner from P/O Garnett's crew survived to fall into enemy hands. This was one of sixteen Lancasters to be shot down on the way out, after the enemy controller easily identified the target, and totally ignored the Mosquito feint at Hamburg. The conditions were no different at the target, which was completely obscured by a layer of ten-tenths cloud with tops in places as high as 19,000 feet. The Path Finders had to employ skymarking (Wanganui), which was somewhat scattered, and the 106 Squadron crews aimed for these parachute flares from 20,000 to 22,000 feet between 03.08 and 03.19. They observed the glow of fires and smoke rising through the cloud tops, and some witnessed a huge explosion at 03.07, which lit up the clouds for three seconds, but it was impossible to assess what was happening on the ground. For most of the Metheringham participants, it was a relatively uneventful trip, but P/O Dickerson and crew were attacked by a night-fighter, and ND332 was slightly damaged at a time when its rear turret was unserviceable. P/O Banfield and crew watched a combat between a Lancaster and a Ju88, which resulted in the enemy aircraft losing an engine. Banfield's gunners also fired at it and claimed it as damaged. It was established, ultimately, that the operation had been a failure, which had scattered bombs across the southern fringes of the city, causing only minor damage, while the main weight of the attack had fallen beyond the city boundaries into wooded and open country. The disappointment was compounded by the loss of twenty-eight Lancasters, among which was 106 Squadron's JB645, which came down near Berlin with the experienced crew of P/O Holbourn on board, and there were no survivors.

During the course of the 2nd, a heavy force of 362 Lancasters and nine of the new Mk III Hercules-powered Halifaxes was made ready for a return to Berlin that night. There was snow on the ground, and many of the crews called to briefing were still tired from being late to bed following the almost-eight-hour round trip the night before. Some of these were in a mutinous frame of mind at being on the Order of Battle again so soon. 5 Group cancelled twenty-five of its intended contribution, leaving 119 to take part, a dozen of them representing 106 Squadron, which began taking off from Metheringham at 23.50 with F/Ls Ginder and Harvey the senior pilots on duty. Eight were safely airborne before one Lancaster put a wheel off the peri-track and became bogged down, and this led to the cancellation of four sorties. The outward route crossed the Dutch coast near Castricum and took the bomber stream to a point south-east of Bremen, followed by a dogleg to the north-west and, finally, a ninety degree change of course to the south-east in the Parchim area to leave a ninety-mile run to the target. On the way home, they would pass south of Hannover and north of the Ruhr to exit at the entry point on the Dutch coast. The presence of the bomber stream was quickly spotted by the night fighter controller, who accurately predicted its destination forty minutes before zero-hour, and a trap was set between Hannover and Bremen. In the event, the two factions failed to come together, and it was not until the night-fighters were sent to Berlin that the combats began. By then, a massive sixty aircraft had turned back, 15.7% of those dispatched, many defeated by severe icing conditions, while others abandoned their sorties because of minor problems that might have seen them carry on had they been fully rested. ND331 was attacked by a night-fighter as it passed through the defensive "hotspot" close to the Mittelland Canal east of Osnabrück, where a number of 106 Squadron aircraft had recently met their end. F/O Cole lost control temporarily, until regaining it at 12,000 feet, by which time he had ordered his crew to prepare to abandon the aircraft. The order was rescinded, but too late to prevent the mid-upper gunner, Sgt Harding, from baling out, and the bombs were jettisoned as they turned for home to claim the enemy aircraft as damaged. The route changes worked well to throw off the night-fighters, until the bombers reached the target area, where ten-tenths cloud with tops at 16,000 feet forced the bombing to take place on the red skymarkers with green stars or on the glow of fires. The remaining 106 Squadron crews delivered their attacks from 20,000 to 22,000 feet between 02.49 and 02.55, and reported smoke rising to 20,000 feet as they turned away, but it was not possible to make an accurate assessment of the outcome, and the impression was of an effective attack, when, in fact, it had been another failure. Bombs had been scattered across the city and destroyed just eighty-two houses for the loss of twenty-seven Lancasters, ten of them belonging to the Path Finder Force, and most had fallen victim to night-fighters in the target area.

After three trips there in five nights, Berlin would now be left to 8 Group Mosquitos to disturb the residents' sleep with cookies until the heavy brigade returned in the final third of the month. This allowed Harris to turn his attention elsewhere on the 5th, and he selected the Baltic port-city of Stettin, which had not been attacked in numbers since the previous April. It was to be another predominantly Lancaster affair, involving 348 of the type accompanied by ten Halifaxes, for which 5 Group put up 120 Lancasters, eleven of them made ready by 106 Squadron at Metheringham. They took off between 23.55 and 00.10 with F/Ls Claridge, Harvey and Poore the senior pilots on duty, and headed for the North Sea to join up with the rest of the bomber stream. In contrast to the seventeen early returns by 5 Group crews during the last Berlin operation, only one came home early on this night, and those continuing on found themselves in thick cloud at cruising altitude, some struggling to find a clear lane even when as high as 23,000 feet. On the plus side, they all benefitted from a Mosquito diversion at Berlin, which kept the night-fighters off the scent. Stettin was found to be partially visible through five-tenths thin cloud with tops at around 10,000 feet, and crews were able to identify some ground features before focusing on

H2S-laid flares and green TIs, which those from 106 Squadron bombed from 18,000 to 22,000 feet between 03.49 and 03.57. They turned for home and were 150 miles from the target when the glow from the burning city faded away, leaving them convinced that the operation had been a success. The crews of F/Ls Claridge and Poore brought back an aiming point photo, while P/O Kirkland and crew reported being attacked by three separate night-fighters, one of which they claimed as damaged. They were able to provide the Intelligence Section with accounts of a highly accurate and concentrated attack, which seemed to leave the entire city on fire. Fourteen Lancasters and two Halifaxes failed to return, in exchange for which, post-raid reconnaissance and local reports confirmed heavy damage in central and western districts, where 504 houses and twenty industrial buildings had been destroyed, a further 1,148 houses and twenty-nine industrial buildings seriously damaged, and eight ships sunk in the harbour.

The arrival of the moon period allowed further respite from operations, and batches of crews were given a forty-eight hour pass over the ensuing week. Snowfalls and freezing conditions made life difficult for ground personnel, but they were able to keep Lancasters flying for training purposes. The tannoys on Lancaster stations called the faithful to prayer on the 14th to tell them of their part in the next operation, and there must have been a degree of relief when the red tape on the wall maps at briefings terminated some way short of Berlin and pointed the way to the medieval city of Braunschweig (Brunswick), situated around fifty miles south-east of Hannover. A garrison city, Braunschweig was a centre of heavy engineering, canneries, research facilities, was a major communications hub, and provided labour, both volunteer and forced, for the Hermann Goering steelworks at nearby Salzgitter and the Volkswagen factory at Fallersleben. A force of 496 Lancasters and two Halifaxes was assembled of which 153 of the former represented 5 Group, thirteen of them made ready at Metheringham for what would be the first major raid on this target. The 106 Squadron participants took off between 16.40 and 17.00 with F/Ls Claridge, Ginder and Harvey the senior pilots on duty, each crew sitting on a cookie and mix of 4lb and 30lb incendiaries. After climbing out, they headed for the North Sea, at which point the German night-fighter controller became aware of the approaching bomber stream and met it at Germany's north-western coast with a proportion of his resources. From that point on, a running battle ensued all the way to the target and back as far as the Dutch coast. Complete cloud cover at the target, in places, up to around 15,000 feet, dictated the use of red skymarkers with green stars, at which the 106 Squadron crews aimed from 20,000 to 22,000 feet between 19.14 and 19.23. The enemy fighters scored consistently and accounted for the majority of the thirty-eight missing Lancasters, many of which came down around Hannover. The attack almost entirely missed the city, falling mostly onto outlying communities to the south, and was reported locally as a light raid. This would be a continuing theme in future attacks up to the autumn, as Braunschweig enjoyed something of a charmed life, leading to a belief among the populace that the surrounding villages were being targeted intentionally, in an attempt to drive the residents into the city, before a major operation destroyed it with them in it! All from Metheringham returned safely, persuaded by the glow of fires beneath the clouds that it had been an effective attack. These first two weeks of 1944 had been particularly bad for the Path Finders, and 156 Squadron alone had lost fourteen aircraft on the Berlin and Braunschweig raids, the equivalent almost of a complete two-flight squadron. Such losses could not be sustained, and many sideways posting took place to maintain a leavening of experience in each 8 Group squadron, while some of the cream among the new recruits leaving training units went straight into 8 Group, rather than gain experience in a main force squadron.

Fog kept the Lincolnshire squadrons on the ground for the next few days and nights, and during this period, on the 16th, the award of a DFC was announced to the popular W/C Baxter. The lull in operations came to an end on the 20th, when orders were received to assemble a maximum effort force for the next round of the Berlin offensive. The Halifax squadrons, which had appeared to be in hibernation since late December, were roused from their slumber, and 264 of them joined 495 Lancasters to constitute the Path Finder and main force elements, while two small Mosquito sections carried out spoof raids on Kiel and

Hannover. 5 Group weighed in with 155 Lancasters, of which sixteen, all of those available, were made ready by 106 Squadron at Metheringham. They took off between 16.25 and 16.45 with F/Ls Claridge and Poore the senior pilots on duty, and experienced a rare pleasure of climbing out with sufficient daylight to observe the dozens of other Lancasters rising up into the dusk to join them from the neighbouring stations. Recent heavy losses had pointed to the need to adopt diversionary tactics, and abandon the straight-in straight-out routing, which led to this night's plan to enter German airspace north-west of Bremen, cross the Schleswig-Holstein peninsula and approach Berlin from the north-west, while small Mosquito feints at Kiel and Hannover hopefully caused confusion in the mind of the night-fighter controller. This did not happen, and night-fighters infiltrated the bomber stream south of Kiel, guided by the tame boar system, based on the orbiting of radio beacons until being vectored by running commentary to where they were needed.

The bomber stream formed up over the North Sea, all the time shedding individual aircraft as a hefty seventy-five crews abandoned their sorties and turned back. The others made landfall on the Nordfriesland coast at a point opposite Kiel, before turning to the south-east on a more-or-less direct course for Berlin, and soon found themselves hounded by night-fighters. The enemy controller had fed a proportion of his resources into the bomber stream east of Hamburg, and they would remain in contact until a point between Leipzig and Hannover on the way home, although, curiously, the 5 Group brigade saw nothing of this and would lose just a single 57 Squadron Lancaster. The two Mosquito diversions had been completely ignored by the Luftwaffe controller, who knew well in advance that Berlin was to be the target. The Path Finders arrived over the Müritzsee to the north of Berlin with a sixty-mile run-in to the aiming point, and they found this to be concealed beneath the same ten-tenths cloud that had accompanied them for the entire outward leg. The tops of the cloud lay beneath the bombers at up to 15,000 feet as the main force crews carried out their attacks on red skymarkers with green stars, those representing 106 Squadron from 20,000 to 22,000 feet between 19.36 and 19.45, before turning south-west to a point north of Leipzig. From here they headed due west, with the night fighters still very much in evidence until south of Brunswick, where most peeled off. North-east of the Ruhr they turned to the north-west to cross northern Holland and exit enemy territory over Terschelling. By this time, twenty-two Halifaxes and thirteen Lancasters had been brought down, representing an 8.3% casualty rate for the former compared with 2.6% for the latter. 106 Squadron came through again without loss, the crews commenting at debriefing on the lack of flak activity over Berlin, and reported the glow of large fires under the cloud and smoke rising through the tops. It took a little time for an assessment of the operation to be made because of continuing cloud over north-eastern Germany, by which time four further raids had taken place. It seems from local reports that the eastern districts had received the heaviest weight of bombs in an eight-mile stretch from Weissesee in the north to Neukölln in the south, although no details of destruction emerged.

On the following day, the city of Magdeburg was posted to host its first major attack of the war. Situated some fifty miles from Braunschweig and slightly to the south of east, it had been a regular destination in 1941 for small forces targeting the Braunkohle A G hydrogenation plant located in the Rothensee district to the north of the city centre, and it was now on an increasingly familiar route as far as the enemy night-fighter controllers were concerned, and within easy striking distance of his assembly beacons. In an attempt to deceive the enemy, a small-scale diversion was planned at Berlin involving twenty-two Lancaster of 5 Group and twelve Mosquitos of 8 Group. 5 Group contributed 122 Lancasters to the main event, 106 Squadron briefing fourteen crews for this and two for Berlin, and they lined up for take-off shortly before 20.00. Seven crews got away safely for Magdeburg and one for Berlin by 20.35 with no senior pilots on duty, before the second Berlin-bound Lancaster became bogged down while taxiing in the darkness and prevented all others from taking off. Having climbed out, they formed into a stream over the North Sea and set course to a point some one hundred miles off the west coast of the Schleswig-

Holstein peninsula, before turning to the south-east to pass between Hamburg and Hannover. Enemy radar was able to detect H2S transmissions during night-flying tests and equipment checks, and the night-fighter controller was, thereby, always aware of an imminent heavy raid. On this night, the night-fighters were able to infiltrate the bomber stream even before the German coast was crossed, and the recently introduced "Tame Boar" night-fighter system provided a running commentary on the bomber stream's progress, enabling the fighters to latch onto it and remain in contact. The final turning-point was twenty-five miles north-east of the target, and this was identified both by Path Finder markers and the bombing of twenty-seven main force aircraft. These had been driven by stronger-than-forecast winds to arrive ahead of schedule, and contained crews anxious to get the job done and get out of the target area as soon as possible. They bombed using their own H2S without waiting for the TIs to go down, and the fires caused by their bombs, along with very effective enemy decoy markers, compromised the Path Finder efforts to achieve concentration after their initial red target indicators went down at 22.50.

The conditions over Magdeburg varied according to the time of arrival, the early birds encountering seven to nine-tenths thin cloud at around 6,000 feet, while those turning up towards the end of the raid found the northern half of the city completely clear with cloud over the southern half only. The 106 Squadron crews experienced a mixture of eight-tenths cloud and relatively clear skies, and, in the face of fairly modest opposition, bombed on clusters of cascading green TIs from 21,000 to 22,000 feet between 22.59 and 23.13, all gaining the impression that the attack had been concentrated around the markers. Returning crews from other groups reported explosions and fires or their glow, and smoke beginning to rise as they turned away. A number reported a flash some twelve minutes after bombing, that lit up the clouds for seven seconds, and two large explosions at 23.15. Fires that initially seemed to be scattered, appeared to become more concentrated as the crews headed for home, and the impression was of a successful operation. While all of this was in progress, the diversionary force arrived at Berlin, some seventy miles away to the north-east, where the sole 106 Squadron representatives, P/O Gibbs and crew, found a layer of eight to ten-tenths cloud at 10,000 feet, through which they bombed from 20,000 feet at 22.54. The 5 Group ORB expressed the opinion that the diversion had succeeded in the early stages in reducing the impact of the Nachtjagd, although this was not borne out by the figures. In the absence of post-raid reconnaissance and a local report, the outcome at Magdeburg was not confirmed, and it is generally believed now that most of the bombing fell outside of the city boundaries. A record fifty-seven aircraft failed to return, thirty-five of them Halifaxes, and this provided another alarming statistic of a 15.6% loss-rate compared with 5.2% for the Lancasters.

The end of the month was to bring the final concerted effort to destroy Berlin, and would involve three trips in the space of an unprecedented four nights. Before this hectic round of operations began on the 27th, however, seventeen Lancasters had been ready to take off from Metheringham for Frankfurt on the evening of the 25th, but a scrub signal came through twenty-five minutes before take-off. This meant that squadrons had enjoyed five nights of rest since the bruising experience of Magdeburg, when Berlin was posted as that night's target on the 27th. The operation involved an all-Lancaster heavy force of 515 aircraft, for which 5 Group detailed a record number of 172, seventeen of them belonging to 106 Squadron, which departed Metheringham between 17.40 and 17.55 with F/L Ginder the senior pilot on duty. After climbing out and rendezvousing with the rest of the 5 Group squadrons, they set course on a complex route that would take the bomber stream towards the north German coast, before swinging to the south-east to enter enemy territory over the Frisians and northern Holland. Having then feinted towards central Germany, suggesting Leipzig as the target, the force was to turn north-east to a point west of Berlin, from where the final run-in would commence. The long return route passed to the west of Leipzig before turning due east to miss Frankfurt on its northern side and traverse Belgium to gain the Channel south of Boulogne. P/O Anderson and crew had both turrets fail before reaching the enemy coast and turned back, leaving the others to press on towards the target, while a mining diversion off

Heligoland and the dispensing of dummy fighter flares and route-markers partially succeeded in reducing the numbers of enemy night-fighters making contact. It was, therefore, a relatively intact bomber force that approached the target over ten-tenths cloud with tops at 15,000 feet, conditions that required the Path Finders to employ sky-marking. Red Wanganui flares with green stars drew the 106 Squadron crews to the aiming point, where all bombed from 20,000 to 22,000 feet between 20.33 and 20.43. F/L Ginder and crew witnessed a large explosion at 20.33, and F/O Perry reported that the glow of fires remained visible for 150 miles into the return journey. Sgt Moxey and crew, who had just joined the squadron, lost their bearings on the way home, and required four fixes from Southampton before they found the south coast and landed at Middle Wallop. They were joined by P/O Rosser and crew, whose navigator had become ill soon after leaving the target, and the bomb-aimer had taken over his duties to guide them home. At debriefings, crews reported the glow of fires and the appearance of a successful raid, but no detailed assessment was forthcoming. Of course, not all would make it back to tell their stories at debriefing, and thirty-three Lancaster dispersal pans stood empty in dawn's early light. Reports from Berlin described bombs falling over a wide area, more so in the south than the north, and damage to fifty industrial premises, a number of them engaged in important war work, while twenty thousand people were bombed out of their homes. A feature of the campaign was the number of outlying communities suffering collateral damage, and, on this night, sixty-one such hamlets recorded bombs falling.

The early time-on-target had allowed crews to get a full night in bed, and they were, hopefully, fully rested, when news came through on the 28th that many of them would be returning to the "Big City" that night. A heavy force of 673 aircraft was assembled, of which 432 were Lancasters and 241 Halifaxes, 155 of the former provided by 5 Group. This number included seventeen Lancasters belonging to 106 Squadron, which departed Metheringham between 00.05 and 00.50 with S/L Crowe the senior pilot on duty. They were routed out over southern Denmark, before turning south-east on a direct course for the target, with an almost reciprocal return and various diversionary measures in place to distract the night-fighter controller, including a Mosquito attack on Berlin, minelaying in Kiel Bay and a spoof attack on Hannover. Sixty-six crews turned back early, suggesting some adverse reaction to the back-to-back operations, and among them were the 106 Squadron crews of F/Sgt Milne and P/O Pezaro, because of engine and rear-turret failure respectively. Those reaching the target area encountered ten-tenths cloud, and a mixture of sky and ground-markers to aim at. The night-fighter controller concentrated his forces over Berlin, where the 106 Squadron crews began to arrive a few minutes after 03.00, S/L Crowe and crew observing one very large explosion in the distance as they closed on the city at 03.15. They bombed ten minutes later from 20,000 feet, and expressed the opinion that this was the most concentrated attack that they had witness at this target, and claimed that fires were still burning from the previous night's raid. The other 106 Squadron crews carried out their bombing runs at 19,000 to 22,000 feet between 03.15 and 03.28, some aiming at release-point flares, while others could see the ground markers through gaps in the clouds, but all were of one mind, that this appeared to be a highly concentrated and destructive operation. Two huge explosions were witnessed at 03.18 and 03.25, the earlier one described by a 10 Squadron crew as lighting up the sky over a radius of fifty miles. Forty-six aircraft failed to return, twenty-six of them Halifaxes, as the defenders fought back to exact another heavy toll of bombers, but Metheringham's dispersals were all occupied as dawn broke over the Lincolnshire Fens. The impression gained from returning crews at debriefing was of a concentrated and effective attack, and this was partly borne-out by local reports of heavy damage in western and southern districts, where 180,000 people had been bombed out of their homes. However, as had been the pattern throughout the campaign against Berlin, seventy-seven outlying communities had also been afflicted.

Before briefings took place for the final operation of the month on the 30th, W/C Baxter carried out a thirty-minute flight to test "Fishpond", an updated H2S system that alerted the crew to the approach of a night-fighter. Then it was back to the war for an operation to Berlin involving 534 aircraft, of which 5

Group contributed 156 Lancasters, seventeen of them belonging to 106 Squadron. They departed Metheringham between 17.10 and 17.45 with W/C Baxter the senior pilot on duty and captain of an experienced all-NCO crew. After climbing out, the Metheringham contingent joined up with the bomber stream over the North Sea, before heading for the Schleswig-Holstein peninsula, and an approach to the target from the north-west. The return route would take them south of Braunschweig, followed by a dash for the Dutch coast via the northern tip of the Ijsselmeer. For the second operation running, P/O Pezaro and crew were forced to turn back, this time with a defective engine, leaving the others to press on and remain relatively free of harassment until approaching the target, where ten-tenths cloud prevailed at around 8,000 feet. Path Finder release-point flares were drifting down, and the 106 Squadron crews bombed on these from 20,000 to 22,000 feet between 20.25 and 20.33, all commenting on the smoke rising through 12,000 feet and the glow of fires beneath the cloud, which, according to some, was still visible from a hundred miles into the return flight. Thirty-two Lancasters and a single Halifax failed to make it home, among them 106 Squadron's ND336, which crashed into the North Sea, and took with it P/O Kirkland RAAF and his crew. His body would wash ashore on the Frisian island of Vlieland some five weeks later, and was the only one from the crew to be recovered. Returning crews mostly reported large areas of fire and a successful attack, and only F/O Forsyth and crew had a brief encounter with a night-fighter, which hit and slightly damaged the bomb bay directly under the pilot's seat. It was reckoned that the odds of surviving a tour were lowest during the first half-dozen sorties, and once through these, chances were that a crew would reach the mid-twenties, before the odds shortened again for the final five, and tension among these crews must have been very high. F/O Forsyth and his crew were on their penultimate operation on this night, and their hearts must have been racing until the enemy fighter broke off the engagement. In return for the significant loss of thirty-three aircraft, and according to local reports, central and south-western districts suffered heavy damage and serious areas of fire. Other parts of the city were also hit, while many bomb loads were again scattered liberally onto outlying communities, and at least a thousand people lost their lives. 112 heavy bombers and their crews had been lost to the Command as a result of these three operations, and, with the introduction of the enemy's highly efficient Tame Boar night-fighter system based on running commentaries, the advantage had swung back in the defenders' favour.

There is no question that Berlin had been sorely afflicted since the resumption of the campaign in November, and, although there would be two further heavy attacks on the city during the next seven weeks, they would be in isolation, and this series at the end of January proved to be the last concerted effort to bring the Capital to its knees. Berlin had not been wrecked from end to end, as Harris had predicted, but there had never been a realistic chance that it could be. Berlin was no Hamburg or Lübeck, which had developed over centuries with narrow streets and tightly-packed residential districts. Berlin was a modern city of concrete and steel, with wide thoroughfares and open spaces acting as natural firebreaks, and the destruction caused by each raid created new firebreaks, invoking the law of diminishing returns. It was also too distant, too big and too well defended, and the campaign came at a time when the Luftwaffe Nachtjagd was at its most efficient and lethal. During the course of the month 106 Squadron operated on nine nights, dispatching 123 sorties for the loss of three aircraft and crews and delivered 497 tons of bombs, the second highest in 5 Group.

February 1944

Bad weather during the first two weeks of February allowed the crews to draw breath and the squadrons to replenish. Harris had intended to maintain the pressure on Berlin, and would have launched a further attack, had he not been thwarted by the conditions, and as a result, the time was filled with training and mining operations.

When the Path Finder and main force squadrons next took to the air, it would be for a record-breaking effort to Berlin on the 15th, and would also be the penultimate operation of the campaign, and, indeed, of the war by Bomber Command's heavy brigade against Germany's capital city. The force of 891 aircraft represented the largest non-1,000 force to date, and, therefore, the greatest-ever to be sent against the Capital, and it would be the first time that more than five hundred Lancasters and three hundred Halifaxes had operated together. 5 Group would surpass its previous best effort by fifty Lancasters when putting 226 of them into the air, and nineteen of them would be representing 106 Squadron. The bomb bays of this huge armada would convey to Berlin the greatest-ever tonnage of bombs to any target to date, and 106 Squadron's contribution would be nineteen cookies and 17,100 x 4lb and 1,196 x 30lb incendiaries. They departed Metheringham between 17.10 and 17.35 with S/L Dunn the senior pilot on duty, and, after joining up with the rest of the 5 Group squadrons, they set course for the western coast of Denmark, before crossing Jutland and entering Germany via the Baltic coast between Rostock and Stralsund, with a direct heading, thereafter, for the target. The return route would require the bombers to pass south of Hannover and Bremen, and cross Holland to the North Sea via Castricum. Extensive diversionary measures included a mining operation in Kiel Bay ahead of the arrival of the bombers, a raid on Frankfurt-an-Oder to the east of Berlin by a small force of 8 Group Lancasters, and Oboe Mosquitos attacking five night-fighter airfields in Holland. The force had been depleted by seventy-five early returns by the time the remainder homed in on the target, where ten-tenths cloud at around 10,000 feet concealed it from their view, but those with H2S were able to confirm their positions, while the others relied on the Path Finders' red release-point flares with green stars and red and green TIs on the ground. The attack was timed to begin at 21.13, and F/L Poore and crew were the first from 106 Squadron to arrive in the spearhead of the main force, and they bombed the skymarkers at 21.15 from 21,000 feet. The attack was supposed to be over by 21.35, and all of the Metheringham crews had delivered their bombs by then from between 20,000 and 23,000 feet, although others continued to arrive right up until almost 22.00. There was another scare for F/O Forsyth and crew after JB641 was hit by incendiaries from above and severely damaged. Fate was determined to give this crew a hard time on their final sortie, but they brought the Lancaster home, where it was declared category AC, which meant that it was beyond unit repair, but could be repaired on site by another unit or contractor. On board with Forsyth and flying as second pilot was P/O Bill Carey, the young Australian who, with his crew, would join 617 Squadron later in the year, and end up temporarily in luxurious internment in Sweden following the second attack on the Tirpitz.

The overlapping circuits of the neighbouring bomber airfields in the region provided numerous opportunities for collisions, and this meant that the tired crews had to maintain vigilance right down to the runway. JB534 had just joined the circuit and was at around 1,000 feet when the bomber-aimer called a terse warning about another aircraft ahead. P/O Dickerson pushed the nose down to avoid a collision, but the Lancaster impacted the ground near Metheringham ten minutes after midnight and broke in two. The pilot and three others in the forward section were killed instantly, and the wireless operator succumbed to his injuries later in the day, while both gunners were taken to hospital and survived. Returning crews reported the markers to be highly effective and well-concentrated, and the burgeoning glow beneath the clouds convinced them that they had taken part in a successful operation. This was borne out by local reports, which confirmed that the 2,642 tons of bombs had caused extensive damage in central and south-western districts, but had also spilled out into surrounding communities. The emergency services had to deal with more than eleven hundred fires, a thousand houses and more than five hundred temporary wooden barracks were destroyed, and important war-industry factories in the Siemensstadt district were damaged. In return, Bomber Command lost forty-three aircraft, twenty-six Lancasters, (4.6%) and seventeen Halifaxes, (5.4%). Perhaps slightly disturbing was the fact that eight of the missing Halifaxes were Mk IIIs, only one fewer than the nine Mk II/Vs. Later on the 16th, the award of a DFC was announced to five pilots, F/Ls Claridge and Harvey, and F/Os Cole, Perry and Forsyth.

The potential for disaster attended every major Bomber Command operation, and on three occasions before the end of the winter campaign, it would be realized in horrific fashion. Despite the recent heavy losses, when orders were received on the 19th to prepare for another major assault that night, this time on Leipzig, the heavy squadrons were able offer 816 aircraft, 561 Lancasters and 255 Halifaxes. 5 Group managed 209 Lancasters and 106 Squadron fifteen, which were spread throughout bomber stream, six in the first wave and three each in the second, third and sixth, and they departed Metheringham between 23.40 and 00.20 with S/L Dunn the senior pilot on duty and the new B Flight commander, S/L Murdoch, flying as second pilot to F/L Ginder. After climbing out, they formed into a stream heading for the Dutch coast, where a proportion of the Luftwaffe Nachtjagd was waiting for them, while others had been drawn away by a mining diversion off Kiel. Barring unforeseen circumstances, the four-hour outward leg was intended to bring the bombers to the target between 04.00 and 04.19. P/O Jardine and crew turned back after an hour or so, while the remainder continued on, some to become embroiled in a running battle with night-fighters all the way into eastern Germany, where inaccurately forecast winds caused some aircraft to arrive at the target early. These were forced to orbit, while they awaited the arrival of the Path Finders to mark the target, and the local flak batteries accounted for around twenty of them, while four others were lost through collisions. The 106 Squadron crews arrived to find ten-tenths cloud with tops at around 10,000 feet, and S/L Dunn and crew located the aiming point by means of Path Finder markers confirmed by their own H2S. They bombed on release-point flares bang on 04.00 from 21,500 feet, and were followed by the others from the squadron, who aimed at the same green Wanganui flares and also red and green TIs from 21,000 to 23,000 feet between 04.00 and 04.10. It seems that there was a brief period during the attack when skymarking stopped and led to some scattering of bombs, but the marker-flares were soon replenished with the arrival of more backers-up, and a considerable glow beneath the cloud remained visible for some fifty minutes into the return journey, giving the impression of a successful assault. When all of those aircraft returning home had been accounted for, there was a massive shortfall of seventy-eight, a record loss by a clear twenty-one aircraft. Among them was 106 Squadron's ME630, which was caught by a night-fighter at 21,000 feet as it approached the target and shot down, although not before F/O Leggett and his crew had managed to take to their parachutes. Sadly, it appears that the pilot fell into water and drowned, while his crew was rounded up and taken into captivity. Forty-four Lancasters and thirty-four Halifaxes had failed to return, with a loss-rate of 7.8% and 13.3% respectively, and this prompted Harris to immediately withdraw the Merlin-powered Mk II and V Halifaxes from further operations over Germany, which, at a stroke, removed a proportion of 4 Group's fire-power from the front line until they could re-equip with the Mk III Halifax. In the meantime, the Mk II and V operators would focus their energies for the remainder of the month on gardening duties.

Despite this depletion of available numbers, a force of 598 aircraft was made ready on the 20th for an operation that night against Stuttgart, which would be the first of three against the city over a three-week period. 5 Group contributed 176 Lancasters, thirteen of them belonging to 106 Squadron, and they were each loaded with a cookie and SBCs of incendiaries, before departing Metheringham between 23.50 and 00.20 with F/L Ginder the senior pilot on duty. Again, the crews had been assigned to specific waves, four in the first, and three each in the second, third and fourth, but the crews of F/O Penman and P/O Anderson returned early with technical problems, leaving the others to press on to the south coast and beyond. They made their way across the Channel to the French coast, from where the cloud remained at ten-tenths with tops at 8,000 feet all the way into southern Germany. A North Sea sweep and a diversionary raid on Munich two hours ahead of the main activity had caused the Luftwaffe to deploy its forces early, and this allowed the bomber stream to push on unmolested to the target. By the time it hove into view, the cloud had thinned to five to eight-tenths at around 6,000 feet, and the excellent visibility enabled the crews to draw a bead on the Path Finder red and green sky-markers and similar-coloured TIs on the ground. The 106 Squadron crews bombed from 22,000 to 24,000 feet between 04.00 and 04.10, observing many large fires, and, on return, there were reports that the glow from the burning city was still visible from 250 miles into the return flight. Despite some scattering of bombs, local reports described central districts and those in a quadrant from north-west to north-east suffering extensive damage, and a Bosch factory was one of the important war industry concerns to be hard-hit. In contrast to twenty-four hours earlier, a modest nine aircraft failed to return.

In an attempt to reduce the prohibitive losses of recent weeks, a new tactic was introduced for the next two operations. A force of 734 aircraft was assembled on the 24th for an assault on the centre of Germany's ball-bearing production, Schweinfurt, situated some sixty miles to the east of Frankfurt in southern Germany. The plan called for 392 aircraft to depart their stations between 18.00 and 19.00, and to be followed into the air two hours later by 342 others in the hope of catching the night-fighters on the ground refuelling and re-arming as the second wave passed through. While this operation was in progress, extensive diversionary measures would be put in hand that involved more than three hundred other aircraft, including 179 from the training units conducting a North Sea sweep, and 110 Halifaxes and Stirlings mining in northern waters. 5 Group contributed 204 Lancasters, of which seventeen represented 106 Squadron, six in the first wave and the remainder in the second, and these were assigned once more to specific waves within each force. W/C Baxter took the early shift with the recently arrived New Zealander, S/L Murdoch and F/L Sprawson, who were both undertaking their first operations with the squadron as crew captains, and also in this first wave were F/O Latham and P/Os Hinkley and Starkey. They got away from Metheringham in a five-minute slot from 18.30, but S/L Murdoch was unable to complete his sortie because of W/T failure. F/L Ginder was the senior pilot among the second phase crews, who took off between 20.20 and 20.40, three of them assigned to Path Finder support duties. This was a new tactic designed to "beef up" the Path Finder presence to prevent individual aircraft from being locked onto by flak, and required the supported crews simply to pass over the aiming point before going round again to release their bombs. The target was found by the first wave crews to be under no more than three-tenths cloud at 3,000 to 4,000 feet, with haze alone spoiling the vertical visibility. W/C Baxter and crew located the target by means of Path Finder TIs and already established fires, and bombed a cluster of red TIs from 22,500 feet at 23.22. They witnessed three large explosions in the target area, while F/L Sprawson and crew described a great column of smoke rising to 10,000 feet. Other crews over the target at this time saw no cloud, and described the visibility as excellent, enabling them to pick out the River Main as they ran in to bomb. Two columns of black smoke were observed to be rising through 5,000 feet as they turned away, and the consensus was of an effective, if, somewhat scattered attack.

Meanwhile, the second phase crews were well on their way, and picked up the glow of fires from the earlier raid at a distance of two hundred miles. The visibility in the target area remained good, despite the rising smoke, and bombing by the 106 Squadron crews took place out of almost cloudless skies onto red and green TIs from 21,000 to 23,000 feet between 01.05 and 01.19. P/O Richards and crew were among these and delivered their five 2,000 pounders at 01.09 from 22,500 feet, before bringing back a bombing photo plotted at two miles from the aiming point. They described the target as a mass of flames, the glow from which could be seen two hundred miles into the return journey. All indications suggested an effective raid, but, unfortunately, both phases of the operation had suffered from undershooting after some Path Finder backers-up had failed to press on to the aiming point. More than 2,200 tons of bombs had been dropped, but photographic reconnaissance was unable to distinguish the RAF results from those of the US Eighth Air Force attack during the previous day. In that regard, it was a disappointing night, but an interesting feature was the loss of 50% fewer aircraft from the second wave in comparison with the first in an overall casualty figure of thirty-three, and this suggested some merit in the tactic. Since the turn of the year a wind-finder system had been in use, in which selected crews monitored wind speed and direction, and passed their findings back to HQ, where the figures were collated, and any changes from the briefed conditions re-broadcast to the bomber stream. This had been found to be extremely useful, but, as would be discovered in the ensuing weeks, the system had its limitations.

The main operation on the following night was directed at the beautiful and culturally significant southern city of Augsburg, situated around thirty miles north-west of Munich. It was home to a major Maschinenfabrik Augsburg Nuremberg (M.A.N) diesel engine factory, which had been the target for the previously mentioned epic low-level daylight raid by 44 and 97 Squadron in April 1942. On this night, 594 aircraft were divided into two waves, and among them were 164 Lancasters of 5 Group, including fifteen representing 106 Squadron. Thirteen of these were assigned to the first wave, taking off between 18.15 and 18.35, with the station commander, G/C McKechnie, the senior pilot on duty, and he was backed up by S/Ls Dunn and Murdoch. They headed for the exit point at Beachy Head to join up with the rest of the force, leaving the crews of P/O Rosser and the recently commissioned P/O Milne on the ground for a further three hours as the only squadron representatives in the second-phase force. The first wave bomber stream flew out over Belgium with ten-tenths cloud beneath them, but that had dissipated by the time the target drew near, and, on arrival, it was possible for crews to gain a visual reference. The Path Finders' red and green TIs were in the bomb sights as the 106 Squadron crews carried out their attacks from 20,000 to 23,000 feet between 22.42 and 23.03, and fires were beginning to take hold as they turned away. The crew of the recently-promoted F/L Gibbs was one of three from the squadron acting as Path Finder supporters, after which they bombed a concentration of red and green TIs from 20,000 feet at 22.45. P/O Hinkley and crew brought back an aiming point photo, and nine others were plotted within a short distance of the target.

The second wave crews were drawn on by the glow in the sky from a hundred miles away, and, by the time they swept in shortly after 01.00, the target was a sea of flames, with smoke rising to 15,000 feet. Despite that, the visibility remained good, and the 106 Squadron duo bombed on existing fires and red and green Wanganui flares and TIs from 22,000 and 23,000 feet at 01.15 and 01.20. The loss of twenty-one aircraft seemed to confirm the benefits of splitting the force, and this tactic would remain an important part of Bomber Command planning for the remainder of the war. It had been a devastatingly destructive operation, in which all facets of the plan had come together in near perfect harmony, spelling disaster for this lightly defended treasure trove of culture. Its heart was torn out by blast and fire that destroyed almost three thousand houses along with buildings of outstanding historical significance, and centuries of irreplaceable culture was lost forever. There was also some industrial damage, and around ninety-thousand people were bombed out of their homes.

The end of the month was characterized by snowfalls, and many of the residents of RAF Metheringham were kept busy wielding shovels. During the course of the month the squadron operated on five nights, dispatching seventy-nine sorties for the loss of two aircraft, one of them crashing at home. The author of the ORB completed the summary for the month by compiling statistics covering the period of operations from the 9th of September 1940 to the 29th of February 1944. Number of nights operated, 368, days 14, sorties 3,531, losses 136, loss rate 3.8%. Bomb tonnage, 8,001.1. Enemy aircraft claimed, (to end of January 1944 only), destroyed 14, probables 3, damaged 23.

March 1944

March would bring an end to the winter campaign, but a long and bitter month would have to be endured first before any respite came from long-range forays into Germany. The crews had enjoyed a few nights off when the second raid of the series on Stuttgart was posted on the 1st, for which a force of 557 aircraft was made ready. This number included 178 Lancasters representing 5 Group, sixteen of which were provided by 106 Squadron, and take-off from Metheringham was accomplished without incident between 23.10 and 23.30 with S/Ls Dunn and Murdoch the senior pilots on duty. Two were allotted to the first wave, three each to the second and third and four to the fourth, while four were designated as Path Finder supporters. They flew out over ten-tenths cloud with tops at between 12,000 and 17,000 feet, which protected the bomber stream from night-fighters, and they encountered similar conditions in the target area, where the Path Finders employed a combination of sky and ground-marking. This, unfortunately, became scattered, and the bombing was directed between two main concentrations, the 106 Squadron crews carrying out their attacks on Wanganui red markers with green stars from 20,000 to 23,000 feet between 03.01 and 03.16. It was not possible to assess the accuracy of the attack, although a column of smoke had reached 25,000 feet by the end of the raid, and large fires were evident from the glow in the sky visible from up to 150 miles away. The continuing presence of thick cloud all the way back made conditions difficult for enemy night-fighters, and a remarkably modest four aircraft failed to return. On their return, the crew of S/L Dunn reported being among the first from the squadron to arrive, and described the visibility above the 15,000-foot cloud as good. They saw no Path Finder flares, and fixed their position by H2S, before delivering five 2,000 pounders at 03.01 from 20,000 feet. They turned for home in the belief that the attack had been scattered and ineffective, and, despite observing a number of large explosions beneath the cloud, most crews returned with the same disappointing impression. It was eventually established that, actually, the raid had been an outstanding success, which had caused extensive damage in central, western and northern districts, where a number of important war-industry factories, including those belonging to Bosch and Daimler-Benz, had sustained damage. 106 Squadron had played its part by dropping sixty-six tons of bombs, and this was the highest in 5 Group.

At the end of the first week, the Halifax brigade, particularly those withdrawn from operations over Germany, fired the opening salvoes of the pre-invasion campaign, the purpose of which was to dismantle by bombing thirty-seven railway centres in France, Belgium and western Germany to prevent their use to counter the Normandy landings. It began on the night of the 6/7th at Trappes marshalling yards, situated some ten miles west-south-west of Paris, and continued at Le Mans in north-western France on the following night. For most of the heavy crews, however, there was no employment following Stuttgart, until a return there in mid-month, but, in the meantime, matters were afoot at 5 Group, and had been ever since a frustrating series of operations against flying bomb launching sites conducted by 617 Squadron since December had failed to realise the desired results. The problem had been an inability to achieve pinpoint accuracy, which was vital to destroy small, precision targets, and Oboe was just not precise enough. Accurate though Oboe undoubtedly was at an urban target, where a margin of error of 400 to 600 yards could be considered pinpoint, precision targets required more. 617 Squadron had obliterated the Oboe markers, only for bombing photos to show that the targets, situated only a matter of yards away, had remained intact. W/C Cheshire and S/L Martin experimented with a dive-bombing technique, which had proved to be successful, but impracticable in a Lancaster, and Cheshire had borrowed a Mosquito for further trials. These were so promising, that the 5 Group A-O-C, AVM Cochrane, authorized a number of operations by the squadron against factory targets in France, before taking the idea to Harris. Harris approved, paving the way for 5 Group to become effectively independent of the main bomber force and begin larger-scale trials.

W/C Baxter took part in an attempt to strike at the Michelin tyre factory at Clermont-Ferrand on the night of the 6/7th, but the crews were recalled when ten minutes from the target because of a fear of inflicting casualties on French civilians. Baxter commented, "A pity", in his log book, but the operation would be rescheduled. His time in command was coming to an end, and, on the 8th, W/C Piercy arrived from 5 Lancaster Finishing School (5LFS) Syerston as the new commanding officer elect. Orders were received at Bardney, Skellingthorpe and Waddington on the 9th to prepare eleven Lancasters each for a

5 Group attack that night against the Lioré et Olivier aircraft factory at Marignane, situated a few miles to the north of Marseilles in southern France. The area was the main pre-war hub for commercial flying boat operations, particularly for the Pan American Clipper Class flights, and the factory had been engaged in the manufacture of the LeO 45 twin-engine medium bomber for the French Air Force. They took off in mid-evening with a round-trip ahead of them of some 1,350 miles if they flew direct, and arrived in the target area under clear skies and bright moonlight. This facilitated an easy identification of the factory buildings, which had been marked by red spotfires, and the bombing was carried out from medium level either side of 01.30. The high-explosives were seen to fall among the buildings, while the incendiaries appeared to be a little scattered, but a large explosion was witnessed at 01.24 and a huge pall of smoke was rising through 6,000 feet as the force turned away. All arrived home safely, most having spent more than nine hours aloft.

The outgoing commanding officer undertook his final operation with the squadron on one of a number of small-scale 5 Group trial operations on the night of the 10/11th. Four small forces were each assigned to attack a specific factory in France that night, the Michelin tyre factory at Clermont-Ferrand, the Bloch aircraft factory at Châteauroux, which was the first to be set up by the famed designer, Marcel Dassault in 1935, the Morane Saulnier aircraft plant at Ossun, just north of the Pyrenese and the Ricamerie needle-bearing works at St-Etienne, the last-mentioned, the objective for sixteen Lancasters from 617 Squadron. Ten 106 Squadron Lancasters joined twenty others from 61 and 619 Squadrons to attack the Bloch factory at Chateauroux in central France, and departed Metheringham between 20.00 and 20.25 with W/C Baxter flying with S/L Dunn, so that he could concentrate on controlling the marking and bombing, while W/C Piercy flew as second pilot with F/O Latham. They arrived in the target area to find clear skies with ground haze, through which S/L Dunn and crew identified the target visually, and dropped three red spotfires from 6,000 feet right on top of the factory. It was the accuracy of these and the controlling by W/C Baxter, which was responsible for the success of the operation, as the squadron participants bombed in a ten-minute slot from 22.44 from between 7,000 and 8,000 feet, and S/L Murdoch brought back an aiming point photo. Reconnaissance confirmed the accuracy of this and the other three attacks, and it brought a fitting conclusion to the tour of the highly popular and greatly respected W/C Baxter.

W/C Baxter departed 106 Squadron on the 13th with a total of 1,170 hours 50 minutes flying time in his log book. His successor, W/C Edmund Keith Piercy, had served in the Middle-East on Wellingtons, and most recently had completed a spell as an instructor at 1661 Conversion Unit at Winthorpe, which had Stirlings on charge. It was here that he inherited his new crew, whose original pilot, F/O Hinton, had failed to return from an operation as a second pilot shortly after they were posted to 9 Squadron. Now headless, they were shipped back to Winthorpe to complete their training and find a new driver. Piercy was a shy man, who was secretive about his Christian names, and never revealed them to his crew. He was also known to be an accomplished drinker, but he did not allow this to impact upon his operational efficiency, and he was recognised to be a first-rate pilot. He quickly acquired the nickname Pluto, which he also applied to his favoured Lancaster. His passion, though, was his Matchless 1,000cc motorcycle, which he raced up and down the runway, much to the consternation of the station commander, G/C McKechnie.

Now that the Mk III Halifax was becoming available in larger numbers, the Command was quickly returning to full strength, and it was a force of 863 aircraft that set out for Stuttgart in the early-evening of the 15th. This number included 206 Lancasters provided by 5 Group, eleven of them departing Metheringham between 19.20 and 19.30 with W/C Piercy and S/L Murdoch the senior pilots on duty. They rendezvoused with the rest of the force as they passed over Reading on their way to the south coast, and an elongated bomber stream crossed the French coast at 20,000 feet over broken cloud with clear conditions above. It maintained a course parallel with the frontiers of Belgium, Luxembourg and Germany as if heading for Switzerland, before turning towards the north-east for the run-in to the target. It was during this final leg that the night-fighters managed to infiltrate a section of the stream and score heavily, although, this was not apparent to the majority of the 5 Group contingent. Adverse winds were responsible for the Path Finders arriving up to six minutes late to open the attack, when they employed both sky and ground-markers in the face of seven to ten-tenths cloud at between 8,000 and 15,000 feet. The Wanganui flares drifted in the wind, marking an area to the north-east of the River Neckar, while the TIs landed far apart in the north and south of the city. The 106 Squadron crews bombed on whatever markers presented themselves, mostly red TIs, from 22,000 to 23,000 feet between 23.15 and 23.31, observing a spread of fires, including two large ones ten miles apart, and smoke rising to bombing altitude. It would be established later that some of the early bombing had been accurate, but, that most of the loads had undershot and fallen into open country, a disappointment compounded by the loss, mostly to night-fighters, of thirty-seven aircraft. The Lancasters of F/L Sprawson and P/O Bartlett almost became casualties after being hit by incendiaries from above, and they needed some repair work. While this operation was in progress six others from Metheringham took off between 20.45 and 21.00 to join a small-scale 5 Group effort against an aero-engine factory at Woippy near Metz in north-eastern France, led by 617 Squadron. The plan was for the 106 Squadron crews under S/L Dunn to illuminate the target, but ten-tenths cloud obscured the ground, and the operation was abandoned.

On the following night, the same six crews joined others from 617 Squadron to attack the Michelin tyre factory at Clermont-Ferrand, in the Auvergne region of central France. S/L Dunn and crew led them away at 19.15, and it took almost four hours to reach the target, which lay under ten-tenths cloud with a base at 13,000 feet. Dropping below, S/L Dunn's bomb-aimer identified the factory visually and by red spotfires, and delivered marker flares to illuminate it. They then flew back across it to deliver ten 1,000 pounders from 12,000 feet at 23.10. The other squadron representatives also carried out accurate attacks, and left the target in flames with smoke rising to 12,000 feet. They returned safely, confident in the effectiveness of their efforts, and F/L Gibbs and crew had an aiming point photo as evidence.

Many operations had been mounted against Frankfurt during the preceding two years, only a small number of which had been really effective. This state of affairs was about to be rectified, however, and the first of two raids against this south-central powerhouse of industry was posted on the 18th, for which a force of 846 aircraft was made ready. 5 Group supported the operation with 212 Lancasters, thirteen of which belonged to 106 Squadron, and they were loaded at Metheringham with a cookie and mix of incendiaries, before taking off between 19.10 and 19.35 with W/C Piercy and S/L Murdoch the senior pilots on duty. F/L Sprawson and crew were soon contending with overheating starboard engines, and were forced to turn back, leaving the others to press on across France and into Germany in good weather conditions. On arrival in the target area, they encountered a layer of haze 20,000 feet thick, and, according to most, no more than three-tenths cloud. This allowed the Path Finders to employ the Newhaven ground marking technique (blind marking by H2S, followed by visual backing-up), which the 106 Squadron crews exploited when carrying out their attacks on red and green TIs from 21,000 to 23,000 feet between 22.01 and 22.07. W/C Piercy and crew picked out three red ground markers, which they bombed from 23,000 feet at 22.04, and, on return, they commented on the late arrival of the Path Finders and sparseness of the marking. The other crews had similar stories to tell, and P/O Hinkley described the Path Finders as very late. The impression given by all at debriefing was of a widely scattered and generally ineffective attack, with few fires. How wrong they were! P/O Bartlett and crew reported that they had mistaken release-point flares for route markers and had overshot Frankfurt, so turned south and attacked Mannheim instead. Despite the doubts of the Metheringham brigade, they had, indeed, contributed to an outstandingly successful raid, during which, 5 Group alone had dropped more than one thousand tons of bombs for the first time at a single target. Local reports calculated that six thousand buildings had been destroyed or seriously damaged in a swathe of destruction across eastern, central and western districts, and a hundred industrial premises had been afflicted to some extent. In return, Bomber Command posted missing twenty-two aircraft and crews, a sustainable 2.6% of those dispatched, and five of them were from 5 Group.

While this operation was in progress, five of the six usual suspects plus F/L Ginder substituting for S/L Dunn, joined thirteen from 617 Squadron to attack the Poudrerie Nationale explosives factory at Bergerac, east of Bordeaux in south-western France. They departed Metheringham in the wake of the Frankfurt element, and arrived in the target area almost four hours later to illuminate the aiming point for the 617 Squadron crews to bomb, six of them employing 12,000lb blockbusters (not to be confused with Wallis's 12,000lb Tallboys, which were not yet in use), as used against the Dortmund-Ems Canal in September of the previous year. The 106 Squadron crews followed up with incendiaries between 23.10 and 23.16 from medium level, and all returned home safely from another highly successful precision attack.

Two nights later the target for 617 Squadron and six Lancasters of 106 Squadron was the nitro-cellulose explosives factory at Angouléme, situated to the north of Bergerac in the Dordogne region of south-western France east of Bordeaux. The 106 Squadron element, led by F/Ls Gibbs and Ginder, was to perform the Path Finder role again, and took off at 19.10 to head for the south coast and the Channel crossing. There was no cloud over the target, and visibility was good as they established their positions, first by H2S and then visually by the light from their own flares. They circled to watch 617 Squadron pound the aiming point with high explosives, before going in themselves to drop 14.9 tons of incendiaries either side of 22.30 from an average of 12,500 feet. Four aiming point photos were brought back and reconnaissance later revealed that most of the factory buildings had been destroyed, and those still standing had sustained damaged to some extent.

Frankfurt was named again on the 22nd as the target for that night, and 217 crews of 5 Group learned that they were to be part of another huge force of 816 aircraft. The eighteen participants from 106 Squadron were to be spread throughout the five waves, with five at the head of the bomber stream to act as Path Finder supporters. They departed Metheringham between 18.45 to 19.10 with S/L Murdoch the senior pilot on duty, and, after climbing out above their stations and forming up, they adopted an unusual route for a target south of the Ruhr, crossing the enemy coast over Vlieland and Teschelling, before passing to the east of Osnabrück on a direct course due south for the target. There were no early returns from the 106 Squadron element, and they arrived at the target to find five to six-tenths thin, low cloud at around 4,000 feet, and Paramatta marking (blind marking by H2S) in progress. They focused their attention on the release-point flares and red and green TIs marking out the aiming point, before bombing from 21,000 to 23,500 feet between 21.45 and 22.00. A massive rectangular area of unbroken fire was observed across the centre of the city, the glow from which could be seen for at least a hundred miles into the return flight. Returning crews reported numerous searchlights lighting up the cloud, and moderate to intense flak that reached up to the bombers' flight level. Local reports confirmed the enormity of the devastation, which was particularly severe in western districts and left this half of the city without electricity, gas and water for an extended period. At 948, the death toll on the ground was more than twice that of the earlier raid, and a further 120,000 were bombed out of their homes at a cost to the Command of twenty-six Lancasters and seven Halifaxes, a loss-rate of 4.2% and 3.8% respectively. 106 Squadron was represented among the missing by JB648, which crashed in the target area after exploding in the air, and only the mid-upper gunner from the crew of P/O Rosser RAAF managed to escape by parachute to fall into enemy hands. The total of 99.2 tons of bombs delivered by the squadron on this night represented a new record for a single target. It was a bad night for senior officers, 207 and 7 Squadrons losing their commanding officers, while Bardney's station commander, G/C Norman Pleasance, failed to return in a

9 Squadron Lancaster. What was about to happen over the next week and a half, however, would overshadow anything that had gone before, and would certainly not fall within what might be considered acceptable.

The squadron continued its Path Finder work on behalf of 617 Squadron on the night of the 23/24th, when the target was the Sigma aero-engine works at Lyon in south-east-central France. The crews of F/Ls Gibbs, Ginder and Lee, F/O Latham and P/Os Anderson and Milne were all safely airborne by 19.30, and arrived in the target area at around 22.45 to find clear skies but poor visibility caused by thick ground haze. They remained in the target area at 13,000 feet dropping illuminator flares at intervals during a twenty-minute slot either side of 23.00, and used up all of their flares in trying to keep the aiming point visible. The plan was for the 106 Squadron crews to then illuminate and attack the nearby transformer station, but having exhausted their supply of flares, they were unable to identify it, and were ordered to abandon the attempt and head for home. According to 617 Squadron records, the 106 Squadron crews actually illuminated the wrong area, firstly four miles to the north, then ten miles to the south and finally ten miles to the north again. There was also an element of unreliability in the flares themselves, which were supposed to burst at 4,000 feet, but often did so at 8,000 feet or on impact with the ground.

It was more than five weeks since the main force had last visited the Capital, and 811 aircraft were made ready on the 24th for what would be the final raid of the war by RAF heavy bombers on the "Big City". 5 Group put up 193 Lancasters, of which fourteen were made ready by 106 Squadron, and they departed Metheringham between 18.35 and 18.50 with W/C Piercy the senior pilot on duty and each carrying a cookie and mix of 4lb and 30lb incendiaries. W/C Piercy lost his instruments very early on, and abandoned his sortie, while the others continued eastwards on a track that would take them across the North Sea to the Danish coast near Ringkøbing and then to a point on the German Baltic coast near Rostock. When north-east of Berlin, they were to adopt a south-westerly course for the bombing run, and, once clear of the defence zone homebound, dogleg to the west and then north-west to pass around Hannover on its southern and western sides, before heading for Holland and an exit via the Castricum coast. The extended outward leg provided a time-on-target of around 22.30, but an unexpected difficulty would be encountered, which would render void all of the meticulous planning. The existence of what we now know as "Jetstream" winds was unknown at the time, and the one blowing from the north with unprecedented strength on this night pushed the bomber stream south of its intended track. Navigators, who were expecting to see the northern tip of Sylt on their H2S screens, were horrified to find the southern end, which meant that they were thirty miles south of track, and about to fly over Germany rather than Denmark. The previously mentioned "wind-finder" system had been set up for precisely this eventuality, but the problem on this night was that the wind-finders refused to believe what their instruments were telling them. Winds in excess of one hundred m.p.h had never been encountered before, and, fearing that they would be disbelieved, many modified the figures downward. The same thing happened at raid control, where the figures were modified again, so that the information rebroadcast to the bomber stream bore no resemblance to the reality of the situation.

There were no further early returns among the 106 Squadron element, and, by the time that the crews had reached Westerhever on the west coast of the Schleswig-Holstein peninsula, most realized that they were some distance south of track, and set course for the north to try to regain the planned route and avoid the defences that would be met if they turned east over Germany. Many commented on the inaccurate wind information received during the outward journey, and having arrived in the target area, some were convinced that the Path Finders were up to ten minutes late in opening the raid. This was confirmed to some by the voice of the Master Bomber exhorting them to hurry up. Crews reported a variety of cloud conditions, from three to ten-tenths at between 6,000 and 15,000 feet, but most were able to pick out the red and green TIs on the ground, and, if not, found red Wanganui flares with green stars to guide them to the aiming point. The 106 Squadron crews confirmed their positions by H2S before bombing from 22,000 to 23,000 feet between 22.28 and 22.50, and observed what appeared to be a scattered attack in the early stages, until fires began to become more concentrated in three distinct areas, and large explosions were witnessed at 22.42 and 22.54. F/O Richards and crew used an H2S-fix because the markers were too scattered, and there were no instructions coming through from the Master Bomber. F/Sgt Hall and crew were on their first operation together, and their first run across Berlin was determined to be south of the city. They made a second run in the face of heavy flak, which knocked out an engine, and were the last from the squadron to deliver their bombs before turning for home. The entire homeward journey was carried out on three engines, and they eventually landed safely at Wing in Buckinghamshire at 02.40. For his perseverance and flying skills F/Sgt Hall received the immediate award of the DFM. At debriefing, crews reported the defences to be very active with moderate flak bursting at up to 24,000 feet, and light flak attempting to shoot out the skymarkers, but night-fighter activity was described by the 5 Group ORB as unusually quiet.

There was a shock awaiting the Command as the returning aircraft landed to leave a shortfall of seventy-two, and it would be established later that two-thirds of them had fallen victim to the Ruhr flak batteries after being driven into that region's defence zone by the wind on the way home. Post-raid analysis revealed that the wind had also played havoc with the marking and bombing, and had pushed the attack towards the south-western districts of the Capital, where most of the damage occurred, while 126 outlying communities also received bombs. 106 Squadron had been present on each of the nineteen main raids to the Capital, and the diversion there on the night of the Magdeburg debacle in January, and had dispatched 281 sorties, the equal second highest number in 5 Group, and only one less than 57 Squadron, and lost just eight Lancasters, the equal second lowest in the group. Fifty-six crewmen were killed, and four survived as PoWs. *(The Berlin Raids, Martin Middlebrook)*.

On the following night, twenty 5 Group Lancasters were invited to take part in an attack on the extensive railway yards at Aulnoye in north-eastern France, while six 106 Squadron crews joined forces yet again with 617 Squadron for a return to the Sigma aero-engine works at Lyons. This time, W/C Piercy was on the Order of Battle, and led them off in a twenty-minute slot from 19.30, each loaded with 184 x 30lb incendiaries and illuminator flares. The visibility in the target area proved to be better on this night, and W/C Piercy and crew identified the target easily before dropping flares for ten minutes, and then circling for twenty minutes awaiting the raid leader's (Cheshire) instructions to bomb on the red spotfires. F/L Gibbs and crew delivered their flares between 23.06 and 23.14, and then circled for thirty-one minutes before dropping their all-incendiary load from 6,000 feet at 23.45. So accurate was the illumination, that F/O Anderson and crew were not called upon to add their flares, but they did deliver their incendiaries at 23.52 before turning for home. F/L Gibbs and Ginder and P/O Milne all brought back aiming point photos. Over at Woodhall Spa there was a debate about the accuracy of the 617 Squadron spotfires delivered by Cheshire, Shannon and McCarthy, and whether or not the crews had bombed the correct ones. By the time that the 617 Squadron crew of F/L Hadland had dropped the last bombs at 00.06, and hour after the raid began, smoke obscured the target, and it was not possible to see if the factory had been hit. Cheshire reported that there were fires covering approximately one square mile, and reconnaissance ultimately revealed that the attack had been concentrated to the south-west of the factory. W/C Piercy reported the glow of fires to be visible for a hundred miles into the return journey.

Although Berlin had now been consigned to the past, the winter campaign still had a week to run, and two more major operations for the crews to negotiate. The first of these was posted on the 26th, and would bring a return to the old enemy of Essen that night, for which a force of 705 aircraft was made ready. 5 Group contributed 172 of the 476 Lancasters, seventeen of them provided by 106 Squadron, which departed Metheringham between 19.40 and 20.00 with F/Ls Gibbs, Ginder and Lee the senior pilots on duty, the first-mentioned undertaking the final sortie of his first tour of operations. They climbed out over the station before joining up with the rest of the bomber stream as it made its way across the North Sea to pass north of Haarlem and Amsterdam, before swinging to the south-east on a direct run to the target. There were no early returns, and all reached the target to find it under eight to ten-tenths cloud with tops in places as high as 14,000 feet. Oboe performed well and enabled the Path Finders to mark the city with red and green TIs and Wanganui flares, which the 106 Squadron crews bombed from 18,000 and 22,500 feet between 22.00 and 22.17, before returning safely, having been unable to assess the results of their efforts. Almost all crews would comment later on the presence of spoof skymarker flares dropped by the enemy, but they were unsuccessful in drawing away the bombing. The impression was of a successful raid, and this was based on a considerable glow developing beneath the clouds as they withdrew. Post-raid reconnaissance soon confirmed another outstandingly destructive operation against this once elusive target, thus continuing the remarkable run of successes here since the introduction of Oboe to main force operations a year earlier. Over seventeen hundred houses were destroyed in the attack, with dozens of war industry factories sustaining serious damage, and, on a night when the night-fighter controllers were caught off guard by the switch to the Ruhr, the success was gained for the modest loss of nine aircraft.

Another attempt to destroy the Sigma aero-engine works at Lyons was mounted on the night of the 29/30th, for which 106 Squadron detailed four crews, led again by W/C Piercy. They took off at 19.40, each carrying twenty flares, and arrived in the target area to find clear skies and visibility assessed at eight miles. F/L Ginder and crew were the first to release their hooded flares, the first batch of three going down at 22.56. The delivery by three 106 Squadron aircraft was co-ordinated to ensure a constant illumination, and W/C Piercy dropped three flares at 23.05, six at 23.13, six more at 23.20 and, finally, four at 23.26. By the time of the arrival of F/O Hinkley and crew, W/C Cheshire was satisfied that the illumination had achieved its aim, and they were told to retain their flares. They returned safely home, and were informed later that the bombing by 617 Squadron had been on the mark, and that sixteen of the twenty-two key buildings on the site had been destroyed.

The period known as the Battle of Berlin, but which was better referred to as the winter campaign, was to be brought to an end on the night of the 30/31st, with a standard maximum-effort raid on Nuremberg. The plan of operation departed from normal practice in only one important respect, and this was to prove critical. It had become standard routine over the winter for 8 Group to plan operations and to employ diversions and feints to confuse the enemy night-fighter controllers. Sometimes they were successful and sometimes not, but with the night-fighter force having clearly gained the upper hand with its "Tame Boar" running commentary system, all possible means had to be adopted to protect the bomber stream. During a conference held early on the 30th, the Lancaster Group A-O-Cs expressed a preference for a 5 Group-inspired route, which would require the bomber stream to fly a long straight leg across Belgium and Germany, to a point about fifty miles north of Nuremberg, from where the final run-in would commence. The Halifax A-O-Cs were less convinced of the benefits, and AVM Bennett, the Path Finder chief, was positively overcome by the potential dangers and predicted a disaster, only to be overruled. A force of 795 aircraft was made ready, of which 201 Lancasters were to be provided by 5 Group, seventeen of them representing 106 Squadron, and the crews attended briefings to be told of the route, wind conditions and the belief that a layer of cloud would conceal them from enemy night-fighters. Before take-off, a Meteorological Flight Mosquito crew radioed in to cast doubts upon the weather conditions, which they could see differed markedly from those that had been forecast. This also went unheeded, and, from around 21.45 for the next hour or so, the crews took off for the rendezvous area, and headed into a conspiracy of circumstances, which would inflict upon Bomber Command its heaviest defeat of the war.

At Metheringham, the 106 Squadron contingent took off between 22.15 and 22.35 with F/Ls Ginder, Lee and Sprawson the senior pilots on duty on what was to be the blackest night in the Command's history. It was not long into the flight before they and the other crews began to notice some unusual features in the conditions, which included uncommonly bright moonlight, and a crystal clarity of visibility that allowed them the rare sight of other aircraft in the stream. On most nights, crews would feel themselves to be completely alone in the sky all the way to the target, until, bang on schedule, TIs would be seen to fall and other aircraft would make their presence known by the turbulence of their slipstreams as they funnelled towards the aiming point. Once at cruising altitude on this night, however, they were alarmed to note that the forecast cloud was conspicuous by its absence, and, instead, lay beneath them as a white tablecloth, against which they were silhouetted like flies. Condensation trails began to form in the cold, clear air to further advertise their presence to the enemy, and the Jetstream winds, which had so adversely affected the Berlin raid a week earlier, were also present, only this time blowing from the south. As then, the wind-finder system would be unable to cope, and this would have a serious impact on the outcome of the operation. The final insult on this sad night was that the route into Germany passed close to two night-fighter beacons, which the enemy aircraft were orbiting while they awaited their instructions, unaware initially that they were about to have the cream of Bomber Command handed to them on a plate.

F/L Lee and P/O Warren would miss the approaching disaster after engine failures forced them to return early before reaching enemy territory. For the others, the carnage began over Charleroi in Belgium, and from there to the target, the route was sign-posted by the burning wreckage on the ground of eighty Bomber Command aircraft. Among these were two from 106 Squadron, the first of them, JB566, containing the crew of F/Sgt Hall DFM, who were on just their second sortie together. They were heading eastwards some twenty miles north-east of Siegen when attacked by a night-fighter, the fire from which caused the Lancaster to explode near Berghausen and become the thirty-fifth victim of the night. The flight engineer and wireless operator were the only survivors, and they were taken into captivity. Just a few minutes later, ND535, "Queen of Sheba", was shot down by the night-fighter of Oblt Martin Becker of I./NJG6 and crashed five miles north of Wetzlar to become the operation's thirty-eighth victim, the only survivors, P/O Starkey and his bomb-aimer, joining their squadron colleagues in enemy hands. By this time, F/O Penman and crew had found themselves to be the quarry of two night-fighters, when some twenty miles south-west of Wetzlar, and had to fend off a number of attacks, during which, extensive damage was inflicted upon ND332. The rear turret was knocked out, and the mid-upper turret then also became unserviceable when the engine providing its power failed. The bombs were jettisoned and the fighters eventually evaded, and the Lancaster was brought back to a landing at Manston, where it became the night's one-hundredth casualty after the undercarriage collapsed on touch-down. The crew walked away from this one, but their reprieve was to be short-lived.

Meanwhile, the wind-finder system had broken down again, and those crews who either failed to detect the strength of the wind, or simply refused to believe the evidence, were driven up to fifty miles north of their intended track, and, consequently, turned towards Nuremberg from a false position. This led to more than a hundred aircraft bombing at Schweinfurt in error, on top of the depletion of the force to enemy action, and this reduced considerably the numbers arriving at the primary target. F/O Lee and crew were among these, having arrived at what was believed to be the approximate location of the target, and finding no markers. Over to the north, however, there were searchlights and incendiaries, and they altered course to bomb there at 01.20, later realising that it was probably Schweinfurt. The twelve 106 Squadron crews reaching the intended target encountered eight to nine-tenths cloud with tops as high as 16,000 feet, and located it mostly by means of release-point flares. They carried out their attacks from 19,250 to 22,000 feet between 01.03 and 01.27, a number after surviving attacks by night-fighters. F/O Anderson and crew were intercepted first by an ME210, which the gunners claimed as damaged, and later by an FW190, which they claimed as destroyed. P/O Moxey RAAF and crew were in ND585, and, it seems, had drifted a little north of the intended track while crossing Belgium on the way home, and had become the ninety-third to be shot down after falling into the clutches of a night-fighter south-west of Namur with no survivors. Many fires were reported by returning crews, the glow from which, according to some, remained visible for 120 miles into the return journey, but ninety-five crews were not able to attend debriefing, twenty-one of them from 5 Group. Some twenty other aircraft did make it home, but were written off in landing crashes or with battle damage too severe to repair. The shock and disappointment were compounded by the fact that the strong wind had driven the marking beyond the city to the east, and Nuremberg had, consequently, escaped serious damage.

During the course of the month the squadron operated on thirteen nights and launched 156 sorties for the loss of four aircraft. The sorties represented the highest monthly figure since converting to Lancasters in May 1942. It was also announced that the statistics for February meant that the squadron had won the 5 Group bombing competition for the third month in a row.

April 1944

Unquestionably, this six-month long campaign had been the toughest faced by the crews during the entire war, and it was their "winter of discontent", probably the only time when their morale had been in question. Harris had failed to wreck Berlin from end to end, and the cost had been greater than he anticipated, and certainly he had not come close to bringing about a collapse in the German will to continue the fight. Now a new campaign lay before the crews, one which had begun, as already mentioned, with attacks on marshalling yards at Trappes and Le Mans during the first week of March. Since then, other marshalling yards at Amiens, Laon, Aulnoye, Courtrai and Vaires had been added to the list and systematically targeted, generally to good effect. That which now lay before the crews was in marked contrast to what had been endured over the preceding months. In place of the long slog to distant German targets on dark, often dirty nights, shorter range trips to the occupied countries would become the order of the day in improving weather conditions. These would prove to be equally demanding in their way, however, and would require of the crews a greater commitment to accuracy, to avoid unnecessary civilian casualties. The main fly in the ointment was a pronouncement from on high, which decreed that most such operations were worthy of counting as just one-third of a sortie towards the completion of a tour, and until this flawed policy was rescinded, an air of discontent and sense of injustice would pervade the bomber stations. With Harris at the helm city-busting would never entirely be shelved in favour of other considerations, but it was to take a back seat for the time being. The size of the force now available to Harris enabled him to succeed in an area where his predecessor had failed, namely, to strike effectively at multiple targets simultaneously. Targets could now be assigned to individual groups, to groups in tandem or to the Command as a whole, as operational requirements dictated, in the sure and certain knowledge that each force had the capacity to deliver a knockout blow at the first attempt.

5 Group returned to the offensive on the 5th, with an operation involving 144 Lancasters and a Mosquito flown by W/C Cheshire of 617 Squadron. The target was the former Dewoitine aircraft factory at Saint-Martin-du-Touch, a suburb of Toulouse in south-western France, which, under a nationalization plan in 1936 involving six aircraft companies, including Lioré et Olivier and Potez, was now operating under the name SNCASE, or Sud Est for short. Cheshire was to mark it with spotfires from low level, using the system that he was instrumental in developing, and one which would become an integral part of 5 Group operations, with refinements, from this point on. This would be Cheshire's first operational flight in a Mosquito, and the first time that he marked a target for 5 Group, rather than just 617 Squadron.

Much depended upon its success if Harris were to become sold on the idea of the low-level visual marking technique and give it his backing. At Metheringham, 106 Squadron loaded a dozen Lancasters with nine 1,000 pounders each and sent them on their way in poor weather conditions between 20.30 and 20.40 with W/C Piercy and S/L Murdoch the senior pilots on duty. Ahead of them lay an outward flight of more than four hours, which all but W/C Piercy and crew would negotiate, after they were forced to return early for an undisclosed reason. The others arrived in time to watch Cheshire lob two red spotfires onto the roof of the factory at 00.17 during his third pass, and, so accurate were they, that the two 617 Squadron Lancaster backers-up were not required. Bombing by the 106 Squadron element took place in bright moonlight from 12,750 and 14,750 feet between 00.22 and 00.41, and large fires were observed with smoke rising through 7,000 feet. One 207 Squadron Lancaster was hit by flak over the target at 00.30 and exploded, killing all on board, and this was the only loss from an outstandingly successful operation involving main force crews, who had no special training in precision bombing. P/O Anderson and crew brought back an aiming point photo, while that of F/L Lee and crew was plotted at fifty feet away. The success of this operation convinced Harris that low-level visual marking was viable, and he now authorized 5 Group to operate independently under appropriate conditions and to take on its own heavy marker force.

It would be almost two weeks before the necessary moves took place, and, in the meantime, the pre-invasion campaign got into full swing with the posting of two operations on the 9th. The Lille-Delivrance goods station in north-eastern France was assigned to 239 aircraft from 3, 4, 6 and 8 Groups, while the marshalling yards at Villeneuve-St-Georges, on the southern outskirts of Paris, were to be targeted by 225 aircraft drawn from all groups. The weather conditions were excellent, and clear skies greeted the latter force as it crossed the French coast at around 14,000 feet. The target could be identified visually, but crews aimed for the red and green TIs that had been accurately placed by the Path Finders, delivering their hardware from between 13,000 and 14,500 feet in the face of little opposition. Many bomb bursts were observed along with orange explosions, and, to those high above, the raid appeared to be highly successful. In fact, many bomb loads had fallen into adjacent residential districts, where four hundred houses had been destroyed or seriously damaged, and ninety-three people killed. This was far fewer than had died in the simultaneous operation at Lille, many miles to the north-east, where over two thousand items of rolling stock had been destroyed, and buildings and installations seriously damaged, but at a collateral cost of 456 French civilian lives. Civilian casualties would prove to be an unavoidable by-product of what was a necessary campaign.

106 Squadron was not involved in either operation, but contributed eight Lancasters to a 1 and 5 Group mining effort of more than a hundred Lancasters operating in various gardens in the Baltic. 5 Group put up fifty-six, eight of them belonging to 106 Squadron and assigned to the Privet garden off the port of Danzig. They were all airborne by 21.30 with W/C Piercy taking the lead, and S/L Murdoch also on the Order of Battle, and each carrying five 1,570lb mines to be delivered from high level. The operation was entirely successful, and all crews delivered their stores into the allotted locations by means of H2S from 15,000 feet, between 01.37 and 01.49, before returning safely home. Meanwhile, F/Os Anderson and Latham and P/O Milne were engaged in low-level mining in the Tangerine garden, specifically the Köningsberg Seekanal, a fifty-four yard-wide stretch of water, which provided the only access to the Baltic at Pillau from the German naval base in the port of Königsberg. Flying as second pilot with F/O Latham was S/L de Belleroche, who had been posted in as a flight commander elect. They took off from Metheringham at the same time as the others for their one thousand-mile outward leg, and found the target without difficulty under clear, moonlit skies. In the interests of accuracy, the mines had to be delivered from 150 feet, and this would require the Lancasters to run the gauntlet of formidable defences. Light flak and heavy machine guns were positioned on both banks of the canal, and many searchlights were brought to bear, some laid horizontally to present an impenetrable dazzle trap to blind the pilots,

bomb-aimers and gunners. Despite this, each Lancaster ran without deviation along the waterway and two of them deposited five mines each into the briefed location. P/O Anderson had a single "hang-up", which he was able to drop in an alternative location, and all returned to land safely after more than nine hours aloft. The ORB proudly stated; "The whole operation was completed with skill, resolution and outstanding courage, and resulted in many congratulatory messages…"

On the following day, Monday the 10th, a further five railway yards, four in France and one in Belgium, were posted as the targets for that night and assigned to individual groups. 5 Group was handed those at Tours in the Loire region of western France, for which 180 Lancasters were made ready, eleven of them at Metheringham. They took off between 22.10 and 22.40 with the station commander, G/C McKechnie, the senior pilot on duty, S/L de Belleroche flying as crew captain for the first time, and S/L Crowe, who, after two operational tours was now the station navigation officer, on board with P/O Harper. They set course for England's south coast and the Channel crossing, and all arrived in the target area after approaching from the west in clear skies and bright moonlight. and observed red spotfires marking the aiming point. Master Bombers were on hand to direct the two phases of the attack, the first against the western side of the yards and the second at the eastern end, and they issued instructions to overshoot the red spotfires by six hundred yards, after they had been delivered short. G/C McKechnie and crew found the target easily, made the necessary adjustments and bombed from 5,000 feet at 01.35, to be followed by the others from 5,000 to 8,000 feet between 01.36 and 01.56, some crews making two passes to deliver the high-explosives and incendiaries separately. The later stages of the second phase bombing were affected by smoke drifting across the target area and rising through 6,000 feet, which persuaded the Master Bomber to call a halt to bombing at 02.48 and send home any crews with bombs still on board. As the above timings suggest, not all crews complied. There were mixed opinions as to the effectiveness of the operation, some gaining the impression that the eastern half of the yards had not been touched, but others claimed the attack to have been accurate and concentrated within the yards, and two large fires were observed. F/O Crosier brought back the squadron's best bombing photo, plotted at 250 yards from the aiming point, and the others were within 500 and 1,300 yards. Post-raid reconnaissance confirmed the success of the attack, but the Germans would round up local civilians and force them into repairing the damage to get the yards working again before long.

Aachen was a major railway centre with marshalling yards at both the western and eastern ends, but the attack planned for the night of the 11/12th was clearly designed as a city-busting exercise for which a force of 341 heavy aircraft was drawn from 1, 3, 5 and 8 Groups. 106 Squadron detailed seven Lancasters, and with thunderstorms over Lincolnshire, they departed Metheringham between 20.30 and 21.15 with S/L Murdoch the senior pilot on duty. They lost the services of P/O Durrant and crew to port-inner engine failure after an hour, while the rest of the bomber stream continued on and had climbed to between 18,000 and 20,000 feet by the time it reached the Belgian coast at 3 degrees east. That altitude was maintained all the way to the target, where six to ten-tenths thin cloud was encountered at 7,000 to 8,000 feet. Red and green TIs identified the aiming point, and the 106 Squadron crews attacked it from 17,000 to 18,000 feet between 22.42 and 22.58, observing many bomb bursts and fires, which suggested to them that the attack was accurate. The crews maintained height on the way home until fifty miles from the coast, at which position they began a gentle descent to exit enemy territory at 15,000 feet or above. F/L Lee and crew brought back a bombing photo plotted at 1,200 yards from the aiming point. Reports coming out of Aachen revealed this to be the city's worst experience of the war to date, with extensive damage in central and southern districts, disruption of its transport infrastructure and a death toll of 1,525 people. However, post-raid reconnaissance revealed that the railway yards had not been destroyed and would require further attention.

On the 14th, the Command became officially subject to the orders coming from the Supreme Headquarters of the Allied Expeditionary Force (SHAEF), under General Dwight D Eisenhower, and would remain thus shackled until the Allied armies were sweeping towards the German frontier at the end of the summer. Among awards to 106 Squadron members announced on the 15th were DFCs for S/L Dunn and navigator F/O Greenhalgh.

On the 18th, the Path Finder Force reluctantly transferred 83 and 97 Squadrons to 5 Group, from whence they had come in August 1942 and April 1943 respectively. It was a loan, but in reality, it amounted to a permanent detachment, along with the Mosquito unit, 627 Squadron. The Lancaster units were to become the 5 Group heavy markers, while the Mosquitos would eventually take over the low-level marking role currently performed by 617 Squadron. This was a major coup for AVM Cochrane and 5 Group and a bitter blow to AVM Bennett, the Path Finder Chief. Relations between Cochrane and Bennett had never been cordial, but this plunged them to new depths. Both were brilliant men, Bennett, an Australian, in particular, a man of the greatest intellect, who, despite his total lack of humour, commanded the deepest respect and loyalty from his men. He and Cochrane possessed vastly different opinions on the subject of target marking, Bennett believing that a low-level method exposed the crews to unnecessary danger, while Cochrane insisted that the risks in a fast-flying Mosquito were negligible and would produce greater accuracy. The 83 and 97 Squadrons crews, though drawn from 5 Group squadrons, immediately became loyal to 8 Group, which they considered to be the pinnacle, and were upset at being removed from what they considered to be an elevated status. Once qualified to do so, they were fiercely proud to wear the Path Finder badge and enjoyed enhanced promotion prospects, privileges which, happily for them, they would retain under the loan arrangement.

Any resentment might have been smoothed over had their reception at Coningsby been handled better, but, as the newly arrived crews tumbled out of their transports, they were summoned immediately to the briefing room, to be lectured by the 54 Base commander, Air Commodore "Bobby" Sharp. Rather than welcoming them as brothers-in-arms, he harangued them over their bad 8 Group habits, and ordered them to buckle down to learning 5 Group ways. This was an insult to experienced airmen, for whom the task of illuminating targets for 5 Group would be a piece of cake compared with the complexities of their 8 Group duties. The fact that the insult was being delivered by a pompous, self-important man with no relevant operational experience, made it doubly unpalatable. From this point on, 5 Group would be known in 8 Group circles somewhat disparagingly as the "Independent Air Force", or "The Lincolnshire Poachers".

The 5 Group target on the 18th was the marshalling yards at Juvisy, situated on the West Bank of the Seine south of Paris, which was one of four similar targets for the night. The intention had been for the new arrivals to participate, but the disgruntled commanding officers, G/C Laurence Deane of 83 Squadron and W/C "Jimmy" Carter of 97 Squadron, announced that they were not yet ready, and the operation would have to go ahead without them. 202 Lancasters and four Mosquitos were made ready, the latter belonging to 617 Squadron, and 8 Group would provide three Oboe Mosquitos to deliver the initial marking. 106 Squadron made ready nine Lancasters, eight of which departed Metheringham between 20.50 and 21.10 with S/Ls Murdoch and de Belleroche the senior pilots on duty and each carrying thirteen 1,000 pounders. The remaining Lancaster swung off the runway, before careering across the grass and bursting a tyre, and its participation had to be scrubbed. As the bombing brigade climbed out before heading towards the south coast in good weather conditions, nine gardeners took off between 21.00 and 21.20 with W/C Piercy leading and turned towards the east for the long trip to the Geranium garden off the Baltic port of Swinemünde in Stettin Bay. Those bound for France all reached the target to find clear skies and ideal bombing conditions, in which they observed W/C Cheshire's red spotfires become backed up by green TIs. Despite black smoke drifting across the aiming point and upwards from the destruction of a fuel dump at 23.32, the 106 Squadron crews were able to hit the markers from 7,000 to 11,000 between 23.32 and 23.50, and, on their return, were enthusiastic about the success of the operation. This was confirmed by post-raid reconnaissance and prompted the crews to make the valid comment that, to count this operation as just one-third of a sortie, was undervaluing it, a sentiment shared by all whose job involved putting their lives on the line. Meanwhile, the gardeners had all arrived in their target area to encounter clear skies but thick haze, which presented some challenges to the establishing of a pinpoint from which to make a timed run. They each delivered five mines from a uniform 15,000 feet between 00.29 and 00.45 and were satisfied that they had fallen in or close to the briefed locations.

Briefings on 5 Group stations on the 20th informed crews of their part in the first operation to include the three newly transferred squadrons, which was a two-phase attack on railway yards at La Chapelle, situated just to the north of Paris, while the night's main event was to be conducted by a force of 357 Lancasters and twenty-two Mosquitos drawn from 1, 3, 6 and 8 Groups against Cologne. A meticulous plan had been prepared for 5 Group, in which the phases were to be separated by an hour, each with its own specific aiming point, and 83 Squadron's W/C Deane was to be the Master Bomber with S/L Sparks his deputy. The plan called for 8 Group Mosquitos to drop cascading flares by Oboe to provide an initial reference, and for a Mosquito element from 627 Squadron to lay a "window" screen ahead of the main force Lancasters. Once the target had been identified, the first members of the 83 Squadron flare force were to provide illumination for the low-level marker Mosquitos of 617 Squadron, which would mark the first aiming point with red spot fires for the main force element to aim at. The whole procedure would then be repeated at the second aiming point. At Coningsby, W/C Deane conducted the briefing, and, at its conclusion, wished the assembled throng good luck, before dismissing them, whereupon a voice from the back declared that the briefing wasn't over, and that the base and station commanders wanted their say. This had not been standard practice in 8 Group, and left Deane mystified and a little humiliated. The senior officers had only waffle to offer, but it made them feel important, while confirming the first impressions of the crews, that A/C Sharp was a self-important and irrelevant link in the chain of command.

106 Squadron made ready eighteen Lancasters as part of the overall force of 247 Lancasters of 5 Group and twenty-two Mosquitos of 5 and 8 Groups, and assigned five each to waves 1 and 3 and four each to waves 2 and 4 as part of the second phase. The departed Metheringham between 23.42 and 23.25 with G/C McKechnie and S/Ls Murdoch and de Belleroche the senior pilots on duty and S/L Crowe flying with F/O Anderson. Each Lancaster was loaded with fourteen 1,000 pounders, every one of which arrived at the target under largely clear skies, with good visibility and only some ground haze to mar the vertical view. Zero hour for the opening phase was set for 00.05, but the Oboe Mosquitos were two minutes late, and some communications problems had to be ironed out before matters began to run smoothly. A large orange explosion at 00.28 sent a column of black smoke skyward, which impaired visibility to some extent, but, those attacking afterwards were able to identify a red spotfire and bomb it, setting off large explosions and creating fires that would be visible to the second phase crews as they approached. By the time of the arrival of the 106 Squadron crews, matters seemed to be proceeding according to plan, but ground haze and smoke from the first attack threatened to impair sight of the markers. Despite this, most were able to see the red spotfires without difficulty, and they dropped their loads from 7,000 to 11,000 feet between 01.21 and 01.45, before bringing back ten photos plotted at between 600 and 2,000 yards from the aiming point. The 113.4 tons of bombs delivered by the squadron was a new record. Following the second phase attack, the fires remained visible for a hundred miles into the return flight, and, at debriefing, crews expressed confidence that they had contributed to a successful operation. Post-raid reconnaissance confirmed the success of both phases of the raid, which had left the

yards severely damaged along with a bridge at the southern end, at a cost of six Lancasters. A congratulatory message from A-O-C AVM Cochrane was received on all participating stations.

The real test for the 5 Group low-level marking system would come at a heavily defended German target, for which Braunschweig was selected on the 22nd, while the rest of the Command targeted the Ruhr city of Düsseldorf. 5 Group put together a force of 238 Lancasters and seventeen Mosquitos, with ten ABC Lancasters of 1 Group's 101 Squadron to provide radio countermeasures (RCM). 106 Squadron contributed twenty Lancasters, which departed Metheringham between 23.05 and 23.25 with W/C Piercy and S/Ls Murdoch and de Belleroche the senior pilots on duty, and F/L Lee undertaking the twenty-ninth and penultimate operation of his first tour. They formed into a stream as they headed for the south coast, before setting course across France towards the south-east and feinting towards Italy. The 617 and 627 Squadron Mosquitos took off three hours after the heavy brigade and adopted a direct route, the latter laying a "window" screen from high level six minutes from the target, masking the arrival of the flare force that was to provide seven minutes of illumination for the 617 marker Mosquitos. P/O Durrant and crew turned back with engine failure before reaching the enemy coast, but the remainder pressed on, guided by route markers, to find the target under six to eight-tenths thin cloud at between 8,000 and 10,000 feet, and ground haze and accurate marking in progress by 617 Squadron. Despite this, the main force crews were unable to properly identify the target, a situation again compounded by communications problems between various controllers, caused by the failure of VHF and the consequent need to pass on instructions instead by W/T. This led to confusion, and many crews were forced to orbit for up to fifteen minutes before bombing. The 106 Squadron crews were in the first wave, and they each delivered a 2,000 pounder and 143 x 30lb incendiaries onto the red spotfires and green TIs from 17,000 to 22,000 feet between 01.56 and 02.07. All but one from Metheringham returned safely to report what appeared to be a successful operation, while also complaining about the dangers of orbiting a target with aircraft heading in a variety of directions. Although some bombs did fall in the city centre, most were directed at reserve H2S-laid TIs to the south of the city, and damage was less severe than might otherwise have been. On the credit side, only four Lancasters were lost, but one of these was 106 Squadron's JB567, which fell to a combination of flak and a night-fighter as it approached the Dutch frontier homebound, and crashed in the Lingen-Ems region killing F/L Lee and five others on board, including a second pilot, P/O Tucker. The flight engineer, F/Sgt Simes, and bomb-aimer, F/O Beven, survived to be taken into captivity. F/Sgt Cunningham and crew were singled out for particular mention for completing their sortie after losing an engine while outbound, and covering the entire homeward leg on three.

When Munich was posted across 5 Group as the target on the 24th for another live test of the low-level visual marking method, it might have been seen as somewhat ambitious to select such a major city, that was protected by two hundred flak guns. The main operation on this night of more than eleven hundred sorties, was to be conducted by a force of 637 aircraft against Karlsruhe, 150 miles to the north-west, which would help to distract the night-fighters. 234 Lancasters were made ready by 5 Group, and supplemented by ten of the ABC variety from 101 Squadron, while four Mosquitos of 617 Squadron were loaded with spotfires to carry out the marking, and twelve of 627 Squadron with "window" to dispense during the final approach to the target. 106 Squadron put up seventeen Lancasters for this operation, and they got away from Metheringham between 20.40 and 21.10 with W/C Piercy and S/L de Belleroche the senior pilots on duty. After climbing out and forming up, they settled into a devious route to try to outwit the defences, losing F/L Sprawson and crew to a dead engine early on. The others pressed on across south-western France, which, along with a feint by six 617 Squadron Lancasters dropping flares and target indicators over Milan, suggested Italy as the destination. The 617 and 627 Squadron Mosquitos took off three hours after the heavy brigade and adopted a direct route, the latter laying a "window" screen from high level six minutes from the target, masking the arrival of the flare force that was to provide seven minutes of illumination for the 617 marker Mosquitos.

The head of the bomber stream arrived in the target area to encounter clear skies and good visibility, and W/C Cheshire dived through the searchlights and flak onto the aiming point at 01.40 to deliver his markers from 1,500 feet, before racing across the rooftops to make good his escape. The main force followed hard on his heels, the 106 Squadron crew delivering their bombs onto the red spotfires and green TIs in the face of intense searchlight and flak activity from 19,000 to 22,000 feet between 01,48 and 02.01, and were soon all on their way home bringing back ten bombing photos plotted at one to three miles from the aiming point. Many fires were seen to take hold, and, as the bombers pointed their snouts back towards France to eventually pass to the north of Paris, Karlsruhe could be seen burning over to starboard. Post-raid reconnaissance and local reports confirmed the success of the raid, which left 1,104 buildings in ruins and a further thirteen hundred severely damaged. It was probably this operation that sealed the award to Cheshire of the Victoria Cross at the conclusion of his operational career of one hundred sorties.

At briefing on the 26th, sixteen 106 Squadron crews were told that Schweinfurt was to be their target that night, after the failure of the RAF to destroy it in February and the American 8th Air Force just two weeks ago. The tone was very much, "leave it to RAF Bomber Command", and, with the satisfaction of Munich still fresh in the mind, and the natural rivalry between the two forces, such attitudes were to be expected. Up to this point, the newly-arrived 627 Squadron had been training and observing, in preparation to take over from 617 Squadron as 5 Group's low-level markers, and now it was time to step up to the plate and assume the role. News of this formed part of the briefing to the crews of 215 Lancasters, including nine from 101 Squadron to provide RCM protection. This was just one of three major operations taking place, the main event at Essen involving 493 aircraft, while the railway yards at Villeneuve-St-Georges were being attended to by a predominantly Halifax force of 217 aircraft. The 106 Squadron crews departed Metheringham between 21.25 and 21.45 with S/Ls de Belleroche and Murdoch the senior pilots on duty, and headed into what, for the squadron, was an unmitigated disaster. They encountered stronger-than-forecast head winds, which delayed the arrival in the target area of the heavy brigade, but they found generally clear skies and good visibility, which the 627 Squadron crews failed to exploit, as their debut marking effort proved to be inaccurate in the face of thick ground haze. The 83 Squadron crews remarked on the lack of illumination, and those carrying hooded flares were called in a number of times to back-up. The 106 Squadron crews bombed from 15,000 to 20,500 feet between 02.26 and 02.44, aiming at red spotfires and green TIs and flares, some following the instructions of the Master Bomber to overshoot by a thousand yards. A large white explosion was witnessed at 02.29, and many fires were reported, but, once again at this location, most of the hardware fell outside of the target area, leaving ball-bearing production more or less unscathed. Night-fighters got amongst the heavy force, and twenty-one Lancasters were shot down, a hefty 9.3%, and five empty dispersal pans at Metheringham next morning told a sorry tale of the squadron's fortunes, which were its unhappiest to date. Numerous bombing photos were brought back, three of them plotted within two miles of the aiming point, and the best, by F/Sgt Cunningham and crew, was just half a mile away.

The eight-man crew of B Flight commander, S/L Murdoch, produced just one survivor, the second pilot, Sgt Bradley, after JB601 "Victory" was brought down over north-eastern France while outbound. S/L Murdoch was a Kiwi from Christchurch, who had joined the pre-war regular RAF. P/O Harper died with four of his crew in JB562, which crashed south-east of Mannheim, and well to the south-west of the target. P/O Fraser's ND850 was attacked by a Me110 over north-eastern France while outbound and may have been hit by a rocket projectile. Whatever the cause, the bomb load caught fire, and the pilot and three others managed to parachute to safely, ultimately to evade capture. ND853 crashed in the general target area, killing P/O Bishop and four of his crew, while the navigator and bomb-aimer were taken into captivity. F/O Mifflin and crew were on their twenty-ninth sortie and were on their way out of the target area in ME660 when they came under attack from a night-fighter. A fire took hold in the starboard wing, inboard of the engines, and F/Sgt Norman Jackson, the flight engineer, undertook the hazardous task of climbing onto the wing with a portable extinguisher, to try to quell the flames. His parachute had accidentally deployed during his exit, and his colleagues inside the aircraft hung on to the rigging lines to secure him. The extinguisher was whipped away by the 200-mph airflow, and, as the fire intensified, Jackson found himself in danger of being engulfed by the flames. He began to sustain burns to his face, hands and clothing, and unable to maintain his tenuous hold, he slid off the trailing edge, followed by his canopy, which showed signs of being alight. As he fell to earth, F/O Mifflin gave the order for the remainder of his crew to abandon the aircraft, and four of them did so safely. Sadly, Mifflin and the rear gunner were killed, and Jackson broke an ankle on landing, leading to a ten-month spell in hospital recovering from his various injuries. On his return to England, he would be awarded the Victoria Cross for his outstanding gallantry.

This was the final operation of the month for 106 Squadron, but 5 Group had further business to attend to and made preparations on the 28th to send a force of eighty-eight Lancasters and four Mosquitos to attack the Alfred Nobel Dynamit A G explosives works at St-Médard-en-Jalles, situated in a wood on the north-western outskirts of Bordeaux in south-western France. A further fifty-one Lancasters and four Mosquitos would head in the opposite direction to target an aircraft maintenance facility at the Kjeller Flyfabrikk, some ten miles north-east of Oslo, which had been occupied by the Germans since April 1940 and was used by Junkers, Daimler-Benz and BMW. The former was abandoned shortly after bombing began because of excessive smoke obscuring the aiming point, while the latter produced explosions on the airfield and runway and among barrack buildings and some of the sheds, and an ammunition dump went up.

Awards of the DFC were announced on the 29th to F/Os Anderson and Latham and P/O Milne for their outstanding performance earlier in the month when delivering mines at low level in the Königsberg Canal in the face of the most fearsome opposition. A further attempt on the Nobel works was scheduled for that night, and the Michelin tyre factory at Clermont-Ferrand was added to the target list. Sixty-eight Lancasters were assigned to the explosives works and fifty-four to the tyre factory, with five 627 Squadron Mosquitos at each to provide the low-level marking. The aiming point at the former was identified both visually and by red spotfires and red and green TIs, which could be seen burning between factory buildings, and returning crews were filled with enthusiasm at the explosions that had ripped the site apart, some commenting that it was the most destructive attack they had taken part in. During the course of the month, 106 Squadron operated on nine nights and dispatched 129 sorties for the loss of six Lancasters.

May 1944

As the invasion of Europe drew ever closer, airfields, fuel and ammunition dumps and coastal defences were added to the burgeoning target list. A dozen 106 Squadron crews were called to briefing at Metheringham on the 1st, to learn that they would be going to southern France that night to attack the Poudrerie explosives works at Toulouse. They would be part of two 5 Group forces totalling 131 Lancasters and eight Mosquitos targeting the city, the other to attack the previously mentioned SNCASE former Dewoitine aircraft assembly factory located in the western suburb of Saint-Martin-du-Touch. A third 5 Group force of forty-six Lancasters and four Mosquitos would be sent against an aircraft repair workshop at Tours in western France. The 106 Squadron crews took off between 21.30 and 21.40 with W/C Piercy and the newly-promoted and freshly appointed B Flight commander, S/L Sprawson, the senior pilots on duty, and employed Gee for the first part of the outward flight until it was jammed.

Thereafter, they relied upon good navigation, green track markers provided by the Path Finders, and H2S, and all reached the target to find moonlight, clear skies and excellent visibility, with flares and red spotfires marking out the aiming point. The 106 Squadron crews identified the target visually in the light of flares, and bombing took place in accordance with the instructions of the Master Bomber on spotfires from between 6,000 and 8,000 feet in a seven-minute slot from 01.32. Once developed, eleven bombing photos showed the target area, with plots up to 1,400 yards from the aiming point, and the best performance was by F/O Bellingham and crew, whose photo was plotted at one hundred yards. The attack was clearly focused on the aiming point, where many bomb bursts were observed and the glow of the burning site remained visible for a hundred miles into the return journey. All crews returned to their respective stations confident of a successful outcome, and post-raid reconnaissance revealed all three factories to have been heavily damaged.

Briefings took place on 1 and 5 Group stations on the 3rd, for what would become a highly contentious operation that night against a Panzer training camp and transport depot at Mailly-le-Camp, situated some seventy-five miles east of Paris in north-eastern France. It was home at the time to a Panzer Divisional HQ, and a number of Panzer battalions and motor transport units that could be brought to bear in defence against the invasion. The events of the operation proved to be so controversial, that recriminations abound to this day concerning the 5 Group leadership provided by W/Cs Cheshire and Deane. Although the grudges by 1 Group aircrew against them can be understood in the light of what happened, they are unjust, and based on emotion and incorrect information, and it is worthwhile to examine the conduct of the operation in some detail. W/C Cheshire was appointed as marker leader, and was piloting one of four 617 Squadron Mosquitos, while 83 Squadron's commanding officer, W/C Deane, was overall raid controller, with S/L Sparks as Deputy. Deane and Cheshire attended separate briefings, and neither seemed aware of the complete plan, particularly the role of the 1 Group Special Duties Flight from Binbrook, which was assigned to mark its own specific aiming point for an element of the 1 Group force.

The twelve 106 Squadron participants departed Metheringham between 21.55 and 22.10 with S/L Sprawson the senior pilot on duty, and all reached the target area to find clear skies, moonlight and excellent bombing conditions, but confusion already beginning to influence events. 617 Squadron's W/C Cheshire and S/L Shannon were in position before midnight, and, as the first flares from the 83 and 97 Squadron Lancasters illuminated the target below, Cheshire released his two red spot fires onto the first aiming point at 00.00½ from 1,500 feet. Shannon backed them up from 400 feet five and a half minutes later, and, as far as Cheshire was concerned, the operation was bang on schedule at this stage. A 97 Squadron Lancaster also laid markers accurately to ensure a constant focal point, and Cheshire passed instructions to Deane to call the bombers in. It was at this stage of the operation that matters began to go awry. A communications problem arose, when a commercial radio station, believed to be an American forces network, jammed the VHF frequencies in use. Deane called in the 5 Group element, elated that everything was proceeding according to plan, but nothing happened. He checked with his wireless operator that the instructions had been transmitted, and called up S/L Sparks, who was also mystified by the lack of bombing, and was reduced to attempting to control the operation by W/T, which also failed. A few crews predominantly from 9, 207 and 467 Squadrons had heard the call to bomb, and did so, but, for most, the instructions were swamped by the interference.

Post raid reports are contradictory, and it is impossible to establish an accurate course of events, particularly when Deane and Cheshire's understanding of the exact time of zero hour differed by five minutes. Remarkably, it also seems, that Deane was unaware that there were two marking points, or three, if one includes 1 Group's Special Duties Flight. Cheshire, initially at least, appeared happy with the early stages of the attack, and described the bombing as concentrated and accurate. It seems certain, however, that many minutes had elapsed between the dropping of Cheshire's markers and the first main force bombs falling, during which period, Deane was coming to terms with the fact that his instructions were not getting through. A plausible scenario is, that in the absence of instructions, and with red spot fires clearly visible within the target, some crews opted to bomb, and others followed suit. These would have been predominantly from 5 Group, but as the 1 Group crews became increasingly agitated at having to wait in bright moonlight, with evidence of enemy night-fighters all around, some of them inevitably joined in.

Now a new problem was arising. Smoke from these first salvoes was obliterating the entire camp, and Cheshire had to decide whether or not to send in Fawke and Kearns to mark the second aiming point. His feeling, and that of Deane, as it later transpired, was, that it was unnecessary, as the volume of bombs still to fall into the relatively compact area of the target would ensure destruction of the entire site. By 00.16, the first phase of bombing should have been completed, leaving a clear run for Fawke and Kearns across the target. In the event, the majority of 5 Group crews were still on their bombing run, a fact unknown to Cheshire, who asked Deane for a pause in the bombing, while the two Mosquitos went in. As far as Cheshire was concerned, there was no response from Deane, who would, anyway, have been confused by mention of a second aiming point. In the event, Deane's deputy, S/L Sparks, eventually found a channel free of interference, and did, in fact, transmit an instruction to halt the bombing, both by W/T and R/T, and some crews reported hearing something. While utter chaos reigned, Kearns and Fawke dived in among the falling cookies at 00.23 and 00.25 respectively, to mark the second aiming point on the western edge of the camp. At 2,000 feet, they were lucky to survive the turbulence created by the exploding 4,000 pounders, when 4,000 feet was considered to be a minimum safe height. They were not entirely happy with their work, but F/O Edwards of 97 Squadron dropped a stick of markers precisely on the mark, and S/L Sparks was then able to call the 1 Group main force in along with any from 5 Group with bombs still on board. Meanwhile, the night fighters continued to create havoc among the Lancasters as they milled around in the target area, and, as burning aircraft were seen to fall all around, some 1 Group crews succumbed to their anxiety and frustration. In a rare breakdown of R/T discipline, they let fly with comments of an uncomplimentary nature, many of which were intended for, and, indeed, heard by Deane.

Despite the problems, the operation was a major success, which destroyed 80% of the camp's buildings, and 102 vehicles, of which thirty-seven were tanks, while over two hundred men were killed. Forty-two Lancasters failed to return, however, two thirds of them from 1 Group, and 50 Squadron was 5 Group's most afflicted unit with four Lancasters and crews unaccounted for. Debriefings on 1 and 5 Group stations were more animated than usual as the stories of the night's events unfolded. The 106 Squadron contingent mostly bombed fairly early on in the proceedings, from 5,500 to 8,000 feet between 00.09 to 00.18 on observing others to do so, by which time smoke was already beginning to drift across the target area. A number of Metheringham crews added their bombs as late as 00.26 and 00.30, but all escaped the carnage to bring back eleven bombing photos plotted within half a mile of the aiming point. Over at Spilsby, S/L Blome-Jones of 207 Squadron described the situation as a complete shambles and chaos, the controller as inefficient and the discipline of some crews as bad. Others voiced the opinion held by all, that this was a trip worthy of counting as more than one-third of a sortie. On the following day, an inquest into the conduct of the raid revealed that the wireless transmitter in Deane's Lancaster had been sufficiently off frequency to allow the interference from the American network to mask the transmission of instructions and prevent the call to bomb from reaching the main force crews. The 1 Group A-O-C, AVM Rice, decided he would not participate in further operations organised by 5 Group, which was probably not a blow to Cochrane, who was confident that his group did not need back-up.

On the 6th, 1 and 5 Groups were invited to send a modest force each to attack ammunition dumps in France, 5 Group detailing sixty-four Lancasters and four Mosquitos for a site at Louailles, situated some four miles south-east of the town of Sable-sur-Sarthe, south-west of Le-Mans. Clear skies and excellent visibility provided ideal conditions, and a Master Bomber was on hand to direct the attack, which resulted in numerous bomb flashes that lit up the long storage sheds. Two enormous explosions were each followed by a large mushroom of smoke rising through 3,000 feet as the force withdrew.

106 Squadron sat this one out, but Metheringham was alerted on the 7th to prepare for its part in five small-scale operations to be mounted against airfields, ammunition dumps and a coastal battery in support of the coming invasion. 5 Group was involved in two raids, the airfield at Tours and an ammunition factory and dump at Salbris, some sixty miles to the east, and it was for the latter that 106 Squadron made ready a dozen Lancasters and sent them on their way between 22.00 and 22.15 with W/C Piercy the senior pilot on duty on what turned out to be another night of perfect conditions and one of great sadness for Metheringham. Each crew was sitting on a cookie and sixteen 500 pounders, which were destined for specific buildings within the complex. They headed south to pass by Reading on their way to Selsey Bill for the Channel crossing, intending to make landfall at Cabourg on the Normandy coast before setting course for the target. Gee working perfectly all the way out, and, with twenty miles horizontal visibility under bright moonlight, the red spotfires were observed well in advance of arrival at the aiming point. They bombed in a seven-minute slot from 00.31 from 5,000 to 7,000 feet, and observed large, vivid explosions and a column of smoke rising through 11,000 feet as they withdrew. Post-raid reconnaissance confirmed that both targets had been bombed accurately and effectively to leave them severely damaged. The success was gained at a cost of seven Lancasters, four of them from Metheringham, and all came down in the area of Loir-et-Cher, just south of Tours, where a second 5 Group operation had been conducted that night against the airfield. They were almost certainly the victims of night-fighters, and the crews of P/O Bartlett in JB292, P/O Rose in JB612, F/O Penman in LL891 and P/O Warren in ND870, were all posted missing. On board LL891 as second pilot to F/O Penman was F/O Steylaerts, a Belgian, and the bomb-aimer, F/O Aaron, was an American from Philadelphia. News would eventually filter through that the bomb-aimer from JB612, Sgt Smith, had been the sole survivor from among the twenty-nine crew members involved, and, thanks to the courage of local civilians, he ultimately evaded capture.

Another small-scale operation was mounted by the group on the 8th against the airfield and seaplane base at Lanveoc-Poulmic, located on the northern side of the peninsula forming the southern boundary of the L'Elorn estuary opposite Brest. A force of fifty-eight Lancasters and six Mosquitos identified the target easily by the coastline and layout of the hangars, which were left on fire along with other buildings and the entire site was enveloped in smoke.

The night of the 9/10th brought attacks on seven coastal batteries in the Pas-de-Calais by four hundred aircraft. The purpose of these operations was to confirm in the mind of the enemy the belief that the Allied invasion forces would land at Calais, and right up to D-Day itself, the coastal region between Gravelines to the east of the port and Berck-sur-Mer to the south-west, would be subjected to constant bombardment. 5 Group, meanwhile, planned a number of operations, one involving fifty-six Lancasters with Mosquito support to attack a foundry and stamping works and the Gnome & Rhone aero-engine factory, both located in Gennevilliers, a north-western district of Paris, while a second force of thirty-nine Lancasters and four Mosquitos targeted a small ball-bearing factory at Annecy, situated in south-eastern France close to the frontiers with Switzerland and Italy. The Gnome & Rhone factory had been bombed previously by elements from the squadron in April and May 1942, but its target on this night was the foundry, for which a dozen Lancasters departed Metheringham in a fifteen-minute slot from 22.10 led by S/L Sprawson. They rendezvoused with the other squadrons over Reading, before beginning the Channel crossing at Shoreham-on-Sea and making landfall on the French coast near Dieppe. Moonlight and clear skies enabled them to map read after Gee was jammed at the French coast, and H2S proved useful as they closed on Paris with the River Seine providing a strong reference point. Yellow TIs and red spotfires identified the aiming point, and the bombing by the 106 Squadron crews took place from 7,000 to 8,000 feet between 00.35 and 00.42. Ten crews returned safely home, bringing back nine bombing photos showing the target. Both operations were successful, but at a cost of five Lancasters, and 106 Squadron again had the sad task of posting missing two of its own. ND851 is believed to have exploded and crashed near Brionne, a location within striking distance of the Normandy coast, and it is reasonable to assume from the manner of its loss that the bombs were still on board and that it was heading south-east to the target. P/O Woodhams RAAF and five of his crew lost their lives, and only the bomb-aimer, Sgt James, survived to become a PoW. ND511 also came down on French soil, and there were no survivors from the crew of P/O Sutherland.

Five railway targets were selected for attention on the night of the 10/11th, among them the marshalling yards at Lille for 5 Group. Bomb bursts were seen across the tracks, and two large explosions were observed, thus confirming a successful assault on this important hub linking north-eastern France with Belgium. Night-fighters were out in force, and most of the night's casualties resulted from this operation, from which a dozen Lancasters failed to return.

5 Group put together a force of 190 Lancasters and eight Mosquitos on the 11th, to target a military camp at Bourg-Leopold in north-eastern Belgium, for which 106 Squadron made ready eight Lancasters. They departed Metheringham between 22.15 and 22.25 with S/L de Belleroche the senior pilot on duty, and all reached the target to find hazy conditions and a little thin cloud at around 10,000 feet, despite which, they would be able to identify ground detail in the form of buildings and huts in the light of illuminating flares. Three Oboe Mosquitos were on hand to deliver the initial marking, but inaccurately forecast winds caused the 83 Squadron element to arrive late, by which time the main force crews had begun to orbit to await instructions. A communications problem prevented some crews from hearing the Master Bomber's broadcasts, but the aiming point could be seen to be marked by red spotfires and green TIs. From the Master Bomber's perspective, the initial Oboe marker had been visible only to a few crews, and quickly burned out, and so he called for another Mosquito to drop a red spot fire onto the aiming point. Before this was accomplished, however, the main force began to bomb, and six from 106 Squadron were among ninety-four to release their loads, doing so from 14,300 and 16,200 feet between 00.18 and 00.31. As smoke began to obscure the ground, the Master Bomber, S/L Mitchell, quickly became uncomfortable about the close proximity of civilian residential property, and called a halt to the bombing at 00.35, before sending the rest of the force home, some of them after circling for more than twenty minutes.

Minor operations occupied elements of the Command for the following week, and, having lost six crews before the first two weeks of the month had elapsed, it gave Metheringham an opportunity to lick its wounds and rebuild. When the station teleprinters sprang to life across the Command on the 19th, they worked overtime to dispense the details of eight operations that night involving nine hundred aircraft targeting marshalling yards, coastal batteries and a radar station. 5 Group detailed 112 Lancasters and eight Mosquitos to attack marshalling yards at Amiens, and 113 Lancasters and four Mosquitos to target the locomotive workshops at Tours 190 miles to the south-west, and it was to the latter that the 106 Squadron element of sixteen was assigned. They departed Metheringham between 22.10 and 22.25 with W/C Piercy and S/L Sprawson the senior pilots on duty, but lost the services of F/Sgt Browne and crew because of defective radio equipment. They set course for their respective targets after crossing the coast near Hastings and found Tours to be shrouded in a layer of ten-tenths cloud at between 6,000 and 11,000 feet. The aiming point was located in the centre of the city, and bearing the responsibility of ensuring as little collateral damage as possible, the Master Bomber brought the force below the cloud base, where the target was easily identified, and the squadron contingent aimed at red spotfires from 5,200 to 7,500 feet between 00.50 and 01.02. The operation took longer to complete than had been intended, but it seems that collateral damage was kept to a minimum, and the yards were badly damaged. All aircraft returned without incident, but fog at Metheringham led to most being diverted, although the recently-installed FIDO fog dispersal system was put into use for the first time, and aided at least one landing. Seven bombing photos were plotted within 750 yards of the aiming point, the best, by P/O Thompson and crew at a mere two hundred yards. Cloud had severely inhibited the Amiens raid, which was halted by the Master Bomber after only thirty-seven aircraft had bombed.

For the first time in a year, Duisburg was posted as the target for a heavy raid on the 21st, for which a force of 510 Lancasters was drawn from 1, 3, 5 and 8 Groups. They would be supported by twenty-two Mosquitos, and, while this operation was in progress, seventy Lancasters, including some from 5 Group, and thirty-seven Halifaxes would undertake gardening duties in the Nectarines and Rosemary gardens around the Frisians and off Heligoland, and in the Forget-me-not, Silverthorn and Quince gardens in the Kattegat and Kiel Bay regions of the Baltic. 106 Squadron would support the main event with six Lancasters, while sending a dozen more to lay mines in the Forget-me-not garden in Kiel harbour. The latter force included the squadron's more experienced crews, with S/Ls de Belleroche and Sprawson the senior pilots on duty, and, with a much greater distance to cover, took off first, departing Metheringham between 22.00 and 22.10. Each carried six mines for delivery from 15,000 feet, and all but one located the target area to make timed runs of two to three minutes from pinpoints at Dovnis Klint, Bocknis Eck and Markelsdorfer Huk. The ORB timings showed F/O Taylor and crew delivering their mines at 00.36, and completing the round trip in six hours, while F/Sgt Fox and crew did not release theirs until 01.50, and their flight time was six hours-forty-five minutes. F/O Bellingham and crew searched long and hard for their pinpoint, but were unable to find it and returned the vegetables to store.

Those bound for the Ruhr took off in poor weather conditions between 22.40 and 22.45 with F/O Harris RCAF the senior pilot on duty, having been told at briefing to adhere to the plan for the outward route, which involved a few aircraft from 3 Group gaining height as they adopted a north-westerly course as far as Sleaford, so as not to cross into enemy radar cover earlier than necessary. The groups would rendezvous at 18,000 feet over the North Sea at 3 degrees east to cross the enemy coast via the western Frisians at 20,000 feet and climb to 22,000 or 23,000 feet, before increasing speed for the run across the target. All of the 106 Squadron participants reached the Ruhr to encounter ten-tenths cloud with tops at between 11,000 and 20,000 feet, into which the red Wanganui markers with-yellow-stars fell almost before they could be seen. F/Sgt Kitto and crew were attacked by a night-fighter ten miles from the target, and jettisoned their bomb load to successfully evade it. Four of the other crews bombed on Path Finder release-point flares and the fifth on a searchlight concentration from 19,000 to 21,000 feet between 01.12 and 01.25, before heading home to report what they felt was a scattered attack. A number of crews commented that the data provided by the wind-finder system was inaccurate, and this made it a challenge to establish positions. The loss of twenty-nine Lancasters was a reminder to the Command that the Ruhr remained a dangerous destination, although most of the missing had come down onto Dutch and Belgian soil or into the sea homebound, after falling victim to night-fighters, Martin Drewes of III./NJG1 alone accounting for at least three Lancasters. Returning crews were not enthusiastic about the outcome, and post-raid reconnaissance confirmed that a modest 350 buildings had been destroyed in the southern half of Duisburg, and 665 others had been seriously damaged.

Just like Duisburg, Dortmund was posted on the 22nd to host its first large-scale visit from the Command for a year, and would face an all-Lancaster heavy force of 361 aircraft drawn from 1, 3, 6 and 8 Groups. While this operation was in progress, 220 Lancasters of 5 Group and five from 101 Squadron were to target Braunschweig, which, thus far, had evaded severe damage at the hands of the Command. 106 Squadron made ready eighteen Lancasters, which departed Metheringham between 22.30 and 22.40 with S/Ls de Belleroche and Sprawson the senior pilots on duty. P/O Stockwell and crew experienced a number of issues as they began the North Sea crossing, but were compelled by two failed generators and Gee and H2S failure, ultimately, to admit defeat. The others pressed on through the clearly evident night-fighter activity from the Dutch coast all the way to the target, and negotiated the patches of ten-tenths cloud over northern Germany, and intense searchlight activity as they passed between Bremen and Osnabrück. The forecast at briefings had suggested clear skies over Braunschweig, but, in fact, the marker force encountered four to seven-tenths drifting cloud with tops up to 7,000 feet. Although highly effective in the right weather conditions, the 5 Group low-level visual marking method could easily be rendered ineffective by cloud cover. The blind heavy marker crews dropped skymarkers by H2S, while the 627 Squadron Mosquito element went in at low level to release red spotfires. Considerable interference over R/T communications added to the problems, and, although the Master Bomber could be heard in discussions with his Deputies, no instructions were received from him, and the attack lacked cohesion. Some crews described "hopeless confusion" with flares and incendiaries spread over a distance, and many had to rely on their own H2S to establish their position. Others found a complete absence of marking and orbited for up to fifteen minutes until a few green TIs appeared, and the 106 Squadron participants released their 2,000 pounder and 168 x 30lb incendiaries each onto whatever marker they could see from 17,000 to 18,000 feet between 01.16 and 01.43. Thirteen Lancasters failed to return, and 106 Squadron welcomed home all but one of its own, S/L Sprawson and crew claiming a Ju88 as damaged after being attacked twice while homebound, having already sustained flak damage over the target. It was the dispersal pan belonging to ME790 which remained unoccupied, and news would come through eventually that it had crashed north of the Ruhr, killing F/L Houlden and six others of the eight occupants, including the second pilot, F/Sgt Scott RCAF, who was probably operating for the first time. The wireless operator, W/O Pringle RAAF, one of four Australians on board, was the sole survivor, and he was taken into captivity. Post-raid reconnaissance confirmed that most of the bombing had fallen onto outlying communities, confirming in the minds of the residents that this was an intentional ploy by the Command.

The main operation on the 24th involved 442 aircraft in an attack on two marshalling yards at Aachen, Aachen-West and Rothe-Erde in the east. As the most westerly city in Germany, sitting on the frontiers of both Holland and Belgium, it was a major link in the railway network that would be a route for reinforcements to the Normandy battle front. Other operations on this night were directed at coastal batteries in the Pas-de-Calais and war-industry factories in Holland and Belgium. 5 Group detailed forty-four Lancasters to attack the Ford Motor works in Antwerp, and fifty-nine for the Philips electronics factory at Eindhoven in southern Holland, while Metheringham remained off the Order of Battle. Those bound for Eindhoven were more than an hour into the outward journey when the Master Bomber sent them home by W/T, presumably after a Met Flight Mosquito crew had found poor visibility in the target area. There were no such difficulties at Antwerp, where the target was identified by illuminating flares, a yellow TI and red spotfires, despite which, post-raid reconnaissance revealed the factory to be intact.

It was announced on the 25th that S/L Crowe had been awarded a well-deserved Bar to his DFC. The night of the 26/27th was devoted to minor operations, including mining off the occupied coasts by forty-two aircraft divided between Nectarine I off the western Frisians and one of the Silverthorn gardens in the Kattegat off the eastern coast of Jutland. Both elements found favourable conditions, with ten-tenths cloud over the Baltic, but good visibility and a light sky, and positions were established on Sjaelland Point by H2S. Almost cloudless conditions over the North Sea also revealed a lighter than normal night sky, and the mines were dropped unopposed into the briefed locations.

The night of the 27/28th was to be one of feverish activity, which would generate more than eleven hundred sorties, reflecting the close proximity of the invasion, now just ten days away. The largest operation would bring a return to the military camp at Bourg Leopold in Belgium, the previous attack on which, two weeks earlier, had been abandoned part-way through. There was also a repeat of the Aachen attack of the 24th, which had failed to destroy the Rothe-Erde marshalling yards at the eastern end of the city and needed further attention. 5 Group was not involved in either of the above, and, instead, prepared forces of one hundred Lancasters and four Mosquitos and seventy-eight Lancasters and five Mosquitos respectively to target marshalling yards and workshops at Nantes and the aerodrome at Rennes, situated some fifty miles apart in north-western France. The 106 Squadron element of ten Lancasters was assigned to the former, and all contained relatively inexperienced crews, who departed Metheringham between 22.45 and 23.15, to be followed into the air between 23.50 and 23.59 by the crews of S/L de Belleroche and four others bound for one of the Rosemary gardens in the Helogoland Bight. The bombing element arrived at its destination to find good conditions and excellent visibility, despite which, only four crews saw any form of markers, and they bombed on red spotfires from 8,400 to 9,500 feet from between 01.43 and 01.46. The others circled for up to twenty-five minutes, before receiving a W/T message at around 02.10 to abandon the operation. P/O Monaghan and crew had delivered their eight 1,000 and eight 500 pounders before LM549 was attacked and extensively damaged by a night-fighter on the way home. The gunners claimed the enemy as damaged, and P/O Monaghan pulled off a masterly one-wheel landing at the emergency strip at Carnaby on the Yorkshire coast. He and his crew walked away from the scene, apparently none the worse for their experience, unaware that an even more testing experience was to come the way of this pilot within six weeks, one that he would also negotiate without dire consequences.

Meanwhile, the gardeners had employed H2S to locate their respective release points situated roughly midway between Heligoland and the Hamburg-owned Scharhörn island some twenty or so miles to the south-east, and each delivered six mines as briefed from 15,000 feet between 02.03 and 02.28, before returning safely. 5 Group also supported operations against coastal batteries, of which there were five on this night, including one at Morsalines, situated on the eastern seaboard of the Cherbourg peninsula, some ten miles north of what, during the forthcoming Operation Overlord, would be the Americans' Utah landing ground.

On the 28th, 181 Lancasters and twenty Mosquitos continued the attacks on coastal batteries overlooking the Normandy beaches, which, a week hence, would be the scene of Operation Overlord. Metheringham was not called into action on this night, or on the following two nights, and it was on the 31st when the next orders were received to prepare for further operations that night against coastal batteries covering the Normandy beaches. 5 Group was to send a force of eighty-two Lancasters and four Mosquitos to attack a railway junction at Saumur in the Loire Valley, and another of sixty-eight Lancasters to a coastal battery at Maisy, overlooking what would be the Americans' Omaha Beach. It was for the latter that 106 Squadron prepared a dozen Lancasters, which departed Metheringham in a violent thunderstorm between 22.50 and 23.25 with W/C Piercy and S/L Sprawson the senior pilots on duty. They had to battle the storm belt as they flew from base to Reading, and the foul weather continued as they passed over Selsey Bill to start the Channel crossing. The leading crews were within seven miles of the French coast when they were recalled by W/T at 00.53, and, while some squadrons were diverted to avoid the bad weather, the 106 Squadron crews all managed to find Metheringham and land safely after jettisoning part of their bomb load. In the event, only six of the sixty-eight participants had bombed by the time that cloud compelled the Master Bomber to abandon proceedings. It was announced that night that S/L Sprawson was to receive the immediate award of a DFC. During the course of the month the squadron carried out ten bombing and two mining operations, dispatching 145 sorties for the loss of seven aircraft and crews.

June 1944

June was to be a hectic month which would make great demands on the crews. The bombing of coastal batteries was to be the priority during the first few days of June leading up to D-Day, but 5 Group would open its account by returning to Saumur to attack a second railway junction on the 1st. The day dawned cloudy and cold, and these conditions would persist throughout the first week of the month, causing concern among the invasion planners. 106 Squadron remained at home, while fifty-eight Lancasters took off in the late evening to find ten-tenths cloud covering the route out to within twenty miles of the town, where it dispersed completely to leave clear skies and good visibility under a three-quarter moon. The flare force was almost superfluous in the conditions, but the first wave was called in by the Master Bomber, W/C Jeudwine, to release from 15,000 feet at 01.08, and the first red spot fire from an Oboe Mosquito fell bang on the aiming point two minutes later. Smoke became a problem as it drifted across the area to obscure the spotfire that was still burning, and a green TI was dropped to maintain the aiming point. Apart from a few scattered sticks to the north, and on an island in the Loire to the south, the attack seemed to be accurate. Returning crews reported little opposition, fires in the yards and a large explosion at 01.35, and the success of the raid was confirmed by photographic reconnaissance, which showed severe damage to the track.

It was important for the Command to continue its attacks on coastal defences in the Pas-de-Calais region to maintain the deception concerning the actual landing grounds, and 106 Squadron opened its month's account with fifteen Lancasters detailed to support one of these on the night of the 2/3rd. The target was a heavy railway-mounted battery at Marquise, situated some eight miles south-west of Calais, for which the squadron participants departed Metheringham between 23.40 and 23.55 with S/L de Belleroche the senior pilot on duty, and climbed immediately into ten-tenths low cloud and drizzle. The unfavourable weather conditions persisted all the way to the target, where the crews of F/Os Bellingham and Mather and W/O Kipfer bombed on the glow of red target indicators from 17,800 to 19,400 feet between 01.40 and 01.42. The other 106 Squadron crews were either awaiting instructions over the target or were on final approach, when they received a message to stop bombing and return home. The outcome, in terms of damage, was unimportant, as long as it reinforced in the mind of the enemy, that Calais was to be the destination of the expected invasion force. Later on the 3rd, the award of the DFC was announced to six squadron officers, including F/L Poore, who was now at 617 Squadron with his crew.

Orders came through on the 4th to prepare for further attacks that night on coastal batteries, three in the Pas-de-Calais to maintain the deception, and the other one at Maisy, overlooking the Utah and Omaha beaches. 259 aircraft of 1, 4, 5, 6 and 8 Groups were made ready, the majority for the deception targets, while fifty-two of the 5 Group Lancasters were assigned to Maisy. 106 Squadron had briefed fifteen crews for these pre-dawn attacks, but worsening weather as take-off time approached caused the withdrawal of all but the three most experienced crews, those of W/C Piercy, S/L Sprawson and W/O Cunningham. They got away from Metheringham by 02.00, each carrying eighteen 500 pounders, and reached the target at Maisy ninety minutes later to find eight to ten-tenths cloud with a base at around 4,000 feet, which necessitated the use of Oboe skymarkers. W/C Piercy and crew came down to 6,200 feet to try to get under the cloud base, and bombed at 03.39 on the glow of red target indicators confirmed by H2S. W/O Cunningham and crew relied on Gee, confirmed by the observation of red TIs on the ground, and they delivered their attack from 8,000 feet at 03.40, while S/L Sprawson and crew remained above the cloud at 9,000 feet, and bombed at 03.44 on the faint glow, the location of which was confirmed by Gee and H2S. It was impossible to assess the outcome, and similar cloudy conditions had thwarted two of the three attempts in the Pas-de-Calais.

The night of the 5/6th was D-Day Eve, and, during the course of the night, a record number of 1,211 sorties would be flown against coastal defences and in support and diversionary and spoof operations. Sixteen 106 Squadron crews attended briefing at Metheringham, where no direct reference was made to the invasion, but, unusually, they were given strict altitudes at which to fly, and were told not to jettison bombs over the sea. They learned also that they would be among more than a thousand aircraft targeting ten heavy gun batteries along the Normandy coast, and that their specific objective as part of a force of 115 Lancasters and four Mosquitos was at Saint-Pierre-du-Mont, which was the closest to Omaha Beach. 97 (Straits Settlement) Squadron would be on hand to provide the illumination led by the commanding officer, W/C Jimmy Carter. Another 5 Group element of 122 Lancasters and four Mosquitos was assigned to a battery at La Pernelle, some three miles north of the one recently attacked at Morsalines, which, although not disclosed to the crews, was also close to Utah Beach, and 83 Squadron would provide the illumination and the marking here. The 106 Squadron contingent departed Metheringham between 02.30 and 02.55 with S/L de Belleroche the senior pilot on duty and each Lancaster carrying 13,000lbs of bombs, made up of eleven 1,000 pounders and four 500 pounders. They reached the target area to find a layer of cloud at around 10,000 feet, and responded to the Master Bomber's instructions to drop beneath the cloud base, from where the red and green target indicators could easily be seen. S/L de Belleroche and crew delivered their attack from 8,250 feet at 04.50, to be followed by the others from 6,500 to 11,500 feet over the ensuing ten minutes. Any homeward-bound crews looking down through the occasional gaps in the clouds were rewarded by the incredible sight of the greatest armada in history, as it ploughed its way sedately southwards through choppy waters towards the French coast at about eight knots. The 106 Squadron ORB stated; "As our crews were returning across the Channel, they saw a vast fleet of miscellaneous craft from battleships to barges, heading towards the coast of Normandy. "D-DAY" HAD ARRIVED!!!" A total of five thousand tons of bombs was dropped during the night, and this was a new record. Only seven aircraft failed to return from these operations, three of them from Sainte-Pierre, including the one containing 97 Squadron's W/C Carter and seven highly experienced crewmen, all but one of whom held either a DFC or DFM.

As the beachheads were being established during the course of the 6th, preparations were put in hand to support the ground forces by attacking nine road and railway communications centres through which the enemy could bring reinforcements. 5 Group was assigned to two targets, Argentan supply depot and railway centre located some thirty miles south-east of Caen, and two road bridges in Caen itself, for which forces of 112 Lancasters and six Mosquitos and 120 Lancasters and four Mosquitos respectively were assembled. 106 Squadron made ready sixteen Lancasters for the latter, and they departed Metheringham between 00.25 and 00.45 with S/L Sprawson the senior pilot on duty. They joined up with the other squadrons as they headed south to begin the Channel crossing at Bridport, and set course for the Channel Islands before turning sharply to the east to cross the Cherbourg peninsula. All reached the target area in bright moonlight to find ten-tenths cloud with a base at 5,000 to 6,000 feet, below which, 627 Squadron Mosquitos ran in at low-level to drop red spotfires, which were then supplemented by red TIs from the heavy marker element. The Metheringham crews attacked the aiming point from below the cloud base from 3,000 to 5,500 feet between 02.41 and 02.48, in accordance with the Master Bomber's instructions and in the face of considerable amounts of light flak, and were able to clearly pick out the river, marshalling yards and town detail despite being impeded by smoke and the glare from fires. Six Lancasters failed to return from the Caen raid, largely as the result of the need for the force to orbit while the markers were assessed. ND680 and NE150 were absent from their dispersal pans, both having come down on French soil, the former close to the target. By this time S/L Sprawson had been B Flight commander for a little over five weeks, and took to heart the responsibility of inspiring those in his charge by leading from the front. A consequence of that was the high rate of loss among squadron and flight commanders, although, the good news would eventually filter through that S/L Sprawson and four of his crew had arrived safely on the ground, and that he and his navigator and bomb-aimer were on their way home, while the flight engineer and wireless operator would have to endure a period of captivity. Both gunners failed to survive, and P/O Arnold, the mid-upper, at forty years of age, was among the oldest officers to lose his life on operations. The latter Lancaster was captained by P/O Warren, and it came down well to the north-east of the target, probably after an encounter with a night-fighter. The pilot and four others died in the wreckage, the bomb-aimer succumbed to his injuries four days later, while the navigator, F/O Drylie, managed to retained his freedom. In some compensation, F/O Mather's gunners claimed the destruction of a Me110. Photo-reconnaissance confirmed that both bridges had been put out of action, and congratulatory messages were received from the C-in-C Army Group.

Four railway targets were earmarked for attention by a force of 337 aircraft on the 7th, while elements of 5 Group were being prepared to join forces with 1 and 8 Groups to attack a six-way road junction at Balleroy, situated fifteen miles west of Caen on the approach to the Foret-de-Cerisy, where it was believed the enemy was concealing a fuel dump and tank units. 106 Squadron was not involved in the operation, which took place in conditions of ten-tenths cloud with a base at 8,000 to 10,000 feet and haze below. The initial Oboe markers appeared to be accurate and on time, but another marker fell simultaneously some five miles to the south-west and attracted some bomb loads. The Master Bomber quickly gained control of the situation and directed the bombing to the correct marker, which was pounded by concentrated bombing. Dense clouds of black smoke and one particularly large explosion were evidence of a successful outcome, during which the gunners in the crew of the 207 Squadron commanding officer shot down three enemy fighters in a twenty-minute period.

The night of the 8/9th was devoted to the disruption of railway communications to prevent the enemy from bring up reinforcements, for which 483 aircraft were detailed and assigned to five centres. Orders were received at Metheringham for 106 Squadron to prepare a dozen Lancasters as part of a 5 Group force of ninety-seven Lancasters and four Mosquitos to attack railway installations at Rennes in Brittany, while fifty-four Lancasters and four Mosquitos attended to a similar target at Pontabault some thirty miles to the north-east. A third 5 Group force consisting of twenty-five Lancasters of 617 Squadron would also operate on this night some 125 miles to the south to deliver the very first Barnes Wallis-designed 12,000lb Tallboy earthquake bombs against the railway tunnel at Saumur, for which four 83 Squadron Lancasters were to provide the illumination. The 106 Squadron element departed Metheringham between 23.05 and 23.25 with F/L Clement the senior pilot on duty, and each Lancaster carrying eighteen 500 pounders, two with delayed action fuses varying from six to thirty-six hours. They had been assigned to three waves, four in each, and arrived in the target area to find complete cloud cover, but excellent visibility beneath. The markers were accurately placed, and the squadron aircraft bombed them at heights ranging from 6,000 to 8,500 feet between 01.34 and 01.50, in accordance with the instructions of the Master Bomber, and all returned safely with six aiming point photos.

A force of 401 aircraft from 1, 4, 6 and 8 Groups was made ready on the 9th to target airfields in the battle area, while 5 Group concentrated on a railway junction at Etampes, south of Paris. 108 Lancasters and four Mosquitos were to take part, while 106 Squadron remained at home. Those reaching the target found eight to ten-tenths cloud with a base at 8,000 feet, and patches of two to three-tenths lower down at 4,000 feet, but this had no effect on the marking. Some crews thought that they had picked up a recall signal, and others a message at around midnight to orbit, until being called in to bomb. Photo-reconnaissance confirmed that all tracks had been cut for a distance of four hundred yards to the north-east of the junction, but it revealed also that the town had sustained collateral damage, which caused many civilian casualties.

It was railways again two nights later, when four targets were to be attacked, including one at Orleans situated some thirty miles south-west of Paris, which was assigned to a 5 Group force of 108 Lancasters and four Mosquitos. Eighteen 106 Squadron Lancasters were made ready, eight for the main raid against the marshalling yards and ten for a subsidiary operation involving only Metheringham crews against a ten-mile stretch of railway line running north from Orleans to Chevilly. While the crews attended briefing, the armourers were busy loading their aircraft with either eighteen or fifteen 500 pounders, a few in each load fitted with long-delay fuses. F/L Taylor DFM was to perform the role of Master Bomber for the special target and would be flying as captain with F/L A.J. Williams and crew as the two elements took off together between 21.50 and 22.35. P/O Thompson and crew of the marshalling yard element were hit by engine failure almost immediately and had to abort their sortie, leaving the others to head for the south coast and the Channel crossing. There was little cloud in the target area, and visibility was good, enabling the marshalling yards to be identified easily, both visually and by the red spotfires burning in their midst. The seven 106 Squadron aircraft bombed from 3,000 to 6,500 feet between 00.42 and 00.48, and the crews of F/Sgt Futcher and P/O Easby brought back aiming point photos, which showed the target to have been obliterated. F/L Taylor assessed the visibility as twenty-to-thirty miles as he closed on the marshalling yards, which he used as a reference before turning north and flying up the railway line. He dropped hooded flares at 00.38, but two of them failed to ignite, and some of those delivered by the crews of P/O Durrant and F/L Clement also proved to be duds. Fortunately, sufficient ignited to provide adequate illumination of the track, and they were supplemented by reconnaissance flares. F/L Taylor bombed from 1,200 feet at 00.50 just south of Cercottes, towards the northern end of the stretch, and then spent the next eight minutes cruising up and down directing the efforts of the other crews, who carried out their attacks from 800 to 1,500 feet between 00.51 and 00.58. A number of sticks were observed to fall along the tracks, and those delivered from 800 feet by F/L A.L. Williams and crew straddled the line south of Artenay. W/O Cunningham and crew dropped their bombs in a series of small salvoes, the first three miles north of Orleans, and the last ten miles north. Reconnaissance photos confirmed that the track was cratered, and that a number of goods trains had sustained damage.

Later, on the 11th, awards of the DFC were announced to the missing F/L Lee, and to F/Os Richards and Lee. The campaign against communications targets continued on the 12th at six locations, including road bridges at Caen and marshalling yards at Poitiers, for which 5 Group detailed forces of 109 Lancasters and four Mosquitos and 112 Lancasters and four Mosquitos respectively. 106 Squadron made ready seventeen Lancasters to take part at the latter, located in west-central France, and they departed Metheringham between 22.25 and 22.45 with W/C Piercy the senior pilot on duty and S/L Marshall DFC flying as second pilot with F/L Clement and crew. It took almost three-and-a-half hours to form up and reach the target area in western France, where the force encountered patchy cloud but good visibility. The target was easily located by means of red spotfires and green TIs, and the squadron element delivered their four 1,000 pounders and twelve 500 pounders at heights ranging from 5,500 to 10,000 feet, and no fewer than thirteen, including W/C Piercy, brought back aiming point photos. The accuracy of the attack was confirmed by reconnaissance, which revealed the Paris to Bordeaux line to have been cut in seven places and was the most successful of the six operations carried out that night against railway objectives. Meanwhile, some 150 miles to the north, six to ten-tenths cloud had created problems, which ate into the strict timing for the duration of the attack, and the Master Bomber called a halt to proceedings with thirty Lancasters still to bomb. A new oil campaign began on this night, prosecuted by 286 Lancasters and seventeen Mosquitos of 1, 3 and 8 Groups, whose target was the Nordstern (Gelsenberg A G) plant at Gelsenkirchen. Such was the accuracy of the attack, that all production of vital aviation fuel was halted for a number of weeks at a cost to the Germans of a thousand tons per day.

The 14th brought the Command's first daylight operation since the departure of 2 Group twelve months earlier. The target was Le Havre, from where the enemy's E-Boats and other fast, light marine craft were posing a threat to Allied shipping supplying the Normandy beachheads. The two-phase operation was conducted by predominantly 1 and 3 Groups with 617 Squadron representing 5 Group, and took place in the evening under the umbrella of a fighter escort. The attack was highly successful, and few craft survived the onslaught. Other operations on this night were directed against railway installations at three locations in France, while elements of 4, 5 and 8 Groups attended to enemy troop and vehicle concentrations at Aunay-sur-Odon and Évrecy near Caen. 5 Group assembled a force of 214 Lancasters and five Mosquitos for the former, of which the twenty representing 106 Squadron departed Metheringham between 22.25 and 22.45 with S/L de Belleroche the senior pilot on duty. The weather was generally clear with some low cloud, but this did not hamper the marking process, which proceeded punctually and accurately. W/C Jeudwine was the Master Bomber, with 83 Squadron's W/C Joe Northrop as Deputy, and the latter made four passes over the target, at 00.30 at 8,000 feet, 00.41 at 10,000 feet, and at 00.54 and 01.00 at 11,000 feet, dropping clusters of flares on the first two, green TIs on the third and red TIs on the fourth. The 106 Squadron crews bombed them with eleven 1,000 and four 500 pounders each from 6,000 to 10,000 feet between 00.35 and 01.04, observing what appeared to be a concentrated attack that produced numerous fires and much black smoke. F/O Crosier and crew were the last to bomb, and were among sixteen to return to Metheringham with an aiming point photo. There had been considerable night-fighter activity, and F/Sgt Fox and crew had to fight off the attentions of two Ju88s and two FW190s, the gunners claiming one of the former as damaged. In all, 1,200 tons of bombs had been delivered, 106 Squadron registering a new squadron record of 116 tons, the most by any individual unit involved.

A force of 297 aircraft from 1, 4, 5, 6 and 8 Groups was assembled on the 15th to try to do to Boulogne what had been done to Le Havre twenty-four hours earlier. It was again left to 617 Squadron to represent 5 Group, and the operation was concluded with equal success. While this was in progress, 5 Group dispatched 110 Lancasters and four Mosquitos to deal with a fuel dump at Châtellerault, situated between Tours and Poitiers in western France. 106 Squadron contributed twenty Lancasters, which departed Metheringham between 21.10 and 21.30 with S/L de Belleroche and new B Flight commander, S/L Marshall, the senior pilots on duty. They were divided equally among the four waves, and all arrived in the target area to find clear skies and good visibility. They each delivered their eighteen 500 pounders onto Path Finder spotfires and green TIs from 7,000 to 10,000 feet between 00.55 and 01.03, and all returned safely. Fourteen of the bombing photos captured the aiming point, and reconnaissance confirmed that the attack had destroyed eight of thirty-five fuel storage sites in the area. The ORB justifiably commended the squadron on launching a total of forty aircraft over two consecutive nights, with no early returns and obtaining thirty aiming point photos.

Plans were put in hand on the 16th, to launch 829 sorties that night against a number of targets. Just three days earlier, the first V-1 flying bombs had landed on London, and this prompted a response in the form of a second new campaign to open during the month, this one against the revolutionary weapon's launching and storage sites in the Pas-de-Calais. Of four targets earmarked for attention, 5 Group was handed a storage site at Beauvoir, located some twenty miles inland from Berck-sur-Mer. The large concrete storage sites, many in various stages of construction, were referred to in Bomber Command parlance as "constructional works", while others, called "ski sites", were small buildings in the shape of a hockey stick and were attached to launching ramps. 112 Lancasters were detailed, and those reaching the target area encountered nine to ten-tenths cloud with tops at 6,000 to 8,000 feet, and bombed on the faint glow of red Oboe markers. It was impossible to assess the outcome, which left crews with little to pass on to the Intelligence Sections at debriefing. The oil campaign continued on this night in the hands of 1, 4, 6 and 8 Groups at Sterkrade-Holten, a district of Oberhausen in the Ruhr, but cloudy conditions caused the bombing to be scattered, and there was little impact on production.

Metheringham had remained inactive since the 15th, and received orders on the 19th to prepare sixteen Lancasters for a 54 Base operation that evening against a storage site in woods at Watten near St-Omer in company with elements of 617 Squadron. An entry in the 106 Squadron ORB for that day mentioned that southern England had "for some days now been subjected to an assault by the much-heralded "secret weapon", variously described as pilotless aircraft, Buzz Bombs or Doodle-Bugs". They took off between 22.45 and 23.00 with F/Ls Williams A G and A L the senior pilots on duty, but were recalled ten minutes later because of the expectation of a dangerously low cloud base at the scheduled landing time. While 617 Squadron went alone to another site at Wizernes on the 20th, and failed to bomb in the face of cloudy conditions, preparations were made at Metheringham for a daylight operation on the following day. In anticipation of regular daylight operations during the summer, tail fins were painted white with a green stripe, and the aircraft letter was also painted in white. In the event, the daylight operation did not take place, but the new colour scheme remained.

5 Group had to wait until Mid-Summer's Night, the 21st, before becoming involved in the oil offensive, and was handed two targets to attack simultaneously. A force of 120 Lancasters from 52 and 55 Bases and six Mosquitos from 54 Base was assembled for the refinery at Wesseling, or to give it its full name, the Union Rheinische Braunkohlen-Kraftstoff Aktien Gesellschaft, situated on the East Bank of the Rhine south of Cologne. On the 53 and 54 Base stations, meanwhile, 120 Lancasters and four Mosquitos were made ready for the Hydrierwerke-Scholven plant in the Buer district of Gelsenkirchen, and both operations would benefit from a sprinkling of ABC Lancasters of 101 Squadron for RCM duties, while a number of Path Finder Oboe Mosquitos would provide the initial marking at the Ruhr target. 106 Squadron made ready twenty Lancasters for Scholven-Buer, and they departed Metheringham between 23.10 and 23.30 with S/L Marshall the senior pilot on duty and S/L Loughborough, who had just been posted in to succeed S/L de Belleroche as A Flight commander, flying as second pilot with the crew of F/O Bellingham. Five early returns reduced the force, and among them was F/L A L Williams and crew, who had turned back after a navigational error caused them to fall fifteen minutes behind the others, all of whom had been assigned to specific waves with strict timings. They arrived in the target area expecting to find clear skies, instead of which, they encountered ten-tenths cloud. This was the only flaw in the highly-effective 5 Group low-level marking method, which required the Mosquito element to go in beneath the cloud base and for the markers to be visible through the cloud. The preliminary Oboe markers were backed up by red and green TIs, the glow from which could be observed only dimly through the cloud, and the crews had to aim for these, those from 106 Squadron from 17,000 to 20,000 feet between 01.40 and 01.49. It was impossible to assess the outcome, and to compound any sense of disappointment at Metheringham, two 106 Squadron crews were among eight from 5 Group to fail to return from this operation. Night-fighters had been waiting to greet them as they crossed Holland outbound, and LM570 was intercepted over central Holland's Gelderland and shot down, killing F/O Bellingham and his crew, including the new A Flight commander elect. LL955 suffered a similar fate, probably also while outbound, and crashed a little further north in the Gelderland, about eleven miles south-west of Zwolle, with no survivors from the crew of P/O Brodie.

Meanwhile, the Wesseling crews had observed many combats as they made their way inland also expecting to find clear skies, instead of which, they encountered up to ten-tenths low cloud at 2,500 to 4,000 feet. It created impossible conditions for the low-level Mosquito crews, who were unable to do their job, and faced with this situation, the Master Bomber, W/C Tait, ordered a blind attack, which required the Lancaster crews to bomb on their own H2S or on the red and green TIs dropped by 83 Squadron also on H2S. They did so in the face of heavy predicted flak, and a large explosion at 01.46 caused an extensive red glow in the cloud, before another one was witnessed at 01.51. There was shock on the 52 and 55 Base stations when thirty-five of the Lancasters that had taken off just a few hours earlier failed to return, 44, 49, 57 and 619 Squadrons each losing six Lancasters, although one from 57

Squadron ditched off the English coast and the crew was rescued. 207 and 630 Squadrons each posted missing five Lancasters and crews. After the war, a secret German report would suggest a 40% loss of production at the site, but this was probably of very short duration as the limited number of casualties on the ground pointed to a scattered and largely ineffective raid.

Losses were a fact of life in Bomber Command, and could not be allowed to interfere with the process of war. A team from the Committee of Adjustment would descend upon the billets of the missing men and remove all trace of them to prepare the way for the next occupants. Such was the size of a bomber squadron, and the constant turnover of arrivals and departures, that close friendships beyond one's own crew were discouraged. Perhaps it was different among officers, who were fewer, and were more frequently in each other's company in the officers' mess, but, generally, the faces of the missing soon faded from memory, and those returning within a matter of months after evading capture, were often shocked to discover how few of their former colleagues were left.

While more than four hundred aircraft of 3, 4, 6 and 8 Groups targeted four flying-bomb sites on the 23rd, elements of 1 and 5 Groups were sent respectively against railway yards at Saintes and Limoges in western France. Ninety-seven Lancasters and four Mosquitos were detailed for the latter, and those reaching the target area found clear skies and good visibility, in which ground features like the River Vienne and the railway sidings stood out prominently. Red spotfires and green TIs marked out the aiming point, and post-raid reconnaissance confirmed a highly accurate and concentrated attack.

617 Squadron had attempted to continue the Tallboy assault on the constructional works at Wizernes in daylight on the 22nd, but the attack had been abandoned in the face of ten-tenths low cloud. The squadron returned the bombs to store, and brought them back to France on the 24th to score a number of direct hits. A further 739 aircraft were detailed to take part in attacks on seven flying bomb launching sites that night, and those at Pommeréval and Prouville, situated respectively some fifteen miles south-east of Dieppe, and east of Abbeville, were handed to 5 Group. 103 Lancasters and four Mosquitos were assigned to each, and it was for the former that 106 Squadron made ready seventeen of its own and sent them on their way between 22.20 and 22.35 with F/L A G Williams the senior pilot on duty. As was now standard practise, they were again allotted to specific waves, six in the first and second, and five in the third. The operation was favoured by excellent weather conditions of clear skies and good visibility, and the 106 Squadron crews passed over the aiming point between 00.04 and 00.12 to deliver their eighteen 500 pounders each, two in each load containing delay fuses. The medium level bombing at between 6,500 and 9,000 feet ensured accuracy, and thirteen aiming point photos were captured. No night-fighters were reported on this night, but flak was quite heavy and accurate, and four Lancasters failed to return. It is believed that LL975 crashed in the target area, probably the victim of flak, and P/O Wright RAAF and four of his crew perished. The flight engineer and bomb-aimer, Sgts McPhail and Knaggs respectively, parachuted to safety, and both ultimately evaded capture. At Prouville, meanwhile, the preliminary Oboe Mosquito was punctual, but the subsequent marking was hampered by intense searchlight activity working in co-operation with flak and night-fighters, and bombing was delayed while the aiming point was positively identified and marked. It took until all of the illuminator flares had been expended before the low-level Mosquitos dropped red spotfires and the heavy brigade from 97 Squadron backed up with red and green TIs. The bombing was controlled by the Master Bomber, but the impression was of a somewhat haphazard attack that lacked concentration, and cost thirteen Lancasters, possibly as a result of the delay in opening the attack.

More than seven hundred aircraft were detailed for operations against six flying-bomb sites on the 27th, while two railway yards would occupy the attention of other elements. There were two targets for 5 Group, a flying-bomb site at Marquise, situated some five miles inland from Cap Gris-Nez, and railway yards at Vitry-le-Francois, situated south-east of Reims also in north-eastern France. 103 Lancaster crews were briefed for the latter, among them sixteen representing 106 Squadron, which departed Metheringham between 21.50 and 22.05 with W/C Piercy the senior pilot on duty. They all reached the target, where varying amounts of cloud were reported between zero to seven-tenths at around 7,000 feet, but the visibility was good, and the aiming point clearly marked by red spot fires and green TIs. Eleven of the 106 Squadron crews delivered their nine 1,000 and three 500 pounders each from 4,800 to 7,500 feet between 01.45 and 01.57, at which point, the Master Bomber called a halt to proceedings and ordered the twenty crews of the final wave to take their bombs home. Three 106 Squadron crews were among these, and 50 Squadron's commanding officer, W/C Frogley, was critical of the decision to abandon the attack, suggesting that, if the first spotfire had not been accurate, the bombing should never even have started. In fact, it had been smoke obscuring the aiming point that had prompted the Master Bomber's actions. Five Metheringham crews came home with aiming point photos, but the operation was only moderately successful, causing damage to the western end of the yards at a cost of two Lancasters, both of which belonged to 106 Squadron. LL974 was shot down by a night-fighter, and crashed near Thibie, north-west of the target, while JB664 crashed near Nemours, north-east of Orleans, also after an encounter with a night-fighter, and there were no survivors from among the crews of F/Sgt Fox and P/O Easby respectively.

Although the month's operational activity was over for some elements of 5 Group, 53 and 54 Bases were alerted on the 29th to provide eighty-five Lancasters and four Mosquitos as part of an overall force of 286 Lancasters and nineteen Mosquitos of 1, 5 and 8 Groups for a daylight attack on two flying-bomb launching sites and one storage site. Fourteen 106 Squadron crews attended briefing to learn of their part in a daylight attack on the previously targeted flying bomb site or "constructional works" at Beauvoir, and this would be the squadron's first daylight foray since Milan on the 24th of October 1942. The target was situated in the Burgundy region of north-central France, and the force of eighty-five Lancasters was to fly out in loose formation, with crews once more assigned to specific waves. There would also be a large and comforting fighter escort to keep them safe from the attentions of the Luftwaffe. W/C Piercy was the senior pilot on duty, and he was supported by S/L Marshall and the newly promoted S/L A L Williams, who had replaced the tour-expired S/L de Belleroche as A Flight commander, and was now well into his second tour with the squadron. They departed Metheringham between 12.10 and 12.20, and flew out in loose formation to join up with the other units before reaching the target to find clear conditions beneath the 15,000-foot cloud level. S/L Williams and crew were in the first wave, and reported being able to pick out concrete buildings and the "ski site" visually, before releasing their eleven 1,000 and four 500 pounders on them, confirmed by a Gee fix, from 17,000 feet at 13.46. Some of those arriving a few minutes later found the aiming point obscured by smoke, but all but one from the squadron carried out an attack at altitudes ranging from 14,000 to 19,000 feet between 13.45 and 13.52. F/O Mather and crew were unable to pin-point the target, and jettisoned their bombs over enemy territory. Flak was heavy and accurate, and F/Sgt Netherwood's ND868 was hit and severely damaged. The pilot displayed fine airmanship by bringing the Lancaster and crew back to a safe landing at the emergency strip at Woodbridge in Suffolk.

During the course of the month the squadron operated on fourteen occasions, dispatching 220 sorties for the loss of seven aircraft and crews. There were also thirty-eight awards to squadron members past and present, including a Bar to the DFC, twenty-two DFCs and fifteen DFMs.

July 1944

Sadly, July would bring further traumas for 5 Group, the first occurring early on, while the disaster of Wesseling was still an open wound. The month began as June had ended, with flying-bomb sites providing employment for over three hundred aircraft on both the 1st and 2nd. It was the 4th before the Independent Air Force was invited to re-enter the fray, when it was called upon to attack a V-Weapon storage site in caves at St-Leu-d'Esserent, some thirty miles north of Paris. The caves had originally been used for growing mushrooms, and they were protected by some twenty-five feet of clay and soft limestone, to say nothing of the anti-aircraft defences brought in by the Germans. The operation involved seventeen Lancasters, a Mustang and a Mosquito from 617 Squadron, and 211 other Lancasters and eleven Mosquitos from the rest of 5 Group, with three ABC Lancasters to provide RCM cover and three Path Finder Oboe Mosquitos to carry out the marking of an initial reference-point. There were actually two aiming points, the road and railway communications to the area dump for the main force, and the tunnel complex at Creil, a settlement located three miles north-east of St Leu, for 617 Squadron.

106 Squadron supported the operation with sixteen Lancasters, which departed Metheringham between 23.15 and 23.30 with S/L Marshall the senior pilot on duty, and arrived in the target area two hours later to find clear skies and good visibility, conditions favourable to attacker and defender alike. There were no searchlights, but the expected volume of flak was thrown up as the 106 Squadron crews ran across the aiming point to deliver eleven 1,000 and four 500 pounders each from 15,000 to 18,000 feet onto accurately placed green TIs between 01.33 and 01.41. Night-fighters pounced on the bombers over the target and on the route home, and thirteen Lancasters failed to return, two of them from Metheringham. 106 Squadron was represented among the missing by ME832 "Hare's Hound", and ND339, and the fortunes of the two crews differed markedly. P/O Futcher and five of his crew lost their lives in the former, which was shot down about five miles west-south-west of Beauvais while approaching the target. F/Sgt McNaughton, the Canadian bomb-aimer, was the only survivor, and he ultimately evaded capture. In contrast, there were six survivors from the crew of F/O Crosier, and four of them also retained their freedom. The fact that F/O Crosier was the single fatality in this crew suggests that he may have remained at the controls in the finest traditions of crew captaincy, to allow his crew time to save themselves. F/O Mavaut RCAF brought a badly damaged ND682 back to a landing at Woodbridge after surviving a night-fighter attack during the bombing run at 17,000 feet. The bombs were delivered as briefed, but the mid-upper gunner, Sgt Ekins, had been fatally wounded. Post-raid reconnaissance revealed that a large area of subsidence had blocked the side entrance to the caves and that the road and railway links had been cut over a distance of four hundred yards.

On the 6th, over five hundred aircraft were engaged on operations against V-Weapons targets, and 617 Squadron was assigned to a V-3 super-gun site at Mimoyecques. Originally planned as one of two sites near Cap Gris Nez containing twenty-five barrels each, angled at 50 degrees and aimed at London, test failures and delays meant that a single three-barrel shaft stretching a hundred metres into the limestone hill, five miles from the coast and 103 miles from its target, was all that existed at the time. Each fifteen-metre-long smooth-bore barrel, which was designed on the multiple-charge principle to progressively boost the acceleration of the one-ton projectile as it travelled towards the muzzle, was to be capable of pounding London at the rate of hundreds per day without let-up. It was protected by a concrete slab thirty metres wide and five-and-a-half metres thick, which was correctly believed by the designers to be impregnable to conventional bombs. It had been attacked on a number of occasions without success, but 617 Squadron scored direct hits with Tallboys, and provisional reconnaissance revealed four deep craters in the immediate target area, one causing a large corner of the concrete slab to collapse. The extent of the damage underground would not be apparent to the planners at Bomber Command, but the shafts and tunnels had been rendered unusable and would remain so. Although Cheshire did not know it, this was to be his final operation, not only with 617 Squadron, but also of the war in Europe. His one hundred-operation career would see him awarded a Victoria Cross, and his successor as commanding officer of 617 Squadron would need to be someone of immense stature, which was found in the person of W/C James "Willie" Tait.

The authorities were not convinced that the site at St-Leu-d'Esserent had received terminal damage, and scheduled another attack on it for the late evening of the 7th. Before the operation got under way, more than 450 aircraft from 1, 4, 6 and 8 Groups had carried out the first major operation in support of the Canadian 1st and British 2nd Armies, which were trying to break out of Caen. The target had been changed from German-fortified villages to an area of open ground north of Caen, where almost 2,300 tons of bombs were dropped somewhat ineffectively, and, ultimately, counter-productively by causing damage to the northern suburbs of the city rather than to German forces. 5 Group detailed 208 Lancasters and fifteen Mosquitos for the return to St-Leu, the 106 Squadron element of sixteen departing Metheringham between 22.30 and 22.45 with S/L Marshall the senior pilot on duty. They arrived in the target area to find medium-level cloud, which prevented the moonlight from providing illumination, although, below the cloud level, the visibility was good. The Master Bomber was the former 207 Squadron officer, W/C Ed Porter, and he oversaw the delivery of the Oboe yellow TI at 01.06, which was followed by the first stick of flares four minutes later. The first red spot fire went down at 01.08, a hundred yards south of the aiming point, but in line with the direction of the bombing run, and backing-up by red and green TIs continued until 01.13. The marking was assessed as sufficiently accurate to call in the main force at 01.15, and the 106 Squadron crews dropped their loads of ten 1,000 and four 500 pounders from 12,000 to 15,000 feet between 01.16 and 01.22. The Master Bomber's VHF was indistinct, so 83 Squadron's S/L Eggins assumed control, and sent the force home at 01.25. It was estimated that the Luftwaffe had committed 130 night-fighters to the battle, and some of these were responsible for most of the twenty-nine Lancasters and two Mosquitos that failed to return, 14% of the force.

It was another sobering night for Metheringham as five empty dispersal pans stood empty as dawn broke. It was a particularly bitter blow, because all of the missing crews were experienced and represented the backbone of the squadron. Although most fell victim to night-fighters, it was flak that brought down PB144 as it was leaving the target area and heading towards Beauvais. It crashed at 01.30 and burst into flames with no survivors from the crew of S/L Marshall DFC, a New Zealander, who had joined the RAF before the war, and had been B Flight commander since the loss of S/L Sprawson a month earlier. He left a widow, Doris, who came from Bradford. F/L Clement DFC and his crew, which included two other holders of the DFC, were in JB641, which, it is believed, was shot down by a night-fighter just after crossing the Normandy coast on the way to the target, and again there were no survivors. ME789 and ME381 ran into night-fighters at about the same time as each other as they headed for the target, and the former had both port engines and rear fuselage ablaze as F/O Mather RCAF and his predominantly Canadian crew took to their parachutes north-west of Beauvais at around 01.00. This was the same time that P/O Monaghan RAAF and his crew hit the silk near Oulins, west of Paris, and both crews arrived safely on the ground. The navigator from ME789, F/O Evans RCAF, managed to evade capture, but his crew mates were picked up by the enemy and packed off to a PoW camp. The bomb-aimer and wireless operator from ME381 suffered a similar fate, while their five colleagues slipped through the net and, thanks to the courage of local civilians, retained their freedom. ME668 had all four engines on fire by the time that F/L Marchant RAAF, his flight engineer and bomb-aimer left it to its fate at 01.15 near the spot where ME831 had come down, and they were all taken prisoner. The remaining four crew members, whose positions were aft of the flight deck, were still on board when the Lancaster crashed. Returning Metheringham crews reported a concentrated attack, confirmed by P/O Durrant's bombing photo, which was plotted at thirty-five yards from the aiming point. F/O Mavaut and crew reported having to orbit the target three times waiting for the time to bomb, and there were echoes of Mailly-le-Camp in their comments. Photo-reconnaissance revealed that both ends of the tunnel complex had collapsed, as had a section in the middle, and the approach road and rail links had been heavily cratered and blocked.

Just three days hence, news would come through that S/L Sprawson and his navigator, F/O Barker, had just returned home after evading capture. There was no immediate opportunity for the afflicted squadrons, particularly 106 and 207, which had lost five crews each, to "get back on the horse", and there must have been a sombre air while the populations of RAF Metheringham and Spilsby came to terms with the loss of thirty-five familiar faces in one night. A special congratulatory message was received from A-O-C, AVM Sir Ralph Cochrane, who considered it the finest effort by 5 Group, successfully pressing home the attack in the face of the fiercest opposition. S/L John Grindon was appointed as the new B Flight commander, and in view of the record of previous incumbents, it could well have been regarded as a poisoned chalice. In the event, and unlike many of his predecessors, he would survive. Born in Cornwall in September 1917, he had served with 150 Squadron in the Advanced Air Striking Force (AASF) in France during the "Phoney War". He was posted home to take a navigation course just as the German advance crushed the Low Countries, and, thereby, he missed the carnage that effectively knocked the Fairey Battle squadrons out of the conflict. Thereafter, he served two tours as an instructor in Canada, before taking up a staff job at Bomber Command HQ. He volunteered for operational duty, and was sent to undergo Lancaster training at 5 LFS.

Operations were posted on 5 Group stations on the 10th and 11th, but were cancelled, and, on the 12th, six 106 Squadron crews were called to briefing to be given the details about that night's operation against railway installations at Culmont-Chalindrey in eastern France. Two aiming points were planned, at the western and eastern ends, for which a force of 157 Lancasters and four Mosquitos was made ready. While this operation was in progress, another by elements of 1 Group further south at a railway junction at Revigny would, hopefully, help to dilute the night-fighter response. The 106 Squadron element departed Metheringham between 21.50 and 21.55 with F/L Taylor the senior pilot on duty, and headed for Bridport to begin the Channel crossing as far as the Channel Islands, before turning east-south-east to pass south of Paris to reach the target. Eight-tenths low cloud attended the outward flight until shortly before reaching the target area, where the conditions improved to provide clear skies, and, promisingly, no sign of defensive activity from the ground. The controller at the eastern aiming point experienced VHF communications problems, which delayed that part of the attack, and eventually, the entire force was directed to the western aiming point. The 106 Squadron crews delivered their eight 1,000 and three 500 pounders each from 5,000 to 8,000 feet onto red spotfires between 02.10 and 02.14, and explosions were observed, followed by fires that remained visible for fifty miles into the return flight. The high proportion of delayed action fuses in use prevented an immediate assessment of results, but there were four aiming point photos to study at Metheringham, and post-raid reconnaissance would confirm an effective operation. Later, on the 13th, on the delivery of the 2,800th Lancaster, A.V. Roe presented 5 Group with a silver model of a Lancaster. Cochrane decided it should be awarded to the squadron with the best non-accident record between January and June 1944, which proved to be 106 Squadron as a result of its magnificent record of just one accident in 6,848 hours of flying.

Ten 106 Squadron crews were detailed to operate on the 14th, and were informed at briefing that their target was to be the huge marshalling yards at Villeneuve-St-Georges, situated on the southern rim of Paris. They would be part of a force of 111 Lancasters, six Mosquitos and an American twin-engine P38 Lightning containing the Master Bomber and former 619 Squadron commanding officer, W/C Jeudwine. They departed Metheringham between 22.05 and 22.15 with with F/L Lines the senior pilot on duty, having just arrived as an experienced replacement to cover recent losses, and followed a similar route to that of forty-eight hours earlier. W/C Jeudwine was having compass trouble, and would arrive on target twelve minutes late, so contacted his Deputy, 83 Squadron's W/C Joe Northrop, to take matters in hand. A large amount of cloud lay over the target area with a base at 5,000 feet, but clear conditions below enabled Northrop to identify the aiming point and judge the Oboe marker to be within fifty yards of it. He called in the 5 Group marker force, which lobbed the TIs within the confines of the yards, and instructed the main force element to bomb from beneath the cloud base to reduce as much as possible the risk of collateral damage. The operation appeared to proceed smoothly and precisely according to plan, and the 106 Squadron crews bombed on red spotfires and red and green TIs from 5,500 to 8,500 feet between 01.36 and 01.53, before returning safely with six aiming point photos between them. Most of bombing hit the yards, but, inevitably, a proportion also fell outside to the east. Meanwhile, 1 Group had returned to Revigny, but had been thwarted by ground haze, which forced the Master Bomber to abandon the attack before any bombing could take place. Seven Lancasters were lost for no gain, and it would fall to 5 Group to finish the job a few nights hence at great expense.

Flying-bomb sites and railways dominated the target list on the 15th, and 5 Group was handed a railway junction at Nevers, a city on the North Bank of the Loire in central France. 106 Squadron contributed nine Lancasters to the force of 104 with four Mosquitos to carry out the low-level marking, and they departed Metheringham between 21.55 and 22.25 with W/C Piercy the senior pilot on duty and S/L Grindon undertaking his first operation as second pilot to F/L Taylor. They each carried seven 1,000 and eight 500 pounders, and arrived at their destination after an outward flight of more than three-and-a-half hours to encounter clear skies and a little haze. The marker force exploited the favourable conditions to mark promptly and accurately, and the 106 Squadron crews delivered their attacks on a red spotfire and green TIs from 4,000 to 5,000 feet between 01.58 and 02.12. The entire force was carrying delayed-action ordnance, and no immediate assessment could be made, but a large explosion suggested, perhaps, that an ammunition train or dump had been hit. Photographic reconnaissance later in the day revealed that the Nevers site had been all but obliterated, and there was much damage to rolling stock.

The 17th was spent by the crews in intensive training for an operation to be mounted on the following morning. Nineteen 106 Squadron crews were then called to briefing at midnight to learn of their part in a tactical support operation to be carried out at dawn by a force of 942 aircraft, of which 201 of the Lancasters were to be provided by 5 Group. It was the start of the ground forces' Operation Goodwood, which was General Montgomery's plan for a decisive breakout into wider France as a prelude to the march towards the German frontier. The aiming points were five enemy-held villages to the east of Caen, Colombelles, Mondeville, Sannerville, Cagny and Manneville, all of which stood in the path of the advancing British 2nd Army. The 106 Squadron element had been assigned to the Mondeville steel works, which the Germans had converted into a strongly defended fortress, and departed Metheringham between 03.55 and 04.16 with station commander G/C McKechnie, W/C Piercy and S/L Williams the senior pilots on duty. They all reached the target area to find their aiming point, already marked with red and yellow TIs, but about to be swallowed up and obscured by drifting smoke. Bombing took place from 6,000 to 10,000 feet between 05.43 and 06.07 in accordance with instructions from the Master Bomber, and, as far as could be determined, each load of eleven 1,000 and four 500 pounders fell accurately onto the markers. All from Metheringham returned safely with sixteen aiming point photos between them, having contributed to the dropping of five thousand tons of bombs by the RAF, much of it to good effect onto the two German divisions in just half an hour. The Americans followed up with a further two thousand tons of bombs.

Operations were not done for the day, and, that night, following two failed attempts by 1 Group to cut a railway junction at Revigny at a combined cost of seventeen Lancasters, the job was handed to a 5 Group element of 109 Lancasters, four Mosquitos and a P38 Lightning containing the Master Bomber, W/C

Jeudwine. It was to be a busy night of operations, which included another railway and two oil targets, along with support and diversionary activities involving a total of 972 sorties. 106 Squadron had been alerted to provide eighteen Lancasters for Revigny, but its participation was cancelled later. The force crossed the French coast near Dieppe and passed through an intense searchlight belt some twenty miles inland, while being harried all the way into eastern France by night-fighters, which had been fed into the stream shortly after it entered enemy airspace. In just forty-five minutes, sixteen Lancasters fell victim to night-fighters and one to flak, before the survivors reached the target to find clear skies, but haze obscuring ground detail. This target continued to present problems, beginning with the first wave of flares, delivered at about 01.30, which were too far to the east. More flares were ordered, and the bombing was put back by five minutes, while Wanganui markers were dropped by Mosquito, and the situation re-assessed. The whole attack seemed chaotic, and the use of many delayed-action bombs meant that it was difficult to see what was happening on the ground. Photo-reconnaissance revealed, that the operation had been successful in cutting the railway link to the battle front, but had cost twenty-four Lancasters, almost 22% of those dispatched. *(For a full and highly detailed account of the three Revigny raids read the amazing book, Massacre over the Marne, by Oliver Clutton-Brock.)*

5 Group crews stood-by on the 19th for a possible daylight operation, and it was evening before orders came through to prepare for an attack on a flying-bomb storage site at Thiverny, situated just to the north of St-Leu-d'Esserent. A force of 103 Lancasters and two Mosquitos was detailed, seventeen of the former provided by 106 Squadron, and they departed Metheringham between 19.20 and 19.35 with F/Ls Jones, Lines and Parry the senior pilots on duty. The attack was to take place in daylight under the protection of a Spitfire escort, which was picked up at the south coast, and all from the squadron reached the target in fine weather conditions, but with ground haze making it difficult to identify the aiming point. Late preliminary marking by the Path Finder element and communications problems between the Master Bomber and his Deputy added to the frustrations and led to most crews having to orbit for five minutes before bombing visually in the face of moderate to intense heavy flak bursting as high as 18,000 feet. The 106 Squadron element carried out their attacks from 14,000 to 18,000 feet between 21.29 and 21.37, and returned safely to make their reports. Post-raid reconnaissance revealed some loose bombing, but sufficient aiming point photographs were brought back, including nine by Metheringham crews, to suggest a successful outcome, and there had been no losses.

Railway yards and a triangle junction at Courtrai (Kortrijk) in Belgium provided the targets for a joint effort by 1, 5 and 8 Groups on the 20th, for which 106 Squadron contributed twenty Lancasters to the 5 Group force of 190 Lancasters and five Mosquitos. They departed Metheringham between 23.10 and 23.25 with the senior pilots of flight lieutenant rank, and all reached the target area to find it free of cloud, but slightly obscured by ground haze. The Oboe marking was well-placed in the marshalling yards, and backed up by green TIs, onto which the squadron participants delivered their eleven 1,000 and four 500 pounders each from 10,000 to 12,500 feet between 00.56 and 01.30. They returned home safely to report a large orange explosion at 00.57 and a successful outcome, which was confirmed by post-raid reconnaissance that revealed both aiming points to have been obliterated in return for the loss of nine Lancasters.

Following two nights at home for 5 Group and a two-month break from city-busting, Harris sanctioned a major raid on the naval port of Kiel on the 23rd, for which a force of 629 aircraft was made ready. 106 Squadron's original requirement of twenty Lancasters was reduced to twelve in a 5 Group force of ninety-nine, and they departed Metheringham between 22.50 and 23.00 with S/L Grindon the senior pilot on duty for the first time. After climbing out, they headed for the rendezvous point to form up behind an elaborate "Mandrel" jamming screen laid on by 100 Group, before setting course for Denmark's western coast. *(In November 1943, 100 Group had been formed to take over the Radio Countermeasures (RCM) role, which had been the preserve of 101 Squadron since its introduction a number of months earlier. 101 Squadron, however, would remain in 1 Group and continue to provide RCM for the remainder of the war.)* When they arrived unexpectedly and with complete surprise in Kiel airspace, they rendered the enemy night-fighter controller confused and unable to bring his night-fighter resources to bear. Kiel was covered by a nine to ten-tenths veil of thin cloud with tops at 4,000 feet, and a skymarking plan was put into action, which enabled the main force to bomb on the glow, first of the flares, and then of fires. The Metheringham crews carried out their attacks from 17,300 to 20,000 feet between 01.27 and 01.36, and, while unable to determine the outcome, the glow of fires visible for a hundred miles into the return journey suggested an effective raid. Local sources conceded that this had been the town's most destructive raid of the war, and had inflicted heavy damage on the port and shipyards, and cut off water supplies for three days and gas for three weeks. Many delayed-action bombs had been dropped, and these continued to cause problems for some time.

5 Group divided its forces on the 24th to enable it to support the first of a three-raid series in five nights on the city of Stuttgart, and an oil refinery and fuel dump at Donges. Situated on the North Bank of the Loire to the east of St-Nazaire, this target had been attacked successfully by elements of 6 and 8 Groups on the previous night, but clearly required further attention. 5 Group detailed ninety-nine Lancasters for southern Germany in an overall force of 614, while 104 Lancasters and four Mosquitos were made ready for western France, with five 8 Group Mosquitos in attendance. 106 Squadron made ready nine Lancasters for each operation, loading those bound for Stuttgart with a 2,000 pounder and twelve "J" cluster incendiaries each, while those heading for France would have eleven 1,000 and 500 pounders in their bomb bays. The Stuttgart element departed Metheringham between 21.45 and 21.50 with F/L Taylor the senior pilot on duty, and was followed into the air between 22.25 and 22.30 by the others, among which, F/Ls Jones, Lines, Parry and Williams were the highest-ranking pilots. Stuttgart was found to be covered by nine to ten-tenths cloud with tops at 4,000 to 7,000 feet, which required the employment of Wanganui flares (skymarking) to mark the aiming point. The 106 Squadron crews bombed on the red glow on the cloud base from 16,000 to 20,000 feet between 01.48 and 01.57 in accordance with the instructions of the Master Bomber, and set course for home fairly satisfied with the outcome, although it was impossible to make an accurate assessment. At debriefings across the Command, crews reported a glow of fires covering an area of perhaps five square miles, which remained visible for eighty miles into the return journey. No local report came out of Stuttgart for this night, but it had been a successful and destructive raid, although gained at a cost of seventeen Lancasters and four Halifaxes.

Meanwhile, some five hundred miles to the west of Stuttgart, clear skies and ground haze greeted the approaching bombers, along with green TIs already burning on the ground. The 106 Squadron crews aimed for these in accordance with the instructions of the Master Bomber from 9,000 to 11,000 feet between 01.43 and 01.52, and observed many explosions followed by developing fires, and at least one storage tank was seen to erupt in flames. They all returned home safely confident in the success of the operation, five of them with aiming point photos, and reconnaissance would reveal the site to have been devastated and to be still burning a number of days later.

5 Group split its forces again on the 25th to support the second of the raids on Stuttgart with eighty-three Lancasters, and a daylight attack on an aerodrome and signals depot at Saint-Cyr involving ninety-four Lancasters and six Mosquitos. *(There are at least four locations called Saint-Cyr, and it is believed that the one targeted on this night was in the Ile-de-France to the west of Paris.)* 106 Squadron briefed twenty crews for the latter, and they departed Metheringham between 17.40 and 18.00 with S/Ls Grindon and Williams the senior pilots on duty. They arrived at the target to find good visibility below the 12,000-foot cloud base and Oboe preliminary marking in progress. Each of the three aiming points was marked by a red spotfire, and, after the bombs had been delivered by the 106 Squadron crews from 9,000 to

12,000 feet between 19.56 and 20.00, a huge pall of smoke rose through the cloud to reach 8,000 feet. All returned safely to Metheringham having delivered a total of nineteen 4,000 and 195 x 500 pounders, and each brought home an aiming point photo, although five of the Lancasters were handed back to their ground crews displaying flak damage. Post-raid reconnaissance would confirm a successful attack at the Saint-Cyr site, which had left all of the buildings severely damaged.

The Stuttgart force, meanwhile, had entered Germany north of Strasbourg accompanied by layers of cloud, which, over the target, was at five to ten-tenths with tops in places as high as 20,000 feet. There was haze below the cloud level to create further challenges for the marker force, and the red and green TIs appeared to the main force crews to be somewhat scattered. Bombing took place from 17,000 to 21,000 feet either side of 02.00, but it was impossible to assess the outcome, and there was little optimism at debriefings that a successful operation had taken place. In fact, this was probably the most destructive of the three raids in this current series, but it would be only after the third one that cumulative reports came out of the city to confirm much destruction and heavy casualties.

The hectic round of operations continued for 5 Group on the 26th with preparations for an attack on two aiming points in the marshalling yards at Givors, situated on the West Bank of the River Rhône, south of Lyon in south-east-central France. 178 Lancasters and nine Mosquitos were made ready, 106 Squadron contributing twenty of the former, which departed Metheringham between 21.15 and 21.30 with an eleven-hundred-mile round-trip ahead of them. S/Ls Grindon and Williams were the senior pilots on duty, and P/O Durrant and crew were embarking on the thirty-sixth and final operation of their first tour. Bad weather had been anticipated, but the conditions during the outward leg over France were even worse than forecast, with heavy ice-bearing cloud, rain, hail, violent thunderstorms and bad visibility persuading fourteen crews to turn back. There were no 106 Squadron crews among these as they covered the almost five-hour outward flight to reach the target to be greeted by continuing severe weather conditions in the form of rain, thunderstorms and lightning. The cloud was down to around 7,000 feet with poor visibility below, and the flare force made a number of runs across the target between 01.42 and 02.07, and orbited in between, awaiting instructions. There were occasional glimpses of the ground, but the Master Bomber was experiencing great difficulty in getting Mosquito TIs onto the two aiming points. Eventually, one of the Deputies managed to put a green TI onto the southern aiming point, and the main force began to bomb at around 02.00. The 106 Squadron crews carried out their attacks from 4,500 to 10,000 feet between 02.14 and 02.27, using the light from flares and aiming at green TIs, all in accordance with instructions. F/L Taylor and crew had arrived at the target at 01.35, but, after searching in vain for thirty minutes, gave up and went home. Returning crews could offer little to the Intelligence Section at debriefing, but S/L Williams and crew reported sticks of bombs falling across the tracks, and they and the crews of F/L Lines and F/L Jones brought back aiming point photos. Post-raid reconnaissance revealed that the attack had fulfilled its aims in closing the tracks to the north of the junction, and damaging the locomotive depot in the yards.

The night of the 28/29th would prove to be busy, eventful and expensive, as the Command prepared for major operations against Stuttgart and Hamburg and a number of smaller undertakings involving a total of 1,126 aircraft. The final raid of the series on Stuttgart was to be an all-Lancaster affair of 494 aircraft drawn from 1, 3, 5 and 8 Groups, while 307 Lancasters and Halifaxes of 1, 6 and 8 Groups carried out the annual last-week-of-July attack on Hamburg, a year and a day after the devastating firestorm of Operation Gomorrah. 5 Group put up 176 Lancasters, eighteen of them made ready by 106 Squadron, and they were each loaded with a 2,000 pounder and twelve 500lb "J" cluster bombs. They departed Metheringham between 22.00 and 22.40 with F/Ls Jones, Lines, Parry and Williams the senior pilots on duty, and joined other elements of the force as they passed over Reading. They made landfall on the French coast south of Fécamp, and flew across France in bright moonlight above the cloud layer, expecting to be protected from the night-fighter hordes by the forecast medium cloud at 18,000 feet. This was absent, however, and the night-fighters infiltrated the bomber stream as it closed on the target. It was the Luftwaffe's Nachtjagd that gained the upper hand on this night, and five 106 Squadron crews were among those to be engaged inconclusively, while ME778 was brought down to crash some thirty miles short of the target near Rastatt at 01.55, with fatal consequences for the crew of F/O Pemberton RAAF. There was a layer of up to ten-tenths thin cloud over the city, with tops in places at around 10,000 feet, and the Path Finders initially employed skymarker flares (Wanganui), and then green TIs, at which the 106 Squadron crews aimed their bombs from 14,000 to 18,500 feet between 01.55 and 02.02. Thirty-nine Lancasters failed to return, fourteen of them from 5 Group, and night-fighters also caught the Hamburg force on its way home, bringing down a further twenty-two aircraft to raise the night's casualty figure to sixty-one aircraft. Although it was difficult to make an accurate assessment of this final Stuttgart raid, the series had severely damaged the city, leaving its central districts devastated, most of its public and cultural buildings in ruins and 1,171 of its inhabitants dead.

Twenty-one 106 Squadron crews were briefed and put on stand-by at Metheringham late on the 29th in anticipation of an early-morning tactical support operation in the Villers Bocage-Caumont region of the Normandy battle area south-west of Caen. They were to be part of an overall force of 692 aircraft, including 185 Lancasters provided by 5 Group, which were to attack six enemy positions facing predominantly American forces. The 106 Squadron element took off for their aiming point at Cahagnes between 05.55 and 06.10 with W/C Piercy and S/L Williams the senior pilots on duty, and approached the target over ten-tenths cloud with tops at 5,000 feet and a base at 3,500 feet. They were five minutes from the bombing run at 07.59, when the Master Bomber assessed the conditions as impossible and sent them home with their bombs. The weather at Metheringham was marginal for the task of safely landing twenty-one Lancasters, so the returning crews were told to adopt a circuitous route home to give time for a forecast improvement in conditions. They arrived safely over England with their eighteen 500 pounders still on board, and it was then that tragedy struck PB304. At around 10.15 the Lancaster was seen to dive out of low cloud and explode on impact on the banks of the River Irwell at Pendleton near Salford in Greater Manchester. F/L Lines and his crew perished, along with two civilians on the ground, one of them a seventy-two year old grandmother.

5 Group prepared for two daylight operations on the 31st, both of them evening attacks, one on a flying bomb storage tunnel at Rilly-la-Montagne, some five miles south of Reims, for which a force of ninety-seven Lancasters and three Mosquitos was assembled that included sixteen Lancasters of 617 Squadron, led by its recently appointed successor to Cheshire, W/C James "Willie" Tait. Tait was well-known to 5 Group crews as a member of the Master Bomber fraternity at Coningsby, but had spent most of his long operational career in 4 Group, and was among the most experienced pilots in the entire Command. 106 Squadron would support this operation with a dozen Lancasters, while sending a further eight to attack locomotive facilities and marshalling yards at Joigny-la-Roche, situated north of Auxerre, some ninety miles south-east of Paris. The latter would involve 127 Lancasters and four Mosquitos drawn from 1 and 5 Groups, and the two 106 Squadron elements departed Metheringham together between 17.25 and 17.45, with G/C McKechnie and S/L Grindon the senior pilots on duty for Rilly. The former was accompanied by F/O Markes as second pilot and S/L Crowe, the station navigation leader, which meant that JB665 was groaning under the weight of nine crew members, eleven 1,000 pounders and three 500 pounders. W/C Piercy and S/L Williams were the senior pilots on duty in the Joigny element, and all headed for the south coast to join up with the rest of the force somewhere near Reading. 83 Squadron formed into two vics, one at 15,000 and the other at 18,000 feet, to lead the Rilly force to the target under a fighter escort, while 97 Squadron performed a similar role for the Joigny-la-Roche force also with a fighter escort.

F/O Fyson returned early with a defective bomb sight, but the remainder arrived in the target area to find clear conditions and 617 Squadron on hand to seal the tunnel entrances with their Tallboys. The task for the remainder of the force was to crater the approaches, and the 106 Squadron crews, assigned to the northern end of the target area, delivered their eleven 1,000 and three 500 pounders each from 15,000 to 18,000 feet between 20.19 and 20.22. A hundred miles to the south, the force encountered no more than three-tenths cloud with tops at 7,000 feet, and good enough visibility to enable a visual identification of the aiming point. The marking was concentrated, as was the bombing onto the red TIs, and the 106 Squadron crews delivered their bomb loads from 12,000 to 15,000 feet between 20.26 and 20.30, some observing the impact and others not. Post-raid reconnaissance confirmed both operations to have been successful for the loss of a single Lancaster from Joigny and two from Rilly, one of the latter containing the 617 Squadron crew of F/L Bill Reid VC, who survived with one of his crew after their Lancaster was hit by bombs from above.

This proved to be the final activity of a second successive hectic month for Metheringham, which had required the squadron to operate on ten nights and five days against sixteen targets. 242 sorties represented a new squadron record, as did the 1,070 tons of bombs delivered. Nine aircraft and crews were lost, but although no one on the squadron could know, the worst was, in fact, now behind them, and in the remaining nine months of the bombing war, there would be only two incidences of multiple losses.

August 1944

August would bring an end to the flying bomb offensive, and also see a return to major night operations against industrial Germany. Flying bomb sites were to dominate the first half of the month, however, and sites would be targeted in daylight on each of the first six days. It began with the commitment of 777 aircraft to operations against numerous flying bomb-related sites on the afternoon of the 1st, although there were serious doubts about the poor weather conditions over England. 5 Group's targets were at La Breteque, situated in Normandy, some ten miles east-south-east of Rouen, Mont Candon, a mile or two south-west of Dieppe, and Siracourt, located some thirty miles east of the coastal town of Berck-sur-Mer. Forces of fifty-three Lancasters, fifty-nine Lancasters and a Lightning and Mosquito and sixty-seven Lancasters and four Mosquitos respectively were made ready, the first and last-mentioned supported by 106 Squadron, to which it contributed five and twelve Lancasters respectively in the late afternoon. The Siracourt element departed Metheringham between 14.50 and 15.10 with F/L Williams the senior pilot on duty, and it was followed into the air between 16.25 and 16.35 by those bound for Breteque led by S/L Grindon, and they joined forces with the others of their respective formations as they made their way towards the south. They lost the cloud as they began the Channel crossing, only for it to build again to nine to ten-tenths stratocumulus with tops at between 2,000 and 5,000 feet over the Pas-de-Calais region. One Lancaster bombed at La Breteque, before the Master Bomber called a halt to proceedings, and the other two attacks were abandoned before any bombing took place. It was a similar story for the other groups, and, in total, only seventy-nine aircraft bombed.

On the following afternoon, 5 Group contributed 194 Lancasters, two Mosquitos and a P38 Lightning to operations by 394 aircraft against one flying bomb launching and three supply sites. Ninety-four Lancasters and two Mosquitos were assigned to a storage site at Trossy-St-Maximin, situated north of Paris and close to St-Leu-d'Esserent, and a hundred Lancasters and the P38 to the Bois-de-Cassan facility. 106 Squadron loaded nineteen Lancasters with a eleven 1,000 and four 500 pounders each destined for the former, and had them ready for take-off at 10.45, only for two delays to keep them on the ground until their eventual departure from Metheringham between 14.10 and 14.25 with W/C Piercy and S/Ls Grindon and Williams the senior pilots on duty. The various elements joined up on the way south, some from other squadrons complaining that the leaders flew too fast, and there were comments about excessive weaving, but all from 106 Squadron reached the target area to find three to seven-tenths patchy cloud. The Oboe proximity markers went down on time, and were backed up with TIs, and, once the bombing started, the defences opened up with accurate flak that caused damage to twenty-seven aircraft including five from Metheringham. Despite that, most of the formation passed over the aiming point and plastered it, the 106 Squadron crews from 15,000 to 18,000 feet between 17.01 and 17.03, and reconnaissance photos revealed many new craters, a large rectangular building stripped of its roof and sides, and the southern end of two road-over-rail bridges demolished. At Bois-de-Cassan, there was three to five-tenths patchy cloud over the target, but few saw the Oboe proximity markers go down, and most bombed on visual reference. The lead aircraft turned suddenly at the last moment and caused a number of those following to overshoot the aiming point, which resulted in their bombs falling wide of the mark. Post-raid reconnaissance revealed fresh damage with many new craters.

Despite the effectiveness of the operation, the Trossy-St-Maximin site was included among targets for more than eleven hundred aircraft on the following day. The 1 and 5 Group crews were told at briefing, that the importance of the site to the Third Reich demanded that no building be left intact, and one or two may have escaped damage during the previous day's attack. 187 Lancasters, one Mosquito and the P38 Lightning were made ready as 5 Group's contribution to the operation, the sixteen 106 Squadron participants departing Metheringham between 11.45 and 11.55 with F/L Williams the senior pilot on duty. Each Lancaster carried the same load as on the previous day, and all but one reached the target area to find unfavourable conditions in the form of complete cloud cover and further intense flak activity. PB191 had been badly damaged by flak as it passed close to Rouen and the mid-upper gunner wounded, and F/O Stewart had little option but to jettison the bombs and return home. The 5 Group element was to attack about fifteen minutes after 1 Group, and, as they closed on the aiming point, smoke could be seen rising to 8,000 feet, which, combined with the flak to present challenges. The 106 Squadron crews bombed on a visual reference from 17,000 to 18,500 feet between 14.30 and 14.33 under instruction from the Master Bomber, having been prevented by the smoke from seeing the markers. Eleven Lancasters returned to Metheringham requiring repairs to flak damage, but it was the dense concentration of aircraft over the aiming point and the risk of being hit by friendly bombs that was the main topic at debriefing, and the consequent need to spread out had led to a scattering of bombs. Photo-reconnaissance was unable to confirm that the site had been obliterated, and it would need to be attacked again on the following day, a job that would be handed to 6 Group, while most of 5 Group stayed at home.

The 5th dawned bright and clear, and brilliant sunshine glinted off the Perspex of eighteen 106 Squadron Lancasters as they took off from Metheringham between 10.30 and 10.45 bound for familiar airspace over St-Leu-d'Esserent with S/L Grindon the senior pilot on duty. The squadron ORB made mention of the unhappy memories associated with this target when attacked twice a month previously. On this morning, they were part of a 5 Group force of 189 Lancasters and one Mosquito, which, in turn, represented about 25% of the effort by 4, 5, 6 and 8 Groups against two flying-bomb sites, the other in the Forét-de-Nieppe, close to the Belgian frontier. F/O Boivin and crew turned back after an hour with a feathered port-outer engine, but it was an almost intact force that homed in on the target to find it partly protected by up to six-tenths patchy cloud with tops at about 12,000 feet. This prevented the Master Bomber from picking up the aiming point until thirty seconds from it, which meant a very late course change to bring the bombers into position. This was achieved, however, although smoke and cloud hid the markers from view, and most crews picked up the aiming point by means of ground features. They 106 Squadron crews ran through a spirited flak defence to bomb from 17,300 to 19,000 feet between 13.31 and 13.33, and at debriefing, a number of crews, including that of S/L Grindon, commented that the lead squadron was too far south of track, and had compromised the bombing run of a number of 106

Squadron aircraft. The crew of F/O Mavaut was among those unable to line up on the target in time, and they had retained their bombs, while F/O Meredith and crew had dropped theirs on marshalling yards north of the target. There were celebrations on landing for W/O Cunningham DFC and crew, who had now completed their first tour of operations on a total of thirty-five, achieved in under five months. The consensus was of a fairly concentrated attack, which PRU photos seemed to confirm with views of fresh damage, and heavily cratered approaches.

Metheringham was not called into action in support of 5 Group's morning activities of the 6th, which involved a force of ninety-nine Lancasters and the P38 Lightning in another swipe at the flying-bomb launching site at Bois-de-Cassan in the L'Isle-Adam, a few miles to the south-west of St-Leu-d'Esserent. 83 Squadron's G/C Deane was the Master Bomber and F/L Drinkall the Deputy, and, after experiencing problems with his navigation homing equipment as he crossed the English coast outbound, Deane decided to hand over to F/L Drinkall while remaining with the formation. When about forty miles inland of the French coast, a large cumulus cloud barred the way up to 20,000 feet, and F/L Drinkall communicated his intention to take the force below it, descending to 16,000 feet. G/C Deane warned him not to go below 15,000, and advised him not to enter the cloud, but to turn to starboard. However, they were immediately enveloped in cloud, and G/C Deane did his best to hang on to F/L Drinkall's tail, as he continued to descend, and the two eventually became separated. Emerging on the other side of the cloud, Deane saw a large formation in the distance, and followed it. Passing through the cloud had caused the formation to become widely scattered, and it could not be reformed. Only thirty-eight aircraft bombed after picking up the aiming point visually, while fifty-eight crews were unable to bomb, but still had to contend with a fierce flak and fighter defence. Three Lancasters failed to return, and among them was that of F/L Drinkall and crew, who failed to survive. Photo-reconnaissance revealed some fresh damage to the eastern side of the target, but two large buildings on the main roadway immediately south of the aiming point remained intact, and further operations would be required.

During that afternoon, sixteen 106 Squadron crews were briefed for a 54 Base attack on the massive K1, K2 and K3 U-Boot pens on the Keroman peninsula at Lorient in support of 617 Squadron, who would be employing Tallboys. One of the unexpected characteristics of the Barnes Wallis-designed weapon was its ability to drill through many feet of reinforced concrete and detonate inside the structure. On the previous day, while attacking a similar target at Brest, 617 Squadron's F/O Don Cheney RCAF and crew, who had begun their operational career at 106 Squadron a year earlier, had been shot down by flak off the French coast, and although three members of the crew lost their lives, Cheney and the others were assisted by local people, and soon returned home. It had been their thirty-ninth sortie. W/C Piercy was the senior pilot on duty as the 106 Squadron crews departed Metheringham between 17.30 and 17.40, each carrying thirteen 1,000 pounders. F/O Kitto and crew turned back with engine failure, but the others pressed on in excellent weather conditions and picked up an escort of Mosquitos provided by 100 Group. The use of "Serrate" Mosquitos of 100 Group as escorts was a new idea, and a departure from their usual role, which was to hunt down enemy night-fighters as they stalked RAF bombers. Through their skill and effectiveness, they quickly became feared as the scourge of the Nachtjagd. There were two aiming points for this evening's attack, the northern end for 617 Squadron and the southern one for the boys from Metheringham. They identified it visually and delivered their bombs from 15,000 to 19,000 feet between 20.28 and 20.30 in the face of an intense flak defence. It was a concentrated and accurate attack, and the squadron participants brought back fourteen aiming point photos. 617 Squadron had achieved two direct hits with Tallboys, but the target would require further attention.

Other than night flying tests (NFTs), there was little activity during the day on the 7th, the first time during the month that no daylight operations had been mounted. It was from teatime onwards that the feverish activity began, to prepare 1,019 aircraft for attacks on five enemy positions facing Allied ground forces in the Normandy battle area. The operation had to be carefully controlled to avoid "friendly fire" incidents, and a Master Bomber and deputy would be on hand at each site. The aiming point for 179 Lancasters and one Mosquito from 5 Group was the fortified village of Secqueville-la-Campagne, situated some fifteen miles east of Le Havre, for which fifteen 106 Squadron Lancasters departed Metheringham between 21.20 and 21.40 with F/L Stewart the senior pilot on duty. They joined up with the others as they travelled south, and the target could be seen by the approaching bombers under clear skies, although haze shrouded ground detail to an extent, and star shells were fired from the ground to illuminate the aiming point. This enabled the Path Finder aircraft to drop red TIs onto it for the main force crews to aim at, and the first phase of bombing proceeded according to plan in concentrated fashion, lasting fifteen minutes. All but one of the 106 Squadron crews carried out their attacks from 6,000 to 9,500 feet between 23.18 and 23.22, only F/O Bumford and crew unable to join in because of a bomb sight malfunction at the last moment. Shortly afterwards, smoke began to obscure the markers, and the Master Bomber called a halt to proceedings before all participants had bombed. LM641 failed to return with the crew of F/O Rabone RNZAF after crashing at Quetteville, ten miles south of the target and south of the Seine estuary near Honfleur. The wireless operator and rear gunner lost their lives, but F/O Rabone and four of his crew parachuted to safety, and all but the flight engineer managed to evade capture. The attacks were generally effective, but the conditions dictated that 360 aircraft were sent home with their bomb loads intact.

The cancellation of an operation on the 8th allowed the crews a rare day off, and the 9th was also operation-free until late afternoon, when briefings took place for that night's attack on an oil storage dump in the Forét-de-Châtellerault, situated south of Tours in western France. It was to be predominantly a 5 Group show involving 171 Lancasters and fourteen Mosquitos, but with five 101 Squadron Lancasters to provide RCM cover. 106 Squadron dispatched fifteen Lancasters from Metheringham between 20.50 and 21.15 with S/Ls Grindon and Allinson the senior pilots on duty, the latter having just been posted in to succeed the tour-expired S/L Williams as A Flight commander. F/O Fyson and P/O Thompson and their crews were designated as "windfinders" for the whole force, and they arrived with their Metheringham colleagues in the target area under clear skies, but with considerable ground haze to create poor visibility for the marker crews attempting to identify the two aiming points. The flares dropped by the first two waves of the marker force were scattered, and prompted the Mosquito marker leader to drop a Wanganui flare as a guide to the third flare-force crews, which, in turn, meant that some crews had to orbit for up to twenty minutes before the Master Bomber was satisfied that the green TIs were in the right spot and called in the main force. They produced accurate bombing, resulting in three large explosions and volumes of black smoke, which, within five minutes, completely obscured the aiming point. A pause in the bombing was called, before it recommenced, until the lack of a verifiable marker compelled the Master Bomber to call a halt. All of the 106 Squadron crews carried out an attack from 4,500 to 8,000 feet between 00.04 and 00.20, and eight brought back an aiming point photo.

The mighty Gironde estuary, situated on France's Biscay coast, narrows as it leads inland towards the south-east, before dividing to become the Garonne River to the west and the Dordogne to the east. Its banks and islands were home to a number of important oil production and storage sites at Pauillac, Blaye, Bec-d'Ambe and Bordeaux, and the region, always a frequent destination for gardening activities, would now become the focus of bombing operations. Bordeaux itself was a vitally important port to the enemy as it contained U-Boot pens and was heavily defended along the entire length of the waterway. Orders were received on 52, 54 and 55 Base stations at teatime on the 10th to prepare sixty-two Lancasters and five Mosquitos to bomb oil storage facilities in Bordeaux itself. 106 Squadron's participation was cancelled, leaving the rest of the force to fly out in daylight, which enabled the Deputy Master Bomber to recognise that the formation had become somewhat disorganized. There were about twenty main force aircraft ahead of the flare force, and the remainder behind it to starboard, but they were catching up, and veering further and further to starboard, until they were some ten to twenty miles off track. Fortunately, the situation rectified itself, and the force arrived in the target area to find clear skies with a little ground haze. As they ran in on the aiming point, a limited amount of heavy flak began to burst at 16,000 to 18,000 feet, while the considerable light flak fell short, and neither proved to be troublesome. Returning crews were confident of a successful attack, but, as few explosions had been observed, it was difficult to accurately assess the outcome.

On the 11th, while 617 Squadron took care of the U-Boot pens at La Pallice, thirty-five other Lancasters from the group, including six from Metheringham, attacked a similar target at Bordeaux under the protection of six Mosquitos of 100 Group. F/Os Browne, Harris and Kipfer and F/Sgt Netherwood took off at 11.50 to place themselves ten minutes ahead of the main force as windfinders, while F/Os Meredith and Mavaut departed twenty minutes later. There were excellent conditions in the target area, and the four 106 Squadron "early birds" awaited the arrival of the others before bombing visually from 19,000 feet shortly after 16.30. There was heavy and intense flak, and LL948 was hit, causing a slight eye injury to F/O Harris's mid-upper gunner, F/Sgt Long. They all arrived home safely between 19.30 and 19.45, each bringing back an aiming point photo. Because of a shortage of Tallboys, even 617 Squadron was forced to employ 2,000lb armour piercing bombs, but photo reconnaissance later showed them to be ineffective against the reinforced concrete structures at both locations. This was the final operation of their tour for F/O Browne and crew, who no doubt filled the remainder of the evening with celebrations in the bar.

For the evening operation, 5 Group was switched to communications targets at Givors, located about twenty miles to the south of Lyon in south-east-central France. There were to be two aiming points for an overall force of 175 Lancasters and ten Mosquitos, the town's marshalling yards to the north, and a railway junction to the south, and a dozen 106 Squadron Lancasters departed Metheringham between 20.40 and 20.55, within an hour of the return of their colleagues from Bordeaux, with S/L Grindon the senior pilot on duty. All arrived in the target area to find favourable conditions of clear skies and a little haze, which the seemingly usual organized chaos of contradictory or confusing instruction via VHF and W/T threatened to waste. Despite the comments later of the participating crews, the 5 Group ORB unaccountably described the W/T control as excellent and the VHF R/T as good. Permission to bomb was not received until 01.12, by which time some crews had been forced to spend fifteen minutes orbiting three times, while the Master Bomber and his Deputy discussed the accuracy of the markers. Despite the wrinkles, both aiming points were well-illuminated and marked, and the bombing was concentrated in the correct place. The 106 Squadron crews confirmed their positions by Gee and H2S-fix, before carrying out their attacks on the marshalling yards on red TIs in accordance with the Master Bomber's instructions from 6,000 to 9,500 feet between 01.14 and 01.19. They all returned to home airspace critical of some aspects of the raid, but confident that it had been concluded successfully, and there were seven aiming point photos at Metheringham. Photo-reconnaissance revealed heavy damage to both aiming points, with the ground badly-cratered and many tracks severed, and the middle span of the railway bridge over the River Rhône was revealed to have received a direct hit.

The main operation on the 12th was an experiment to gauge the ability of main force crews to locate and attack an urban target on the strength of their own H2S equipment in the absence of a Path Finder element. This resulted from the huge volume of operations generated by the four concurrent campaigns, each of which called upon the finite resources of 8 Group, compelling it, in the short term at least, to spread itself more and more thinly. The conclusion of the flying-bomb campaign at the end of the month, together with the end of tactical support for the ground forces, would remove the pressure, and the planned independence of 3 Group through the G-H bombing system from the autumn would solve the problem altogether. In the meantime, however, no one knew what demands might be made of the

Command, and it would be useful to see what main force crews could do when left to their own devices. The target was to be Braunschweig, for which a force of 379 aircraft was assembled, seventy-two of the Lancasters provided by 5 Group. 106 Squadron made ready a dozen Lancasters, and, as they were preparing to leave, a "rush" job was announced, and a further seven crews were briefed for an operation against German troop concentrations and a road junction north of Falaise in an area south of Caen, for which they would take off after midnight.

In the meantime, the Braunschweig-bound crews departed Metheringham between 21.15 and 21.30 with W/C Piercy the senior pilot on duty on a night of heavy Bomber Command activity at numerous locations involving more than eleven hundred sorties. A second large operation over Germany was directed at the Opel motor works at Rüsselsheim two hundred miles to the south, and involved 297 aircraft, but, as events were to prove, this would not weaken the enemy night-fighter defences, and powerful elements of the Nachtjagd were waiting for the Braunschweig force as it crossed the German coast at around 18,000 feet. Night-fighter flares were in evidence from then until the coast was crossed again on the way home, and it would prove to be an expensive night for the Command as a whole. The Brunswick force made its way eastwards under clear skies, before encountering nine to ten-tenths thin cloud in the target area with tops at 7,000 feet. This was not a problem, as the whole purpose of the operation was to locate and bomb the target blind by H2S. Ten of the 106 Squadron crews bombed from 18,000 to 22,000 feet between 23.58 and 00.08, and observed the glow of fires beneath the cloud, while two others bombed on e.t.a over a built-up area, which was believed later to be Hildesheim, a little over thirty miles short of the primary target. W/C Piercy's ND682 was hit by heavy flak somewhere near Emden on the way home, but they got back without further incident. Photo-reconnaissance confirmed that some of the bombing had, indeed, hit Braunschweig, but there was no concentration, and many outlying towns also reported bombs falling. Twenty-seven aircraft failed to return from this operation and a further twenty from the disappointing raid on the Opel factory, demonstrating that the Nachtjagd still had sufficient resources to effectively divide its strength.

The seven crews briefed for Falaise were led away at 00.15 by F/L Parry, to join up with the rest of the 144-strong mixed force of which twenty-five Lancasters represented 5 Group. A blanket of ten-tenths stratus cloud lay over the target area with tops at 2,000 feet, through which the green TIs were clearly visible. The 106 Squadron Lancasters were each carrying twelve 1,000lb GP (general purpose) or SAP (semi-armour piercing) bombs and a single 1,000lb MC (medium capacity) with a six-hour delay fuse. These were delivered from 6,000 to 8,000 feet between 02.18 and 02.21, and post-raid reconnaissance confirmed that the area around the junction had been heavily cratered and the roads leading from it mostly blocked. The ORB entry for the 14th stated that; "After two months of severe fighting, the Allied armies have at last broken out from their Normandy bridgehead, and the German army is now in full retreat".

A major operation was mounted on the afternoon of the 14th to bomb seven German troop positions in the Falaise area ahead of the advancing Canadian 3rd Division. Over eight hundred aircraft were involved, including ten from 106 Squadron, whose crews were briefed to bomb at Quesnay, a village close to the previous night's effort north of Falaise. W/C Piercy led them away at noon, on what would be his final operation as the squadron's commanding officer. They located the target easily, and bombed on target indicators in accordance with the Master Bomber's instructions from 10,000 to 11,000 feet between 14.20 and 14.21, and returned safely with nine aiming point photos. Master Bombers were on hand to control the bombing at each aiming point because of the close proximity of the opposing armies, but despite the most stringent efforts to avoid friendly fire incidents, some bombs did fall into a quarry occupied by Canadian troops, killing thirteen, injuring fifty-three others and destroying a large number of vehicles.

Later that evening, 128 Lancasters from 5 Group were sent to attack ships in Brest harbour. Thirty-one were assigned to a hulk, possibly the Clemenceau, thirty-seven to an oil tanker and fifty, including the 106 Squadron element, to the French cruiser Gueydon. This vessel had been attacked during the morning by elements from 617 and 9 Squadrons, but was found to be still afloat, as was its companion, the Clemenceau. Eight 106 Squadron Lancasters took part in the operation, departing Metheringham between 17.20 and 17.45 with S/L Allinson the senior pilot on duty. They found the vessels under clear skies but protected by intense and accurate flak, despite which, they pressed home their attacks from 17,000 to 18,000 feet between 20.26 and 20.31, and returned safely with an aiming point photo each. They reported smoke rising from the cruiser, and observing it to be "down at one end", and the tanker was also seen to be on fire. The Photographic Reconnaissance Unit (PRU) produced evidence on the following day that Gueydon had settled on the bottom and its decks were awash.

In preparation for his new night offensive against Germany, Harris called for operations against enemy night-fighter airfields in Holland and Belgium. In response, a list of nine such targets was prepared for attention by daylight on the 15th, and they would involve a thousand aircraft. 5 Group was handed Deelen in central Holland and Gilze-Rijen in the south, and prepared forces of ninety-four Lancasters and five Mosquitos for the former and 103 Lancasters, four Mosquitos and the P38 Lightning for the latter. The P38 contained S/L "Count" Ciano and W/C Guy Gibson, who was desperate to get back onto operations. The 106 Squadron contingent of seventeen was selected to form the spearhead of the force for Gilze-Rijen, situated to the west of Tilburg, and S/L Allinson led them away from Metheringham between 09.55 and 10.15. On board with the A Flight commander was Mr V Lewis, a war correspondent with the Daily Sketch newspaper, while a Mr T Wilson represented the BBC in the Lancaster of F/L Williams and crew, complete with state-of-the-art recording equipment. They arrived in the target area to find clear skies and excellent visibility, and delivered their eleven 1,000 pounders and four 500 pounders each across the airfield from 17,000 to 19,000 feet between 12.07 and 12.10. Returning crews brought back fifteen aiming point photos and reported smoke rising to 6,000 feet over the target. The success was confirmed by PRU photos, which revealed eight hundred craters across the airfield and at least a hundred on the runways. Mr Lewis devoted several columns to the squadron in praise of its efforts, but Mr Wilson's recording equipment let him down, and there would be no broadcast by the BBC.

The new offensive would begin with simultaneous attacks on Stettin and Kiel on the night of the 16/17th, 5 Group contributing 145 aircraft to the overall all-Lancaster force of 461 assigned to the former. 106 Squadron made ready ten Lancasters for the main event and six to join twenty-four others for mining duties in the Young Geranium garden off the Baltic port of Swinemünde, some thirty miles to the north. The latter was actually the 150-yard-wide Stettin Canal, which provided access from the Stettiner Haff inland sea to the Baltic. The bombers departed Metheringham first between 21.20 and 21.30 with S/L Allinson the senior pilot on duty and accompanied by the newly-arrived F/L Fee as second pilot, and the gardening brigade followed between 21.30 and 21.55 with F/Ls Jones, Stewart and Williams taking the lead. W/O Donkin and crew turned back with the Jutland coast in sight through an inability to climb, leaving the others to complete the three-and-a-half-hours flight to reach the target area, where the bombing brigade was greeted by up to nine-tenths high cloud with a base at 18,000 to 20,000 feet and sufficient breaks to register clear visibility below. Concentrated red and green TIs could be seen marking out the aiming point, which the 106 Squadron crews bombed from 17,000 to 19,000 feet between 01.07 and 01.16, and reported fires taking hold.

Two of the 106 Squadron gardening crews, those of F/L Stewart and F/O Kitto, had taken off late, and, unable to make up the time, abandoned their sorties on instructions from the controller. The remaining four made their way to the canal, where a low-level run-in was required to ensure accuracy. F/L Jones and crew identified the target area first by flares and then by flame floats, and then, somehow, two of the five mines were jettisoned accidentally. Pressing on, they approached at 300 feet and two hundred miles per hour i.a.s. (indicated air speed), and delivered the remaining three mines in the correct location in the face of intense light flak from both banks. F/O Sayeau RCAF and crew went in at 250 feet and dropped two mines at 190 i.a.s. at 01.19. F/L Williams and crew released a single mine from 300 feet, while F/O Kipfer RCAF and crew made two runs, both at 350 feet, delivering two mines on each occasion into the briefed locations. All returned safely, and there were immediate awards of the DFC to F/O Sayeau and F/O Kipfer, and also to the latter's bomb-aimer, F/O Redman. The Admiralty was impressed by the efforts of these crews, and sent a message of congratulations. Not all returning crews were confident about the outcome at Stettin, some suggesting the raid had been scattered, when, in fact, it had been highly successful, destroying fifteen hundred houses, numerous industrial premises, and sinking five ships in the harbour, while seriously damaging eight more.

Fifteen 106 Squadron crews were called to briefing early on the 18th to be told of that morning's operation against two flying-bomb dumps in the Forét-de-L'Isle Adam, north of Paris. 158 Lancasters, six Mosquitos and the P38 Lightning were to be involved, with 83 Squadron leading, and providing the back-up marking on the heels of the low-level Mosquitos at the two aiming points in the east and west. The Metheringham element took off between 11.20 and 12.01 with F/Ls Jones, Stewart, Parry and Fee the senior pilots on duty, the last-mentioned on his first operation with the squadron as crew captain. The BBC reporter, Mr I Wilson, occupied a position in the Lancaster of F/L Jones. Each Lancaster was carrying eleven 1,000 and four 500 pounders as they headed south in squadron formation to rendezvous with the rest of the force and pick up the fighter escort. When over the mid-point of the Channel at 13.15, sixty or seventy American Liberators passed across the bows of the gaggle, heading east a thousand feet higher, prompting the lead Lancaster to change course. This may have been the cause of comments by some crews on return, that not all had observed station keeping as set out at briefing, a situation that would result in aircraft bombing out of the planned sequence and on wrong headings. There was five to seven-tenths cloud in the target area with tops at around 8,000 feet, which hampered identification of both aiming points, and instructions were issued to not bomb unless a clear view of the target had been established. Some were able to pick out the aiming points assisted by smoke markers, and the 106 Squadron crews bombed visually from 9,000 to 10,000 feet between 14.10 and 14.12. F/O Meredith and crew were about to bomb when cloud slid across the aiming point, and they abandoned their sortie. There was intense flak, causing damage to four 106 Squadron aircraft, and W/O Donkin's flight engineer was wounded in the foot. Bombing photos suggested that the attack had overshot to the north, and this was confirmed later by PRU pictures.

Shortly before they arrived home, four other Lancasters departed Metheringham between 15.25 and 15.35 to join up with twenty-two Lancasters and five Mosquitos from 5 Group to attack an oil storage depot at Bordeaux. S/L Allinson was the senior pilot on duty as they headed for the south coast, and all was well until F/L Williams noticed an excessive oil leak in his port-inner engine, and decided to turn back from a position south-east of Peterborough. The others reached the target, which was easily identified under clear skies, and bombed it from an average of 15,300 to 16,000 feet at 20.10 in the face of intense flak. S/L Allinson's aircraft was holed, but made it home safely with an aiming point photo to add to those of the other two crews.

The stations of 53 Base, Waddington, Skellingthorpe and Bardney, were called into action on the 19th to provide fifty-two Lancasters for an attack on La Pallice, and reached the target area to find six to nine-tenths cloud hanging over the western aiming point, and seven to eight-tenths over the eastern one, with tops at 15,000 feet. This created challenging conditions in which to identify the targets, made more so by intense light flak, but crews claimed to have done so visually before carrying out their attacks. This was the first day of a spell of wet, cloudy and, sometimes, windy weather, which would last for the next week, and, apart from a number of small-scale operations, 5 Group remained largely on the ground.

Having operated against eighteen targets over fourteen days and nights, 106 Squadron was happy to spend the following week at home, where it could rest and recuperate while minor operations held sway. In some ways it was an advantage to be so busy, as it allowed crews to complete a tour of operations much more quickly than earlier in the war, when it might have taken a year or more to amass thirty operations, whereas now, it could be completed in two months or less. W/C Piercy's time as commanding officer was up after completing his second tour of twenty-five operations. He had been with the squadron for just five months, and had put himself on the Order of Battle more frequently even than Gibson, and this at a time when commanding officers were expected to operate perhaps just once per month. He was officially posted out on the 25th, and would eventually be sent to the Middle East, where he apparently lost his life in an accident in 1945. He was succeeded on the 26th by W/C M M J Stevens.

Major operations resumed on the 25th, when preparations were put in hand to make ready more than nine hundred aircraft to launch against three targets, Rüsselsheim and nearby Darmstadt in southern Germany, and the port of Brest, while a further four hundred would be engaged in a variety of smaller endeavours. The largest operation was to be the all-Lancaster affair involving 461 aircraft from 1, 3, 6 and 8 Groups in a return to the Opel motor works, while 334 others attended to eight coastal batteries around Brest. 5 Group was assigned to Darmstadt, a university city and centre of scientific research and development, and one of a few almost virgin targets considered to be worthy of attention. 5 Group assembled a force of 191 Lancasters and six Mosquitos, seventeen of the former made ready by 106 Squadron, and they departed Metheringham between 20.45 and 21.10 with F/Ls Jones, Stewart, Williams, Parry and Fee the senior pilots on duty. The Master Bomber was one of five crews to return early, leaving his two Deputies from 83 Squadron, F/L Meggeson DFC and S/L Williams DFC to step into the breach. The target area was found to be free of cloud, and some ground haze was present, but this was not responsible for matters going awry early on. VHF communication proved to be weak, which made it difficult for the Deputy Master Bombers to pass on instructions, and five aircraft dropped flares at 01.05, which turned out to be too far to the west, and, consequently, the low-level Mosquito crews reported at 01.07, that they were unable to find the aiming point. H-hour was pushed back to 01.22, although bombing actually began at 01.19, and, soon after, someone left their VHF on transmit, creating a noise that drowned out all voice communications, at the same time that W/T became jammed. One of the Deputies was heard indistinctly instructing the crews to "bomb on the box" (H2S), and then he and the other Deputy were shot down. The main force crews did their best to comply, among them those from 106 Squadron, who were over what they believed was the aiming point at 8,000 to 10,000 feet between 01.20 and 01.53, some after orbiting for almost thirty minutes. Some crews from other squadrons came upon Rüsselsheim, fifteen miles to the north-west of Darmstadt, and either joined in the attack there or found other alternative targets. Typical of the reports at debriefing was that by the crew of F/O Mavaut, whose H2S had failed and who arrived over Darmstadt at 01.15 to see some flares but no markers. At 01.20 they received orders by VHF to bomb, but no code word was mentioned, and it was decided to bomb the first alternative target they came upon, which turned out to be scattered while lights and a fire at 01.44. One Metheringham crew's photo was plotted at fifteen hundred yards from the aiming point, but others were between five and eight miles away.

The German port of Königsberg, now Kaliningrad in Lithuania, is located on the eastern side of the Bay of Danzig, and was being used by the enemy to supply its eastern front. It lay some 860 miles in a straight line from the bomber stations surrounding Lincoln, which increased to a round trip of 1,900 miles when the routing across Denmark was taken into account. This made it the most distant location ever targeted by the Command, and was exceeded only by SOE flights to Poland. Such a distance required the sacrifice of bombs for fuel, and it was a reduced load of a single 2,000 pounder and twelve 500lb "J" cluster bombs that was loaded into each of 106 Squadron's fourteen participating Lancasters, which were part of an overall heavy force of 174. Having been briefed for this target twice before without going, there was some doubt as to whether or not this one would go ahead, but it did, and the first Lancasters began to roll at Metheringham at 20.15 to be followed by the others over the ensuing ten minutes with F/Ls Fee, Jones, Stewart and Williams the senior pilots on duty. Accompanying the force to the target area and taking off at the same time were ten Lancasters carrying mines for delivery into the Tangerine garden, the sea-lanes off Pillau at the entrance to the estuary serving Königsberg. The crews of F/L Parry and F/Os Thompson and Fyson were handed this exacting and demanding task as the 106 Squadron representatives, and they set off alongside the bombing element with a ten-hour marathon ahead of them.

When they arrived in the target area almost five hours later, after flying through electrical storms and icing conditions over Denmark, the skies were clear and the visibility good, and they were greeted by around a hundred searchlights and an intense flak defence. The flare force went in at 14,000 to 15,000 feet between 01.05 and 01.12, to be followed minutes later by the heavy markers at a lower level. The Metheringham crews identified the aiming point by red TIs, and confirmed their positions by H2S before bombing them from 10,000 to 11,800 feet between 01.17 and 01.25, the latter time just as the Master Bomber issued the order to cease bombing. Returning crews were fairly enthusiastic about the outcome, reporting punctual marking, concentrated bombing and fires that could be seen, according to some, from 250 miles into the return journey. Meanwhile, the crews of F/Os Thompson and Fyson were off the coast, homing in on the narrow and well-defended Königsberg Seekanal, and delivered their four mines each from 13,000 feet at 01.00 and 01.06 respectively, while F/L Parry and crew went in at 90 feet in what were described as perfect conditions, and, in the face of intense light flak from both banks, delivered five mines into the briefed location. On his return, F/L Parry received the immediate award of the DFC to add to the AFC (Air Force Cross) already in his possession. Photo-reconnaissance revealed that the main weight of the attack had fallen into the town's north-eastern districts, where fire had ripped through many building blocks at a cost of just four Lancasters. However, the job was not yet done, and a second operation would have to be mounted.

The final operations in the long-running flying-bomb campaign were conducted by small Oboe-led forces against twelve sites on the 28th, and Allied ground forces took control of the Pas-de-Calais a few days later.

It was clear, that a decisive blow had not been delivered on Königsberg, and, at 17.30 on the 29th, briefings took place on the participating 5 Group stations for the return. Sixteen 106 Squadron crews learned that they were to be part of a 5 Group force of 189 Lancasters, which, because of the extreme range, again carried between them only 480 tons of bombs to deliver onto four aiming points. Station commanders were not supposed to operate, but it was difficult to keep G/C McKechnie away from a Lancaster with a bomb load, and he was the senior pilot to depart Metheringham on this night between 20.10 and 20.45, supported by S/L Grindon., with the crews of F/Os Archer and Mavaut, who were among the ten assigned to the Tangerine garden, bringing up the rear. The bomber stream made its way across the North Sea and Denmark and reached the target to encounter eight to ten-tenths cloud with a base at around 10,000 feet. The Master Bomber, W/C Woodroffe, one of 5 Group's most experienced raid controllers, and having decided on a visual attack, instructed the first flare force wave to drop below the cloud, while keeping the spearhead of the main force circling for twenty minutes before the marking began. The later arrivals could see the markers going down as they approached for what was a complex plan of attack and observed the first flares going down at around 01.05 and continuing at regular intervals thereafter. At 01.24, the third flare force wave was instructed to illuminate the red spot fire, and, a minute later, an instruction was given to overshoot by 400 yards to the east of the aiming point. At 01.26, a marker aircraft was told to run over the red marker and overshoot by 300 yards, while, at 01.27, another was ordered to overshoot by 600 yards east of the aiming point, before the visual backers-up were sent to track over the reds and greens and overshoot by 300 yards. The flare force was invited to go home at 01.30, and, at 01.34, the visual marker crews were instructed first to back up the greens by 600 yards on a westerly heading, and, two minutes later, the concentrations of reds and greens. The 106 Squadron crews identified the target by the red and green TIs and searchlight concentrations, and confirmed their positions by H2S before bombing from 8,000 to 10,400 feet between 01.39 and 01.50. The Master Bomber called a halt to bombing at 01.52 and sent the crews home, where the absence of four 50 Squadron Lancasters at Skellingthorpe prompted a scathing review of W/C Woodroffe's performance, blaming his stubbornness for the high casualty rate of fifteen Lancasters, 7.9% of those dispatched. They maintained that the backers-up had confirmed the marking to be accurate, despite which, he kept some crews orbiting for up to forty minutes. At the Metheringham debriefing, F/O Marks and crew reported that they had orbited for twenty-four minutes, before eventually bombing from 10,000 feet at 01.44, while the crews of S/L Grindon and a number of others bombed towards the tail end of the attack, following the Master Bomber's instructions to aim at a concentration of red and green TIs and allow a twenty-two second overshoot. LM215 was hit by light flak during the bombing run and lost the use of its port-outer engine, but F/O Kitto and crew brought it back on three. F/Os Archer and Mavaut delivered four Mk VI mines each from 13,000 feet into the Königsberg Seekanal at 01.25 and 01.28 respectively, and returned to report a successful outcome.

Two Lancasters were absent from their Metheringham dispersal pans, one of them JB593 "Admiral Dombo", which had contained G/C McKechnie and crew. McKechnie, who had been awarded a George Cross in 1940, had been an inspiration to the crews at Metheringham for putting his life on the line when he didn't have to. As no trace of the Lancaster and crew was ever located, it must be assumed that it went into the sea. On board was flight engineer Ron Clarke, who had been a member of W/C Piercy's crew. Also missing was ND331, from which the flight engineer and bomb-aimer managed to escape by parachute to fall into enemy hands, but F/O Boivin and the rest of his crew also disappeared into the cold waters of the Baltic. Post-raid reconnaissance confirmed that the operation had been an outstanding success, which destroyed over 40% of the town's residential and 20% of its industrial buildings. W/C Piercy took temporary command of Metheringham pending the appointment of G/C Heath as the permanent successor to G/C McKechnie. This, of course allowed, him the freedom to ride his motor bike up and down the runway without any disapproving looks from higher up the food chain.

The flying-bomb campaign may now have ended, but a new one against V-2 rocket storage and launching sites began on the 31st with raids on nine suspected locations in northern France. 5 Group sent three forces of forty-nine, forty-six and fifty-two Lancasters with two Mosquitos each to respectively target sites at Auchy-les-Hesdin, Rollancourt and Bergueneuse, all situated some twenty miles inland from the coast at Berck-sur-Mer. Elements from 52 and 54 Bases was assigned to the first-mentioned, for which 106 Squadron made ready sixteen Lancasters, and dispatched them from Metheringham between 15.30 and 16.10 with S/L Allinson the senior pilot on duty. All reached the target area to find five to eight-tenths cloud with a base at 6,000 feet and tops as high as 18,000 feet, out of which issued occasional heavy rain showers. The force was told to orbit until the cloud bank moved away to allow the Mosquitos to drop smoke markers, which failed to ignite. The Master Bomber directed the attack to be carried out visually, and the 106 Squadron crews complied with his instructions to bomb from 10,500 and 15,000 feet between 18.04 and 18.18, and the effort seemed to be fairly concentrated on the markers. There was little opposition, and all of the participants returned home safely with reports of an uneventful trip and a large explosion at 18.10. The operation appeared to be a little scattered, but largely successful, as were those at the other sites. This concluded a month of feverish and record activity for most heavy squadrons, during which 106 Squadron had taken part in twenty-three operations, including mining, on ten days and eight nights, and had dispatched a record 288 sorties for the loss of three aircraft and crews.

September 1944

The destructive power of the Command was now almost beyond belief. Each of its heavy bomber groups was capable of laying waste to a German town and city at one go, and, from now until the end of the war, this would be demonstrated in awesome and horrific fashion. Much of the Command's effort during the new month would be directed towards the liberation of the three French ports remaining in enemy hands, but operations began for 5 Group with an attack on shipping at Brest on the 2nd, for which sixty-seven Lancasters were detailed from 52 and 55 Bases.

Preparations were put in hand on the following morning to launch attacks on six Luftwaffe-occupied aerodromes in southern Holland. A total of 675 aircraft were to be involved, 5 Group detailing 103 Lancasters and two Mosquitos for its target at Deelen, of which 106 Squadron dispatched seventeen Lancasters from Metheringham between 15.20 and 15.35 with W/C Stevens the senior pilot on duty for the first time. F/O Archer and crew were forced to turn back with a faulty bomb sight, leaving the others to reach the target area without incident, although cloud on the way out had created challenging conditions for formation-keeping. Over enemy territory they encountered varying amounts of cloud up to nine-tenths with tops at 7,000 feet, and orbited while they awaited gaps through which to identify the aiming point visually. The marking was assessed to be accurate, and twelve of the 106 Squadron crews bombed from 13,800 to 16,000 feet between 17.33 and 17.43 in the face of a spirited flak defence from the airfield, while four others were unable to identify the aiming point through the cloud and brought their bombs home. Some crews were critical of the use of smoke-puffs as inadequate for the purpose, and would have preferred TIs. Returning crews were relatively confident that they had fulfilled their brief and there were no losses, although F/Sgt Thomas and crew handed PB122 back to the ground crew with damage from heavy flak. There were eight aiming point photos to confirm that the operation had been successful, but it would be the 6th before photo-reconnaissance provided a partial cover of the target area and revealed at least sixty craters around runway intersections and taxiways. In fact, the damage was so severe, that the Luftwaffe abandoned the aerodrome. There were celebrations for the popular F/O Kitto RNZAF and crew, who, although bringing their bombs home on this occasion, had now completed their first tour of operations.

Most of 5 Group remained at home over the ensuing five days, while enemy strong-points in and around Le Havre received daylight visitations from other elements of the Command on the 5th, 6th, 8th and 9th. These operations took place during a spell of unhelpful weather conditions, and the attacks of the 8th and 9th were not fully pressed home. Mönchengladbach was posted as the target for 113 Lancasters and fourteen Mosquitos on the 9th, for which operation briefings took place at 01.30. The eighteen 106 Squadron crews learned that they were to attack the centre of the town, which, with Operation Market Garden looming, was expected soon to be within striking distance of the advancing Allied forces. In the event, they would have to wait until the early hours of the 10th before departing Metheringham between 02.35 and 03.05 with S/L Grindon the senior pilot on duty. There would be no early returns as they made their way via Ostend to the target on the heels of the flare forces, which had started dispensing illumination a little early at 05.05 and had continued until 05.14, at which point they were sent home. The main force was called in to attack under clear skies and in good visibility, the Metheringham crews identifying the aiming point by means of red TIs, which they bombed in accordance with instructions from the Master Bomber from 16,500 to 17,000 feet between 05.18 and 05.24. A number of large explosions occurred at 05.21 and 05.23, and a heavy pall of smoke was rising to meet the crews as they turned away, continuing to observe the glow of fires from the Dutch coast up to eighty miles away. There were no losses, and photo-reconnaissance confirmed the claims of the crews, revealing a highly successful raid, which had left the town centre in ruins.

A further attack on German positions around Le Havre was carried out on the evening of the 10th and involved almost a thousand aircraft, 5 Group supporting the effort with 108 Lancasters and two Mosquitos, but none from Metheringham. The operation took place under clear skies and just a little ground haze, which enabled crews to identify the target visually, and with no opposition, plaster the aiming points until they became enveloped in smoke. The 11th would bring the final attacks on the environs of the port, and would involve 218 aircraft drawn from 4, 5, 6 and 8 Groups in an early morning attack. 5 Group contributed ninety-three Lancasters from 53, 54 and 55 Bases, of which eleven were provided by 106 Squadron. Nineteen had actually been snaking their way to the Metheringham runway threshold, when one put a wheel off the concrete and became bogged down, preventing the seven following from progressing further. The eleven at the head of the snake took off between 05.40 and 06.20 with W/C Stevens the senior pilot on duty, and they arrived in the target area under clear skies with slight haze to locate their aiming points, which had all been named after car manufacturers. The aiming points for the 5 Group element were to the north and south of the outer defences and were coded Cadillac 1 and 2, and it was at the latter that the bombing by the Metheringham crews took place on red TIs from 11,500 to 12,000 feet between 07.34 and 07.42. All returned safely with aiming point photos, and photo-reconnaissance would confirm an accurate and concentrated attack, within hours of which, the German garrison surrendered to British forces.

Many of the crews involved in the morning activity, found themselves on the Order of Battle and back in the briefing room later in the day to learn of their part in 5 Group's return to Darmstadt, which had escaped serious damage during the last week of August. A force of 221 Lancasters and fourteen Mosquitos was made ready, and the 106 Squadron element of twenty departed Metheringham between 20.50 and 21.05 with F/Ls Jones, Mavaut, Parry and Stewart the senior pilots on duty. They began the Channel crossing at Beachy Head, aiming for the French coast near Berck-sur-Mer, before traversing France to enter Germany in the Strasbourg area and turning north to the target. They arrived to find the skies over southern Germany clear of cloud, and, despite some ground haze, good visibility prevailing as the flare force went in at 17,000 feet at 23.52, homing in on a green Mosquito-laid TI. The Master bomber seemed satisfied with the illumination, and required no further flares, leaving the backers-up to drop their TIs over the ensuing four minutes, before being sent home at 23.59. The main force crews followed up with extreme accuracy and concentration, F/O Bumford and crew the first from Metheringham to bomb on red TIs at 00.02, by which time the city was already burning. The others followed up over the ensuing ten minutes, aiming at red and green TIs from 11,800 to 12,500 feet, and observed the city centre become engulfed in flames, which spread outwards to consume large parts of the built-up area. The glow, according to some, could be seen from the French coast, 250 miles away. The conditions had been ideal for the 5 Group marking method, and photo-reconnaissance confirmed the main weight of the attack to have fallen in the central and surrounding districts to the south and east. It was learned after the war, that the attack had resulted in a genuine firestorm, only the third to be recorded after Hamburg and Kassel in 1943, although a number of local ones may have occurred in other cities like Berlin and Stuttgart. More than twelve thousand people died in the inferno, and a further seventy thousand, 60% of a total population of 120,000, were made homeless. There had been considerable night-fighter activity, and F/O Kipfer's Lancaster sustained extensive damage in an encounter with one of them. The operation cost 5 Group twelve Lancasters, among them 106 Squadron's PB203, which crashed in the target area at midnight killing F/L Mavaut RCAF DFC and three others of his highly experienced crew, while his navigator and bomb-aimer, both also Canadians, survived to be taken into captivity.

Orders were received on 5 Group stations on the 12th to prepare for a return to southern Germany that night, this time to target Stuttgart. Thirteen 106 Squadron crews attended the briefing at Metheringham to learn that they were to be part of a force of 195 Lancasters and fourteen Mosquitos, which would be accompanied by nine ABC Lancasters from 1 Group's 101 Squadron. A simultaneous operation by 378 Lancasters and nine Mosquitos of 1, 3 and 8 Groups would take place at Frankfurt, a hundred miles to the north. The Metheringham element took off between 18.55 and 19.15 with W/C Stevens and S/Ls Allinson and Grindon the senior pilots on duty, and joined the bomber stream as they headed south to adopt a course similar to that of twenty-four hours earlier. They mostly enjoyed an uneventful flight across France to Stuttgart, which was found to be under clear skies with moderate visibility and ground haze, and, therefore, ideal conditions for the low-level markers. The marking and backing up was very accurate, and the main force bombing concentrated upon the city centre, with a slight tendency to creep back towards the north-eastern district of Bad Canstatt and beyond into Feuerbach. The 106 Squadron crews bombed on well-placed red TIs from 17,000 to 19,000 feet between 23.12 and 23.18, and a huge explosion was reported at 23.25, which lasted for about five seconds. All from Metheringham returned safely, the crews of W/C Stevens and F/L Fee with an aiming point photo each, and, when a PRU aircraft photographed the city on the following morning, the entire centre was obscured by the smoke from numerous and widespread fires. Local sources described the central districts as "erased", and it seems that a firestorm had erupted in northern and west-central districts, wiping them from the map. Almost twelve hundred people lost their lives, the highest death toll ever in this much-bombed city, at a cost to Bomber Command of four Lancasters.

After four years to the week of operating on the front line, 106 Squadron was given a new role, acting as a training unit for 5 Group's Path Finder element. It would continue to take part in the bombing offensive, but, perhaps, with a little less intensity, and its orders would come through principally from Coningsby, the home of 83 and 97 Squadrons and the base commander Air Commodore Bobby Sharp. In future it would receive crews recommended by their training units as suitable for entry to the Path Finders, and they would complete five operational sorties with the squadron, before moving on to the Navigation Training Unit (NTU) at Warboys in Cambridgeshire for training in Path Finder methods. Thereafter, they would return to Metheringham for further operations until being posted to either 83 or 97 Squadrons. *(It should be remembered, that although these squadrons were now on permanent loan to 5 Group, they remained officially Path Finder/8 Group units)*. Crews currently serving with the squadron would be given the opportunity to volunteer for Path Finder duties, and most of those who declined would be posted to other front-line units, while the "few" would be retained as "hardcore". This would mean a reduced level of activity for the squadron, but it would gain the privilege and responsibility of being a Path Finder nursery.

Other than the first of 617 Squadron's three attacks on Tirpitz on the 15th, launched from Yagodnik in Russia, 5 Group undertook no further operations until the morning of the 17th, when contributing to a total of 762 aircraft assembled to attack troop positions at seven locations around the port of Boulogne. The raids would be staggered over a four-hour period and benefit from a 5 Group effort of 195 Lancasters and four Mosquitos, sixteen of the former representing 106 Squadron and departing Metheringham between 08.15 and 08.30 with S/L Allinson the senior pilot on duty. He was accompanied by the new station commander, G/C Heath, an officer with no previous operational experience, whose stock would now rise in the eyes of the aircrew. By the time they were all safely airborne, the operation was just getting under way on the other side of the Channel as the first of seven aiming points was attacked at 08.30. The squadron contingent arrived to find clear skies and good visibility, and they delivered their standard loads of eleven 1,000 pounders and four 500 pounders from 8,000 to 9,000 feet between 09.46 and 09.52, before returning home with an aiming point photo each. Some crews in the later waves were hampered by drifting smoke, but, a total of three thousand tons of bombs was sufficient to pave the way for Allied ground forces to move in shortly afterwards to accept the surrender of the German garrison. This left only Calais of the major French ports still under enemy occupation.

5 Group stations received orders on the 18th to prepared for an operation that night against the port of Bremerhaven, located on the East Bank at the mouth of the River Weser, some thirty miles north of Bremen. It was to be a classic 5 Group-style attack, employing the low-level visual marking method and involved 206 Lancasters and seven Mosquitos. At Metheringham, 106 Squadron loaded sixteen Lancasters with 2,700 x 4lb incendiaries, and sent them off between 18.15 and 18.45 with W/C Stevens and S/L Allinson the senior pilots on duty. There were no early returns, allowing the squadron to arrive at full strength in the target area to find favourable weather conditions and good visibility. The bombing brigade ran in on the aiming point at medium level, the 106 Squadron participants releasing their loads onto red TIs from 12,000 to 12,800 feet between 21.02 and 21.12, mostly in accordance with the Master Bomber's instructions. A number of huge explosions were witnessed at 21.02 and 21.07, and, as they headed out of the target area, they could see many large fires spreading throughout the built-up area, the glow from which remained visible for at least 150 miles. Post-raid reconnaissance revealed that this first major attack on the port, carried out by what, at the time, could be considered to be a modest force, had devasted the built-up areas north and south of the harbour entrance, wiping out installations and warehousing, and only the most northerly and southerly suburbs had escaped complete destruction. Local reports produced a figure of 2,670 buildings reduced to rubble and thirty-thousand people bombed out of their homes, all at the modest cost to 5 Group of a single Lancaster and a Mosquito.

Eighteen 106 Squadron crews assembled for briefing at Metheringham on the 19th, and learned that they were to be part of a predominantly 5 Group attack on the twin towns of Mönchengladbach and Rheydt, and that the latter was to be their specific aiming point. This represented a shallow penetration into Germany, just ten minutes from the Dutch border, and, therefore, a short round trip of four-and-a-half to five hours, followed by a night in bed. 217 Lancasters and ten Mosquitos were made ready, along with ten ABC Lancasters from 101 Squadron, and the Metheringham contingent took off between 19.00 and 19.15 with W/C Stevens and S/L Grindon the senior pilots on duty, each Lancaster carrying a 2,000 pounder and a dozen 500 pounders. The Master Bomber for the operation was W/C Guy Gibson VC, DSO, DFC, who was currently serving as the Base Operations Officer at Coningsby and had been agitating to get back into the war before it was over. His great fear was that his service would end in a backwater, while others gained the glory by being in at the death, and he had racked up a number of sorties unofficially by flying as a second pilot. Gibson was a warrior, and the war had brought out of him qualities, which, in peacetime, may have lain dormant. War had also given him a direction, and he revelled in the company of fellow operational types, particularly those of the officer class, and, having been torn away from the operational scene following the success of the Dams operation, his purpose had gone, and he had become listless, frustrated and discontented. His time in the operational wilderness had not, however, deprived him of his arrogance and self-belief, and, when the opportunity to fly as Master Bomber on the coming raid presented itself, he grabbed it. He was driven the three miles from Coningsby to Woodhall Spa to collect his 627 Squadron Mosquito, which, for whatever reason, he rejected, and swapped with F/L Mallender, causing a degree of resentment. Gibson had already set the tone for the evening by rejecting the advice of W/C Charles Owen, who had been Master Bomber at this target ten nights earlier. Owen had advised him to leave the target by a south-westerly route, and cross north-eastern France to the coast, and also to observe orders to remain above 10,000 feet. Gibson insisted that he would fly home via a direct route across Holland at low level, and would not be dissuaded. He took off ahead of the 627 Squadron element at 19.51, to meet up with the main force over the target, where two aiming points were to be marked.

Some crews reported icing clouds at around 9,000 feet, which happened to be the cruising altitude to the target over Belgium, and most chose to keep below, before climbing fast to 15,000 feet as the cloud dispersed. The marking was complex, with a green marker to be dropped on a factory in a western district of Mönchengladbach, and a yellow marker on railway yards in the north, while a red marker was to be placed on railway yards in Rheydt, two miles to the south. It would have been a demanding plan even for an experienced Master Bomber, which Gibson was not, but, even so, his instructions were heard clearly. All seemed to be going to plan, with accurate and punctual marking for the green and yellow forces, but late, though accurate marking for the red force, and some of the red force crews were diverted to the green aiming point. The crews of F/O Kelley and F/L Stewart were instructed to bomb on green TIs, but none was visible to the former, who aimed instead at fires burning in the centre of the target area, while the latter found greens, and brought home an aiming point photo to prove it. F/O Sayeau and crew were ordered also to bomb greens, only to have that instruction cancelled and changed to reds, while those not identifying their briefed aiming point, bombed on whatever markers presented themselves. The 106 Squadron crews carried out their attacks from 10,000 to 11,500 feet between 21.50 and 21.59, and sixteen of them returned home. F/L Barron and crew employed Gee to find Metheringham, but were unable to locate it precisely in cloudy conditions, and, while circling to get their bearings, Barron had to take evasive action to avoid another aircraft. He was unable to maintain control, and pulled off a successful crash-landing near Fulbeck airfield, from which he and his crew walked away unscathed, leaving PB298 a write-off. The operation cost four Lancasters and a Mosquito, two of the former belonging to 106 Squadron, PB347 crashing on the west-north-westerly approach to the target shortly after crossing the frontier with Holland. F/O Brindley and five of his crew lost their lives, while only the bomb-aimer, F/O Ayres, escaped to fall into enemy hands. PB359 crashed east-south-east of the target after bombing, and F/L Fee RAAF managed to evade capture, while the three other survivors did not. Post-raid reconnaissance confirmed a highly destructive attack on both towns, and Gibson did, indeed attempt to return low over Holland, just as he said he would, but crashed on the outskirts of Steenbergen in south-western Holland with fatal consequences for him and Coningsby's recently appointed station navigation officer, S/L James Warwick.

It was now time to turn attention upon Calais as the final port still under enemy occupation. 5 Group was not involved in the first round of attacks on enemy positions on the 20th, the day on which the award of a DFC was announced to W/C Piercy and F/O Durrant. AVM Cochrane visited the station on the 21st, accompanied by the 54 Base commander, Air Commodore Sharp, and the former squadron commanding officer, W/C Baxter. Orders came through on that morning of the 23rd to prepare 136 Lancasters and five Mosquitos for an attack that night on the aqueduct section of the Dortmund-Ems Canal south of Ladbergen. It had been the scene of a disaster for 617 Squadron in September 1943, when five of eight crews had failed to return. An element from 617 Squadron would be on scene also on this night, to open the attack with Tallboys, to which the raised banks containing the waterway were particularly vulnerable. Germany's canal system was a vital component in the transport network, and facilitated the import of raw materials and the export of finished goods to support the war effort. Its wide thoroughfares allowed the passage of large barges, and, as the slack in Germany's war production was taken up during 1944, traffic was being pushed through at increasing levels. While this operation was in progress, a second 5 Group force of 108 Lancasters, four Mosquitos and the P38 Lightning would hit Handorf aerodrome some ten miles to the south to prevent it from interfering. The main operation on this night, however, would be conducted by 549 aircraft from 1, 3, 4 and 8 Groups seventy miles to the south-west at Neuss, situated on the southern edge of the Ruhr facing Düsseldorf across the Rhine, and this, hopefully, might help to split the enemy defences.

Sixteen Lancasters were made ready at Metheringham and loaded with fourteen 1,000 pounders, each with a half-hour delay fuse, and W/C Stevens again put himself at the top of the Order of Battle, thus maintaining the tradition of 106 Squadron commanding officers to lead from the front. S/L Allinson was the other senior pilot on duty as they became airborne in ten minutes from 19.10, but F/O Kelley and crew returned early after the mid-upper gunner reported sick. The others arrived in the target area shortly before 22.00 to find complete cloud cover over the canal, but good visibility below the cloud base at around 8,000 feet. 617 Squadron went in first, and direct hits by two Tallboys breached both branches of the section, leaving a six mile stretch of the waterway drained. The challenge of identifying a specific pinpoint in this region was intensified by the presence nearby of the Mittelland Canal, which joined the Dortmund-Ems Canal in a triangular basin called Das Nasse Dreieck (the Wet Triangle) near Ibbenbüren a few miles further north, and the Glane, a river which passed under the Dortmund-Ems Canal at the twin aqueduct section. Features were easily confused, and some aircraft strayed north of the intended aiming point, to a spot beyond the town of Ladbergen, where a similar-looking section of the Mittelland Canal was attacked near Gravenhorst. The crews arriving first bombed on the glow of markers through the cloud, while later arrivals came below the cloud base on instructions from the Master Bomber. Four of the 106 Squadron crews bombed from between 14,000 and 15,000 feet on target markers, while those of W/C Stevens, F/O Meredith and S/L Allinson were below 8,000 feet as they carried out their attacks on what they believed to be the correct location, but, according to their bombing photos, was actually a location six miles north. F/O Symes and crew joined in the bombing of Handorf aerodrome as an alternative, while F/L Sexton and crew abandoned their sortie over the target on instructions from the Master Bomber.

The attack on Handorf was also not proceeding according to plan as the Master Bomber found himself unable to direct the attack, and experienced great difficulty in communicating the fact to his Deputy because of intense interference on VHF. Identification and marking of the aiming points proved to be difficult, and only two green TIs could be seen by a few crews. There would be complaints later that there was no control, and some crews orbited and remained in the target area for up to thirty-five minutes before bombing either on green TIs at Handorf or on yellows at Münster, which had been selected as the last-resort target. Night-fighters were active towards the end of the raid, and contributed to the loss of fourteen Lancasters, more than 10% of those dispatched. 106 Squadron was represented among the missing by ND868, which crashed near Ibbenbüren, killing seven of the eight men on board, including the newly-arrived second pilot, F/O Isaac, and only the pilot, F/L Jones, survived to fall into enemy hands. F/O Meredith RCAF and crew arrived back in a night-fighter-damaged PB248, and thus completed their first tour of operations.

The second of the series of raids on enemy positions around Calais was mounted by 188 aircraft on the 24th, for which 5 Group detailed thirty Lancasters from the 53 Base stations of Skellingthorpe and Waddington. In the event, only 126 aircraft bombed, eight of them from 5 Group, and they attacked either on a reference provided by Oboe skymarkers or came below the cloud base to bomb visually. At such a height, they were sitting ducks for the heavy and light flak batteries, which accounted for seven Lancasters and a Halifax. It was a similar story on the following day, when only a third of more than eight hundred aircraft were able to deliver their bombs, before the Master Bomber called a halt to proceedings in the face of low cloud. The campaign continued on the 26th, with two separate raids against seven enemy positions around Cap Gris Nez and nearer Calais involving more than seven hundred aircraft. This time the conditions were favourable, and bombing was observed to be concentrated around the aiming points.

On the afternoon of the 26th, thirteen 106 Squadron crews attended briefing, and learned that the night's operation was to be against the city of Karlsruhe in southern Germany, for which 216 Lancasters of 5 Group were made ready, along with ten of the ABC variety from 101 Squadron and eleven Mosquitos. It was to be a two-wave attack, and the 106 Squadron element was to be divided between the two, eight for the first and five for the second. They departed Metheringham between 00.55 and 01.20 with W/C Stevens the senior pilot on duty, and flew out over France with ten-tenths cloud beneath them, which persisted all the way to the target, but thinned to a narrow band with the base estimated to be at between 6,000 and 7,000 feet. The plan was to bomb through the cloud on H2S, guided by Wanganui flares, and some approaching crews observed a red TI cascade above the cloud at 03.54. The 106 Squadron crews focused on the glow of red and green TIs, and bombed them from 10,700 to 12,300 between 04.02 and 04.10 in accordance with the instructions of the Master Bomber. All returned safely to report what appeared to be a city in flames and the glow of fires visible for up to 150 miles into the return journey. There were no plottable bombing photos, but reconnaissance confirmed that the attack had been spread throughout the city and had left a large part of it devastated.

As the crews returned to their stations after 07.00, elements of 1, 3, 4 and 8 Groups were preparing to leave theirs for a further attack on the Calais area. On arrival, the Master Bomber ordered the 340-strong force to come below the cloud base to bomb visually, and another successful operation ensued. Later that day, thirteen 106 Squadron crews attended briefing for an operation that night against Kaiserslautern, an historic city on the edge of the Palatinate Forest, some thirty miles west of Mannheim. It would be the first major attack of the war on this location, for which a force of 217 Lancasters, including ten from 101 Squadron, and ten Mosquitos, was made ready. The Metheringham Lancasters were provided with all-incendiary bomb loads, which they lifted into the air between 22.05 and 22.15 with S/L Allinson the senior pilot on duty, accompanied again by the station commander, G/C Heath. Clear skies over England gave way to a build-up of cloud over the Channel, and, from the French coast to near the target, the bomber stream encountered ten-tenths cumulus with a base at 2,800 feet. The target was partially covered by a thin layer of five to eight-tenths cloud with tops at 3,000 feet, with a further layer at 6,000 to 7,000 feet. The marking with red and green TIs was punctual and accurate, and a green TI visible in the centre of the town became the objective for the main force crews in accordance with the Master Bomber's instructions at 00.58. The railway workshops were of particular interest to the 106 Squadron crews, but this was an area attack, and most carried all-incendiary loads, while some others had a single 2,000 pounder and a dozen 500lb incendiaries, which they delivered from 4,000 to 5,100 feet between 01.03 and 01.10. The bombing appeared to be concentrated, causing two yellow explosions at 01.02, and fires were beginning to take hold as the force retreated towards the west. Reconnaissance revealed massive damage within the city caused by more than nine hundred tons of bombs, and an estimated 36% of the built-up area had been reduced to ruins.

The final raids on German positions around Calais were carried out by 490 aircraft of 1, 3, 6 and 8 Groups on the 28th, and the garrison surrendered to Canadian forces shortly thereafter. A change in organization at 5 Group brought about the disbandment of 52 Base at the end of the month, and the transfer of 44 and 619 Squadrons from Dunholme Lodge to Spilsby and Strubby respectively, which, with East Kirkby, formed 55 Base. There was no further activity for 106 Squadron during the month, which had brought eleven operations on three days and eight nights, and generated 171 sorties at a cost of five Lancasters and four crews.

October 1944

A theme running throughout October was a campaign against the island of Walcheren in the Scheldt estuary, where heavy gun emplacements were barring the approaches to the much-needed port of Antwerp some forty miles upstream. Attempts to bomb these positions in September had proved unsuccessful, and it was decided to flood the land, both to inundate the batteries, and to render the terrain difficult to defend when the ground forces moved in. 252 Lancasters were drawn from 1, 5 and 8 Groups and made ready on the 3rd to attack the seawalls at Westkapelle, the most westerly point of the island. 5 Group contributed 128 Lancasters, allotted to four of eight waves of thirty aircraft each, with the Tallboy-carrying 617 Squadron Lancasters standing off to be called in only if required. A breach was opened by the fifth wave, which was extended by those following behind, and the flood waters had reached the town by the time the last Lancasters turned for home. 106 Squadron had not been invited to take part, and it was the 4th when orders were received at Metheringham to prepare five Lancasters for mining duties in the Silverthorn III garden in the Kattegat as part of a seventeen-strong 5 Group force. The crews of W/C Stevens, F/Ls Parry and Stewart and F/Os Daniel and Sayeau took off between 17.15 and 17.30 bound for Sejerø Bay off the north-western coast of Denmark's Sjælland island, which they reached to find good visibility and varying amounts of cloud between zero and eight-tenths. They encountered no opposition and delivered their six vegetables each from 11,000 feet between 20.58 and 21.08 to be the only squadron to achieve a 100% success.

5 Group's first major outing of the month was posted on the 5th, and was a daylight attempt to bomb the port of Wilhelmshaven through ten-tenths cloud on H2S. A force of 227 Lancasters, one Mosquito and the P38 Lightning was assembled with 106 Squadron providing nine aircraft for what would be its first daylight foray over Germany. They departed Metheringham between 07.55 and 08.00 with S/L Allinson the senior pilot on duty and each Lancaster carrying ten 1,000 pounders and four 500lb "J" cluster incendiaries. Whether or not it was part of the plan, the controller led the force around the northern side of Heligoland, before heading for Jade Bay, where they found the forecast layer of ten-tenths cloud between 3,000 and 5,000 feet with good visibility above. The 106 Squadron crews established their positions by H2S-fix or by observing others, and all but one delivered their payloads from 17,000 to 18,300 feet between 11.04 and 11.08. A technical problem prevented S/L Allinson and crew from releasing their load, and repeated attempts to jettison it on the way home failed, leaving them with no choice but to land with it still on board on what was the final operation of their first tour. No results were observed, and there was no possibility of making an assessment, but the impression of a scattered attack was confirmed later when photo-reconnaissance became possible.

From this point until the end of the war, German towns and cities were to be subjected to a new and terrible bomber offensive, beginning with a second Ruhr campaign, which was to open at Dortmund, and for which a 3, 6 and 8 Group force of 523 aircraft was made ready on the 6th. 5 Group, meanwhile, had its own target, and prepared 237 Lancasters and seven Mosquitos for what would prove to be the thirty-second and final raid of the war on the city of Bremen. 106 Squadron loaded thirteen Lancasters with 2,700 x 4lb incendiaries, while F/L Parry and crew were sitting on a cookie and six 1,000 pounders as they departed Metheringham between 17.40 and 17.45 with S/L Grindon the senior pilot on duty and F/L Stewart and crew undertaking the final sortie of their tour with F/L Barlow RAAF on board as second pilot. Having climbed out and set course, they left the cloud behind and headed into crystal clear skies over the North Sea with a three-quarter moon. The perfect conditions held firm in the target area, which was ideal for the 5 Group low-level marking method, and handed the hapless city on a plate to the bombers. The 106 Squadron crews carried out their attacks in the face of many searchlights and the usual flak response, and aimed for the red and green TIs from 16,000 to 16,800 feet between 20.29 and 20.34, before turning away from a city in flames, the glow from which remained visible for 150 miles into the return flight. The success of the operation was confirmed by post-raid reconnaissance and local reports, which described a huge area of fire, and catalogued the destruction of more than 4,800 houses and apartment blocks, and severe damage to war industry factories, all achieved at the modest cost of five aircraft. Tragically, among these was PD214, which crashed into the sea, taking with it the eight-man crew of F/L Stewart. It was a bitter pill for the 106 Squadron and Metheringham communities to swallow, to see one of their own crews robbed of the prize of survival on the very last operation of their tour. The squadron was also about to bid farewell to S/L Grindon, for whom this had been the sixteenth and final operation before their posting on the 8th to take command of 57 Squadron at East Kirkby. His success in that post would see him succeed G/C Johnny Fauquier as commanding officer of 617 Squadron at the end of April, after the bombing war had ended. He was succeeded as B Flight commander by the newly-promoted S/L Parry DFC, AFC. Now that the focus of operations had moved from France to Germany, the number of sorties to complete a tour had been reduced from thirty-five to thirty-three, and this meant an unexpected bonus to some.

The squadron was not involved in any operations over the following week, when much of the Command's effort was directed towards coastal defences around the Scheldt Estuary, and the softening up of enemy resistance in the Eifel region of Germany ahead of the advancing Allied ground forces. Following the failure of Operation Market Garden, the German frontier towns of Cleves (Kleve) and Emmerich, separated by the Rhine and just five miles apart, were earmarked for attention by daylight on the 7th, and both suffered massive damage at the hands of large forces from 1, 3, 4 and 8 Groups. 5 Group, meanwhile, returned to Walcheren to target the seawalls near Flushing with 121 Lancasters and three Mosquitos, many carrying bombs with a thirty-minute delay fuse. The dyke was already beginning to crumble as the bombers headed home, where confirmation of a successful outcome would catch up with them.

During the few rest periods over the summer months, the squadrons of 54 Base had competed for a handsome bronze sports trophy awarded for points won in cricket, swimming, athletics, badminton, rifle-shooting and other pursuits. On the morning of the 8th, Air Commodore Sharp presented it to the winners, 106 Squadron. Focus remained on the Scheldt defences, and the gun battery at Fort Frederik Hendrik near Breskens on the East Scheldt was targeted by elements of 1 and 8 Groups on the 11th, while 115 Lancasters from 5 Group were assigned to others near Flushing on the North Bank of the West Scheldt. At the same time, sixty-one Lancasters and two Mosquitos from the group were to attempt to breach the seawalls at Veere, situated on the eastern side of Walcheren opposite Westkapelle. Post-raid reconnaissance revealed an area of flooding of 800 x 250 yards at Veere, but no new damage to the gun positions.

Early on the 14th, the opening salvoes were fired of Operation Hurricane, a terrifying demonstration to the enemy of the overwhelming superiority of the Allied air forces ranged against it. Bomber Command ordered a maximum effort from all but 5 Group to attack Duisburg, for which 1,013 Lancasters, Halifaxes and Mosquitos answered the call. The American 8th Air Force would also be in business on this day, targeting the Cologne area further south with 1,250 bombers escorted by 749 fighters. The RAF force took off at first light, picked up its own fighter escort, and delivered 4,500 tons of high-explosives and incendiaries into Duisburg shortly after breakfast time, causing unimaginable destruction. That night, similar numbers returned to press home the point about superiority, bringing the total weight of bombs over the two raids to 9,000 tons from 2,018 sorties in fewer than twenty-four hours. The only involvement by 5 Group were single sorties by a Lancaster and a Mosquito to conduct a photo-reconnaissance of the operation.

However, 5 Group took advantage of the evening activity over the Ruhr to return to Braunschweig, the scene of quite a number of unsatisfactory previous attempts to land a really telling blow. A force of 232 Lancasters and eight Mosquitos was made ready, of which a dozen of the former were provided by 106 Squadron. They departed Metheringham between 22.55 and 23.05 with no senior pilots on duty and every one bearing the rank of flying officer. All reached the target area to find conditions ideal for low-level marking, and approached at 18,000 feet from the south-west over Hallendorf and Salzgitter, the latter the home to the Reichswerke Hermann Göring steelworks. The bombers had to run the gauntlet of searchlight cones and heavy flak for the three minutes it took to pass through to the start of the bombing run, where they were greeted by clear skies and good visibility, which facilitated accurate marking with red and green TIs. The early bombing tended to undershoot, but the Master Bomber quickly brought it back on track, calling for crews to overshoot by up to nineteen seconds. The 106 Squadron contingent passed over the aiming point at 17,400 to 18,000 feet between 02.30 and 02.36, and delivered their loads accurately to contribute to a highly effective raid. 83 Squadron's F/O Price complained that main force crews were jettisoning incendiaries all the way back as far as the Rhine, and thereby illuminating the track for any stalking night-fighters. Returning crews reported fires visible from a hundred miles away, and bombing photos were plotted at between 1,300 and 3,300 yards from the aiming point. In the event, only a single Lancaster failed to return from what was, indeed, confirmed to be an outstanding result, which had wiped out the entire centre of this historic city, and visited damage on almost every district. Such was the level of destruction that local authorities believed a thousand bombers had taken part.

Stubborn resistance by the occupiers on Walcheren demanded further operations against the seawalls at Westkapelle, for which 5 Group detailed forty-seven Lancasters and three Mosquitos on the 17th. 106 Squadron loaded each of eight Lancasters with fourteen 1,000 pounders fitted with delay fuses of varying lengths and dispatched them from Metheringham between 12.40 and 13.00 again with all pilots of flying officer rank. They arrived at the target to find favourable conditions and bombed from 4,500 to 6,000 feet between 14.04 and 14.09, before returning safely home with an aiming point photo each, leaving a reconnaissance aircraft over the target from 14.55 to 15.10 to record the delayed-action bomb blasts. Its photos would reveal no extension to the breach in the dyke.

Following a night off, thirteen 106 Squadron crews assembled in the briefing room at Metheringham on the 19th, to receive details of the 5 Group operation that night against Nuremberg, while 560 aircraft from the other groups plied their trade at Stuttgart, some ninety miles to the south-west. A new record 5 Group force of 263 Lancasters and seven Mosquitos stood ready in the early evening, and the 106 Squadron element took off between 17.30 and 17.45, with W/C Stevens the senior pilot on duty and each bearing aloft a cookie and thirteen 500lb "J" Cluster bombs, the latter made up of 106 x 4lb incendiaries. The outward flight across France was uneventful, and the target was found to be covered by a wedge of eight to ten-tenths cloud between 3,000 and 10,000 feet, with poor visibility below. The marker force laid down flares and backed them up with others along with red and green TIs, which were observed to be somewhat scattered, and bombing had to take place on their glow seen through the cloud. The 106 Squadron crews carried out their attacks from 13,000 to 17,200 feet between 20.57 and 21.05 in accordance with the Master Bomber's instructions, before returning home uncertain as to the outcome. The impression given by the glow of fires was of an effective attack, but post-raid reconnaissance revealed the bombing to have fallen not on the intended city-centre aiming point, but predominantly into the more industrial southern districts, where almost four hundred houses were destroyed, along with forty-one industrial buildings.

It was back to Walcheren on the 23rd for 112 Lancasters of 5 Group, this time to target the coastal battery at Flushing. They were greeted at the target by eight to ten-tenths cloud with a base at between 3,000 and 5,000 feet, and poor visibility below caused by haze and rain. The force was led in on what appeared to be a decent approach, but was ordered to "orbit port" as the lead crews experienced great difficulty in identifying their respective aiming points. A second run was no more revealing, even for those crews who ventured down as low as 2,000 feet, and twenty would still have their bombs on board when ordered to go home.

That evening, a new record force of 1,055 aircraft was sent against Essen as part of the Hurricane "message", and dropped 4,538 tons of bombs, more than 90% of which was high explosive. This number was achieved without 5 Group, which took the night off, and committed only twenty-five Lancasters to gardening duties in northern waters on the following night. The gardens were all in the western Baltic, Kraut, Yew Tree and Silverthorn, and it was for the last mentioned that 106 Squadron contributed ten aircraft, which departed Metheringham between 17.15 and 17.30 with W/C Stevens the senior pilot on duty. They encountered ten-tenths cloud in the target area with tops at 8,000 feet, and employed H2S to locate Anholt Island, from where timed runs were made, and all aircraft dropped six mines each from an average height of 12,000 feet between 21.47 and 22.04. There was no opposition of any kind, and all landed safely at Lossiemouth after eight to nine hours in the air.

Essen was pounded again by more than seven hundred aircraft in daylight on the 25th, after which it ceased to be an important source of war production. Operation Hurricane moved on to Cologne on the 28th, when two districts east of the centre were totally devastated by more than seven hundred aircraft. 5 Group occupied the day with the preparation of a force of 237 Lancasters and seven Mosquitos for an operation that night against the U-Boot pens at Bergen in Norway. 106 Squadron made ready sixteen Lancasters, and dispatched them between 22.25 and 23.00 with F/Ls Bretherton, Daniel and Marks the senior pilots on duty, and the cosmopolitan make-up of the squadron was demonstrated by the presence of two South African Air Force pilots, Capt Pechey and Lt Addison, along with two almost all-Australian crews, whose flight engineers were RAF. There were only two early returns from the entire force, which reached the target area after a three-and-a-half-hour outward flight, having battled their way through electrical storms. They had been told to expect clear conditions, although some doubts had been expressed about the forecast, and these were confirmed when the force was met by eight-to ten-tenths cloud between 4,000 and 14,000 feet, which obscured the aiming point. This would not have been a problem over Germany, but the risk to Norwegian civilians was uppermost in the mind of the Master Bomber as he pondered his options before calling for the main force to descend. Even then, most were unable to pick out any markers, and the situation was exacerbated by intermittent VHF reception, which persuaded 83 Squadron's F/L Cornish to fly up and down the coast acting as a communications link between the Master Bomber and the main force. The flare force crews did what they could from between 12,500 and 15,000 feet, and the main force supporters flew as low as 4,500 feet, without being able to identify the target. The operation was abandoned after only forty-seven aircraft had bombed, among which were five from Metheringham, who carried out their attacks on red TIs from 5,000 to 6,000 feet between 02.08 and 02.23. While this operation was in progress, the crews of F/Os Symes and Dodson laid six mines each into the Onion garden in Oslo harbour from 8,000 feet at 00.07 and 00.30 respectively.

The final operations against Walcheren were undertaken by 5 Group on the 30th, when two forces of fifty-one Lancasters and four Mosquitos each were sent against coastal batteries at Westkapelle and Flushing. 106 Squadron contributed six Lancasters to the Westkapelle attack, and they departed Metheringham between 10.35 and 10.40 with no senior pilots on duty, and were in position ninety minutes later with loads of fourteen 1,000 pounders with delay fuses of thirty minutes to an hour. Visibility was compromised by four to seven-tenths cloud at 6,000 feet, but the Zouteland battery, situated some 2½ miles to the south-east of Westkapelle, was identified visually and by red TIs, and the squadron participants bombed from 2,500 to 4,000 feet between 12.10 and 12.19, before returning safely with five aiming point photos. Ground forces went in on the following day, and a week of heavy fighting preceded the island's capture. Even then, the clearing of mines from the approaches to Antwerp kept the port out of commission for a further three weeks.

Later, on that evening of the 30th, nine hundred aircraft returned to Cologne, and almost five hundred went back again twenty-four hours later to complete the destruction of the Rhineland Capital. It had been a good month for 106 Squadron, which had lost just a single Lancaster and crew from seven night operations, including two mining, and three in daylight involving a total of ninety-five sorties.

November 1944

The new month began for 5 Group with a daylight operation on the afternoon of the 1st, against a synthetic oil plant referred to by the raid planners simply as Homberg, a name with an evil reputation among 3 Group squadrons, which had suffered heavy casualties in repeated attacks on the plant during the summer. The Gewerkschaft Rheinpreussen A G production site lay in the Meerbeck district of the town of Moers, which is situated a mile-and-a-half to the west of Homberg on the West Bank of the Rhine opposite Duisburg. Its reputation probably meant less to the men of 5 Group Squadrons, whose hearts were more likely to be set racing by the mention of the Wesseling refinery south of Cologne. 106 Squadron briefed twenty crews as part of an overall 5 Group force of 226 Lancasters and two Mosquitos, which were to be joined by fourteen 8 Group Mosquitos to provide the Oboe marking. Some good news before the crews made their way to their aircraft, was that the number of sorties for a tour had been reduced again to thirty, which would be a cause for celebration among a select few who had already reached that milestone. The Metheringham element took off between 13.55 and 14.10 with S/L Parry the senior pilot on duty, and all reached the target to find it completely obscured by cloud with tops at between 6,000 and 9,000 feet. The skymarkers were scattered, and the first bombers to arrive on scene either failed to see them or watched them falling behind, and these brought their bombs home, but 159 crews did deliver their payloads, among them the 106 Squadron contingent from 16,000 to 18,000 feet between 16.09 and 16.13 without being able to assess the results. Arriving on the scene towards the end of the raid, these found the skymarkers well-scattered over a circle with a ten-mile radius, prompting a backer-up from 83 Squadron to drop a yellow TI over the built-up area in the hope of attracting some bombing. Some crews caught a glimpse of the target area through a chink in the cloud, while others carried out a time-and-distance run from the last visual pinpoint, before aiming at red skymarkers with green stars. A lack of clear communication with the Master Bomber and the wide spread of the markers were other factors in the failure of the operation. Flak was intense and accurate, and a burst shot away one of PB303's engines, while probably inflicting other serious damage. This resulted in the Lancaster crashing near Steenbergen in southern Holland, the scene of Gibson's fatal crash six weeks earlier, and there were no survivors from the crew of F/O Symes, who were well into their first tour and would be missed at Metheringham. While the engine and airframe fitters began the task of repairing flak damage, the crews attended debriefing, many of them to report that the Master Bomber's VHF transmissions had been jammed by someone in another aircraft leaving the transmit button on.

Düsseldorf's turn to face a massive force came on the 2nd, when 992 aircraft were made ready for what would prove to be the final major raid of the war on this much-bombed city on the southern edge of the Ruhr. 5 Group put up 187 Lancasters, sixteen provided by 106 Squadron for this rare experience for the "Lincolnshire Poachers" to operate with the rest of the Command. They departed Metheringham between 16.25 and 17.00 with F/L Bretherton the senior pilot on duty, and all arrived at the target to find clear skies, moonlight and only ground haze to slightly mar the vertical visibility. The moonlight nullified the glare of the searchlights ringing the city, but, of greater concern was the heavy flak bursting at 17,000 to 20,000 feet. The main force crews found the aiming point to be well illuminated and marked with red and green TIs, those representing 106 Squadron observing the scene from a variety of altitudes between 15,500 and 21,000 feet, and well spread out in the bomber stream. F/O Scott and crew were all-Australian, with the exception of the "Pom" flight engineer, and were among the first to deliver their mixed payload of a cookie, six 1,000 pounder and six 500 pounders, which went down from 19,800 feet at 19.15, when it was too early in the raid to assess what was happening below. By the time that F/O May RAAF and crew dropped theirs from 17,000 feet at 19.41, however, there were very large areas of fire and the whole city was covered by smoke. In between, the other 106 Squadron participants carried out their attacks from 15,500 to 20,750 feet between 19.16 and 19.33, and watched fires beginning to take hold and smoke rising to 2,000 feet as they turned away confident of a successful attack. PB248 was severely damaged by cannon fire from a night-fighter, but F/O Day and crew brought the Lancaster home. Many returning crews reported a large explosion, and the glow of fires still visible from up to two hundred miles away, and F/O Stanfield and crew brought back an aiming point photo. The success of the operation was confirmed by post-raid reconnaissance, which revealed that the northern half of the city had received the main weight of bombs, and that five thousand houses had been destroyed or seriously damaged.

The continuing campaign against Ruhr cities would be prosecuted by 749 aircraft at Bochum on the 4th, while 5 Group renewed its acquaintance with the Dortmund-Ems Canal, which had been repaired following the successful breaching of its banks near Münster in September. Now that Germany's railways were being pounded, the Dortmund-Ems and the nearby Mittelland Canal took on a greater significance as vital components in the transportation system, particularly with regard to the movement of raw materials like coal and coke to the steel works of the Ruhr region. A force of 168 Lancasters and two Mosquitos contained a dozen of the former belonging to 106 Squadron, whose ORB specified embankment rather than aqueduct, possibly referring to the section south of the aqueducts closer to Greven, which had been the target for the ill-fated 617 Squadron attack in September 1943. However, the bomb load of fourteen 1,000 pounders carried by each Lancaster was more suited to the aqueduct section, and it was these structures that received mention in the post-raid reports. The Metheringham contingent lined up for take-off at 17.40, and all got away safely in around ten minutes with F/L Bretherton the senior pilot on duty. They hoped to sneak in under cover of the main operation sixty miles to the south, thereby, avoiding the attentions of night-fighters. The first marker aircraft of 83 Squadron arrived at the target at 19.19, after making a GPI run (ground position indicated) by means of H2S from Münster, and encountered clear skies with ground haze. A blind-dropped green TI burst on the canal bank four hundred yards short of the aiming point, which the flare force crews employed as a reference for their runs between 19.20 and 19.28. Red TIs were observed to fall between the two aqueducts, after which, the Master Bomber cancelled the third wave of flares and sent them all home to leave the way clear for the main force. The first bombs tended to overshoot, but, thereafter, the attack became accurate and concentrated, and the 106 Squadron crews bombed in accordance with the instructions from the Master Bomber from 10,000 to 13,000 feet in a six-minute slot from 19.30. Photo-reconnaissance confirmed that both branches of the canal had been breached and drained, leaving barges stranded and the waterway unnavigable. This had been the one-hundredth operation for Lancaster JB663, which had been taken on squadron charge on the 18th of November 1943, and, on this night, contained the crew of F/O Day.

To capitalize on this success, an attack was planned for the 6th against the Mittelland Canal at Gravenhorst, a point about a mile north of Das Nasse Dreieck, the "Wet Triangle" at Bergeshövede. This was a triangular basin, where the two waterways converge about ten miles north of Ladbergen, before the Dortmund-Ems continues to the west, and the Mittelland north and then to the east. It was a 5 Group show involving 239 Lancasters and seven Mosquitos, eighteen of the former representing 106 Squadron, which departed Metheringham between 16.30 and 16.45 with F/Ls Barden, Barron and Sexton the senior pilots on duty. All reached the target area to find clear skies but haze up to around 4,000 feet that affected the vertical visibility. The Master Bomber called in the flare force, and, despite the illumination, the low-level Mosquito markers experienced great difficulty in identifying the aiming point, and only a single Mosquito piloted by F/L De Vigne eventually delivered a target indicator accurately onto the aiming point, only for it to fall into the water and become extinguished. Only thirty-one aircraft had bombed before the Master Bomber called a halt to proceedings, and all from 106 Squadron withheld their loads, jettisoning the delayed-action 1,000 pounders before setting course for home and encountering not only night-fighter activity, but also very challenging weather conditions of electrical storms and low cloud. Ten Lancasters failed to return, a high rate of loss with nothing to show for it, and among them was 106 Squadron's LL953, which crashed on German soil, killing F/O Neale and his crew. LL948 was almost another grim statistic after sustaining heavy damage, but Lt Howes and crew nursed it home to a safe landing. Mention was made at some debriefings of the presence of jet-propelled fighters, one of which was claimed as destroyed.

Earlier on the 6th, a series of raids on Ruhr oil refineries had begun with an area attack by more than seven hundred aircraft at Gelsenkirchen, where the Nordstern plant (Gelsenberg A G) and the city centre were the aiming points, and this was followed by smaller-scale operations at Homberg on the 8th, Wanne-Eickel on the 9th and Castrop-Rauxel on the morning of the 11th, none of which involved 5 Group.

Later, on the 11th, twenty 106 Squadron crews assembled in the briefing room to learn that fourteen of them would shortly be attacking the Rhenania-Ossag synthetic oil plant at Harburg, while six targeted the town, situated on the South Bank of the Elbe opposite Hamburg. It had been attacked by American bombers on a number of occasions, and was always well defended. It was another all-5 Group show involving 237 Lancasters and eight Mosquitos, while elements of 1 and 8 Groups targeted a similar plant at Dortmund. The Metheringham Lancasters targeting the refinery were each loaded with a cookie and five 1,000 and seven 500 pounders, while the others had a cookie and fourteen SBCs of incendiaries in the bomb bays as they took off between 16.25 and 16.40, with W/C Stevens the senior pilot on duty. They reached the target area to find largely clear conditions, with only a thin layer of stratus at 8,000 feet and another at 17,000 to 18,000 feet between them and the aiming point. This they identified either by H2S or red and green TIs, before delivering their loads from 16,300 to 19,000 feet between 19.15 and 19.28 in accordance with instructions from the Master Bomber. The defenders threw up a heavy flak barrage, which reached as high as 23,000 feet, and seven Lancasters failed to return. At debriefing, crews reported a large explosion at 19.28, followed by an oil fire, and local reports would confirm that heavy damage had been inflicted upon the town's residential and industrial districts.

The 16th was devoted to the erasure from the map of the three small towns of Heinsberg, Jülich and Düren, located respectively in an arc from north to east of Aachen, and close to the German lines upon which American ground forces were advancing. A total of 1,188 aircraft was involved, and 1, 5 and 8 Groups provided the heavy bombing and marking force of 485 Lancasters for the last-mentioned. 106 Squadron contributed nineteen aircraft to the 5 Group force of 214, and they got away from Metheringham between 12.40 and 13.00 with S/L Parry the senior pilot on duty, and no fewer than five pilots serving in the SAAF. Each Lancaster lifted eleven 1,000 and four 500 pounders through the ten-tenths cloud which accompanied them most of the way to the target, before it thinned to three-tenths stratus above 6,000 feet as they approached the aiming point in the final wave of the attack. They bombed in accordance with the instructions of the Master Bomber from 10,000 to 12,500 feet between 15.37 and 15.45, and observed smoke rising through 9,000 feet as they turned for home, confident in the success of the attack. Most of the bombing photos were unplottable because of the smoke covering the area, but the operation was a complete success at a cost of just three aircraft, post-raid reconnaissance confirming that the town had been destroyed. Local sources reported a death toll in excess of three thousand inhabitants, needlessly sacrificed, as, in the event, unfavourable ground conditions prevented the American advance from succeeding anyway.

Twenty-one 106 Squadron crews were called to briefing on the 21st, to be told, that elements of 53 and 54 Bases would be going back to the Dortmund-Ems Canal on a night of multiple operations involving 1,345 sorties. 1, 4, 6 and 8 Groups were involved in three operations, each by 270 aircraft, against railway yards at Aschaffenburg, situated about twenty miles south-east of Frankfurt, and oil plants at Castrop-

Rauxel and Sterkrade in the Ruhr. 5 Group prepared two forces of 137 and 123 Lancasters respectively, with Mosquito support, for the Mittelland and Dortmund-Ems Canals, while a whole host of minor operations would complete the Order of Battle. The 106 Squadron element departed Metheringham for the latter between 17.35 and 17.55 with F/Ls Barden, Bretherton and Marks the senior pilots on duty. They encountered a layer of six to ten-tenths cloud in the target area between 4,000 and 8,000 feet, which did not inhibit the accuracy of the marking, and the canal could be identified visually during the run-up anyway, although could not be seen from directly above. That mattered little, as clear instructions from the Master Bomber kept the attack on track and brought the bombers down to below the cloud, where the red TIs were clearly visible. The 106 Squadron crews bombed from 2,500 to 6,000 feet between 21.03 and 21.12 and observed the attack to be accurate, but no photographs were taken because of the low-level aspect of the operation. PRU photos, however, confirmed that the embankment had been breached again, and a section of the canal had drained, and there were many complimentary comments concerning the performance of the Master Bomber.

In contrast, his opposite number at Gravenhorst was accused of causing confusion by issuing contradictory instructions, despite which, post-raid reconnaissance revealed that the canal had been breached over a distance of fifty feet on the western bank, south of the road bridge, and had been drained over a thirty-mile stretch to leave fifty-nine vessels stranded and damaged by direct hits. Reconnaissance at Ladbergen revealed success also, showing the left-hand channel, which was the only one repaired since the last attack, to have been breached again where it crossed the River Glane, the inability of which to cope with the volume of water released had led to extensive flooding on both sides of the canal. The two operations were concluded for the loss of just two 49 Squadron Lancasters. The Germans recognized that repairing the canals was an open invitation to Bomber Command to return, and, so vital were they to the transportation system, that they could not be abandoned. The answer was to complete repairs, but to leave the sections drained and apparently still under repair, until sufficient traffic had built up to push through in one night. They would then be flooded and re-emptied to dupe RAF reconnaissance flights and maintain the deception.

On the following night, 5 Group dispatched 171 Lancasters and seven Mosquitos to attack the U-Boot pens at Trondheim in Norway, a straight-line distance from Metheringham of some eight hundred miles. 106 Squadron launched fourteen Lancasters into the air between 15.50 and 16.15 with F/Ls Barden and Pritchard the senior pilots on duty, and all arrived in the target area some five-and-a-half hours later to find clear skies and excellent visibility. However, an effective smoke screen prevented the marker force from finding the aiming point, and the Master Bomber had no option but to send the force home, where they arrived between 01.30 and 03.05 after more than ten hours aloft. They were probably on their way to bed when a further six 106 Squadron crews took off at 04.50 to join others in laying mines in the Rosemary garden in Heligoland Bay. F/L Marks found ten-tenths cloud in the target area, but good horizontal visibility, and, using H2S, made an eleven-mile run north from the western tip of Wangerooge Island, before releasing six mines from 12,000 feet at 06.40. Within minutes of each other, their Metheringham colleagues had carried out similar runs of varying distances from the same height to leave a chain of mines across the important sea lane, and all returned without major incident. Later, on the 23rd, awards of the DFC were announced to F/Os Thompson, Harris, Browne Kitto, Fyson and Archer, and W/O Carmichael.

The weather was mainly responsible for curtailing operations over the next few days until the 26th, when briefings took place on 5 Group stations at 20.00. The record twenty-three attending 106 Squadron crews learned that Munich was to be their target for an all-5 Group affair involving 270 Lancasters and eight Mosquitos, which represented a maximum effort. They departed Metheringham between 23.35 and 00.05 with S/L Parry the senior pilot on duty, undertaking the final sortie of his tour, and each Lancaster carrying a 4,000lb cookie and thirteen SBCs of 4lb Nº14 "J" cluster bombs. Forming up and climbing to operational altitude was a time-consuming business, and it would be five hours before the target was reached, while, in the meantime, isolated aircraft turned back, although none from Metheringham. The target area was found to be under clear skies with good visibility, and crews confirmed their positions by means of H2S before beginning their bombing runs. Aside from one errant red TI, the low-level Mosquito marking was accurate, and the Master Bomber ensured that the crews focused upon the reds and greens on and close to the planned aiming point, calling on some to carry out a twenty-two second overshoot. The 106 Squadron crews bombed from 15,000 to 17,600 feet between 05.00 and 05.06, and all returned safely with reports of a successful operation. F/O Vallance and crew brought back an aiming point photo, to go with many others plotted within two miles, and other returning crews praised the quality of the route, the target marking and the performance of the Master Bomber. They reported smoke rising through 18,000 feet as they turned away, and fires visible for a hundred miles into the return flight. The confidence in a concentrated and effective attack was justified, when post-raid reconnaissance confirmed it as such, and a local report singled out railway installations as being particularly hard-hit. The squadron ORB made much of what had, perhaps, been the squadron's most outstanding operation of the war, in which all twenty-three crews had reached and bombed the target as briefed and returned safely home.

Thereafter, other elements of the Command carried out heavy and destructive attacks on Freiburg and Neuss on the 27/28th, Essen on the 28/29th and Duisburg on the 30th. 106 Squadron operated on seven nights and two days during the month, dispatching 169 sorties for the loss of two aircraft and crews. This was the second month in succession that the squadron had operated without a single early return.

December 1944

There were no operations for 5 Group for the first three nights of the new month, largely because of the weather, and, in the meantime, 1, 4, 6 and 8 Groups pounded the Ruhr town of Hagen on the night of the 2/3rd. Worthwhile targets were becoming more and more scarce at a time when the Command was at its most powerful, and this final period of the war would bring the most devastating attacks to date on the German homeland. 5 Group returned to action in the early evening of the 4th, to target the city of Heilbronn, situated thirty miles due north of Stuttgart, which had the River Neckar and a north-south rail link running through it, but, otherwise, was of no genuine strategic importance, and would not have been expecting to be attacked. 106 Squadron made ready twenty-two Lancasters as part of a record 5 Group force of 282 of the type and ten Mosquitos. The main operation on this night was actually by 535 aircraft of 1, 6 and 8 Groups at Karlsruhe, some fifty-six miles west-south-west of Heilbronn, and the concentration of aircraft in this area would be certain to bring out the night-fighters. The 106 Squadron element departed Metheringham between 16.30 and 16.50 with F/Ls Barden, Daniel and Marks the senior pilots on duty, and, with no early returns to reduce their number, they made their way across France in good conditions to find three to five-tenths thin stratus over the target at around 12,000 feet. The aiming points were the marshalling yards and the town, which were illuminated by the flare force ahead of the low-level Mosquitos' run to drop red TIs for the visual markers to back up. The marshalling yards were marked with yellows, which the main force element was unable to distinguish in the burgeoning fires, and this persuaded them to focus on the town instead. F/O J N Scott, one of two pilots of that name serving with the squadron, and his crew had just started their bombing run when engaged by a night-fighter, which attacked six times and forced them off track and beyond the target. Too late to turn back, they jettisoned their cookie and incendiaries two miles south-west of the target and turned for home. The other 106 Squadron crews bombed on red TIs from 10,500 to 11,500 feet between 19.30 and 19.38, contributing to the 1,200 tons of bombs raining down onto the target and adding to the general destruction. As the force retreated westwards into electrical storms, 82% of the city's built-up area was in the process of being destroyed by what probably amounted to a firestorm. It cost 5 Group twelve aircraft, including 106 Squadron's PB281, which came down near the target with fatal consequences for all but the rear gunner in the crew of F/O Thompson, who, with the exception of the flight engineer, were all members of the RAAF. F/O Dodson and crew were attacked by a Ju88, which the gunners claimed as destroyed. The post-war British Bombing Survey estimated 351 acres of destruction, and a death toll of at least seven thousand people.

The town of Giessen was 5 Group's objective on a night of heavy Bomber Command activity on the 6/7th. Other operations centred on the oil refinery at Leuna (Merseburg), which was the target for 475 Lancasters of 1, 3 and 8 Groups, while 450 aircraft from predominantly 4 and 6 Groups attacked railway installations at Osnabrück, north of the Ruhr. 106 Squadron briefed twenty crews as part of an overall 5 Group heavy force of 255 Lancasters, and they set off from Metheringham between 17.05 and 17.25 with F/L Daniel the senior pilot on duty, and each Lancaster carrying a dozen 1,000 pounders. Their destination lay some eighty-five miles south-east of Cologne in west-central Germany, and thirty-five miles north of Frankfurt, and all but one of the 106 Squadron element made it all the way, after F/O Hamilton and crew were forced to turn back with an unserviceable rear turret. The others found varying amounts of cloud in the target area at between three and seven-tenths, but visibility was good, and the target indicators clearly visible. The main force crews had been assigned to two aiming points, two-thirds of them to the town, and the remainder to the marshalling yards, and, although the flare force began illuminating three minutes early and to the west of the target, the Mosquito-laid red TIs fell close to the aiming points, and the Master Bomber ensured that they were backed up by greens. The 106 Squadron crews carried out their attacks on the marshalling yards in accordance with instructions from the Master Bomber from 9,000 to 10,800 feet between 20.18 and 20.26, and all returned safely to report another successful raid. Returning crews spoke of large fires, and F/Os Norton, Scott and Simpson brought back aiming point photos, while several others were plotted within a short distance. Reconnaissance confirmed later that both aiming points had sustained severe damage at a cost of eight Lancasters.

The Urft Dam was one of a number of similar structures in the beautiful Eifel region of western Germany, close to the Belgian frontier. There was a fear that the enemy might strategically release flood water to hamper the American advance into Germany, and it was decided to attempt to breach the dam, to allow any excess water to drain away. The first of a number of attacks on the region began on the 3rd at Heimbach, the small town nestling against the northern reaches of the reservoir, but the 1 and 8 Group force failed to identify it, and no bombs fell. On the following day, a small 8 Group effort against the dam was unsuccessful, as was a 3 Group attack on the nearby Schwammenauel dam on the 5th. The job was handed to 5 Group on the 8th, for which a force of 205 Lancasters was made ready, fourteen of them by 106 Squadron and nineteen from 617 Squadron, the latter carrying Tallboys. The Metheringham element took off in a sleet storm between 09.00 and 09.15 with F/L Barden the senior pilot on duty and all reached the target to be greeted by six to nine-tenths cloud at between 6,000 and 8,000 feet and moderate visibility, which partially obscured the aiming point for some as they ran in to bomb. Eleven of the 106 Squadron crews caught glimpses of the target through gaps in the cloud and delivered their fourteen 1,000 pounders each from 8,000 to 11,500 feet between 11.04 and 11.20, while three others returned their loads to store. The conditions were too marginal for the 617 Squadron element, and they returned home with their valuable Tallboys still on board. 129 aircraft did release their bombs before the Master Bomber called a halt to proceedings, but the attack was scattered and the dam escaped damage. The weather remained bad in Lincolnshire, forcing many crews to divert to airfields in the south, like Ford, but not so at Metheringham, where the 106 Squadron element managed to land without issue. P/O

Phelan RCAF and F/L Barden brought back aiming point photos, and a number of others were plotted within two thousand yards.

The conditions had prevented any assessment of results, which meant that another attempt on the dam would be necessary, and preparations were put in hand on the 10th to return with a force of 217 Lancasters. 106 Squadron launched fifteen of its own between 04.25 and 04.45 on a cold and frosty morning, but the entire force was recalled before it reached the English coast. Like a dog with a bone, 5 Group would not leave the Urft dam alone, and assembled a force of 233 Lancasters and a Mosquito for an early morning take-off on the 11th to join five 8 Group Mosquitos at the target. In the event, take-off was postponed until early afternoon, when the fifteen 106 Squadron participants departed Metheringham between 12.30 and 12.45 with F/Ls Barden and Bretherton the senior pilots on duty. They met icing conditions at the French coast, and found that the weather in the target area was hardly an improvement on the previous day, with up to nine-tenths cloud topping out at 8,000 feet making life difficult for the Master Bomber. He tried to bring the crews down to below the cloud base, and some complied, while others were able to identify the aiming point through a four-mile-long gap. Twelve of those from Metheringham were able to carry out an attack with fourteen 1,000 pounders from 4,000 to 7,500 feet between 14.59 and 15.02, while three others were thwarted by the conditions. Bombs were observed to detonate on the stepped apron in front of the dam wall, and aiming point photos were obtained by F/Os Arnot RAAF and Hamilton, with most of the others plotted within a mile. Reconnaissance confirmed some hits on the dam and much cratering of the surrounding area, but no actual breach.

The award of a DFC was announced on the 12th to the now departed S/L Allinson and to F/Os Netherwood and Coen. The final heavy night raid of the war on Essen was carried out by 540 aircraft from 1, 4 and 8 Groups on the 12/13th, and was sufficiently accurate to be complimented by Albert Speer in his diaries. Centred upon the Krupp complex, the attack inflicted severe industrial damage and also destroyed almost seven hundred houses, while damaging thirteen hundred more.

On the following night, a 54 Base force of fifty-two Lancasters and seven Mosquitos from 106, 83, 97 and 627 Squadrons was dispatched to attack a German light cruiser, Emden according to the squadron ORB, while other sources stated that it was the Köln at berth at Horten in Oslo Fjord. Both vessels were present in the area at the time, having been deployed as part of the Kriegsmarine's Baltic mine-laying force. 106 Squadron supported the operation with twenty Lancasters, which took off between 15.30 and 15.45 with F/Ls Bretherton and Marks the senior pilots on duty, to act as the main force element, each carrying eleven 1,000 pounders. They reached the target to find cloudless conditions and good visibility, but the target vessel could not be identified, possibly because it had been moved to a new location. Nine crews withheld their bombs after failing to positively identify the vessel, but eleven others bombed by the light of flares from 7,000 to 9,000 feet between 19.03 and 19.18 in accordance with the raid controller's instructions. Some crews aimed at ships moored off Bluecher Quay, but no results were observed, and all of the participants returned safely home. F/O Stanfield brought back a photo of a cruiser, which was presumed to be the target vessel, lying just north of Ostoya, an island a short distance to the north of Horten.

The main operation on the night of the 15/16th was directed at Ludwigshafen in southern Germany, home to a number of I G Farben factories, which, as mentioned a number of times before, were major and brutal employers of slave workers in the production of synthetic oil and other products. The attack by elements of 1, 6 and 8 Groups was highly destructive, and had a greater effect on synthetic oil production at this plant than any previous raid. 106 Squadron was the only 5 Group unit active on this night, providing fifteen Lancasters for a mining effort in the Spinach garden off the port of Gdynia in Danzig Bay. They departed Metheringham between 00.25 and 00.45 with F/Ls Bretherton and Daniel the senior pilots on duty, and each Lancaster carrying either five Mk IV or four Mk VI mines. F/O Anderson and crew turned back with a dead engine and a number of other equipment failures, leaving the remainder to arrive in the target area to find ten-tenths cloud with tops averaging out at 15,000 feet. Using H2S, thirteen crews located their drop zones and successfully delivered their stores from 14,000 to 17,500 feet between 05.06 and 05.41. ND682 failed to return to Metheringham after crashing in the Baltic, and there were no survivors from the crew of F/O Barratt. It is interesting to note that the rear gunner, Sgt Green, was thirty-nine years old, and well beyond the normal age of aircrew. It was later that morning, that German ground forces began a new offensive in the Ardennes, in an attempt to break through the American lines and reach the port of Antwerp in what would become known as the Battle of the Bulge.

Munich had become something of a 5 Group preserve during the year, and a further operation against it was planned for the night of the 17/18th, which would turn out to be another night of heavy Bomber Command activity. The main raid was to be by more than five hundred aircraft, predominantly of 4 and 6 Groups, at Duisburg, while 1 Group targeted Ulm with over three hundred Lancasters, leaving 5 Group to send 280 Lancasters some seventy miles beyond to the Bavarian capital city. 106 Squadron briefed thirteen crews, while their Lancasters were being prepared for the 1,300-mile round-trip, and they departed Metheringham between 16.30 and 16.50 with W/C Stevens the senior pilot on duty. They crossed the French coast near Berck-sur-Mer, and reached the target to find generally clear skies and good visibility, which the marker crews exploited. The red and green TIs fell with accuracy and concentration upon the city-centre and marshalling yards aiming points, and the Metheringham crews bombed a cluster of red TIs with a twenty-three-second overshoot from 11,000 to 12,000 feet between 22.00 and 22.10 in accordance with instructions from the Master Bomber, who declared himself satisfied with the results. F/O Newenham and crew failed to deliver an attack after arriving too late. The resultant fires were visible from a hundred miles into the return journey, and, while, as usual, no local report was available to confirm or deny, the Command claimed severe and widespread damage to the city.

On the following night, it was the turn of the distant Baltic port of Gdynia to play host to 5 Group, for which 106 Squadron made ready fourteen Lancasters in an overall force of 236 of the type. The intention was to catch elements of the German fleet at anchor, in particular the Lützow, and also to destroy harbour installations, as well as cause damage within the town. *(The original Lützow was actually never completed, and was sold to the Russian navy in 1940 as a hull minus superstructure. The pocket battleship, Deutschland, was renamed Lützow, to avoid humiliation for the nation should she be lost in battle.)* While this operation was in progress, fourteen other Lancasters of 5 Group were to sneak in under cover of the main activity to deliver mines to the Privet and Spinach gardens in Danzig (Gdansk) Bay. A dozen of the 106 Squadron crews were briefed to attack the shipping, aiming point A, while the crews of F/Os Arnott and Stanfield were to focus on the Lützow, aiming point B, and all reached the target area after an outward flight of almost five hours to find clear skies and good visibility. As was usually the practise, the initial identification was by H2S, but the harbour and town could be picked out visually until a smoke screen was activated. The illumination and marking proceeded according to plan, and the 106 Squadron crews delivered their eight 1,000 pounders each on red and green TIs from 11,000 to 14,000 feet between 21.58 and 22.13 in accordance with the Master Bomber's instructions, and in the face of intense light flak. The smoke screen eventually obscured the Lützow, and crews with bombs still to deliver turned their attention to the port area and town. It was not possible to make an accurate assessment of results, but F/Os Arnott and Stanfield brought back aiming point photos of the Lützow, and there were aiming point A photos from the crews of Capt Pechey and F/O Newenham. Reconnaissance confirmed that damage had been inflicted upon shipping, port installations and residential property in the waterfront districts, at a cost of four Lancasters. Sadly, the squadron's NN726 was one of those failing to return after being brought down in the target area. F/L Pritchard was killed with four of his crew, while both gunners escaped with their lives to be taken into captivity.

Thick fog kept the crews on the ground on the 20th, and threatened to do so also on the 21st, but an operation was called on the basis that the weather over Scotland after midnight would be clear for returning aircraft, even if Lincolnshire remained fogbound. In briefing rooms across southern and south-eastern Lincolnshire, crews learned that their target would require them to retrace their recent steps to Germany's eastern Baltic region, although the Wintershall oil refinery at Politz, situated fewer than ten miles north of the port of Stettin, was some two hundred miles short of their trip to Gdynia. *(This location is often wrongly spelled Pölitz, which is a town in Germany's Schleswig-Holstein region at the western end of the Baltic.)* A force of 207 Lancasters and a single Mosquito was assembled, and, unusually, it included an element from 617 Squadron carrying Tallboys. 106 Squadron did not take part in the main operation, but sent two Lancasters to a railway junction at Schneidemühl (believed to lie between Berlin and Stettin) as a diversion, and ten others to lay mines in the Silverthorn III garden in the Kattegat. The crews of F/L Gilbert and F/O Scott took off in thick fog at 16.35 and 16.55 respectively, and found their way to the target area, where they arrived some three-and-a-half hours later to deliver four 1,000 and seven 500 pounders each from 15,000 feet.

The gardeners had been led away by W/C Stevens between 16.45 and 17.15, by which time only a quarter of the length of the runway was visible through the murk. They found ten-tenths cloud in the target area with tops at 8,000 feet, which was not a problem as they were delivering their Mk VI mines from medium-level by means of H2S. W/C Stevens and crew, however, having flown all the way to the waters off eastern Demark, found their H2S to be malfunctioning, and jettisoned the stores "safe". The others all successfully pinpointed on Sejerø island before dropping their vegetables from 10,000 to 12,000 feet between 20.30 and 21.13, and were diverted to Banff and Dallachy in Scotland on return. Meanwhile, the main 5 Group element had located the Wintershall plant under clear skies but with ground haze, which may have been a smoke screen, and found the highly important war-industry asset to be protected by around fifty searchlights. Heavy flak accompanied the Lancasters as they ran in on the red and green TIs, which had fallen some two thousand yards north-north-west of the plant, a situation recognized by the Master Bomber, but he was unable to persuade the backers-up to shift the point of aim accordingly, and most of the bombing would miss the mark. Fires remained visible for almost a hundred miles into the return journey, at the end of which, tired crews were faced with fogbound airfields and five aircraft were involved in crashes. The oil plant had been damaged but not destroyed, and it would be necessary to mount further raids.

The final wartime Christmas period was celebrated on 5 Group stations undisturbed by operational activity between the 22nd and Boxing Day, which was not necessarily the case for the other groups. The peace came to an end on the 26th, when three hundred crews from all groups were roused from any resulting stupor to attend briefings for operations against enemy troop positions at St Vith in Belgium. The German advance towards Antwerp had run out of steam after its earlier successes, and, starved of fuel and ammunition, it was now attempting to withdraw back into Germany. 5 Group contributed twenty-six Lancasters to the force of 296 aircraft for the first joint operation since October, and the crews found the target to be under clear skies with visibility sufficiently good to enable them to identify the aiming point visually by a red TI. When this became obscured by smoke, the Master Bomber ordered them to descend to 10,000 feet and bomb the upwind edge of the smoke, and all indications suggested the attack to be well concentrated and effective.

53 Base was called into action on the 27th, to provide aircraft for a daylight attack on marshalling yards at Rheydt, for a which a force of two hundred Lancasters and eleven Mosquitos was drawn from 1, 3, 5 and 8 Groups. The target was found to be under clear skies, and the aiming point could be identified visually, although red and green TIs marked it out to provide a more solid reference. The attack took

place under the control of a Master Bomber and was well concentrated, but no explosions or fires were reported, and, it seems, there was no post-raid reconnaissance. A 5 Group force of sixty-seven Lancasters was made ready on the 28th to target shipping, specifically the light cruiser Köln, at Horten in Oslo Fjord. The target area was reached after an outward flight of four-and-a-half hours, and conditions were relatively clear and the visibility good, but a thin layer of alto-cumulus cloud at between 15,000 and 20,000 feet reduced the brightness of the moonlight and cast deceptive shadows on the water to prevent a clear identification of the target. The aiming point was marked by Wanganui flares, but most crews followed the Master Bomber's instructions after establishing their own reference point. A patch of light flak to the north-east of the harbour mole was thought to be concealing a large naval unit, and this area was marked and bombed. Some crews would claim to have attacked a large vessel moving from this area in a southerly direction, and other shipping in the harbour, all in the face of intense shipboard and shore-based light flak. No direct hits were claimed and the operation produced inconclusive results.

Following its long absence from operations, 106 Squadron was also active on this night, the ORB making the point that it was the first time for a week that both sides of the airfield had been visible at the same time. Eleven crews were briefed for mining duties in the Baltic, five for the Silverthorn VI garden and six for Yew Tree, respectively to the east of Anholt island and between Læsø island and the northern coast of Jutland. They departed Metheringham between 19.20 and 19.50 with W/C Stevens the senior pilot on duty, and located their target areas without difficulty in ideal conditions, those in the Silverthorn garden pinpointing on the eastern tip of Anholt Island, while, some sixty miles across the freezing water to the north-west, the port of Frederikshavn provided the reference for the timed runs. They delivered between them a total of sixty-five mines by H2S from 13,900 to 14,600 feet in a thirty-minute slot to 00.02, before returning safely home.

A dozen 106 Squadron crews were called to briefing late on the 30th to learn that they were to be part of a 5 Group force of 154 Lancasters and thirteen Mosquitos to attack an enemy supply line at Houffalize in the Ardennes region of Belgium. They took off between 02.25 and 02.40 with F/Ls Bretherton and Gilbert the senior pilots on duty, and found the target area to be under five to seven-tenths stratus cloud at 5,000 to 6,000 feet, with another layer of eight-tenths with tops at 9,000 feet, all of which made identification very difficult. The marking was punctual and accurate, but the red TIs were observed only by a proportion of the crews, who chanced upon a gap in the clouds directly over the aiming point. Five of the 106 Squadron participants bombed from 9,000 to 11,500 feet between 05.00 and 05.04, but seven others were unable to establish the location of the aiming point and aborted their sorties. A number of crews in the force descended to below the cloud base and confirmed that the bombing was concentrated around the markers, but it would be deemed necessary to revisit this objective within a short time.

During the course of the month the squadron carried out operations on two days and ten nights, and dispatched 184 sorties for the loss of three aircraft and crews. Confidence was high that the New Year would bring the long-awaited victory, although no one knew how long the resistance of the tenacious enemy would last. What could be confidently stated, however, was that the Command had risen phoenix-like from the dark days of Berlin, and had contributed magnificently to the success of the land campaign, while maintaining a stranglehold on Germany's capacity to produce vital munitions and fuel stuffs.

Before and after - Gnome et Rhône Factory, Paris on 9/10th May 1944

Sgt R Bradley was shot down on 26/27th April 1944 on a raid on Schweinfurt. He was the only survivor and became a PoW. Crew who died: Pilot S/L Anthony Murdoch, Sgt Henry Clark, P/O William Collins, F/Sgt William Evans, Sgt Ernest Hatch, Sgt Leonard Izod, Sgt John Rees.

106 Squadron Metheringham July August 1944. S/L Grindon and crew
L-R: Sgt P J Hollands (FE), Sgt J Painting RCAF (RG), F/O G L Mortiboys (BA), W/C J E Grindon, Sgt J Pappin RCAF (MUG), Sgt R E Holding (W.Op), Sgt J Swaffield (Nav).

Crew of F/O F.C.W. Clement. August 1944

Ground crew huts at dispersal, Metheringham 1944.

Bombardment of Gilze Rijen air base August 1944 by 106 Squadron

A villager cutting the rubber from wheel of Lancaster JB601
(For making shoes and clothes)

F/O Louis Steylaerts   *F/O Elmer Aaron RCAF*
Both killed in Lancaster LL891 on Salbris operation 8th May 1944

G/C Maurice Heath with WAAF's of Administration group

P/O E Holbourn   *Sgt H V Walmsley*   *F/Sgt S R Mattick DFM*

Sgt E N Burton   Sgt T T Powell   Sgt J H Dyer   Sgt T H Mallett
All killed 2nd January 1944 on a Berlin raid in Lancaster JB645 ZN-F.

Photoflash taken over the target from the Holbourn crew's Lancaster DV272 during a raid on Kassel 3/4th October 1943.   *German type VII and IX U-boats at Trondheim, Norway. (1945)*

P/O Don Evans leaving for overseas (Garth Evans)

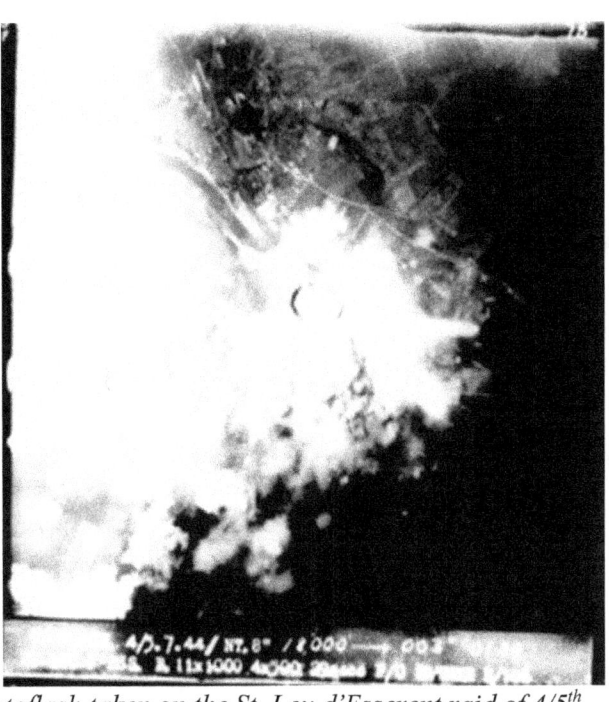
Photoflash taken on the St. Leu d'Esserent raid of 4/5th July 1944 from Lancaster ME789 flown by Gordon Mather and crew.

Aerial photograph showing the entrances to the subterranean tunnels at St. Leu d'Esserent, north of Paris, which were used by the Germans to store flying bombs. An accurate attack by aircraft mainly from 5 Group on the 7/8th July 1944, succeeded in causing a landslide which blocked the entrances.

The bomb bay of a Lancaster loaded with 4000lb blast bomb or 'Cookie' and 2832 4lb incendiary bombs contained in 12 small bomb containers.

AVM Sir Ralph Cochrane

ACM Sir Arthur Harris

Dortmund Ems Canal – Before and After

12,000lb HC bomb first used by 617 Squadron on Dortmund-Ems Canal

*Celebrating the end of a tour with a bottle of beer -
F/O Victor Cole and his crew on the 21st January 1944 after returning from Magdeburg.*

Crew of F/O Jack Netherwood
Back row: Glen Hendrey (BA), Al Parisani (MUG), Len Lucas (W/Op).
Front row: Bill Lloyd (RG), Jack Netherwood (Pilot), and Harry Winter (Nav).

Lancaster ND331 30th August 1944. The Boivin crew.
Crashed on 30th August 1944 while raiding Konigsberg. Those crew who were not taken prisoner are remembered on the Runnymede Memorial to the Missing.
Sgt E G L Parker(KIA), F/Sgt R H McLean KIA, ?Sgt A Hargill KIA, ?Sgt J P Nicol (PoW)
?Sgt S Bell (PoW), F/O L C W Boivin KIA, Sgt W S Bryson KIA.

Sgt J J Kearney   *The Futcher Crash Site, France*

P/O S M Futcher, Sgt R Bentley, Sgt A Bradley, Sgt J J Kearney, F/O W H C Ramsay, F/Sgt F H Stokeld were all killed when Lancaster ME832 crashed on the 4/5th July 1944. F/Sgt O J McNaughton survived and was taken into captivity.

(Photo Regis Biaux - Aerosteles)
Memorial to the Futcher Crew at the crash site at Saint-Germain-la-Poterie.

106 Squadron Lancaster ND339 'Admiral Shyte-Awke II'
F/O W R P (Bill) Perry

F/L Stewart with two ground crew

Crew of F/L (acting S/L) Arthur Barden

Lancaster JB663 ZN-A 'King of the Air'

Lancaster PB303 ZN-R F/O G.J. Symes & crew all KIA. Aircraft going down 1st November 1944
F/O George Jeffrey Symes RCAF, Sgt Alfred Harris, F/Sgt Cyril Ernest Bayliss, F/O John Arthur Smith, F/O Leslie W Perry, Sgt John Anthony Crisp, F/Sgt Clifford Eugene Leroy Cook

Crash site of Lancaster PD214 ZN-D. 6th October 1944
Crew killed -F/L J C Barlow RAAF (2nd pilot), F/L D Stewart, (Pilot), Sgt R P Barton, (F/E), F/Sgt Kirby, G B, RAF (Nav), P/O C J Service, RCAF (BA), Sgt G S Grogan, (WOp/AG), F/Sgt J Fell, (MUG), Sgt R J Paul (RG).

Raid on Mailly-le-camp.

Badly damaged Lancaster returns from Mailly-le-camp raid (Not 106 Squadron)

A low flying Lancaster is seen through the glare of a burning Mailly-le-Camp

Heavily-laden Avro Lancaster B Mark IIIs of 106 Squadron RAF taxi from their dispersals to the runway at Metheringham, Lincolnshire, for take-off on a raid to Frankfurt, Germany. The resulting attack on 22/23rd March 1944 caused extensive destruction to eastern, central and western districts of the city, including the Opera House.

Target photograph of industrial area top right with roads and buildings. Submitted with description 'Target photo of the Signa aero engine works, Lyons, taken 25/26th March 1944. The pilot was W/C E K Piercy, 106 Squadron's newly-appointed Commanding Officer'.

Focke-Wulf Plant in the Hemelingen district of Bremen

U-Boot Pens Brest

Above and below: F/O Richardson and Crew

Darmstadt after the 11/12th Setpember 1944 raid.

G/C W N Mcechnie (right) and crew.
All seven crew members on board Lancaster JB593 ZN-T died after it was shot down in the Konigsberg area of Germany on 30th August 1944. Crew: G/C W.N.McKechnie, Sgt R.B.Clarke, F/Sgt H.W.T.Carter RCAF, F/O E.E.Fletcher, Sgt C.C.Jeffrey, Sgt D.Forster, F/Sgt E.L.Collins

Group Captain William Neil McKechnie GC

Flak battery, 88mm with crew, France, 1944.

Railway mounted flak battery on the coast. The white rings around the barrels of the main guns represent eleven RAF bombers claimed shot down by this battery. Wellington, a sterling six six Halifax's and three Lancasters.

Damage to the SNCA aircraft factory at Chateauoux/Deols airfield. 10/11th March 1944.

View inside the tram terminus at Dusseldorf, Germany, wrecked as a result of repeated Bomber Command raids on the city in 1943 and 1944.

F/L Ian Harvey,

F/O Philip George navigator

Crew of W/C E K Piercy. Third left PO Philip George (Nav)

Maisy Coastal Battery Command Bunker attacked 31st May 1944.

F/O Freddie Mifflin, 106 Squadron pilot in 1943-44

F/O Freddie Mifflin tragically died when his Lancaster was shot down leaving the target area at Schweinfurt. His flight engineer, Sgt Norman Jackson, (below right, with G/C Leonard Cheshire) received the VC for climbing out onto the wing of their burning Lancaster in an attempt to extinguish the flames, in what was one of Bomber Command's most famous episodes. G/C Cheshire was also the recipient of the Victoria Cross for sustained gallantry in the course of 102 operations.

106 Squadron Metheringham January 1944. De-briefing with P/O F Mifflin
F/Sgt F Higgins, F/Sgt M H Toft, F/Sgt N Johnson, F/Sgt E Sandelands F/O F Mifflin

Hookes crew 1944-45.

F/L James Fee   *Mother Philomena and son Joseph Ophoven 1944*

On the 19th September 1944, James Fee was pilot of Lancaster PB359. As he was running in to bomb the target at Rheydt, the aircraft was attacked by a night fighter. With the whole of the port wing on fire, Jim gave the order to bale out. He landed just to the east of Monchengladbach. and set off walking towards Holland. Jim reached the River Roer on 24th September where he was shot in the hip by a German soldier. The wound was a gaping hole, exposing bone. He managed to reach an isolated farmhouse to ask if he was in Holland. An old lady quickly took him inside, fed him and sent for Doctor Staapert who supplied him with a false identity His assistant, Lenie Peters visited the house many times to tend to his wound. These four people risked their own lives to shelter Jim as German troops regularly came to the house to search for radios and food. The underground also called in regularly trying to arrange an escape route. Jim was hidden by the Ophovens for four months until January 1945 when he was picked up by a unit of the armoured division of the British Army.

S/L A G Williams and crew
Back L-R: A H Horry, P A Morgan, Lloyd, H High
Front L-R: A B Waff, S/L Ailliams, R C Harvey

106 Squadron Lancaster JB601 ZN-V shot down by a Me 109 on the way to Schweinfurt 26/27th April 1944 in France. The pilot S/L A D Murdoch (below) was killed.

106 Squadron Lancaster PB248. Shattered H2S blister and turret

106 Squadron Metheringham YMCA Tea Van – Driver Ann

Clermont Ferrand – Michelin Factory raid 16/17th March 1944

Urft Dam – Attacked December 1944 (David Fell)

Crew of F/O D.W Meredith. July 1944

F/O PJ Richards pictured after a raid and celebrating being awarded a DFC

Wetton Crew

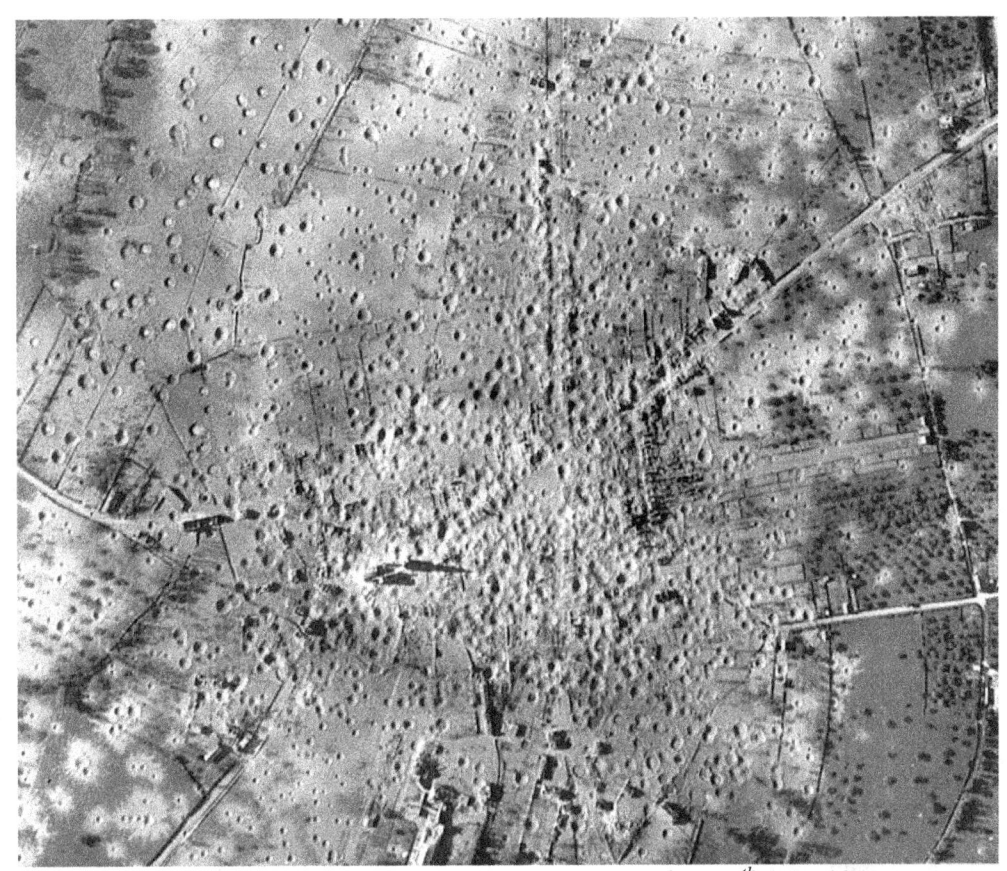
Aerial photo during the bombing of Aunay-sur-Odon, 14th June 1944

A reconnaissance photograph showing some of the severe damage to the Bergerac Powder works, Angoulême. (Crown Copyright)

Above and below - Bergen U-Boot pens
A major attack was carried out on 29th October 1944 and saw almost 250 RAF aircraft involved, though less than 50 eventually found and bombed the target. During this raid, Lancaster bomber ND332, was hit by AA shells and crashed in Store Lungegårdsvann after dropping its bombs over Nøstet causing a lot of destruction.

January 1945

The final year of the war began with a flourish, as the Luftwaffe launched its ill-conceived and, ultimately, ill-fated, Operation Bodenplatte (Baseplate) at first light on New Year's Day. The intention to destroy the Allied air forces on the ground at the recently liberated airfields in France, Holland and Belgium was only modestly realized, and it cost the German day fighter force around 250 aircraft. Many of the pilots were killed, wounded or fell into Allied hands, and it was a setback from which the Tagjagd would never fully recover, while the Allies could make good their losses within hours from their enormous stockpiles.

5 Group was also active that morning, having roused the crews early from their beds to attend briefings for an attack on the embankments of the recently repaired Dortmund-Ems Canal near Ladbergen, for which 102 Lancasters and two Mosquitos were made ready. 106 Squadron loaded ten Lancasters with the appropriate canal-busting ironware, namely a dozen 1,000 pounders and a single delay-fused 500 pounder, and dispatched them between 07.50 and 08.10 with F/L Daniel the senior pilot on duty. The 54 Base squadrons from Coningsby and Metheringham fell in line behind 83 Squadron, with the 55 Base squadrons from East Kirkby, Spilsby and Strubby about three miles further back, and a third section, made up of 53 Base units from Waddington, Skellingthorpe and Bardney some twenty miles to the rear. The last-mentioned were allowed to catch up, putting the force two minutes behind schedule at point C over the North Sea. It was between points C and D that the fighter escort was expected to join them, and, although it was not immediately apparent, it did eventually put in an appearance. Lt Howes SAAF and crew turned back after the port-inner engine failed, making it impossible for them to maintain height and keep pace with the rest of the stream. The others maintained their positions in the gaggle, which held together fairly well, although the controller would complain later that the legs were too short to keep the gaggle tight, and some aircraft were seen to break formation. When about eight minutes from the target, smoke from a Mosquito-laid red TI could be seen, which was assessed as being on the southern tip of the island between the two branches of the canal. It was clearly visible to all crews, who were able to home in on it without difficulty. A six-gun flak battery greeted their arrival with accurate salvoes, but this did not inhibit the bombing runs, and the 106 Squadron crews carried out their attacks from 11,000 to 11,550 feet between 11.16 and 11.18, aiming at the aqueduct section or the raised embankments. On return, a number of crews complained that the gaggle was too tight and put crews at risk from "friendly" bombs. The impression was of an effective operation, the use of delay fuses having prevented an immediate assessment of the results, but eight aiming point photos were brought back to Metheringham, and photo-reconnaissance revealed later, that the canal had been breached again, and the surrounding fields had become flooded. It was during this operation that an heroic F/Sgt Thompson of 9 Squadron earned the award of the Victoria Cross, although sadly, it would have to be conferred posthumously, after he succumbed to his burns three weeks later.

Operations on this day for 5 Group were not yet done, as it now had an appointment with the Mittelland Canal at Gravenhorst, for which 152 Lancasters and five Mosquitos were made ready. 106 Squadron dispatched nine Lancasters between 16.55 and 17.00 with W/C Stevens the senior pilot on duty, and all reached the target area to find that the clear conditions enjoyed during the morning raid nearby, had persisted, and so accurate were the initial TIs and illumination delivered visually or by H2S, that the third flare force was not required and was sent home. The main force was called in ahead of H-Hour at around 19.10, and the 106 Squadron element bombed on red TIs from 9,300 to 11,800 feet between 19.13 and 19.16, claiming good results, although an accurate assessment could not be made as most of the bombs contained delay fuses. Bad weather at Metheringham caused a diversion to northern stations on return either side of midnight, and when the photos were plotted, seven were found to be of the aiming point. One of the perils of operating on New Year's Day was the risk of falling victim to trigger-happy American flak gunners, who had been spooked by the German raids at dawn, and now fired at anything that moved. Sadly, a number of RAF aircraft and crews would be lost in such "friendly fire" incidents. A highly successful operation was confirmed later by photo-reconnaissance.

5 Group remained on the ground when Nuremberg and Ludwigshafen were raided by large forces on the night of the 2/3rd, and both operations were hugely destructive. A controversial attack was planned against the small French town of Royan in the early hours of the 5th, in response to requests from Free French forces, which were laying siege. Situated on the east bank at the mouth of the Gironde Estuary, it was occupied by a German garrison, and was in the way of an advance towards the port of Bordeaux. The inhabitants had been offered an opportunity by the German garrison commander to evacuate the area, but around two thousand had declined, and would suffer the consequences. 1, 5 and 8 Groups put together a force of 347 Lancasters and seven Mosquitos, of which sixteen of the former represented 106 Squadron. They departed Metheringham between 00.25 and 00.40 with the recently promoted and new A Flight commander, S/L Bretherton, the senior pilot on duty, and each Lancaster carrying a cookie and sixteen 500 pounders. 5 Group represented the spearhead of the two waves heading for the unsuspecting target, with 1 Group following on an hour to the rear, and it was approaching 04.00 as they lined up for the bombing run in cloudless skies and excellent visibility. The start of the attack was delayed for two minutes to allow misplaced markers to be corrected, but a red TI went down at 04.01 very close to the aiming point, and another fell in the middle of the town, near the beach, at which point, the Master Bomber called in the main force. The 106 Squadron crews delivered their attacks from 8,500 to 11,200 feet on Path Finder markers between 04.03 and 04.08, and witnessed an oil fire emitting volumes of black smoke and a number of large explosions, and the resultant fires would act as a distant beacon to the 1 Group force. Four Lancasters crashed after becoming involved in mid-air collisions, and F/O A H Scott's PB617 was lost in this manner after colliding with 463 Squadron's PB695 in the target area, and all fourteen men lost their lives. F/O Scott was a member of the RAAF, as were the others in his crew with the exception of the RAF flight engineer. Over fifteen hundred tons of high explosives reduced around 85% of the town to rubble, and killed an estimated 30% of the civilian inhabitants. In the event, the French forces did not capture the town until mid-April.

5 Group was not involved in a major attack on Hannover by more than 650 aircraft on the night of the 5/6th, the first on this northern city since the series in the autumn of 1943. However, a rushed battle order came through to 5 Group stations at 18.30, which would lead to another late briefing and take-off for 131 crews, and it was actually between 00.20 and 00.40 on the 6th that a dozen 106 Squadron crews departed Metheringham bound for a German supply column trapped at Houffalize in the Belgian Ardennes. There were no senior pilots on duty, but four of those taking part were members of the SAAF. F/O Bence RAAF and crew were flying south over Bedfordshire when a coolant leak ended their interest in proceedings, leaving the others to continue on their way on a clear night above low cloud, which, over the target, formed thin layers of eight to ten-tenths cover between 4,000 and 10,000 feet. The marker force crews were able to identify the aiming point visually, and the first red Mosquito-laid TIs were seen to go down close together, followed by greens at H-3. They were backed up to leave a compact group of reds and greens visible by their glow through the clouds, and the Master Bomber, who was circling at 10,000 feet, called in the main force to bomb. Eight of the 106 Squadron crews complied from 9,100 to 11,400 feet between 03.04 and 03.10, while the crews of F/O Penney and Lts Howes and Lourens were among around one-third of the force unable to establish the location of the aiming point and withheld their bombs in accordance with instructions at briefing. Afterwards, one of the marker crews descended to 3,500 feet between the cloud layers, where they saw two large columns of smoke, the source of which could not be identified. Post-raid reconnaissance confirmed that the target had been bombed with great accuracy, and the success had been gained for the loss of two Lancasters. The Hannover raid had caused

damage across the city and destroyed almost five hundred residential buildings containing 3,600 apartments.

Hanau and Neuss were the main targets on the night of the 6/7th, neither of them involving 5 Group, but twenty Lancasters were sent mining off Baltic ports, and among these were five from 106 Squadron, whose crews were assigned to the Spinach garden on the approaches to the port of Gdynia in Danzig Bay. S/L Bretherton led them away in the gathering dusk between 15.55 and 16.15, and they all arrived in the target area some four-and-a-half-hours later to find good visibility above the complete cloud cover. They located their drop zones by H2S, and each delivered five mines as briefed from 14,000 to 14,500 feet between 20.41 and 21.03, before returning safely home, in the case of F/O Laidlaw RAAF and crew, after 10¾ hours aloft.

A major operation against Munich was planned for the 7th, for which a two-wave force of 645 aircraft was drawn from all five of the Lancaster-equipped groups. 5 Group, which was unused to sharing this target, would lead the way with 213 Lancasters and three Mosquitos, leaving the second wave to follow on two hours later, the tanks of the heavy brigade containing sufficient fuel for a nine-hour round-trip. The 106 Squadron element of sixteen Lancasters departed Metheringham as darkness closed in between 16.35 and 17.15 with W/C Stevens the senior pilot on duty. F/L Barron and crew lost the use of their Loran and Gee equipment as they closed on the German frontier south-west of Strasbourg, and dropped out of the bomber stream to head home. They jettisoned their cookie "safe", but, as frequently was the case, it detonated on impact. The others pressed on to find broken medium-level cloud at 14,000 feet above the target, with haze or thin cloud below, by which time, the Master Bomber had made a visual identification of the aiming point and had sent the first two primary blind markers in to deliver their TIs at the same time thirty seconds ahead of the planned opening of the attack. The flare force followed on immediately, and illuminated the city very effectively, allowing ground detail to be identified. Red TIs went down west and east of the River Isar, bracketing the aiming point, and the Master Bomber ordered the backers-up to drop their TIs between the reds, after which, the next batch of flares formed a circle around the aiming point. The main force was then called in, and the 106 Squadron participants bombed on clusters of green TIs from 18,000 to 20,000 feet between 20.23 and 20.35. The city was seen to be burning well as the force withdrew, and the glow of fires could be seen from up to 130 miles away. PB724 encountered a snowstorm and severe icing conditions on the way home, and, while trying to get underneath it, crashed at Meligny-le-Grand, thirty-five miles west of Nancy in north-eastern France, after hitting trees. F/O J N Scott and four of the others on board were killed, while the wireless operator and rear gunner sustained severe injuries from which they would ultimately recover. Two hours after the 5 Group attack, in what had become an established pattern, the 1, 3, 6 and 8 Group force arrived to complete the destruction of the central and some industrial districts, and this proved to be the final large-scale attack of the war on Munich.

With the exception of 617 Squadron, 5 Group remained on the ground for the ensuing six days, with snow-clearing providing exercise for all capable of wielding a shovel. The crews were, therefore, no doubt relieved to be called to briefing on the 13th, when they learned that 5 Group would be operating alone against the Wintershall oil refinery at Politz near Stettin. The plant had sustained damage in the previous attack in December, but production had not been halted, and a force of 218 Lancasters and seven Mosquitos was assembled for the return, of which ten of the Lancasters were provided by 106 Squadron. Another dusk departure saw them taking off between 16.15 and 16.30 with F/L Barden the senior pilot on duty, an officer being groomed for promotion in the near future to take over as B Flight commander. A further four Lancasters had followed in their wake by 16.35 led by F/L Daniel and bound for the distant Geranium garden off the Baltic port of Swinemünde. The bombing brigade arrived in the target area punctually to find clear skies with slight haze, by which time the blind marker crews had identified the target by means of H2S, and delivered their green TIs in a line approaching the target shortly after 22.00. The illuminators then dropped their flares, which caused ground detail to stand out, highlighted by the snow on the ground. A blind-bombing attack had been planned, but, because of the excellence of the conditions, Mosquitos were able to go in at low level. The main force was called in, and the 106 Squadron crews bombed in accordance with instructions from the Master Bomber from 17,000 to 18,100 feet between 22.15 and 22.27 to help seal the fate of the plant, and all returned without incident with bombing photos plotted at 550 to 2,400 yards from the aiming point. Meanwhile, some thirty miles to the north, the gardeners had encountered ten-tenths low cloud, but, employing H2S to establish their positions, they successfully delivered their stores from 14,000 feet shortly before 22.00. Photographic reconnaissance confirmed that the oil refinery site had been severely damaged, and Bomber Command claimed it to be in ruins.

Oil targets would continue to dominate during the remainder of the month, and a two-phase attack was planned for the following night against the refinery at Leuna, near Merseburg in eastern Germany, as previously mentioned, one of many similar sites situated in an arc from north to south to the west of Leipzig. The first phase would be carried out by 5 Group, which detailed 210 Lancasters and nine Mosquitos, a dozen of the former representing 106 Squadron. They departed Metheringham between 16.10 and 16.30 with S/L Bretherton the senior pilot on duty, and headed for the Sussex coast near Brighton to begin the Channel crossing for the southern approach to eastern Germany. F/O Day and crew turned back after reaching the Abbeville area after the rear turret became unserviceable, but the others pressed on to find clear skies but poor vertical visibility due to a layer of haze, which, in the event, was no hindrance to the primary blind markers, whose job was to establish their position over the aiming point by means of H2S. They delivered their TIs from 18,000 feet, after which, the first element of the flare force was called in. The Master Bomber ordered ground marking only, which was carried out by the low-level Mosquito element, and, by 20.50, he was satisfied and sent the marker aircraft home. The main force produced what appeared to be concentrated bombing, those from 106 Squadron dropping their loads of a cookie and nine 500 pounders each onto red and green TIs from 14,000 to 16,500 feet between 21.00 and 21.07 with a fourteen-second overshoot in accordance with the Master Bomber's instructions. Returning crews reported explosions and two columns of smoke rising up through 8,000 feet as they turned for home, and left behind a beacon for the second wave of 363 Lancasters and five Mosquitos of 1, 6 and 8 Groups following three hours behind. They would add to the massive destruction, which effectively put the plant out of action for the remainder of the war. PB122 did not arrive back with the others, and it was learned later that it had flown into the ground at an acute angle near Vignacourt at 23.59 when approaching Abbeville homebound, and there had been no survivors from the crew of F/O McIntosh RAAF.

Three oil plants were selected for attention on the night of the 16/17th, at Zeitz, near Liepzig, Wanne-Eickel in the Ruhr, and Brux in north-western Czechoslovakia (now Most in the Czech Republic), some 140 miles due south of Berlin. It was for the last-mentioned that fourteen 106 Squadron crews were briefed as part of a 5 Group force of 224 Lancasters and six Mosquitos, which would be accompanied by seven 101 Squadron ABC Lancasters for RCM duties. They were each carrying a cookie and nine 500 pounders, one of the latter with a 72-hour delay fuse, as they departed Metheringham between 17.55 and 18.10 with F/Ls Barden, Daniel and Gilbert the senior pilots on duty on what would be a nine-hour round-trip. There were ten early returns from the force, and among them was the crew of F/L Barden with a failed starboard-inner engine. The others reached the target area to encounter nine to ten-tenths low cloud with tops at 3,000 feet, which interfered with the low-level marking system. The four primary blind markers identified the target by means of H2S, and dropped green TIs, and they were followed by the first illuminators, who also relied on H2S to deliver their flares. It seems that a number of Mosquitos managed to get below the cloud base to put red TIs onto the aiming point and reported that the greens were among the oil tanks. However, the reds were not generally visible through the clouds, and the Master Bomber called for skymarking, while informing flare force 3 that it would not be required. The 106 Squadron participants bombed either on the glow of the red TIs or on the cascading greens from 14,200 to 16,700 feet between 22.32 and 22.37, and observed many explosions and large columns of thick, black smoke emerging through the cloud tops. All returned safely from what was confirmed by photo-reconnaissance to be an outstanding success, and another major setback to the enemy's oil production.

The Group was involved in just one more operation before the end of the month, and this was a smallish area attack on Gelsenkirchen in company with elements of 4 and 8 Groups on the night of the 22/23rd. 106 Squadron was not involved in this operation, and finished the month with a tally of 108 sorties from operations on one day and eight nights, during which three aircraft and crews had been lost. On the 24th, the squadron was notified that it had won the coveted silver Lancaster trophy for the fewest avoidable accidents in 5 Group during the final quarter of the year. There was not a single avoidable accident during the period, despite the squadron flying more hours than any other 5 Group unit. Having already held the trophy for the January to June period, the squadron had been "Top Dogs" in this category for nine months of 1944.

February 1945

The weather at the start of February provided difficult conditions for marking and bombing, particularly for 5 Group, and a number of operations would struggle to achieve their aims in the face of thick, low cloud and strong winds. 5 Group was back in harness immediately at the start of the new month following the long lay-off, and 271 Lancaster and eleven Mosquito crews were called to briefings on all 5 Group stations on the 1st to learn that their target was to be the marshalling yards in the town of Siegen, situated some fifty miles east of Cologne. This was a 5 Group show, and was one of three major operations planned for the night, the others, by larger forces, taking place at Ludwigshafen and Mainz further into southern Germany. A high wind during the night had helped to clear some of the snow, and the fifteen 106 Squadron Lancasters took off without incident between 16.03 and 16.18 with no fewer than six pilots of flight lieutenant rank on the Order of Battle. Each of the Metheringham crews was sitting on a cookie and thirteen SBCs of incendiaries, all of which reached the target area shortly after 19.00, where ten-tenths cloud between 3,000 and 7,000 feet caused problems for the flare and marker forces, some of which were finding it difficult to obtain a clear H2S image on their screens. Eventually, one of the primary blind markers ran in and dropped green TIs at 19.05 from 15,000 feet, and their glow was visible through the clouds. This prompted the first flares, followed by an attempt to mark at low-level with red TIs, which were not visible through the clouds, and, when the Master Bomber called for skymarking at 19.10, the remaining illuminators were superfluous to requirements and were sent home. The bombing phase was put back by four minutes until 19.20, forcing crews to either orbit or dogleg to waste time if they were still on approach, and then instructions were issued to aim at the skymarkers, which were being driven by the strong wind across the intended aiming point and beyond the target. The glow of red target indicators was faintly visible through the clouds, but this was most likely a decoy fire site prepared by the Germans. It attracted many bomb loads, perhaps some from the 106 Squadron participants, who delivered their attacks from 8,000 to 12,000 feet between 19.29 and 19.33, contributing to what became a widely scattered raid. Much of the effort fell into open and wooded country, and, although the railway station sustained damage, the marshalling yards escaped. Three Lancasters were shot down during the operation, and a fourth, 106 Squadron's LM215, crash-landed at Juvincourt airfield on the way home after sustaining damage from flak, but no injuries were reported among the crew of F/O Gray.

The next briefing revealed the bad news that a tour of operations was to be increased again to thirty-six sorties. Fifteen 106 Squadron crews were in attendance at 15.00 on a drizzly afternoon on the 2nd, to be told further, that the night's operation was to be against Karlsruhe in southern Germany. This was to be another 5 Group effort involving 250 Lancasters and eleven Mosquitos, and was again, only one of three major operations taking place. Wiesbaden was to receive its one and only major raid of the war at the hands of almost five hundred aircraft, while a 320-strong predominantly Halifax force dealt with an oil plant at Wanne-Eickel in the Ruhr. The 106 Squadron element departed Metheringham between 20.05 and 20.25 again strongly represented by pilots of flight lieutenant rank, and headed for the assembly point over Reading. The winds turned out to be lighter than forecast, and this caused a change in route, which now took the force directly from Reading to the target, straddling the Franco-Belgian frontier all the way to Germany, where they encountered heavy cloud between 3,000 and 15,000 feet. The flare force arrived over the target at 17,500 to 18,500 feet between 23.03 and 23.28, and tried to perform their assigned tasks in difficult conditions, some with malfunctioning H2S boxes. The Mosquito crews tried to establish an aiming point, but the illumination was not getting through to the ground, and, even had they dropped red TIs, it is unlikely that they would have been visible. At 23.11 the Master Bomber called for skymarking and sent the Mosquitos and remaining illuminators home. The Metheringham crews bombed on the glow of markers as instructed by the Master Bomber from 12,000 to 16,000 feet between 23.19 and 23.26, and all returned safely. This final raid of the war on Karlsruhe was a complete failure, and cost fourteen Lancasters, four of them from 189 Squadron at Fulbeck, a station located a dozen miles to the south-west of Metheringham.

Three main operations were posted again on the 4th, against the Gutehoffnunugshütte Oberhausen A G benzol plant at Osterfeld near Leipzig, the Gelsenkirchener Bergwerke A G (Nordstern) coking plant in the Ruhr and an area attack on the city of Bonn, which, together involved 480 aircraft from 4, 6 and 8 Groups.

While the frontier towns of Goch and Cleves were being pounded by the other groups on the night of the 7/8th, ahead of the advancing British XXX Corps, 5 Group returned to the Dortmund-Ems Canal with 177 Lancasters and eleven Mosquitos, the former carrying delayed action bombs. A dozen 106 Squadron Lancasters departed Metheringham between 21.05 and 21.15 with F/Ls Barden, Dodwell, Eakins and Robertson the senior pilots on duty, each crew with twelve 1,000 pounders and two 500 pounders beneath their feet. F/L Robertson and crew had noticed excessive fuel consumption from the start, and abandoned their sortie while flying south over Bedfordshire. The others reached the target to find seven to ten-tenths cloud at between 6,000 and 9,000 feet, and bombed through gaps from 8,500 to 11,500 feet between 00.01 and 00.08 on the instructions of the Master Bomber, but could not assess the outcome as all bombs contained delay fuses. It turned out to be a rare unsuccessful attack on this target, photographic reconnaissance revealing that the bombs had fallen into fields, and had failed to cause any breach.

Briefings took place on 5 Group stations on the 8th for another long round-trip to the Wintershall oil refinery at Politz, for which a force of 227 Lancasters and seven Mosquitos was assembled. They were to act as the first wave in a two-phase attack, which would be completed two hours later by 248 Lancasters from 1 and 8 Groups. 106 Squadron was not involved in the main operation, but made ready nine Lancasters to send to Neubrandenburg in north-eastern Germany as a diversion. They took off between 16.45 and 17.05, with F/Ls Dodwell and Gilbert the senior pilots on duty, but F/O Laidlaw RAAF acting as raid controller, and set out for the target, which was only sixty miles short of Politz. While these crews were spoofing the enemy, six others from the squadron were to plant vegetables in the Geraniums garden off Swinemünde, for which they departed Metheringham between 17.20 and 17.25 led by S/L Bretherton and his crew. The bombing element arrived at its destination shortly before 21.00 and delivered flares and target markers from 12,500 feet to simulate a full raid, while, to add a little more realism, the crews also dropped fifteen-and-a-half tons-worth of bombs in the form of seventy 500 pounders. The gardeners picked up coastal pinpoints visually, confirmed by H2S, and F/O Hamilton and crew employed the now largely defunct rocket research site of Peenemünde on the island of Usedom as the starting point for their timed run. A total of twenty-four mines were successfully planted from 12,000 to 12,800 feet between 21.13 and 21.36, and all aircraft returned safely home.

Meanwhile, at Politz, the blind markers and the flare force crews went in at 13,000 to 14,500 feet between 21.03 and 21.15 to carry out their assigned tasks in the face of an ineffective smoke screen, but, more seriously, fierce night-fighter activity on approach to and over the target. The main force reached the target area to find clear skies and excellent visibility, and delivered their loads onto red TIs in accordance with the Master Bomber's instructions. A number of crews reported up to six explosions and smoke rising through 3,000 feet as they turned away to the west, confident in the quality of their work, and the second wave completed the destruction to ensure that no further production at the site was possible in what remained of the war. Ten Lancasters failed to arrive back in home airspace, but there were no absentees at Metheringham, and so successful was the diversion deemed to be, that the A-O-C sent a congratulatory message.

Briefings took place on the 13th for the first round of Operation Thunderclap, the Churchill inspired offensive against Germany's eastern cities, which was devised partly to act in support of the advancing Russians, and also as a demonstration to Stalin of RAF air power, should he turn against the Allies after the war. The historic and culturally significant city of Dresden was selected to open the offensive in another two-phase affair, with a 5 Group force of 246 Lancasters and nine Mosquitos leading the way, to be followed three hours later by 529 Lancasters of 1, 3, 6 and 8 Groups. It had proved to be a successful policy thus far, with the 5 Group low-level marking system and main force attacks providing a beacon for the second force, and, should it be required on this night, 8 Group would provide any necessary marking for phase two from high level. The 106 Squadron contingent of seventeen Lancasters departed Metheringham between 18.05 and 18.20 with W/C Stevens the senior pilot on duty, and the crews had absolutely no concept of the ramifications of the operation, both in terms of its outcome on the ground, and its hysterical aftermath. Dresden was Germany's seventh largest city, and its largest remaining largely un-bombed built-up area, which, according to American sources, contained more than a hundred factories and fifty thousand workers contributing to the war effort. It was also an important railway hub, to the extent that the marshalling yards had been attacked twice in late 1944 by the USAAF.

The heavy force was two hours out when W/C Maurice Smith of 54 Base, the Master Bomber for the 5 Group attack, lifted off the Woodhall Spa runway at a few minutes before 20.00 hours in Mosquito KB401 AZ-E, a 627 Squadron aircraft, and he was followed away by eight others from 627 Squadron. F/L Plenderleith and crew had to contend with a lack of power from the starboard-outer engine, and they abandoned their sortie after little more than an hour. The heavy brigade and the Mosquitos arrived in the target area at the same time to encounter three layers of cloud, between 3,000 and 5,000 feet, 6,000 to 8,000 feet and 15,000 to 16,000 feet, but otherwise good visibility. The first primary blind marker delivered green TIs from 15,000 feet at 22.03, and was followed in by the flare force, which lit the way for the low-level Mosquitos. The main force Lancasters were carrying eight hundred tons of bombs, those representing 106 Squadron in the form of a cookie supplemented by either eight 500 pounders or eleven SBCs of incendiaries, which were delivered from 13,000 to 15,250 feet between 22.13 and 22.25 with a thirty-second overshoot from the glow of red TIs in accordance with the Master Bomber's instructions. They were on their way home by 22.30, and, as far as they were concerned, this attack was no different from any other, and the fires visible for a hundred miles into the return journey nothing out of the ordinary. At debriefing, F/O Newenham and crew reported their failure to bomb after an error left their bombs unselected and unfused.

By the time that the second force of 1, 3, 6 and 8 Group Lancasters arrived over Dresden three hours after 5 Group, the skies had cleared, and the fires created by the earlier attack provided the expected beacon. A further eighteen hundred tons of bombs rained down onto the historic and beautiful old city, setting off the same chain of events that had devastated parts of Hamburg in July 1943, and a number of other cities since. Dresden's population had been swelled by masses of refugees fleeing from the eastern front, and many were engulfed in the ensuing firestorm. As daylight settled over the city, three hundred American bombers carried out a separate attack under the umbrella of a fighter escort, and completed the destruction. There were claims that RAF aircraft had strafed the streets and open spaces to increase the level of terror, and such accusations abound in the city to this day. In fact, American fighters were responsible, and were trying to add to the general confusion and chaos. Initial propaganda-inspired reports from the Office of the Propaganda Minister, Joseph Goebbels, falsely claimed a death toll of 250,000 people, but an accurate figure of twenty-five thousand has been settled upon since.

The destruction of Dresden has been used by some in this country also as a weapon with which to beat Bomber Command and Harris, and label them as war criminals. Curiously, no accusations have been levelled at the Americans. It should also be understood that Harris had no interest in attacking Dresden, and had to be nagged by Chief-of-the-Air-Staff Portal to fulfil Churchill's wishes. The aircrew simply did the job asked of them, and Dresden was no different from any other urban target. The death toll at Hamburg was much higher, and yet, there has been no similar outcry. The legacy of this operation served to deny Harris and the men under his Command their due recognition for the massive part they played in the ultimate victory, and only in recent times has a monument been erected in Green Park in London and a campaign clasp awarded, sadly, far too late for the majority. Churchill, with his eyes set on a peacetime election, betrayed Harris and the Command in a typical politically motivated U-turn, in which he accused Harris of bombing solely for the purpose of inflicting terror. In the post-war honours, Harris was the only commander in the field to be omitted.

Round two of Thunderclap was planned for the following night, when Chemnitz was posted as the target for 717 aircraft drawn from 1, 3, 4, 6 and 8 Groups, while 224 Lancasters and eight Mosquitos of 5 Group targeted an oil refinery in the small town of Rositz, situated twenty-five miles due south of Leipzig and thirty miles north-west of Chemnitz. Seventeen 106 Squadron Lancasters were made ready, and departed Metheringham between 16.45 and 17.25 with S/L Bretherton the senior pilot on duty. They all reached the target area to be greeted by six to ten-tenths thin cloud in two layers, one at 6,000 to 8,000 feet, and the other at 10,000 to 12,000 feet, but the primary blind marker made a good run on H2S at 15,000 feet at 20.48 to drop green TIs, and the illuminators followed up between 20.51 and 20.58 from a similar height. The main force crews arriving on time carried out support runs with the marker element, before being called in to bomb at 21.07, those from 106 Squadron releasing their cookie and up to eleven 500 pounders each onto red and green TIs, or on their glow, from 8,000 to 11,500 feet between 21.05 and 21.18 in accordance with the controller's instructions. F/O Dennis RCAF and crew had lost the aiming point during their first two runs and were on their third when the Master Bomber called a halt to proceedings. Three or four large fires were evident in the oil plant, and black smoke was rising through 5,000 feet as the force turned away. It was established afterwards, that the southern part of the site had been damaged, but it would be necessary to return to finish the job. The Chemnitz raid had been compromised by adverse weather conditions, and it would be March before success was achieved against this target.

On the night of the 15/16th, the squadron sent four Lancasters to join others from 5 Group mining in the Silverthorn III garden in the Kattegat Channel. They took off at 16.45 led by S/L Bretherton and crew, who lost their starboard-outer engine shortly afterwards. Undaunted, they pressed on to the target, using

H2S to pinpoint on Anholt Island, before making a timed run to the release point. The others were equally successful, pinpointing on Sjaellands Point or Hessel Island, and all returned safely having delivered six mines each from 14,000 feet between 20.00 and 20.14.

An oil refinery at Böhlen was posted as the target on the 19th for a 5 Group force of 264 Lancasters and six Mosquitos. It was another of the collection of similar plants in the Leipzig area and some ten miles north of Rositz, for which 106 Squadron dispatched seventeen Lancasters in a late take-off between 23.30 and 23.50 with W/C Stevens and S/Ls Barden and Bretherton the senior pilots on duty. They all completed the three-and-a-half-hour flight out, and would meet up with the later-departing Mosquito element at the target, which included the Master Bomber for the occasion, 54 Base's W/C Benjamin, who was flying the same Mosquito used by W/C Smith at Dresden six nights earlier. They encountered ten-tenths cloud over the target in two layers at 5,000 to 8,000 feet and 10,000 to 14,000 feet, and this would introduce a challenging element to the operation. The illuminators went in at around 15,000 feet between 04.05 and 04.13, and the VHF chatter suggested that a Mosquito had been able to mark a factory building with a red TI, and that it had been backed up. The main force was called in, before W/C Benjamin's VHF was suddenly cut off, and his Deputy took over. It would be established later, that the Master Bomber's Mosquito had been shot down by flak, and that W/C Benjamin DFC & Bar had died alongside his navigator. The 106 Squadron crews carried out their attacks in accordance with confusing instructions from 15,850 to 16,900 feet between 04.19 and 04.41, aiming mostly at the glow in the cloud of red and green TIs, and none was able to make an assessment of results. Post-raid reconnaissance revealed only superficial damage to the site, which would have to be attacked again.

The following night, the 20th, proved to be a busy one, with more than five hundred Lancasters targeting Dortmund, while 268 Halifaxes from 4 and 6 Groups provided the heavy elements for raids on Rhenania-Ossag oil refineries in Düsseldorf and Monheim. 5 Group, meanwhile, prepared itself for a further attempt on the Mittelland Canal at Gravenhorst, for which ten 106 Squadron crews were briefed as part of an overall force of 154 Lancasters and eleven Mosquitos. They departed Metheringham between 21.50 and 22.05 with F/Ls Daniel, Gilbert, Mawer and Simpson the senior pilots on duty, and all reached the target area to find ten-tenths cloud between them and the aiming point. The primary blind marker succeeded in delivering two green TIs by H2S from 12,000 feet at 00.53, and they fell on the starboard side of the canal. After the flare force had done its job, the Mosquito element descended to 400 feet, but could not identify the aiming point, and, just before H-Hour, the Master Bomber sent the markers home, to be followed almost immediately by the main force as he abandoned the operation.

The operation was rescheduled for twenty-four hours later, when Duisburg and Worms were also to be attacked by heavy forces of 362 and 349 aircraft respectively. 5 Group detailed 165 Lancasters and twelve Mosquitos, and, among those attending the briefing at Coningsby was G/C Evans-Evans, the station commander, who would be taking the bulk of the 83 Squadron commanding officer's highly experienced crew with him. Evans-Evans was 43 and a larger-than-life character, who had commanded 115 Squadron for a spell earlier in the war during its Wellington era and had never lost the enthusiasm to be "one of the boys" and take part in operations. A number of years of good living had widened his girth, and it must have been a struggle to fit into the cramped confines of a Lancaster cockpit. The ten 106 Squadron participants took off between 17.15 and 17.30 with S/L Bretherton the senior pilot on duty, and reached the target area to find moonlight beaming down from clear skies with some ground haze. One of the primary blind markers was able to deliver his green TIs two minutes late because of a change in the wind, and they fell about a mile south of the aiming point, quite close to the Wet Triangle meeting point of the Mittelland and Dortmund-Ems Canals. After the flare force had done its job, the Mosquitos delivered their red TIs, which were backed up successfully, before the main force was called in at 20.25. The 106 Squadron crews released their loads of a dozen 1,000 pounders each from 8,300 to

11,000 feet between 20.27 and 20.40, and brought back eight aiming point photos. The presence of night-fighters was clearly evident by the number of combats taking place, and among nine missing Lancasters was the one belonging to 83 Squadron containing G/C Evans-Evans and seven others. Only the rear gunner survived, and, among those killed was the twenty-two-year-old navigator, S/L Wishart DSO, DFC & Bar, who had completed sixty-one operations in Lancasters with 97 Squadron and eighteen in Mosquitos as navigator to Master Bombers. 83 Squadron's commanding officer, G/C Ingham, was left deeply saddened by the loss of his crew. The photos from the whole force suggested a concentrated attack, but as all of the bombs contained half-hour delay fuses, it was necessary to wait for reconnaissance to be carried out to gain confirmation that the canal had been breached again, and, according to Bomber Command, "rendered 100% unserviceable".

It was announced on the 23rd that W/C Stevens was to receive a DFC, a highly merited award in recognition of his determination to lead from the front, particularly on the more testing operations against heavily-defended targets. That night, 5 Group went north with a modest force of seventy-three Lancasters, including a dozen from 106 Squadron, to attack what was believed to be a U-Boot base at Horten in Oslo Fjord. They departed Metheringham between 17.20 and 17.30 with F/Ls Dodwell and Ruff the senior pilots on duty, and arrived in the target area to find clear skies and good visibility. The marking was accurate, and bombing took place from 10,000 to 11,500 feet between 20.45 and 20.54 in accordance with the Master Bomber's instructions. Whether or not a U-Boot base existed is uncertain, but no shipping was seen by the crews, and a local report described heavy damage in the port area and a shipyard, and the sinking of a tanker and floating crane. Crews returning from mining sorties in the same area reported smoke climbing through 8,000 feet over Horten, and large fires visible for eighty miles into the return journey. F/O Hamilton and crew returned on three engines, and PB296 was ultimately declared a write-off, although there was no explanation for its demise in the ORB.

While the above operation was in progress, some 770 miles to the south a force of 366 Lancasters, plus one from the Film Unit, and thirteen Mosquitos drawn from 1, 6 and 8 Groups was attacking the city of Pforzheim, situated in southern Germany between Karlsruhe to the north-west and Stuttgart to the south-east. This would be the first area raid on the city, which was known as a centre for jewellery and watch manufacture, but was believed by the Allies to be involved in the production of precision instruments in support of Germany's war effort. They were greeted by clear skies and bright moonlight in the target area, and the thin veil of ground haze proved to be no impediment as the first red Oboe TIs went down at 19.52, to be followed quickly by illuminator flares and salvoes of concentrated reds and greens. Fires rapidly took hold until the whole town north of the river looked like a sea of flames, and, by 20.06, the fires were too dazzling for the TIs to be visible, after which, the Master Bomber ordered the smoke to be bombed. The raid lasted twenty-two minutes, during which 1,825 tons of bombs fell into the built-up area, reducing 83% of it to ruins and setting off a firestorm in which 17,600 people lost their lives. This was the highest death toll to result from a single attack on a German city after Hamburg (40,000) and Dresden (25,000). It was during this operation that the final Victoria Cross was earned by a member of RAF Bomber Command. It went posthumously to the Master Bomber from 582 Squadron, Captain Ed Swales of the South African Air Force, who continued to control the attack in a Lancaster severely damaged by a night-fighter, before sacrificing his life to allow his crew to abandon the stricken aircraft.

The squadron concluded its operational activities for the month on the night of the 24/25th, when sending nine Lancasters to lay mines in the Onion garden in Oslo Fjord, and was the only 5 Group unit operating. They departed Metheringham between 17.05 and 17.15 led by W/C Stevens, and found three to five-tenths cloud in the target area, but excellent visibility. H2S was used to locate the garden, and each crew planted six mines as briefed from around 11,200 to 11,500 feet between 20.26 and 20.50. The presence of a seventy-mile-per-hour wind required the aircraft to be over land as the mines were released, and this demanded the crews' highest skills, while also exposing them to danger from the local defences, and seven reported being coned by searchlights. During the course of the month the squadron undertook ten bombing and three gardening operations and dispatched 153 sorties without loss.

March 1945

The new month would see the Command bludgeon its way across Germany, concentrating on oil, rail and road targets, along with the few towns still boasting a built-up area. Mannheim was raided for the last time in numbers by a large force from 1, 6 and 8 Groups on the 1st, while 5 Group remained at home. Later, on the 2nd, Cologne was pounded for the final time, first by a force of seven hundred aircraft, which inflicted huge destruction across the city, particularly west of the Rhine, and, later, by a 3 Group force, of which only fifteen bombed because of a faulty G-H station in England. The city ceased to function, thereafter, and was still paralyzed when American forces marched in four days later. Just when it seemed that German resistance to air attack might end, March would prove that the defenders were still capable of mounting a challenge, even though they were stretched beyond their capacity to protect every corner of the Reich.

5 Group opened its March account with a return to the Ladbergen aqueduct section of the Dortmund-Ems Canal on the evening of the 3rd, for which 212 Lancasters and ten Mosquitos were made ready. The force encountered eight to ten-tenths cloud in the target area at between 3,500 and 6,000 feet, and it was noted that the defences had been strengthened since the last attack, and were throwing up a curtain of intense light flak as high as 15,000 feet. H2S allowed the two 83 Squadron primary blind markers to locate the canal and deliver their green TIs from 14,000 feet at 21.47 and 21.49, and the first illuminators went in a minute later to light the way for the Mosquitos, after which, a large red glow could be seen through the clouds. At 21.59, the Master Bomber called in the main force to bomb on the glow or on sight of the TIs through gaps in the thin cloud, and the crews complied to contribute to the breaching of both branches, which rendered the waterway unnavigable and out of action for the remainder of the war.

While the above was in progress, 5 Group sent a small force back to Oslo Fjord to mine the waters of the Onions garden. The six 106 Squadron Lancasters took off between 17.10 and 17.15 with S/L Bretherton the senior pilot on duty, but lost the services of F/L Simpson and crew to an engine issue early on. The others reached the target area to find visibility at twenty miles, and located their dropping points by means of H2S, before delivering thirty mines between them from 10,000 to 10,500 feet between 20.58 and 21.26. When they arrived home between 01.30 and 02.10 they were diverted to avoid a number of enemy intruders stooging around Metheringham, which shot the place up, but, somehow, inflicted no damage.

Fourteen 106 Squadron crews attended briefing on the 5th, to learn that 5 Group would be sending 248 Lancasters and ten Mosquitos back to Böhlen, for another crack at the Deutsche Erdöl A G synthetic oil refinery. A simultaneous operation by a Thunderclap force of 760 aircraft would attempt to redress the recent failure at Chemnitz, some thirty-five miles to the south. Take-off from Metheringham was accomplished without incident either side of 17.30 with W/C Stevens and S/Ls Barden and Bretherton the senior pilots on duty. F/L Eakins turned back with a fuel leak, but the remainder reached the target to find ten-tenths cloud in layers between 2,000 and 12,000 feet. Uncertainty concerning the prevailing conditions on arrival had led to the preparation of two marking plans, low-level and skymarking, and the lead primary blind marker made his first run at 14,000 feet to drop green TIs at 21.40. He did not see them burst because of the cloud, but thought that the illuminator flares were well-placed. Some of the Coningsby crews had H2S difficulties, and not all were able to pinpoint on Leipzig for the run-in. This meant that they were unsure of their position, and, when the Master Bomber called for Wanganui flares at 21.45, they withheld them, rather than risk dropping them inaccurately and attracting some of the bombing. A large explosion was witnessed at 21.50, and, three minutes later, Wanganui flares were observed by those in the approaching main force element. The 106 Squadron crews delivered their cookie and eleven 500 pounders each from 11,100 to 13,200 feet between 21.55 and 22.02, observing another large explosion at 21.57, before the Master Bomber called a halt at 22.01 and sent everyone home, leaving evidence of fires and smoke behind them. Post-raid reconnaissance revealed extensive damage to the coal-drying plant, and some hits in other areas of the site, but it was still not a knockout blow. Meanwhile, the Thunderclap force had succeeded in inflicting severe fire damage in central and southern districts of Chemnitz.

Briefings took place on the 6th for 191 crews of 5 Group for an operation that night against the small port of Sassnitz on the north-eastern corner of the island of Rügen, about fifty miles north of Peenemünde. 150 aircraft were to attack the port and its installations, while the remainder went for shipping in or near the harbour. 106 Squadron put up ten aircraft to attack shipping, and they departed Metheringham between 18.20 and 18.30 with F/L Eakins the senior pilot on duty, and arrived in the target area to find five to nine-tenths drifting cloud with tops up to 8,000 feet. An 83 Squadron blind marker crew made a run at 22.50 to drop green TIs over the port from 12,000 feet, and the flare force maintained illumination of the town and outer harbour for the next twenty-five minutes. Apart from a short break, when cloud slid across the aiming point, the markers remained visible to the main force crews, and those representing 106 Squadron carried out their attacks from 3,500 to 9,400 feet between 23.00 and 23.45. As F/O Penney and crew ran up on a passenger liner, which they assessed to be of fifteen to twenty-five thousand tons, they saw it straddled by the bombs from two other aircraft. They followed up with their own from 8,200 feet at 23.00, but cloud immediately obscured their view, and the results of their efforts were missed. F/O Roberts and crew attacked the same vessel nine minutes later, and watched their bombs fall alongside, at which point the Lancaster sustained damage from an unknown cause, that left a large hole in the pilot's Perspex. F/O Barrow and crew lost their hydraulics immediately after bombing, and flew all the way back to the emergency strip at Carnaby with the bomb doors open. F/O Hill and crew reported a warship heading eastwards into open sea with a list to port, while the crew of F/O Kiesling spotted white smoke and flame issuing forth from a vessel anchored amongst others just offshore. Reconnaissance revealed later that three ships had been sunk, and part of the town had suffered extensive damage.

It was back to the oil campaign for 5 Group on the following night, for an attack on an oil refinery at Harburg, south of Hamburg, for which a force of 234 Lancasters and seven Mosquitos was made ready. They would not be alone over Germany, however, as more than a thousand other aircraft would be engaged against similar targets at Dessau and Hemmingstedt and in minor and support operations. 106 Squadron provided thirteen Lancasters, which departed Metheringham between 18.20 and 18.30 with S/L Barden the senior pilot on duty. They arrived over the target to find eight-tenths thin cloud and red and yellow target indicators clearly visible, which they bombed in accordance with the Master Bomber's instructions with a seven-second overshoot from 10,750 to 11,500 feet between 21.58 and 22.04. Bomb bursts were clearly seen, along with explosions and black smoke rising through 10,000 feet, and all from Metheringham returned safely to make their reports. 5 Group crews distinguished themselves on this night by claiming the destruction of seven enemy fighters. Post-raid reconnaissance confirmed further damage to this previously attacked target, with oil storage tanks taking the most hits, and revealed that a rubber factory had also been severely damaged.

An all-time record was set on the 11th, when 1,079 aircraft, the largest Bomber Command force ever for a single target, was assembled to attack Essen for the last time. 5 Group contributed 199 Lancasters and a single Mosquito, 106 Squadron loading fourteen Lancasters with a cookie and sixteen 500 pounders each, and dispatching them between 12.05 and 12.30 with W/C Stevens with S/L Bretherton the senior pilots on duty. The city was covered by ten-tenths cloud with tops at 6,000 feet, which required the Path Finder element to employ skymarkers in the form of red and blue smoke puffs, and these were bombed by the 106 Squadron crews from 16,000 to 19,000 feet between 15.18 and 15.23. More than 4,600 tons of bombs were dropped into the already ravaged city and former industrial powerhouse, and left it with smoke rising through 10,000 feet as the force turned away. It would still be in a state of paralysis when the American ground forces captured it unopposed on the 10th of April.

A little over twenty-four hours later, the short-lived record was surpassed by the departure from their stations in the early afternoon of 1,108 aircraft, which had Dortmund as their destination. This time 5 Group provided 211 Lancasters, fourteen of them representing 106 Squadron, which departed Metheringham between 13.30 and 13.40 with S/L Barden the senior pilot on duty and the station commander, G/C Heath, performing the role of second pilot on board SW248. They found the Ruhr still under a blanket of ten-tenths cloud, this time with tops at 6,000 feet, but H2S allowed the Path Finders to mark the target with green and blue smoke puffs, and it was to the latter that the main force crews were directed by the Master Bomber. The 106 Squadron crews complied from 15,500 to 16,800 feet between 16.47 and 16.54, and returning crews spoke of brown smoke climbing through the clouds to 8,000 feet from the northern end of the city, and also a ring of smoke encircling the area so dense, that it remained visible for 120 miles into the return flight. F/O Penney and crew reported losing an engine while outbound, and arriving later than the others to eventually bomb from 13,300 feet at 16.57. One 500 pounder had hung-up, and they brought it back home on three engines, having contributed to another devastating attack, which left the city broken and in chaos. Just two aircraft failed to return, and one of them was the first to be posted missing by 106 Squadron for six weeks. RA508 was lost without trace, and it was a tragedy that P/O Baker and his crew should lose their lives so close to the end. A new record of 4,800 tons of bombs had been delivered, and photo-reconnaissance revealed that the central and southern districts of the city had received the greatest weight, and had been left in chaos with all industry silenced permanently and railway tracks torn up.

5 Group's next objective was the Wintershall oil refinery at Lützkendorf, another site to the west of Leipzig and south-west of Leuna in the Geiseltal. *(Lützkendorf no longer exists on a map of Germany, and is now known as either Mücheln or Krumpa)*. The briefing of 244 Lancaster and eleven Mosquito crews took place on the 14th, fifteen of the former representing 106 Squadron, and they departed Metheringham between 17.00 and 17.15 with F/Ls Daniel, Robertson and Ruff the senior pilots on duty. They headed out over the Wash and the bulge of East Anglia en-route to the Scheldt Estuary, before crossing Belgium to swing south of Cologne, and embark on the long leg eastwards to the target. They were met on arrival by conditions described variously as ten-tenths cloud, no cloud, thin layer of cloud, thin banks of stratus with tops at 12,000 feet, a little medium cloud, poor visibility and good visibility, but there was unanimity with regard to the haze. Ahead, the primary blind marker aircraft could be seen delivering their green TIs at 21.49, followed by the illuminators immediately afterwards between 21.51 and 22.00 to drop flares and bombs. Finally, the low-level Mosquitos did their job to accurately mark the aiming point before the main force was called in, those from 106 Squadron bombing on red and green TIs in accordance with the Master Bomber's instructions from 8,000 to 11,000 feet between 22.02 and 22.07. Returning crews claimed an accurate attack, reporting explosions and fires, and thick black smoke drifting across the plant and ascending through 7,000 feet, which rendered impossible a detailed assessment. Night-fighters were very much in evidence over the target and during the return flight, and 106 Squadron's LL948 was among eighteen failures to return, 7.4% of those dispatched. It had come down near Karlsruhe, and only the rear gunner survived to be taken into captivity, while the remains of the rest of the crew of F/O Barrow RAAF were not recovered, and their names are commemorated on

the Runnymede Memorial, having the sad distinction of being the last to lose their lives while operating on behalf of 106 Squadron. The other fourteen 106 Squadron aircraft arrived safely in English air space, but conditions over Lincolnshire led to them being diverted to a number of airfields further south, including Silverstone, Chelveston and Gransden Lodge. Post-raid reconnaissance revealed that a partially successful operation had taken place, which meant that a further visit would be required.

Later that day, W/C Levis became the squadron's final wartime commanding officer on the departure of W/C Stevens, who was promoted to group captain and posted to Coningsby, presumably as station commander. George Levis was a fine sportsman, who had represented the RAF College at athletics, cross-country, boxing, football and cricket. He presided over his first operation on the night of the 16/17th, when the squadron provided a dozen Lancasters as part of an overall 5 Group heavy force of 225 aircraft, with eleven Mosquitos to carry out the marking. The target was Würzburg, a small city on the River Main, some ninety miles north-north-east of Stuttgart, which had not been attacked before, and where the railway infrastructure in the south was to be the point of focus for 106 Squadron. They were airborne from Metheringham between 17.50 and 18.00 with no fewer than five pilots of flight lieutenant rank leading the way, and arrived in the target area to find clear skies and good visibility, and red and yellow target indicators already marking the aiming point. The Master Bomber called for a thirty-second overshoot, with which they complied, delivering their cookies and incendiaries from 12,000 to 12,300 feet between 21.33 and 21.40. This was in the early stages of the attack, before there was much to observe on the ground, but, as the 106 Squadron crews turned for home, it was clear that fires were developing around the main aiming point further to the north. The bombing lasted just seventeen minutes, during which period 1,127 tons of bombs fell into the historic old cathedral city, destroying an estimated 89% of the built-up area and killing four to five thousand people. The Nuremberg operation had also been highly destructive, but had cost 1 Group twenty-four Lancasters, thus proving, that the enemy defences were not yet spent and could still give the Command a bloody nose.

There was further business to attend to at the Böhlen oil refinery, and 5 Group prepared a force of 236 Lancasters and eleven Mosquitos on the 20th, to deal what was hoped to be the knockout blow. Briefings began at 20.00, and, at Metheringham, was attended by sixteen 106 Squadron crews, who learned that a small-scale diversionary raid would be directed at Halle, situated some twenty miles to the north-west of Leipzig. They took off between 23.30 and 23.50, each carrying a cookie and twelve 500 pounders, and set out on the now familiar path to eastern Germany, where conditions in the target area were fairly good, with three to six-tenths cloud topping out at 6,000 to 8,000 feet. The bomber stream arrived early because of stronger-than-forecast winds, and the main force had to orbit while the first primary blind marker delivered green TIs at 03.33. They fell 750 yards south of the plant, to be followed at H-16 by a yellow TI bursting two miles short of the target. A cluster of illuminator flares ignited ahead, revealing that a smoke screen had been activated and was generating much smoke to create difficulties for the Mosquito low-level markers, despite which, they deposited red TIs on the button, and the main force was called in. A few dummy TIs attracted a number of bomb loads, but the 106 Squadron crews complied with the instructions of the Master Bomber to bomb on specific reds and yellows from 11,100 to 12,800 feet between 03.46 and 03.51. The main weight of the attack was concentrated around the target, and numerous explosions were witnessed, as was smoke rising through 5,000 feet as they turned away. The operation put the oil plant out of action, and it was still idle when American forces moved in a few weeks later.

Briefings on 5 Group stations on the 21st took place in the later evening, when 151 Lancaster and eight Mosquito crews were informed that the Deutsche Erdölwerke synthetic oil refinery at Hamburg was to be their target that night. 106 Squadron loaded fifteen Lancasters with a cookie and sixteen 500 pounders each, and sent then into the air between 01.15 and 01.35 with F/Ls Eakins, Mawer and Ruff the senior pilots on duty. The force pinpointed on the Danish coast to approach the target from the north, and found thin stratus cloud at around 2,000 feet, through which the primary blind marker crew dropped green TIs on H2S from 14,000 feet at 03.55. The first illuminators went in thirty seconds later, and continued to light up the aiming point until 04.01, by which time the Mosquitos had marked, allowing the main force to be called in at 04.05. The 106 Squadron crews bombed from 15,500 to 18,000 feet between 04.07 and 04.13, observing many fires and a large explosion at 04.11, from which red flame shot up 4,000 feet accompanied by black smoke. Another was reported at 04.16, and it was clear to the homebound crews that the attack had been successful, a fact confirmed by post-raid reconnaissance, which revealed that twenty storage tanks had been destroyed, and would remain out of action for the remainder of the war.

Metheringham was not involved in 5 Group's operations against railway bridges at Nienburg and Bremen on the 22nd and 23rd, but fourteen 106 Squadron crews were called to briefing on the afternoon of the 23rd to learn of their part in a raid that night on the town of Wesel. This had the misfortune to lie close to the Rhine and in the path of advancing British ground forces, which, since the 16th of February, had caused it to be systematically reduced to rubble by repeated air attacks, and now had one final onslaught to face, having already endured one by 3 Group earlier in the day. 195 Lancasters and eleven Mosquitos were made ready, those representing 106 Squadron departing Metheringham between 19.25 and 19.35 with the usual flight lieutenant-ranked suspects the senior pilots on duty. Most crews were sitting on fourteen 1,000 pounders and a single 500 pounder, and all reached the target area to find clear skies with slight ground haze, through which they were able to identify it visually. The aiming point was well-marked by red and green TIs, which were bombed by the Metheringham crews from 8,000 to 12,000 feet between 22.35 and 22.42 in accordance with the Master Bomber's instructions. It was noticed, that, despite the Master Bomber ending the attack at H+8, bombing had continued. The only incident of note was a bird-strike on NG397, which smashed the Perspex windscreen and caused injury to the pilot, F/O Richardson. The bird probably also sustained a headache! P/O Richardson landed at Manston, and was treated in the sick bay before being transferred to hospital. Reconnaissance confirmed the effectiveness of the attack, which added to the previous destruction and left only 3% of Wesel's buildings standing. After the war it would claim, justifiably, to be the most completely destroyed town in Germany.

On the 25th, it was announced that the now departed S/L Parry had been awarded a Bar to his DFC. The month's final operations for 5 Group took place on the 27th, when twenty Lancasters of 617 Squadron were sent with Tallboys and Grand Slams to attack the U-Boot pens at Farge, a small port on the eastern bank of the Weser, northwest of Bremen. In his classic book, The Dambusters, Paul Brickhill described the target as the largest concrete structure in the world, measuring some 1,450 by 300 yards, which boasted a reinforced-concrete roof twenty-three-feet thick. The massive structure contained a tank large enough for completed U-Boots to be tested under water. It was still under construction and had not yet become operational, and, in fact, the concrete for the roof had only recently been poured, and had not had time to set before 617 Squadron arrived overhead with evil intent. A simultaneous operation by ninety-five Lancasters against a nearby underground oil storage facility involved fourteen crews from 106 Squadron, which departed Metheringham between 09.55 and 10.05 with W/C Levis and S/L Barden the senior pilots on duty. They all arrived at the target to find clear skies and good visibility, and identified the aiming point visually by the river and railway lines, and F/L Gilbert also picked out a canal on the western bank and a PoW camp on the eastern bank. They aimed their bombs at marshalling yards or sidings, which were apparently concealing the storage tanks, releasing them from 15,700 to 17,000 feet between 13.02 and 13.07. They were unable to assess the outcome, but three explosions and thick, brown smoke suggested a successful attack, and their attention was drawn inevitably to the 617 Squadron activity, where a sheet of flame was observed. The 617 Squadron attack was another masterly display of precision bombing, and photo-reconnaissance confirmed two direct hits by Grand Slams, which had penetrated the partially completed roof and caused a great deal of it to collapse. The structure was still incomplete at the end of hostilities, having never been used, and its enormous bulk remains to this day as a permanent monument to a failed regime.

During the course of the month the squadron operated on three days and nine nights, dispatching 157 sorties for the loss of two Lancasters and their crews.

April 1945

The new month began for 106 Squadron with a rare accident involving ND501, which crashed on landing at Metheringham at 02.30 on the 3rd on return from a night training exercise. It was declared a write-off, but, happily, there were no injuries to F/O Smythe and his crew. There would be a gentle introduction to April for 5 Group, and it was not until the 4th that the "Independent Air Force" was called into action. The operation was against what was believed to be a military barracks at Nordhausen, situated in the Harz Mountains between Hannover to the north-west and Leipzig to the south-east. The site was actually a pair of enormous parallel tunnels under the Kohnstein Hill, which had been developed originally by the BASF Company to mine gypsum between 1917 and 1934. Following the destruction of Peenemünde, smaller tunnels had been created as a link between them to form a horizontal ladder effect, and the site turned over to the Mittelwerk GmbH (Gesellschaft mit beschrenkter Haftung, or Limited Company) for the manufacture of V-2 rockets and other secret projects. The "barracks" were part of the Mittelwerk-Dora forced workers camp, where inmates existed under the most horrendous conditions and brutal treatment, while they were starved, worked to death or simply executed by an increasingly desperate regime seeking to change the course of the war. The camp had been attacked on the previous day by 1 Group, and many casualties inflicted on the occupants, while those in the tunnels had been protected. The 5 Group attack, by 243 Lancasters, was to be divided between the barracks and the town, ninety-three to the former and 150 to the latter, and it was to the latter that the eighteen crews representing 106 Squadron were assigned. Each Lancasters was loaded with a cookie and sixteen 500 pounders and departed Metheringham between 06.15 and 06.30 with S/L Bretherton the senior pilot on duty. They arrived at the target to encounter five-to-seven-tenths cloud with tops as high as 7,000 feet, and those assigned to the barracks were able to identify them visually, along with the marshalling yards serving the site, until smoke began to obscure the area, at which point, those still with bombs were redirected to the town. The 106 Squadron crews bombed the town from 12,000 to 16,000 feet between 09.16 and 09.21, and, while some of the early bombing was seen to undershoot, the Master Bomber corrected this by calling for a five-second overshoot, and, thereafter, the markers were soon obscured by smoke. F/O Boyd RAAF and crew were not at debriefing, but news soon arrived to explain their absence. Having had one engine fail shortly before reaching the target, they lost another on the way home, and had to land at Brussels. The other crews were able to report a concentrated attack on both aiming points, claiming severe damage, but, tragically and inevitably, further heavy casualties were suffered by the unfortunate slave workers. The camp and production facilities were evacuated immediately, and, despite orders by Hitler to destroy the site utterly to prevent the Allies from recovering anything of use, Speer ignored his Führer and it was left intact, allowing the Americans to capture examples of Germany's revolutionary technology.

The only sizeable effort on the night of the 7/8th was by 175 Lancasters and eleven Mosquitos of 5 Group, which had a benzol plant at Molbis, near Leipzig, as their target. Situated south of the city, and less than two miles east of Böhlen, it was becoming a familiar destination for 5 Group via a well-trodden route across Belgium to pass south of Cologne. 106 Squadron made ready nine Lancasters, which departed Metheringham between 18.05 and 18.15 with W/C Levis the senior pilot on duty, and, after being delayed by inaccurately forecast head winds, they reached the target area some five hours later in time to participate in the operation. Two 83 Squadron primary blind markers formed the tip of the spear, and identified Zeitz on H2S, before making the ten-mile north-easterly run from there to the target. Green TIs were released from 15,000 feet at 22.48, and the flare force followed up between 22.50 and 22.57 to enable the low-level Mosquitos to drop red and green TIs among the chimneys of the plant. The following main force crews were greeted by clear skies with ground haze, or, perhaps, a smoke screen in operation, but this proved to be no impediment, and the highly accurate and visible marking was an invitation for the main force crews to plaster the site with high explosives. W/C Levis and crew were among the first to arrive over the aiming point, by which time they had already been coned in searchlights and damaged by flak as they turned to start the bombing run. They bombed on red and green TIs from 16,300 feet shortly after 23.00, and immediately thereupon, were attacked by a night-fighter, which inflicted extensive damage to the starboard main-plane, inner fuel tank, fuselage, mid-upper turret and bomb sight. The gunners scored hits to drive the enemy off, and RA567 would make it home on dwindling fuel reserved to land at Wing. F/O Boyd and crew were also coned by about twenty searchlights as they approached the target, and they spotted a BF109 lurking about nine hundred feet above. They took violent evasive action, which completely wrecked the bomb-run, and the load was ultimately jettisoned three miles west of the target. The remaining 106 Squadron crews delivered their cookies and 500 pounders each from 16,200 to 17,000 feet between 23.03 and 23.07, and the Master Bomber called "Cease bombing", at 23.11, before some from other squadrons had been able to bomb. Returning crews were confident in the effectiveness of their work, and photo-reconnaissance confirmed that the raid had been a complete success, which ended all production at the plant.

Two major operations were scheduled for the 8th, the larger one involving 440 aircraft from 4, 6 and 8 Groups to be directed against Hamburg's shipyards, where the new Type XXI U-Boots were under construction. 5 Group, meanwhile, would take on the Lützkendorf refinery, following a failed attempt on the 4th by 1 and 8 Groups to conclusively end production at the site. A force of 231 Lancasters and eleven Mosquitos was put together, of which seventeen belonged to 106 Squadron, and they departed Metheringham between 17.55 and 18.20 with S/L Bretherton the senior pilot on duty. They all reached the target area, where conditions were as they had been twenty-four hours earlier, with clear skies and either ground haze or generated smoke. The primary blind markers ran in at 14,000 feet at 22.33 to deliver green TIs, and the illuminators followed between 22.35 and 22.42, after which, the main force was called in. The 106 Squadron crews attacked in accordance with the Master Bomber's instructions to bomb the southerly red and yellow TIs after an eleven second overshoot. They ran in at 13,000 to 16,000 feet between 22.45 and 22.51, before returning safely to a diversion airfield at Long Marston, just south of Stratford-upon-Avon in Warwickshire, confident that it would not be necessary to return to that particular target. They described their experiences to the intelligence section at debriefing, reporting many explosions, including a large one at 22.47, which was surpassed in size by another one two minutes later, and flames were said to have reached up to 3,000 feet. The complete destruction of the site was confirmed by photo-reconnaissance, and the plant would remain out of action for what remained of the war. Earlier in the day, the length of a tour had been reduced from thirty-six to thirty-three sorties, and those with that number already under their belt, would, no doubt, get drunk in celebration that night.

The squadron sat out a modest 5 Group raid on oil storage tanks and U-Boot pens at Hamburg in daylight on the 9th, and an attack on a stretch of railway track linked to the Wahren marshalling yards, situated to the north-west of Leipzig on the night of the 10/11th. A larger operation on this night, involving more than three hundred aircraft from 1 and 8 Groups was directed at the Plauen marshalling yards to the south-west of Dresden, and the two forces would adopt a similar route until shortly before reaching Leipzig. 5 Group contributed all seventy-six Lancasters for Leipzig and eleven Mosquitos, with 8 Group providing the other eight Oboe Mosquitos, which, now that mobile Oboe stations had been set up on the Continent, could operate over the whole of Germany. The force was greeted in the target area by clear skies and excellent conditions for bombing and also a forest of ineffective searchlights co-operating with light flak only, because of the presence of night-fighters. The marking and bombing were accurate, and photographic-reconnaissance confirmed serious damage to the eastern half of the targeted stretch of track.

A major attack on Kiel by elements of 3, 6 and 8 Groups was planned for the night of the 13/14th, while a simultaneous mining effort involving over a hundred aircraft went ahead in Kiel Bay and the Kattegat. 5 Group detailed eighteen Lancasters to lay mines in the Forget-me-not garden in Kiel harbour, the five representing 106 Squadron departing Metheringham between 20.25 and 20.30 with S/L Barden the senior pilot on duty. F/O Gray and crew had a mine shake off its carrier during take-off, and, thereafter, it rolled around in the bomb bay, threatening to push the doors open. This one was jettisoned safe in the North Sea, leaving five more Mk VI devices to deliver to the target area, which they found underneath six to ten-tenths stratus with tops up to 7,000 feet. Employing H2S to establish their positions, the 106 Squadron crews fulfilled their briefs from 10,500 to 10,900 feet between 23.27 and 23.41, and returned safely to report successfully planting twenty-nine lethal vegetables.

5 Group was used to being handed the most distant targets, and, as the final days of the bombing war approached, it found itself facing three long-range trips on consecutive nights, all to railway targets. The first of these was at Pilsen in Czechoslovakia, for which a force of 222 Lancasters and eleven Mosquitos was made ready. Fourteen 106 Squadron crews attended briefing in the early evening, and the first eleven took off without incident between 23.25 and 23.40. NG414 was next in line with the crew of F/O Dean on board, but the Lancaster swung out of control as it gathered speed and crashed on the airfield. Happily, the occupants scrambled clear before the bomb load went up to register the squadron's final aircraft casualty of the war, but the incident prevented the remaining two sorties from taking off. The others found clear skies in the target area, and only slight haze, and, ahead, watched the first primary blind marker Lancaster deliver green TIs at 03.38, before the flare forces followed between 03.51 and 03.56. The main force was called in at 03.58, and the 106 Squadron participants bombed from 15,100 to 16,000 feet between 04.00 and 04.09, aiming at the north-westerly red and yellow TIs with an eight-second overshoot in accordance with the Master Bomber's instructions. Two large explosions were observed at 04.05, and other vivid explosions and smoke could be seen as they headed away from the target. F/O Harvey and crew were confused by another operation on this night, taking place against railway yards at Schwandorf on the German side of the frontier, south-west of Pilsen, and by the time they identified the correct location, the Master Bomber had called a halt to proceedings. Metheringham remained unserviceable because of the accident, and returning aircraft landed at Harwell and Manston.

There was good news to celebrate on the 17th, when the length of a tour was reduced yet again to thirty sorties, releasing many crews to contemplate a long future. That evening, the target posted for ninety 5 Group Lancasters and eleven Mosquitos was the marshalling yards at Cham, on Germany's border with Czechoslovakia. It took more than four hours to reach the target area, where the force was greeted by clear skies with slight ground haze and the 5 Group marking method prepared the target for destruction. The employment of delay-fused bombs meant that no immediate assessment would be possible, but photo-reconnaissance later confirmed that tracks had been torn up and rolling stock damaged, and it was another success for 5 Group.

Metheringham had not been called into action for the above operation, and remained inactive also while elements of 5 Group contributed to a force of more than nine hundred aircraft, which reduced the island of Heligoland to the appearance of a cratered moonscape on the 18th. 114 Lancasters from 5 Group returned to Czechoslovakia to deal with the railway yards at Komotau on the night of the 18/19th, and this brought to an end the campaign against communications begun more than a year earlier in preparation for D-Day. It was the afternoon of the 23rd before the squadron next flew in anger, when seventeen Lancasters took off between 15.40 and 15.50 to attack the railway yards and port facilities at Flensburg on the Baltic side of the Schleswig-Holstein peninsula. W/C Levis and S/L Barden were the senior pilots on duty, but the operation was thwarted by cloud conditions during the bombing run, and the 149-strong force was recalled. The final major operation of the war to involve 5 Group took place on the morning of the 25th, when eighty-eight Lancasters took off at first light to join elements of 1 and 8 Groups in an overall force of 359 Lancasters and sixteen Mosquitos to attack Hitler's Eaglesnest retreat at Berchtesgaden in the Bavarian mountains, and the nearby SS barracks.

106 Squadron was not invited to take part in the above somewhat symbolic operation, but contributed fourteen Lancasters to 5 Group's and, indeed, the Command's final offensive operation of the war by heavy bombers. It was an attack by 107 Lancasters and twelve Mosquitos on oil storage tanks at Tonsberg in the mouth of Oslo Fjord that same night. The 106 Squadron contingent departed Metheringham between 20.30 and 20.40 with S/L Bretherton the senior pilot on duty, but lost the services of F/L Davis and crew to an unserviceable a.s.i. This prevented the pilot from accurately assessing his landing speed, and persuaded him to use the long runway at the emergency landing strip at Carnaby. Twelve others found the target under eight to ten-tenths cloud, below which, the visibility was excellent, and the controller called them down to bomb on clearly visible red and yellow TIs. They complied from 7,900 to 9,900 feet between 23.46 and 23.52, and reported many explosions and black smoke. F/O Smythe and crew had to make a course correction and arrived over the target at 23.55, three minutes after the controller had called a halt, and they brought their bombs home. While this operation was in progress, S/L Barden and F/O Rowley RAAF delivered twelve mines between them into the waters of Oslo Fjord. Sadly, the ORB entry for this night is too corrupted to make out which crew had the honour to be the last to land and bring to an end 106 Squadron's outstanding operational career as part of Bomber Command's massive contribution to victory. During the course of the month the squadron operated on two days and five nights, dispatching ninety-three sorties without loss. The squadron learned that it had been awarded the silver Lancaster trophy for the January to March 1945 quarter for the fewest avoidable accidents, the third time that the squadron had been so honoured, and it reflected massively on the squadron and on the Metheringham service community.

As soon as the bombing war concluded, elements of the Command were put on to humanitarian duties, the most urgent of which was Operation Manna, the delivery of food to the starving Dutch people still under enemy occupation. From the end of April through to the 8th of May, hundreds of sorties were carried out, although 106 Squadron did not participate. Operation Exodus also began before the war had officially ended, to repatriate the many thousands of PoWs. 106 Squadron was involved in these flights on the 4th of May, when seventeen of its Lancasters brought home 402 former prisoners from Juvincourt, and on the 8th, the day on which the war officially ended, when six aircraft returned 144 men from Rheine. These operations would continue into the summer.

Once 106 Squadron entered the bombing war on the 9th of September 1940, it played a major role in all of the Command's campaigns and produced a record of service equal to any and surpassed by none. A list of some of those personalities associated with 106 Squadron serves to justify its tremendous spirit. W/C Allen laid the foundations of efficiency, and this was built upon by his successors. W/C Guy Gibson went on to fame as a Dambuster and earned a Victoria Cross, and his former 106 Squadron colleagues, John Hopgood, Lewis Burpee and David Shannon went with him into bomber folklore. John Searby, who gained fame as the Master Bomber at Peenemünde, also enjoyed a glittering career, as did John (Dim) Wooldridge, whom Searby replaced as flight commander at 106 Squadron. W/Cs Baxter, Piercy, Stevens and Levis understood that effective leadership came from the front, and they were supported admirably by their flight commanders, many of whom paid the ultimate price for their devotion to duty.

106 Squadron was, without doubt, one of the finest in Bomber Command, and, had Harris decided to take a squadron out of the line to tackle the dams operation, it seems likely that 106 would have been given the job. It carried out the fourth highest number of overall Lancaster operations in Bomber Command, and the third highest number of Lancaster overall operations and sorties in 5 Group.

The memory of this magnificent squadron and its final station of residence is perpetuated by the Metheringham Airfield Visitors' Centre at Westmoor Farm, Martin Moor, Metheringham, Lincolnshire. It is a vibrant community of volunteer enthusiasts and members, who keep alive the memory of those who graced the squadron through five unrelenting years of war. Close by lies the former airfield, now returned to farmland, whereon stands a monument to the memory of all who served there.

Thirteen 106 Squadron Lancasters over clouds early 1945.

106 Squadron at Metheringham. View from Lancaster LM690 ZN-R. February 1945.

F/O W (Ted) Hamilton clearing snow in January 1945

Lancaster JB663 ZN-A 'King of the Air'. 100+ operations. Believed to be F/O Day's crew

F/Sgt F W Berry (W.Op) in cockpit of 106 Squadron at Metheringham Lancaster PB284 ZN-U. 48 operations. Winter 1944/45

The Daniel Crew
Back: Sgt F W Berry (W.Op), Sgt J F Keating (MUG), Sgt K King (FE), Sgt P Waight (RG)
Front: P/O J C D Howie RCAF (BA), F/O J M Daniel (Pilo)t, Sgt P S Zolty (Nav)

106 Squadron at Metheringham early 1945. Baker Crew.
J L Fish (BA), G Clarke (RG), H K Baker, G Naylor (Nav), S Mason (FE), F Crabtree, (MUG), T Glasper (W.Op)

L – R: J L Fish, Cpl Peacey, H K Baker, G Naylor, G Clarke, T Glasper, S Mason

106 Squadron at Metheringham early 1945.
L – R: J L Fish, T Glasper, S Mason (in cockpit), H K Baker (in cockpit),
G Naylor, G Clarke.

106 Squadron Lancaster ND333 ZN-S 'Unbeatable' March 1945.

F/L G H Eakins and crew just before taking off on daylight raid to Essen. The insignia is three playing cards. This was taken at 90 operations, the aircraft completed at least 93.

F/L G H Eakins' Groundcrew. Sgt Buchanan in charge.

Lancaster ND333 ZN-S
Crew: L – R: H C Winsor, C T R White, E P Dryden, W Hesketh-Gibson, R P Moulds, F/L G H Eakins, N W H Thomas.

Dresden February 1945

106 Squadron at Metheringham November 1944-April 1945. S/L Bretherton and Crew. Lancaster PB618 ZN-G 'Let George Do It'. 51 Operations. Back L-R: E Peters, E Dickenson, DB Bretherton, AEG Smith, L Kendall, W D Hill, RCAF, E Carney RCAF

106 Squadron Disbandment

106 Squadron

Top L – R: S/L D B Bretherton, OC A Flight; W/C L G Levis, OC 106 Squadron, S/L G O McGregor OC B Flight.
2nd Row L – R: F/L Stevens, F/L Sanford, F/L Rowe, F/L L J B Blood, F/L Ronaldson
3rd Row L – R: F/L B R Marks, F/O Pilkington, F/O K R Richardson, F/O Schneider, F/O Harvey.
4th Row L – R: F/O Palowker, F/L J H Barnes, F/O Bannister, F/O Topping, F/O Mosby,
5th Row L – R: F/O Wilston, F/O Edwards, F/O H K Baker, F/L Burroughs, F/L Sievwright.
6th Row L – R: F/O Dobbie, W/O Middleton, F/O H Anderson.

106 Squadron crew 20th June 1945 at Metheringham

W/C L G Levis and Crew

Crew of W/C MMJ Stevens in front of Lancaster LM690, ZN-P, 'Come on Steve'

A group of the intelligence boffins

106 Squadron Lancaster ND616 ZN-J pranged 17th July 1945. Note the FIDO pipes.

Sulzer pumps installed at Graveley, Huntingdonshire, to supply the FIDO (Fog Investigation and Dispersal Operation) petrol pipes on either side of the main runway, 28th May 1945. Similar pumps would have operated at Metheringham.

Skoda Works in Pilsen, Czechoslovakia.

Lützkendorf oil refinery after bombing, 1945.

VE Day – 8th May 1945. Streams of 'Window' decorate the Repair & Maintenance Hangar.

106 Squadron Memorial
Metheringham

106 SQUADRON

MOTTO **PRO LIBERTATE** (For freedom)   Code **ZN**

Stations

COTTESMORE	01.09.39. to 06.10.39.
FINNINGLEY	06.10.39. to 23.02.41.
CONINGSBY	23.02.41. to 01.10.42.
SYERSTON	01.10.42. to 11.11.43.
METHERINGHAM	11.11.43. to 18.02.46.

Commanding Officers

WING COMMANDER G R MONTGOMMERIE	08.10.38. to 16.06.40.
SQUADRON LEADER R D STUBBS DFC (Temp)	16.06.40. to 02.11.40.
WING COMMANDER W J H LINDLAY	02.11.40. to 28.02.41.
WING COMMANDER P J POLGLASE	01.03.41 to 05.04.41.
SQUADRON LEADER R.P. NELMS (Temp)	09.04.41. to 04.05.41.
WING COMMANDER R S ALLEN DFC	04.05.41. to 20.03.42.
WING COMMANDER G P GIBSON DSO DFC	20.03.42. to 14.03.43.
WING COMMANDER J H SEARBY DFC	14.03.43. to 09.05.43.
WING COMMANDER R E BAXTER DFC	09.05.43. to 30.03.44.
WING COMMANDER E K PIERCY DFC	30.03.44. to 25.08.44.
WING COMMANDER M M J STEVENS DFC	25.08.44. to 15.03.45.
WING COMMANDER L G LEVIS	15.03.45. to 18.02.46.

Flight Commanders

A FLIGHT

Flying Officer C E Johnson	24.10.38. to 01.11.39.
Squadron Leader W Sheen (temp)	01.11.39. to 01.12.39.
Squadron Leader T C Weir	01.12.39. to 04.09.40.
Squadron Leader Cooper	04.09.40. to 02.03.41.
Squadron Leader R P Nelms	02.03 41. to 01.04.42.
Squadron Leader F H Robertson	01.04.42. to 28.07.42.
Squadron Leader C M Howell	28.07.42. to 17.09.42.
Squadron Leader C E Hill	17.09.42. to 18.10.42.
Flight Lieutenant W N Whamond	18.10.42. to 16.11.42.
Squadron Leader A J McDougall	16.11.42. to 01.03.43.
Squadron Leader P Ward-Hunt	01.03.43. to 01.04.43.
Squadron Leader J Latimer	01.04.43. to 17.04.43.
Squadron Leader E A Williamson	17.04.43. to 01.07.43.
Squadron Leader P Brandon-Trye	01.07.43. to 19.07 43.

Squadron Leader D S Howroyd							19.07.43. to 21.10.43.
Squadron Leader A R Dunn							21.10.43. to 10.04.44.
Squadron Leader H R Belleroche						10.04.44. to 10.07.44.
Squadron Leader A L Williams						10.07.44. to 10.08.44.
Squadron Leader W J Allinson						10.08.44. to 30.12.44.
Squadron Leader D B Bretherton						30.12.44.

B FLIGHT

Squadron Leader Parker							1939. to c 06.40.
Squadron Leader Stubbs							06.40. to 28.10.40.
Squadron Leader Norris							28.10.40. to
Squadron Leader Parker							to 16.03.41.
Squadron Leader S O Tudor							16.03.41. to 01.10.41.
Squadron Leader C D Stenner							01.10.41. to 10.06.42.
Squadron Leader J de L Wooldridge						10.06.42. to 01.11.42.
Squadron Leader J Searby							01.11.42. to 15.03.43.
Squadron Leader E L Hayward							15.03.43. to 01.04.43.
Squadron Leader A M Young							01.04.43. to 27.06.43.
Squadron Leader A H Crowe							27.06.43. to 15.02.44.
Squadron Leader A O S Murdoch						15.02.44. to 28.04.44.
Squadron Leader E A Sprawson						28.04.44. to 08.06.44.
Squadron Leader T O Marshall						08.06.44. to 09.07.44.
Squadron Leader J E Grindon							09.07.44. to 08.10.44.
Squadron Leader M Parry							08.10.44. to 10.01.45.
Squadron Leader A Barden							10.01.45.

Aircraft

HAMPDEN							05.39. to 03.42.
MANCHESTER							02.42. to 06.42.
LANCASTER I/III							05.42. to 02.46.

Operational Record

OPERATIONS	SORTIES	AIRCRAFT LOSSES	% LOSSES
557	5745	169	2.9

CATEGORY OF OPERATIONS

BOMBING	MINING	OTHER
471	82	4

HAMPDEN

OPERATIONS	SORTIES	AIRCRAFT LOSSES	% LOSSES
150	1230	55	4.5

CATEGORY OF OPERATIONS

BOMBING	MINING
106	44

MANCHESTER

OPERATIONS	SORTIES	AIRCRAFT LOSSES	% LOSSES
36	151	9	6.0

CATEGORY OF OPERATIONS

BOMBING	MINING	OTHER
19	14	3

LANCASTER

OPERATIONS	SORTIES	AIRCRAFT LOSSES	% LOSSES
371	4364	105	2.4

CATEGORY OF OPERATIONS

BOMBING	MINING	OTHER
346	24	1

Aircraft Histories

HAMPDEN.	**To March 1942.**

L4038	From 49 Squadron. To 25 OTU.
L4042	From 44 (Rhodesia) Squadron. To 408 (Goose) Squadron RCAF.
L4100	From 44 (Rhodesia) Squadron. To 14 OTU.
L4103	From 61 Squadron. Crashed in circuit at Finningley during night training 7.12.40.
L4120	From 61 Squadron. Crashed at Finningley while training 16.12.40.
L4139	From 76 Squadron. To 7 Squadron.
L4149	From 76 Squadron. To 50 Squadron.
L4150	To 50 Squadron.
L4174 ZN-A	Crashed near Finningley while training 31.5.40.
L4175 ZN-B	Crashed while trying to land at Finningley 24.10.39.
L4176	To 7 Squadron.
L4177	To 7 Squadron.
L4178	To 44 (Rhodesia) Squadron.
L4180 ZN-F	FTR from mining sortie 29/30.10.40.
L4181	Crashed on landing at Finningley while training 6.7.40.
L4182 ZN-K	To 1 AAS.
L4183 ZN-P	Crashed on take-off at Finningley while training 29.11.40.
L4184 ZN-Q	Crashed on take-off at Finningley while training 13.10.40.
L4185 ZN-S	Crashed in the Thames Estuary on return from Dortmund 4/5.7.41.
L4186 ZN-T	Crashed in Lincolnshire while training 11.11.39.
L4187 ZN-U	Crashed in Lincolnshire while training 7/8.8.40.
L4188 ZN-V	Blew up over Buckinghamshire while training 1.9.40.
L4189	Crashed in Derbyshire while training 30.9.40.
L4194	From 195 Squadron. FTR from mining sortie 22/23.11.40
P1198	To 144 Squadron.
P1228 ZN-L	From 50 Squadron. FTR Hamburg 30.11/1.12.41.
P1253	To 61 Squadron.
P1254	To 14 OTU.
P1255	To BTU.
P1256	Crashed near Finningley during training 27.9.40.
P1258	To 25 OTU.
P1259	FTR from mining sortie 18/19.9.40.
P1290	FTR from mining sortie 7/8.11.41.
P1303	To 5 Group TF.
P1304 ZN-Y	Crashed in Yorkshire while training 21.12.40.
P1311	To 32 OTU.
P1320 ZN-B	Crashed in Lincolnshire during training 25.11.40.
P1321	To 50 Squadron.
P1322	To 44 (Rhodesia) Squadron.
P1336	Crashed at Coventry during training 24.5.40.
P1337	To 5 Group TF.
P1341	From 16 OTU. FTR Hamburg 15/16.1.42.
P2071	Abandoned over Shropshire while training 23.12.40.

P2073	To 408 (Goose) Squadron RCAF.
P2083	To 5 Group TF and back. Force-landed at Wellesbourne Mountford on return from mining sortie 27.5.41.
P2098	FTR from mining sortie 27/28.12.40.
P2099 ZN-K	Force-landed in Rutland during training 17.5.41.
P2129	To 16 OTU.
P4302	To 25 OTU.
P4314	From 14 OTU. Crashed near Finningley while training 3.1.41.
P4318	To 25 OTU.
P4323	From 16 OTU. FTR from mining sortie 23/24.2.42.
P4377	To 49 Squadron.
P4398	From 83 Squadron. FTR Münster 28/29.1.42.
P4413 ZN-J	Crashed while landing at Pocklington on return from Hamburg 16.9.41.
P4414	From 44 (Rhodesia) Squadron. FTR from an intruder operation to the Cologne area 21/22.2.42.
P5323	From 7 AAU. Converted for use as torpedo bomber. To 455 Squadron RAAF.
P5330	From 7 AAU. To 420 (Snowy Owl) Squadron RCAF.
X2914	Abandoned over Somerset on return from mining sortie 27.9.40.
X2921	To 44 (Rhodesia) Squadron.
X2960	Force-landed near Finningley while training 18.9.40.
X2970	To 25 OTU.
X2986 ZN-F	FTR Cologne 20/21.4.41.
X3002	FTR Cologne 3/4.3.41.
X3021	From 49 Squadron. FTR Schiphol 29/30.10.41.
X3058	From 61 Squadron. FTR Münster 28/29.1.42.
X3131	From 83 Squadron. Converted for use as torpedo bomber. To 455 Squadron RAAF.
X3148 ZN-E	FTR Düsseldorf 10/11.4.41.
X3152	To 5 Bombing and Gunnery School.
X3153	FTR Düsseldorf 10/11.4.41.
X3154 ZN-A	Crashed in Derbyshire during navigation exercise 21.12.40.
AD735 ZN-R	FTR Mönchengladbach (97 (Straits Settlement) Squadron crew) 7/8.7.41.
AD736	To 16 OTU.
AD738	FTR Brest 4/5.4.41.
AD743	To 25 OTU.
AD746 ZN-Z	Crashed on approach to Coningsby on return from Bremen 21.10.41.
AD749	To 14 OTU.
AD750	FTR from mining sortie 4/5.2.41.
AD756	FTR Düsseldorf 16/17.8.41.
AD758	To 44 (Rhodesia) Squadron.
AD760 ZN-W	FTR from mining sortie 7/8.11.41.
AD763	Crashed on landing at Coningsby during a ferry flight 1.3.41.
AD765	To 144 Squadron.
AD768	Abandoned over Ireland on return from Karlsruhe 1/2.10.41.
AD785	Blew up over Yorkshire on return from Hamburg 27.10.41.
AD790	Crashed on take-off at Coningsby while training 25.2.41.
AD799	To 49 Squadron.
AD802	To 14 OTU.

AD803	To 455 Squadron RAAF and back. To 408 (Goose) Squadron RCAF.
AD848	From 16 OTU. To 14 OTU.
AD855	To 44 (Rhodesia) Squadron.
AD857	To 408 (Goose) Squadron RCAF.
AD861	Crashed off Plymouth on return from Brest (97 (Straits Settlement) Squadron crew) 7.7.41.
AD862	FTR Duisburg 2/3.7.41.
AD863	FTR Cologne 15/16.6.41.
AD873	FTR Duisburg 2/3.7.41.
AD895	FTR Bremen 29/30.6.41.
AD914	FTR Dortmund 4/5.7.41.
AD919	Force-landed soon after take-off from Coningsby when bound for Cologne 18.8.41.
AD925	To A&AEE.
AD929	To 50 Squadron.
AD932	FTR from mining sortie 7/8.11.41.
AD970	Crashed off Skegness during air test 30.7.41.
AD984	FTR Bremen 20/21.10.41.
AD986	FTR Dortmund 4/5.7.41.
AD988	To 14 OTU.
AE120	FTR Mannheim 5/6.8.41.
AE123 ZN-D	From 49 Squadron. FTR Bremen 21/22.1.42.
AE134	FTR Düsseldorf 16/17.8.41.
AE136	FTR Hamburg 26/27.10.41.
AE144	FTR Essen 10/11.10.41.
AE151 ZN-F	FTR from intruder sortie over Germany 21.12.41.
AE186	From 420 (Snowy Owl) Squadron RCAF. To 408 (Goose) Squadron RCAF.
AE193 ZN-A	FTR Duisburg 28/29.8.41.
AE220	FTR Mannheim 22/23.8.41.
AE232	FTR Hamburg 15/16.9.41.
AE246	To 420 (Snowy Owl) Squadron RCAF.
AE255	To 5 OTU.
AE261	To 49 Squadron.
AE292	Crashed in Lincolnshire during training 14.1.42.
AE293	From 97 (Straits Settlement) Squadron. To 408 (Goose) Squadron RCAF.
AE299	From 207 Squadron. FTR Berlin 7/8.9.41.
AE300	From 97 (Straits Settlement) Squadron. FTR Rostock 11/12.9.41.
AE301 ZN-N	From 97 (Straits Settlement) Squadron. FTR from mining sortie 26/27.8.41.
AE302	From 97 (Straits Settlement) Squadron. FTR Cologne 26/27.8.41.
AE307	Converted for use as torpedo bomber. To 455 Squadron RAAF.
AE317	FTR Emden 26/27.11.41.
AE378	To 420 (Snowy Owl) Squadron RCAF.
AE391	FTR Gelsenkirchen 12.12.41.
AE425	Crashed on take-off from Coningsby en-route to Mannheim 11.2.42.
AE426	To 408 (Goose) Squadron RCAF.
AT115	FTR Hamburg 30.11/1.12.41.
AT121	FTR Münster 28/29.1.42.
AT122 ZN-A	FTR Münster 28/29.1.42.
AT123 ZN-K	FTR from mining sortie 3/4.1.42.

AT131	To 455 Squadron RAAF.
AT141	To 408 (Goose) Squadron RCAF.
AT146	From 50 Squadron. FTR from mining sortie 22/23.1.42.
AT178	To 49 Squadron.
AT190	To 49 Squadron.
AT191	To 49 Squadron.
AT219	To 420 (Snowy Owl) Squadron RCAF.

MANCHESTER. **From February 1942 to June 1942.**

L7291	From 97 (Straits Settlement) Squadron. No operations. To 50 Squadron.
L7301 ZN-D	FTR Cologne 30/31.5.42, (50 Squadron crew of P/O Manser VC).
L7305	From 25 OTU. Became ground instruction machine.
L7315	From 61 Squadron. No operations.
L7317	From 207 Squadron. Force-landed near Lee-on-Solent on return from Dortmund 15.4.42 after twenty-one operations.
L7319	From 207 Squadron. Completed at least 25 operations. Fate not recorded.
L7376	From 25 OTU. To 1654 Conversion Unit.
L7378	From 207 Squadron. Completed thirty-two operations. To 1654 Conversion Unit.
L7389	From 49 Squadron. To 106 Squadron Conversion Flight. Became ground instruction machine.
L7390	FTR Essen 25/26.3.42.
L7391 ZN-F	From 207 Squadron. To 1485 Flight.
L7394	From 83 Squadron. FTR from mining sortie 29/30.3.42.
L7398	To 49 Squadron.
L7399 ZN-X	FTR from mining sortie 2/3.5.42.
L7417 ZN-V	From 207 Squadron. Crashed on cross-country excercise 19.5.42.
L7418	FTR from training flight, presumed lost in the Irish Sea 19.5.42.
L7434 ZN-U/J	To 1656 Conversion Unit.
L7456 ZN-T	FTR Cologne 30/31.5.42. (50 Squadron crew).
L7457	From 97 Straits Settlement) Squadron Conversion Flight. To 83 Squadron Conversion Flight via 106 Squadron Conversion Flight.
L7461	From 97 (Straits Settlement) Squadron. To 1660 Conversion Unit.
L7463 ZN-L	From 97 (Straits Settlement) Squadron. FTR Rostock 23/24.4.42.
L7467	From 97 (Straits Settlement) Squadron Conversion Flight. To 1661 Conversion Unit.
L7474	From 97 (Straits Settlement) Squadron. Abandoned over Lincolnshire while training 12.3.42.
L7485	From 207 Squadron. FTR from mining sortie 16/17.4.42.
L7488 ZN-E	From 207 Squadron. Became ground instruction machine.
L7515 ZN-O	From 207 Squadron. To 49 Squadron.
R5769	From 25 OTU. To 50 Squadron.
R5770 ZN-G	From 25 OTU. To 1660 Conversion Unit.
R5780 ZN-G	From 83 Squadron. Returned to 83 Squadron.
R5796 ZN-K	From 207 Squadron. Eighteen operations. To 1654 Conversion Unit.
R5839	To 1661 Conversion Unit.
R5840 ZN-X	FTR from mining sortie 2/3.5.42.
R5841	To 1660 Conversion Unit.

LANCASTER.   **From May 1942.**

L7569	From 44 (Rhodesia) Squadron. Became ground instruction machine.
L7577	From 97 Straits Settlement) Squadron on loan for one operation. Returned to 97 (Straits Settlement) Squadron. To 1654 Conversion Unit via 106 Squadron Conversion Flight.
L7579 ZN-Z	From A.V.Roe. To 1654 Conversion Unit via 106 Squadron Conversion Flight.
L7582 ZN-P	From 207 Squadron. To 100 Squadron.
R5492 ZN-S/Y	From 44 (Rhodesia) Squadron. To 1661 Conversion Unit.
R5551 ZN-V	From 97 (Straits Settlement) Squadron. FTR Oberhausen 14/15.6.43.
R5572 ZN-M	From 97 (Straits Settlement) Squadron. FTR Gelsenkirchen 25/26.6.43.
R5573 ZN-B	FTR Cologne 8/9.7.43.
R5574 ZN-H	FTR Munich 21/22.12.42.
R5575	From 97 (Straits Settlement) Squadron. 106 Squadron Conversion Flight only. Returned to 97 (Straits Settlement) Squadron.
R5576 ZN-J	To 106 Conversion Flight. Crashed on take-off from Coningsby while training 21.7.42.
R5604 ZN-X	FTR Düsseldorf 31.7/1.8.42. Was carrying first 8,000lb bomb.
R5608 ZN-Y	FTR from mining sortie 25/26.7.42.
R5609 ZN-L	From 97 (Straits Settlement) Squadron. To 1LFS.
R5611 ZN-D/W	From R.A.E. FTR Pilsen 13/14.5.43.
R5614 ZN-Z	From 97 (Straits Settlement) Squadron. Crashed at Syerston while training 1.8.43.
R5631	From 44 (Rhodesia) Squadron. 106 Squadron Conversion Flight only. To 1660 Conversion Unit.
R5637 ZN-D	FTR Düsseldorf 27/28.1.43.
R5638	FTR Düsseldorf 10/11.9.42.
R5665 ZN-D	From 44 (Rhodesia) Squadron. FTR Remscheid 30/31.7.43.
R5668	To 207 Squadron.
R5676 ZN-E	To 1660 Conversion Unit via 106 Squadron Conversion Flight.
R5677 ZN-B/A	FTR Wuppertal 29/30.5.43.
R5678	FTR Düsseldorf 15/16.8.42.
R5680 ZN-C/T	FTR Essen 13/14.1.43.
R5681 ZN-Y/O	Flown by W/C Gibson on his first Lancaster operation. FTR Essen 16/17.9.42.
R5683	Exploded over The Wash when bound for Duisburg 26.7.42.
R5684 ZN-P	FTR Frankfurt 24/25.8.42.
R5697 ZN-J	From 44 (Rhodesia) Squadron. FTR Duisburg 20/21.12.42.
R5700 ZN-G	Completed thirty-four operations. To 9 Squadron via 5MU.
R5702	From 50 Squadron. To 460 Squadron RAAF.
R5731 ZN-M	FTR Hamburg 3/4.3.43.
R5742	To 61 Squadron.
R5748 ZN-R	FTR Hamburg 26/27.7.42.
R5749 ZN-G	FTR Essen 12/13.3.43.
R5750 ZN-Z	FTR Wilhelmshaven 18/19.2.43.
R5844 C4	From 50 Squadron Conversion Flight. Conversion Flight only. FTR Essen 1/2.6.42. First operational loss of 106 Squadron Lancaster.

R5848 C7	From 207 Squadron via 106 Squadron Conversion Flight. To 1660 Conversion Unit.
R5854 C3	Conversion Flight only. To 97 (Straits Settlement) Squadron.
R5861 ZN-Q	FTR Wilhelmshaven 8/9.7.42.
R5864 ZN-K	To 61 Squadron and back. Returned to 61 Squadron.
R5899 ZN-F	FTR from mining sortie 18/19.9.42.
R5900 ZN-X	Crashed while landing at Syerston on return from Berlin 18.1.43.
R5901 ZN-U	To 44 (Rhodesia) Squadron.
R5906	106 Conversion Flight only. To XV Squadron.
R5910	To 61 Squadron and back. To 1654 Conversion Unit.
R5914	FTR Munich 21/22.12.42.
W4102 ZN-E	Crashed on approach to Langar after early return from Aachen 5.10.42.
W4109	FTR Mainz 11/12.8.42.
W4118 ZN-Y/Z	FTR Turin 4/5.2.43.
W4127 C2	From 97 (Straits Settlement) Squadron. Conversion Flight only. To 619 Squadron.
W4156 ZN-J	FTR Duisburg 8/9.4.43.
W4178	FTR Essen 16/17.9.42.
W4179	FTR Essen 16/17.9.42.
W4195 ZN-W	FTR Cologne 15/16.10.42.
W4238 ZN-C	Crashed at Newton following early return from Krefeld 2.10.42.
W4242 ZN-A/F	FTR Hannover 8/9.10.43.
W4253	To 1661 Conversion Unit.
W4256 ZN-V/D	FTR Gelsenkirchen 25/26.6.43.
W4261 ZN-C	FTR Essen 13/14.1.43.
W4302	FTR Cologne 15/16.10.42.
W4367 ZN-C	From 50 Squadron. FTR Gelsenkirchen 25/26.6.43.
W4381	From 467 Squadron RAAF. To 61 Squadron.
W4768	FTR Krefeld 2/3.10.42.
W4770 ZN-O	FTR Hamburg 3/4.2.43.
W4771	FTR Cologne 15/16.10.42.
W4778	To 44 (Rhodesia) Squadron via 106 Squadron Conversion Flight.
W4826 ZN-D	From 467 Squadron RAAF. FTR Hamburg 30/31.1.43.
W4842 ZN-O/H	FTR Essen 27/28.5.43.
W4886 ZN-X	FTR Nuremberg 25/26.2.43.
W4897 ZN-X	From 156 Squadron. To 463 Squadron RAAF.
W4918 ZN-D	FTR Essen 5/6.3.43.
W4921 ZN-Z	To 617 Squadron for training purposes.
W4922 ZN-J	From 156 Squadron. FTR Mannheim 5/6.9.43.
DV181 ZN-E	FTR Turin 12/13.7.43.
DV182 ZN-S	FTR Mannheim 5/6.9.43.
DV195	FTR Nuremberg 10/11.8.43.
DV196 ZN-K	FTR Milan 7/8.8.43.
DV229 ZN-Z	Admiral Shyte-'Awk. To 463 Squadron RAAF.
DV271	FTR Mannheim 23/24.9.43.
DV272 ZN-F	FTR Hannover 8/9.10.43.
DV273 ZN-L	To Bombing Development Unit.
DV274 ZN-K	To 463 Squadron RAAF.
DV297 ZN-O	To 61 Squadron.

DV339	To 61 Squadron.
DV344 ZN-S	To 61 Squadron.
ED303 ZN-A/J	From 467 Squadron RAAF. FTR Hamburg 27/28.7.43.
ED358 ZN-T	From 50 Squadron. FTR Leipzig 20/21.10.43.
ED360 ZN-K	From 467 Squadron RAAF. Crashed near Wisbech on return from Cologne 9.7.43.
ED385	From 57 Squadron. FTR Berlin 3/4.9.43.
ED409 ZN-B/E	From 50 Squadron. FTR Berlin 31.8/1.9.43.
ED420	From 9 Squadron. To 463 Squadron RAAF.
ED451 ZN-O	FTR Essen 30.4/1.5.43.
ED542	FTR Essen 3/4.4.43.
ED593 ZN-T/Y	To 5LFS after at least 71 operations.
ED596 ZN-H	FTR Berlin 29/30.3.43.
ED649 ZN-X	FTR Oberhausen 14/15.6.43.
ED708	FTR Hamburg 27/28.7.43.
ED720 ZN-R	FTR Cologne 8/9.7.43.
ED752 ZN-H/P	FTR Stuttgart 14/15.4.43.
ED801 ZN-N	To 207 Squadron via 1661 Conversion Unit.
ED819 ZN-U	FTR Munich 6/7.9.43.
ED873	From 97 (Straits Settlement) Squadron. Crashed while landing at Metheringham following early return from Berlin 26.11.43.
ED874 ZN-O/D	From 97 (Straits Settlement) Squadron. FTR Berlin 2/3.12.43.
EE125 ZN-R	FTR Gelsenkirchen 25/26.6.43.
EE186	From 49 Squadron. To 61 Squadron.
EE191 ZN-R/G	To 463 Squadron RAAF.
JA845	From SIU. No operations. To Bombing Development Unit.
JA871	FTR Leverkusen 22/23.8.43.
JA876 ZN-R	To 1661 Conversion Unit.
JA893 ZN-C	Ditched in North Sea on return from Berlin 3/4.9.43.
JA973 ZN-F/E	To 463 Squadron RAAF.
JB146 ZN-F	Crash-landed at Romney Marsh on return from Berlin 1.9.43.
JB292 ZN-R	From 1660 Conversion Unit. FTR Salbris 7/8.5.44.
JB534 ZN-K	From 61 Squadron. Crashed in Lincolnshire on return from Berlin 16.2.44.
JB562 ZN-M	Completed eleven Berlin operations. FTR Schweinfurt 26/27.4.44.
JB566 ZN-C	Completed ten Berlin operations. FTR Nuremberg 30/31.3.44.
JB567 ZN-E	Completed ten Berlin operations. FTR Braunschweig 22/23.4.44.
JB592 ZN-W	FTR Berlin 26/27.11.43.
JB593 ZN-T	Completed thirteen Berlin operations. FTR Königsburg 29/30.8.44.
JB601 ZN-V	Completed eleven Berlin operations. FTR Schweinfurt 26/27.4.44.
JB612 ZN-U/G	FTR Salbris 7/8.5.44.
JB638 ZN-G	FTR Berlin 16/17.12.43.
JB641 ZN-X	Completed eleven Berlin operations. FTR St-Leu-d'Esserent 7/8.7.44.
JB642 ZN-J	FTR Berlin 1/2.1.44.
JB645 ZN-F	FTR Berlin 1/2.1.44.
JB648 ZN-B	FTR Frankfurt 22/23.3.44.
JB663 ZN-A	Completed 111 operations. To 24 Maintenance Unit.
JB664 ZN-N	FTR Vitry-le-Francois 27/28.6.44.
LL891 ZN-S/B	FTR Salbris 7/8.5.44.
LL948 ZN-V	FTR Lützkendorf 14/15.3.45.

LL953 ZN-C/O	FTR Gravenhorst 6/7.11.44.	
LL955 ZN-E	FTR Gelsenkirchen 21/22.6.44.	
LL974 ZN-F	FTR Vitry-le-Francois 27/28.6.44.	
LL975 ZN-H	FTR Pommerval 24/25.6.44.	
LM211 ZN-Z	To 7 Squadron.	
LM215 ZN-F	Crash-landed at Juvincourt on return from Siegen 1.2.45.	
LM303 ZN-M	FTR Wilhelmshaven 11/12.2.43.	
LM310	From 467 Squadron RAAF. To 61 Squadron.	
LM377 ZN-F	To 61 Squadron.	
LM549 ZN-R	Crash-landed at Carnaby on return from Nantes 28.5.44.	
LM570 ZN-Z	FTR Scholven-Buer 21/22.6.44.	
LM641 ZN-D	FTR Secqueville 7/8.8.44.	
LM690 ZN-P	To 7 Squadron.	
ME313	From 582 Squadron via Navigation Training Unit.	
ME324 ZN-R	To 1661 Conversion Unit.	
ME355 ZN-P/S	From 514 Squadron. To 50 Squadron.	
ME336	From 514 Squadron.	
ME630 ZN-P	From 97 (Straits Settlement) Squadron. FTR Leipzig 19/20.2.44.	
ME668 ZN-L	FTR St-Leu-d'Esserent 7/8.7.44.	
ME669 ZN-O	FTR Schweinfurt 26/27.4.44.	
ME778 ZN-O	FTR Stuttgart 28/29.7.44.	
ME789 ZN-B/R	FTR St-Leu-d'Esserent 7/8.7.44.	
ME790 ZN-U	FTR Braunschweig (Brunswick) 22/23.5.44.	
ME831 ZN-R	FTR St-Leu-d'Esserent 7/8.7.44.	
ME832 ZN-J	FTR St-Leu-d'Esserent 4/5.7.44.	
ND331 ZN-G/C	FTR Königsburg 29/30.8.44.	
ND332 ZN-B	Crash-landed at Manston on return from Nuremberg 30/31.3.44.	
ND333 ZN-R/S	From 83 Squadron.	
ND336 ZN-Q	FTR Berlin 30/31.1.44.	
ND339 ZN-Z/U	Detached to 617 Squadron. Returned to 106 Squadron. FTR St-Leu-d'Esserent 4/5.7.44.	
ND501 ZN-K/O	From 97 (Straits Settlement) Squadron. Crashed while landing at Metheringham during training 3.4.45.	
ND511 ZN-N/E	FTR Gennevilliers 9/10.5.44.	
ND535 ZN-Q	FTR Nuremberg 30/31.3.44.	
ND585 ZN-J/Q	FTR Nuremberg 30/31.3.44.	
ND680 ZN-P	FTR Coutances (Caen) 6/7.6.44.	
ND682 ZN-X/K	FTR from mining sortie 15/16.12.44.	
ND850 ZN-C	FTR Schweinfurt 26/27.4.44.	
ND851 ZN-H	FTR Gennevilliers 9/10.5.44.	
ND853 ZN-J	FTR Schweinfurt 26/27.4.44.	
ND868 ZN-Q	FTR Dortmund Ems Canal 23/24.9.44.	
ND870 ZN-S	FTR Salbris 7/8.5.44.	
NE150 ZN-H	FTR Coutances (Caen) 6/7.6.44.	
NG222 ZN-T	To 1654 Conversion Unit.	
NG397 ZN-T	From 1661 Conversion Unit.	
NG414 ZN-K	From 1661 Conversion Unit. Crashed on take-off from Metheringham when bound for Pilsen 16.4.45.	
NN719 ZN-Q	To 7 Squadron.	

NN725	To 7 Squadron.
NN726 ZN-D	FTR Gdynia 18/19.12.44.
PA194 ZN-D	From 1661 Conversion Unit.
PA232 ZN-H	To RWA.
PA267 ZN-N	To 7 Squadron.
PA310	To 7 Squadron.
PA331	To 7 Squadron.
PB122 ZN-Y	FTR Leuna 14/15.1.45.
PB144 ZN-P	FTR St-Leu-d'Esserent 7/8.7.44.
PB145 ZN-L/M	Damaged and written-off.
PB191 ZN-H	How's Hare.
PB203 ZN-M	FTR Darmstadt 11/12.9.44.
PB232 ZN-N	Twice damaged and written-off.
PB248 ZN-E	To 5LFS.
PB281 ZN-J	FTR Heilbronn 3/4.12.44.
PB284 ZN-U/S	To RAE for use in mine experiments.
PB296 ZN-X	Damaged beyond repair 23/24.2.45.
PB298 ZN-B	Force-landed near Fulbeck on return from Bremerhaven 19.9.44.
PB303 ZN-R	FTR Homburg 1.11.44.
PB304 ZN-Z/S	Crashed in Lancashire on return from operation to the Normandy battle area 30.7.44.
PB347 ZN-G	From 49 Squadron. FTR Rheydt 19/20.9.44.
PB359 ZN-T	From 49 Squadron. FTR Rheydt 19/20.9.44.
PB617 ZN-B	FTR Royan 5.1.45.
PB618 ZN-G	
PB645	To 227 Squadron.
PB676 ZN-E	From 35 (Madras Presidency) Squadron. To 189 Squadron.
PB682	From 405 (Vancouver) Squadron RCAF.
PB724 ZN-L/M	FTR Munich 7/8.1.45.
PB732 ZN-K	From 189 Squadron.
PB734 ZN-E	Crash-landed at Metheringham 1.2.45.
PD214 ZN-D	FTR Bremen 6/7.10.44.
PD429	To 186 Squadron.
RA508 ZN-B	FTR Dortmund 12.3.45.
RA567	To 7 Squadron.
RA581 ZN-B	To 35 (Madras Presidency) Squadron.
RE130	To 7 Squadron.
RF130 ZN-F	To 7 Squadron.
RF151 ZN-E	From 189 Squadron.
RF215	To 7 Squadron.
RF235	Crashed at Rheine air base in Germany 9.5.45.
RF236 ZN-V	To the Middle East.
SW248 ZN-R	From 1661 Conversion Unit.
SW265 ZN-O	From 49 Squadron.

HEAVIEST SINGLE LOSS.

Schweinfurt   26/27.04.44. 5 Lancasters FTR.
St-Leu-d'Esserent 07/08.07.44. 5 Lancasters FTR.

Roll of Honour

F/O	Elmer Oscar	AARON	08.05.44.
Sgt	Sydney	ABEL	01.05.43.
Sgt	Leonard	ACRES	17.08.41.
F/O	Juan Alberto	ADAMS-LANGLEY	08.07.44.
F/Sgt	Ross Maddaugh	AGNEW	11.02.43.
Sgt	John Gordon	ALDERSON	01.05.43.
Sgt	Frank Henry	ALDRIDGE	22.06.44.
W/OII	Joseph	ALEO	13.01.43.
F/Sgt	George	ALLANSON	04.04.41.
F/Sgt	Douglas George	ALLBON	04.12.44.
Sgt	Dennis Geoffrey	ALLEN	08.05.44.
Sgt	William	ALTON	20.10.41.
Sgt	Edward William John	AMOR	09.07.43.
Sgt	George Stewart	ANDERSON	20.12.42.
Sgt	Reginald Stephen	ANDERSON	24.02.42.
F/Sgt	Walter Mowbray	ANDREWS	11.09.42.
Sgt	Ernest	ANTHONY	10.05.44.
Sgt	John Richard	ANYAN	28.01.42.
F/Sgt	Geoffrey	APPLEYARD	26.07.42.
Sgt	Ian George	ARMET	28.07.43.
Sgt	George Henry	ARMSTRONG	15.03.45.
Sgt	Robert Lionel	ARMSTRONG	06.11.44.
F/O	Philip Sydney	ARNOLD	07.06.44.
Sgt	Lewis Ernest	ASHFORTH	01.09.40.
F/O	Graham Leslie	ASHMAN	02.12.43.
Sgt	Francis Langhorne	BACKHOUSE	28.07.43.
Sgt	John Warren	BADLEY	12.08.42.
F/Sgt	Ronald Stanley	BAGNALL	05.07.41.
Sgt	Garnet James	BAILEY	26.07.42.
Sgt	Wilfred	BAILEY	09.07.43.
P/O	Alfred George	BAKE	02.06.42.
P/O	Frank Ernest	BAKER	12.03.45.
Sgt	Frederick William	BAKER	28.01.42.
Sgt	George William Frederick	BAKER	30.03.43.
P/O	Murray Richard Frederick	BAKER	30.06.41.
Sgt	Wilfred Eric	BAKER	04.02.43.
Sgt	Joseph Smillie	BALFOUR	16.09.42.
Sgt	Robert William	BALL	13.07.43.
Sgt	Wilfred Langdon	BALL	26.11.43
Sgt	Angus Granger	BALLANTYNE	15.06.43.
F/Sgt	James	BALMER	08.07.44.
Sgt	Eric George	BANKS	08.07.44.

Rank	Name	Surname	Date
Sgt	Alfred Lionel	BARBER	01.05.43.
F/L	John Colclough	BARLOW	06.10.44.
Sgt	Raymond	BARNES	30.07.44.
Sgt	Douglas Allen	BARNFATHER	28.07.43.
F/O	Elgar	BARRATT	16.12.44.
Sgt	Ronald Charles	BARRETT	09.07.43.
F/O	Bruce Ernest	BARROW	14.03.45.
Sgt	Kenneth Walter	BARRY	30.01.44.
P/O	Cyril Alfred	BARTLETT	08.05.44.
Sgt	Ronald Pascoe	BARTON	06.10.44.
Sgt	John Frederick	BATES	26.06.43.
F/Sgt	Cyril Ernest	BAYLISS	01.11.44.
Sgt	Douglas Stanley	BAZELEY	30.10.40.
Sgt	Ernest George Ronald	BEACHAM	13.05.43.
Sgt	Robert Lovie	BEADDIE	26.07.42.
Sgt	Robert Allen	BEATON	15.06.43.
Sgt	William Robert Noel	BEAVERS	28.01.40
F/Sgt	Harold	BEDFORD	14.03.45.
Sgt	George Hutchinson Rennie	BELL	06.09.43.
W/O	Hilton Craig	BELL	08.07.44.
F/O	James	BELL	26.06.43.
Sgt	Richard	BELL	17.09.42.
Sgt	Robert Ernest	BELL	15.06.43.
Sgt	John Ernest	BELLAMY	15.10.42.
F/O	Kenneth George	BELLINGHAM	22.06.44.
Sgt	Ronald	BENTLEY	05.07.44.
F/Sgt	Arnold	BERRY	16.12.44.
F/Sgt	William	BEUTEL	25.06.44.
Sgt	John Henry	BEVANS	30.06.41.
P/O	Peter Edward	BEVIS	26.06.43.
Sgt	Robert William Antony	BIDDLECOMBE	28.01.42.
Sgt	Henry Stuart Fell	BISHELL	12.03.43.
P/O	Cyril Arthur	BISHOP	27.04.44.
Sgt	Peter Derek	BISHOP	21.02.42.
F/Sgt	Stanley Kevin	BLACK	11.06.44.
Sgt	Albert William	BLAKE	24.02.42.
Sgt	Edward Albert	BLAKE	15.10.42.
Sgt	James William	BLANCHARD	22.06.44.
Sgt	Alfred Maurice (Bob)	BLYTH	21.07.42.
Sgt	George Henry	BOFFEY	16.02.44.
Sgt	James Joseph Aloysius	BOGUE	27.09.40.
F/O	Leslie Claude William	BOIVIN	30.08.44.
Sgt	James Edward	BONSON	05.03.43.
F/Sgt	Kenneth Charles James	BOTSFORD	08.07.41.
P/O	David Roy	BOWDEN	27.10.41.

F/Sgt	Norman Edward	BOWERING	04.07.41.
Sgt	Irvin	BOWLEY	29.07.44.
Sgt	John Fred Reginald	BOYALL	10.04.41.
P/O	Harold Arthur	BRAD	27.04.44.
Sgt	Alfred	BRADLEY	05.07.44.
Sgt	Ernest	BRADLEY	26.07.42.
Sgt	George Edwin	BRADLEY	29.10.41.
Sgt	Alexander	BRAID	30.12.43.
Sgt	Ralph Hollesley	BRECKELL	26.11.42
Sgt	Kenneth Ernest	BRIGHT	04.09.43.
F/O	Anthony Harley	BRINDLEY	19.09.44.
F/Sgt	John Derrick	BRINKHURST	21.12.42.
F/Sgt	Arthur George	BRISTOW	09.07.43.
P/O	Kenneth James	BRODERICK	09.07.42.
P/O	James	BRODIE	22.06.44.
F/Sgt	John Hooper	BROOKS	15.10.42.
P/O	Harold Selwyn	BROUGH	29.03.42.
Sgt	Dennis	BROWN	30.03.43.
Sgt	Douglas	BROWN	01.05.43.
P/O	Douglas Stewart	BROWN	15.06.43.
Sgt	John Downie	BROWN	02.06.42.
P/O	Walter	BROWN	04.04.41.
Sgt	Albert Edward	BROWNBILL	05.07.41.
Sgt	Edward Whitby Henry	BROWNE	26.06.43.
F/Sgt	William	BROWNLEE	22.06.44.
Sgt	Wallace	BRUCE	31.08.43.
F/O	Gerald George	BRYAN	23.09.44.
W/O	Alexander Collingwood	BRYCE	02.05.42.
W/OII	George	BRYSON	27.04.44.
Sgt	William Sutherland	BRYSON	30.08.44.
Sgt	Alan Stewart	BURGESS	23.09.43.
Sgt	Roy Eric	BURGESS	09.10.43.
Sgt	William Ezra	BURRELL	21.04.41.
Sgt	Raymond Benjamin	BURROWS	25.03.42.
Sgt	Aaron	BURSON	03.04.43.
Sgt	Eric	BURT	30.09.40.
Sgt	Edward Nichols	BURTON	02.01.44.
F/Sgt	Henry Chaytor	BUSSELL	29.03.42.
Sgt	Eric James	BUTLER	10.04.41.
Sgt	Richard William	BUTLER	26.07.42.
F/Sgt	Warren Henry	BUTT	14.01.45.
F/O	Ernest Rex	BUTTERWORTH	02.10.42.
Sgt	Harold	BUXTON	15.04.43.
F/Sgt	James Reginald	CALDER	09.07.43.
F/Sgt	Clive Percival	CALVERT	16.12.44.

F/O	Donald Allister	CAMPBELL	28.07.43.
Sgt	William Archibald	CAMPBELL	17.05.41.
P/O	Arthur Mussendine	CAMPLIN	21.12.42.
P/O	Peter Norman	CANN	25.03.42.
Sgt	James	CANNIFF	25.08.42.
Sgt	Ernest Albert	CANNON	04.09.43.
Sgt	Robert	CAPELING	01.09.40.
P/O	Walter Beattie	CARLYLE	21.07.42.
F/Sgt	Douglas John	CARMICHAEL	26.10.41.
Sgt	Andrew Steel	CARSCADDEN	04.09.43.
P/O	Anthony	CARTER	21.12.41.
Sgt	Donovan Yukin	CARTER	12.03.45.
P/O	Henry William Tilson	CARTER	30.08.44.
Sgt	Stanley Arthur	CARTER	12.08.42.
Sgt	Eric Frank	CARTHEW	25.11.40.
F/Sgt	Robin William	CASKEY	12.08.42.
F/O	Clyde Allen	CASSIDY	05.01.45.
Sgt	Herbert	CASTLE	14.03.45.
Sgt	Gerald Graham	CHALMERS	11.09.42.
Sgt	William	CHAMBERS	28.12.40.
Sgt	Arthur Stuart	CHANTRELL	22.01.42
Sgt	Anthony William	CHAPMAN	30.05.43.
Sgt	Frank	CHAPMAN	19.05.42.
Sgt	Douhlas Stanley Knox	CHAPPELL	09.10.43.
F/Sgt	John Bennett	CHARTERS	28.07.43.
Sgt	Robert John	CHARTERS	30.01.44.
P/O	Robert Fleming	CHASE	17.09.42.
Sgt	Rex Joseph	CHATWIN	19.09.44.
P/O	Lorne Smith	CHRISTMAN	05.07.41.
F/Sgt	Edward Blake	CLAMPITT	12.03.43.
Sgt	Henry David	CLARK	27.04.44.
F/Sgt	Terence George	CLARK	16.09.42.
Sgt	Arthur Tracey	CLARKE	25.06.44.
F/Sgt	John Frederick William	CLARKE	23.09.44.
Sgt	Joseph Gordon	CLARKE	06.09.43.
P/O	Robert Barclay	CLARKE	30.08.44.
F/O	Andrew	CLARKSON	29.07.44.
F/L	Frederick Cecil Walter	CLEMENT	08.07.44.
Sgt	William	CLYDE	06.11.44.
F/O	John Edward	COATES	16.08.42.
Sgt	John	COLE	08.08.43.
Sgt	John Raymond	COLLINGHAM	24.05.40.
Sgt	Eric	COLLINGWOOD	25.08.42.
F/Sgt	Ernest Lewis	COLLINS	30.08.44.
Sgt	Peter Robert	COLLINS	31.08.43.

Rank	First Names	Surname	Date
P/O	William Frederick	COLLINS	27.04.44.
Sgt	George Alec	COLLISON	28.06.44.
Sgt	Frederick Arnold	COLSON	04.02.41.
Sgt	Charles Owen	COOK	30.09.40.
F/Sgt	Clifford Eugene Leroy	COOK	01.11.44.
F/O	Grimwood Choke	COOKE	21.12.42.
Sgt	Roy Edward	COOKE	03.02.43.
F/Sgt	James Daniel O'Leary	COONEY	16.08.42.
F/L	Gerald Charles	COOPER	20.10.43.
Sgt	Joseph John	COOPER	27.07.42.
Sgt	Kenneth John	COOPER	01.08.42.
F/Sgt	William Joseph	COOPER	12.03.45.
Sgt	Sidney	CORDERY	09.04.43.
Sgt	Frank Leonard	CORNER	07.06.44.
Sgt	Eric William	COSNETT	30.05.43.
W/O	James Bowes	COSSART	14.03.45.
Sgt	Willie	COTTON	31.01.43.
F/Sgt	Joseph Rosario Arthur	COULOMBE	03.02.43.
F/Sgt	James	COULTON	16.12.43.
Sgt	Kenneth Owen	COURT	25.02.43.
Sgt	Reginald Francis	COVERDALE	30.05.43.
Sgt	Stanley	COWGILL	26.06.43.
Sgt	Donald	COY	31.01.43.
Sgt	Reginald Herbert	COZENS	23.05.44.
F/O	James Edgar Donald	CRAIGIE	26.06.43.
Sgt	David Charles	CRANSTON	29.10.41.
P/O	Vernon	CRESSWELL	11.08.43.
Sgt	John Anthony	CRISP	01.11.44.
F/Sgt	Arthur Cornelius	CROFT	28.06.44.
F/O	Peter Frederick	CROFT	18.12.44.
Sgt	James MacGregor	CROLL	06.11.44.
F/Sgt	Leslie William	CRONK	13.01.43.
Sgt	Eric Charles	CROOK	26.06.43.
F/O	Frank	CROSIER	05.07.44.
Sgt	Lennox Ashton	CROSSLEY	17.09.42.
Sgt	David Arthur Donald	CROUCH	04.03.41.
P/O	Thomas Bernard	CROWFOOT	15.10.42.
F/Sgt	Samuel Victor	CROWHURST	12.12.41.
P/O	David Macleod	CROZIER	13.01.43.
Sgt	James	CUNLIFFE	06.09.43.
Sgt	Alexander	CURRIE	29.03.42.
F/Sgt	William	CURRIE	08.05.44.
F/L	Donald Joseph	CURTIN	25.02.43.
Sgt	William Henry	CURTIS	08.07.42.
P/O	Jack	CUTMORE	21.04.41.

Rank	Name	Surname	Date
Sgt	Arthur Stuart	DALGRESS	07.08.40.
F/O	Leslie John	DARBY	19.09.44.
Sgt	Keith Edward	DARE	09.07.42.
F/O	Kenneth Charles	DARKE	07.01.45.
F/Sgt	Frank Lawrence	DARLINGTON	04.02.43.
F/Sgt	Montague	DARVILL	26.07.42.
Sgt	John Bruce Thornley	DAVENPORT	30.07.44.
Sgt	Derrick Joseph	DAVEY	21.12.40.
Sgt	James Douglas	DAVIE	26.07.42.
Sgt	Edgar William	DAVIES	26.11.43.
F/Sgt	Hiram Edwin	DAVIES	25.06.43.
Sgt	Richard George	DAVIES	02.05.42.
P/O	Thomas Herbert	DAVIES	09.10.43.
Sgt	Percy John	DAW	27.04.44.
Sgt	Douglas Edward	DAY	20.10.43.
Sgt	Edward George Havelock	DAY	09.10.43.
Sgt	Raymond Edward Buckenham	DAY	16.12.44.
Sgt	Aubrey Wilfred	DEERE	21.01.42.
W/OII	Joseph Charles Edward	DELLAR	05.03.43.
Sgt	Louis Thomas	DELORME	30.05.43.
Sgt	Maurice John	DEMBREY	27.07.42.
Sgt	Frank Henry	DENTON	21.02.42.
P/O	Duncan Hugh Alexander	DEWAR	13.01.43.
Sgt	Alfred James	DICKERSON	28.01.42.
P/O	Reginald William	DICKERSON	16.02.44.
P/O	David Gray	DICKIE	15.06.41.
Sgt	John Dundas	DICKIE	16.08.42.
F/Sgt	Albert William	DICKISON	26.06.43.
Sgt	Francis Arthur	DIGBY	17.09.42.
Sgt	John	DIGGORY	03.07.41.
F/Sgt	Edgar Robert	DIMOND	29.03.42.
P/O	Geoffrey Francis	DISBURY	09.07.43.
F/Sgt	John Arthur Glanville	DIXON	28.06.44.
P/O	Desmond James	DOWNER	17.09.42.
Sgt	David William	DOWNES	28.07.43.
Sgt	Joseph William	DOYLE	28.07.43.
Sgt	Maurice	DRANSFIELD	18.02.43.
Sgt	Thomas	DUFFY	23.09.43.
Sgt	Alexander	DUNBAR	13.01.43.
Sgt	Alexander	DUNCAN	01.09.40.
Sgt	Stanley Albert	DUNGEY	28.01.42.
F/O	Robert Duncan	DUNLOP	07.01.45.
F/L	Robert Jack	DUNLOP-MACKENZIE	25.03.42.
Sgt	Leslie Allan	DUNMORE	13.05.43.
Sgt	Desmond Colbert Kent	DUNNE	03.07.41.

Sgt	John Harold	DYER	02.01.44.
P/O	Norman Wilson	EASBY	28.06.44.
Sgt	William Moss	EATON	28.12.40.
Sgt	Bernard James	ECKETT	12.03.43.
Sgt	Eric	EDGE	02.01.44.
Sgt	Frank John	EDWARDS	13.01.43.
Sgt	Edward Henry	EKINS	05.07.44.
Sgt	Maitland	ELLICK	31.03.44.
F/Sgt	John Francis	ELLINS	09.10.43.
Sgt	Horace Spencer Edward	ELLIS	22.01.42
F/O	Kenneth Hector	ELLIS	03.03.43.
Sgt	Basil Lionel	ELLIS-BUXTON	01.08.42.
Sgt	John Frederick	ELSON	07.01.45.
Sgt	John Frederick Wallace	EMERSON	16.12.44.
Sgt	Ronald Jack	EMMS	15.10.42.
P/O	Gerard William Board	ENRIGHT	26.06.43.
P/O	James Paul	ERLY	22.08.41.
Sgt	Victor Thomas	ESSEX	04.03.41.
F/Sgt	William Frederick	EVANS	27.04.44.
Sgt	William Herbert Arthur	EVERSON	11.10.41.
F/O	Leonard Marvin	FALKINS	08.05.44.
F/O	Ralph Enrique	FAVIER	07.09.43.
F/Sgt	James Anthony	FELL	06.10.44.
Sgt	Peter Bernard	FELTHAM	19.09.44.
P/O	Desmond Charles	FIRTH	08.11.41.
Sgt	Harry	FISHER	04.09.43.
F/O	Edward Eric	FLETCHER	30.08.44.
Sgt	George	FLETCHER	14.01.45.
Sgt	Dennis Samuel	FORD	14.01.45.
Sgt	Morgan	FORD	30.06.41.
F/Sgt	Douglas	FORSTER	30.08.44.
Sgt	Laurence Arthur	FORTY	27.05.41.
F/Sgt	Ernest Clive	FOX	28.06.44.
Sgt	John Albert	FRANCIS	26.06.43.
Sgt	Jack Lewis	FRANCO	04.02.41.
Sgt	Charles	FRANKISH	16.12.43.
F/O	Alexander James	FRASER	03.01.42
P/O	George Eitaro	FRASER	23.08.43.
Sgt	John McLean	FRASER	19.09.40.
Sgt	Diamond	FREEMAN	26.07.42.
F/Sgt	Gordon Albert	FRENCH	11.08.43.
Sgt	Patrick	FRIEL	08.05.44.
F/Sgt	John Bert	FROST	18.02.43.
F/Sgt	Edward Charles	FRY	08.05.44.
Sgt	Francis Alfred	FRY	29.03.42.

Rank	Name	Surname	Date
P/O	William Alfred John	FULLER	27.07.42.
P/O	Stanley Montague	FUTCHER	05.07.44.
Sgt	David Douglas	GARBETT	15.10.42.
Sgt	Albert Harry	GARDNER	03.01.42
F/Sgt	John	GARDNER	20.12.42.
P/O	Frederick Horace	GARNETT	02.01.44.
Sgt	Henry Elliott	GASKELL	01.08.42.
F/O	Norman Vincent	GAUTSCHI	08.07.44.
F/Sgt	Howard	GAVIN	22.06.44.
P/O	John Vicary Frank	GIBBS	30.10.40.
F/Sgt	Albert Graham	GIBSON	21.07.42
Sgt	Reginald Aubrey	GILBERT	05.07.41.
F/O	Christopher James John	GILL	31.01.43.
F/Sgt	Joseph Thomas	GILL	31.03.44.
Sgt	Kenneth John	GILL	19.05.42.
F/Sgt	Hunter	GILLENDER	12.03.45.
Sgt	Robert Alfred	GLADEN	26.10.41.
Sgt	William Bert	GLADSTONE	08.07.44.
Sgt	Albert Leslie	GLAVES	15.06.41.
Sgt	Thomas William	GLENN	22.11.40.
Sgt	Derek Humphrey	GLOVER	12.08.42.
Sgt	James Walter	GODDARD	22.08.41.
F/O	Aaron George William	GODLEY	11.08.43.
Sgt	William Claude	GOLDSMITH	07.08.40.
Sgt	Kenneth	GOOD	04.03.41.
Sgt	Arthur	GOODACRE	22.06.44.
Sgt	Jack	GOODBRAND	30.11.41.
P/O	Bernard Cuthbert	GOODWIN	21.12.42.
Sgt	Thomas George	GOODWIN	07.09.43.
P/O	George Arthur Ormond	GORDON	11.10.41.
Sgt	Norman Joseph	GOSS	23.03.44.
Sgt	John Gray	GOW	30.09.40.
Sgt	Thomas Francis	GOWAN	30.11.41.
F/O	John Crichton	GRAHAM	26.11.43.
F/Sgt	Harry	GRAINGER	23.04.44.
P/O	James	GRANT	17.08.41.
P/O	Frank Stanford	GREEN	06.09.43.
Sgt	George Edward	GREEN	03.03.43.
Sgt	John	GREEN	23.08.43.
Sgt	Lawrence	GREEN	23.08.43.
Sgt	Percy Edward	GREEN	16.12.44.
P/O	George Frederick Edward	GREENHALGH	05.07.41.
F/Sgt	Victor	GREENWOOD	21.12.42.
Sgt	Robert Sidney	GREEP	18.02.43.
P/O	Bernard Edward	GREIN	12.08.42.

Sgt	Duncan	GREY	13.05.43.
Sgt	Patrick Michael	GRIFFIN	07.07.41.
Sgt	Henry	GRIFFITHS	30.11.41.
Sgt	Leslie Thomas	GRIMSHAW	01.08.42.
Sgt	James William	GRIMWADE	26.07.42.
F/Sgt	Gordon Stuart	GROGAN	06.10.44.
Sgt	Alan Peter James	GRUNDY	26.08.41.
F/Sgt	Eric Granville	GRUNDY	16.12.43.
F/O	James	GUILE	08.05.44.
Sgt	Henry Noble	GUSTARD	09.10.43.
F/Sgt	Roy Edward	HACKETT	16.12.43.
Sgt	Edward Ralph	HALL	15.06.41.
F/Sgt	Thomas William John	HALL	31.03.44.
Sgt	William	HALL	10.05.44.
Sgt	Oliver	HALWARD	27.10.41.
F/O	Harry Douglas	HAM	01.09.43.
Sgt	Harold Charles	HAMBLING	13.07.43.
F/L	Richard Alfred Charles	HAMMOND	10.05.44.
P/O	Philip	HANAVAN	20.10.43.
Sgt	Gordon William	HANCOCK	15.04.43.
P/O	George Robert	HANNA	21.07.42.
Sgt	Edward	HANNELL	09.07.43.
F/Sgt	Donald Edwin	HANSCOMBE	04.12.44.
F/O	William Gordon	HARDCASTLE	08.07.44.
Sgt	Edwin Thomas	HARDING	26.06.43.
F/Sgt	Herbert George	HARDING	12.03.45.
Sgt	Sidney George	HARDING	28.01.42.
F/Sgt	Walter	HARDY	06.11.44.
Sgt	Allen	HARGILL	30.08.44.
Sgt	John Frederick	HARMES	03.12.43.
P/O	Edward Charles Bisset	HARPER	27.04.44.
Sgt	Alfred	HARRIS	01.11.44.
Sgt	Ernest Charles Elam	HARRIS	23.03.44.
Sgt	Jack Frank	HARRIS	31.03.44.
P/O	John Alfred	HARRIS	31.03.44.
P/O	Lloyd George	HARRIS	11.08.43.
Sgt	Charles Malcolm	HARROWER	01.05.43.
Sgt	Robert Isaac	HART	02.06.42.
Sgt	Edward	HARTLEY	27.01.43.
Sgt	Bernard	HARVEY	27.09.40.
P/O	Stuart James	HARVEY	17.05.41.
Sgt	Wilfred Gerald	HARVEY	09.04.43.
F/O	Michael James Carr	HARWOOD	26.08.41.
Sgt	Eric	HASTE	26.10.41.
Sgt	Ernest Ambrose	HATCH	27.04.44.

Sgt	Kenneth Robert	HAW	12.03.45.
P/O	John Edwin	HAY	09.10.43.
Sgt	John Reginald	HAYLE	26.06.43.
F/O	Colin	HAYLEY	13.07.43.
S/L	Eric Lewis	HAYWARD	30.03.43.
W/OII	Victor Charles	HAYWARD	11.02.43.
F/L	Everard Frank Gray	HEALEY	13.01.43.
Sgt	Harry Reginald	HEALEY	27.04.44.
Sgt	Leslie James	HEMUS	09.04.43.
Sgt	Edward Hamilton	HENDERSON	16.09.42.
F/Sgt	John Lawrence	HENDRY	31.08.43.
F/O	William	HENRY	11.02.43.
F/L	Thomas Brodie	HERD	08.11.41.
Sgt	David	HETHERINGTON	28.06.44.
F/Sgt	Sydney Napier	HILDER	06.11.44.
Sgt	Arthur Edward	HILL	30.11.41.
S/L	Charles Ernest	HILL	15.10.42.
F/O	James Jewill	HILL	30.10.40.
Sgt	Kimber	HILL	25.03.42.
F/Sgt	William Hiram	HILL	13.05.43.
Sgt	Walter Charles	HILLS	16.02.44.
Sgt	James	HINDLEY	15.06.43.
Sgt	Reginald Frank William	HIRST	21.02.42.
Sgt	Alfred Edward	HISCOCK	19.09.42.
F/O	Jacques Robert Christiaan	HOBOKEN	26.11.43.
G/C	Francis Samuel	HODDER	06.09.43.
Sgt	Duncan Edwward	HODGKINSON	28.01.42.
Sgt	Thomas Ernest	HODGSON	02.06.42.
P/O	Edwin Cecil	HOLBOURN	02.01.44.
Sgt	Albert Edward	HOLLAND	27.01.43.
Sgt	William	HOLLAND	22.01.42
Sgt	Edward J	HOLMAN	04.04.41.
Sgt	Charles Albert	HOLMES	16.08.42.
Sgt	Ernest Frank	HOLMES	01.08.42.
Sgt	James Breeds	HOOD	13.01.43.
Sgt	Cecil Bruce	HORNE	15.10.42.
F/O	Alan James	HOROBIN	09.10.43.
Sgt	Ernest	HORTON	13.07.43.
P/O	Ronald Elmer	HORTON	22.06.44.
Sgt	Jack	HOUGHAM	09.07.43.
F/L	Sisney Jack	HOULDEN	23.05.44.
F/O	Melvin Olaf	HOVINEN	13.07.43.
P/O	Donald Arthur	HOWARD	03.01.42
Sgt	George Lawson	HOWE	30.10.40.
S/L	Cecil Moreton	HOWELL	16.09.42.

Rank	Name	Surname	Date
Sgt	Francis James	HOWELL	13.05.43.
P/O	Gordon Robert	HOWELL	08.07.44.
S/L	David William Southam	HOWROYD	09.10.43.
P/O	Michael	HUBBARD	21.12.40.
F/Sgt	Laurence Gilbert	HUDSON	05.03.43.
F/Sgt	Philip	HUDSON	08.07.41.
Sgt	Norman William	HULL	22.11.40.
Sgt	Raymond Cecil	HULME	23.05.44.
P/O	James Turner	HUNT	11.02.43.
Sgt	Maurice	HUNTER	23.08.43.
Sgt	Gerald George	HUTSON	05.07.41.
Sgt	Peter Arthur	INGRAM	08.11.41.
P/O	George Harold Frederick	INNISS	04.02.41.
F/O	John	INSTON	30.01.44.
P/O	James Melville Dundas	IRVINE	24.05.40.
P/O	John Lawrence	IRVINE	09.04.43.
F/O	James	ISAAC	23.09.44.
F/O	Canon Frederick	ISAACS	24.08.42.
Sgt	Leonard George Alfred	IZOD	27.04.44.
Sgt	Vincent Edward	JACK	25.02.43.
Sgt	Vernon Russell	JACOB	28.07.43.
F/Sgt	Joseph Alfred	JACOBSON	28.01.42.
Sgt	Frederick Thomas	JAMES	12.09.44.
Sgt	Howard	JAMES	12.08.42.
Sgt	Andrew Patton	JAMIESON	11.09.42.
Sgt	John	JAMIESON	31.03.44.
Sgt	Charles Colin	JEFFREY	30.08.44.
F/O	James Peter Julian	JENKINS	26.11.43.
Sgt	James Stuart	JOHNS	09.07.43.
Sgt	Howard Edward	JOHNSON	31.01.43.
F/Sgt	Leslie Ronald	JOHNSON	09.07.43.
Sgt	Norman Francis	JOHNSON	25.08.42.
F/Sgt	Norman Hugh	JOHNSON	27.04.44.
Sgt	Robert Newton	JOHNSON	08.05.44.
F/Sgt	Hubert Clodomir	JOHNSTON	17.09.42.
Sgt	Norman Burt	JOHNSTONE	04.02.43.
F/O	Cecil Gordon	JONES	03.02.43.
Sgt	Dan Davies	JONES	30.11.41.
Sgt	Francis Terence Pargeter	JONES	16.09.42.
Sgt	Kenneth Victor	JONES	03.03.43.
Sgt	Sidney James Holroyd	JONES	08.11.41.
Sgt	Thomas Gronwy	JONES	20.10.41.
Sgt	Eric Bernard	JORDAN	28.07.43.
Sgt	Richard Henry	JULIAN	23.09.44.
Sgt	Caspar Harold	JURGENSEN	13.01.43.

F/O	George Donald	KAIN	23.08.43.
Sgt	James Joseph	KEARNEY	05.07.44.
Sgt	Sidney Bertie	KEATS	19.09.40.
F/Sgt	James Philip	KEENAN	27.04.44.
F/Sgt	David Robinson Neill	KEITH	22.06.44.
Sgt	Francis Clifford	KELLY	11.02.43.
F/Sgt	Ronald Glendinning	KELLY	09.10.43.
F/Sgt	Sydney Norris	KELLY	23.05.44.
Sgt	Francis Alderson	KENDALL	14.01.45.
Sgt	Colin	KENMURE	19.09.40.
Sgt	William Richard	KENNEDY	08.05.44.
Sgt	Stanley Arthur	KENT	24.02.42.
Sgt	Walter	KING	08.11.41.
F/Sgt	George Bowering	KIRBY	06.10.44.
Sgt	James	KIRBY	27.01.43.
P/O	Kenneth Herbert William	KIRKLAND	30.01.44.
Sgt	Frederick William	KITE	16.12.43.
Sgt	Leslie David	KNAPMAN	07.01.45.
Sgt	Charles Henry George	KNIGHT	01.09.40.
Sgt	William Leslie	KNOWLES	06.08.41.
P/O	Ronald Maurice Alexander	LAKIN	21.04.41.
Sgt	Frederick Victor	LAMB	20.12.42.
Sgt	William Lewis	LAMBERT	02.06.42.
Sgt	Francis Roland	LAMIN	29.10.41.
Sgt	Peter Anthony	LANE	05.01.45.
Sgt	James	LANGRELL	31.01.43.
F/O	Harold Keith	LANGRISH	23.04.44.
Sgt	William Hamilton	LAPSLEY	05.07.41.
P/O	Robert Dive	LARGE	07.09.43.
S/L	Jerrard	LATIMER	15.04.43.
Sgt	Donald	LAWTON	14.01.42.
Sgt	Joseph	LEADBETTER	30.05.43.
Sgt	Leonard Arthur	LEADBITTER	05.03.43.
P/O	Antony Frederick	LEAR	25.02.43.
Sgt	Jack	LEE	11.02.43.
F/L	James Henry Stallwood	LEE	23.04.44.
Sgt	Kenneth Richard	LEES	11.02.43.
F/O	Edward Richard Freeman	LEGGETT	20.02.44.
Sgt	Samuel	LEIGH	09.07.43.
Sgt	Ralph Thomas Gurden	LESTER	09.10.43.
P/O	David	LEVENE	23.09.44.
F/O	Ronald Hugh	LEWIS	16.02.44.
F/Sgt	Frederick William George	LIMBRICK	09.04.43.
F/L	Peter	LINES	30.07.44.
Sgt	Sidney	LINLEY	05.07.41.

Sgt	Robert	LITTERICK	19.09.44.
Sgt	Robert William	LITTLEFAIR	13.05.43.
F/O	Joseph William	LLOYD	19.09.44.
Sgt	Kenneth	LOACH	03.02.43.
F/Sgt	Reginald Kingsley	LOCKE	14.03.45.
Sgt	John Lawson	LOCKWOOD	20.10.41.
Sgt	Ottiwell Francis	LODGE	09.07.42.
Sgt	Ernest	LONG	08.05.44.
P/O	Henry William	LONG	16.09.42.
F/Sgt	Robert Antoine Frederick	LORETAN	08.05.44.
F/Sgt	Brian Gordon	LOUCH	21.12.42.
S/L	Arthur James	LOUGHBOROUGH	22.06.44.
P/O	John Edgecombe	LOWE	27.09.40.
Sgt	George Emile Garton	LUCAS	26.11.43.
Sgt	William George	LUDBROOK	03.03.43.
F/O	Michal Hope	LUMLEY	13.01.43.
F/Sgt	Noel	LUSHER	26.08.41.
Sgt	William Snowball	MABEN	28.07.43.
Sgt	James Melven	MACILWRAITH	06.08.41.
Sgt	Julian Pelham	MACKILLIGIN	31.03.44.
Sgt	Henry	MacLEAN	02.05.42.
P/O	John Donald	MacLEOD	16.09.42.
F/Sgt	John	MACMILLAN	25.06.43.
Sgt	Robert Blair	MacWILLIAM	27.01.43.
P/O	Pierre Joseph Benoit Morel	MADORE	27.04.44.
Sgt	Matthew Coutts	MAIR	25.11.40.
Sgt	Sidney Joseph	MALABAND	22.06.44.
F/Sgt	Charles Lucas	MALLETT	26.06.43.
Sgt	Thomas Henry	MALLETT	02.01.44.
F/Sgt	Charles Richard	MANGNALL	05.01.45.
Sgt	Horace	MANN	08.09.41.
Sgt	William George	MANN	30.01.44.
P/O	Eric Harry	MANTLE	30.03.43.
P/O	Edward Roy	MARKLAND	18.02.43.
Sgt	Alfred	MARLOW	12.09.44.
Sgt	Charles Kenneth	MARSH	23.08.43.
Sgt	Giles Bacchus	MARSH	27.01.43.
F/O	John Frank Vale	MARSHALL	19.09.44.
Sgt	Norman	MARSHALL	31.01.43.
P/O	Raymond Keith	MARSHALL	15.10.42.
S/L	Trevor Owen	MARSHALL	08.07.44.
Sgt	John Kenneth	MARSHMAN	21.07.42.
Sgt	Maurice Jack	MARTIN	16.12.43.
Sgt	Peter Richard	MARTIN	11.10.41.
Sgt	Reginald Arthur	MARTIN	15.06.43.

Sgt	Robert Muir	MATHIESON	21.07.42.
F/Sgt	Frederick Joseph	MATKIN	08.09.41.
Sgt	Cecil Arthur William	MATTHEWS	31.03.44.
F/Sgt	Stanley Richard	MATTICK	02.01.44.
F/L	Paul Raymond Murray	MAVAUT	12.09.44.
P/O	Andrew	MAXWELL	16.08.42.
Sgt	Alan Joseph	McALLISTER	10.05.44.
F/O	George Richard	McCLEAVE	06.09.43.
F/Sgt	Robert	McCORMACK	07.07.41.
F/Sgt	George Roger	McCULLUM	04.12.44.
P/O	Arthur Lennox	McDONALD	12.03.43.
Sgt	William Grant	McDONALD	25.03.42.
P/O	George	McDOUGALL	10.05.44.
Sgt	John Alexander Johnstone Mills	McGHIE	29.07.44.
F/Sgt	Leslie James	McGREGOR	25.06.44.
P/O	Allan Frederick	McGRUER	22.08.41.
Sgt	Alexander Joseph	McHARDY	19.05.42.
F/O	Donald Robert	McINTOSH	14.01.45.
F/Sgt	John Jacob	McINTYRE	15.09.41
Sgt	William Meikle	McINTYRE	06.11.44.
F/O	Bruce Gordon	McIVER	08.11.41.
Sgt	William Fraser	McKAY	03.07.41.
G/C	William Neil	McKECHNIE	30.08.44.
F/Sgt	Kenneth	McKENZIE	03.01.42.
Sgt	Leslie John Andrew	McKENZIE	03.09.43
Sgt	John Matthew	McLACHLAN	08.07.44.
P/O	Kenneth Alexander	McLAUGHLIN	23.09.44.
Sgt	David	McLEAN	02.01.44.
F/Sgt	Kenneth Hector	McLEAN	09.07.43.
F/Sgt	Robert Hudson	McLEAN	30.08.44.
Sgt	William Thomas	McLEAN	15.04.43.
F/Sgt	Donald Hugh	McLEOD	09.07.43.
F/Sgt	Ellis George	McLEOD	28.07.43.
Sgt	Lloyd Haig Beatty	McLEOD	27.09.40.
Sgt	Stanley Ronald	McLEOD	24.02.42.
Sgt	Ewen Cameron	McMILLAN	15.06.43.
Sgt	Francis	McNEIL	03.02.43.
Sgt	Ray Douglas	McPHERSON	11.09.42.
Sgt	Trevor	MELLORS	21.12.42.
W/O	Neil MacDonald	MENZIES	04.12.44.
W/O	Peter Ernest	MERRALLS	01.08.42.
F/O	Frank Manuel	MIFFLIN	27.04.44.
Sgt	Harry Walker	MILLAR	13.07.43.
W/O	Kenneth Thomas	MILLIKAN	23.05.44.
Sgt	Alan	MITCHELL	26.08.41.

Rank	Name	Surname	Date
W/OII	Douglas Seldon	MITCHELL	13.05.43.
P/O	James Agnew (Donald)	MOFFAT	27.04.44.
Sgt	Thomas	MONTEITH	23.04.44.
Sgt	Arthur John	MOORE	30.11.41.
Sgt	Maurice William	MOORE	30.05.43.
F/L	Richard William George	MOORE	20.10.43.
Sgt	Fred	MORRELL	21.12.42.
Sgt	Frank	MORRIS	11.10.41.
Sgt	Joseph Hebden	MORRISON	29.07.44.
F/Sgt	Stewart Alexander	MORRISON	22.01.42
Sgt	Stanley Carlton	MORSE	05.07.41.
Sgt	Walter James	MOSS	26.11.41
P/O	Wilfred George	MOXEY	31.03.44.
Sgt	Reginald William Lingfield	MUIR	09.07.43.
S/L	Anthony O'Shea	MURDOCH	27.04.44.
F/Sgt	Kenneth William	MURPHY	09.07.43.
F/O	Peter Rodney Vincent	MYERS	18.02.43.
Sgt	Donald	NAYLOR	30.01.44.
F/O	Conrad Denis	NEALE	06.11.44.
F/O	William Sidney	NEATHWAY	07.09.43.
P/O	Ronald Frederick	NEIL	02.12.43.
F/Sgt	Ronald	NELSON	28.06.44.
Sgt	John	NEWLANDS	29.07.44.
Sgt	Alec William	NEWTON	22.11.40.
P/O	John Frederick	NICOLLE	11.09.42.
P/O	Vincent Anthony	NONO	01.05.43.
Sgt	Frank	NORMAN	12.12.41.
F/Sgt	George John Patrick	O'BRIEN	12.03.45.
F/Sgt	George Francis Leo	O'CONNELL	22.06.44.
Sgt	George Ernest Patrick	O'CONNOR	13.01.43.
F/O	Patrick Joseph	O'LEARY	08.07.44.
P/O	Michael Joseph	O'SULLIVAN	16.09.42.
F/Sgt	William Alexander	OASTLER	26.08.41.
F/O	Harold Denis	OATES	15.06.43.
F/O	Charles Jack	OSMOND	02.10.42
Sgt	Robin Cecil Carrow	OWEN	12.03.43.
P/O	Peter John	PAGE	26.06.43.
F/O	Alan Cairns	PALMER	03.04.43.
Sgt	James	PALMER	08.07.44.
Sgt	Thomas Leslie	PANTING	29.10.41.
Sgt	Anthony Joseph William	PARKER	30.11.41.
Sgt	Edward George Lancelot	PARKER	30.08.44.
F/Sgt	Ronald Henry George	PARKER	31.03.44.
F/O	Robert Henry	PARR	15.06.43.
Sgt	Edward	PARRY	19.02.43.

Rank	Name	Surname	Date
F/Sgt	Joseph	PASS	25.06.43.
F/O	Frank Gordon	PATERSON	08.07.44.
Sgt	Ronald McLay	PATERSON	20.12.42.
F/Sgt	Alexander Granton	PATRICK	28.01.42.
F/Sgt	Samuel Roger	PATTI	08.05.44.
Sgt	Ronald James	PAUL	06.10.44.
F/Sgt	Felix Owen Warboys	PAULEY	16.02.44.
Sgt	Roland	PAYNE	19.09.42.
Sgt	Leslie	PEACE	29.07.44.
Sgt	Ernest Montague John	PEASE	02.01.44.
P/O	Henry Thomas	PEEBLES	27.04.44.
Sgt	George Henry	PEEL	26.06.43.
F/O	Lloyd Lewis	PEMBERTON	29.07.44.
F/O	Ernest Richard (Dickie)	PENMAN	08.05.44.
Sgt	Dennis William	PENNEY	19.02.43.
F/O	John Ray	PENNINGTON	13.01.43.
Sgt	Jack Desmond	PEPPER	28.06.44.
Sgt	Kenneth Walsingham Boyd	PERKINS	21.12.40.
F/O	Leslie W	PERRY	01.11.44.
W/OII	Maurice Andrew	PHAIR	13.01.43.
F/L	William James	PICKEN	05.03.43.
Sgt	Thomas Leonard Hill	PIDDOCK	15.10.42.
F/Sgt	Peter John	PITCHFORD	07.10.42.
F/O	Leslie Charles	PITMAN	23.09.43.
Sgt	John	PLANT	08.09.41.
P/O	Stanley	PLASKETT	01.05.43.
Sgt	Eric John	PLUMRIDGE	20.10.43.
W/C	Patrick Julyan	POLGLASE	04.04.41.
Sgt	Gilbert Anthony	POOLE	31.03.44.
F/O	Allister Wilson	PORTER	20.10.43.
F/Sgt	Ralph Ainsworth	POST	19.05.42.
Sgt	Ralph Desmond	POTTER	08.07.44.
F/O	George Roland	POWELL	04.02.43.
Sgt	Graham James	POWELL	05.03.43.
Sgt	Thomas Trevor	POWELL	02.01.44.
F/O	Vernon Douglas	POWELL	05.01.45.
Sgt	Thomas Henry	POWER	16.04.42.
Sgt	Kenneth Sidney	POWERS	06.10.40.
F/Sgt	Herbert Gordon	PRATT	08.05.44.
F/Sgt	Hubert Everard	PRESTON	21.04.41.
F/Sgt	Alexander Philip	PRICE	06.08.41.
F/L	Marcus Sydney Francis	PRITCHARD	18.12.44.
Sgt	Raymond Price	PROTHERO	02.12.43.
P/O	Geoffrey Victor	PRYOR	30.03.43.
Sgt	Ralph Lionel	PUCKETT	07.06.44.

Rank	Name	Surname	Date
Sgt	Hugh Patrick	PURDY	06.09.43.
F/Sgt	Ronald Albert	QUINEY	14.01.45.
W/OII	James Edward	QUINN	13.01.43.
Sgt	Frederick George	RALPH	08.08.44.
F/O	William Hannah Clingen	RAMSAY	05.07.44.
F/O	Charles Buckingham	RANDALL	08.11.41.
Sgt	Kenneh Graham	RATHBONE	13.07.43.
Sgt	Anthony Leonard Powell	RAWLINSON	22.08.41.
F/O	Aubrey William	READ	26.11.43.
Sgt	Philip Noel	REED	03.02.43.
Sgt	John Howard	REES	27.04.44.
Sgt	William Leslie Schlater	REES	09.07.42.
Sgt	Stanley Rickard	REEVE	27.04.44.
F/O	Harry	REID	30.07.44.
P/O	Kenneth Maxime	REID	31.07.43.
Sgt	Russell Addisson	REID	03.07.41.
Sgt	Thomas Allen	REID	16.08.42.
Sgt	Ian Leslie Toynton	REIS	05.07.41.
Sgt	Walter Leo Arthur	RESTELL	10.05.44.
Sgt	Michael	REYNOLDS	21.12.42.
Sgt	Cecil	RHODES	06.08.41.
Sgt	Herbert Wilfred	RICHARDSON	31.03.44.
Sgt	Eric Philip	RICHOMME	28.06.44.
Sgt	Thomas John	RIDD	03.04.43.
Sgt	Henry	RIGBY	25.02.43.
F/O	Bruce Thomas	ROBERTS	05.01.45.
Sgt	Colin	ROBERTS	31.03.44.
Sgt	John Andrew	ROBERTS	08.05.44.
Sgt	John Robert	ROBERTS	16.09.42.
Sgt	Phillip	ROBERTS	06.09.43.
Sgt	Sidney Arthur	ROBERTS	09.07.42.
P/O	Angus Alan	ROBERTSON	06.09.43.
S/L	Francis Harold	ROBERTSON	27.07.42.
Sgt	Frank	ROBERTSON	28.07.43.
Sgt	George Smith	ROBERTSON	31.03.44.
Sgt	Robert	ROBERTSON	16.04.42.
F/Sgt	Thomas Jack	ROBERTSON	02.12.43.
F/Sgt	Anthony	ROBINSON	28.06.44.
F/Sgt	Stanley	ROBINSON	18.12.44.
F/O	Terence Myles	ROBINSON	10.10.41.
W/O	George	ROBSON	02.06.42.
Sgt	T	ROBSON-SCOTT	12.12.41.
W/OII	Thomas Joseph	ROCHE	28.07.43.
Sgt	William Valentine	ROGERSON	16.04.42.
Sgt	Frank Edwin	ROLFE	30.11.41.

Sgt	Norman Charles Vezey	ROOKER	07.06.44.
F/O	Leslie Walter	ROPER	04.09.43.
P/O	Harold Kenty	ROSE	08.05.44.
P/O	Stanley	ROSENBERG	25.08.42.
Sgt	Saul Austin Roy	ROSENTHAL	11.08.43.
1Lt	Eugene Leon	ROSNER	09.07.43.
P/O	Edward Walters	ROSSER	22.03.44.
Sgt	Bernard	ROYANS	23.09.43.
Sgt	Kenneth Frederick	RUNCORN	26.08.41.
Sgt	John	RUSSELL	11.09.42.
Sgt	Ronald Sidney	SABELL	03.04.43.
Sgt	William McPhie	SAMUEL	26.07.42.
Sgt	William Stewart	SANDOM	14.04.41.
Sgt	Henry Selwyn	SANDS	04.12.44.
Sgt	Kenneth	SAUNDERS	09.10.43.
Sgt	Derrick William	SAVOY	07.09.43.
F/O	Thomas William Allan	SAXBY	04.09.43.
P/O	Charles	SCATCHARD	16.04.42.
F/O	Andrew Hawkins	SCOTT	05.01.45.
Sgt	Clarence Elgy	SCOTT	22.06.44.
F/O	James Neil	SCOTT	07.01.45.
P/O	Walter Hugh	SCOTT	23.05.44.
F/O	Ernest George	SEALL	15.06.43.
Sgt	Edward Gordon	SEARS	23.03.44.
F/Sgt	John	SEERY	29.03.42.
P/O	Robert Vincent	SELFE	28.01.42.
Sgt	Horace	SELL	08.11.41.
P/O	Clyde James	SERVICE	06.10.44.
Sgt	Malcolm Charles	SEWELL	08.05.44.
F/O	Ronald Reginald	SHADBOLT	06.09.43.
F/O	Eric Lewis	SHARP	08.05.44.
F/L	John Francis	SHARP	03.07.41.
P/O	Charles Hugh	SHAW	10.05.44.
Sgt	Ronald	SHAW	27.01.43.
Sgt	Robert William	SHEARON	27.01.43.
Sgt	Eric Henry William	SHELFER	27.09.40.
F/Sgt	Eric	SHEPHERD	10.05.44.
P/O	Henry Ian	SHEPHERD	23.09.44.
F/Sgt	Henry Wright	SHEPHERD	12.08.42.
Sgt	James Patrick	SHERIDAN	06.09.43.
Sgt	Malcolm James	SHERYN	02.12.43.
Sgt	Reginald	SHIPLEY	08.05.44.
Sgt	Charles Edward Richad	SIDEBOTHAM	28.12.40.
Sgt	Clifford	SIMM	09.07.43.
F/O	Joseph William	SIMPSON	03.04.43.

Rank	First Names	Surname	Date
F/Sgt	Cecil Horace	SINCLAIR	26.06.43.
Sgt	Mohna	SINGH	30.07.44.
Sgt	Donald	SKENE	10.04.41.
Sgt	Frederick Newman	SKINNER	20.12.42.
Sgt	Edward Wilfred	SKIPPER	18.12.44.
Sgt	George Rowland	SLACK	28.07.43.
Sgt	Royston	SLEEP	22.06.44.
F/O	Peter David	SMALE	15.10.42.
Sgt	Alfred Geoffrey	SMITH	11.09.42.
F/Sgt	Arnold George	SMITH	01.08.42.
Sgt	David	SMITH	07.09.43.
Sgt	David William	SMITH	21.12.40.
Sgt	Edward Boucher	SMITH	27.10.41.
Sgt	Francis Andrew	SMITH	09.04.43.
P/O	Francis Charles	SMITH	16.09.42
Sgt	Frederick George	SMITH	20.10.43.
Sgt	George Edward	SMITH	30.06.41.
F/Sgt	Hugh McPherson	SMITH	25.06.44.
F/O	John Arthur	SMITH	01.11.44.
P/O	Ray Branton	SMITH	26.07.42.
Sgt	Reginald John	SMITH	10.05.44.
P/O	Royal Joseph	SMITH	10.05.44.
F/O	Stanley	SMITH	20.10.43.
Sgt	Edward John	SNELLING	28.01.42.
Sgt	Peter	SOMERS	15.06.41.
Sgt	C. Henry	SOUTHWORTH	28.06.44.
W/O	Lawson Frederick	SPARLING	26.06.43.
Sgt	John	SPENCER	10.04.41.
Sgt	Antoni	SPORNY	28.01.42.
F/Sgt	Darrel Barry	STABLES	27.10.41.
F/O	John Harvey	STEEL	30.07.44.
Sgt	Herbert Dennis	STEELE	22.03.44.
Sgt	Cecil	STEPHENSON	08.05.44.
P/O	William George	STEVENS	27.04.44.
F/O	Donald Leslie	STEVENSON	15.06.43.
F/L	Douglas	STEWART	06.10.44.
Sgt	John Joseph	STEWART	25.03.42.
F/O	Louis David	STEYLAERTS	08.05.44.
P/O	Harry Murdoch	STOFFER	24.04.42.
F/Sgt	Francis Henry	STOKELD	05.07.44.
Sgt	Frederick James	STOKER	15.06.43.
Sgt	Reginald (Reg)	STONE	31.01.43.
F/Sgt	Melvin Harold	STONER	28.06.44.
P/O	Colin Harrison	STORER	16.12.43.
Sgt	Donald Neale	STORER	16.04.42.

Rank	Name	Surname	Date
F/Sgt	Benjamin George	STRETCH	15.10.42.
Sgt	George Henry	STUBBS	02.12.43.
F/Sgt	Robert Ford	STUBELT	08.05.44.
F/O	Harry George	STUFFIN	26.11.43.
P/O	Hugh Alastair	SUTHERLAND	10.05.44.
Sgt	Donald	SWAINE	29.03.42.
F/Sgt	James Vincent	SWEENEY	15.06.43.
F/O	George Jeffrey	SYMES	01.11.44.
Sgt	Hugh	TAIT	08.07.41.
Sgt	James Francis	TARRAN	26.11.44
Sgt	Lawrence James	TATE	09.04.43.
Sgt	Leslie	TATE	16.09.42.
Sgt	Alan Armitage	TAYLOR	08.05.44.
P/O	Arthur Edwin	TAYLOR	06.09.43.
F/Sgt	Jack	TAYLOR	06.09.43.
F/O	Jack	TAYLOR	08.08.44.
Sgt	John	TEEVIN	21.07.42
F/Sgt	Kenneth Valentine Frank	TERRY	23.04.44.
P/O	Arthur Evans Cosdett	THOMAS	28.06.44.
Sgt	Arthur William	THOMAS	03.02.43.
Sgt	John	THOMAS	31.08.43.
F/Sgt	Theophilus John	THOMAS	02.01.44.
F/O	William Kelman Burr	THOMAS	04.02.41.
F/Sgt	Frank	THOMPSON	31.03.44.
F/O	George Austin	THOMPSON	19.09.44.
F/O	Harold John	THOMPSON	04.12.44.
F/O	Ian James	THOMPSON	08.07.44.
F/Sgt	Reginald Hamilton	THOMSON	14.01.45.
Sgt	Stanley Edward	THURSTON	30.07.41
Sgt	Raymond Foster	TOLAND	10.05.44.
F/Sgt	Leo	TOOMEY	22.06.44.
Sgt	Stanley	TOPHAM	16.08.42.
F/Sgt	Edward George	TOWLE	16.12.44.
P/O	Stanley Richard	TRILL	23.09.43.
P/O	John Lovelace	TUCKER	23.04.44.
F/Sgt	Frederick John	TURKENTINE	18.12.44.
F/Sgt	Dalton Arnold	TURNER	09.07.43.
Sgt	Edward Ernest	TYLER	25.06.43.
Sgt	Frederick William	TYSALL	06.09.43.
P/O	Alexander	URQUHART	30.03.43.
P/O	Lawrence Ross	VAN HORNE	12.09.44.
P/O	George Francis	WADESON	05.07.41.
Sgt	Graham	WALE	02.05.42.
Sgt	George William	WALKER	31.03.44.
F/Sgt	John Edward Stuart	WALKER	21.07.42

Rank	Name	Surname	Date
Sgt	Herbert Vincent	WALMSLEY	02.01.44.
F/Sgt	Percy William Keith	WALTER	05.01.45.
Sgt	Albert John Wallace	WARD	04.03.41.
Sgt	Derek Charles	WARD	15.10.42.
F/O	George William	WARD	16.04.42.
Sgt	John Montague	WARD	22.11.40.
P/O	Kenneth Rowe	WARREN	08.05.44.
P/O	Merrick George Munday	WARREN	07.06.44.
Sgt	Ralph Ernest	WARREN	19.05.42.
P/O	Eric Thomas	WATKIN	19.09.40.
Sgt	Richard George	WATSON	03.03.43.
Sgt	Edwin James Duguid	WATT	20.12.42.
F/Sgt	Maxwell Birdwood	WATT	26.06.43.
P/O	Gordon Geoffrey	WATTS	17.08.41.
F/Sgt	Frank	WEAVER	07.09.43.
Sgt	Leonard Keith	WEBB	28.06.44.
Sgt	Robert Charles Henry	WEBB	03.04.43.
F/L	Harold Dudley	WEBBER	12.12.41.
F/Sgt	John Charles	WELCH	25.06.43.
F/Sgt	Wilfred Deryck	WELHAM	25.03.42.
W/OII	Kenneth Douglas	WELLWOOD	04.09.43.
F/O	Ralph Eric	WESLEY	03.03.43.
Sgt	Brian Douglas	WEST	08.05.44.
W/O	Lindsay William	WHEELER	19.09.44.
F/Sgt	Douglas	WHITE	23.03.44.
Sgt	Stephen George	WHITE	26.06.43.
F/Sgt	Thomas	WHITE	23.09.43.
Sgt	Hugh Richard Belcher	WHYATT	30.05.43.
W/O	Cecil Harold	WHYTE	23.05.44.
F/Sgt	Raymond Daniel	WIBERG	20.12.42.
Sgt	Edward Ernest James	WIGGINS	07.06.44.
Sgt	Maurice Hardy	WIGHAM	07.06.44.
Sgt	Douglas	WIGHTMAN	16.04.42.
Sgt	Kenneth	WILCOCK	15.06.43.
Sgt	Harold	WILD	27.04.44.
Sgt	Huch Vernon	WILKINSON	26.08.41.
F/O	William Bertram	WILKINSON	08.07.44.
Sgt	Alan	WILLIAMS	09.10.43.
Sgt	Alcwyn	WILLIAMS	17.09.42.
Sgt	Bernard Wayne	WILLIAMS	16.09.42.
Sgt	Ernest	WILLIAMS	03.04.43.
Sgt	Geoffrey Fraser	WILLIAMS	20.10.41.
F/Sgt	John Arthur	WILLIAMS	16.08.42.
Sgt	John Gareth Vaughan	WILLIAMS	26.06.43.
Sgt	Raymond George	WILLIAMS	08.05.44.

P/O	William Ogwyn	WILLIAMS	16.09.42.
Sgt	Frederick Roy	WILLS	23.08.43.
Sgt	George William	WILSON	11.08.43.
Sgt	James Ferguson Lindsay	WILSON	05.03.43.
Sgt	Roy Fleming	WILSON	07.08.40.
F/O	Reginald John Frederick	WINDSOR	25.02.43.
Sgt	Robert John	WINFINDALE	30.01.44.
Sgt	Philip	WITCOMB	16.09.42.
Sgt	John Alfred	WITHINGTON	02.01.44.
F/O	Frank George	WODEHOUSE	08.08.43.
F/Sgt	George William	WOODD	08.05.44.
P/O	Jack Sainsbury	WOODHAMS	10.05.44.
Sgt	Edward Harold	WOODS	31.03.44.
F/Sgt	Robert Ward	WOOLNER	08.07.42.
Sgt	Ronald Clifford	WOOLNOUGH	04.09.43.
P/O	John Allan	WORSWICK	02.06.42.
Sgt	Wilfred	WORTHINGTON	09.07.43.
Sgt	Charles Wilson	WRIGHT	14.01.42.
Sgt	Gordon	WRIGHT	11.08.43.
Sgt	John	WRIGHT	07.07.41.
Sgt	John Henry Bernard	WRIGHT	03.03.43.
Sgt	John Thompson	WRIGHT	10.04.41.
Sgt	Norman Duke	WRIGHT	21.02.42.
P/O	Stanley Mountford	WRIGHT	25.06.44.
S/L	Alfred Markham	YOUNG	26.06.43.
Sgt	Arthur Wilmot	YOUNG	30.07.44.
F/L	John Oswald	YOUNG	30.03.43.
Sgt	Kenneth Roland Joseph	YOUNG	13.03.43.
Sgt	Leonard Walter	YOUNG	26.07.42.
Sgt	Robert McKay	YOUNG	28.01.42.
W/O	Rodney Frederick Harling	YOUNG	25.08.42.
F/Sgt	William Lewis Johnston	YOUNG	02.05.42.
W/OII	Russell	ZAVITZ	13.01.43.
F/O	Leslie Charles	ZEFFERTT	08.07.44.

Key to Abbreviations

A&AEE	Aeroplane and Armaments Experimental Establishment.
AA	Anti-Aircraft fire.
AACU	Anti-Aircraft Cooperation Unit.
AAS	Air Armament School.
AASF	Advance Air Striking Force.
AAU	Aircraft Assembly Unit.
ACM	Air Chief Marshal.
ACSEA	Air Command South-East Asia.
AFDU	Air Fighting Development Unit.
AFEE	Airborne Forces Experimental Unit.
AFTDU	Airborne Forces Tactical Development Unit.
AGS	Air Gunners School.
AMDP	Air Members for Development and Production.
AOC	Air Officer Commanding.
AOS	Air Observers School.
ASRTU	Air-Sea Rescue Training Unit.
ATTDU	Air Transport Tactical Development Unit.
AVM	Air Vice-Marshal.
BAT	Beam Approach Training.
BCBS	Bomber Command Bombing School.
BCDU	Bomber Command Development Unit.
BCFU	Bomber Command Film Unit.
BCIS	Bomber Command Instructors School.
BDU	Bombing Development Unit.
BSTU	Bomber Support Training Unit.
CF	Conversion Flight.
CFS	Central Flying School.
CGS	Central Gunnery School.
C-in-C	Commander in Chief.
CNS	Central Navigation School.
CO	Commanding Officer.
CRD	Controller of Research and Development.
CU	Conversion Unit.
DGRD	Director General for Research and Development.
EAAS	Empire Air Armament School.
EANS	Empire Air Navigation School.
ECDU	Electronic Countermeasures Development Unit.
ECFS	Empire Central Flying School.
ETPS	Empire Test Pilots School.
F/L	Flight Lieutenant.
Flt	Flight.
F/O	Flying Officer.
FPP	Ferry Pilots School.
F/S	Flight Sergeant.
FTR	Failed to Return.
FTU	Ferry Training Unit.

G/C	Group Captain.
Gp	Group.
HCU	Heavy Conversion Unit.
HGCU	Heavy Glider Conversion Unit.
LFS	Lancaster Finishing School.
MAC	Mediterranean Air Command.
MTU	Mosquito Training Unit.
MU	Maintenance Unit.
NTU	Navigation Training Unit.
OADU	Overseas Aircraft Delivery Unit.
OAPU	Overseas Aircraft Preparation Unit.
OTU	Operational Training Unit.
P/O	Pilot Officer.
PTS	Parachute Training School.
RAE	Royal Aircraft Establishment.
SGR	School of General Reconnaissance.
Sgt	Sergeant.
SHAEF	Supreme Headquarters Allied Expeditionary Force.
SIU	Signals Intelligence Unit.
S/L	Squadron Leader.
SOC	Struck off Charge.
SOE	Special Operations Executive.
Sqn	Squadron.
TF	Training Flight.
TFU	Telecommunications Flying Unit.
W/C	Wing Commander.
Wg	Wing.
WIDU	Wireless Intelligence Development Unit.
W/O	Warrant Officer.

www.ingramcontent.com/pod-product-compliance
Lightning Source LLC
Chambersburg PA
CBHW080236170426
43192CB00014BA/2465